GRAPHIC DESIGN DISCOURSE
Evolving Theories, Ideologies, and Processes of Visual Communication

Edited by
Henry Hongmin Kim

Foreword by
Steff Geissbühler

Princeton Architectural Press
New York

Published by
Princeton Architectural Press
A McEvoy Group company
202 Warren Street, Hudson, NY 12534
Visit our website at www.papress.com

Editor: Jenny Florence
Designer: Henry Hongmin Kim

Special thanks to: Ryan Alcazar, Janet Behning, Nolan Boomer, Nicola Brower,
Abby Baxter, Abby Bussel, Benjamin English, Jan Cigliano Hartman,
Susan Hershberg, Kristen Hewitt, Lia Hunt, Valerie Kamen, Simone Kaplan-Senchak,
Sara McKay, Eliana Miller, Nina Pick, Wes Seeley, Rob Shaeffer, Sara Stemen,
Marisa Tesoro, Paul Wagner, and Joseph Weston of Princeton Architectural Press
—Kevin C. Lippert, publisher

Library of Congress
Cataloging-in-Publication Data
Kim, Henry Hongmin, editor.
Graphic design discourse: evolving theories, ideologies, and processes of visual
communication
ISBN 978-1-61689-639-3 (hardcover)
ISBN 978-1-61689-558-7 (paperback)
1. Visual communication—Methodology. 2. Graphic arts—Methodology.
LCC P93.5 .G725 2017 | DDC 302.2/22—dc23

Everything belongs to design, everything springs from it,
whether it says so or not: the body is designed,
sexuality is designed, political, social, human relations
are designed, just as are needs and aspirations, etc.
This "designed" universe is what properly constitutes
the environment.

Jean Baudrillard
Design and Environment   1981

Table of Contents

*The bud disappears when the blossom breaks through,
and we might say that the former is refuted by the latter;
in the same way when the fruit comes, the blossom may
be explained to be a false form of the plant's existence, for
the fruit appears as its true nature in place of the blossom.
The ceaseless activity of their own inherent nature makes
these stages moments of an organic unity, where they
not merely do not contradict one another, but where one
is as necessary as the other; and constitutes thereby
the life of the whole.*

Georg Wilhelm Friedrich Hegel
The Phenomenology of Mind 1807

Steff Geissbühler

Foreword
| Design Is Beautiful

Steff Geissbühler was a partner and principal at Chermayeff & Geismar Inc. for thirty years and the designer of some of the most memorable posters and corporate identity programs of the late twentieth century. He was awarded the American Institute of Graphic Arts Medal for his sustained contribution to design excellence and the development of the profession. He is also the recipient of the Federal Achievement Design Award.

....

I am a practicing graphic designer and problem solver. I am involved in every part of a design project, from research and analysis through thinking and sketching to design and execution; from developing a visual language and establishing specifications and guidelines to rolling out applications and programs. We designers communicate visually, no matter the language, country, or culture of our target audience. We like to think of what we do as being fluent in the universal language of graphic design. We are hired to "speak" for the client because we can interpret and translate the words into images, which in turn express what our client wants to say, project, or be.

This book is about revolutions leading to evolutions in design. The manifestos, philosophies, and writings included here are about change and progress. Most argue against the old and urge us to discard the former and embrace the new. "We must…" "We can no longer…" "We reject…" We are implored to destroy the cult of the past, and along with it ornamentation, decoration, and the unnecessary. But we are also pressed to return to craft and go back to purity and absolute clarity.

Modern design appeals for simplicity, immediacy, and economy of form and function. The story it tells must be abbreviated for a fast-moving world. Design becomes more abstract, mathematically constructed, organized, rational, standardized, and streamlined for mass production and consumption. Designers communicate using a shorthand of simple words and abbreviations. Designers are designing symbols, pictures, and visual codes for our audiences to express or communicate anything from facts to opinions and emotions.

But as design becomes more mechanized, it gets more predictable and sterile. And we come to realize that the hand, controlled by our brain, can give our communications more personality and character. There has been, and always will be, a demand for craft and illustration, a return to the hand-drawn and the handmade. The pendulum will always swing back to the human. Perhaps more than anything else, design is about rational thinking, innovation, meaningfulness, honesty, and, last but not least, beauty.

Graphic Design Discourse is an anthology of important historical documents that speak to our origins as designers, a collection of writings that have influenced the course and discourse of design. With the addition of his own brilliant texts and analysis, Henry Hongmin Kim has passed a tremendous assembly of critical thinking throughout the ages into the hands of professionals and students. It is a joy to revisit and understand the discourse we are building on today.

PROCESS 0-2

Henry Hongmin Kim

End of Design, Beginning of Process | Manifesto[FM] of Process[AW] Design

Graphic design is a problem-solving[MV] methodology driven by analytical and structural[FS] thinking. A graphic designer is not merely a utilitarian visual mechanic but a consilient,[EW] transdiscursive auteur[RB] [MF2] of the "desire of the other."[JL] Our creativity comes from a critical analysis of communication and prehension[AW] processes[AW] through structural[FS] and post-structural[RB MF] understanding of discourses on ontology, epistemology,[IK] semiotics,[RB] and linguistics.[FS]

Confrontation,[RD FM] which is a process of radical doubt[RD]—antithesis[GH] against a generic thesis[GH]—leads us to a constructive and productive synthesis.[GH] The visual outcome is simply a natural result of this evolution, but it is neither what graphic design is nor what defines a graphic designer.

The process[AW] itself cannot be a solution either. The solution is the visual outcome, the signifier.[FS] Design is language,[FS] visual language. Thus, execution requires craftsmanship[JT] built upon a strong syntactical foundation.[MV] Like language, design cannot exist in a vacuum; like language, design is a social phenomenon.[JB]

Thinking without pragmatics[MV] cannot be considered design.

A design without thinking is just visual rubbish.

Screw design thinkers.

Screw visual polluters.[MV]

It is all about process![AW]

Our faith in an engineered[JT] process[AW] of dissection and construction lets us approach every step of a creative challenge with passion, enthusiasm, and excitement. We can imagine our life in the continuous thrall of a Stendhal syndrome of our own making, an essential[GH] superject.[AW]

Structural[MF] Process[AW] Designers of the World, Unite![KM]

Graphic Design Discourse[VM]
2017

Everything is design.

We design everything.

Design is everything.

Deucalion and Pyrrha, *engraving by Virgil Solis*
Ovid's Metamorphoses, *Book I, 347–415. Fol. 7v, image 11. 1563*

HENRY HONGMIN KIM, END OF DESIGN, BEGINNING OF PROCESS

AT | Aristotle. *Rhetoric. 4th Century* BCE.

RD | Descartes, René. *The Discourse on Method; And, Metaphysical Meditations.* 1635.

IK | Kant, Immanuel. *Critique of Pure Reason.* 1781.

GH | Hegel, Georg Wilhelm Friedrich. *Science of Logic.* 1812.

KM | Marx, Karl. *Manifesto of the Communist Party.* 1848.

FM | Marinetti, F. T. *The Joy of Mechanical Force: Futuristic Manifesto.* 1909.

FS | Saussure, Ferdinand de. *Course in General Linguistics.* 1916.

JT | Tschichold, Jan. *The New Typography.* 1928.

AW | Whitehead, Alfred North. *Process and Reality: An Essay in Cosmology.* 1929.

KP | Popper, Karl. *The Logic of Scientific Discovery.* 1934.

WB | Benjamin, Walter. *Illuminations.* 1936.

AB | Bazin, André. *On the Auteur Theory.* 1957.

JI | Itten, Johannes. *The Art of Color: The Subjective Experience and Objective Rationale of Color.* 1960.

JL | Lacan, Jacques. *The Seminar. Book XI. The Four Fundamental Concepts of Psychoanalysis.* 1964.

MF | Foucault, Michel. *The Order of Things: An Archaeology of the Human Sciences.* 1966.

RB | Barthes, Roland. "The Death of the Author." 1968.

MF2| Foucault, Michel. "What Is an Author?" 1969.

RB2 | Barthes, Roland. *Camera Lucida: Reflections of Photography.* 1980.

JB | Baudrillard, Jean. *For a Critique of the Political Economy of the Sign.* 1981.

JM | Müller-Brockmann, Josef. *Grid and Design Philosophy.* 1981.

PB | Bourdieu, Pierre. "The Forms of Capital." 1986.

VM | Margolin, Victor. *Design Discourse.* 1989.

EW | Wilson, Edward O. *Consilience: The Unity of Knowledge.* 1998.

MV | Vignelli, Massimo. *The Vignelli Canon.* 2010.

PROCESS 0-3

Henry Hongmin Kim

Introduction
| Graphic Design Discourse

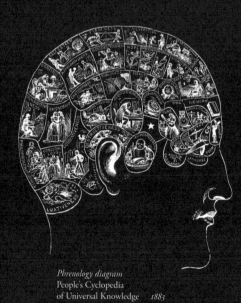

Phrenology diagram
People's Cyclopedia
of Universal Knowledge   *1883*

Process

The aim of graphic design is simple: graphic design is visual communication. And yet, in spite of the relatively straightforward goal of communicating information, the field of graphic design has struggled to situate itself between two aesthetic antipodes. On the one hand, graphic design tends toward the studio arts. Such design unabashedly bears the eccentric mark of an individual designer. At its extreme, this mode of graphic design can fail to successfully—that is, unambiguously—communicate with its audience. On the other hand, graphic design can be rigorously systematized and eschew the authorial imprint in favor of clear, objective information. At its most extreme, structural graphic design becomes rote and predictable, the bland output of an algorithmic design vending machine.

Modernism provided a gospel for the age of information and communication after the Industrial Revolution. The modernist doctrine has proved to be a universally sophisticated approach, enabling design to traverse cultures, but it can also limit a designer's aesthetic. In reaction, postmodern designers sought ways of embedding their aura into their work by circumventing the structural foundations of modernist design.

Over the years, designers have claimed various new roles, with a strong emphasis today on design thinking. However, a designer is typically also able to practice skilled craftsmanship based on design principles. In the age of information, graphic designers must be all things—thinker and technician, problem solver and practitioner. We must be goal oriented and process driven. However, our role hinges on our ability to not only produce successful outcomes but also to think rationally, to argue reasonably, and to give shape to the desire of others within a given system. We are not studio artists; we are engineers of communication. We create not because we are creative but because we are radical believers in the value of a structurally sound and well-delivered message.

If we allow ourselves to submit to confrontation as a method of truth finding—if we allow our ideas to be challenged and negated ad infinitum—we will discover a positive means of systematically yielding a productive synthesis. No designer is an island; our dominion is found in the act of letting go and trusting the process—a process that is always heteronomous and never solitary, one that should stand upon the shoulders of sound theoretical discourse. We are collaborators, transdiscursive authors, and engineers. Graphic design is in its infancy.

Therefore, we must take this opportunity to define our identity, as it will shape our influence moving forward.

Is it possible to design information in an expressive way without undermining the design's purpose—clear and concise visual communication based on an intelligent structural methodology and a coherent visualization process? Before considering this approach, we must glean insights from the history, theory, and discourse of design.

Graphic Design Discourse

Most existing design theory or history books present either (1) the overarching personal view of a single author, (2) a collection of essays by several designers, or (3) a single author's interpretation of texts from other disciplines, such as semiotics or linguistics, considered within design pragmatics. *Graphic Design Discourse* is a collection of discourses—canonical ideologies and practices that have been observed, gathered, and recorded to provide a new generation of designers with a collection of interpretative teachings—a design(ed) doctrine.

Graphic Design Discourse presents a chronological progression of in-depth theories to create a sophisticated dialogue. Over five hundred articles and books by philosophers, designers, architects, artists, and critics were reviewed, and over seventy texts have been selected and arranged based on the evolution of design discourse throughout history. *Graphic Design Discourse* groups articles into seven categories. Each section presents another approach to design, another moment in its evolution. Processes serve as individual anchor points, chronologically ordered, secured by the designers and philosophers who conceived them, and organized into accessible sections to be devoured. A new anchor acts as a turn of prehension relative to the previous point, allowing for the evolution of design history through a wider process of deduction. Thus, an individual design methodology should be a deductive process, and not an inductive process drenched in generalized empirical knowledge. Each process is extremely important to understanding how we as designers have landed in our current position. Without the anchor points we would free fall; with them we have the ability to strengthen our resolve and to push design into the future.

Graphic Design Discourse is not a proclamation of a singular truth but an analysis of multiple understandings. As graphic designers, we must consider our role in this process more critically; we must broaden our scope of knowledge and develop a clear theoretical understanding of what it means to communicate.

Graphic Design Discourse is the manifestation of the pursuit of unity in knowledge—concrescence among philosophers, academics, and designers. It is a collection of expansive discourses that will guide us to a more critical and learned understanding of what we do and what our role in society will be in the future. We are not spontaneous beings: nothing is natural; everything is designed. It is our responsibility to fully understand the breadth and influence of our field and to, in turn, derive our creativity from a comprehensive understanding of the discourse that surrounds it.

We believe that this is the right moment to create the ultimate canon of design theory and discourse in order to ensure a bright future for design and design education.

Disruption of Convention
| Against Humanism

Traditional forms of art—including painting, sculpture, and architecture—have been integral to human civilization since its inception. They defined and advanced human creativity through centuries of evolving discourse, theory, and ideology. In comparison, the history of graphic design as a discrete field is infinitesimal. After the long development of traditional art forms over thousands of years, graphic design—unfathomable prior to the advent of the printing press and mass communication—emerged as one of the most advanced forms of visual communication and expression.

The birth of the field of graphic design—both its visual form and its conceptual foundations—and its continuation into the modern era depended on upheavals brought by political and social revolutions and two world wars. The avant-garde artistic movements that came to the fore in the early twentieth century are significant in the history of art, as they consciously integrated ethico-political criticism and sought to shape the concept of modernity through expressive design that deliberately upset convention. The originality of the avant-garde also lay in its attempts to visualize highly abstract scientific and philosophical attributes of the modern age—speed, perspectivism, general relativity, anonymity, and a nascent globalization. Movements such as Futurism and Cubism embodied these abstract concepts formally. The political thrust of the avant-garde was driven by revolutionary originality, the individual as political agent, and the capacity for art to mobilize the masses. By bolstering these three presuppositions with ingenuity and technical skill, the avant-garde aimed at nothing less than large-scale social change.

As the modern age progressed, the ideological positions of the early avant-garde movements were reinterpreted and reimagined by subsequent generations, allowing for a free-flowing redefinition of the idea of creativity. The disruptions caused by these evolving artistic practices led to increasing cross-disciplinarity. The manifestos of these movements suggest the ideological changes required to advance the interpretation and conceptual understanding of creativity within graphic design.

1-1

F. T. Marinetti

The Founding and Manifesto of Futurism
1909

"we intend to sing the love of danger, the habit of energy and fearlessness"

Filippo Tommaso Marinetti (1876–1944) was an Italian poet, editor, and art theorist. He was a founder of Futurism, which rejected the past and celebrated industry, machinery, speed, violence, and youth. The Futurist movement came to be considered a turning point in the advancement of modernism in art and design. Marinetti's Futurist manifesto first appeared as the preface to a 1909 volume of his poems. It was published later that year in the Italian news-paper Gazzetta dell'Emilia *and the French newspaper* Le Figaro.

We had stayed up all night, my friends and I, under hanging mosque lamps with domes of filigreed brass, domes starred like our spirits, shining like them with the prisoned radi-ance of electric hearts. For hours we had trampled our atavistic ennui into rich oriental rugs, arguing up to the last confines of logic and blackening many reams of paper with our frenzied scribbling.

An immense pride was buoying us up, because we felt ourselves alone at that hour, alone, awake, and on our feet, like proud beacons or forward sentries against an army of hostile stars glaring down at us from their celestial encampments. Alone with stokers feeding the hellish fires of great ships, alone with the black spectres who grope in the red-hot bellies of locomotives launched on their crazy courses, alone with drunkards reeling like wounded birds along the city walls.

Suddenly we jumped, hearing the mighty noise of the huge double-decker trams that rumbled by outside, ablaze with colored lights, like villages on holiday suddenly struck and uprooted by the flooding Po and dragged over falls and through gorges to the sea.

Then the silence deepened. But, as we listened to the old canal muttering its feeble prayers and the creaking bones of sickly palaces above their damp green beards, under the win-dows we suddenly heard the famished roar of automobiles.

"Let's go!" I said. "Friends, away! Let's go! Mythology and the Mystic Ideal are defeated at last. We're about to see the Centaur's birth and, soon after, the first flight of Angels!... We must shake at the gates of life, test the bolts and hinges. Let's go! Look there, on the earth, the very first dawn! There's nothing to match the splendor of the sun's red sword, slashing for the first time through our millennial gloom!"

We went up to the three snorting beasts, to lay amorous hands on their torrid breasts. I stretched out on my car like a corpse on its bier, but revived at once under the steering wheel, a guillotine blade that threatened my stomach.

The raging broom of madness swept us out of ourselves and drove us through streets as rough and deep as the beds of torrents. Here and there, sick lamplight through window glass taught us to distrust the deceitful mathematics of our perishing eyes.

I cried, "The scent, the scent alone is enough for our beasts."

And like young lions we ran after Death, its dark pelt blotched with pale crosses as it escaped down the vast violet living and throbbing sky.

But we had no ideal Mistress raising her divine form to the clouds, nor any cruel Queen to whom to offer our bodies, twisted like Byzantine rings! There was nothing to make us wish for death, unless the wish to be free at last from the weight of our courage!

And on we raced, hurling watchdogs against doorsteps, curling them under our burning tires like collars under a flatiron. Death, domesticated, met me at every turn, gracefully holding out a paw, or once in a while hunkering down, making velvety caressing eyes at me from every puddle.

"Let's break out of the horrible shell of wisdom and throw ourselves like pride-ripened fruit into the wide, contorted mouth of the wind! Let's give ourselves utterly to the Unknown, not in desperation but only to replenish the deep wells of the Absurd!"

The words were scarcely out of my mouth when I spun my car around with the frenzy of a dog trying to bite its tail, and there, suddenly, were two cyclists coming towards me, shaking their fists, wobbling like two equally convincing but nevertheless contradictory arguments. Their stupid dilemma was blocking my way—Damn! Ouch!... I stopped short and to my disgust rolled over into a ditch with my wheels in the air...

O maternal ditch, almost full of muddy water! Fair factory drain! I gulped down your nourishing sludge; and I remembered the blessed black breast of my Sudanese nurse... When I came up—torn, filthy, and stinking—from under the capsized car, I felt the white-hot iron of joy deliciously pass through my heart!

A crowd of fishermen with handlines and gouty naturalists were already swarming around the prodigy. With patient, loving care those people rigged a tall derrick and iron grapnels to fish out my car, like a big beached shark. Up it came from the ditch, slowly, leaving in the bottom, like scales, its heavy framework of good sense and its soft upholstery of comfort.

They thought it was dead, my beautiful shark, but a caress from me was enough to revive it; and there it was, alive again, running on its powerful fins!

And so, faces smeared with good factory muck—plastered with metallic waste, with senseless sweat, with celestial soot—we, bruised, our arms in slings, but unafraid, declared our high intentions to all the living of the earth:

Manifesto of Futurism

1. We intend to sing the love of danger, the habit of energy and fearlessness.
2. Courage, audacity, and revolt will be essential elements of our poetry.
3. Up to now literature has exalted a pensive immobility, ecstasy, and sleep. We intend to exalt aggressive action, a feverish insomnia, the racer's stride, the mortal leap, the punch and the slap.
4. We affirm that the world's magnificence has been enriched by a new beauty: the beauty of speed. A racing car whose hood is adorned with great pipes, like serpents of explosive breath—a roaring car that seems to ride on grapeshot is more beautiful than the *Victory of Samothrace*.
5. We want to hymn the man at the wheel, who hurls the lance of his spirit across the Earth, along the circle of its orbit.
6. The poet must spend himself with ardor, splendor, and generosity, to swell the enthusiastic fervor of the primordial elements.
7. Except in struggle, there is no more beauty. No work without an aggressive character can be a masterpiece. Poetry must be conceived as a violent attack on unknown forces, to reduce and prostrate them before man.
8. We stand on the last promontory of the centuries!… Why should we look back, when what we want is to break down the mysterious doors of the Impossible? Time and Space died yesterday. We already live in the absolute, because we have created eternal, omnipresent speed.
9. We will glorify war—the world's only hygiene—militarism, patriotism, the destructive gesture of freedom-bringers, beautiful ideas worth dying for, and scorn for woman.
10. We will destroy the museums, libraries, academies of every kind, will fight moralism, feminism, every opportunistic or utilitarian cowardice.
11. We will sing of great crowds excited by work, by pleasure, and by riot; we will sing of the multicolored, polyphonic tides of revolution in the modern capitals; we will sing of the vibrant nightly fervor of arsenals and shipyards blazing with violent electric moons; greedy railway stations that devour smoke-plumed serpents; factories hung on clouds by the crooked lines of their smoke; bridges that stride the rivers like giant gymnasts, flashing in the sun with a glitter of knives; adventurous steamers that sniff the horizon; deep-chested locomotives whose wheels paw the tracks like the hooves of enormous steel horses bridled by tubing; and the sleek flight of planes whose propellers chatter in the wind like banners and seem to cheer like an enthusiastic crowd.

It is from Italy that we launch through the world this violently upsetting incendiary manifesto of ours. With it, today, we establish Futurism, because we want to free this land from its smelly gangrene of professors, archaeologists, *ciceroni* and antiquarians. For too long has Italy been a dealer in second-hand clothes. We mean to free her from the numberless museums that cover her like so many graveyards.

Museums: cemeteries!... Identical, surely, in the sinister promiscuity of so many bodies unknown to one another. Museums: public dormitories where one lies forever beside hated or unknown beings. Museums: absurd abattoirs of painters and sculptors ferociously slaughtering each other with color-blows and line-blows, the length of the fought-over walls!

That one should make an annual pilgrimage, just as one goes to the graveyard on All Souls' Day—that I grant. That once a year one should leave a floral tribute beneath the *Gioconda*, I grant you that...But I don't admit that our sorrows, our fragile courage, our morbid restlessness should be given a daily conducted tour through the museums. Why poison ourselves? Why rot?

And what is there to see in an old picture except the laborious contortions of an artist throwing himself against the barriers that thwart his desire to express his dream completely?...Admiring an old picture is the same as pouring our sensibility into a funerary urn instead of hurtling it far off, in violent spasms of action and creation.

Do you, then, wish to waste all your best powers in this eternal and futile worship of the past, from which you emerge fatally exhausted, shrunken, beaten down?

In truth I tell you that daily visits to museums, libraries, and academies (cemeteries of empty exertion, Calvaries of crucified dreams, registries of aborted beginnings!) are, for artists, as damaging as the prolonged supervision by parents of certain young people drunk with their talent and their ambitious wills. When the future is barred to them, the admirable past may be a solace for the ills of the moribund, the sickly, the prisoner...But we want no part of it, the past, we the young and strong Futurists!

So let them come, the gay incendiaries with charred fingers! Here they are! Here they are!... Come on! Set fire to the library shelves! Turn aside the canals to flood the museums!... Oh, the joy of seeing the glorious old canvases bobbing adrift on those waters, discolored and shredded!... Take up your pickaxes, your axes and hammers and wreck, wreck the venerable cities, pitilessly!

The oldest of us is thirty: so we have at least a decade for finishing our work. When we are forty, other younger and stronger men will probably throw us in the wastebasket like useless manuscripts—we want it to happen!

They will come against us, our successors, will come from far away, from every quarter, dancing to the winged cadence of their first songs, flexing the hooked claws of predators, sniffing doglike at the academy doors the strong odor of our decaying minds, which will have already been promised to the literary catacombs.

But we won't be there…At last they'll find us—one winter's night—in open country, beneath a sad roof drummed by a monotonous rain. They'll see us crouched beside our trembling aeroplanes in the act of warming our hands at the poor little blaze that our books of today will give out when they take fire from the flight of our images.

They'll storm around us, panting with scorn and anguish, and all of them, exasperated by our proud daring, will hurtle to kill us, driven by a hatred the more implacable the more their hearts will be drunk with love and admiration for us.

Injustice, strong and sane, will break out radiantly in their eyes.

Art, in fact, can be nothing but violence, cruelty, and injustice.

The oldest of us is thirty: even so we have already scattered treasures, a thousand treasures of force, love, courage, astuteness, and raw will-power; have thrown them impatiently away, with fury, carelessly, unhesitatingly, breathless, and unresting…Look at us! We are still untired! Our hearts know no weariness because they are fed with fire, hatred, and speed!… Does that amaze you?

It should, because you can never remember having lived! Erect on the summit of the world, once again we hurl our defiance at the stars!

You have objections?—Enough! Enough! We know them…We've understood!… Our fine deceitful intelligence tells us that we are the revival and extension of our ancestors— Perhaps!… If only it were so!—But who cares? We don't want to understand!…Woe to anyone who says those infamous words to us again!

Lift up your heads!

Erect on the summit of the world, once again we hurl defiance to the stars!

1-2

Umberto Boccioni

Futurist Painting: Technical Manifesto

1910

"destroy the cult of the past, the obsession with the ancients, pedantry and academic formalism"

Umberto Boccioni (1882–1916) was an Italian painter and sculptor. As one of the leading figures of Italian Futurism, he created dynamic and frenetic compositions that helped define the Futurist aesthetic. His manifesto for painters was first published as a leaflet in the Futurist magazine Poesia. *In addition to Boccioni, the artists Gino Severini, Luigi Russolo, Carlo Carrà, and Giacomo Balla signed and endorsed it.*

....

TO THE YOUNG ARTISTS OF ITALY!

The cry of rebellion which we utter associates our ideals with those of the Futurist poets. These ideals were not invented by some aesthetic clique. They are an expression of a violent desire which boils in the veins of every creative artist today.

We will fight with all our might the fanatical, senseless and snobbish religion of the past, a religion encouraged by the vicious existence of museums. We rebel against that spineless worshipping of old canvases, old statues and old bric-a-brac, against everything which is filthy and worm-ridden and corroded by time. We consider the habitual contempt for everything which is young, new and burning with life to be unjust and even criminal.

Comrades, we tell you now that the triumphant progress of science makes profound changes in humanity inevitable, changes which are hacking an abyss between those docile slaves of past tradition and us free moderns, who are confident in the radiant splendor of our future.

We are sickened by the foul laziness of artists, who, ever since the sixteenth century, have endlessly exploited the glories of the ancient Romans.

In the eyes of other countries, Italy is still a land of the dead, a vast Pompeii, white with sepulchres. But Italy is being reborn. Its political resurgence will be followed by a cultural resurgence. In the land inhabited by the illiterate peasant, schools will be set up; in the land where doing nothing in the sun was the only available profession, millions of machines are already roaring; in the land where traditional aesthetics reigned supreme, new flights of artistic inspiration are emerging and dazzling the world with their brilliance.

Living art draws its life from the surrounding environment. Our forebears drew their artistic inspiration from a religious atmosphere which fed their souls; in the same way we must breathe in the tangible miracles of contemporary life—the iron network of speedy communications which envelops the earth, the transatlantic liners, the dreadnoughts, those marvelous flights which furrow our skies, the profound courage of our submarine navigators and the spasmodic struggle to conquer the unknown. How can we remain insensible to the frenetic life of our great cities and to the exciting new psychology of night-life; the feverish figures of the bon viveur, the cocotte, the apache and the absinthe drinker?

We will also play our part in this crucial revival of aesthetic expression: we declare war on all artists and all institutions which insist on hiding behind a façade of false modernity, while they are actually ensnared by tradition, academicism and, above all, a nauseating cerebral laziness.

We condemn as insulting to youth the acclamations of a revolting rabble for the sickening reflowering of a pathetic kind of classicism in Rome; the neurasthenic cultivation of hermaphroditic archaism which they rave about in Florence; the pedestrian, half-blind handiwork of '48 which they are buying in Milan; the work of pensioned-off government clerks which they think the world of in Turin; the hotchpotch of encrusted rubbish of a group of fossilized alchemists which they are worshipping in Venice. We are going to rise up against all superficiality and banality—all the slovenly and facile commercialism which makes the work of most of our highly respected artists throughout Italy worthy of our deepest contempt.

Away then with hired restorers of antiquated incrustations. Away with affected archaeologists with their chronic necrophilia! Down with the critics, those complacent pimps! Down with gouty academics and drunken, ignorant professors!

Ask these priests of a veritable religious cult, these guardians of old aesthetic laws, where we can go and see the works of Giovanni Segantini today. Ask them why the officials of the Commission have never heard of the existence of Gaetano Previati. Ask them where they can see Medardo Rosso's sculpture, or who takes the slightest interest in artists who have not yet had twenty years of struggle and suffering behind them, but are still producing works destined to honor their fatherland?

These paid critics have other interests to defend. Exhibitions, competitions, superficial and never disinterested criticism, condemn Italian art to the ignominy of true prostitution.

And what about our esteemed "specialists"? Throw them all out. Finish them off! The Portraitists, the Genre Painters, the Lake Painters, the Mountain Painters. We have put up with enough from these impotent painters of country holidays.

Down with all marble-chippers who are cluttering up our squares and profaning our cemeteries! Down with the speculators and their reinforced-concrete buildings! Down with laborious decorators, phoney ceramicists, sold-out poster painters and shoddy, idiotic illustrators!

These are our final CONCLUSIONS:

With our enthusiastic adherence to Futurism, we will:

1. Destroy the cult of the past, the obsession with the ancients, pedantry and academic formalism.

2. Totally invalidate all kinds of imitation.

3. Elevate all attempts at originality, however daring, however violent.

4. Bear bravely and proudly the smear of "madness" with which they try to gag all innovators.

5. Regard art critics as useless and dangerous.

6. Rebel against the tyranny of words: "Harmony" and "good taste" and other loose expressions which can be used to destroy the works of Rembrandt, Goya, Rodin...

7. Sweep the whole field of art clean of all themes and subjects which have been used in the past.

8. Support and glory in our day-to-day world, a world which is going to be continually and splendidly transformed by victorious Science.

The dead shall be buried in the earth's deepest bowels! The threshold of the future will be swept free of mummies! Make room for youth, for violence, for daring!

Antonio Sant'Elia

Manifesto of Futurist Architecture

1914

"words-in-freedom, plastic dynamism, music without quadrature and the art of noises, and for which we fight without respite against traditionalist cowardice"

Antonio Sant'Elia (1888–1916) was an architect and the originator of Futurism in architecture. He realized almost no built works but is known for his bold architectural drawings, which envisioned an industrialized and technologically advanced city of monolithic skyscrapers. The "Manifesto of Futurist Architecture" was published in August 1914, the year he met Filippo Tommaso Marinetti.

No architecture has existed since 1700. A moronic mixture of the most various stylistic elements used to mask the skeletons of modern houses is called modern architecture. The new beauty of cement and iron are profaned by the superimposition of motley decorative incrustations that cannot be justified either by constructive necessity or by our (modern) taste, and whose origins are in Egyptian, Indian or Byzantine antiquity and in that idiotic flowering of stupidity and impotence that took the name of NEOCLASSICISM.

These architectonic prostitutions are welcomed in Italy, and rapacious alien ineptitude is passed off as talented invention and as extremely up-to-date architecture. Young Italian architects (those who borrow originality from clandestine and compulsive devouring of art journals) flaunt their talents in the new quarters of our towns, where a hilarious salad of little ogival columns, seventeenth-century foliation, Gothic pointed arches, Egyptian pilasters, rococo scrolls, fifteenth-century cherubs, swollen caryatids, take the place of style in all seriousness, and presumptuously put on monumental airs. The kaleidoscopic appearance and reappearance of forms, the multiplying of machinery, the daily increasing needs imposed by the speed of communications, by the concentration of population, by hygiene, and by a hundred other phenomena of modern life, never cause these self-styled renovators of architecture a moment's perplexity or hesitation. They persevere obstinately with the rules of Vitruvius, Vignola and Sansovino plus gleanings from any published scrap of information on German architecture that happens to be at hand. Using these, they continue to stamp the image of imbecility on our cities, our cities which should be the immediate and faithful projection of ourselves.

And so this expressive and synthetic art has become in their hands a vacuous stylistic exercise, a jumble of ill-mixed formulae to disguise a run-of-the-mill traditionalist box of bricks and stone as a modern building. As if we who are accumulators and generators of movement, with all our added mechanical limbs, with all the noise and speed of our life, could live in streets built for the needs of men four, five or six centuries ago.

This is the supreme imbecility of modern architecture, perpetuated by the venal complicity of the academies, the internment camps of the intelligentsia, where the young are forced into the onanistic recopying of classical models instead of throwing their minds open in the search for new frontiers and in the solution of the new and pressing problem: THE FUTURIST HOUSE AND CITY. The house and the city that are ours both spiritually and materially, in which our tumult can rage without seeming a grotesque anachronism.

The problem posed in Futurist architecture is not one of linear rearrangement. It is not a question of finding new moldings and frames for windows and doors, of replacing columns, pilasters and corbels with caryatids, flies and frogs. Neither has it anything to do with leaving a façade in bare brick, or plastering it, or facing it with stone or in determining formal differences between the new building and the old one. It is a question of tending the healthy growth of the Futurist house, of constructing it with all the resources of technology and science, satisfying magisterially all the demands of our habits and our spirit, trampling down all that is grotesque and antithetical (tradition, style, aesthetics, proportion), determining new forms, new lines, a new harmony of profiles and volumes, an architecture whose reason for existence can be found solely in the unique conditions of modern life, and in its correspondence with the aesthetic values of our sensibilities. This architecture cannot be subjected to any law of historical continuity. It must be new, just as our state of mind is new.

The art of construction has been able to evolve with time, and to pass from one style to another, while maintaining unaltered the general characteristics of architecture, because in the course of history changes of fashion are frequent and are determined by the alternations of religious conviction and political disposition. But profound changes in the state of the environment are extremely rare, changes that unhinge and renew, such as the discovery of natural laws, the perfecting of mechanical means, the rational and scientific use of material. In modern life the process of stylistic development in architecture has been brought to a halt. ARCHITECTURE NOW MAKES A BREAK WITH TRADITION. IT MUST PERFORCE MAKE A FRESH START.

Calculations based on the resistance of materials, on the use of reinforced concrete and steel, exclude "architecture" in the classical and traditional sense. Modern constructional materials and scientific concepts are absolutely incompatible with the disciplines of historical styles, and are the principal cause of the grotesque appearance of "fashionable" buildings in which attempts are made to employ the lightness, the superb grace of the steel beam, the delicacy of reinforced concrete, in order to obtain the heavy curve of the arch and the bulkiness of marble.

The utter antithesis between the modern world and the old is determined by all those things that formerly did not exist. Our lives have been enriched by elements the possibility of whose existence the ancients did not even suspect. Men have identified material contingencies, and revealed spiritual attitudes, whose repercussions are felt in a thousand ways. Principal among these is the formation of a new ideal of beauty that is still obscure and embryonic, but whose fascination is already felt even by the masses. We have lost our predilection for the monumental, the heavy, the static, and we have enriched our sensibility with a taste for the light, the practical, the ephemeral and the swift. We no longer feel ourselves to be the men of the cathedrals, the palaces and the podiums. We are the men of the great hotels, the railway stations, the immense streets, colossal ports, covered markets, luminous arcades, straight roads and beneficial demolitions.

We must invent and rebuild the Futurist city like an immense and tumultuous shipyard, agile, mobile and dynamic in every detail; and the Futurist house must be like a gigantic machine. The lifts must no longer be hidden away like tapeworms in the niches of stairwells; the stairwells themselves, rendered useless, must be abolished, and the lifts must scale the lengths of the façades like serpents of steel and glass. The house of concrete, glass and steel, stripped of paintings and sculpture, rich only in the innate beauty of its lines and relief, extraordinarily "ugly" in its mechanical simplicity, higher and wider according to need rather than the specifications of municipal laws. It must soar up on the brink of a tumultuous abyss: the street will no longer lie like a doormat at ground level, but will plunge many stories down into the earth, embracing the metropolitan traffic, and will be linked up for necessary interconnections by metal gangways and swift-moving pavements.

THE DECORATIVE MUST BE ABOLISHED. The problem of Futurist architecture must be resolved, not by continuing to pilfer from Chinese, Persian or Japanese photographs or fooling around with the rules of Vitruvius, but through flashes of genius and through scientific and technical expertise. Everything must be revolutionized. Roofs and underground spaces must be used; the importance of the façade must be diminished; issues of taste must be transplanted from the field of fussy moldings, finicky capitals and flimsy doorways to the broader concerns of BOLD GROUPINGS AND MASSES, AND LARGE-SCALE DISPOSITION OF PLANES. Let us make an end of monumental, funereal and commemorative architecture. Let us overturn monuments, pavements, arcades and flights of steps; let us sink the streets and squares; let us raise the level of the city.

I COMBAT AND DESPISE:

1. All the pseudo-architecture of the avant-garde, Austrian, Hungarian, German and American;

2. All classical architecture, solemn, hieratic, scenographic, decorative, monumental, pretty and pleasing;

3. The embalming, reconstruction and reproduction of ancient monuments and palaces;

4. Perpendicular and horizontal lines, cubical and pyramidical forms that are static, solemn, aggressive and absolutely excluded from our utterly new sensibility;

5. The use of massive, voluminous, durable, antiquated and costly materials.

AND PROCLAIM:

1. That Futurist architecture is the architecture of calculation, of audacious temerity and of simplicity; the architecture of reinforced concrete, of steel, glass, cardboard, textile fiber, and of all those substitutes for wood, stone and brick that enable us to obtain maximum elasticity and lightness;

2. That Futurist architecture is not because of this an arid combination of practicality and usefulness, but remains art, i.e. synthesis and expression;

3. That oblique and elliptic lines are dynamic, and by their very nature possess an emotive power a thousand times stronger than perpendiculars and horizontals, and that no integral, dynamic architecture can exist that does not include these;

4. That decoration as an element superimposed on architecture is absurd, and that the decorative value of Futurist architecture depends solely on the use and original arrangement of raw or bare or violently colored materials;

5. That, just as the ancients drew inspiration for their art from the elements of nature, we—who are materially and spiritually artificial—must find that inspiration in the elements of the utterly new mechanical world we have created, and of which architecture must be the most beautiful expression, the most complete synthesis, the most efficacious integration;

6. That architecture as the art of arranging forms according to pre-established criteria is finished;

7. That by the term architecture is meant the endeavor to harmonize the environment with Man with freedom and great audacity, that is, to transform the world of things into a direct projection of the world of the spirit;

8. From an architecture conceived in this way no formal or linear habit can grow, since the fundamental characteristics of Futurist architecture will be its impermanence and transience. THINGS WILL ENDURE LESS THAN US. EVERY GENERATION MUST BUILD ITS OWN CITY. This constant renewal of the architectonic environment will contribute to the victory of Futurism, which has already been affirmed by WORDS-IN-FREEDOM, PLASTIC DYNAMISM, MUSIC WITHOUT QUADRATURE AND THE ART OF NOISES, and for which we fight without respite against traditionalist cowardice.

Tristan Tzara

Dada Manifesto

1918

"Dada was born of a need for independence, of a distrust toward unity. Those who are with us preserve their freedom. We recognize no theory"

Tristan Tzara (1896–1963) was a French-Romanian writer, poet, playwright, literary critic, performance artist, and founding member of Dada, an international avant-garde and anti-establishment art movement that developed in response to the horrors of World War I.

The magic of a word—Dada—which has brought journalists to the gates of a world unforeseen, is of no importance to us.

To put out a manifesto you must want: ABC
to fulminate against 1, 2, 3,
to fly into a rage and sharpen your wings to conquer and disseminate little abcs and big ABCs, to sign, shout, swear, to organize prose into a form of absolute and irrefutable evidence, to prove your non plus ultra and maintain that novelty resembles life just as the latest appearance of some whore proves the essence of God. His existence was previously proved by the accordion, the landscape, the wheedling word. To impose your ABC is a natural thing—hence deplorable. Everybody does it in the form of crystalbluff-madonna, monetary system, pharmaceutical product, or a bare leg advertising the ardent sterile spring. The love of novelty is the cross of sympathy, demonstrates a naive je m'enfoutisme, it is a transitory, positive sign without a cause.

But this need itself is obsolete. In documenting art on the basis of the supreme simplicity: novelty, we are human and true for the sake of amusement, impulsive, vibrant to crucify boredom. At the crossroads of the lights, alert, attentively awaiting the years, in the forest. I write a manifesto and I want nothing, yet I say certain things, and in principle I am against manifestos, as I am also against principles (half-pints to measure the moral value of every phrase too too convenient; approximation was invented by the impressionists). I write this manifesto to show that people can perform contrary actions together while taking one fresh gulp of air; I am against action; for continuous contradiction, for affirmation too, I am neither for nor against and I do not explain because I hate common sense.

DADA—this is a word that throws up ideas so that they can be shot down; every bourgeois is a little playwright, who invents different subjects and who, instead of situating suitable characters on the level of his own intelligence, like chrysalises on chairs, tries to find causes or objects (according to whichever psychoanalytic method he practices) to give weight to his plot, a talking and self-defining story.

Every spectator is a plotter, if he tries to explain a word (to know!). From his padded refuge of serpentine complications, he allows his instincts to be manipulated. Whence the sorrows of conjugal life.

To be plain: The amusement of redbellies in the mills of empty skulls.

 DADA DOES NOT MEAN ANYTHING

If you find it futile and don't want to waste your time on a word that means nothing...
The first thought that comes to these people is bacteriological in character: to find its etymological, or at least its historical or psychological, origin. We see by the papers that the Kru Negroes call the tail of a holy cow Dada. The cube and the mother in a certain district of Italy are called: Dada. A hobby horse, a nurse both in Russian and Rumanian: Dada. Some learned journalists regard it as an art for babies, other holy Jesuscallingthelittlechildrenuntohims of our day, as a relapse into a dry and noisy, noisy and monotonous primitivism. Sensibility is not constructed on the basis of a word; all constructions converge on perfection which is boring, the stagnant idea of a gilded swamp, a relative human product. A work of art should not be beauty in itself, for beauty is dead; it should be neither gay nor sad, neither light nor dark to rejoice or torture the individual by serving him the cakes of sacred aureoles or the sweets of a vaulted race through the atmospheres. A work of art is never beautiful by decree, objectively and for all. Hence criticism is useless, it exists only subjectively, for each man separately, without the slightest character of universality. Does anyone think he has found a psychic base common to all mankind? The attempt of Jesus and the Bible covers with their broad benevolent wings: shit, animals, days. How can one expect to put order into the chaos that constitutes that infinite and shapeless variation: man? The principle: "love thy neighbor" is a hypocrisy. "Know thyself" is utopian but more acceptable, for it embraces wickedness. No pity. After the carnage we still retain the hope of a purified mankind. I speak only of myself, since I do not wish to convince, I have no right to drag others into my river, I oblige no one to follow me, and everybody practices his art in his own way, if he knows the joy that rises like arrows to the astral layers, or that other joy that goes down into the mines of corpse-flowers and fertile spasms. Stalactites: seek them everywhere, in mangers magnified by pain, eyes white as the hares of the angels.

And so Dada was born of a need for independence, of a distrust toward unity. Those who are with us preserve their freedom. We recognize no theory. We have enough cubist and futurist academies: laboratories of formal ideas. Is the aim of art to make money and cajole the nice nice bourgeois? Rhymes ring with the assonance of the currencies, and the inflexion slips along the line of the belly in profile. All groups of artists have arrived at this trust company after riding their steeds on various comets. While the door remains open to the possibility of wallowing in cushions and good things to eat.

Here we are dropping our anchor in fertile ground.

Here we really know what we are talking about, because we have experienced the trembling and the awakening. Drunk with energy, we are revenants thrusting the trident into heedless flesh. We are streams of curses in the tropical abundance of vertiginous vegetation, resin and rain is our sweat, we bleed and burn with thirst, our blood is strength.

Cubism was born out of the simple way of looking at an object: Cézanne painted a cup 20 centimetres below his eyes, the cubists look at it from above, others complicate appearance by making a perpendicular section and arranging it conscientiously on the side. (I do not forget the creative artists and the profound laws of matter which they established once and for all.) The futurist sees the same cup in movement, a succession of objects one beside the others, and maliciously adds a few force lines. This does not prevent the canvas from being a good or bad painting suitable for the investment of intellectual capital.

The new painter creates a world, the elements of which are also its implements, a sober, definite work without argument. The new artist protests: he no longer paints (symbolic and illusionist reproduction) but creates directly in stone, wood, iron, tin, boulders—locomotive organisms capable of being turned in all directions by the limpid wind of momentary sensation. All pictorial or plastic work is useless: let it then be a monstrosity that frightens servile minds, and not sweetening to decorate the refectories of animals in human costume, illustrating the sad fable of mankind.

A painting is the art of making two lines, which have been geometrically observed to be parallel, meet on a canvas, before our eyes, in the reality of a world that has been transposed according to new conditions and possibilities. This world is neither specified nor defined in the work, it belongs, in its innumerable variations, to the spectator. For its creator it has neither case nor theory. Order=disorder; ego=non-ego; affirmation=negation: the supreme radiations of an absolute art. Absolute in the purity of its cosmic and regulated chaos,

eternal in that globule that is a second which has no duration, no breath, no light and no control. I appreciate an old work for its novelty. It is only contrast that links us to the past. Writers who like to moralise and discuss or ameliorate psychological bases have, apart from a secret wish to win, a ridiculous knowledge of life, which they may have classified, parcelled out, canalised; they are determined to see its categories dance when they beat time. Their readers laugh derisively, but carry on: what's the use?

TRISTAN TZARA, DADA MANIFESTO

There is one kind of literature which never reaches the voracious masses. The work of creative writers, written out of the author's real necessity, and for his own benefit. The awareness of a supreme egoism, wherein laws become significant. Every page should explode, either because of its profound gravity, or its vortex, vertigo, newness, eternity, or because of its staggering absurdity, the enthusiasm of its principles, or its typography. On the one hand there is a world tottering in its flight, linked to the resounding tinkle of the infernal gamut; on the other hand, there are: the new men. Uncouth, galloping, riding astride on hiccups. And there is a mutilated world and literary medicasters in desperate need of amelioration.

I assure you: there is no beginning, and we are not afraid; we aren't sentimental. We are like a raging wind that rips up the clothes of clouds and prayers, we are preparing the great spectacle of disaster, conflagration and decomposition. Preparing to put an end to mourning, and to replace tears by sirens spreading from one continent to another. Clarions of intense joy, bereft of that poisonous sadness. DADA is the mark of abstraction; publicity and business are also poetic elements.

I destroy the drawers of the brain, and those of social organisation: to sow demoralisation everywhere, and throw heaven's hand into hell, hell's eyes into heaven, to reinstate the fertile wheel of a universal circus in the Powers of reality, and the fantasy of every individual.

Philosophy is the question: from which side shall we look at life, God, the idea or other phenomena. Everything one looks at is false. I do not consider the relative result more important than the choice between cake and cherries after dinner. The system of quickly looking at the other side of a thing in order to impose your opinion indirectly is called dialectics, in other words, haggling over the spirit of fried potatoes while dancing method around it.

If I shout:

Ideal, Ideal, Ideal

Knowledge, Knowledge, Knowledge

Boomboom, Boomboom, Boomboom

I have given a pretty faithful version of progress, law, morality and all other fine qualities that various highly intelligent men have discussed in so many books, only to conclude that after all everyone dances to his own personal boomboom, and that the writer is entitled to his boomboom: the satisfaction of pathological curiosity a private bell for inexplicable needs; a bath; pecuniary difficulties; a stomach with repercussions in tile; the authority of the mystic wand formulated as the bouquet of a phantom orchestra made up of silent fiddle bows greased with filters made of chicken manure. With the blue eye-glasses of an angel they have excavated the inner life for a dime's worth of unanimous gratitude. If all of them are right and if all pills are Pink Pills, let us try for once not to be right. Some people think they can explain rationally, by thought, what they think. But that is extremely relative. Psychoanalysis is a dangerous disease, it puts to sleep the anti-objective impulses of man and systematizes the bourgeoisie. There is no ultimate Truth. The dialectic is an amusing mechanism which guides us / in a banal kind of way / to the opinions we had in the first place. Does anyone think that, by a minute refinement of logic, he had demonstrated the truth and established the correctness of these opinions? Logic imprisoned by the senses is an organic disease. To this element philosophers always like to add: the power of observation. But actually this magnificent quality of the mind is the proof of its impotence. We observe, we regard from one or more points of view, we choose them among the millions that exist. Experience is also a product of chance and individual faculties. Science disgusts me as soon as it becomes a speculative system, loses its character of utility that is so useless but is at least individual. I detest greasy objectivity, and harmony, the science that finds everything in order. Carry on, my children, humanity…Science says we are the servants of nature: everything is in order, make love and bash your brains in. Carry on, my children, humanity, kind bourgeois and journalist virgins…I am against systems, the most acceptable system is on principle to have none. To complete oneself, to perfect oneself in one's own littleness, to fill the vessel with one's individuality, to have the courage to fight for and against thought, the mystery of bread, the sudden burst of an infernal propeller into economic lilies.

Dadaist Spontaneity

What I call the I-don't-give-a-damn attitude of life is when everyone minds his own business, at the same time as he knows how to respect other individualities, and even how to stand up for himself, the two-step becoming a national anthem, a junk shop, the wireless transmitting Bach fugues, illuminated advertisements for placards for brothels, the organ broadcasting carnations for God, all this at the same time, and in real terms, replacing photography and unilateral catechism.

Active Simplicity

Inability to distinguish between degrees of clarity: to lick the penumbra and float in the big mouth filled with honey and excrement. Measured by the scale of eternity, all activity is vain—(if we allow thought to engage in an adventure the result of which would be infinitely grotesque and add significantly to our knowledge of human impotence). But supposing life to be a poor farce, without aim or initial parturition, and because we think it our duty to extricate ourselves as fresh and clean as washed chrysanthemums, we have proclaimed as the sole basis for agreement: art. It is not as important as we, mercenaries of the spirit, have been proclaiming for centuries. Art afflicts no one, and those who manage to take an interest in it will harvest caresses and a fine opportunity to populate the country with their conversation. Art is a private affair, the artist produces it for himself, an intelligible work is the product of a journalist, and because at this moment it strikes my fancy to combine this monstrosity with oil paints: a paper tube simulating the metal that is automatically pressed and poured hatred cowardice villainy. The artist, the poet rejoice at the venom of the masses condensed into a section chief of this industry, he is happy to be insulted: it is a proof of his immutability. When a writer or artist is praised by the newspapers, it is a proof of the intelligibility of his work: wretched lining of a coat for public use; tatters covering brutality, piss contributing to the warmth of an animal brooding vile instincts. Flabby, insipid flesh reproducing with the help of typographical microbes.

We have thrown out the cry-baby in us. Any infiltration of this kind is candied diarrhoea. To encourage this act is to digest it. What we need is works that are strong straight precise and forever beyond understanding. Logic is a complication. Logic is always wrong. It draws the threads of notions, words, in their formal exterior, toward illusory ends and centres. Its chains kill, it is an enormous centipede stifling independence. Married to logic, art would live in incest, swallowing, engulfing its own tail, still part of its own body, fornicating within itself, and passion would become a nightmare tarred with protestantism, a monument, a heap of ponderous grey entrails. But suppleness, enthusiasm and even the joy of injustice, that little truth that we practise as innocents and that makes us beautiful: we are cunning, and our fingers are malleable and glide like the branches of that insidious and almost liquid plant; this injustice is the indication of our soul, say the cynics. This is also a point of view; but all flowers aren't saints, luckily, and what is divine in us is the awakening of anti-human action. What we are talking about here is a paper flower for the buttonhole of gentlemen who frequent the ball of masked life, the kitchen of grace, our white, lithe or fleshy girl cousins. They make a profit out of what we have selected. The contradiction and unity of opposing poles at the same time may be true. IF we are absolutely determined to utter this platitude, the appendix of libidinous, evil-smelling morality. Morals have an atrophying effect, like every other pestilential product of the intelligence. Being governed by morals and logic has made it impossible for us to be anything other than impassive towards policemen—the cause of slavery—putrid rats with whom the bourgeois are fed up to the teeth, and who have infected the only corridors of clear and clean glass that remained open to artists.

Let each man proclaim: there is a great negative work of destruction to be accomplished. We must sweep and clean. Affirm the cleanliness of the individual after the state of madness, aggressive complete madness of a world abandoned to the hands of bandits, who rend one another and destroy the centuries. Without aim or design, without organization: indomitable madness, decomposition. Those who are strong in words or force will survive, for they are quick in defence, the agility of limbs and sentiments flames on their faceted flanks.

Morality has determined charity and pity, two balls of fat that have grown like elephants, like planets, and are called good. There is nothing good about them. Goodness is lucid, clear and decided, pitiless toward compromise and politics. Morality is an injection of chocolate into the veins of all men. This task is not ordered by a supernatural force but by the trust of idea brokers and grasping academicians. Sentimentality: at the sight of a group of men quarrelling and bored, they invented the calendar and the medicament wisdom. With a sticking of labels the battle of the philosophers was set off (mercantilism, scales, meticulous and petty measures), and for the second time it was understood that pity is a sentiment like diarrhoea in relation to the disgust that destroys health, a foul attempt by carrion corpses to compromise the sun. I proclaim the opposition of all cosmic faculties to this gonorrhoea of a putrid sun issued from the factories of philosophical thought, I proclaim bitter struggle with all the weapons of—

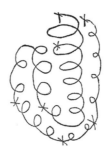

Dadaist Disgust

Every product of disgust capable of becoming a negation of the family is *dada*; a protest with the fists of its whole being engaged in destructive action: DADA ; knowledge of all the means rejected up until now by the shamefaced sex of comfortable compromise and good manners: DADA ; abolition of logic, which is the dance of those impotent to create: **DADA** ; of every social hierarchy and equation set up for the sake of values by our valets: DADA: every object, all objects, sentiments, obscurities, apparitions and the precise clash of parallel lines are weapons for the fight: **DADA** ; abolition of memory: *DADA* ; abolition of archaeology: **DADA** ; abolition of prophets: **DADA** ; abolition of the future: *DADA* ; absolute and unquestionable faith in every god that is the immediate product of spontaneity: DADA ; elegant and unprejudiced leap from a harmony to the other sphere; trajectory of a word tossed like a screeching phonograph record; to respect all individuals in their folly of the moment: whether it be serious, fearful, timid, ardent, vigorous, determined, enthusiastic; to divest one's church of every useless cumbersome accessory; to spit out disagreeable or amorous ideas like a luminous waterfall, or coddle them—with the extreme satisfaction that it doesn't matter in the least—with the same intensity in the thicket of core's soul pure of insects for blood well-born, and gilded with bodies of archangels. Freedom: **DADA DADA DADA**, a roaring of tense colors, and interlacing of opposites and of all contradictions, grotesques, inconsistencies:
LIFE.

TRISTAN TZARA, DADA MANIFESTO

PROCESS 2A

Modernism, the Beginning
| Rational and Critical Thinking

PROCESS 2B

Artist, Designer, and Engineer
| An Age of New Aesthetics

The genesis of graphic design lies with the birth of modern thinking and modern technology. Before the Industrial Revolution, mass
communication could not exist, and thus most human interaction took
place on a localized scale, with little possibility of cultural or linguistic
heterogeneity. As the world became industrialized, these differences
came to the forefront of daily life. Suddenly, a universal language was
needed to traverse cultural boundaries that were no longer easily contained by physical barriers. To safeguard against chaos and confusion,
the role of professional communicator was born.

Graphic communication in the modern era relied on the divestment of
emotion and personal expression in favor of the rational and technical
interpretation of ideas, more akin to the logical approach taken by engineers. This antihumanist method called for a strong understanding of a
new culture—mass culture—as conveying information visually became
the most efficient and progressive way to communicate across cultural
and geographic frontiers.

During the modern era, members of the avant-garde developed systematic methodologies based on their theories and ideologies. The Bauhaus, a school formed under the guidance of architect Walter Gropius in Germany in 1919, became a leading proponent of modernism—indeed, an institution synonymous with modernism—by promoting a unified vision of the arts and crafts. It did so through a curriculum that included architecture, sculpture, painting, industrial design, graphic design, typography, weaving, metalworking, and pottery, as well as by encouraging design for mass production.

The rational and objective approach to communication that was developed during the modern era defined the methodology of graphic design as a practice of visualization and problem solving. The pathfinders who birthed this creed also defined the profession's social obligation—that is, its basic function as a mode of communication—and expressed the value of graphic design for modern society. Understanding their philosophies and ideologies is of great importance to contemporary designers in order to grasp the fundamental meaning and mere existence of the profession.

René Descartes

Discourse on Method

1635

"never to accept anything for true which I did not clearly know to be such"

René Descartes (1596–1650), a French philosopher and mathematician, is widely considered the father of modern Western philosophy. He is generally believed to be the first philosopher to apply reason to the development of the natural sciences. Descartes employed methodological skepticism to evaluate ideas in order to establish a foundation of knowledge.

Part II

I was then in Germany, attracted thither by the wars in that country, which have not yet been brought to a termination; and as I was returning to the army from the coronation of the Emperor, the setting in of winter arrested me in a locality where, as I found no society to interest me, and was besides fortunately undisturbed by any cares or passions, I remained the whole day in seclusion,[1] with full opportunity to occupy my attention with my own thoughts. Of these one of the very first that occurred to me was, that there is seldom so much perfection in works composed of many separate parts, upon which different hands have been employed, as in those completed by a single master. Thus, it is observable that the buildings which a single architect has planned and executed, are generally more elegant and commodious than those which several have attempted to improve, by making old walls serve for purposes for which they were not originally built. Thus also, those ancient cities which, from being at first only villages, have become, in course of time, large towns, are usually but ill-laid out compared with the regularly constructed towns which a professional architect has freely planned on an open plain; so that although the several buildings of the former may often equal or surpass in beauty those of the latter, yet when one observes their indiscriminate juxtaposition, there a large one and here a small, and the consequent crookedness and irregularity of the streets, one is disposed to allege that chance rather than any human will guided by reason, must have led to such an arrangement. And if we consider that nevertheless there have been at all times certain officers whose duty it was to see that private buildings contributed to public ornament, the difficulty of reaching high perfection with but the materials of others to operate on, will be readily acknowledged. In the same way I fancied that those nations which, starting

---

1   *Literally, in a room heated by means of a stove.—Tr.*

from a semi-barbarous state and advancing to civilisation by slow degrees, have had their laws successively determined, and, as it were forced upon them simply by experience of the hurtfulness of particular crimes and disputes, would by this process come to be possessed of less perfect institutions than those which, from the commencement of their association as communities, have followed the appointments of some wise legislator. It is thus quite certain that the constitution of the true religion, the ordinances of which are derived from God, must be incomparably superior to that of every other. And, to speak of human affairs, I believe that the past preeminence of Sparta was due not to the goodness of each of its laws in particular, for many of these were very strange, and even opposed to good morals, but to the circumstance that, originated by a single individual, they all tended to a single end. In the same way I thought that the sciences contained in books, (such of them at least as are made up of probable reasonings, without demonstrations,) composed as they are of the opinions of many different individuals massed together, are farther removed from truth than the simple inferences which a man of good sense using his natural and unprejudiced judgment draws respecting the matters of his experience. And because we have all to pass through a state of infancy to manhood, and have been of necessity, for a length of time, governed by our desires and preceptors, (whose dictates were frequently conflicting, while neither perhaps always counselled us for the best,) I further concluded that it is almost impossible that our judgments can be so correct or solid as they would have been, had our Reason been mature from the moment of our birth, and had we always been guided by it alone.

It is true, however, that it is not customary to pull down all the houses of a town with the single design of rebuilding them differently, and thereby rendering the streets more handsome; but it often happens that a private individual takes down his own with the view of erecting it anew, and that people are even sometimes constrained to this when their houses are in danger of falling from age, or when the foundations are insecure. With this before me by way of example, I was persuaded that it would indeed be preposterous for a private individual to think of reforming a state by fundamentally changing it throughout, and overturning it in order to set it up amended; and the same I thought was true of any similar project for reforming the body of the Sciences, or the order of teaching them established in the Schools: but as for the opinions which up to that time I had embraced, I thought that I could not do better than resolve at once to sweep them wholly away, that I might afterwards be in a position to admit either others more correct, or even perhaps the same when they had undergone the scrutiny of Reason. I firmly believed that in this way I should much better succeed in the conduct of my life, than if I built only upon old foundations, and leant upon principles which, in my youth, I had taken upon trust. For although I recognised various difficulties in this undertaking, these were not, however, without remedy, nor once to be compared with such as attend the slightest reformation in public affairs. Large bodies, if once overthrown are with great difficulty set up again, or even kept erect when once seriously shaken, and the fall of such is always disastrous. Then if there are any imperfections in the constitutions of states, (and that many such exists the diversity of constitutions is alone sufficient to assure us,) custom has without doubt materially smoothed their inconveniences, and has even managed to steer altogether clear of, or sensibly corrected a number which sagacity could not have provided against with equal effect; and, in fine, the defects are almost always more tolerable than the change necessary for their removal; in the same manner that highways which wind among mountains, by being much frequented, become gradually so smooth and commodious, that it is much better to follow them than to seek a straighter path by climbing over the tops of rocks and descending to the bottoms of precipices.

Hence it is that I cannot in any degree approve of those restless and busy meddlers who, called neither by birth nor fortune to take part in the management of public affairs, are yet always projecting reforms; and if I thought that this Tract contained aught which might justify the suspicion that I was a victim of such folly, I would by no means permit its publication. I have never contemplated anything higher than the reformation of my own opinions, and basing them on a foundation wholly my own. And although my own satisfaction with my work has led me to present here a draft of it, I do not by any means therefore recommend to every one else to make a similar attempt. Those whom God has endowed with a larger measure of genius will entertain, perhaps, designs still more exalted; but for the many I am much afraid lest even the present undertaking be more than they can safely venture to imitate. The single design to strip one's self of all past beliefs is one that ought not to be taken by every one. The majority of men is composed of two classes, for neither of which would this be at all a befitting resolution: in the first place, of those who with more than a due confidence in their own powers, are precipitate in their judgments and want the patience requisite for orderly and circumspect thinking; whence it happens, that if men of this class once take the liberty to doubt of their accustomed opinions, and quit the beaten highway, they will never be able to thread the bye-way that would lead them by a shorter course, and will lose themselves and continue to wander for life; in the second place, of those who, possessed of sufficient sense or modesty to determine that there are others who excel them in the power of discriminating between truth and error, and by whom they may be instructed, ought rather to content themselves with the opinions of such than trust for more correct to their own Reason.

For my own part, I should doubtless have belonged to the latter class, had I received instruction from but one master, or had I never known the diversities of opinion that from time immemorial have prevailed among men of the greatest learning. But I had become aware, even so early as during my college life, that no opinion, however absurd and incredible, can be imagined, which has not been maintained by some one of the philosophers; and afterwards in the course of my travels I remarked that all those whose opinions are decidedly repugnant to ours are not on that account barbarians and savages, but on the contrary that many of these nations make an equally good, if not a better, use of their Reason than we do. I took into account also the very different character which a person brought up from infancy in France or Germany exhibits, from that which, with the same mind originally, this individual would have possessed had he lived always among the Chinese or with savages, and the circumstance that in dress itself the fashion which pleased us ten years ago, and which may again, perhaps, be received into favour before ten years have gone, appears to us at this moment extravagant and ridiculous. I was thus led to infer that the ground of our opinions is far more custom and example than any certain knowledge. And, finally, although such be the ground of our opinions, I remarked that a plurality of suffrages is no guarantee of truth where it is at all of difficult discovery, as in such cases it is much more likely that it will be found by one than by many. I could, however, select from the crowd no one whose opinions seemed worthy of preference, and thus I found myself constrained, as it were, to use my own Reason in the conduct of my life.

But like one walking alone and in the dark, I resolved to proceed so slowly and with such circumspection, that if I did not advance far, I would at least guard against falling. I did not even choose to dismiss summarily any of the opinions that had crept into my belief without having been introduced by Reason, but first of all took sufficient time carefully to satisfy myself of the general nature of the task I was setting myself, and ascertain the true Method by which to arrive at the knowledge of whatever lay within the compass of my powers.

Among the branches of Philosophy, I had, at an earlier period, given some attention to Logic, and among those of the Mathematics to Geometrical Analysis and Algebra,—three Arts or Sciences which ought, as I conceived, to contribute something to my design. But, on examination, I found that, as for Logic, its syllogisms and the majority of its other precepts are of avail rather in the communication of what we already know, or even as the Art of Lully, in speaking without judgment of things of which we are ignorant, than in the investigation of the unknown; and although this Science contains indeed a number of correct and very excellent precepts, there are, nevertheless, so many others, and these either injurious or superfluous, mingled with the former, that it is almost quite as difficult to effect a severance of the true from the false as it is to extract a Diana or a Minerva from a rough block of marble. Then as to the Analysis of the ancients and the Algebra of the moderns, besides that they embrace only matters highly abstract, and, to appearance, of no use, the former is so exclusively restricted to the consideration of figures, that it can exercise the Understanding only on condition of greatly fatiguing the Imagination;[2] and, in the latter, there is so complete a subjection to certain rules and formulas, that there results an art full of confusion and obscurity calculated to embarrass, instead of a science fitted to cultivate the mind. By these considerations I was induced to seek some other Method which would comprise the advantages of the three and be exempt from their defects. And as a multitude of laws often only hampers justice, so that a state is best governed when, with few laws, these are rigidly administered; in like manner, instead of the great number of precepts of which Logic is composed, I believed that the four following would prove perfectly sufficient for me, provided I took the firm and unwavering resolution never in a single instance to fail in observing them.

The first was never to accept anything for true which I did not clearly know to be such; that is to say, carefully to avoid precipitancy and prejudice, and to comprise nothing more in my judgment than what was presented to my mind so clearly and distinctly as to exclude all ground of doubt.

The second, to divide each of the difficulties under examination into as many parts as possible, and as might be necessary for its adequate solution.

The third, to conduct my thoughts in such order that, by commencing with objects the simplest and easiest to know, I might ascend by little and little, and, as it were, step by step, to the knowledge of the more complex; assigning in thought a certain order even to those objects which in their own nature do not stand in a relation of antecedence and sequence.

2   *The Imagination must here be taken as equivalent simply to the Representative Faculty.—Tr.*

And the last, in every case to make enumerations so complete, and reviews so general, that I might be assured that nothing was omitted.

The long chains of simple and easy reasonings by means of which geometers are accustomed to reach the conclusions of their most difficult demonstrations, had led me to imagine that all things, to the knowledge of which man is competent, are mutually connected in the same way, and that there is nothing so far removed from us as to be beyond our reach, or so hidden that we cannot discover it, provided only we abstain from accepting the false for the true, and always preserve in our thoughts the order necessary for the deduction of one truth from another. And I had little difficulty in determining the objects with which it was necessary to commence, for I was already persuaded that it must be with the simplest and easiest to know, and, considering that of all those who have hitherto sought truth in the Sciences, the mathematicians alone have been able to find any demonstrations, that is, any certain and evident reasons, I did not doubt but that such must have been the rule of their investigations. I resolved to commence, therefore, with the examination of the simplest objects, not anticipating, however, from this any other advantage than that to be found in accustoming my mind to the love and nourishment of truth, and to a distaste for all such reasonings as were unsound. But I had no intention on that account of attempting to master all the particular Sciences commonly denominated Mathematics: but observing that, however different their objects, they all agree in considering only the various relations or proportions subsisting among those objects, I thought it best for my purpose to consider these proportions in the most general form possible, without referring them to any objects in particular, except such as would most facilitate the knowledge of them, and without by any means restricting them to these, that afterwards I might thus be the better able to apply them to every other class of objects to which they are legitimately applicable. Perceiving further, that in order to understand these relations I should sometimes have to consider them one by one, and sometimes only to bear them in mind, or embrace them in the aggregate, I thought that, in order the better to consider them individually, I should view them as subsisting between straight lines, than which I could find no objects more simple, or capable of being more distinctly represented to my imagination and senses; and on the other hand, that in order to retain them in the memory, or embrace an aggregate of many, I should express them by certain characters the briefest possible. In this way I believed that I could borrow all that was best both in Geometrical Analysis and in Algebra, and correct all the defects of the one by help of the other.

And, in point of fact, the accurate observance of these few precepts gave me, I take the liberty of saying, such ease in unravelling all the questions embraced in these two sciences, that in the two or three months I devoted to their examination, not only did I reach solutions of questions I had formerly deemed exceedingly difficult, but even as regards questions of the solution of which I continued ignorant, I was enabled, as it appeared to me, to determine the means whereby, and the extent to which, a solution was possible; results attributable to the circumstance that I commenced with the simplest and most general truths, and that thus each truth discovered was a rule available in the discovery of subsequent ones. Nor in this perhaps shall I appear too vain if it be considered that, as the truth on any particular point is one, whoever apprehends the truth, knows all that on that point can be known. The child, for example, who has been instructed in the elements of Arithmetic, and has made a particular addition, according to rule, may be assured that he has found, with respect to the sum of the numbers before him, all that in this instance is within the reach of human genius. Now, in conclusion, the Method which teaches adherence to the true order, and an exact enumeration of all the conditions of the thing sought includes all that gives certitude to the rules of Arithmetic.

But the chief ground of my satisfaction with this Method, was the assurance I had of thereby exercising my reason in all matters, if not with absolute perfection, at least with the greatest attainable by me: besides, I was conscious that by its use my mind was becoming gradually habituated to clearer and more distinct conceptions of its objects; and I hoped also, from not having restricted this Method to any particular matter, to apply it to the difficulties of the other Sciences, with not less success than to those of Algebra. I should not, however, on this account have ventured at once on the examination of all the difficulties of the Sciences which presented themselves to me, for this would have been contrary to the order prescribed in the Method, but observing that the knowledge of such is dependent on principles borrowed from Philosophy, in which I found nothing certain, I thought it necessary first of all to endeavour to establish its principles. And because I observed, besides, that an inquiry of this kind was of all others of the greatest moment, and one in which precipitancy and anticipation in judgment were most to be dreaded, I thought that I ought not to approach it till I had reached a more mature age, (being at that time but twenty-three,) and had first of all employed much of my time in preparation for the work, as well by eradicating from my mind all the erroneous opinions I had up to that moment accepted, as by amassing variety of experience to afford materials for my reasonings, and by continually exercising myself in my chosen Method with a view to increased skill in its application.

Immanuel Kant

Critique of Pure Reason
1781

"proper mathematical propositions are always judgments a priori, and not empirical, because they carry along with them the conception of necessity, which cannot be given by experience"

Immanuel Kant (1724–1804) was a German philosopher whose writings on metaphysics, ethics, and epistemology changed the course of modern Western philosophy. Kant argued that human experience is determined by the structure of the mind and that there are therefore commonalities in our perceptions. He pointed to our shared experience of space and time and of cause and effect as examples. Kant's Critique of Pure Reason *remains one of the most influential works in the history of Western philosophy.*

Introduction

1. Of the difference between pure and empirical knowledge.

That all our knowledge begins with experience there can be no doubt. For how is it possible that the faculty of cognition should be awakened into exercise otherwise than by means of objects which affect our senses, and partly of themselves produce representations, partly rouse our powers of understanding into activity, to compare, to connect, or to separate these, and so to convert the raw material of our sensuous impressions into a knowledge of objects, which is called experience? In respect of time, therefore, no knowledge of ours is antecedent to experience, but begins with it.

But, though all our knowledge begins with experience, it by no means follows that all arises out of experience. For, on the contrary, it is quite possible that our empirical knowledge is a compound of that which we receive through impressions, and that which the faculty of cognition supplies from itself (sensuous impressions giving merely the occasion), an addition which we cannot distinguish from the original element given by sense, till long practice has made us attentive to, and skilful in separating it. It is, therefore, a question which requires close investigation, and not to be answered at first sight, whether there exists a knowledge altogether independent of experience, and even of all sensuous impressions? Knowledge of this kind is called *à priori*, in contradistinction to empirical knowledge, which has its sources *à posteriori*, that is, in experience.

But the expression, "*à priori*," is not as yet definite enough adequately to indicate the whole meaning of the question above started. For, in speaking of knowledge which has its sources in experience, we are wont to say, that this or that may be known *à priori*, because we do not derive this knowledge immediately from experience, but from a general rule, which, however, we have itself borrowed from experience. Thus, if a man undermined his house, we say, "he might know *à priori* that it would have fallen;" that is, he needed not to have waited for the experience that it did actually fall. But still, *à priori*, he could not know even this much. For, that bodies are heavy, and, consequently, that they fall when their supports are taken away, must have been known to him previously, by means of experience.

By the term "knowledge *à priori*," therefore, we shall in the sequel understand, not such as is independent of this or that kind of experience, but such as is absolutely so of *all* experience. Opposed to this is empirical knowledge, or that which is possible only *à posteriori*, that is, through experience. Knowledge *à priori* is either pure or impure. Pure knowledge *à priori* is that with which no empirical element is mixed up. For example, the proposition, "Every change has a cause," is a proposition *à priori*, but impure, because change is a conception which can only be derived from experience.

2. The human intellect, even in an unphilosophical state, is in possession of certain cognitions *à priori*.

The question now is as to a criterion, by which we may securely distinguish a pure from an empirical cognition. Experience no doubt teaches us that this or that object is constituted in such and such a manner, but not that it could not possibly exist otherwise. Now, in the first place, if we have a proposition which contains the idea of necessity in its very conception, it is a judgment *à priori*; if, moreover, it is not derived from any other proposition, unless from one equally involving the idea of necessity, it is absolutely *à priori*. Secondly, an empirical judgment never exhibits strict and absolute, but only assumed and comparative universality (by induction); therefore, the most we can say is,—so far as we have hitherto observed, there is no exception to this or that rule. If, on the other hand, a judgment carries with it strict and absolute universality, that is, admits of no possible exception, it is not derived from experience, but is valid absolutely *à priori*.

Empirical universality is, therefore, only an arbitrary extension of validity, from that which may be predicated of a proposition valid in most cases, to that which is asserted of a proposition which holds good in all; as, for example, in the affirmation, "All bodies are heavy." When, on the contrary, strict universality characterizes a judgment, it necessarily indicates another peculiar source of knowledge, namely, a faculty of cognition *à priori*. Necessity and strict universality, therefore, are infallible tests for distinguishing pure from empirical knowledge, and are inseparably connected with each other. But as in the use of these criteria the empirical limitation is sometimes more easily detected than the contingency of the judgment, or the unlimited universality which we attach to a judgment is often a more convincing proof than its necessity, it may be advisable to use the criteria separately, each being by itself infallible.

Now, that in the sphere of human cognition we have judgments which are necessary, and in the strictest sense universal, consequently pure *à priori*, it will be an easy matter to show. If we desire an example from the sciences, we need only take any proposition in mathematics. If we cast our eyes upon the commonest operations of the understanding, the proposition, "every change must have a cause," will amply serve our purpose. In the latter case, indeed, the conception of a cause so plainly involves the conception of a necessity of connection with an effect, and of a strict universality of the law, that the very notion of a cause would entirely disappear, were we to derive it, like Hume, from a frequent association of what happens with that which precedes; and the habit thence originating of connecting representations—the necessity inherent in the judgment being therefore merely subjective. Besides, without seeking for such examples of principles existing *à priori* in cognition, we might easily show that such principles are the indispensable basis of the possibility of experience itself, and consequently prove their existence *à priori*. For whence could our experience itself acquire certainty, if all the rules on which it depends were themselves empirical, and consequently fortuitous? No one, therefore, can admit the validity of the use of such rules as first principles. But, for the present, we may content ourselves with having established the fact, that we do possess and exercise a faculty of pure *à priori* cognition; and, secondly, with having pointed out the proper tests of such cognition, namely, universality and necessity.

Not only in judgments, however, but even in conceptions, is an *à priori* origin manifest. For example, if we take away by degrees from our conceptions of a body all that can be referred to mere sensuous experience—colour, hardness or softness, weight, even impenetrability—the body will then vanish; but the space which it occupied still remains, and this it is utterly impossible to annihilate in thought. Again, if we take away, in like manner, from our empirical conception of any object, corporeal or incorporeal, all properties which mere experience has taught us to connect with it, still we cannot think away those through which we cogitate it as substance, or adhering to substance, although our conception of substance is more determined than that of an object. Compelled, therefore, by that necessity with which the conception of substance forces itself upon us, we must confess that it has its seat in our faculty of cognition *à priori*.

3. Philosophy stands in need of a science which shall determine the possibility, principles, and extent of human knowledge *à priori*.

Of far more importance than all that has been above said, is the consideration that certain of our cognitions rise completely above the sphere of all possible experience, and by means of conceptions, to which there exists in the whole extent of experience no corresponding object, seem to extend the range of our judgments beyond its bounds. And just in this transcendental or supersensible sphere, where experience affords us neither instruction nor guidance, lie the investigations of Reason, which, on account of their importance, we consider far preferable to, and as having a far more elevated aim than, all that the understanding can achieve within the sphere of sensuous phenomena. So high a value do we set upon these investigations, that even at the risk of error, we persist in following them out, and permit neither doubt nor disregard nor indifference to restrain us from the pursuit. These unavoidable problems of mere pure reason are God, Freedom (of will), and Immortality. The science which, with all its preliminaries, has for its especial object the solution of these problems is named metaphysics—a science which is at the very outset dogmatical, that is, it confidently takes upon itself the execution of this task without any previous investigation of the ability or inability of reason for such an undertaking.

Now the safe ground of experience being thus abandoned, it seems nevertheless natural that we should hesitate to erect a building with the cognitions we possess, without knowing whence they come, and on the strength of principles, the origin of which is undiscovered. Instead of thus trying to build without a foundation, it is rather to be expected that we should long ago have put the question, how the understanding can arrive at these *à priori* cognitions, and what is the extent, validity, and worth which they may possess? We say, this is natural enough, meaning by the word natural, that which is consistent with a just and reasonable way of thinking; but if we understand by the term, that which usually happens, nothing indeed could be more natural and more comprehensible than that this investigation should be left long unattempted. For one part of our pure knowledge, the science of mathematics, has been long firmly established, and thus leads us to form flattering expectations with regard to others, though these may be of quite a different nature. Besides, when we get beyond the bounds of experience, we are of course safe from opposition in that quarter; and the charm of widening the range of our knowledge is so great that, unless we are brought to a standstill by some evident contradiction, we hurry on undoubtingly in our course. This, however, may be avoided, if we are sufficiently cautious in the construction of our fictions, which are not the less fictions on that account.

Mathematical science affords us a brilliant example, how far, independently of all experience, we may carry our *à priori* knowledge. It is true that the mathematician occupies himself with objects and cognitions only in so far as they can be represented by means of intuition. But this circumstance is easily overlooked, because the said intuition can itself be given *à priori*, and therefore is hardly to be distinguished from a mere pure conception. Deceived by such a proof of the power of reason, we can perceive no limits to the extension of our knowledge. The light dove cleaving in free flight the thin air, whose resistance it feels, might imagine that her movements would be far more free and rapid in airless space. Just in the same way did Plato, abandoning the world of sense because of the narrow limits it sets to the understanding, venture upon the wings of ideas beyond it, into the void space of pure intellect. He did not reflect that he made no real progress by all his efforts; for he met with no resistance which might serve him for a support, as it were, whereon to rest, and on which he might apply his powers, in order to let the intellect acquire momentum for its progress. It is, indeed, the common fate of human reason in speculation, to finish the imposing edifice of thought as rapidly as possible, and then for the first time to begin to examine whether the foundation is a solid one or no. Arrived at this point, all sorts of excuses are sought after, in order to console us for its want of stability, or rather, indeed, to enable us to dispense altogether with so late and dangerous an investigation. But what frees us during the process of building from all apprehension or suspicion, and flatters us into the belief of its solidity, is this. A great part, perhaps the greatest part, of the business of our reason consists in the analysation of the conceptions which we already possess of objects. By this means we gain a multitude of cognitions, which although really nothing more than elucidations or explanations of that which (though in a confused manner) was already thought in our conceptions, are, at least in respect of their form, prized as new introspections; whilst, so far as regards their matter or content, we have really made no addition to our conceptions, but only disinvolved them. But as this process does furnish real *à priori* knowledge,[1] which has a sure progress and useful results, reason, deceived by this, slips in, without being itself aware of it, assertions

1. *Not synthetical.—Tr.*

of a quite different kind; in which, to given conceptions it adds others, *à priori* indeed, but entirely foreign to them, without our knowing how it arrives at these, and, indeed, without such a question ever suggesting itself. I shall therefore at once proceed to examine the difference between these two modes of knowledge.

4. Of the difference between analytical and synthetical judgments.

In all judgments wherein the relation of a subject to the predicate is cogitated (I mention affirmative judgments only here; the application to negative will be very easy), this relation is possible in two different ways. Either the predicate B belongs to the subject A, as somewhat which is contained (though covertly) in the conception A; or the predicate B lies completely out of the conception A, although it stands in connection with it. In the first instance, I term the judgment analytical, in the second, synthetical. Analytical judgments (affirmative) are therefore those in which the connection of the predicate with the subject is cogitated through identity; those in which this connection is cogitated without identity are called synthetical judgments. The former may be called explicative, the latter augmentative[2] judgments; because the former add in the predicate nothing to the conception of the subject, but only analyse it into its constituent conceptions, which were thought already in the subject, although in a confused manner; the latter add to our conceptions of the subject a predicate which was not contained in it, and which no analysis could ever have discovered therein. For example, when I say, "all bodies are extended," this is an analytical judgment. For I need not go beyond the conception of body in order to find extension connected with it, but merely analyse the conception, that is, become conscious of the manifold properties which I think in that conception, in order to discover this predicate in it: it is therefore an analytical judgment. On the other hand, when I say, "all bodies are heavy," the predicate is something totally different from that which I think in the mere conception of a body. By the addition of such a predicate, therefore, it becomes a synthetical judgment.

Judgments of experience, as such, are always synthetical. For it would be absurd to think of grounding an analytical judgment on experience, because in forming such a judgment I need not go out of the sphere of my conceptions, and therefore recourse to the testimony of experience is quite unnecessary. That "bodies are extended" is not an empirical judgment, but a proposition which stands firm *à priori*. For before addressing myself to experience, I already have in my conception all the requisite conditions for the judgment, and I have only to extract the predicate from the conception, according to the principle of contradiction, and thereby at the same time become conscious of the necessity of the judgment, a necessity which I could never learn from experience. On the other hand, though at first I do not at all include the predicate of weight in my conception of body in general, that conception still indicates an object of experience, a part of the totality of experience, to which I can still add other parts; and this I do when I recognize by observation that bodies are heavy. I can cognize beforehand by analysis the conception of body through the characteristics of extension, impenetrability, shape, etc., all of which are cogitated in this conception. But now I extend my knowledge, and looking back on experience from which I had derived this conception of body, I find weight at all times connected with the above characteristics, and therefore I synthetically add to my concep-

2. *That is, judgments which really add to, and do not merely analyse or explain, the conceptions which make up the sum of our knowledge.—Tr.*

tions this as a predicate, and say, "all bodies are heavy." Thus it is experience upon which rests the possibility of the synthesis of the predicate of weight with the conception of body, because both conceptions, although the one is not contained in the other, still belong to one another (only contingently, however), as parts of a whole, namely, of experience, which is itself a synthesis of intuitions.

But to synthetical judgments *à priori*, such aid is entirely wanting. If I go out of and beyond the conception A, in order to recognize another B as connected with it, what foundation have I to rest on, whereby to render the synthesis possible? I have here no longer the advantage of looking out in the sphere of experience for what I want. Let us take, for example, the proposition, "everything that happens has a cause." In the conception of something that happens, I indeed think an existence which a certain time antecedes, and from this I can derive analytical judgments. But the conception of a cause lies quite out of the above conception, and indicates something entirely different from "that which happens," and is consequently not contained in that conception. How then am I able to assert concerning the general conception—"that which happens"—something entirely different from that conception, and to recognize the conception of cause although not contained in it, yet as belonging to it, and even necessarily? what is here the unknown = X, upon which the understanding rests when it believes it has found, out of the conception A a foreign predicate B, which it nevertheless considers to be connected with it? It cannot be experience, because the principle adduced annexes the two representations, cause and effect, to the representation existence, not only with universality, which experience cannot give, but also with the expression of necessity, therefore completely *à priori* and from pure conceptions. Upon such synthetical, that is augmentative propositions, depends the whole aim of our speculative knowledge *à priori*; for although analytical judgments are indeed highly important and necessary, they are so, only to arrive at that clearness of conceptions which is requisite for a sure and extended synthesis, and this alone is a real acquisition.

5. In all theoretical sciences of reason, synthetical judgments *à priori* are contained as principles.

1. Mathematical judgments are always synthetical. Hitherto this fact, though incontestably true and very important in its consequences, seems to have escaped the analysts of the human mind, nay, to be in complete opposition to all their conjectures. For as it was found that mathematical conclusions all proceed according to the principle of contradiction (which the nature of every apodeictic certainty requires), people became persuaded that the fundamental principles of the science also were recognized and admitted in the same way. But the notion is fallacious; for although a synthetical proposition can certainly be discerned by means of the principle of contradiction, this is possible only when another synthetical proposition precedes, from which the latter is deduced, but never of itself.

Before all, be it observed, that proper mathematical propositions are always judgments *à priori*, and not empirical, because they carry along with them the conception of necessity, which cannot be given by experience. If this be demurred to, it matters not; I will then limit my assertion to pure mathematics, the very conception of which implies that it consists of knowledge altogether non-empirical and *à priori*.

We might, indeed, at first suppose that the proposition 7 + 5 = 12 is a merely analytical proposition, following (according to the principle of contradiction) from the conception of a sum of seven and five. But if we regard it more narrowly, we find that our conception of the sum of seven and five contains nothing more than the uniting of both sums into one, whereby it cannot at all be cogitated what this single number is which embraces both. The conception of twelve is by no means obtained by merely cogitating the union of seven and five; and we may analyse our conception of such a possible sum as long as we will, still we shall never discover in it the notion of twelve. We must go beyond these conceptions, and have recourse to an intuition which corresponds to one of the two,—our five fingers, for example, or like Segner in his "Arithmetic," five points, and so by degrees, add the units contained in the five given in the intuition, to the conception of seven. For I first take the number 7, and, for the conception of 5 calling in the aid of the fingers of my hand as objects of intuition, I add the units, which I before took together to make up the number 5, gradually now by means of the material image of my hand, to the number 7, and by this process, I at length see the number 12 arise. That 7 should be added to 5, I have certainly cogitated in my conception of a sum = 7 + 5, but not that this sum was equal to 12. Arithmetical propositions are therefore always synthetical, of which we may become more clearly convinced by trying large numbers. For it will thus become quite evident that, turn and twist our conceptions as we may, it is impossible, without having recourse to intuition, to arrive at the sum total or product by means of the mere analysis of our conceptions. Just as little is any principle of pure geometry analytical. "A straight line between two points is the shortest" is a synthetical proposition. For my conception of straight contains no notion of quantity, but is merely qualitative. The conception of the shortest is therefore wholly an addition, and by no analysis can it be extracted from our conception of a straight line. Intuition must therefore here lend its aid, by means of which, and thus only, our synthesis is possible.

Some few principles preposited by geometricians are, indeed, really analytical, and depend on the principle of contradiction. They serve, however, like identical propositions, as links in the chain of method, not as principles,—for example, a = a, the whole is equal to itself, or (a + b) > a, the whole is greater than its part. And yet even these principles themselves, though they derive their validity from pure conceptions, are only admitted in mathematics because they can be presented in intuition. What causes us here commonly to believe that the predicate of such apodeictic judgments is already contained in our conception, and that the judgment is therefore analytical, is merely the equivocal nature of the expression. We must join in thought a certain predicate to a given conception, and this necessity cleaves already to the conception. But the question is, not what we must join in thought to the given conception, but what we really think therein, though only obscurely, and then it becomes manifest that the predicate pertains to these conceptions, necessarily indeed, yet not as thought in the conception itself, but by virtue of an intuition, which must be added to the conception.

2. The science of Natural Philosophy (Physics) contains in itself synthetical judgments *à priori*, as principles. I shall adduce two propositions. For instance, the proposition, "in all changes of the material world, the quantity of matter remains unchanged;" or, that, "in all communication of motion, action and re-action must always be equal." In both of these,

not only is the necessity, and therefore their origin *à priori* clear, but also that they are synthetical propositions. For in the conception of matter, I do not cogitate its permanency, but merely its presence in space, which it fills. I therefore really go out of and beyond the conception of matter, in order to think on to it something *à priori*, which I did not think in it. The proposition is therefore not analytical, but synthetical, and nevertheless conceived *à priori*; and so it is with regard to the other propositions of the pure part of natural philosophy.

3. As to metaphysics, even if we look upon it merely as an attempted science, yet, from the nature of human reason, an indispensable one, we find that it must contain synthetical propositions *à priori*. It is not merely the duty of metaphysics to dissect, and thereby analytically to illustrate the conceptions which we form *à priori* of things; but we seek to widen the range of our *à priori* knowledge. For this purpose, we must avail ourselves of such principles as add something to the original conception—something not identical with, nor contained in it, and by means of synthetical judgments *à priori*, leave far behind us the limits of experience; for example, in the proposition, "the world must have a beginning," and such like. Thus metaphysics, according to the proper aim of the science, consists merely of synthetical propositions *à priori*.

6. The universal problem of pure reason.

It is extremely advantageous to be able to bring a number of investigations under the formula of a single problem. For in this manner, we not only facilitate our own labour, inasmuch as we define it clearly to ourselves, but also render it more easy for others to decide whether we have done justice to our undertaking. The proper problem of pure reason, then, is contained in the question: "How are synthetical judgments *à priori* possible?"

That metaphysical science has hitherto remained in so vacillating a state of uncertainty and contradiction is only to be attributed to the fact that this great problem, and perhaps even the difference between analytical and synthetical judgments, did not sooner suggest itself to philosophers. Upon the solution of this problem, or upon sufficient proof of the impossibility of synthetical knowledge *à priori*, depends the existence or downfall of the science of metaphysics. Among philosophers, David Hume came the nearest of all to this problem; yet it never acquired in his mind sufficient precision, nor did he regard the question in its universality. On the contrary, he stopped short at the synthetical proposition of the connection of an effect with its cause (*principium causalitatis*), insisting that such proposition *à priori* was impossible. According to his conclusions, then, all that we term metaphysical science is a mere delusion, arising from the fancied insight of reason into that which is in truth borrowed from experience, and to which habit has given the appearance of necessity. Against this assertion, destructive to all pure philosophy, he would have been guarded, had he had our problem before his eyes in its universality. For he would then have perceived that, according to his own argument, there likewise could not be any pure mathematical science, which assuredly cannot exist without synthetical propositions *à priori*,—an absurdity from which his good understanding must have saved him.

In the solution of the above problem is at the same time comprehended the possibility of the use of pure reason in the foundation and construction of all sciences which contain theoretical knowledge *à priori* of objects, that is to say, the answer to the following questions:

How is pure mathematical science possible?
How is pure natural science possible?

Respecting these sciences, as they do certainly exist, it may with propriety be asked, how they are possible?—for that they must be possible is shown by the fact of their really existing.[3] But as to metaphysics, the miserable progress it has hitherto made, and the fact that of no one system yet brought forward, far as regards its true aim, can it be said that this science really exists, leaves any one at liberty to doubt with reason the very possibility of its existence.

Yet, in a certain sense, this kind of knowledge must unquestionably be looked upon as given; in other words, metaphysics must be considered as really existing, if not as a science, nevertheless as a natural disposition of the human mind (*metaphysica naturalis*). For human reason, without any instigations imputable to the mere vanity of great knowledge, unceasingly progresses, urged on by its own feeling of need, towards such questions as cannot be answered by any empirical application of reason, or principles derived therefrom; and so there has ever really existed in every man some system of metaphysics. It will always exist, so soon as reason awakes to the exercise of its power of speculation. And now the question arises—How is metaphysics, as a natural disposition, possible? In other words, how, from the nature of universal human reason, do those questions arise which pure reason proposes to itself, and which it is impelled by its own feeling of need to answer as well as it can?

But as in all the attempts hitherto made to answer the questions which reason is prompted by its very nature to propose to itself, for example, whether the world had a beginning, or has existed from eternity, it has always met with unavoidable contradictions, we must not rest satisfied with the mere natural disposition of the mind to metaphysics, that is, with the existence of the faculty of pure reason, whence, indeed, some sort of metaphysical system always arises; but it must be possible to arrive at certainty in regard to the question whether we know or do not know the things of which metaphysics treats. We must be able to arrive at a decision on the subjects of its questions, or on the ability or inability of reason to form any judgment respecting them; and therefore either to extend with confidence the bounds of our pure reason, or to set strictly defined and safe limits to its action. This last question, which arises out of the above universal problem, would properly run thus: How is metaphysics possible as a science?

Thus, the critique of reason leads at last, naturally and necessarily, to science; and, on the other hand, the dogmatical use of reason without criticism leads to groundless assertions, against which others equally specious can always be set, thus ending unavoidably in scepticism.

Besides, this science cannot be of great and formidable prolixity, because it has not to do with objects of reason, the variety of which is inexhaustible, but merely with Reason

---

3. *As to the existence of pure natural science, or physics, perhaps many may still express doubts. But we have only to look at the different propositions which are commonly treated of at the commencement of proper (empirical) physical science—those, for example, relating to the permanence of the same quantity of matter, the vis inertiae, the equality of action and reaction, &c.—to be soon convinced that they form a science of pure physics (physica pura, or rationalis), which well deserves to be separately exposed as a special science, in its whole extent, whether that be great or confined.*

herself and her problems; problems which arise out of her own bosom, and are not proposed to her by the nature of outward things, but by her own nature. And when once Reason has previously become able completely to understand her own power in regard to objects which she meets with in experience, it will be easy to determine securely the extent and limits of her attempted application to objects beyond the confines of experience.

We may and must, therefore, regard the attempts hitherto made to establish metaphysical science dogmatically as non-existent. For what of analysis, that is, mere dissection of conceptions, is contained in one or other, is not the aim of, but only a preparation for metaphysics proper, which has for its object the extension, by means of synthesis, of our *à priori* knowledge. And for this purpose, mere analysis is of course useless, because it only shows what is contained in these conceptions, but not how we arrive, *à priori*, at them; and this it is her duty to show, in order to be able afterwards to determine their valid use in regard to all objects of experience, to all knowledge in general. But little self-denial, indeed, is needed to give up these pretensions, seeing the undeniable, and in the dogmatic mode of procedure, inevitable contradictions of Reason with herself, have long since ruined the reputation of every system of metaphysics that has appeared up to this time. It will require more firmness to remain undeterred by difficulty from within, and opposition from without, from endeavouring, by a method quite opposed to all those hitherto followed, to further the growth and fruitfulness of a science indispensable to human reason—a science from which every branch it has borne may be cut away, but whose roots remain indestructible.

7. Idea and division of a particular science, under the name of a Critique of Pure Reason.

From all that has been said, there results the idea of a particular science, which may be called the Critique of Pure Reason. For reason is the faculty which furnishes us with the principles of knowledge *à priori*. Hence, pure reason is the faculty which contains the principles of cognizing anything absolutely *à priori*. An Organon of pure reason would be a compendium of those principles according to which alone all pure cognitions *à priori* can be obtained. The completely extended application of such an organon would afford us a system of pure reason. As this, however, is demanding a great deal, and it is yet doubtful whether any extension of our knowledge be here possible, or, if so, in what cases; we can regard a science of the mere criticism of pure reason, its sources and limits, as the propaedeutic to a system of pure reason. Such a science must not be called a doctrine, but only a critique of pure reason; and its use, in regard to speculation, would be only negative, not to enlarge the bounds of, but to purify, our reason, and to shield it against error,—which alone is no little gain. I apply the term transcendental to all knowledge which is not so much occupied with objects as with the mode of our cognition of these objects, so far as this mode of cognition is possible *à priori*. A system of such conceptions would be called Transcendental Philosophy. But this, again, is still beyond the bounds of our present essay. For as such a science must contain a complete exposition not only of our synthetical *à priori*, but of our analytical *à priori* knowledge, it is of too wide a range for our present purpose, because we do not require to carry our analysis any farther than is necessary to understand, in their full extent, the principles of synthesis *à priori*, with which alone we have to do. This investigation, which we cannot properly call a doctrine, but only a transcendental critique, because it aims not at the enlargement, but at the correction and guidance, of our knowledge, and is to serve as a touchstone of the worth or worthlessness of all knowledge *à priori*, is the sole object of our present essay. Such a critique is consequently, as far as possible, a preparation for an organon; and if this new organon should be found to fail, at least for a canon of pure reason, according to which the complete system of the philosophy of pure reason, whether it extend or limit the bounds of that reason, might one day be set forth both analytically and synthetically. For that this is possible, nay, that such a system is not of so great extent as to preclude the hope of its ever being completed, is evident. For we have not here to do with the nature of outward objects, which is infinite, but solely with the mind, which judges of the nature of objects, and, again, with the mind only in respect of its cognition *à priori*. And the object of our investigations, as it is not to be sought without, but, altogether within, ourselves, cannot remain concealed, and in all probability is limited enough to be completely surveyed and fairly estimated, according to its worth or worthlessness. Still less let the reader here expect a critique of books and systems of pure reason; our present object is exclusively a critique of the faculty of pure reason itself. Only when we make this critique our foundation, do we possess a pure touchstone for estimating the philosophical value of ancient and modern writings on this subject; and without this criterion, the incompetent historian or judge decides upon and corrects the groundless assertions of others with his own, which have themselves just as little foundation.

Transcendental philosophy is the idea of a science, for which the Critique of Pure Reason must sketch the whole plan architectonically, that is, from principles, with a full guarantee for the validity and stability of all the parts which enter into the building. It is the system of all the principles of pure reason. If this Critique itself does not assume the title of transcendental philosophy, it is only because, to be a complete system, it ought to contain a full analysis of all human knowledge *à priori*. Our critique must, indeed, lay before us a complete enumeration of all the radical conceptions which constitute the said pure knowledge. But from the complete analysis of these conceptions themselves, as also from a complete investigation of those derived from them, it abstains with reason; partly because it would be deviating from the end in view to occupy itself with this analysis, since this process is not attended with the difficulty and insecurity to be found in the synthesis, to which our critique is entirely devoted, and partly because it would be inconsistent with the unity of our plan to burden this essay with the vindication of the completeness of such an analysis and deduction, with which, after all, we have at present nothing to do. This completeness of the analysis of these radical conceptions, as well as of the deduction from the conceptions *à priori* which may be given by the analysis, we can, however, easily attain, provided only that we are in possession of all these radical conceptions, which are to serve as principles of the synthesis, and that in respect of this main purpose nothing is wanting.

To the Critique of Pure Reason, therefore, belongs all that constitutes transcendental philosophy; and it is the complete idea of transcendental philosophy, but still not the science itself; because it only proceeds so far with the analysis as is necessary to the power of judging completely of our synthetical knowledge *à priori*.

The principal thing we must attend to, in the division of the parts of a science like this, is: that no conceptions must enter it which contain aught empirical; in other words, that the knowledge *à priori* must be completely pure. Hence, although the highest principles and fundamental conceptions of morality are certainly cognitions *à priori*, yet they do not belong to transcendental philosophy; because, though they certainly do not lay the conceptions of pain, pleasure, desires, inclinations, &c., (which are all of empirical origin), at the foundation of its precepts, yet still into the conception of duty,—as an obstacle to be overcome, or as an incitement which should not be made into a motive,—these empirical conceptions must necessarily enter, in the construction of a system of pure morality. Transcendental philosophy is consequently a philosophy of the pure and merely speculative reason. For all that is practical, so far as it contains motives, relates to feelings, and these belong to empirical sources of cognition.

If we wish to divide this science from the universal point of view of a science in general, it ought to comprehend, first, a Doctrine of the Elements, and, secondly, a Doctrine of the Method of pure reason. Each of these main divisions will have its subdivisions, the separate reasons for which we cannot here particularize. Only so much seems necessary, by way of introduction of premonition, that there are two sources of human knowledge (which probably spring from a common, but to us unknown root), namely, sense and understanding. By the former, objects are given to us; by the latter, thought. So far as the faculty of sense may contain representations *à priori*, which form the conditions under which objects are given, in so far it belongs to transcendental philosophy. The transcendental doctrine of sense must form the first part of our science of elements, because the conditions under which alone the objects of human knowledge are given must precede those under which they are thought.

PROCESS 2A

Modernism, the Beginning
| Rational and Critical Thinking

PROCESS 2B

Artist, Designer, and Engineer
| An Age of New Aesthetics

2B-1

Louis H. Sullivan

The Tall Office Building Artistically Considered

1896

"the life is recognizable in its expression, that form ever follows function. This is the law"

Louis H. Sullivan (1856–1924) was an American architect, often considered the father of the skyscraper, as he codified the construction and appearance of the multistory steel-framed building. Sullivan was a mentor to Frank Lloyd Wright, who was head draftsman for Sullivan's firm, Adler & Sullivan, and an inspiration to the Prairie School of architects. The axiom "form follows function" is credited to Sullivan.

....

1.

The architects of this land and generation are now brought face to face with something new under the sun—namely, that evolution and integration of social conditions, that special grouping of them, that results in a demand for the erection of tall office buildings.

It is not my purpose to discuss the social conditions; I accept them as the fact, and say at once that the design of the tall office building must be recognized and confronted at the outset as a problem to be solved—a vital problem pressing for a true solution.

Let us state the conditions in the plainest manner. Briefly, they are these: offices are necessary for the transaction of business; the invention and perfection of the high-speed elevators make vertical travel, that was once tedious and painful, now easy and comfortable, development of steel manufacture has shown the way to safe, rigid, economical constructions rising to a great height; continued growth of population in the great cities, consequent congestion of centers and rise in value of ground, stimulate an increase in number of stories; these successfully piled one upon another, react on ground values;-and so on, by action and reaction, interaction and inter-reaction. Thus has come about the form of lofty construction called the "modern office building." It has come in answer to a call, for in it a new grouping of social conditions has found a habitation and a name.

Up to this point all in evidence is materialistic, an exhibition of force, of resolution, of brains in the keen sharp sense of the word. It is the joint product of the speculator, the engineer, the builder.

Problem: How shall we impart to this sterile pile, this crude, harsh, brutal agglomeration, this stark, staring exclamation of eternal strife, the graciousness of those higher forms of sensibility and culture that rest on the lower and fiercer passions? How shall we proclaim from the dizzy height of this strange, weird, modern housetop the peaceful evangel of sentiment, of beauty, the cult of a higher life?

This is the problem; and we must seek the solution of it in a process analogous to its own evolution—indeed, a continuation of it—namely, by proceeding step by step from general to special aspects, from coarser to finer considerations.

It is my belief that it is of the very essence of every problem that it contains and suggests its own solution. This I believe to be natural law. Let us examine, then, carefully the elements, let us search out this contained suggestion, this essence of the problem.

The practical conditions are, broadly speaking, these:

Wanted—1st, a story below-ground, containing boilers, engines of various sorts, etc.—in short, the plant for power, heating, lighting, etc. 2nd, a ground floor, so called, devoted to stores, banks, or other establishments requiring large area, ample spacing, ample light, and great freedom of access. 3rd, a second story readily accessible by stairways—this space usually in large subdivisions, with corresponding liberality in structural spacing and expanse of glass and breadth of external openings. 4th, above this an indefinite number of stories of offices piled tier upon tier, one tier just like another tier, one office just like all the other offices—an office being similar to a cell in a honeycomb, merely a compartment, nothing more. 5th and last, at the top of this pile is placed a space or story that, as related to the life and usefulness of the structure, is purely physiological in its nature—namely, the attic. In this the circulatory system completes itself and makes its grand turn, ascending and descending. The space is filled with tanks, pipes, valves, sheaves, and mechanical et cetera that supplement and complement the force-originating plant hidden below-ground in the cellar. Finally, or at the beginning rather, there must be on the ground floor a main aperture or entrance common to all the occupants or patrons of the building.

This tabulation is, in the main, characteristic of every tall office building in the country. As to the necessary arrangements for light courts, these are not germane to the problem, and, as will become soon evident, I trust, need not be considered here. These things, and such others as the arrangement of elevators, for example, have to do strictly with the economics of the building, and I assume them to have been fully considered and disposed of to the satisfaction of purely utilitarian and pecuniary demands. Only in rare instances does the plan or floor arrangement of the tall office building take on an aesthetic value, and this usually when the lighting court is external or becomes an internal feature of great importance.

As I am here seeking not for an individual or special solution, but for a true normal type, the attention must be confined to those conditions that, in the main, are constant in all tall office buildings, and every mere incidental and accidental variation eliminated from the consideration, as harmful to the clearness of the main inquiry.

The practical horizontal and vertical division or office unit is naturally based on a room of comfortable area and height, and the size of this standard office room as naturally predetermines the standard structural unit, and, approximately, the size of window-openings. In turn, these purely arbitrary units of structure form in an equally natural way the true basis of the artistic development of the exterior. Of course the structural spacings and openings in the first or mercantile story are required to be the largest of all; those in the second or quasi-mercantile story are of a somewhat similar nature. The spacings and openings in the attic are of no importance whatsoever (the windows have no actual value), for light may be taken from the top, and no recognition of a cellular division is necessary in the structural spacing.

Hence it follows inevitably, and in the simplest possible way, that if we follow our natural instincts without thought of books, rules, precedents, or any such educational impedimenta to a spontaneous and "sensible" result, we will in the following manner design the exterior of our tall office building—to wit:

Beginning with the first story, we give this a main entrance that attracts the eye to its location, and the remainder of the story we treat in a more or less liberal, expansive, sumptuous way—a way based exactly on the practical necessities, but expressed with a sentiment of largeness and freedom. The second story we treat in a similar way, but usually with milder pretension. Above this, throughout the indefinite number of typical office tiers, we take our cue from the individual cell, which requires a window with its separating pier, its sill and lintel, and we, without more ado, make them look all alike because they are all alike. This brings us to the attic, which, having no division into office-cells, and no special requirement for lighting, gives the power to show by means of its broad expanse of wall, and its dominating weight and character, that which is the fact—namely, that the series of office-tiers has come definitely to an end.

This may perhaps seem a bald result and a heartless, pessimistic way of stating it, but even so we certainly have advanced a most characteristic stage beyond the imagined sinister building of the speculator-engineer-builder combination. For the hand of the architect is now definitely felt in the decisive position at once taken, and the suggestion of a thoroughly sound, logical, coherent expression of the conditions is becoming apparent.

When I say the hand of the architect, I do not mean necessarily the accomplished and trained architect. I mean only a man with a strong, natural liking for buildings, and a disposition to shape them in what seems to his unaffected nature a direct and simple way. He will probably tread an innocent path from his problem to its solution, and therein he will show an enviable gift of logic. If he have some gift for form in detail, some love for that, his result in addition to its simple straightforward naturalness and completeness in general statement will have something of the charm of sentiment.

However, thus far the results are only partial and tentative at best; relatively true, they are but superficial. We are doubtless right in our instinct, but we must seek a fuller justification, a finer sanction, for it.

2.

I assume now that in the study of our problem we have passed through the various stages of inquiry, as follows: 1st, the social basis of the demand for tall office buildings; 2nd, its literal material satisfaction; 3rd, the elevation of the question from considerations of literal planning, construction, and equipment, to the plane of elementary architecture as a direct outgrowth of sound, sensible building; 4th, the question again elevated from an elementary architecture to the beginnings of true architectural expression, through the addition of a certain quality and quantity of sentiment.

But our building may have all these in a considerable degree and yet be far from the adequate solution of the problem I am attempting to define. We must now heed the imperative voice of emotion.

It demands of us, what is the chief characteristic of the tall office building? And at once we answer, it is lofty. This loftiness is to the artist-nature its thrilling aspect. It is the very open organ-tone in its appeal. It must be in turn the dominant chord in his expression of it, the true excitant of his imagination. It must be tall, every inch of it tall. The force and power of altitude must be in it, the glory and pride of exaltation must be in it. It must be every inch a proud and soaring thing, rising in sheer exultation that from bottom to top it is a unit without a single dissenting line—that it is the new, the unexpected, the eloquent peroration of most bald, most sinister, most forbidding conditions.

The man who designs in this spirit and with the sense of responsibility to the generation he lives in must be no coward, no denier, no bookworm, no dilettante. He must live of his life and for his life in the fullest, most consummate sense. He must realize at once and with the grasp of inspiration that the problem of the tall office building is one of the most stupendous, one of the most magnificent opportunities that the Lord of Nature in His beneficence has ever offered to the proud spirit of man. That this has not been perceived—indeed, has been flatly denied—is an exhibition of human perversity that must give us pause.

3.

One more consideration: Let us now lift this question into the region of calm, philosophic observation. Let us seek a comprehensive, a final solution: let the problem indeed dissolve.

Certain critics, and very thoughtful ones, have advanced the theory that the true prototype of the tall office building is the classical column, consisting of base, shaft and capital—the molded base of the column typical of the lower stories of our building, the plain or fluted shaft suggesting the monotonous, uninterrupted series of office-tiers, and the capital the completing power and luxuriance of the attic.

Other theorizers, assuming a mystical symbolism as a guide, quote the many trinities in nature and in art, and the beauty and conclusiveness of such trinity in unity. They aver the beauty of prime numbers, the mysticism of the number three, the beauty of all things that are in three parts—to wit, the day, subdividing into morning, noon, and night; the limbs, the thorax, and the head, constituting the body. So they say, should the building be in three parts vertically, substantially as before, but for different motives.

Others, of purely intellectual temperament, hold that such a design should be in the nature of a logical statement; it should have a beginning, a middle, and an ending, each clearly defined—therefore again a building, as above, in three parts vertically.

Others, seeking their examples and justification in the vegetable kingdom, urge that such a design shall above all things be organic. They quote the suitable flower with its bunch of leaves at the earth, its long graceful stem, carrying the gorgeous single flower. They point to the pine tree—its messy roots, its lithe, uninterrupted trunk, its tuft of green high in the air. Thus, they say, should be the design of the tall office building: again in three parts vertically.

Others still, more susceptible to the power of a unit than to the grace of a trinity, say that such a design should be struck out at a blow, as though by a blacksmith or by mighty Jove, or should be thought-born, as was Minerva, full-grown. They accept the notion of a triple division as permissible and welcome, but non-essential. With them it is a subdivision of their unit; the unit does not come from the alliance of the three; they accept it without murmur, provided the subdivision does not disturb the sense of singleness and repose.

All of these critics and theorists agree, however, positively, unequivocally, in this, that the tall office building should not, must not, be made a field for the display of architectural knowledge in the encyclopedic sense; that too much learning in this instance is fully as dangerous, as obnoxious, as too little learning; that miscellany is abhorrent to their sense; that the sixteen story building must not consist of sixteen separate, distinct, and unrelated buildings piled one upon the other until the top of the pile is reached.

To this latter folly I would not refer were it not the fact that nine out of every ten tall office buildings are designed in precisely this way in effect, not by the ignorant, but by the educated. It would seem, indeed, as though the "trained" architect, when facing this problem, were beset at every story, or, at most, every third or fourth story, by the hysterical dread lest he be in "bad form;" lest he be not bedecking his building with sufficiency of quotation from this, that, or the other "correct" building in some other land and some other time; lest he be not copious enough in the display of his wares; lest he betray, in short, a lack of resources. To loosen up the touch of this cramped and fidgity hand, to allow the nerves to calm, the brain to cool, to reflect equably, to reason naturally, seems beyond him; he lives, as it were, in a waking nightmare filled with the *disjecta membra* of architecture. The spectacle is not inspiriting.

As to the former and serious views held by discerning and thoughtful critics, I shall, with however much of regret, dissent from them for the purpose of this demonstration, for I regard them as secondary only, non-essential, and as touching not at all upon the vital spot, upon the quick of the entire matter, upon the true, the immovable philosophy of the architectural art.

This view let me now state, for it brings to the solution of the problem a final, comprehensive formula:

All things in nature have a shape, that is to say, a form, an outward semblance, that tells us what they are, that distinguishes them from ourselves and from each other.

Unfailingly in nature these shapes express the inner life, the native quality, of the animal, tree, bird, fish, that they present to us; they are so characteristic, so recognizable, that we say simply, it is "natural" it should be so. Yet the moment we peer beneath this surface of things, the moment we look through the tranquil reflection of ourselves and the clouds above us, down into the clear, fluent, unfathomable depth of nature, how startling is the silence of it, how amazing the flow of life, how absorbing the mystery! Unceasingly the essence of things is taking shape in the matter of things, and this unspeakable process we call birth and growth. Awhile the spirit and the matter fade away together, and it is this that we call decadence, death. These two happenings seem jointed and interdependent, blended into one like a bubble and its iridescence, and they seem borne along upon a slowly moving air. This air is wonderful past all understanding.

Yet to the steadfast eye of one standing upon the shore of things, looking chiefly and most lovingly upon that side on which the sun shines and that we feel joyously to be life, the heart is ever gladdened by the beauty, the exquisite spontaneity, with which life seeks and takes on its forms in an accord perfectly responsive to its needs. It seems ever as though the life and the form were absolutely one and inseparable, so adequate is the sense of fulfillment.

Whether it be the sweeping eagle in his flight, or the open apple-blossom, the toiling workhorse, the blithe swan, the branching oak, the winding stream at its base, the drifting clouds, over all the coursing sun, form ever follows function, and this is the law. Where function does not change, form does not change. The granite rocks, the ever-brooding hills, remain for ages; the lightning lives, comes into shape, and dies in a twinkling.

It is the pervading law of all things organic and inorganic, of all things physical and metaphysical, of all things human and all things superhuman, of all true manifestations of the head, of the heart, of the soul, that the life is recognizable in its expression, that form ever follows function. This is the law.

Shall we, then, daily violate this law in our art? Are we so decadent, so imbecile, so utterly weak of eyesight, that we cannot perceive this truth so simple, so very simple? Is it indeed a truth so transparent that we see through it but do not see it? It is really, then, a very marvelous thing, or is it rather so commonplace, so everyday, so near a thing to us, that we cannot perceive that the shape, form, outward expression, design, or what-ever we may choose, of the tall office building should in the very nature of things follow the functions of the building, and that where the function does not change, the form is not to change?

Does this not readily, clearly, and conclusively show that the lower one or two stories will take on a special character suited to the special needs, that the tiers of typical offices, having the same unchanging function, shall continue in the same unchanging form, and that as to the attic, specific and conclusive as it is in its very nature, its function shall equally be so in force, in significance, in continuity, in conclusiveness of outward expression? From this results, naturally, spontaneously, unwittingly, a three-part division—not from any theory, symbol, or fancied logic.

And thus the design of the tall office building takes its place with all other architectural types made when architecture, as has happened once in many years, was a living art. Witness the Greek temple, the Gothic cathedral, the medieval fortress.

And thus, when native instinct and sensibility shall govern the exercise of our beloved art; when the known law, the respected law, shall be that form ever follows function; when our architects shall cease strutting and prattling handcuffed and vainglorious in the asylum of a foreign school; when it is truly felt, cheerfully accepted, that this law opens up the airy sunshine of green fields, and gives to us a freedom that the very beauty and sumptuousness of the outworking of the law itself as exhibited in nature will deter any sane, any sensitive man from changing into license; when it becomes evident that we are merely speaking a foreign language with a noticeable American accent, whereas each and every architect in the land might, under the benign influence of this law, express in the simplest, most modest, most natural way that which it is in him to say: that he might really and would surely develop his own characteristic individuality, and that the architectural art with him would certainly become a living form of speech, a natural form of utterance, giving surcease to him and adding treasures small and great to the growing art of his land; when we know and feel that Nature is our friend, not our implacable enemy—that an afternoon in the country, an hour by the sea, a full open view of one single day, through dawn, high noon, and twilight, will suggest to us so much that is rhythmical, deep, and eternal in the vast art of architecture, something so deep, so true, that all the narrow formalities, hard-and-fast rules, and strangling bonds of the schools cannot stifle it in us— then it may be proclaimed that we are on the high-road to a natural and satisfying art, an architecture that will soon become a fine art in the true, the best sense of the word, an art that will live because it will be of the people, for the people, and by the people.

2B-2

Hermann Muthesius and Henry van de Velde

Werkbund Theses and Antitheses

1907

"standardization, to be understood as the result of a beneficial concentration, will alone make possible the development of a universally valid, unfailing good taste"

"they will protest against every suggestion for the establishment of a canon and for standardization"

Hermann Muthesius (1861–1927) was a German architect and a leader of the Deutscher Werkbund, a state-sponsored group of artists, designers, and architects who sought to merge traditional crafts with mass production. Through his work with the Werkbund, Muthesius would have a significant influence on early modernism in Germany.

Henry van de Velde (1863–1957) was a Belgian architect and interior designer who was a leading proponent of Art Nouveau.

Hermann Muthesius

1. Architecture, and with it the whole area of the Werkbund's activities, is pressing towards standardization, and only through standardization can it recover that universal significance which was characteristic of it in times of harmonious culture.

2. Standardization, to be understood as the result of a beneficial concentration, will alone make possible the development of a universally valid, unfailing good taste.

3. As long as a universal high level of taste has not been achieved, we cannot count on German arts and crafts making their influence effectively felt abroad.

4. The world will demand our products only when they are the vehicles of a convincing stylistic expression. The foundations for this have now been laid by the German movement.

5. The creative development of what has already been achieved is the most urgent task of the age. Upon it the movement's ultimate success will depend. Any relapse and deterioration into imitation would today mean the squandering of a valuable possession.

6. Starting from the conviction that it is a matter of life and death for Germany constantly to ennoble its production, the Deutscher Werkbund, as an association of artists, industrialists, and merchants, must concentrate its attention upon creating the preconditions for the export of its industrial arts.

7. Germany's advances in applied art and architecture must be brought to the attention of foreign countries by effective publicity. Next to exhibitions the most obvious means of doing this is by periodical illustrated publications.

8. Exhibitions by the Deutscher Werkbund are only meaningful when they are restricted radically to the best and most exemplary. Exhibitions of arts and crafts abroad must be looked upon as a national matter and hence require public subsidy.

9. The existence of efficient large-scale business concerns with reliable good taste is a prerequisite of any export. It would be impossible to meet even internal demands with an object designed by the artist for individual requirements.

10. For national reasons, large distributive and transport undertakings whose activities are directed abroad ought to link up with the new movement, now that it has shown what it can do, and consciously represent German art in the world.

Henry van de Velde

1. So long as there are still artists in the Werkbund and so long as they exercise some influence on its destiny, they will protest against every suggestion for the establishment of a canon and for standardization. By his innermost essence the artist is a burning idealist, a free spontaneous creator. Of his own free will he will never subordinate himself to a discipline that imposes upon him a type, a canon. Instinctively he distrusts everything that might sterilize his actions, and everyone who preaches a rule that might prevent him from thinking his thoughts through to their own free end, or that attempts to drive him into a universally valid form, in which he sees only a mask that seeks to make a virtue out of incapacity.

2. Certainly, the artist who practises a "beneficial concentration" has always recognized that currents which are stronger than his own will and thought demand of him that he should acknowledge what is in essential correspondence to the spirit of his age. These currents may be very manifold; he absorbs them unconsciously and consciously as general influences; there is something materially and morally compelling about them for him. He willingly subordinates himself to them and is full of enthusiasm for the idea of a new style *per se*. And for twenty years many of us have been seeking forms and decorations entirely in keeping with our epoch.

3. Nevertheless it has not occurred to any of us that henceforth we ought to try to impose these forms and decorations, which we have sought or found, upon others as standards. We know that several generations will have to work upon what we have started before the physiognomy of the new style is established, and that we can talk of standards and standardization only after the passage of a whole period of endeavours.

4. But we also know that as long as this goal has not been reached our endeavours will still have the charm of creative impetus. Gradually the energies, the gifts of all, begin to combine together, antitheses become neutralized, and at precisely that moment when individual strivings begin to slacken, the physiognomy will be established. The era of imitation will begin and forms and decorations will be used, the production of which no longer calls for any creative impulse: the age of infertility will then have commenced.

5. The desire to see a standard type come into being before the establishment of a style is exactly like wanting to see the effect before the cause. It would be to destroy the embryo in the egg. Is anyone really going to let themselves be dazzled by the apparent possibility of thereby achieving quick results? These premature effects have all the less prospect of enabling German arts and crafts to exercise an effective influence abroad, because foreign countries are a jump ahead of us in the old tradition and the old culture of good taste.

6. Germany, on the other hand, has the great advantage of still possessing gifts which other, older, wearier peoples are losing: the gifts of invention, of brilliant personal brainwaves. And it would be nothing short of castration to tie down this rich, many-sided, creative élan so soon.

7. The efforts of the Werkbund should be directed toward cultivating precisely these gifts, as well as the gifts of individual manual skill, joy, and belief in the beauty of highly differentiated execution, not toward inhibiting them by standardization at the very moment when foreign countries are beginning to take an interest in German work. As far as fostering these gifts is concerned, almost everything still remains to be done.

8. We do not deny anyone's good will, and we are very well aware of the difficulties that have to be overcome in carrying this out. We know that the workers' organization has done a very great deal for the workers' material welfare, but it can hardly find an excuse for having done so little towards arousing enthusiasm for consummately fine workmanship in those who ought to be our most joyful collaborators. On the other hand, we are well aware of the need to export that lies like a curse upon our industry.

9. And yet nothing, nothing good and splendid, was ever created out of mere consideration for exports. Quality will not be created out of the spirit of export. Quality is always first created exclusively for a quite limited circle of connoisseurs and those who commission the work. These gradually gain confidence in their artists; slowly there develops first a narrower, then a national clientele, and only then do foreign countries, does the world slowly take notice of this quality. It is a complete misunderstanding of the situation to make the industrialists believe that they would increase their chances in the world market if they produced *a priori* standardized types for this world market before these types had become well tried common property at home. The wonderful works being exported to us now were none of them originally created for export: think of Tiffany glasses, Copenhagen porcelain, jewellery by Jensen, the books of Cobden-Sanderson, and so on.

10. Every exhibition must have as its purpose to show the world this native quality, and it is quite true that the Werkbund's exhibitions will have meaning only when, as Herr Muthesius so rightly says, they restrict themselves radically to the best and most exemplary.

Adolf Loos

Ornament and Crime

1908

"the enormous damage and devastation caused in aesthetic development by the revival of ornament would be easily made light of, for no one, not even the power of the state, can halt mankind's evolution"

Adolf Loos (1870–1933) was a Czech-Austrian architect and architectural theorist whose critical essays would have a major impact on the development of modern architecture and interiors. "Ornament and Crime" was first delivered as a lecture in Vienna in 1910 and was subsequently published in 1913 in Les Cahiers d'Aujourd'hui.

The human embryo in the womb passes through all the evolutionary stages of the animal kingdom. When man is born, his sensory impressions are like those of a newborn puppy. His childhood takes him through all the metamorphoses of human history. At 2 he sees with the eyes of a Papuan, at 4 with those of an ancient Teuton, at 6 with those of Socrates, at 8 with those of Voltaire. When he is 8 he becomes aware of violet, the colour discovered by the eighteenth century, because before that the violet was blue and the purple-snail red. The physicist points today to colours in the solar spectrum which already have a name but the knowledge of which is reserved for the men of the future.

The child is amoral. To our eyes, the Papuan is too. The Papuan kills his enemies and eats them. He is not a criminal. But when modern man kills someone and eats him he is either a criminal or a degenerate. The Papuan tattoos his skin, his boat, his paddles, in short everything he can lay hands on. He is not a criminal. The modern man who tattoos himself is either a criminal or a degenerate. There are prisons in which eighty per cent of the inmates show tattoos. The tattooed who are not in prison are latent criminals or degenerate aristocrats. If someone who is tattooed dies at liberty, it means he has died a few years before committing a murder.

The urge to ornament one's face and everything within reach is the start of plastic art. It is the baby talk of painting. All art is erotic.

The first ornament that was born, the cross, was erotic in origin. The first work of art, the first artistic act which the first artist, in order to rid himself of his surplus energy, smeared on the wall. A horizontal dash: the prone woman. A vertical dash: the man penetrating her. The man who created it felt the same urge as Beethoven, he was in the same heaven in which Beethoven created the Ninth Symphony.

But the man of our day who, in response to an inner urge, smears the walls with erotic symbols is a criminal or a degenerate. It goes without saying that this impulse most frequently assails people with such symptoms of degeneracy in the lavatory. A country's culture can be assessed by the extent to which its lavatory walls are smeared. In the child this is a natural phenomenon: his first artistic expression is to scribble erotic symbols on the walls. But what is natural to the Papuan and the child is a symptom of degeneracy in the modern adult. I have made the following discovery and I pass it on to the world: The evolution of culture is synonymous with the removal of ornament from utilitarian objects. I believed that with this discovery I was bringing joy to the world; it has not thanked me. People were sad and hung their heads. What depressed them was the realization that they could produce no new ornaments. Are we alone, the people of the nineteenth century, supposed to be unable to do what any Negro, all the races and periods before us have been able to do? What mankind created without ornament in earlier millennia was thrown away without a thought and abandoned to destruction. We possess no joiner's benches from the Carolingian era, but every trifle that displays the least ornament has been collected and cleaned and palatial buildings have been erected to house it. Then people walked sadly about between the glass cases and felt ashamed of their impotence. Every age had its style, is our age alone to be refused a style? By style, people meant ornament. Then I said: Weep not! See, therein lies the greatness of our age, that it is incapable of producing a new ornament. We have outgrown ornament; we have fought our way through to freedom from ornament. See, the time is nigh, fulfilment awaits us. Soon the streets of the city will glisten like white walls. Like Zion, the holy city, the capital of heaven. Then fulfilment will be come.

There were black albs, clerical gentlemen, who wouldn't put up with that. Mankind was to go on panting in slavery to ornament. Men had gone far enough for ornament no longer to arouse feelings of pleasure in them, far enough for a tattooed face not to heighten the aesthetic effect, as among the Papuans, but to reduce it. Far enough to take pleasure in a plain cigarette case, whereas an ornamented one, even at the same price, was not bought. They were happy in their clothes and glad they didn't have to go around in red velvet hose with gold braid like fairground monkeys. And I said: See, Goethe's death-chamber is finer than all Renaissance splendour and a plain piece of furniture more beautiful than any inlaid and carved museum pieces. Goethe's language is finer than all the ornaments of Pegnitz's shepherds.

The black albs heard this with displeasure, and the state, whose task it is to halt the cultural development of the peoples, made the question of the development and revival of ornament its own. Woe to the state whose revolutions are in the care of the *Hofrats*! Very soon we saw in the Wiener Kunstgewerbe museum [Vienna Museum of Applied Art] a sideboard known as "the rich haul of fish," soon there were cupboards bearing the name "the enchanted princess" or something similar referring to the ornament with which this unfortunate piece of furniture was covered. The Austrian state took its task so seriously that it is making sure the foot-rags used on the frontiers of the Austro-Hungarian monarchy do not disappear. It is forcing every cultivated man of 20 for three years to wear foot-rags instead of manufactured footwear. After all, every state starts from the premise that a people on a lower footing is easier to rule.

Very well, the ornament disease is recognized by the state and subsidized with state funds. But I see in this a retrograde step. I don't accept the objection that ornament heightens a cultivated person's joy in life, don't accept the objection contained in the words: "But if the ornament is beautiful!" Ornament does not heighten my joy in life or the joy in life of any cultivated person. If I want to eat a piece of gingerbread I choose one that is quite smooth and not a piece representing a heart or a baby or a rider, which is covered all over with ornaments. The man of the fifteenth century won't understand me. But all modern people will. The advocate of ornament believes that my urge for simplicity is in the nature of a mortification. No, respected professor at the school of applied art, I am not mortifying myself! The show dishes of past centuries, which display all kinds of ornaments to make the peacocks, pheasants and lobsters look more tasty, have exactly the opposite effect on me. I am horrified when I go through a cookery exhibition and think that I am meant to eat these stuffed carcasses. I eat roast beef.

The enormous damage and devastation caused in aesthetic development by the revival of ornament would be easily made light of, for no one, not even the power of the state, can halt mankind's evolution. It can only be delayed. We can wait. But it is a crime against the national economy that it should result in a waste of human labour, money, and material. Time cannot make good this damage.

The speed of cultural evolution is reduced by the stragglers. I perhaps am living in 1908, but my neighbour is living in 1900 and the man across the way in 1880. It is unfortunate for a state when the culture of its inhabitants is spread over such a great period of time. The peasants of Kais are living in the twelfth century. And there were peoples taking part in the Jubilee parade [of the Emperor Franz Joseph] who would have been considered backward even during the migration of the nations. Happy the land that has no such stragglers and marauders. Happy America!

Among ourselves there are unmodern people even in the cities, stragglers from the eighteenth century, who are horrified by a picture with purple shadows because they cannot yet see purple. The pheasant on which the chef has been working all day long tastes better to them and they prefer the cigarette case with Renaissance ornaments to the smooth one. And what is it like in the country? Clothes and household furniture all belong to past centuries. The peasant isn't a Christian, he is still a pagan.

The stragglers slow down the cultural evolution of the nations and of mankind; not only is ornament produced by criminals but also a crime is committed through the fact that ornament inflicts serious injury on people's health, on the national budget and hence on cultural evolution. If two people live side by side with the same needs, the same demands on life and the same income but belonging to different cultures, economically speaking the following process can be observed: the twentieth-century man will get richer and richer, the eighteenth-century man poorer and poorer. I am assuming that both live according to their inclinations. The twentieth-century man can satisfy his needs with a far lower capital outlay and hence can save money. The vegetable he enjoys is simply boiled in water and has a little butter put on it. The other man likes it equally well only when honey and nuts have been added to it and someone has spent hours cooking it. Ornamented plates are very expensive, whereas the white crockery from which the modern man likes to eat is cheap. The one accumulates savings, the other debts. It is the same with whole nations. Woe when a people remains behind in cultural evolution! The British are growing wealthier and we poorer....

Even greater is the damage done by ornament to the nation that produces it. Since ornament is no longer a natural product of our culture, so that it is a phenomenon either of backwardness or degeneration, the work of the ornamentor is no longer adequately remunerated.

The relationship between the earnings of a woodcarver and a turner, the criminally low wages paid to the embroideress and the lacemaker are well known. The ornamentor has to work twenty hours to achieve the income earned by a modern worker in eight. Ornament generally increases the cost of an article; nevertheless it happens that an ornamented object whose raw material cost the same and which demonstrably took three times as long to make is offered at half the price of a smooth object. Omission of ornament results in a reduction in the manufacturing time and an increase in wages. The Chinese carver works for sixteen hours, the American worker for eight. If I pay as much for a smooth cigarette case as for an ornamented one, the difference in the working time belongs to the worker. And if there were no ornament at all—a situation that may perhaps come about in some thousands of years—man would only have to work four hours instead of eight, because half of the work done today is devoted to ornament. Ornament is wasted labour power and hence wasted health. It has always been so.

Since ornament is no longer organically linked with our culture, it is also no longer the expression of our culture. The ornament that is manufactured today has no connexion with us, has absolutely no human connexions, no connexion with the world order. It is not capable of developing. What happened to Otto Eckmann's ornament, or van de Velde's? The artist has always stood at the forefront of mankind full of vigour and health. But the modern ornamentalist is a straggler or a pathological phenomenon. He himself will repudiate his own products three years later. To cultivated people they are immediately intolerable; others become aware of their intolerable character only years later. Where are Otto Eckmann's works today? Modern ornament has no parents and no progeny, no past and no future. By uncultivated people, to whom the grandeur of our age is a book with seven seals, it is greeted joyfully and shortly afterwards repudiated.

Mankind is healthier than ever; only a few people are sick. But these few tyrannize over the worker who is so healthy that he cannot invent ornament. They force him to execute in the most varied materials the ornaments which they have invented.

Changes of ornament lead to a premature devaluation of the labour product. The worker's time and the material employed are capital goods that are wasted. I have stated the proposition: the form of an object lasts, that is to say remains tolerable, as long as the object lasts physically. I will try to explain this. A suit will change its form more often than a valuable fur. A lady's ball gown, intended for only one night, will change its form more quickly than a desk. But woe if a desk has to be changed as quickly as a ball gown because the old form has become intolerable; in that case the money spent on the desk will have been lost.

This is well known to the ornamentalist, and Austrian ornamentalists are trying to make the best of this shortcoming. They say: "We prefer a consumer who has a set of furniture that becomes intolerable to him after ten years, and who is consequently forced to refurnish every ten years, to one who only buys an object when the old one is worn out. Industry demands this. Millions are employed as a result of the quick change."

This seems to be the secret of the Austrian national economy. How often do we hear someone say when there is a fire: "Thank God, now there will be work for people to do again." In that case I know a splendid solution. Set fire to a town, set fire to the empire, and everyone will be swimming in money and prosperity. Manufacture furniture which after three years can be used for firewood, metal fittings that have to be melted down after four years because even at an auction sale it is impossible to get a tenth of the original value of the material and labour, and we shall grow wealthier and wealthier.

The loss does not hit only the consumer; above all it hits the producer. Today ornament on things that have evolved away from the need to be ornamented represents wasted labour and ruined material. If all objects would last aesthetically as long as they do physically, the consumer could pay a price for them that would enable the worker to earn more money and work shorter hours. For an object I am sure I can use to its full extent I willingly pay four times as much as for one that is inferior in form or material. I happily pay forty kronen for my boots, although in a different shop I could get boots for ten kronen. But in those trades that groan under the tyranny of the ornamentalist no distinction is made between good and bad workmanship. The work suffers because no one is willing to pay its true value.

And this is a good thing, because these ornamented objects are tolerable only when they are of the most miserable quality. I get over a fire much more easily when I hear that only worthless trash has been burned. I can be pleased about the trash in the Künstlerhaus because I know that it will be manufactured in a few days and taken to pieces in one. But throwing gold coins instead of stones, lighting a cigarette with a banknote, pulverizing and drinking a pearl create an unaesthetic effect.

Ornamented things first create a truly unaesthetic effect when they have been executed in the best material and with the greatest care and have taken long hours of labour. I cannot exonerate myself from having initially demanded quality work, but naturally not for that kind of thing.

The modern man who holds ornament sacred as a sign of the artistic superabundance of past ages will immediately recognize the tortured, strained, and morbid quality of modern ornaments. No ornament can any longer be made today by anyone who lives on our cultural level.

It is different with the individuals and peoples who have not yet reached this level.

I am preaching to the aristocrat, I mean the person who stands at the pinnacle of mankind and yet has the deepest understanding for the distress and want of those below. He well understands the Kaffir who weaves ornaments into his fabric according to a particular rhythm that only comes into view when it is unravelled, the Persian who weaves his carpet, the Slovak peasant woman who embroiders her lace, the old lady who crochets wonderful things with glass beads and silk. The aristocrat lets them be; he knows that the hours in which they work are their holy hours. The revolutionary would go to them and say: "It's all nonsense." Just as he would pull down the little old woman from the wayside crucifix and tell her: "There is no God." The atheist among the aristocrats, on the other hand, raises his hat when he passes a church.

My shoes are covered all over with ornaments consisting of scallops and holes. Work done by the shoemaker for which he was never paid. I go to the shoemaker and say: "You ask thirty kronen for a pair of shoes. I will pay you forty kronen." I have thereby raised this man to heights of bliss for which he will thank me by work and material infinitely better than would be called for by the additional price. He is happy. Happiness rarely enters his house. Here is a man who understands him, who values his work and does not doubt his honesty. He already sees the finished shoes in his mind's eye. He knows where the best leather is to be found at the present time; he knows which craftsman he will entrust the shoes to; and the shoes will be so covered in scallops and holes as only an elegant shoe can be. And then I say to him: "But there's one condition. The shoes must be completely smooth." With this I have cast him down from the heights of bliss to the pit of despondency. He has less work, but I have taken away all his joy.

I am preaching to the aristocrat. I tolerate ornaments on my own body, when they constitute the joy of my fellow men. Then they are my joy too. I can tolerate the ornaments of the Kaffir, the Persian, the Slovak peasant woman, my shoemaker's ornaments, for they all have no other way of attaining the high points of their existence. We have art, which has taken the place of ornament. After the toils and troubles of the day we go to Beethoven or to Tristan. This my shoemaker cannot do. I mustn't deprive him of his joy, since I have nothing else to put in its place. But anyone who goes to the Ninth Symphony and then sits down and designs a wallpaper pattern is either a confidence trickster or a degenerate. Absence of ornament has brought the other arts to unsuspected heights. Beethoven's symphonies would never have been written by a man who had to walk about in silk, satin, and lace. Anyone who goes around in a velvet coat today is not an artist but a buffoon or a house painter. We have grown finer, more subtle. The nomadic herdsmen had to distinguish themselves by various colours; modern man uses his clothes as a mask. So immensely strong is his individuality that it can no longer be expressed in articles of clothing. Freedom from ornament is a sign of spiritual strength. Modern man uses the ornaments of earlier or alien cultures as he sees fit. He concentrates his own inventiveness on other things.

2B-4

Theo van Doesburg

Concrete Art Manifesto

1918

"the old one is directed towards the individual…the new one is directed towards the universal"

Theo van Doesburg (1883–1931) was a Dutch artist and one of the founders of the De Stijl movement, along with Piet Mondrian. Followers of De Stijl advocated pure abstraction; the restriction of formal elements to essential forms and primary colors; and the integration of design, architecture, and painting.

1. There is an old and a new consciousness of the age. The old one is directed towards the individual. The new one is directed towards the universal. The struggle of the individual against the universal may be seen both in the world war and in modern art.

2. The war is destroying the old world with its content: individual predominance in every field.

3. The new art has brought to light that which is contained in the new consciousness of the age: a relationship of equality between the universal and the individual.

4. The new consciousness of the age is prepared to realize itself in everything, including external life.

5. Tradition, dogmas and the predominance of the individual stand in the way of this realization.

6. Therefore the founders of the new culture call upon all who believe in reform of art and culture to destroy these obstacles to development, just as in the plastic arts—by doing away with natural form—they have eliminated that which stood in the way of pure artistic expression, the logical conclusion of every artistic concept.

7. The artists of today, all over the world, impelled by one and the same consciousness, have taken part on the spiritual plane in the world war against the domination of individualism, of arbitrariness. They therefore sympathize with all who are fighting spiritually or materially for the formation of an international unity in life, art, and culture.

8. The organ *De Stijl*, founded for this purpose, seeks to contribute towards setting the new conception of life in a clear light. The collaboration of all is possible by:
Sending in (to the editorial board) as a proof of agreement the (exact) name, address, and profession.
Contributions in the broadest sense (critical, philosophical, architectural, scientific, literary, musical, etc., as well as reproductions) to the monthly magazine *De Stijl*.
Translation into other languages and propagation of the views published in *De Stijl*

Signatures of the contributors:

Theo van Doesburg, Painter.   *Robt. van't Hoff, Architect.*
Vilmos Huszar, Painter.   *Antony Kok, Poet.*
Piet Mondriaan, Painter.   *G. Vantongerloo, Sculptor.*
Jan Wils, Architect.

PROCESS 2B   81

2B-5

Walter Gropius

Programme of the Staatliches Bauhaus in Weimar

1919

"the old art schools were unable to produce this unity…we must all return to crafts"

Walter Gropius (1883–1969) was a German architect who founded the Bauhaus, a school whose curriculum was based on the union of craft, art, and technology. Gropius had an enormous influence on the development and expansion of modern design and architecture.

The ultimate aim of all visual arts is the complete building! To embellish buildings was once the noblest function of the fine arts; they were the indispensable components of great architecture. Today the arts exist in isolation, from which they can be rescued only through the conscious, co-operative effort of all craftsmen. Architects, painters, and sculptors must recognize anew and learn to grasp the composite character of a building both as an entity and in its separate parts. Only then will their work be imbued with the architectonic spirit which it has lost as 'salon art'.

The old schools of art were unable to produce this unity; how could they, since art cannot be taught. They must be merged once more with the workshop. The mere drawing and painting world of the pattern designer and the applied artist must become a world that builds again. When young people who take a joy in artistic creation once more begin their life's work by learning a trade, then the unproductive 'artist' will no longer be condemned to deficient artistry, for their skill will now be preserved for the crafts, in which they will be able to achieve excellence.

Architects, sculptors, painters, we all must return to the crafts! For art is not a 'profession'. There is no essential difference between the artist and the craftsman. The artist is an exalted craftsman. In rare moments of inspiration, transcending the consciousness of his will, the grace of heaven may cause his work to blossom into art. But proficiency in a craft is essential to every artist. Therein lies the prime source of creative imagination.

Let us then create a new guild of craftsmen without the class distinctions that raise an arrogant barrier between craftsman and artist! Together let us desire, conceive, and create the new structure of the future which will embrace architecture and sculpture and painting in one unity and which will one day rise toward heaven from the hands of a million workers like the crystal symbol of a new faith.

2B-6

Naum Gabo and Norton Pevsner

The Realistic Manifesto (Constructivist Manifesto)

1920

"art is called upon to accompany man everywhere where his tireless life takes place and acts"

Naum Gabo (1890–1977) was a Russian Constructivist sculptor and a pioneer of kinetic art.

Above the tempests of our weekdays,

Across the ashes and cindered homes of the past,

Before the gates of the vacant future,

We proclaim today to you artists, painters, sculptors, musicians, actors, poets...to you people to whom Art is no mere ground for conversation but the source of real exaltation, our word and deed.

The impasse into which Art has come to in the last twenty years must be broken.

The growth of human knowledge with its powerful penetration into the mysterious laws of the world which started at the dawn of this century,

The blossoming of a new culture and a new civilization with their unprecedented-in-history surge of the masses towards the possession of the riches of Nature, a surge which binds the people into one union, and last, not least, the war and the revolution (those purifying torrents of the coming epoch), have made us face the fact of new forms of life, already born and active.

What does Art carry into this unfolding epoch of human history?

Does it possess the means necessary for the construction of the new Great Style?

Or does it suppose that the new epoch may not have a new style?

Or does it suppose that the new life can accept a new creation which is constructed on the foundations of the old?

In spite of the demand of the renascent spirit of our time, Art is still nourished by impression, external appearance, and wanders helplessly back and forth from Naturalism to Symbolism, from Romanticism to Mysticism.

The attempts of the Cubists and the Futurists to lift the visual arts from the bogs of the past have led only to new delusions.

Cubism, having started with simplification of the representative technique, ended with its analysis and stuck there.

The distracted world of the Cubists, broken in shreds by their logical anarchy, cannot satisfy us who have already accomplished the Revolution or who are already constructing and building up anew.

One could heed with interest the experiments of the Cubists, but one cannot follow them, being convinced that their experiments are being made on the surface of Art and do not touch on the bases of it seeing plainly that the end result amounts to the same old graphic, to the same old volume and to the same decorative surface as of old.

One could have hailed Futurism in its time for the refreshing sweep of its announced Revolution in Art, for its devastating criticism of the past, as in no other way could have assailed those artistic barricades of "good taste"…powder was needed for that and a lot of it…but one cannot construct a system of art on one revolutionary phrase alone.

One had to examine Futurism beneath its appearance to realize that one faced a very ordinary chatterer, a very agile and prevaricating guy, clad in the tatters of worn-out words like "patriotism," "militarism," "contempt for the female," and all the rest of such provincial tags.

In the domain of purely pictorial problems, Futurism has not gone further than the renovated effort to fix on the canvas a purely optical reflex which has already shown its bankruptcy with the Impressionists. It is obvious now to every one of us that by the simple graphic registration of a row of momentarily arrested movements, one cannot re-create movement itself. It makes one think of the pulse of a dead body.

The pompous slogan of "Speed" was played from the hands of the Futurists as a great trump. We concede the sonority of that slogan, and we quite see how it can sweep the strongest of the provincials off their feet. But ask any Futurist how does he imagine "speed," and there will emerge a whole arsenal of frenzied automobiles, rattling railway depots, snarled wires, the clank and the noise and the clang of carouseling streets… does one really need to convince them that all that is not necessary for speed and for its rhythms?

Look at a ray of sun...the stillest of the still forces, it speeds more than 300 kilometers in a second...behold our starry firmament...who hears it...and yet what are our depots to those depots of the Universe? What are our earthly trains to those hurrying trains of the galaxies?

Indeed, the whole Futurist noise about speed is too obvious an anecdote, and from the moment that Futurism proclaimed that "Space and Time died yesterday," it sunk into the obscurity of abstractions.

Neither Futurism nor Cubism has brought us what our time has expected of them.

Besides those two artistic schools our recent past has had nothing of importance or deserving attention.

But Life does not wait and the growth of generations does not stop and we go to relieve those who have passed into history, having in our hands the results of their experiments, with their mistakes and their achievements, after years of experience equal to centuries... we say...

No new artistic system will withstand the pressure of a growing new culture until the very foundation of Art will be erected on the real laws of Life.

Until all artists will say with us...

All is a fiction...only life and its laws are authentic and in life only the active is beautiful and wise and strong and right, for life does not know beauty as an aesthetic measure... efficacious existence is the highest beauty.

Life knows neither good nor bad nor justice as a measure of morals...need is the highest and most just of all morals.

Life does not know rationally abstracted truths as a measure of cognizance, deed is the highest and surest of truths.

Those are the laws of life. Can art withstand these laws if it is built on abstraction, on mirage, and fiction?

We say...

Space and time are re-born to us today.

Space and time are the only forms on which life is built and hence art must be constructed.

States, political and economic systems perish, ideas crumble, under the strain of ages...but life is strong and grows and time goes on in its real continuity.

Who will show us forms more efficacious than this…who is the great one who will give us foundations stronger than this?

Who is the genius who will tell us a legend more ravishing than this prosaic tale which is called life?

The realization of our perceptions of the world in the forms of space and time is the only aim of our pictorial and plastic art.

In them we do not measure our works with the yardstick of beauty, we do not weigh them with pounds of tenderness and sentiments.

The plumb-line in our hand, eyes as precise as a ruler, in a spirit as taut as a compass…we construct our work as the universe constructs its own, as the engineer constructs his bridges, as the mathematician his formula of the orbits.

We know that everything has its own essential image; chair, table lamp, telephone, book, house, man…they are all entire worlds with their own rhythms, their own orbits.

That is why we in creating things take away from them the labels of their owners…all accidental and local, leaving only the reality of the constant rhythm of the forces in them.

1. *Thence in painting we renounce color as a pictorial element, color is the idealized optical surface of objects; an exterior and superficial impression of them; color is accidental and has nothing in common with the innermost essence of a thing.*

   We affirm *that the tone of a substance, i.e. its light-absorbing material body is its only pictorial reality.*

2. We renounce *in a line, its descriptive value; in real life there are no descriptive lines, description is an accidental trace of a man on things, it is not bound up with the essential life and constant structure of the body. Descriptiveness is an element of graphic illustration and decoration.*

   We affirm *the line only as a direction of the static forces and their rhythm in objects.*

3. We renounce *volume as a pictorial and plastic form of space; one cannot measure space in volumes as one cannot measure liquid in yards: look at our space…what is it if not one continuous depth?*

   We affirm *depth as the only pictorial and plastic form of space.*

4. We renounce *in sculpture, the mass as a sculptural element. It is known to every engineer that the static forces of a solid body and its material strength do not depend on the quantity of the mass…for example a rail, a T-beam, etc.*

   But you sculptors of all shades and directions, you still adhere to the age-old prejudice that you cannot free the volume of mass. Here (in this exhibition) we take four planes and we construct with them the same volume as of four tons of mass.

Thus we bring back to sculpture the line as a direction and in it we affirm depth as the one form of space.

5. We renounce *the thousand-year-old delusion in art that held the static rhythms as the only elements of the plastic and pictorial arts.*

   We affirm *in these arts a new element the kinetic rhythms as the basic forms of our perception of real time.*

These are the five fundamental principles of our work and our constructive technique.

Today we proclaim our words to you people. In the squares and on the streets we are placing our work convinced that art must not remain a sanctuary for the idle, a consolation for the weary, and a justification for the lazy.

Art should attend us everywhere that life flows and acts…at the bench, at the table, at work, at rest, at play; on working days and holidays…at home and on the road…in order that the flame to live should not extinguish in mankind.

We do not look for justification, neither in the past nor in the future.

Nobody can tell us what the future is and what utensils does one eat it with.

Not to lie about the future is impossible and one can lie about it at will.

We assert that the shouts about the future are for us the same as the tears about the past: a renovated day-dream of the romantics.

A monkish delirium of the heavenly kingdom of the old attired in contemporary clothes.

He who is busy today with the morrow is busy doing nothing.

And he who tomorrow will bring us nothing of what he has done today is of no use for the future.

Today is the deed.

We will account for it tomorrow.

The past we are leaving behind as carrion.

The future we leave to the fortune-tellers.

We take the present day.

Moscow, 5 August 1920

2B-7

Alexander Rodchenko and Varvara Stepanova

Programme of the First Working Group of Constructivists

1922

"prove theoretically and practically the incompatibility of aesthetic activity with the functions of intellectual and material production"

Alexander Rodchenko (1891–1956) was a Russian painter, sculptor, graphic designer, photographer, and one of the founders of Constructivism. His work heavily inspired twentieth-century graphic design.

Varvara Stepanova (1894–1958) was a Russian Constructivist artist and a prominent figure of the avant-garde whose cross-disciplinary work included graphic design, set design, and costume and textiles.

....

The Group of Constructivists has set itself the task of finding *the communistic expression of material structures*.

In approaching its task the group insists on the need to synthesize the ideological aspect with the formal for the real transference of laboratory work onto the rails of practical activity.

Therefore, at the time of its establishment, the group's programme in its ideological aspect pointed out that:

1. Our sole ideology is scientific communism based on the theory of historical materialism.

2. The theoretical interpretation and assimilation of the experience of Soviet construction must impel the group to turn away from experimental activity 'removed from life' towards real experimentation.

3. In order to master the creation of practical structures in a really scientific and disciplined way the Constructivists have established three disciplines: *Tectonics*, *Faktura* and *Construction*.
    A. Tectonics or the tectonic style is tempered and formed on the one hand from the properties of communism and on the other from the expedient use of industrial material.

B. *Faktura* is the organic state of the worked material or the resulting new state of its organism. Therefore, the group considers that *faktura* is material consciously worked and expediently used, without hampering the construction or restricting the tectonics.

C. Construction should be understood as the organizational function of Constructivism.

If tectonics comprises the relationship between the ideological and the formal which gives unity to the practical design, and *faktura* is the material, the Construction reveals the very process of that structuring.

In this way the third discipline is the discipline of the realization of the design through the use of the worked material.

The Material. The material as substance or matter. Its investigation and industrial application, properties and significance. Furthermore, time, space, volume, plane, color, line and light are also material for the Constructivists, without which they cannot construct material structures.

The Immediate Tasks of the Group

1. In the ideological sphere:
   To prove theoretically and practically the incompatibility of aesthetic activity with the functions of intellectual and material production.
   The real participation of intellectual and material production as an equal element in the creation of communist culture.
2. In the practical sphere:
   To publish a statement.
   To publish a weekly paper, VIP [*Vestnik Intellektual'nogo Proizvodstva; The Herald of Intellectual Production*].
   To print brochures and leaflets on questions relating to the activities of the group.
   To construct designs.
   To organize exhibitions.
   To establish links with all the Production Boards and Centres of that unified Soviet machine which in fact practically shapes and produces the emergent forms of the communist way of life.
3. In the agitational sphere:
   i. The Group declares uncompromising war on art.
   ii. It asserts that the artistic culture of the past is unacceptable for the communistic forms of Constructivist structures.

2B-8

László Moholy-Nagy

Constructivism and the Proletariat

1922

"our task to carry the revolution toward reformation, to fight for a new spirit to fill the forms stamped out by the monstrous machine"

László Moholy-Nagy (1895–1946) was a Hungarian painter and photographer, as well as the director of the foundation course at the Bauhaus. After fleeing Europe for the United States in 1937, he went on to found the School of Design in Chicago, which was later absorbed into the Illinois Institute of Technology. Moholy-Nagy's work examines human interaction with the forces of time and light.

....

Reality is the measure of human thinking. It is the means by which we orient ourselves in the Universe. The actuality of time—the reality of this century—determines what we can grasp and what we cannot understand.

And this reality of our century is *technology*—the invention, construction and maintenance of the machine. To be a user of machines is to be of the spirit of this century. It has replaced the transcendental spiritualism of past eras.

Before the machine, everyone is equal—I can use it, so can you—it can crush me and the same can happen to you. There is no tradition in technology, no consciousness of class or standing. Everybody can be the machine's master or its slave.

This is the root of socialism, the final liquidation of feudalism. It is the machine that woke up the proletariat. In serving technology the worker discovered a changed world. We have to eliminate the machine if we want to eliminate socialism. But we all know there is no such thing. This is our century-technology, machine, socialism. Make your peace with it. Shoulder its task.

Because it is our task to carry the revolution toward reformation, to fight for a new spirit to fill the forms stamped out by the monstrous machine. Material well-being does not depend on manufactured goods. Look around. The proletariat isn't happy today in spite of the machine.

Material well-being is caused by the spirit that is superior to the demand of routine work; it is a socialism of the mind, a dedication to the spirit of the group. Only a proletariat, educated to this grasp of essential community, can be satisfied.

Who will teach them? Words are heavy, obscure. Their meaning is evasive to the untrained mind. Past traditions hang on to their meaning. But there is art. Art expresses the spirit of the times; it is art that crystallizes the emotional drive of an age. The art of our century, its mirror and its voice, is Constructivism.

Constructivism is neither proletarian nor capitalist. Constructivism is primordial, without class and without ancestor. It expresses the pure form of nature, the direct color, the spatial element not distorted by utilitarian motifs.

The new world of the proletariat needs Constructivism; it needs fundamentals that are without deceit. Only the natural element, accessible to all eyes, is revolutionary. It has never before been the property of civilized man.

In Constructivism form and substance are one. Not substance and tendency, which are always identified. Substance is essential, but tendency is intentional. Constructivism is pure substance—not the property of one artist alone who drags along under the yoke of individualism. Constructivism is not confined to the picture frame and the pedestal. It expands into industrial design, into houses, objects, forms. It is the socialism of vision— the common property of all men.

Only the today is important for the Constructivist. He cannot indulge in the luxurious speculations of either the Utopian Communist who dreams of a future world domination, or of the bourgeois artist who lives in splendid isolation. It cannot be either proletarian art or art of the precious salons. In Constructivism the process and the goal are one—the spiritual conquest of a century of technology.

2B-9

Le Corbusier

Aesthetic of the Engineer, Architecture
1923

Argument
1923

"the engineer, inspired by the law of economy and governed by mathematical calculation, puts us in accord with universal law"

Le Corbusier (1887–1965) was a Swiss French urban planner, designer, painter, writer, and one of the preeminent architects of the twentieth century. Over his five-decade career as an architect, during which he realized buildings throughout Europe, the Americas, and India, Le Corbusier helped define modernism. Toward an Architecture *is a collection of seven of the architect's essays, most of which had been previously published in* L'Esprit Nouveau, *a journal he had cofounded in 1920.*

···

Aesthetic of the Engineer, Architecture
1923

The Engineer's Aesthetic and Architecture—two things that march together and follow one from the other—the one at its full height, the other in an unhappy state of retrogression.

The Engineer, inspired by the law of Economy and governed by mathematical calculation, puts us in accord with universal law. He achieves harmony.

The Architect, by his arrangement of forms, realizes an order which is a pure creation of his spirit; by forms and shapes he affects our senses to an acute degree, and provokes plastic emotions; by the relationships which he creates he wakes in us profound echoes, he gives us the measure of an order which we feel to be in accordance with that of our world, he determines the various movements of our heart and of our understanding; it is then that we experience the sense of beauty.

The Engineer's aesthetic and Architecture—two things that march together and follow one from the other—the one at its full height, the other in an unhappy state of retrogression. A QUESTION of morality; lack of truth is intolerable, we perish in untruth.

Architecture is one of the most urgent needs of man, for the house has always been the indispensable and first tool that he has forged for himself. Man's stock of tools marks out the stages of civilization, the stone age, the bronze age, the iron age. Tools are the result of successive improvement; the effort of all generations is embodied in them. The tool is the direct and immediate expression of progress; it gives man essential assistance and essential freedom also. We throw the out-of-date tool on the scrap-heap: the carbine, the culverin, the growler and the old locomotive. This action is a manifestation of health, of moral health, of *morale* also; it is not right that we should produce bad things because of a bad tool; nor is it right that we should waste our energy, our health and our courage because of a bad tool; it must be thrown away and replaced.

But men live in old houses and they have not yet thought of building houses adapted to themselves. The lair has been dear to their hearts since all time. To such a degree and so strongly that they have established the cult of the home. A roof! then other household gods. Religions have established themselves on dogmas, the dogmas do not change; but civilizations change and religions tumble to dust. Houses have not changed. But the cult of the house has remained the same for centuries. The house will also fall to dust.

A man who practices a religion and does not believe in it is a poor wretch; he is to be pitied. We are to be pitied for living in unworthy houses, since they ruin our health and our morale. It is our lot to have become sedentary creatures; our houses gnaw at us in our sluggishness, like a consumption, We shall soon need far too many sanatoriums. We are to be pitied. Our houses disgust us; we fly from them and frequent restaurants and night clubs; or we gather together in our houses gloomily and secretly like wretched animals; we are becoming demoralized.

Engineers fabricate the tools of their time. Everything, that is to say, except houses and moth-eaten boudoirs.

There exists in France a great national school of architecture, and there are, in every country, architectural schools of various kinds, to mystify young minds and teach them dissimulation and the obsequiousness of the toady. National schools!

Our engineers are healthy and virile, active and useful, balanced and happy in their work. Our architects are disillusioned and unemployed, boastful or peevish. This is because there will soon be nothing more for them to do. We no longer have the money to erect historical souvenirs. At the same time, we have got to wash!

Our engineers provide for these things and they will be our builders.

Nevertheless there does exist this thing called ARCHITECTURE, an admirable thing, the loveliest of all. A product of happy peoples and a thing which in itself produces happy peoples.

The happy towns are those that have an architecture.

Architecture can be found in the telephone and in the Parthenon. How easily could it be at home in our houses! Houses make the street and the street makes the town and the town is a personality which takes to itself a soul, which can feel, suffer and wonder. How at home architecture could be in street and town!

The diagnosis is clear.

Our engineers produce architecture, for they employ a mathematical calculation which derives from natural law, and their works give us the feeling of HARMONY. The engineer therefore has his own aesthetic, for he must, in making his calculations, qualify some of the terms of his equation; and it is here that taste intervenes. Now, in handling a mathematical problem, a man is regarding it from a purely abstract point of view, and in such a state, his taste must follow a sure and certain path.

Architects, emerging from the Schools, those hot-houses where blue hortensias and green
chrysanthemums are forced, and where unclean orchids are cultivated, enter into the town in the spirit of a milkman who should, as it were, sell his milk mixed with vitriol or poison.[1]

People still believe here and there in architects, as they believe blindly in all doctors. It is very necessary, of course, that houses should hold together! It is very necessary to have recourse to the man of art! Art, according to Larousse, is the application of knowledge to the realization of a conception. Now, to-day, it is the engineer who knows, who knows the best way to construct, to heat, to ventilate, to light. It is not true? Our diagnosis is that, to begin at the beginning, the engineer who proceeds by knowledge shows the way and holds the truth. It is that architecture, which is a matter of plastic emotion, should in its own domain BEGIN AT THE BEGINNING ALSO, AND SHOULD USE THOSE ELEMENTS WHICH ARE CAPABLE OF AFFECTING OUR SENSES, AND OF REWARDING THE DESIRE OF OUR EYES, and should dispose them in such a way THAT THE SIGHT OF THEM AFFECTS US IMMEDIATELY by their delicacy or their brutality, their riot or their serenity, their indifference or their interest; these elements are plastic elements, forms which our eyes see clearly and which our mind can measure. These forms, elementary or subtle, tractable or brutal, work physiologically upon our senses (sphere, cube, cylinder, horizontal, vertical, oblique, etc.), and excite them. Being moved, we are able to get beyond the cruder sensations; certain relationships are thus born which work upon our perceptions and put us into a state of satisfaction (in consonance with the laws of the universe which govern us and to which all our acts are subjected), in which man can employ fully his gifts of memory, of analysis, of reasoning and of creation.

Architecture to-day is no longer conscious of its own beginnings.

Architects work in "styles" or discuss questions of structure in and out of season; their clients, the public, still think in terms of conventional appearance, and reason on the foundations of an insufficient education. Our external world has been enormously transformed in its outward appearance and in the use made of it, by reason of the machine. We have gained a new perspective and a new social life, but we have not yet adapted the house thereto.

1 *I have not felt it incumbent upon me to modify somewhat rhetorical passages such as the above. -Trans.*

The time has therefore come to put forward the problem of the house, of the street and of the town, and to deal with both the architect and the engineer. For the architect we have written our "THREE REMINDERS."

- MASS which is the element by which our senses perceive and measure and are most fully affected.
- SURFACE which is the envelope of the mass and which can diminish or enlarge the sensation the latter gives us.
- PLAN which is the generator both of mass and surface and is that by which the whole is irrevocably fixed.

Then, still for the architect, "REGULATING LINES" showing by these one of the means by which architecture achieves that tangible form of mathematics which gives us such a grateful perception of order. We wished to set forth facts of greater value than those in many dissertations on the soul of stones. We have confined ourselves to the natural philosophy of the matter, to things that can be known.

We have not forgotten the dweller in the house and the crowd in the town. We are well aware that a great part of the present evil state of architecture is due to the client, to the man who gives the order, who makes his choice and alters it and who pays. For him we have written "EYES WHICH DO NOT SEE."

We are all acquainted with too many big business men, bankers and merchants, who tell us: "Ah, but I am merely a man of affairs, I live entirely outside the art world, I am a Philistine." We protest and tell them: "All your energies are directed towards this magnificent end which is the forging of the tools of an epoch, and which is creating throughout the whole world this accumulation of very beautiful things in which economic law reigns supreme, and mathematical exactness is joined to daring and imagination. That is what you do; that, to be exact, is Beauty."

One can see these same business men, bankers and merchants, away from their businesses in their own homes, where everything seems to contradict their real existence—rooms too small, a conglomeration of useless and disparate objects, and a sickening spirit reigning over so many shams—Aubusson, Salon d'Automne, styles of all sorts and absurd bric-á-brac. Our industrial friends seem sheepish and shriveled like tigers in a cage—it is very clear that they are happier at their factories or in their banks. We claim, in the name of the steamship, of the airplane, and of the motor-car, the right to health, logic, daring, harmony, perfection.

We shall be understood. These are evident truths. It is not foolishness to hasten forward a clearing up of things.

Finally, it will be a delight to talk of ARCHITECTURE after so many grain-stores, workshops, machines and sky-scrapers. ARCHITECTURE is a thing of art, a phenomenon of the emotions, lying outside questions of construction and beyond them. The purpose of construction is TO MAKE THINGS HOLD TOGETHER; of architecture To MOVE US. Architectural emotion exists when the work rings within us in tune with a universe whose laws we obey, recognize and respect. When certain harmonies have been attained, the work captures us. Architecture is a matter of "harmonies," it is "a pure creation of the spirit."

Today, painting has outsped the other arts.

It is the first to have attained attunement with the epoch.[2] Modern painting has left on one side wall decoration, tapestry and the ornamental urn and has sequestered itself in a frame-flourishing, full of matter, far removed from a distracting realism; it lends itself to meditation.
Art is no longer anecdotal, it is a source of meditation; after the day's work it is good to meditate.

On the one hand the mass of people look for a decent dwelling, and this question is of burning importance.

On the other hand the man of initiative, of action, of thought, the LEADER, demands a shelter for his meditations in a quiet and sure spot; a problem which is indispensable to the health of specialized people.

Painters and sculptors, champions of the art of to-day, you who have to bear so much mockery and who suffer so much indifference, let us purge our houses, give your help that we may reconstruct our towns. Your works will then be able to take their place in the framework of the period and you will everywhere be admitted and understood. Tell yourselves that architecture has indeed need of your attention. Do not forget the problem of architecture.

---

2   *I mean, of course, the vital change brought about by cubism and later researches, and not the lamentable fall from grace which has for the last two years seized upon painters, distracted by lack of sales and taken to task by critics as little instructed as sensitive (1921).*

"we must create the mass-production spirit"

Argument
1923

....

THREE REMINDERS TO ARCHITECTS

MASS

Our eyes are constructed to enable us to see forms in light.

Primary forms are beautiful forms because they can be clearly appreciated.

Architects today no longer achieve these simple forms.

Working by calculation, engineers employ geometrical forms, satisfying our eyes by their geometry and our understanding by their mathematics; their work is on the direct line of good art.

SURFACE

A mass is enveloped in its surface, a surface which is divided up according to the directing and generating lines of the mass; and this gives the mass its individuality.

Architects today are afraid of the geometrical constituents of surfaces.

The great problems of modern construction must have a geometrical solution.

Forced to work in accordance with the strict needs of exactly determined conditions, engineers make use of generating and accusing lines in relation to forms. They create limpid and moving plastic facts.

PLAN

The Plan is the generator.

Without a plan, you have lack of order, and willfulness.

The Plan holds in itself the essence of sensation.

The great problems of to-morrow, dictated by collective necessities, put the question of "plan" in a new form.

Modern life demands, and is waiting for, a new kind of plan, both for the house and for the city.

REGULATING LINES

An inevitable element of Architecture.

The necessity for order. The regulating line is a guarantee against willfulness. It brings satisfaction to the understanding.

The regulating line is a means to an end; it is not a recipe. Its choice and the modalities of expression given to it are an integral part of architectural creation.

EYES WHICH DO NOT SEE

LINERS

A great epoch has begun.

There exists a new spirit.

There exists a mass of work conceived in the new spirit; it is to be met with particularly in industrial production.

Architecture is stifled by custom.

The "styles" are a lie.

Style is a unity of principle animating all the work of an epoch, the result of a state of mind which has its own special character.

Our own epoch is determining, day by day, its own style.

Our eyes, unhappily, are unable yet to discern it.

AIRPLANES

The airplane is the product of close selection.

The lesson of the airplane lies in the logic which governed the statement of the problem and its realization.

The problem of the house has not yet been stated.

Nevertheless there do exist standards for the dwelling house.

Machinery contains in itself the factor of economy, which makes for selection. The house is a machine for living in.

AUTOMOBILES

We must aim at the fixing of standards in order to face the problem of perfection.

The Parthenon is a product of selection applied to a standard.

Architecture operates in accordance with standards.

Standards are a matter of logic, analysis and minute study; they are based on a problem which has been well "stated." A standard is definitely established by experiment.

ARCHITECTURE

THE LESSON OF ROME

The business of Architecture is to establish emotional relationships by means of raw materials.

Architecture goes beyond utilitarian needs.

Architecture is a plastic thing.

The spirit of order, a unity of intention.

The sense of relationships; architecture deals with quantities.

Passion can create drama out of inert stone.

The Plan proceeds from within to without; the exterior is the result of an interior.

The elements of architecture are light and shade, walls and space.

Arrangement is the gradation of aims, the classification of intentions.

Man looks at the creation of architecture with his eyes, which are 5 feet 6 inches from the ground. One can only deal with aims which the eye can appreciate, and intentions which take into account architectural elements. If there come into play intentions which do not speak the language of architecture, you arrive at the illusion of plans, you transgress the rules of the Plan through an error in conception, or through a leaning towards empty show.

PURE CREATION OF THE MIND

Contour and profile[1] are the touchstone of the architect.

Here he reveals himself as artist or mere engineer.

Contour is free of all constraint.

There is here no longer any question of custom, nor of tradition, nor of construction nor of adaptation to utilitarian needs.

Contour and profile are a pure creation of the mind; they call for the plastic artist.

MASS-PRODUCTION HOUSES

A great epoch has begun.

There exists a new spirit.

Industry, overwhelming us like a flood which rolls on towards its destined ends, has furnished us with new tools adapted to this new epoch, animated by the new spirit. Economic law inevitably governs our acts and our thoughts.

The problem of the house is a problem of the epoch. The equilibrium of society to-day depends upon it. Architecture has for its first duty, in this period of renewal, that of bringing about a revision of values, a revision of the constituent elements of the house. Mass-production is based on analysis and experiment.

Industry on the grand scale must occupy itself with building and establish the elements of the house on a mass-production basis.

1 *Modénature. The nearest equivalent of Le Corbusier's use of this word.—Trans.*

We must create the mass-production spirit.

The spirit of constructing mass-production houses.

The spirit of living in mass-production houses. The spirit of conceiving mass-production houses.

If we eliminate from our hearts and minds all dead concepts in regard to the house, and look at the question from a critical and objective point of view, we shall arrive at the "House-Machine," the mass-production house, healthy (and morally so too) and beautiful in the same way that the working tools and instruments which accompany our existence are beautiful.

Beautiful also with all the animation that the artist's sensibility can add to severe and pure functioning elements.

ARCHITECTURE OR REVOLUTION

In every field of industry, new problems have presented themselves and new tools have been created capable of resolving them. If this new fact be set against the past, then you have revolution.

In building and construction, mass-production has already been begun; in the face of new economic needs, mass-production units have been created both in mass and detail; and definite results have been achieved both in detail and in mass. If this fact be set against the past, then you have revolution, both in the method employed and in the large scale on which it has been carried out.

The history of Architecture unfolds itself slowly across the centuries as a modification of structure and ornament, but in the last fifty years steel and concrete have brought new conquests, which are the index of a greater capacity for construction, and of an architecture in which the old codes have been overturned. If we challenge the past, we shall learn that "styles" no longer exist for us, that a style belonging to our own period has come about; and there has been a Revolution.

Our minds have consciously or unconsciously apprehended these events and new needs have arisen, consciously or unconsciously.

The machinery of Society, profoundly out of gear, oscillates between an amelioration, of historical importance, and a catastrophe.

The primordial instinct of every human being is to assure himself of a shelter. The various classes of workers in society to-day no longer have dwellings adapted to their needs; neither the artizan nor the intellectual.

It is a question of building which is at the root of the social unrest of to-day: architecture or revolution.

Ludwig Mies van der Rohe

Architecture and the Times
1924

Aphorisms on Architecture and Form
1923

On Form in Architecture
1927

"our utilitarian buildings can become worthy of the name of architecture only if they truly interpret their time by their perfect functional expression"

Ludwig Mies van der Rohe (1886–1969) was a pioneer of modernism. His designs, which integrated industrial materials and employed open plans, established a minimalist vocabulary for modern architecture.

....

Architecture and the Times
1924

Greek temples, Roman basilicas and medieval cathedrals are significant to us as creations of a whole epoch rather than as works of individual architects. Who asks for the names of these builders? Of what significance are the fortuitous personalities of their creators? Such buildings are impersonal by their very nature. They are pure expressions of their time. Their true meaning is that they are symbols of their epoch.

Architecture is the will of the epoch translated into space. Until this simple truth is clearly recognized, the new architecture will be uncertain and tentative. Until then it must remain a chaos of undirected forces. The question as to the nature of architecture is of decisive importance. It must be understood that all architecture is bound up with its own time, that it can only be manifested in living tasks and in the medium of its epoch. In no age has it been otherwise.

It is hopeless to try to use the forms of the past in our architecture. Even the strongest artistic talent must fail in this attempt. Again and again we see talented architects who fall short because their work is not in tune with their age. In the last analysis, in spite of their great gifts, they are dilettantes; for it makes no difference how enthusiastically they do the wrong thing. It is a question of essentials. It is not possible to move forward and look backwards; he who lives in the past cannot advance.

The whole trend of our time is toward the secular. The endeavors of the mystics will be remembered as mere episodes. Despite our greater understanding of life, we shall build no cathedrals. Nor do the brave gestures of the Romantics mean anything to us, for behind them we detect their empty form. Ours is not an age of pathos; we do not respect flights of the spirit as much as we value reason and realism.

The demand of our time for realism and functionalism must be met. Only then will our buildings express the potential greatness of our time; and only a fool can say that it has no greatness.

We are concerned today with questions of a general nature. The individual is losing significance; his destiny is no longer what interests us. The decisive achievements in all fields are impersonal and their authors are for the most part unknown. They are part of the trend of our time toward anonymity. Our engineering structures are examples. Gigantic dams, great industrial installations and huge bridges are built as a matter of course, with no designer's name attached to them. They point to the technology of the future.

If we compare the mammoth heaviness of Roman aqueducts with the web-like lightness of modern cranes or massive vaulting with thin reinforced concrete construction, we realize how much our architecture differs from that of the past in form and expression. Modern industrial methods have had a great influence on this development. It is meaningless to object that modern buildings are only utilitarian.

If we discard all romantic conceptions, we can recognize the stone structures of the Greeks, the brick and concrete construction of the Romans and the medieval cathedrals, all as bold engineering achievements. It can be taken for granted that the first Gothic buildings were viewed as intruders in their Romanesque surroundings.

Our utilitarian buildings can become worthy of the name of architecture only if they truly interpret their time by their perfect functional expression.

"form is not the aim of our work, but only the result"

Aphorisms on Architecture and Form
1923

We reject all aesthetic speculation, all doctrine, all formalism.

Architecture is the will of an epoch translated into space; living, changing, new.

Not yesterday, not tomorrow, only today can be given form.

Only this kind of building will be creative.

Create form out of the nature of our tasks with the methods of our time.

This is our task.

We refuse to recognize problems of form, but only problems of building.

Form is not the aim of our work, but only the result.

Form, by itself, does not exist.

Form as an aim is formalism; and that we reject.

Essentially our task is to free the practice of building from the control of aesthetic speculators and restore it to what it should exclusively be: building.

"we do not evaluate the result but the starting point of the creative process"

On Form in Architecture
1927

....

I do not oppose form, but only form as a goal.
And I do this as the result of a number of experiences and the insight I have gained from them.

Form as a goal always ends in formalism.
For this striving is directed not towards an inside, but towards an outside.
But only a living inside has a living outside.

Only intensity of life has intensity of form.
Every How is carried by a What.
The unformed is not worse than the over-formed.
The former is nothing; the latter is mere appearance.
Real form presupposes real life.
But not something that has already existed, nor something thought out.

Here lies the criterion.

We do not evaluate the result but the starting point of the creative process.
Precisely this shows whether the form was discovered by starting from life, or for its own sake.

That is why I consider the creative process so essential.
Life is for us the decisive factor.
In all its fullness, in its spiritual and real commitments.

Is not one of the Werkbund's most important tasks to illuminate, to make visible, the spiritual and real situation in which we stand, to order its currents and thereby to lead the way? Must we not leave everything else to the creative powers?

Hannes Meyer

Building

1928

"building is a biological process. building is not an aesthetic process"

Hannes Meyer (1889–1954) was a Swiss architect who became director of the Bauhaus following the departure of the school's founding director, Walter Gropius. Meyer's doctrine rejected aesthetics in favor of functionalism that would support all people rather than just the elite.

....

building
all things in this world are a product of the formula: (function times economy).

all these things are, therefore, not works of art:
all art is composition and, hence, is unsuited to achieve goals.
all life is function and is therefore unartistic.
the idea of the "composition of a harbour" is hilarious!
but how is a town plan designed? or a plan of a dwelling? composition or function? art or
life?????

building is a biological process. building is not an aesthetic process.
in its design the new dwelling becomes not only a "machine for living", but also a biological apparatus serving the needs of body and mind.
the new age provides new building materials for the new way of building houses:

reinforced concrete	aluminium	ripolin
synthetic rubber	euböolith	viscose
synthetic leather	plywood	asbestos concrete
porous concrete	hard rubber	bitumen
woodmetal	torfoleum	canvas
wire-mesh glass	silicon steel	asbestos
pressed cork	cold glue	acetone
synthetic resin	cellular concrete	casein
synthetic horn	rolled glass	trolite
synthetic wood	xelotect	tombac

we organize these building materials into a constructive whole based on economic principles. thus the individual shape, the body of the structure, the colour of the material and the surface texture evolve by themselves and are determined by life. (snugness and prestige are not leitmotifs for dwelling construction.) (the first depends on the human heart and not on the walls of a room...) (the second manifests itself in the manner of the host and not by his persian carpet!)

architecture as "an emotional act of the artist" has no justification.
architecture as "a continuation of the traditions of building" means being carried along by the history of architecture.
this functional, biological interpretation of architecture as giving shape to the functions of life, logically leads to pure construction: this world of constructive forms knows no native country. it is the expression of an international attitude in architecture. internationality is a privilege of the period.
pure construction is the basis and the characteristic of the new world of forms.

1. sex life	5. personal hygiene	9. cooking
2. sleeping habits	6. weather protection	10. heating
3. pets	7. hygiene in the home	11. exposure to the sun
4. gardening	8. car maintenance	12. service

these are the only motives when building a house. we examine the daily routine of everyone who lives in the house and this gives us the function-diagram for the father, the mother, the child, the baby and the other occupants. we explore the relationships of the house and its occupants to the world outside: postman, passer-by, visitor, neighbour, burglar, chimney-sweep, washerwoman, policeman, doctor, charwoman, playmate, gas inspector, tradesman, nurse, and messenger boy. we explore the relationships of human beings and animals to the garden, and the interrelationships between human beings, pets, and domestic insects. we determine the annual fluctuations in the temperature of the ground and from that calculate the heat loss of the floor and the resulting depth required for the foundation blocks. the geological nature of the soil informs us about its capillary capability and determines whether water will naturally drain away or whether drains are required. we calculate the angle of the sun's incidence during the course of the year according to the latitude of the site. with that information we determine the size of the shadow cast by the house on the garden and the amount of sun admitted by the window into the bedroom. we estimate the amount of daylight available for interior working areas. we compare the heat conductivity of the outside walls with the humidity of the air outside the house. we already know about the circulation of air in a heated room. the visual and acoustical relationships to neighbouring dwellings are most carefully considered. knowing the atavistic inclinations of the future inhabitants with respect to the kind of wood finish we can offer, we select the interior finish for the standardized, prefabricated dwelling accordingly: marble-grained pine, austere poplar, exotic okumé or silky maple. colour to us is merely a means for intentional psychological influence or a means of orientation. colour is never a false copy of various kinds of material. we loathe variegated colour. we consider paint to be a protective coating. where we think colour to be psychically indispensable, we include in our calculation the amount of light reflection it offers. we avoid using a purely white finish on the house. we consider the body of the house to be an accumulator of the sun's warmth...

the new house is a prefabricated building for site assembly; as such it is an industrial product and the work of a variety of specialists: economists, statisticians, hygienists, climatologists, industrial engineers, standardization experts, heating engineers...and the architect?... he was an artist and now becomes a specialist in organization!

the new house is a social enterprise. it frees the building industry from partial seasonal unemployment and from the odium of unemployment relief work. by rationalized house-keeping methods it saves the housewife from household slavery, and by rationalized gardening methods it protects the householder from the dilettantism of the small gardener. it is primarily a social enterprise because it is—like every government standard—the standardized, industrial product of a nameless community of inventors.

the new housing project as a whole is to be the ultimate aim of public welfare and as such is an intentionally organized, public-spirited project in which collective and individual energies are merged in a public-spiritedness based on an integral, co-operative foundation. the modernness of such an estate does not consist of a flat roof and a horizontal-vertical arrangement of the façade, but rather of its direct relationship to human existence. in it we have given thoughtful consideration to the tensions of the individual, the sexes, the neighbourhood and the community, as well as to geophysical relationships.

building   is the deliberate organization of the processes of life.
building   as a technical process is therefore only one part of the whole process. the functional diagram and the economic programme are the determining principles of the building project.
building   is no longer an individual task for the realization of architectural ambitions.
building   is the communal effort of craftsmen and inventors. only he who, as a master in the working community of others, masters life itself...is a master builder.
building   then grows from being an individual affair of individuals (promoted by unemployment and the housing shortage) into a collective affair of the whole nation.
building   is nothing but organization:
social, technical, economic, psychological organization.

Theo van Doesburg

Manifesto of Concrete Art

1930

"an effort toward absolute clarity is mandatory"

Theo van Doesburg (1883–1931) was a Dutch artist and one of the founders of the De Stijl movement, along with Piet Mondrian. Followers of De Stijl advocated pure abstraction; the restriction of formal elements to essential forms and primary colors; and the integration of design, architecture, and painting.

BASIS OF CONCRETE PAINTING

We say:

1. Art is universal.

2. A work of art must be entirely conceived and shaped by the mind before its execution. It shall not receive anything of nature's or sensuality's or sentimentality's formal data. We want to exclude lyricism, drama, symbolism, and so on.

3. The painting must be entirely built up with purely plastic elements, namely surfaces and colors. A pictorial element does not have any meaning beyond "itself"; as a consequence, a painting does not have any meaning other than "itself".

4. The construction of a painting, as well as that of its elements, must be simple and visually controllable.

5. The painting technique must be mechanic, i.e., exact, anti-impressionistic.

6. An effort toward absolute clarity is mandatory.

Carlsund, Doesbourg, Helion, Tutundjian, and Wantz.

Alexey Brodovitch

What Pleases the Modern Man

1930

"present-day life: industrialization, mechanization, standardization and consequently, competition and speed, requires astuteness and intensity of thought"

Alexey Brodovitch (1898–1971) was a Russian-born photographer and art director who oversaw Harper's Bazaar from 1934 to 1958. His innovative graphic design often employed montage, playful typography, and full-page bleeds.

....

Present-day life: industrialization, mechanization, standardization and consequently, competition and speed, requires astuteness and intensity of thought. The man of today is of an extremely inventive nature and is seeking for the improvement of living. The precepts of comfort, utility and standardization come first in every field.

Standardization and ever-increasing competition, two factors of modern life, disclose a new and interesting chapter in the history of culture, at the same time bringing into it elements of a paradox: standardization—competition, simplification—elaboration. The solving of these problems in Publicity is of primary importance.

Publicity is full of contrast and paradox. Publicity is born of life and life is learned through publicity. Publicity no longer serves merely for the pushing of single products such as soap, sewing machines and spaghetti. Publicity is bigger, deeper and more universal.

If we think of Publicity as art, I would prefer not to call it Applied-Art, as it is generally known, but rather, I should call it Deep-Art as in contrast to the term Fine-Art.

We are living in the age of research and great achievements: electricity, radio, television, aviation, movies, automobiles, and Einstein, Edison, Marconi, Mussolini, Lenin, and Lindberg.

These achievements, on the one hand, have changed our psychology, giving us new images and new understanding; on the other hand, because of the ever accelerating tempo of life they have dulled our sensitivity to thrills and exclamation. No longer do we marvel at fantastic possibilities when each day on picking up the paper we read of record-breaking cars, or that Marconi on his luxurious yacht near Naples has touched a button which turns on myriads of electric lights in Australia to announce the opening of the electrical exposition, or again an article on the project of drying up the North Sea.

How much of this new understanding of form, mass, plastic, dynamic, color, light, and shadow and perspective is given us by engineering!

The eye of man is trained and sharpened by his daily work, and has become too much the slave of tradition and atavism.

The projector, the lens, even the simple prism, give us a new aspect of the things about us.

The ray of the spotlight piercing the darkness proves the existence of profundity, it shows the third dimension and possibly even the fourth dimension. It reveals and explains the variety of textures, forms, and reliefs.

The lens of a Kodak presents a new understanding of foreshortening and perspective. The movie camera solves the problems of plastic, dynamic, rhythm, and the aesthetic of deformation of objects in motion.

The spectroscope, or the prism, demolishes the existing signification of color, and offers the possibility of explaining form by a different use of color.

The telescope and the microscope reveal to us the infinity of the greatest and the least.

The airplane forces upon us the understanding of cosmic velocity and space.

The television apparatus proves, with lightning speed, a new and definite idea of distance.

In the monotony and drudgery of our work-a-day world there is to be found new beauty and a new aesthetic:

The blinking lights of the city.

The surface of a revolving phonograph record.

The fantastic reflection of the red taillight and the tread of an automobile tire on the wet pavement.

The romanticism of a night landscape revealed by the light of an automobile.

The lyricism of the steel pistons, connection-rods and cogwheels in motion.

The heroism and daring in the silhouette of an airplane.

The harmonious grace of the wireless tower.

The moving static and grandeur of a liner.

The dynamic immensity of a locomotive.

The aesthetic of duco-lacquer, concrete, and chromium steel.

The rhythm of the barographical or statistical diagram.

The primitive precision of the hieroglyphs of stenography.

The science of the underground railway.

The semaphores, traffic lights, and policemen.

The symbol of the circle on the face of a clock.

The deformation of the wheel circle in becoming an ellipse on the photograph of a racing automobile.

Consider the new aesthetic, the new understanding, rhythm, movement, matter…Consider the endless possibilities of these new ideas.

Industry today gives the publicity artist not only a new vision but also a variety of new materials and instruments as a means for realizing advertising ideas.

Zinc, hard rubber, glass, sensitive film and paper, celluloid, galalith, lumarith, and ebonoid can easily and adequately take the place of cumbersome lithographic stone, expensive box-wood and steel and copper which are difficult to work. At the same time these materials offer a new medium of expression and may give entirely new effects.

Industrial lacquers, air brush, a thin ray of light, perfected hard, flexible steel needles, surgical knives, and even dental implements may also adequately take the place of watercolors, undurable and clumsy brushes, and charcoal pens and crayons.

Hand-made engraving and printing are things of the past, and while they have not yet become anachronisms, their proper place should be on the dusty shelves of snobbish collectors.

Modern and contemporary technical methods of reproduction and printing such as tepo, helio, and offset open up colossal potentialities for the publicity artist.

Study the screens and plates, watch the revolutions of cylinders in a printing press, follow the work of the linotypist, examine even the discarded first proofs and we may find many new and purely graphic possibilities which may endlessly enlarge the horizon of artistic conception.

The publicity artist of today must be not only a fine craftsman with the faculty for finding new means of presentation but he must also be a keen psychologist. He must be able to perceive and preconceive the tastes, aspirations and habits of the consumer-spectator and the mob. The modern publicity artist must be a pioneer and a leader, he must fight against routine and the bad taste of the mob.

Man today lives, works, and revolves in a realm created by himself, finding in it utility and comfort. Tradition has compelled him to search for beauty and art in history, museums, expositions, and on the Rue de la Paix; and subconsciously, he loves and cherishes the fruits of his utilitarian efforts, not even suspecting that by so doing he admits their beauty. To force a realization of this on the man of today is the task of the modern publicity artist.

We are living in an age of industry and mechanization. Standardized images and, at the same time, endlessly diversified images, born of human ingenuity, not only simplify our daily tasks but also mark the path for the understanding and the serving of the new aesthetic, rhythm, construction, conception and composition.

We are learning to see and to feel new images, we are using new tools to work new materials: new and unexpected possibilities are opened up and a new aesthetic is born. This is an achievement. To deepen this achievement is the problem of the publicity artist.

To make a summary of the foregoing, the maxims to be developed by the publicity artist of today are:

1. Individuality.

2. Universality.

3. Feeling and understanding for modern life.

4. Feeling and understanding of the psychology of the consumer-spectator and the mob.

5. Facility to juggle with all the graphic possibilities which come with the study and improvement of modern materials and technique and of modern methods of presentation and reproduction.

6. Facility for realizing the advertising idea in materials by the use of elementary methods of enforcement and by presenting publicity in a utilitarian, simple, new, unusual, and logical manner.

2B-14

Paul Rand

The Beautiful and the Useful

1947

*"the designer experiences, perceives, analyzes, organizes, symbolizes,
synthesizes"*

*Paul Rand (1914–1996) was an American designer who created often-playful variations on
Swiss Style graphic design. He was a professor at Yale University and is best known for the
design of logos for corporations such as* IBM, UPS, *Enron, Westinghouse,* ABC, *and NeXT.*

....

The Beautiful and the Useful

To interpret the modern approach to visual communication as mere sensationalism is to
misunderstand the very spirit of our time. In advertising, the contemporary approach
to art is based on a simple concept, a concept of the advertisement as an organic and
functional unit, each element of which is integrally related to the others, in harmony
with the whole, and essential to the execution of the idea. From this standpoint, copy,
art, and typography are indissoluble. Editorial layout, promotional matter, direct mail,
packaging, book designing, and industrial design are governed by the same considerations:
function...form...production process...integrated product. Such an evolution logically
precludes extraneous trimmings and "streamlined" affectations.

That which makes for good *advertising* is one thing, and that which makes for good *art*
another; but that which makes for good *advertising art* is an harmonious resolution of
both, integrating as a whole the utilitarian and formal requirements of the problem.

Commenting on the distinction between fine art and useful or technological art, John
Dewey states: "That many, perhaps most, of the articles and utensils made at present for
use are not genuinely esthetic happens, unfortunately, to be true. But it is true for reasons
that are foreign to the relation of the 'beautiful' and 'useful' as such. Wherever conditions
are such as to prevent the act of production from being an experience in which the whole
creature is alive and in which he possesses his living through enjoyment, the product will
lack something of being esthetic. No matter how useful it is for special and limited ends,
it will not be useful in the ultimate degree—that of contributing directly and liberally to
an expanding and enriched life."[1]

1 *John Dewey,* Art as Experience; *"Etherial Things"; p. 26.*

This philosophy is demonstrated in the life of the Shakers, whose history reveals the love of, and strict adherence to, the principles of harmony, beauty, and utility. It is not surprising that such ideals should have found expression in the production of much furniture and many utensils of great aesthetic value, characterized by a keen sensitivity to form and a constant awareness of function. These products are a document of the every-day life of the sect, their asceticism, their devotion to fine craftsmanship, their feeling for fine proportion, space, and order, and their sincerity and naturalness. This fusion of spiritual and material values is also evidenced in Oriental art. The genuine pleasure we derive from the best examples of early Chinese art testifies to these same qualities.

Interpreted in the light of our own experience and of the transition from manual to machine production, these basic truths still prevail. To realize the production of modern advertising and industrial art in terms of functional-aesthetic perfection is to realize the oneness of art and living.

The Designer's Problem

An erroneous conception of the advertising designer's function is that all he need do to produce a successful "layout"[2] is to make a pleasing arrangement of the materials furnished him. This is actually putting the cart before the horse, for the arrangement or layout is almost always an effect and not a cause. I say "almost," for at times the layout is the be-all and end-all of the advertisement simply because the material is such that it requires the consideration only of pure plastic elements to evoke certain predetermined effects, without regard to any immediate selling problem. This is particularly true of editorial layout and institutional advertising. But the designer does not, as a rule, begin with a preconceived idea. His idea is the result of subjective and objective thought, and the design a product of the idea. In order, therefore, to achieve an honest and effective solution he necessarily passes through some sort of mental process. (It may be of interest to the reader to refer to R.H. Wilenski's *The Modern Movement in Art* for a description of the artist's mental processes in creating a work of art.)

Consciously or not, he analyzes, interprets, translates. He apprizes himself of the new scientific and technological developments in his own and kindred fields. He improvises, invents new techniques and combinations. He coordinates and integrates his material so that he may restate his problem in terms of ideas, pictures, forms, and shapes. He unifies, simplifies, eliminates superfluities. He *symbolizes*...abstracts from his material by association and analogy. He intensifies and reinforces his symbol with appropriate accessories to achieve clarity and interest. He draws upon instinct and intuition. He considers the spectator, his feelings and predilections.

Briefly, the designer experiences, perceives, analyzes, organizes, symbolizes, synthesizes.

As the material furnished the designer is often inadequate, vague, uninteresting, or otherwise unsuitable for visual interpretation, his task is to re-create or restate the problem. This may involve a complete revision or total elimination of much of the initial material.

---

2 *For want of a more suitable term and because of general acceptance, the term "layout" is used. Unfortunately, a "layout" is generally looked down upon as meaning a blue print for an illustration. I should prefer to use "composition" in the same sense in which it is used in painting.*

By analysis (breaking down of the complex material into its simplest components…the how, why, when, and where) the designer is able to begin to pose his problem.

The original material is merely one facet of the advertising designer's problem. He is really confronted with three classes of material: a) the original material: product, copy, slogan, logotype, format, medium; b) the formal material: proportion, balance, line, color, harmony, mass, shape, texture, space, rhythm, volume, weight; c) the psychological material: his own, as well as the spectators' instinct, intuition, emotion. He must, therefore, fuse these heterogeneous elements into a homogeneous unit.

The problem of fusing psychological (dramatic) and plastic (formal) experiences in a single picture is one which both easel painter and advertising designer must cope with. The following statement by Roger Fry[3] is intended to supplement the preceding paragraph: "… This may, perhaps, give us a hint as to the nature of such combinations of two arts, namely, that cooperation is most possible where neither of them are pushed to the fullest possibilities of expression, where in both a certain freedom is left to the imagination, where we are moved rather by suggestion than statement."

3   *Roger Fry,* Transformations, *1926; "Some Questions in Esthetics"; p. 24.*

Language, Type, and Typography
| Dissemination of Information

Typography is one of the most rational methodologies of human communication. Understanding typography requires strong knowledge of verbal and written communication, as well as the symbolic origins of written language.

A design decision should reflect the meaning of language and the message the designer wishes to communicate. Technical knowledge of typographic elements—typefaces, hierarchy, legibility, layout—is fundamental for a designer. However, the strongest foundation for a wise designer combines semiotics, linguistics, anthropology, and ontology. Consideration of an assignment within these arenas allows for basic comprehension to be established prior to concerning oneself with a project's formal demands and visual details.

Helvetica Neue LT Std		Adobe Garamond Pro	
55 Roman	7/14	Italic	13/15
	9/10.8		10/12
	13/15	Regular	10/11.5
Column	5	Top Margin	5p0
Gutter	0p6	Bottom Margin	5p6
Rows	8	Inside Margin	4p6
Module	5·8=40	Outside Margin	4p0
Folios	Flushed Outside	Running Feet	Centered

The mechanization of written language by the printing press necessitated the creation of the first reusable letter system and thus the first typeface. As this form matured, typefaces multiplied, each with its own characteristics and requirements for effectively facilitating communication. During the nineteenth century, an overabundance of elaborate typography and eclectic letterforms produced compositions that were chaotic, difficult-to-read visual smorgasbords. This approach had peaked by the beginning of the twentieth century and was followed by the subversive, expressionist typography of the avant-garde art, literary, and design movements that dominated the interwar period.

The International Typographic Style, which originated in Switzerland during and after World War II, can be understood as both a pragmatic response to a vast increase in informational complexity and a reaction to the expressionist typography that came before it. Graphic artists endeavored to present information clearly and objectively in order to facilitate its consumption by an increasingly diverse public, and good design became synonymous with successful mass communication. Aided by their analytical acumen, midcentury typographers formulated a rigorously methodical approach to visual communication that drew from a rich historical lineage of stylistic movements for both philosophical and visual inspiration. The International Typographic Style, by integrating formal qualities from the Bauhaus, the New Typography, Constructivism, and concrete art, provided a clearly delineated and systematic methodology based around unambiguous grid-based layouts.

The success of the New Typographic Style—or the Swiss Style—is beyond dispute. Swiss-inspired graphic design was capable of clearly and effectively disseminating information to a large audience. Systematic design that promoted efficient communication in the age of information was the modernist designers' main concern. However, the success of this pragmatic approach came at a price: in many ways, the individual designer was subsumed, and the expressivity and emotional resonance that had imbued avant-garde design became seen as something to be eradicated. Many designers became anonymous workers churning out template-based design that, while competent, was ultimately rote, uninspired, and unimaginative.

3-1

El Lissitzky

Topography of Typography

1923

"the supernatural reality of the perfected eye"

El Lissitzky (1890–1941) was a Russian designer, photographer, typographer, and conceptual architect. He adapted the Suprematism of his mentor, Kazimir Malevich, resulting in paintings that resemble geometric architectural renderings.

1. The words on the printed surface are taken in by seeing, not by hearing.

2. One communicates meanings through the convention of words; meaning attains form through letters.

3. Economy of expression: optics not phonetics.

4. The design of the book-space, set according to the constraints of printing mechanics, must correspond to the tensions and pressures of content.

5. The design of the book-space using process blocks which issue from the new optics. The supernatural reality of the perfected eye.

6. The continuous sequence of pages: the bioscopic book.

7. The new book demands the new writer. Inkpot and quill-pen are dead.

8. The printed surface transcends space and time. The printed surface, the infinity of books, must be transcended.
THE ELECTRO-LIBRARY.

3-2

László Moholy-Nagy

The New Typography
1923

Contemporary Typography
1926

"legibility-communication must never be impaired by an a priori esthetics"

László Moholy-Nagy (1895–1946) was a Hungarian painter and photographer, as well as the director of the foundation course at the Bauhaus. After fleeing Europe for the United States in 1937, he went on to found the School of Design in Chicago, which was later absorbed into the Illinois Institute of Technology. Moholy-Nagy's work examines human interaction with the forces of time and light.

....

The New Typography
1923

Typography is a tool of communication. It must be communication in its most intense form. The emphasis must be on absolute clarity, since this distinguishes the character of our own writing from that of ancient pictographic forms. Our intellectual relationship to the world is individual-exact (e.g., this individual-exact relationship is in a state of transition toward a collective-exact orientation). This is in contrast to the ancient individual-amorphous and later collective-amorphous mode of communication. Therefore priority: unequivocal clarity in all typographical compositions. Legibility—communication must never be impaired by an *a priori* esthetics. Letters may never be forced into a preconceived framework, for instance a square.

The printed image corresponds to the contents through its specific optical and psychological laws, demanding their typical form. The essence and the purpose of printing demand an uninhibited use of all linear directions (therefore not only horizontal articulation). We use all typefaces, type sizes, geometric forms, colors, etc. We want to create a new language of typography whose elasticity, variability and freshness of typographical composition is exclusively dictated by the inner law of expression and the optical effect.

The most important aspect of contemporary typography is the use of zincographic techniques, meaning the mechanical production of photoprints in all sizes. What the

Egyptians started in their inexact hieroglyphs whose interpretation rested on tradition and personal imagination has become the most precise expression through the inclusion of photography into the typographic method. Already today we have books (mostly scientific ones) with precise photographic reproductions; but these photographs are only secondary explanations of the text. The latest development supersedes this phase, and small or large photos are placed in the text where formerly we used inexact, individually interpreted concepts and expressions. The objectivity of photography liberates the receptive reader from the crutches of the author's personal idiosyncrasies and forces him into the formation of his own opinion.

It is safe to predict that this increasing documentation through photography will lead in the near future to a replacement of literature by film. The indications of this development are apparent already in the increased use of the telephone, which makes letterwriting obsolete. It is no valid objection that the production of films demands too intricate and costly an apparatus. Soon the making of a film will be as simple and available as now printing books.

An equally decisive change in the typographical image will occur in the making of posters, as soon as photography has replaced posterpainting. The effective poster must act with immediate impact on all psychological receptacles. Through an expert use of the camera, and of all photographic techniques, such as retouching, blocking, superimposition, distortion, enlargement, etc., in combination with the liberated typographical line, the effectiveness of posters can be immensely enlarged.

The new poster relies on photography, which is the new storytelling device of civilization, combined with the shock effect of new typefaces and brilliant color effects, depending on the desired intensity of the message.

The new typography is a simultaneous experience of vision and communication.

"an essential component of typographical order is the harmonious arrangement of the surface spaces, the invisible and yet clearly perceivable tension-laden linear relationships that permit various possibilities of balance apart from symmetrical equilibrium"

Contemporary Typography

1926

Typography is modern in concept if it derives its design from its own laws.... The utilization of the possibilities offered by the machine is characteristic and, for the purposes of historical development, essential to the techniques of today's productions. Thus, our modern printing products will, to a large extent, be commensurate with the latest machines; that is, they will have to be based on clarity, conciseness, and precision.

The development of printing methods from setting the type by hand to setting it by machine was long and complicated; and the final and unequivocal adjustment to machine-set type will yet lead to greater tensions. The future form of typographical communication will be to a large extent dependent on the development of machine methods; on the other hand, the development of typographical machines will, in some respect, be determined by a reorientation of typography, which today is still largely influenced by handsetting. The typographical process is based on the effectiveness of visual relationships. Every age possesses its own visual forms and its own corresponding typography. A visual experience that allows itself to be articulated depends on light and dark contrasts or color contrasts.... The old incunabula, and also even the first typographical works, made ample use of the contrasting effects of color and form (initials, multicolored lettering, colored illustrations). The widespread application of the printing process, the great demand for printed works, along with the economical and money-oriented utilization of paper, of the small format, of cast letters, of the single-color print, etc., have changed the vital, contrast-rich layouts of the old printed works into the generally quite monotonous gray of later books.

This monotone of our books has resulted in disadvantages: first, a visually clear articulation of the text has become more difficult to achieve, despite the significant possibilities for articulation offered by the paragraph indent; second, the reader tires much more easily than he would by looking at a layout built on contrasts of light and dark or contrast of color. Thus, the majority of our books today have come no further in their typographical, visual, synoptical form than the Gutenberg production, despite the technological transformation in their manufacture.... The situation is much more favorable with newspapers, posters, and job printing, since typographical progress has been almost entirely devoted to this area.

All of today's known attempts at typographical reform consciously or unconsciously start with these facts. The monotony and the lack of contrast in modern books were…grasped intuitively, but the reaction to this was nothing but a retrospective demonstration. [These typographers] by the use of hand-set type…have produced curious effects, and have called attention to hitherto unknown charms of typographical material—such as lines, rules, circles, squares, crosses, etc. With these structures they "stuccoed"—with a purely craftlike mentality—illustrations, objects, figures, all very interesting because of their uniqueness. But on the whole they were far from influencing significantly any possible future development of typography. This will be left to those typographers who can not only grasp the developmental possibilities and the flexibility of typographical machines and materials, but who can also understand the larger horizon of today's visual experiences. Innovations (such as the wider distribution of photography, of film, and of photoengraving and electroplating techniques) have yielded a new, constantly developing creative basis also for typography. The invention of photogravure, its further development, the photographic typesetting machine, the use of advertising with light, the experience of the visual continuity of the cinema, the simultaneous effects of perceptual events (the city), all these make possible and call for an entirely new level in the field of the visual-typographical. The gray text will change into a colored picture book and will be understood as a continuous visual design (a coherent sequence of many individual pages). With the expansion of the reproduction technique…all, possibly even philosophical works, will be printed using the same means for illustrations.…

Whereas typography, from Gutenberg up to the first posters, was merely a (necessary) intermediary link between the content of a message and the recipient, a new stage of development began with the first posters.…One began to count on the fact that form, size, color, and arrangement of the typographical material (letters and signs) contain a strong visual impact. The organization of these possible visual effects gives a visual validity to the content of the message as well; this means that by means of printing the content is also being defined pictorially.… This…is the essential task of visual-typographical design.

What is necessary, for example, is a unitary type of lettering, without small and capital letters; letters unified not only in size but also in form.…Of course here one could also put up ideal demands which would go far beyond a modernization of our present day type forms. Our lettering, aside from the very few phonetically derived symbols, is based on a time-honored convention. The origin of these signs is hard to ascertain today. They are very often no more than formal stylistic (or practical) modifications of traditional forms which are no longer recognizable. So, one will be able to speak of an actual reorganization of (printed) lettering only when this reorganization has been carried out in an objective, scientific manner. Perhaps on the basis of opto-phonetical experiments.… The adoption of basic forms—such as the circle, square, and triangle—in the reform of lettering admittedly leads today to interesting formal, and even essential practical results. [Seen] from what is today still a Utopian point of view, they are, however, not to be taken as the correct understanding of the problem.… [It] is very likely that this kind of investigation will [lead] at first to the construction of automatic typewriters and typesetting machines working from dictation. But for the time being we do not even have a practical type face of the right size that is clearly legible, has no individual peculiarities, is based on a functional, visual form, and has neither distortions nor curlicues. We have, on the other hand, good fonts of type that are sometimes suitable for labels and title pages...but when used in larger quantities they begin to "swim." The tensions that stem from contrasting visual effects are most thoroughly created by opposites: empty—full, light—dark, polychrome—monochrome, vertical—horizontal, upright—oblique, etc. These contrasts are primarily produced by means of the type (letters). Today, we seek to create the "style" for our works—not from borrowed requisites but out of this...typographical material. There are [but] a few well-suited forms, [however] there are many ways of using them, a fact which contributes to the precision [and] clarity...of the visual image. The whole field of the photoengraving techniques also belongs in this area. In order to bring typographical design into conformity with the purposes of typography, it might possibly be well even to use various line directions and the like (thus not just horizontal arrangements). The nature and the purpose of the communication (leaflet or poster) determine the manner and the use of the typographical material. Typographical signs (like points, lines, and other geometrical forms) can also be used to advantage....

An essential component of typographical order is the harmonious arrangement of the surface spaces, the invisible and yet clearly perceivable tension-laden linear relationships that permit various possibilities of balance apart from symmetrical equilibrium. In contrast to the centuries-old static-concentric equilibrium, one seeks today to produce a dynamic-eccentric equilibrium. In the first case the typographical object is captured at a glance, with all the centrally focused elements, including the peripheral ones; in the second case, the eye is led step by step from point to point, whereby [the awareness of] the mutual relationships of the individual elements must not suffer (posters, job printing, titles of books, etc.).

One could point out many more possibilities for achieving new effects that lie in the same direction as the essential typographical development mentioned here.

3-3

Jan Tschichold

The New Typography
1928

New Life in Print
1930

"the engineer shapes our age. Distinguishing marks of his work: economy, precision, use of pure constructional forms that correspond to the functions of the object"

Jan Tschichold (1902–1974) was a German typographer and teacher. In his early career he advocated for a standardized, hierarchical typography restricted to sans serif typefaces, although he eventually renounced many of his early principles and went on to design the popular serif face Sabon.

....

The New Typography
1928

The New World-View

The revolutionary technical discoveries of the late 19th and early 20th centuries have been only slowly followed by man's ability to make use of his new opportunities and develop them into a new pattern of life. "Civilization" and the too-rapid penetration of all classes by these new technical discoveries have led to complete cultural chaos, caused by the failure of the affected generation to draw the right conclusions for a new way of life from the new facts.

The new generation facing this state of affairs is free of the prejudices against the New that obsessed the previous generation. The technical advances in every tool and service used by man have been enthusiastically accepted by the younger generation and have brought about a completely new attitude to their surroundings.

The objects in use by the new generation suffer from the fatal compromise between a supposedly "artistic" intention and the dictates of technical manufacture; from a feeble turning back to historical parallels; from the conflict between essence and appearance. Instead of recognizing and designing for the laws of machine production, the previous generation contented itself with trying anxiously to follow a tradition that was in any case only imaginary. Before them stand the works of today, untainted by the past, primary shapes which identify the aspect of our time: Car Aeroplane Telephone Wireless Factory

Neon-advertising New York! These objects, designed without reference to the aesthetics of the past, have been created by a new kind of man: **the engineer!**

The engineer shapes our age. Distinguishing marks of his work: economy, precision, use of pure constructional forms that correspond to the functions of the object. Nothing could be more characteristic of our age than these witnesses to the inventive genius of the engineer, whether one-off items such as: airfield, department store, underground railway; or mass-produced objects like: typewriter, electric light-bulb, motor cycle. They have created a new—our own—attitude to our surroundings. An immense enrichment of our lives comes from the new inventions which confront us at every step. The collective whole already largely determines the material existence of every individual. The individual's identical fundamental needs are met by standardized products: electric light-bulbs, gramophone records, Van Heusen collars, Zeiss bookcases, tinned milk, telephones, office furniture, typewriters. Gillette razors. The standardization and electro-mechanization of the things we use daily will be further increased. Economies in production and use of materials will lead to constant improvements. But electro-mechanization as an end in itself is nonsense: its true purpose, by satisfying basic needs through mass-produced objects of highest quality, is to make possible for the first time a true and unlimited awakening of all the creative powers of man.

In some fields, standardization, rationalization, and mechanization have made great progress, but in most others almost everything remains to be done. Where no tradition existed, and where therefore there was the least amount of restraint on design, record progress was made, e.g. in Rumpler-Tropfen cars, in giant aircraft, in typewriters. Further rationalization in the manufacture of the parts of these engineering products will allow even more energy to be harnessed that today is going to waste. But in most spheres of human activity, progress towards the shapes expressive of our time is slow indeed. Thus in the field of housing, the projects of Gropius and Le Corbusier have only very recently been recognized, achieving in an unpromising-looking area a high degree of standardization and series-production. The design and construction of homes for people who live the same sort of lives can be planned so as to meet the economic demands of our time for rationalization and standardization.

Modern engineering and standardized machine manufacture have of necessity led to the use of precise geometric forms. The final and purest shape of a product is always built up from geometric forms. The new age has created an entirely new visual world, and has guided us to the primary elements of human expression: geometric shape and pure exact form. Our sympathy for the shapes derived from geometry and science is part of our inborn striving for order, both in things and in events, which is redoubled when we are confronted by chaos. We, who require the utmost purity and truth in our surroundings, arrive everywhere at forms which do not, as previously, deny the necessary elements of their construction, but openly reveal and affirm them. Such shapes must by necessity transcend individualism and nationalism in their appearance. The value of an object is not measured by its origin, but by its approach to perfection of form, the highest and purest design. The creator disappears completely behind his work. People of today regard the arrogant thrusting forward of the man before his work as aesthetically embarrassing. Just as every human being is part of a greater whole, and is conscious of his connection with it, so his work should also be an expression of this general feeling of wholeness. An analogy in the field of sport is the excitement shared by millions in a victory by Tunney over Dempsey. Every new record means, to the individual, a higher achievement in which all have participated; it shows how successfully the dashing new generation is replacing middle-aged stuffiness by movement and action. Contemplative introversion has given way to new realities, the thrills of active modern life. The theatre, an illusion of life, has lost its drawing power, for life itself has become a play: city street, neon signs, stadium. A few clear heads, the avant-garde of all nations, are leading the way here. Their achievements in painting and architecture have led to a new vision and a new activity in all other fields of human creativity. Their exemplars were works of the engineers, expressing purity and clarity in their construction. Construction is the basis of all organic and organized form: the structure and form of a rose are no less logical than the construction of a racing car—both appeal to us for their ultimate economy and precision.

Thus the striving for purity of form is the common denominator of all endeavour that has set itself the aim of rebuilding our life and forms of expression in every individual activity we recognize the single way, the goal.

Unity of Life!
So the arbitrary isolation of a part is no longer possible for us—every part belongs to and harmonizes with the whole. Where slackness is still the rule, we must make it our work to fight against laziness, envy, and narrow-mindedness.

Typography too must now make itself part of all the other fields of creativity. The purpose of this book is to show these connections and explain their consequences, to state clearly the principles of typography, and to demand the creation of a contemporary style. The connection between typography and all other fields of creativity, especially architecture, has been accepted in all progressive periods. Today we are witnessing the birth of a new and splendid architecture, which will set its stamp on our period. Anyone who has recognized the deep underlying similarity between typography and architecture and has understood the true nature of the new architecture can no longer doubt that the future will belong to the new typography and not the old.

And it is impossible for both the old and the new typography to continue to exist together, as some think they can. The great period of design that is coming would not be one if the Renaissance style continued to exist beside the modern, in whatever field, whether of printing or architecture. The romanticism of the previous generation, however understandable, never hindered the birth of a new style. Just as it is absurd today to build villas like Rococo palaces or Gothic castles, so people tomorrow will smile at those who continue to practise the old typography.

In the battle between the old and the new, it is not a question of creating a new style for its own sake. But new needs and new contents create new forms which look utterly unlike the old. And it is just as impossible to argue away these new needs as it is to deny the need for a truly contemporary style of typography.

That is why printers today have a duty to concern themselves with these questions. Some have forged ahead with energy and creative success: for the rest, however, it seems that there is still almost **EVERYTHING** to do!

"design is the most legible ordering and the correct choice of type dimensions according to their value within the logical bounds of the text"

New Life in Print

1930

....

The general term "The New Typography" embraces the activities of a few of the younger typographers working principally in Germany, the Soviet Union, Holland, Czechoslovakia, and in Switzerland and Hungary. The inception of the movement in Germany reaches back into the war period. The existence of the New Typography can be said to be due to the personal achievement of its initiators; but to me it seems more accurate to regard these as the exponents of the tendencies and practical needs of our time, a view which by no means attempts to underestimate their extraordinary achievements and creative power or the inestimable value of their individual pioneer work. The movement would never have been so widespread, as in Central Europe it incontestably is, had it not served practical contemporary needs, and this it does so excellently because its primary aim is the unprejudiced adaptation of typography to the purposes of the task in hand.

Here I think it necessary briefly to describe the state of prewar typographical development. Following upon the stylistic confusion of the eighties, England gave birth to the Arts and Craft movement (Morris 1892), which at least from a typographical standpoint, was mainly influenced by traditional tendencies (limitation of incunabula). In the "Youth style" (Jugendstil, ca. 1900) an attempt was made, without however any permanent success, to break away from traditional models, arriving at a misunderstood off-shoot of the Natural Form (Eckmann), finally to end in a renovated Biedermeier type (Wieynck)—in a word, in a new traditionalism. Then the traditional models were rediscovered and further imitated, albeit on this occasion with better understanding (German Book Production 1911-14-20). The reverence for traditional forms evoked by a more intensive research-work resulted naturally in a limitation of creative freedom and forced it at length into inanition. Contrary to expectation, the most important gain resulting from these years was the rediscovery of original traditional faces (Walbaum, Unger, Didot, Bodoni, Garamond, etc.), which for some time and with every justification have been preferred above their "precursors," in reality their imitators.

The natural reaction to the inanition of prewar typography was the New Typography aiming above all at suppleness in its methods of design.

Two aims can be discerned in all typographical work: the recognition and fulfillment of practical requirements—and the visual design. (Visual design is a question of aesthetic; it is senseless to attempt to avoid this expression.) At this point typography differs not a little from architecture: it is possible (and it has indeed been done by the best architects) that the form of a house may be determined by its practical purpose but in the case of typography the aesthetic side in the question of design makes itself clearly manifest. This factor relates typography far more nearly to the domain of "free" design on a plane surface (painting, drawing) than to that of architectural art. Both typography and the graphic arts are always concerned with surface (plane) design. Here at this stage the reason why none other than the "new" painters, the "abstract" painters, were destined to be the initiators of the New Typography. It is too wide a subject here to give any account of the development of abstract painting in this connection: visit any exhibition of their work, and its relation to the New Typography is immediately discernible. This connection is not, as many believe, a formalist one but is genetic, a fact which abstract painters themselves have failed to understand. Abstract painting is the "unpurposing" relating of pure color and form without any literary admixtures. Typography signifies the visual (or aesthetic) ordering of given elements (practical requirements, type, pictures, color, etc.), on a plane surface. The difference between painting and typography exists only inasmuch as in the former there is a free choice of elements and the resulting design has no practical purpose. Modern typography therefore cannot be better occupied than with an intensive study of surface composition in abstract painting.

Let us examine the principles followed by prewar typography. The majestic traditional model knew of only one scheme of design—the medial axis, the axial symmetry whose plainest example was the title page. The whole of typography followed this scheme, whatever its immediate task might be, whether printing a newspaper or a circular, letterheads or advertisements.

Only in the postwar period did the dim realization dawn that all these were quite different tasks, making entirely different practical demands to be met creatively by the typographer.

A distinction between the New Typography and the old can only be drawn by means of a negation—the New Typography does not traditionalize. And at the door of the old, whose tendency was purely traditional, the blame for this negation must be laid. But at the same time the New Typography, because of its utter rejection of any formalist limitations, is less antitraditional than nontraditional. For instance, to achieve typographical design it is permissible to use every traditional and nontraditional face, every manner of plane relationship and every direction of line. The sole aim is design: the creative harmonious ordering of the practical requirements. Therefore there exist no limitations such as are imposed by the positing of "permissible" and "forbidden" type conjunctions. The old, unique aim of design to present a "restful" page is also reversed—we are at liberty to present a designed "unrest."

The swift tempo of modern business forces us further to a most accurate calculation of economic presentation. Typography had not only to find a simpler and more easily realizable constructive form (than the medial axis) but at the same time had to make this itself more visually attractive and varied in design. Dadaism, through Marinetti in Italy with his

"Les mots en liberté futuriste (1919)" and even earlier in Germany, gave the first impulse to the new development in typography. Even today Dadaism is looked upon as sheer idiocy by many who have not taken the trouble to understand its dynamic; only in time to come will the important pioneer work done by those in the schools of Hausmann, Heartfield, Gross, Hulsenbeck, and other Dadaists be estimated at their proper value. In any case, the handbills and other publications of the Dadaists (which date back into the wartime) were the earliest documents of the New Typography. In 1922 the movement spread; a few abstract painters began typographical experiments. A further impulse was given by the author's supplement ("Elementare Typographie") of the "Typographische Mitteilungen" (1925, out of print), in which the efforts made and results achieved were demonstrated for the first time and which, published in an edition of 28,000, was broadcast to the printing world. The views of the New Typography were the object of savage attack on all sides—today none but a few disgruntled die-hards ever think of raising their voice against them. The New Typography has won through.

Next to its nontraditional attitude the New Typography is characterized by its preference for new technical processes. It prefers:

typefounder's type	to engraved type
machine setting	to hand setting
machine-made paper	to handmade paper
machine presses	to hand presses
photographs	to drawings
photo process blocks	to woodcuts
standardization	to individualization, etc.

Further, the New Typography, by virtue of its methods of design, embraces the whole domain of printing and not merely the narrow field of pure type. Thus in photography we possess an objective means of reproducing objectivity and one which is comprehensible to all. Photography because it is merely another method of visual speech is also regarded as type.

The method of the New Typography is based upon a clear realization of purpose and the best means of achieving it. No modern typography, be it never so "beautiful," is "new" if it sacrifices purpose to form. "Form" is the result of work done and not the realization of an external conception of form. This fact has not been grasped by a whole troupe of pseudo-moderns. The chief demand of the New Typography is the most ideal adaptation to purpose.

This makes the omission of any decorative ingredients self-understood. Purpose further demands, and this cannot be too strongly emphasized, really good legibility. Lines too narrowly or too widely spaced and set are difficult to read and therefore, if for no other reason, to be avoided. The proper use of the various new processes produces in nearly every case specific forms, and it is the typographer's proper study to recognize these and adapt his design to them. Thus a good typographer without a most thorough knowledge of technical requirements is unthinkable.

The present mass of printed matter, circulars (a thing which closely affects the individual as he receives no small part of them), renders the use of a standardized format necessary.

Of the available standing types, the New Typography is most partial to the "grotesque" or "block" type, as this is simply formed and easy to read. The use of others, easily legible, or even traditional faces, in the new sense is quite admissible, as they are "evaluated" one against the other, i.e., if the contrast between them be designed. It is not therefore demanded that everything be set in "grotesque," although in most cases this is indicated as most fitting. This face in its many variations (thin, semi-bold, bold-faced, condensed, expanded, hair-spaced, etc.) is open to many effects which in juxtaposition are capable of rich and varied contrasts. Varying contrasts can be obtained by the introduction of antique faces (Egyptienne, Walbaum, Garamond, Italic, etc.), and there is no reason why these effects should not be used in conjunction. Typescript is also a very peculiar and effective face.

Design is the most legible ordering and the correct choice of type dimensions according to their value within the logical bounds of the text (which can be intensified or diminished). The conscious use of movement by means of type or now and again a thick or thin rule, or group of rules, the visual agitated contrast of upper and lower case, thin and bold face, condensed and expanded type, gray and colored patches, slanting and horizontal, compact, and loose groups of type, etc., are further means of design. They represent the "aesthetic" side of typographical composition. Within the definite limits set by practical requirement and logical structure it is possible to tread various paths so that from this point onwards the visual sensibilities of the typographer must be the deciding factor. Thus it comes about that when several typographers are engaged upon the one definite task, they each achieve a varying result, each of which may have the same practical advantages. The various men whose work is illustrated in this article reveal tremendously varying possibilities, in spite of the use of the same means and methods of design. Thus, means which are practically identical meet with an extraordinary variety of usage. And these examples show that modern methods, in spite of frequent surmise, do not lead to monotony of expression, but on the contrary to results of extreme dissimilarity and which above all possess more originality than those of prewar typography.

Color is just such another effective element as type. In a certain sense the unprinted surface must be reckoned in with it and the discovery of its effectiveness must be put to the credit of the New Typographers. The white surface is not regarded as a passive background but as an active element. Among actual colors preference is given to red; as "The" color it forms the most effective contrast to the normal black. The clear tones yellow and blue must also be given place in the foreground of interest, as these two are not diffuse. Color is not used as a decorative, "beautifying" ingredient, but the peculiar psychophysical properties of each are used as a means to heighten (or tone down) effects.

Illustration is supplied by photography. By this means we are given the most objective rendering of the object.

Whether photography is in itself an art or not an art need not concern us here; in conjunction with type and a plane surface it can be an art, as then it is purely a matter of values, of fitness in structural contrasts and relationships. Many people incline to mistrust graphic illustrations; the old (often falsifying) graphic illustrations no longer convince us, and their individualistic pose and mannerisms affect us unpleasantly. If it be desired to give several pictorial impressions at the same time, to display several contrasting things, montage must be called into service. For this the same general methods of design as in typography hold good; used in conjunction with type, the photograph becomes a part of the whole and must be properly evaluated in this connection so as to achieve harmonious design. A rare but very attractive photographic possibility is the photogram of which an example is shown. A photogram is taken without a camera simply by placing a more or less transparent object on a sensitized medium (paper, film or plates). Typography + Photography is termed "Typophoto."

The extraordinary adaptability of the New Typography to every conceivable purpose renders it an important phenomenon in contemporary life. Its very attitude and position reveal that it is no mere fashion of a moment but is destined to form the basis of all further typographical progress.

Karel Teige of Prague has formulated the main characteristics of the New Typography as follows:

"Constructivist Typography" (a synonym for the New Typography) means and requires:

1. Freedom from tradition and prejudice; overthrow of archaicism and academicism and the rejection of decoration. No respect for academic and traditional rules unsupported by visual reason and which are here lifeless form ("the golden section," unity of type).

2. A choice of type, more perfect, more legible and cut with more geometric simplicity. Understanding of the spirit of the types suitable and their use in accord with the character of the text, contrast of typographical material to emphasize content.

3. Constant appreciation of purpose and fulfillment of requirement. Differentiation in special aims. Advertisements meant to be seen from a distance require different treatment to a scientific work or a volume of verse.

4. Harmonious disposition of surface and text in accordance with objective visual law; surveyable structure and geometric organization.

5. Exploitation of all means, which are or may be offered by present and future technical discoveries; conjunction of illustration and text by typophoto.

6. The closest cooperation between typographers and experts in the composing room is desirable, just as the designing architect cooperates with the constructional engineer, etc., specialization and division of labor are quite as necessary as close contact.

7. There is nothing to be added to the above beyond that the "golden section" together with other exact proportional formulas are often far more effective than chance relationships and should therefore not suffer fundamental exclusion.

Beatrice Warde

The Crystal Goblet

1932

"the book typographer has the job of erecting a window between the reader inside the room and that landscape which is the author's words"

Beatrice Warde (1900–1969), a well-known American writer and expert on typography, first earned her reputation with a meticulously researched essay on the origins of the Garamond typefaces. She was a prolific lecturer and the longtime publicity manager of the Monotype Corporation in London, where she edited the Monotype Recorder.

Imagine that you have before you a flagon of wine. You may choose your own favorite vintage for this imaginary demonstration, so that it be a deep shimmering crimson in color. You have two goblets before you. One is of solid gold, wrought in the most exquisite patterns. The other is of crystal-clear glass, thin as a bubble, and as transparent. Pour and drink; and according to your choice of goblet, I shall know whether or not you are a connoisseur of wine. For if you have no feelings about wine one way or the other, you will want the sensation of drinking the stuff out of a vessel that may have cost thousands of pounds; but if you are a member of that vanishing tribe, the amateurs of fine vintages, you will choose the crystal, because everything about it is calculated to reveal rather than hide the beautiful thing which it was meant to contain.

Bear with me in this long-winded and fragrant metaphor; for you will find that almost all the virtues of the perfect wine-glass have a parallel in typography. There is the long, thin stem that obviates fingerprints on the bowl. Why? Because no cloud must come between your eyes and the fiery heart of the liquid. Are not the margins on book pages similarly meant to obviate the necessity of fingering the type-page? Again: the glass is colorless or at the most only faintly tinged in the bowl, because the connoisseur judges wine partly by its color and is impatient of anything that alters it. There are a thousand mannerisms in typography that are as impudent and arbitrary as putting port in tumblers of red or green glass! When a goblet has a base that looks too small for security, it does not matter how cleverly it is weighted; you feel nervous lest it should tip over. There are ways of setting lines of type which may work well enough, and yet keep the reader subconsciously worried by the fear of "doubling" lines, reading three words as one, and so forth.

Now the man who first chose glass instead of clay or metal to hold his wine was a "modernist" in the sense in which I am going to use that term. That is, the first thing he asked of his particular object was not "How should it look?" but "What must it do?" and to that extent all good typography is modernist.

Wine is so strange and potent a thing that it has been used in the central ritual of religion in one place and time, and attacked by a virago with a hatchet in another. There is only one thing in the world that is capable of stirring and altering men's minds to the same extent, and that is the coherent expression of thought. That is man's chief miracle, unique to man. There is no "explanation" whatever of the fact that I can make arbitrary sounds which will lead a total stranger to think my own thought. It is sheer magic that I should be able to hold a one-sided conversation by means of black marks on paper with an unknown person half-way across the world. Talking, broadcasting, writing, and printing are all quite literally forms of thought transference, and it is the ability and eagerness to transfer and receive the contents of the mind that is almost alone responsible for human civilization.

If you agree with this, you will agree with my one main idea, i.e. that the most important thing about printing is that it conveys thought, ideas, images, from one mind to other minds. This statement is what you might call the front door of the science of typography. Within lie hundreds of rooms; but unless you start by assuming that printing is meant to convey specific and coherent ideas, it is very easy to find yourself in the wrong house altogether.

Before asking what this statement leads to, let us see what it does not necessarily lead to, let us see what it does not necessarily lead to. If books are printed in order to be read, we must distinguish readability from what the optician would call legibility. A page set in 14-pt Bold Sans is, according to the laboratory tests, more "legible" than one set in 11-pt Baskerville. A public speaker is more "audible" in that sense when he bellows. But a good speaking voice is one which is inaudible as a voice. It is the transparent goblet again! I need not warn you that if you begin listening to the inflections and speaking rhythms of a voice from a platform, you are falling asleep. When you listen to a song in a language you do not understand, part of your mind actually does fall asleep, leaving your quite separate aesthetic sensibilities to enjoy themselves unimpeded by your reasoning faculties. The fine arts do that; but that is not the purpose of printing. Type well used is invisible as type, just as the perfect talking voice is the unnoticed vehicle for the transmission of words, ideas.

We may say, therefore, that printing may be delightful for many reasons, but that it is important, first and foremost, as a means of doing something. That is why it is mischievous to call any printed piece a work of art, especially fine art: because that would imply that its first purpose was to exist as an expression of beauty for its own sake and for the delectation of the senses. Calligraphy can almost be considered a fine art nowadays, because its primary economic and educational purpose has been taken away; but printing in English will not qualify as an art until the present English language no longer conveys ideas to future generations, and until printing itself hands its usefulness to some yet unimagined successor.

There is no end to the maze of practices in typography, and this idea of printing as a conveyor is, at least in the minds of all the great typographers with whom I have had the privilege of talking, the one clue that can guide you through the maze. Without this essential humility of mind, I have seen ardent designers go more hopelessly wrong, make more ludicrous mistakes out of an excessive enthusiasm, than I could have thought possible. And with this clue, this purposiveness in the back of your mind, it is possible to do the most unheard-of things, and find that they justify you triumphantly. It is not a waste of time to go to the simple fundamentals and reason from them. In the flurry of your individual problems, I think you will not mind spending half an hour on one broad and simple set of ideas involving abstract principles.

I once was talking to a man who designed a very pleasing advertising type that undoubtedly all of you have used. I said something about what artists think about a certain problem, and he replied with a beautiful gesture: "Ah, madam, we artists do not think—we feel!" That same day I quoted that remark to another designer of my acquaintance, and he, being less poetically inclined, murmured: "I'm not feeling very well today, I think!" He was right, he did think; he was the thinking sort, and that is why he is not so good a painter, and to my mind ten times better as a typographer and type designer than the man who instinctively avoided anything as coherent as a reason.

I always suspect the typographic enthusiast who takes a printed page from a book and frames it to hang on the wall, for I believe that in order to gratify a sensory delight he has mutilated something infinitely more important. I remember that T. M. Cleland, the famous American typographer, once showed me a very beautiful layout for a Cadillac booklet involving decorations in color. He did not have the actual text to work with in drawing up his specimen pages, so he had set the lines in Latin. This was not only for the reason that you will all think of, if you have seen the old type foundries' famous Quousque Tandem copy (i.e., that Latin has few descenders and thus gives a remarkably even line). No, he told me that originally he had set up the dullest "wording" that he could find (I daresay it was from Mansard), and yet he discovered that the man to whom he submitted it would start reading and making comments on the text. I made some remark on the mentality of boards of directors, but Mr. Cleland said, "No, you're wrong; if the reader had not been practically forced to read—if he had not seen those words suddenly imbued with glamour and significance-then the layout would have been a failure. Setting it in Italian or Latin is only an easy way of saying, 'This is not the text as it will appear.'"

Let me start my specific conclusions with book typography, because that contains all the fundamentals, and then go on to a few points about advertising. The book typographer has the job of erecting a window between the reader inside the room and that landscape which is the author's words. He may put up a stained-glass window of marvelous beauty, but a failure as a window; that is, he may use some rich superb type like text Gothic that is something to be looked at, not through. Or he may work in what I call transparent or invisible typography. I have a book at home, of which I have no visual recollection whatever as far as its typography goes; when I think of it, all I see is the Three Musketeers and their comrades swaggering up and down the streets of Paris. The third type of window is one in which the glass is broken into relatively small leaded panes; and this corresponds to what is called "fine printing" today, in that you are at least conscious that there is a window there, and that someone has enjoyed building it. That is not objectionable, because of a very important fact which has to do with the psychology of the subconscious mind. That is that the mental eye focuses through type and not upon it. The type which, through any arbitrary warping of design or excess of "color," gets in the way of the mental picture to be conveyed, is a bad type. Our subconsciousness is always afraid of blunders (which illogical setting, tight spacing and too-wide unleaded lines can trick us into), of boredom, and of officiousness. The running headline that keeps shouting at us, the line that looks like one long word, the capitals jammed together without hair-spaces—these mean subconscious squinting and loss of mental focus.

And if what I have said is true of book printing, even of the most exquisite limited editions, it is fifty times more obvious in advertising, where the one and only justification for the purchase of space is that you are conveying a message—that you are implanting a desire, straight into the mind of the reader. It is tragically easy to throw away half the reader-interest of an advertisement by setting the simple and compelling argument in a face which is uncomfortably alien to the classic reasonableness of the book-face. Get attention as you will by your headline, and make any pretty type pictures you like if you are sure that the copy is useless as a means of selling goods; but if you are happy enough to have really good copy to work with, I beg you to remember that thousands of people pay hard-earned money for the privilege of reading quietly set book-pages, and that only your wildest ingenuity can stop people from reading a really interesting text.

Printing demands a humility of mind, for the lack of which many of the fine arts are even now floundering in self-conscious and maudlin experiments. There is nothing simple or dull in achieving the transparent page. Vulgar ostentation is twice as easy as discipline. When you realize that ugly typography never effaces itself, you will be able to capture beauty as the wise men capture happiness by aiming at something else. The "stunt typographer" learns the fickleness of rich men who hate to read. Not for them are long breaths held over serif and kern, they will not appreciate your splitting of hair-spaces. Nobody (save the other craftsmen) will appreciate half your skill. But you may spend endless years of happy experiment in devising that crystalline goblet which is worthy to hold the vintage of the human mind.

3-5

Herbert Bayer

On Typography
1959

"it became clear that typography is not self-expression within predetermined aesthetics, but that it is conditioned by the message it visualizes"

Herbert Bayer (1900–85) was an Austrian American designer who studied mural painting and typography at the Bauhaus and later returned to the school to teach advertising and typography. His signature typeface, Universal, consisted of a single geometric sans serif alphabet with no capital letters.

....

typography is a service art, not a fine art, however pure and elemental the discipline may be.

the graphic designer today seems to feel that the typographic means at his disposal have been exhausted. accelerated by the speed of our time, a wish for new excitement is in the air. "new styles" are hopefully expected to appear.

nothing is more constructive than to look the facts in the face. what are they? the fact that nothing new has developed in recent decades? the boredom of the dead end without signs for a renewal? or is it the realization that a forced change in search of a "new style" can only bring superficial gain?

it seems appropriate at this point to recall the essence of statements made by progressive typographers of the 1920s:

previously used largely as a medium for making language visible, typographic material was discovered to have distinctive optical properties of its own, pointing toward specifically typographic expression. typographers envisioned possibilities of deeper visual experiences from a new exploitation of the typographic material itself.

they called for clarity, conciseness, precision; for more articulation, contrast, tension in the color and black and white values of the typographic page.

typography was for the first time seen not as an isolated discipline and technique, but in context with the ever-widening visual experiences that the picture symbol, photo, film, and television brought.

they recognized that in all human endeavors a technology had adjusted to man's demands; while no marked change or improvement had taken place in man's most profound invention, printing-writing, since gutenberg.

the manual skill and approach of the craftsman was seen to be inevitably replaced by mechanical techniques.

once more it became clear that typography is not self-expression within predetermined aesthetics, but that it is conditioned by the message it visualizes.

that typographic aesthetics were not stressed in these statements does not mean a lack of concern with them. but it appears that the searching went beyond surface effects into underlying strata.

it is a fallacy to believe that styles can be created as easily and as often as fashions change. more is involved than trends of taste devoid of inner substance and structure, applied as cultural sugar-coating.

moreover, the typographic revolution was not an isolated event but went hand in hand with a new social, political consciousness and consequently, with the building of new cultural foundations.

the artist's acceptance of the machine as a tool for mass production has had its impression on aesthetic concepts. since then an age of science has come upon us, and the artist has been motivated more than ever, to open his mind to the new forces that shape our lives.

new concepts will not grow on mere design variations of long-established forms such as the book. the aesthetic restraint that limits the development of the book must finally be overcome, and new ideas must logically be deduced from the function of typography and its carriers. although i realize how deeply anchored in tradition and how petrified the subject of writing and spelling is, a new typography will be bound to an alphabet that corresponds to the demands of an age of science. it must, unfortunately, be remembered that we live in a time of great ignorance and lack of concern with the alphabet, writing, and typography. with nostalgia we hear of times when literate people had knowledge, respect, and understanding of the subject. common man today has no opinion at all in such matters. it has come to a state where even the typesetter, the original typographer, as well as the printer, has lost this culture, responsibility has been shifted onto the shoulders of the designer almost exclusively.

in the united states the art of typography, book design, visual communication at large, in its many aspects, is being shelved as a minor art. it has no adequate place of recognition in our institutions of culture, the graphic designer is designated with the minimizing term "commercial" and is generally ignored as compared to the prominence accorded by the press to architecture and the "fine arts." visual communication has made revolutionary strides and real contributions to the contemporary world picture. yet, the artist-typographer represents a small number of typography producers compared to the output of the nation. their efforts must be valued as they keep the aesthetic standards from falling, and because they alone set the pace in taste.

there can be no doubt that our writing-printing-reading methods are antiquated and inefficient as compared to the perfection attained in other areas of human endeavor.

the history of our alphabet and any probing into its optical effectiveness expose a lack of principle and structure, precision and efficiency which should be evidenced in this important tool.

attempts have been made to design visually (to distinguish from aesthetically) improved alphabets. but redesigning will result in just another typeface unless the design is primarily guided by optics as well as by a revision of spelling. this, in turn, reveals the need for a clearer relation of writing-printing to the spoken word, a reorganization of the alphabetic sound-symbols, the creation of new symbols. the type designer is not usually a language reformer, but a systematic approach will inevitably carry him to a point where he will ask for nothing less than a complete overhaul of communication with visual sound.

however unlikely the possibilities for the adoption of such far-reaching renovation appears at the moment, revitalization of typography will come:

a. from the increased demands made on the psychophysiological apparatus of our perceptive senses;

b. from a new alphabet;

c. from the different physical forms that the carriers of typography will take. the more we read, the less we see. constant exposure to visual materials has dulled our sense of seeing. overfed with reading as we are, the practice of reading must be activated. a new effort is needed to recapture and retain freshness. little known is the fact that the act of seeing is work, that it demands more than a quarter of the nervous energy the human body burns up. during waking hours your eyes almost never rest. in reading this article you must refocus as you skip from word to word. much energy is required for blinking and turning the eyeballs. more is needed by the tiny ciliary muscles to alter the shape of the crystalline lens for focusing. the effort of seeing contributes a large share to physical tiredness.

taking a closer look at present-day typographic customs, i make the following suggestions, believing that they offer immediate possibilities for both improvement and change.

HERBERT BAYER, ON TYPOGRAPHY

visual research

the eye seldom focuses for long on one point in a design. it flits back and forth from one element to another in haphazard sequence, unless the design is skillfully arranged to focus its orderly progress from one idea to the next. it is a vital part of the designer's job to make sure that the eye sees first things first and that it is made to dwell as long as possible on areas of special importance, such as the name of a product.

graphic design will more than ever be determined by its purpose. the designer-typographer can find new impetuses from research in vision such as the above exemplifies.

universal communication

for a long time to come we will accept the existence of the different languages now in use. this will continue to pose barriers to communication, even after improved (possibly phonetic) writing methods have been adopted within all the languages. therefore, a more universal visual medium to bridge the gap between them must eventually evolve. first steps in this direction have, strangely enough, been made by the artist. now science must become a teammate and give him support with precise methods for a more purposeful handling of visual problems.

the book has been a standard form for a long time. a new spirit invaded the stagnant field of rigidity with the adoption of the dynamic page composition. an important extension was introduced with the recognition of supra-national pictorial communication. with its combination of text and pictures, today's magazine already represents a new standard medium. while pictorial communication in a new sense has lived through a short but inspiring childhood, typography has hardly aspired to become an integrated element.

exploration of the potentialities of the book of true text-picture integration has only begun and will, by itself, become of utmost importance to universal understanding.

communication of selling

recently certain american national advertising pages have expressed a remarkable trend to planning. these pages contain and operate with a conglomeration of ugly, differently styled, contrasting or conflicting alphabets. the advertising agencies (no artist-designer's reasoning or taste could produce these pages) that produced this concept clearly must have been motivated by attention-getting-by-all-means aggressiveness and provocation. the result is irritation to the reader, who, therefore, reacts. this ignoring of aesthetics, in fact this twisting of unaesthetics into a function, provides a lesson to be learned. here is bad taste under the disguise of functionalism par excellence.

but new typographic life may come from such a ruthless technique, as is exemplified in many of america's "hard-sell" advertising pages. the reason for this speculation is that here typography clearly serves an intended purpose. the means by which the purpose is obtained are wrong and bear none of the aesthetic restraint that dominates much typographic thinking.

the narrow column

sizes of typefaces must be proportionate to the length of the line. the smaller the type, the shorter the line (for a standard measurement, 10 point typeface should not be set wider than 20 to 25 pica). adoption of the narrow column, which has proven itself to be considerably easier and faster to read, as newspaper readers can testify, would change the shape of the book. a "one column" book would be high and narrow, would not lend itself to binding on the long side, but might be divided into separate chapters in accordion folds collected in binders or boxes.

square span

tradition requires that sentences follow each other in a horizontal continuous sequence. paragraphs are used to ease perception by a slight break. there is no reason for this to be the only method to transmit language to the eye. sentences could as well follow each other vertically or otherwise, if it would facilitate reading.

following is an excerpt of a letter from the reporter of direct mail advertising: "square span" is putting words into thought groups of two or three short lines, such as

"after a short time	you will begin thinking	in easily understood	groups of words
you will automatically stop	confusing your sentences	with complicated phrases	and unnecessary words"

typewriters and typesetting machines would have to be adjusted to this method. text written in logical, short thought groups lends itself best. the advantages of grouping words support the theory that we do not read individual letters, but words or phrases. this poses a new challenge for the typographer.

text in color

black printing on white stock, because of its extreme opposites, is not entirely satisfactory. the eye forms complementary images. flickering and optical illusions occur, however minimized they may be in a small typeface. they can be reduced if the contrast of black on white is softened by gray printing on white stock; black printing on gray, yellow, light blue, or light green stock; brown, dark green, or dark blue printing on light colored stock. the colors of printing in relation to the colors of stock need not necessarily be chosen for harmonies; it is the power of controlled contrast that must be retained.

HERBERT BAYER, ON TYPOGRAPHY

change of impact

furthermore, a great easing of reading is effected and freshness of perception is prolonged if a book is made up with a sequence of pages of different colored stock printed in various colors. which color follows another is less important than that the hues be approximately of equal value to safeguard continuity.

dr. w. h. bates has recommended a frequent shifting to aid in refocusing a fixed stare caused by the eye-tiring monotony of reading matter. the typographer can support this recommendation by the above change of impact through color.

new slaves

speculation into the future (perhaps not so distant) leads me to assume that methods of communication will change drastically.

the storage of books will be replaced by microfilms, which in turn will change the design of libraries. computing machines can already substitute for printed matter by storing knowledge. they will have any and all desired information available and ready when needed on short call, faster, more completely than research teams could, relieving and unburdening our brains of memory ballast. this suggests that we will write and read less and less, and the book may be eliminated altogether. the time may come when we have learned to communicate by electronic or extrasensory means.

formalism and the straightjacket of a style lead to a dead end. the self-changing pulse of life is the nature of things with its unlimited forms and ways of expression. this we must recognize and not make new cliches out of old formulas.

3-6

Emil Ruder

Typography

1967

"typography has one plain duty before it and that is to convey information in writing. No argument or consideration can absolve typography from this duty."

Emil Ruder (1914–1970) was a Swiss typographer who, along with Armin Hofmann, established the Swiss Style of minimalist, objective, and formalist design. His work was informed by a deliberate focus on typographic form to convey meaning.

....

Introduction

[...]

The present age knows many of the underlying assumptions and hypotheses of modernism, and it looks as if good design has become something taken for granted. Yet appearances are deceptive, for shoddy craftsmanship and modernistic affectation got up in contemporary garb cause no little confusion. Even taking the optimistic view, it is certain that a great deal of work remains to be done before the knowledge we have acquired gains acceptance and receives its ultimate refinement.

There are two essential aspects to the work of the typographer: he must take into account knowledge already acquired and keep his mind receptive to novelty. It is notoriously easy for satisfaction with what has been already achieved to degenerate into complacency. For this reason training in experimental typography, which involves the workshop becoming a laboratory and testing station, is more necessary than ever before if typography is not to congeal round principles that have long been recognized. There must be no letting up in the determination to produce vital work reflecting the spirit of the times; doubt and perturbation are good antidotes against the tendency to follow the line of least resistance.

It is the intention of this book to bring home to the typographer that perhaps it is precisely the restriction of the means at his disposal and the practical aims he has to fulfill that make the charm of his craft. It is hoped that the book will elicit those strict and inherent laws of the craft of typography which wields such influence in determining the visual aspect of our world today.

It is left to the reader and the future to decide whether the author has succeeded in banishing from his text and examples the excessively modish and the whims and fancies peculiar to our day and age.

Typography has one plain duty before it and that is to convey information in writing. No argument or consideration can absolve typography from this duty. A printed work which cannot be read becomes a product without purpose.

From the invention of printing in the 15th century down to the printed work of the 20th efforts have been directed exclusively to one end: to disseminate information in the cheapest and quickest possible way. The only exceptions were the fine editions printed at the turn of the century at a time when technical progress and the industrialization that went with it commanded unqualified admiration. To impress upon that age the beauty of work which was true to material and the craft, something happened which was quite contrary to the essential nature of typography: editions were artificially limited in order to confer rarity and therefore greater value upon the individual copy. Nevertheless we are indebted to these limited editions for obtaining recognition for certain prerequisites in typography: a feeling for the written form and an understanding of its nature; a proper division of the type into word, line, page and a compact area of type unequivocally related to the blank areas; the double-spread as the starting point for work on a book; unity of typeface and limitations as regards kind and size.

At the beginning of the 20th century the bibliophile was already under criticism: the limited edition of a "merely" beautiful book is absurd; a book must be beautiful and cheap. And this calls for as big an edition as possible. Book production for the bibliophile is ridiculed as antiquated and obsolete.

Today the book has become a cheap consumer article and has made its way from the bookshop through to the department store to the kiosk in the street, side by side with the newspaper, leaflet and poster. It is here, no doubt, that typography has found its fulfilment as a means to mass communication.

The typographer chooses the printing types he requires from a large variety of typefaces, none of which he has designed himself. He often considers his dependence on the founts the type designer and founder have created for him to be a disadvantage. This dependence is particularly inconvenient when the variety of types available does not meet his requirements either artistically or technically.

The typographer has to realize that he occupies a place in the printing trade in which, on the one hand, he is dependent on the finished work of others (type, paper, ink, tools, machines) and, on the other, he has to enable others to put his work through subsequent additional processes (printing, finishing). He is not free to make his own independent decisions; he must depend on what went beforehand and take into account what is to come.

The fact that the typographer has no contribution of his own to make to the form of the typeface but takes these ready-made is of the essence of typography and must not be regarded as a detraction from the craft. Quite the contrary. It is not merely that type design involves aesthetic problems; the forms are largely determined by technical factors which are quite unknown to the typographer.

The type designer should avoid idiosyncrasies as far as possible in his typefaces, since these are detrimental to the universal use of the type. The designer of type is often found to be the very man who is not invariably successful in his application of type, since he often lacks the necessary critical distance from his own creation. But the typographer does possess this ability to stand back from the work, and it is very useful to him in his craft, since critical distance is a virtue in a typographer. The typographer must be able to take the impersonal view; wilful individuality and emotion have little place in his work.

The sum total of all these prefabricated elements is so large that there is an almost infinite number of possible ways of arranging them in ever-new patterns. There can be no question of the typographer exhausting all the potential combinations. There would have to be a systematic effort to narrow down typographical forms and reduce them to a few formulae before typography became rigid and lifeless.

The written character is and remains the basis of every typographical activity. It is not a creation of our century. The written character goes far back in time, spanning the vast distance from early hieroglyphics to the abstract written symbols of today and involving many contradictions. The typographer must be familiar with this evolution and recognize its problems so that he can do justice to the tasks of the future.

Our direction of reading was developed in Early Greek lapidary writing (by way of the boustrophedonic intermediate stage), and the transformation of capitals into lower-case letters can also be followed as a parallel phenomenon. Some of the ancient majuscules underwent a charming metamorphosis into lower-case letters; a smaller number remained in the majuscule form. Lower-case letters, initially used in Carolingian minuscule, make for more rapid reading when composed into a word by virtue of their ascenders and descenders. The evolution of written characters was concluded; all the rest is variation and confusion.

Variation: Carolingian minuscule appears in variant forms in the characters of Gothic, the Italian and German Renaissance, and the sans-serif of our time, but there have been no drastic changes in its basic forms.

Confusion: *Littera umanistica* grew into a heterogeneous alphabet; its lower-case letters were supplemented by capitals taken from the classical world, and figures from Arabic were added to the Western hand. Not only the type designer but also the typographer ought to be alive to the complex nature of written characters. Perhaps we are in much the same position as Charlemagne, who felt constrained to order the creation of his minuscule in which the many transitional forms of the past were amalgamated. The many active contacts between people from every country today leave no scope for typefaces with a pronounced national character.

The neutral typeface, aloof from all national considerations, has already to some extent become reality. Simplicity is the goal of technical progress, and there is hardly any warrant for using five different alphabets to set an ordinary text: capitals, roman and italic; lower-case, roman and italic; and small capitals. Direct lines right round the world are used for teleprinters, and alphabets are being evolved which can be read automatically by a machine. Technology compels us to think afresh and calls for new forms as a living expression of the age in which we live.

The craft of the typographer, like any other, necessarily reflects the times. The age gives him the means with which to satisfy the needs the age creates. There are two sides to typography. First, it does a practical job of work; and second, it is concerned with artistic form. Both these aspects, the utilitarian and the formal, have ever been true children of their day and age; sometimes form has been accentuated, sometimes function, and in particularly blessed periods form and function have been felicitously balanced.

In recent years specialist literature has been very insistent in its call for typographical design matched to modern times. In 1931 Paul Renner wrote: "The printing works is not a place that hires out fancy dress. It is not our task to fit out any literary content with a fashionable costume; we have done our job if we see that it gets a dress in the style of our day. For what we want is typographical life and not a typographical theatre or masked ball." In 1948 Stanley Morison wrote: "Printing does not want primarily to be art but the most responsible part of our social, economic and intellectual structure."

Seen over a tract of years, any period makes a solid, uniform impression. The typography of the Gothic age bears a striking similarity to other works of the same epoch, the "yachting style" at the turn of the century is reflected in the fount of Otto Eckmann, and the Constructivism of the twenties in the typography of the Bauhaus. For contemporary man the present is never simple, it confuses him with its multifariousness; yet we ought to recognize the features of the twentieth century clearly enough. These characteristics come into being by way of our efforts to find the best possible answer to the problems facing us; only then will the printed work become a genuine document marked with the unmistakable traits of our day. The different fields of creative activity have not yet become autonomous, and typography cannot be segregated from the general flux of events. This would be tantamount to condemning it to sterility. But it has laws of its own, imposed by its technical nature, and these can and should preserve its identity even when it is closely bound up with other fields. One may sometimes regret the way typography becomes all too easily involved in the fits and moods of the age, but it is better than standing by aloof. The creative worker, on the other hand, spares little thought for contemporary style, for he realizes that style is not something that can be deliberately created; it comes all unawares!

More than graphic design, typography is an expression of technology, precision and good order. Typography is no longer concerned with meeting the lofty and difficult demands of art but with satisfying, formally and functionally, the everyday requirements of a craft. The mechanical production of printing types and composition within a right angled system of fixed dimensions makes a clear structure and cleanly ordered relationships imperative.

What the typographer has to do first and foremost is to sort out and organize things which are of a very disparate nature. The whole text of a book is so unwieldy that it has to be divided up in such a way that the reader can manage each page comfortably and follow the print without impediment. A line of more than 60 characters is hard to read; too little space between lines destroys the pattern they make, too much exaggerates it.

Tabular works afford the typographer his best opportunity to show his skill in arranging his material, but he must not let such purely formal requirements get out of hand. The composition of tables has a beauty and technical charm of its own, and a simple page of a railway timetable may well be a better piece of craftsmanship than jobbing work replete with colours and fancy shapes. But advertising is also a challenge to the typographer.

Our age needs printed works which catch the eye when ideas and products are forever competing for our attention. With an enormous range of typefaces available, thin or thick, large or small, it is a question of selecting the right one, composing the copy with these faces and interpreting it. The typographer should have founts at his disposal which combine agreeably, and mention might be made in this connection of the Univers family, which is very well graded and embodies a great deal of careful thought. Let us hope that this achievement will show the way to better things and help to sort out the more or less chaotic state of affairs in typefounding today.

Many pieces of printing are attractive for the simple reason that the typographer put aside artistic ambitions and tried to make the print do its job well. They are just what Stanley Morison wanted when he said that a printed work, being a means of communication, should be thought out to the last detail and made superlatively fit for the purpose it serves.

In the architecture of the Baroque, in modern architecture and sculpture, and in oriental philosophy and art the significance of created form and the effect of the counter-form arising in space are held to be of equal value.

The re-assessment of Baroque architecture by the modern age is partly based on the fact that the incorporation of empty space into the whole is consistent with the axioms of modern art. Living space is articulated into large cubes, and the empty space between the buildings is fitted into the overall scheme. This gives rise to an unencumbered area for that "activity of standing together or strolling which derives variously from business, conversation and sweet leisure" (Jakob Burckhardt).

The oriental philosophers hold that the essence of created form depends on empty space. Without its hollow interior a jug is merely a lump of clay, and it is only the empty space inside that makes it into a vessel. Thus we read in the eleventh aphorism of Lao-Tse:

"Thirty spokes meet the hub,
but it is the emptiness between them that makes the essence of the wheel.
From clay pots are made,
but it is the emptiness inside them that makes the essence of the pot.
Walls with windows and doors form the house,

but it is the emptiness between them that makes the essence of the house.
The principle: The material contains usefulness, the immaterial imparts essence."

These are considerations which can and should be transferred to typography. Unlike the Renaissance, when the unprinted blank was merely a background for what was printed thereon, contemporary typographers have long recognized the empty space of the unprinted surface to be an element of design. The typographer is familiar with white as a value in design and he is familiar with the visual changes of white.

[...]

Without rhythm there would be no life, there would be no creation at all. Each creature passes rhythmically through its stages of growth; under the wind's influence, forests, corn fields and the shifting sands move in rhythm. The advent of the machine has brought home to us again the value of a working rhythm, and we know that the health of the worker, his mental equilibrium, depends on his working in rhythm. Every shade of rhythmic awareness can be seen reflected in works of art down the ages. And in the twentieth century in particular, artists have again become alive to the significance and power of rhythm in design.

In typography there are many opportunities of working with rhythmic values. Take a typeface for instance. The straights and curves, verticals and horizontals, sloping elements, starts and finishes work together to produce a rhythmic pattern. There is an abundance of rhythmic values in an ordinary piece of composition: ascenders and descenders, round and pointed forms, symmetry and asymmetry. The word spaces divide the line and type matter into words of unequal size, into a rhythmic interplay of varying lengths and values of different weight. Break and blank lines also add accents of their own to the pattern of composition, and finally the graded sizes of the type are another excellent means of bringing rhythm into the typographer's work. If a simple piece of text is well composed, it will of its own accord give the work a rhythmic appeal.

The format of the paper is another rhythmic pattern, whether it is the symmetry of the equilateral square, or the stressed rhythm of the edges and sides of the rectangle. The typographer has endless possibilities of creating rhythms by the way he disposes his composition on the page. The shape of the composition can harmonize or contrast in its rhythm with the format of the paper. In designing composition, the typographer should examine every possible means of getting away from rigid systems and dull repetition, not merely for the sake of vitalizing the form but also in the interests of legibility.

3-7

Josef Müller-Brockmann

Grid Systems in Graphic Design
1981

"the reduction of the number of visual elements used and their incorporation in a grid system creates a sense of compact planning, intelligibility, and clarity, and suggests orderliness of design"

Josef Müller-Brockmann (1914–1996) was a Swiss graphic designer and a leading proponent of Swiss Style typography. His books, which include The Graphic Artist and His Design Problems *and* Grid Systems in Graphic Design, *remain influential today.*

Grid and Design Philosophy

The use of the grid as an ordering system is the expression of a certain mental attitude inasmuch as it shows that the designer conceives his work in terms that are constructive and oriented to the future.

This is the expression of a professional ethos: the designer's work should have the clearly intelligible, objective, functional, and aesthetic quality of mathematical thinking.

His work should thus be a contribution to general culture and itself form part of it.

Constructive design which is capable of analysis and reproduction can influence and enhance the taste of a society and the way it conceives forms and colors. Design which is objective, committed to the common weal, well composed, and refined constitutes the basis of democratic behavior. Constructivist design means the conversion of design laws into practical solutions. Work done systematically and in accordance with strict formal principles makes those demands for directness, intelligibility, and the integration of all factors which are also vital in sociopolitical life.

Work with the grid system means submitting to laws of universal validity.
The use of the grid system implies
the will to systematize, to clarify
the will to penetrate to the essentials, to concentrate
the will to cultivate objectivity instead of subjectivity

the will to rationalize the creative and technical production processes
the will to integrate elements of color, form, and material
the will to achieve architectural dominion over surface and space
the will to adopt a positive, forward-looking attitude
the recognition of the importance of education and the effect of work devised in a
constructive and creative spirit.

Every visual creative work is a manifestation of the character of the designer. It is a
reflection of his knowledge, his ability, and his mentality.

The Typographic Grid

The grid divides a two-dimensional plane into smaller fields or a three-dimensional space
into smaller compartments. The fields or compartments may be the same or different in
size. The fields correspond in depth to a specific number of lines of text and the width of
the fields is identical with the width of the columns. The depths and the widths are indicated in typographic measures, in points and ciceros.

The fields are separated by an intermediate space so that on the one hand pictures do not
touch each other and legibility is thus preserved and on the other that captions can be
placed below the illustrations.

The vertical distance between the fields is one, two, or more lines of text, the horizontal
space depending on the size of the type character and of the illustrations. By means of this
division into grid fields the elements of design, viz. typography, photography, illustration,
and color, can be disposed in a better way. These elements are adjusted to the size of the
grid fields and fitted precisely into the size of the fields. The smallest illustration corresponds to the smallest grid field.

The grid for a $^1/_1$ page comprises a smaller or larger number of such grid fields. All illustrations, photographs, statistics, etc., have the size of one, two, three, or four grid fields.
In this way a certain uniformity is attained in the presentation of visual information.

The grid determines the constant dimensions of space. There is virtually no limit to the
number of grid divisions. It may be said in general that every piece of work must be studied
very carefully so as to arrive at the specific grid network corresponding to its requirements.

The rule: The fewer the differences in the size of the illustrations, the quieter the impression
created by the design. As a controlling system, the grid makes it easier to give the surface or
space a rational organization.

Such a system of arrangement compels the designer to be honest in his use of design
resources. It requires him to come to terms with the problem in hand and to analyse it. It
fosters analytical thinking and gives the solution of the problem a logical and material basis.
If the text and pictures are arranged systematically, the priorities stand out more clearly.

A suitable grid in visual design makes it easier

a

to construct the argument objectively with the means of visual communication

b

to construct the text and illustrative material systematically and logically

c

to organize the text and illustrations in a compact arrangement with its own rhythm

d

to put together the visual material so that it is readily intelligible and structured with a high degree of tension.

There are various reasons for using the grid as an aid to the organization of text and illustration:

economic reasons: a problem can be solved in less time and at lower cost;

rational reasons: both simple and complex problems can be solved in a uniform and characteristic style;

mental attitude: the systematic presentation of facts, of sequences of events, and of solutions to problems should, for social and educational reasons, be a constructive contribution to the cultural state of society and an expression of our sense of responsibility.

What Is the Purpose of the Grid?

The grid is used by the typographer, graphic designer, photographer, and exhibition designer for solving visual problems in two and three dimensions. The graphic designer and typographer use it for designing press advertisements, brochures, catalogs, books, periodicals, etc., and the exhibition designer for conceiving his plan for exhibitions and show-window displays.

By arranging the surfaces and spaces in the form of a grid the designer is favorably placed to dispose his texts, photographs, and diagrams in conformity with objective and functional criteria. The pictorial elements are reduced to a few formats of the same size. The size of the pictures is determined according to their importance for the subject.

The reduction of the number of visual elements used and their incorporation in a grid system creates a sense of compact planning, intelligibility, and clarity, and suggests orderliness of design. This orderliness lends added credibility to the information and induces confidence.

Information presented with clear and logically set out titles, subtitles, texts, illustrations, and captions will not only be read more quickly and easily but the information will also be better understood and retained in the memory. This is a scientifically proved fact, and the designer should bear it constantly in mind.

The grid can be successfully used for the corporate identities of firms. This includes all visual media of information from the visiting card to the exhibition stand: all printed forms for internal and external use, advertising matter, vehicles for goods and passenger transport, name-plates and lettering on buildings, etc.

Postmodernism and De(con)structionism
| Expressing Subjectivity

Deconstruction refers to the notion, formulated by the philosopher
Jacques Derrida, that text necessarily undoes itself. That is, any text
tacitly undermines its own position by inviting interpretation and
analysis, and therefore cannot be stable, systematic, or unified. The
term has been co-opted by popular culture and can now describe
any act that self-consciously eschews normative standards in order to
challenge convention.

The graphic design movement known as deconstructive typography draws upon a generalized understanding of the term rather than an in-depth comprehension of all it encompasses. Deconstructive typography purposefully ignores conventional, grid-based typographic practices by championing intuition, randomness, and personal preference above rationality and systemization. As a result of this approach, deconstructive typography simultaneously disrupts the work's semiotic field and hinders the viewer's ability to generate a stable, univocal, and unambiguous interpretation.

It can be argued that deconstructionism's celebration of polysemy—a sign's ability to have several meanings—is problematic for the purposes of visual communication, and rarely does one find a nuanced, philosophical underpinning to late twentieth-century and early twenty-first-century graphic design. Instead, design that revels in the shallow play of stochastic surface forms, design that celebrates the idiosyncratic, expressive whim of the designer, proliferates. Perhaps such design should therefore be understood as "destructive" rather than "deconstructive"; like the avant-garde designs of previous movements, destructive typography often disregards coherent design principles meant to foster understanding in favor of visual egotism. Therefore, while these designs can be appreciated for their aesthetic innovation, one is hard-pressed to view them as exemplars of visual communication.

Derrida warned that deconstruction cannot be used as a methodological practice. Deconstruction is and is not everything simultaneously. However, postmodernity and the ideologies underlined by true deconstruction can be beneficial within a structure-oriented design program, as long as it is seen as part of the design process and not as the final product. Within these parameters, deconstruction can serve as a useful design tool, allowing for an antithetical approach to a challenging design equation.

4-1

Robert Venturi

Complexity and Contradiction in Architecture
1966

"where simplicity cannot work, simpleness results. Blatant simplification means bland architecture. Less is a bore"

Robert Venturi (1925–) is a Pritzker Architecture Prize–winning American postmodern architect and a founding principal of the firm Venturi, Scott Brown and Associates. Learning from Las Vegas, *the treatise on populist architecture and Las Vegas he cowrote with the architect Denise Scott Brown, remains a foundational text. He coined the maxim "Less is a bore," a retort to Mies van der Rohe's famous modernist dictum "Less is more."*

....

1. Nonstraightforward Architecture : A Gentle Manifesto
I like complexity and contradiction in architecture. I do not like the incoherence or arbitrariness of incompetent architecture nor the precious intricacies of picturesqueness or expressionism. Instead, I speak of a complex and contradictory architecture based on the richness and ambiguity of modern experience, including that experience which is inherent in art. Everywhere, except in architecture, complexity and contradiction have been acknowledged, from Gödel's proof of ultimate inconsistency in mathematics to T. S. Eliot's analysis of "difficult" poetry and Joseph Albers' definition of the paradoxical quality of painting.

But architecture is necessarily complex and contradictory in its very inclusion of the traditional Vitruvian elements of commodity, firmness, and delight. And today the wants of program, structure, mechanical equipment, and expression, even in single buildings in simple contexts, are diverse and conflicting in ways previously unimaginable. The increasing dimension and scale of architecture in urban and regional planning add to the difficulties. I welcome the problems and exploit the uncertainties. By embracing contradiction as well as complexity, I aim for vitality as well as validity.

Architects can no longer afford to be intimidated by the puritanically moral language of orthodox Modern architecture. I like elements which are hybrid rather than "pure," compromising rather than "clean," distorted rather than "straightforward," ambiguous rather than "articulated," perverse as well as impersonal, boring as well as "interesting," conventional rather than "designed," accommodating rather than excluding, redundant rather than simple, vestigial as well as innovating, inconsistent and equivocal rather than direct and clear. I am for messy vitality over obvious unity. I include the non sequitur and proclaim the duality.

I am for richness of meaning rather than clarity of meaning; for the implicit function as well as the explicit function. I prefer "both-and" to "either-or," black and white, and sometimes gray, to black or white. A valid architecture evokes many levels of meaning and combinations of focus: its space and its elements become readable and workable in several ways at once.

But an architecture of complexity and contradiction has a special obligation toward the whole: its truth must be in its totality or its implications of totality. It must embody the difficult unity of inclusion rather than the easy unity of exclusion. More is not less.

2. Complexity and Contradiction vs. Simplification or Picturesqueness

Orthodox Modern architects have tended to recognize complexity insufficiently or inconsistently. In their attempt to break with tradition and start all over again, they idealized the primitive and elementary at the expense of the diverse and the sophisticated. As participants in a revolutionary movement, they acclaimed the newness of modern functions, ignoring their complications. In their role as reformers, they puritanically advocated the separation and exclusion of elements, rather than the inclusion of various requirements and their juxtapositions. As a forerunner of the Modern movement, Frank Lloyd Wright, who grew up with the motto "Truth against the World," wrote: "Visions of simplicity so broad and far-reaching would open to me and such building harmonies appear that... would change and deepen the thinking and culture of the modern world. So I believed." And Le Corbusier, co-founder of Purism, spoke of the "great primary forms" which, he proclaimed, were "distinct...and without ambiguity." Modern architects with few exceptions eschewed ambiguity.

But now our position is different: "At the same time that the problems increase in quantity, complexity, and difficulty they also change faster than before," and require an attitude more like that described by August Heckscher: "The movement from a view of life as essentially simple and orderly to a view of life as complex and ironic is what every individual passes through in becoming mature. But certain epochs encourage this development; in them the paradoxical or dramatic outlook colors the whole intellectual scene....Amid simplicity and order rationalism is born, but rationalism proves inadequate in any period of upheaval. Then equilibrium must be created out of opposites. Such inner peace as men gain must represent a tension among contradictions and uncertainties....A feeling for paradox allows seemingly dissimilar things to exist side by side, their very incongruity suggesting a kind of truth."

Rationalizations for simplification are still current, however, though subtler than the early arguments. They are expansions of Mies van der Rohe's magnificent paradox, "less is more." Paul Rudolph has clearly stated the implications of Mies' point of view: "All problems can never be solved....Indeed it is a characteristic of the twentieth century that architects are highly selective in determining which problems they want to solve. Mies, for instance, makes wonderful buildings only because he ignores many aspects of a building. If he solved more problems, his buildings would be far less potent."

The doctrine "less is more" bemoans complexity and justifies exclusion for expressive purposes. It does, indeed, permit the architect to be "highly selective in determining which problems [he wants] to solve." But if the architect must be "committed to his particular way of seeing the universe," such a commitment surely means that the architect determines how problems should be solved, not that he can determine which of the problems he will solve. He can exclude important considerations only at the risk of separating architecture from the experience of life and the needs of society. If some problems prove insoluble, he can express this: in an inclusive rather than an exclusive kind of architecture there is room for the fragment, for contradiction, for improvisation, and for the tensions these produce. Mies' exquisite pavilions have had valuable implications for architecture, but their selectiveness of content and language is their limitation as well as their strength.

I question the relevance of analogies between pavilions and houses, especially analogies between Japanese pavilions and recent domestic architecture. They ignore the real complexity and contradiction inherent in the domestic program—the spatial and technological possibilities as well as the need for variety in visual experience. Forced simplicity results in oversimplification. In the Wiley House, for instance, in contrast to his glass house, Philip Johnson attempted to go beyond the simplicities of the elegant pavilion. He explicitly separated and articulated the enclosed "private functions" of living on a ground floor pedestal, thus separating them from the open social functions in the modular pavilion above. But even here the building becomes a diagram of an oversimplified program for living—an abstract theory of either-or. Where simplicity cannot work, simpleness results. Blatant simplification means bland architecture. Less is a bore.

The recognition of complexity in architecture does not negate what Louis Kahn has called "the desire for simplicity." But aesthetic simplicity which is a satisfaction to the mind derives, when valid and profound, from inner complexity. The Doric temple's simplicity to the eye is achieved through the famous subtleties and precision of its distorted geometry and the contradictions and tensions inherent in its order. The Doric temple could achieve apparent simplicity through real complexity. When complexity disappeared, as in the late temples, blandness replaced simplicity.

Nor does complexity deny the valid simplification which is part of the process of analysis, and even a method of achieving complex architecture itself. "We oversimplify a given event when we characterize it from the standpoint of a given interest." But this kind of simplification is a method in the analytical process of achieving a complex art. It should not be mistaken for a goal.

An architecture of complexity and contradiction, however, does not mean picturesqueness or subjective expressionism. A false complexity has recently countered the false simplicity of an earlier Modern architecture. It promotes an architecture of symmetrical picturesqueness—which Minoru Yamasaki calls "serene"—but it represents a new formalism as unconnected with experience as the former cult of simplicity. Its intricate forms do not reflect genuinely complex programs, and its intricate ornament, though dependent on industrial techniques for execution, is dryly reminiscent of forms originally created by handicraft techniques. Gothic tracery and Rococo rocaille were not only expressively valid in relation to the whole, but came from a valid showing-off of hand skills and expressed a vitality derived from the immediacy and individuality of the method. This kind of complexity through exuberance, perhaps impossible today, is the antithesis of "serene" architecture, despite the superficial resemblance between them. But if exuberance is not characteristic of our art, it is tension, rather than "serenity," that would appear to be so.

The best twentieth-century architects have usually rejected simplification—that is, simplicity through reduction—in order to promote complexity within the whole. The works of Alvar Aalto and Le Corbusier (who often disregards his polemical writings) are examples. But the characteristics of complexity and contradiction in their work are often ignored or misunderstood. Critics of Aalto, for instance, have liked him mostly for his sensitivity to natural materials and his fine detailing, and have considered his whole com-position willful picturesqueness. I do not consider Aalto's Imatra church picturesque. By repeating in the massing the genuine complexity of the triple-divided plan and the acous-tical ceiling pattern, this church represents a justifiable expressionism different from the willful picturesqueness of the haphazard structure and spaces of Giovanni Michelucci's recent church for the Autostrada. Aalto's complexity is part of the program and structure of the whole rather than a device justified only by the desire for expression. Though we no longer argue over the primacy of form or function (which follows which?), we cannot ignore their interdependence.

The desire for a complex architecture, with its attendant contradictions, is not only a reaction to the banality or prettiness of current architecture. It is an attitude common in the Mannerist periods: the sixteenth century in Italy or the Hellenistic period in Classical art, and is also a continuous strain seen in such diverse architects as Michelangelo, Palladio, Borromini, Vanbrugh, Hawksmoor, Soane, Ledoux, Butterfield, some architects of the Shingle Style, Furness, Sullivan, Lutyens, and recently, Le Corbusier, Aalto, Kahn, and others.

Today this attitude is again relevant to both the medium of architecture and the program in architecture.

First, the medium of architecture must be re-examined if the increased scope of our architecture as well as the complexity of its goals is to be expressed. Simplified or super-ficially complex forms will not work. Instead, the variety inherent in the ambiguity of visual perception must once more be acknowledged and exploited.

Second, the growing complexities of our functional problems must be acknowledged. I refer, of course, to those programs, unique in our time, which are complex because of their scope, such as research laboratories, hospitals, and particularly the enormous projects at the scale of city and regional planning. But even the house, simple in scope, is complex in purpose if the ambiguities of contemporary experience are expressed. This contrast between the means and the goals of a program is significant. Although the means involved in the program of a rocket to get to the moon, for instance, are almost infinitely complex, the goal is simple and contains few contradictions; although the means involved in the program and structure of buildings are far simpler and less sophis-ticated technologically than almost any engineering project, the purpose is more complex and often inherently ambiguous.

Wim Crouwel and Jan van Toorn

The Debate

1972

"the designer has freedom, but it also comes with certain formal restrictions… come on, boys, stop it! You go too far as a designer"

"the acts you perform take place through you, and you are a subjective link. But you deny this subjectivity, meaning"

Wim Crouwel (1928–) is a Dutch graphic designer and educator who has created typefaces, corporate identities, posters, and album covers. He is best known for his graphic design work for the Stedelijk Museum in Amsterdam.

Jan van Toorn (1932–) is a graphic designer, educator, and self-proclaimed "visual journalist." He conveys meaning through unconventional design that privileges semantic message over style.

....

Wim Crouwel

My first remark is a generalizing one. When as a designer you respond to a topical social or cultural pattern, this may give rise to, first, an analytical approach, in order to arrive at an objective participation in a process of communication; this is an approach, in my view of lasting value and longevity. And, second, it may give rise to a spontaneous approach that strongly appeals to current opinion and therefore has powerful communicative effects. But I believe this is a short-lived communication.

In my opinion, these are the two things that move us, and I would like to clarify them. Designer A, who favors the analytical approach to arrive at a maximally objective message, will be inclined to make use of solidly tested means only and will not be easily tempted to experiment for the sake of novelty. For this reason, he is also likely to end up in a place that is sometimes characterized as rather dry. By contrast, Designer B is more likely to make use of trendy means, and he will not reject experiments in order to arrive at new results.

Further, Designer A will be inclined to position himself professionally, without surrendering his sense of responsibility vis-à-vis society, and therefore he will refrain from engaging in specialties that are not his. Through his specific work, he will provide a contribution to the problem articulated. I think that Designer B, based on his large sense of responsibility towards society, will tend to become so absorbed by the problem posed that he enters into specialties that are not his. He runs the risk of wasting his expertise by resorting to an amateurish contribution to the problem at hand.

Our colleagues know which side I'm on, for I believe that as a designer I must never stand between the message and its recipient. Instead, I try to present the issue as neutrally as possible.

Jan van Toorn

I think that as a specialization graphic design, just like other forms of design, has begun to fall short under the pressure of industrial developments in our society and all their various consequences. The designer falls short not only because through his use of form he programs rather than informs, but also because he no longer questions his goal and responsibility. His design influences and conditions users, rather than supporting its content.

I start from more or less the same two types of designers as Wim. But what you call the analytical designer, I call the technologist-designer, because he works with methods derived from technology and science. The analytical strand, of which you are a characteristic exponent, is determined by a technological-organizational attitude. I do not believe that a designer can adopt, as you put it, the position of neutral intermediary. The acts you perform take place *through* you, and you are a subjective link. But you deny this subjectivity, meaning: you view your occupation as a purely neutral one.

Wim says that he uses a particular graphic means as a neutral thing, but in my view it is always used subjectively. Its use, after all, has social meaning! It has a social goal and that is why it is subjective. It is there that your influence lies, be it your personal influence or your influence as a group. It all depends on how you use your means.

Those in graphic design, just like people in other specialties, are inclined not only to exaggerate their own value, but also to start seeing their dealings and their means as a goal in itself, thus losing sight of the actual goal. This is why I once again looked up what you wrote in the 1961 Christmas issue[1]. The first thing you say there about design is that form is determined by content. But in the remainder of this short article I do not read a single word on the relation between content and form, yet there is an awful lot about formal options, techniques, and technology, so about means in general. But today, I feel, the relationship between form and content is in fact highly relevant. It is perhaps more so than in 1961, for it comes with a responsibility. And maybe we should be adventurous in facing the challenge, without perhaps sufficiently knowing the means we have at our disposal.

1   *The Christmas issue of* Drukkersweekblad en Autolijn, *a weekly trade publication for the printing and publishing industries.*

Wim Crouwel

When you say that my approach is technological and observe that I constantly talk about technology, this is an effect of my fondness for technology. I was at times strongly influenced by technical innovations. But I do not have the sense of being led by technology to such a degree that I've ever become an extension of the machine. Technology is a source of wonder to me, and I have long believed that it would be able to free us from a great many difficulties.

After all, the amount of information fired at people has grown so large that it can no longer be processed. In this predicament a particular technology may offer a solution, if you apply it well. To apply technology well, I once made a proposal for a new basic alphabet. And this implied larger freedom for the designer than before, when alphabets were forced upon us and handed down to us from the Renaissance, the baroque, and neoclassicism.

To be sure, the designer has freedom, but it also comes with certain formal restrictions. Formal restrictions can be stretched according to your needs. So when I show admiration for technology, this does not automatically lead to technological work.

I would like to cite a recent statement by Jan from the newspaper: "The function of a graphic designer is to convey information. This should happen in a way that makes it possible for the reader or viewer to arrive at a view of his own, rather than imposing the mind-set of the messenger."

When Jan says that design is a subjective activity, he adopts—as a designer—the role of intermediary. I'm afraid, however, to adopt such a subjective role, and rather try to take an objective stance.

At first glance, Jan van Toorn, as he put it in the newspaper quote, views the designer as a coordinator who, without defining views of his own, merely provides assistance in realizing some communication of information. But this is not the case with Jan, because he does not operate without taking a position in between sender and receiver. Jan quite consciously participates subjectively in that process.

Jan van Toorn

Let us first briefly talk about this subjectivity. In my view, there are two important issues. To convey content does not mean that the design itself does not represent particular values. Any design has a certain content, an emotional value. It has specific features. It has a clear goal. You have to convey something to somebody. Perhaps a political conviction, perhaps only a report on a meeting. Any design is addressed to someone. The double duty of the messenger, the designer, is to convey the content without interfering with it. On the other hand, there is the designer's inescapable input and subjectivity. You cannot deny this dialectic, and you should rather see it as an advantage.

You are afraid of it, and you used the word "fear." You do not want to inflict harm onto either the content or the identity [of the message], which is why you always design in the same way—this, at least, is what I think your work will show over a longer period. By giving the same design response in all situations, you produce work of great uniformity, in which any sense of identity is lost. In my opinion, however, identity is a most essential feature of all human contact, including the communication of any kind of message.

Wim Crouwel

I agree with you when you say that you can never step outside of yourself. As the designer of the message, you stand in between the sender and the receiver. And when I claim to be afraid to put myself in between them, that is because I feel it's never productive for me to add a vision of my own on top of it. I believe you can separate the two.

When a designer works for a political party or wants to promote his own political convictions, he goes at it in a very subjective way, because he then chooses a perspective. He will shape this perspective through his own personal input in order to get his point across as optimally as possible. This implies that a designer should only do work that he can fully agree with. Well, it is impossible for me to concur with that position. In particular with regard to work involving a political dimension, I say: "It's okay to do it subjectively." But then you run the risk of ending up with a rather narrow range of assignments.

When you take a position like mine, I say: "Guys, I do not want to contribute to what the man says, because I want to be able to offer my services as a designer in a wider area." After all, when as a designer I adopt a subjective position and I'm constantly aware of it, this is automatically visible in my designs. However, this is possible in specific cases only, and not in a very broad area, or you risk lapsing into that amateurism I mentioned previously, something I do not believe in. At the time I had an extensive conversation with René[2] about a program aimed at doing something about educational materials for developing countries. In this context, one designer felt motivated to immerse himself completely in the problem of educational materials, and subsequently he began to design based on that knowledge. My response would be: Come on, boys, stop it! You go too far as a designer. This is something you really shouldn't do, because in this instance you'd better engage an educational specialist to supply the specific know-how. You are the designer, and you shouldn't come anywhere near that specific know-how. Instead, based on your know-how, you start tackling the problem from your professional attitude and approach, after you've been given a thorough briefing. And this is the part someone else should stay away from, because this is your territory. Of course there has to be an ongoing conversation, unquestionably, but I strongly believe in specialties.

I fear, then, that for instance standard typography, meaning book typography, cannot be done by someone who adopts such a subjective stance, for a book, any book, will never become a better one just through its typography. Never ever. Even the admirable achievement of the *Nieuwe Zakelijkheid*[3], a typography that follows the text closely and emphasizes it, is way too subjective to my taste already. I find it altogether wrong. But let me not exaggerate the word "subjective." The subjective designer has a much more limited scope of work, and he'd better accept it. His talents will never be done full justice while there is a demand for designers in many more domains.

2 *René de Jong, then director of the organization for Dutch Graphic Designers (GVN).*
3 *The Nieuwe Zakelijkheid (New Objectivity) is a term used in the Netherlands for modernism and functionalism in architecture and design in the interwar years.*

Jan van Toorn

First let me address your specialties and the reference to the New Objectivity. A specialist attitude such as yours, whereby you get in touch with other disciplines but do not want to immerse yourself in their backgrounds and expect to be briefed, produces a proxy. You create a disconnect, whereas there are in fact connections. Moreover, general human experience, which can't be reduced to a single operational denominator, spans more territory than that covered by the rational disciplines. Still it is quite possible to approach, to come nearer to such a human dimension, and this is something you ignore.

The designer should approach his vocation from the angle of the artist and the origin of his métier, *and* from an industrial-technological angle. For me, however, it is not relevant at all to articulate the different methods and their corresponding means. It is about one's attitude regarding social relations. This is what should be center stage, but you see it only once in a while.

You impose your design on others and level everything. You were at the forefront, and now our country is inundated by waves of trademarks and house styles and everything looks the same. Yet there are challengers as well, and they come from designers who take a much more sensitive approach. To me, your approach is not relevant, and in my view you should not propagate it as the only possible solution for a number of communication problems, because it's not true. What your approach does is basically confirm existing patterns. This is not serving communication—it is conditioning human behavior.

Katherine McCoy

Typography as Discourse
1988

Rethinking Modernism, Revising Functionalism
1994

"the focus now is on expression through semantic content, utilizing the intellectual software of visual language as well as the structural hardware and graphic grammar of modernism"

Katherine McCoy (1945–) is a renowned American graphic designer and educator. With her husband, Michael McCoy, she formed the practice McCoy & McCoy Associates in 1971. She has served on the faculty of various academic institutions, notably as cochair with Michael McCoy of the Cranbrook Academy of Art graduate design program from 1971 to 1995.

....

Typography as Discourse
1988

The recent history of graphic design in the U.S. reveals a series of actions and reactions. The fifties saw the flowering of U.S. graphic design in the New York School. This copy-concept and image-oriented direction was challenged in the sixties by the importation of Swiss minimalism, a structural and typographic system that forced a split between graphic design and advertising. Predictably, designers in the next decade rebelled against Helvetica and the grid system that had become the official American corporate style.

In the early seventies, Robert Venturi's *Complexity and Contradiction in Architecture* emerged alongside the study of graphic design history as influences on American graphic design students. Simultaneously, Switzerland's Basel school was transformed by Wolfgang Weingart's syntactical experimentation, an enthusiasm that quickly spread to U.S. schools. Academia's rediscovery of early 20th century Modernism, the appearance of historicized and vernacular architectural postmodernism and the spread of Weingartian structural expressionism all came together in the graphic explosion labeled as New Wave.

Shattering the constraints of minimalism was exhilarating and far more fun than the antiseptic discipline of the classical Swiss school. After a brief flurry of diatribes in the graphic design press, this permissive new approach quickly moved into the professional mainstream. Today, however, the maverick has been tamed, codified into a formalistic style that fills our design annuals with endlessly sophisticated renditions. What was originally a revolution is now an institution, as predictable as Beaux Arts architecture. It is the new status quo—the New Academy, as Phil Meggs calls it.

Determining whether New Wave is postmodernism or just late Modernism is important in understanding new work today. New Wave extends the classical Swiss interest in structure to dissections and recombinations of graphic design's grammar. Layered images and textures continue the collage aesthetic begun by Cubism, Constructivism, and Dada. But the addition of vernacular imagery and colors reflects postmodern architecture's discovery of popular culture, and the reintroduction of the classic serif typefaces draws on pre–20th century history. Taken as a whole, however, New Wave's complex arrangements are largely syntactical, abstracting type and images into baroquely Modern compositions.

The New Academy's knowing, often slick iterations have left some graphic designers dissatisfied. As a result, long neglected design elements, such as semantic expression in form, text and imagery, are beginning to resurface. Much of this recent work steps outside the lineage of Bauhaus/Basel/New Wave, and not surprisingly, some of its practitioners come from fine art, photographic or literary backgrounds rather than graphic design training.

When one looks for experimental typography today, what one finds is not so much new typography, as new relationships between text and image. In fact, the typography so celebrated over the past ten years of structuralist dissection is disappearing. The look and structure of the letter is underplayed, and verbal signification, interacting with imagery and symbols, is instead relied upon. The best new work is often aformal and sometimes decidedly anti-formal, despite the presence of some New Wave elements. Reacting to the technical perfection of mainstream graphic design, refinement and mastery are frequently rejected in favor of the directness of unmannered, hand-drawn or vernacular forms—after all, technical expertise is hardly a revelation anymore. These designers value expression over style.

Here on the edges of graphic design, the presence of the designer is sometimes so oblique that certain pieces would seem to spring directly from our popular culture. Reflecting current linguistic theory, the notion of "authorship" as a personal, formal vocabulary is less important than the dialogue between the graphic object and its audience; no longer are there one-way statements from designer. The layering of content, as opposed to New Wave's formal layering of collage elements, is the key to this exchange. Objective communication is enhanced by deferred meanings, hidden stories and alternative interpretations.

Sources for much current experimentation can be traced to recent fine art and photography, and to literary and art criticism. Influenced by French post-structuralism, critics and artists deconstruct verbal language as a filter or bias that inescapably manipulates the reader's response. When this approach is applied to art and photography, form is treated as a visual language to be read as well as seen. Both the texts and the images are to be read in detail, their meanings decoded. Clearly, this intellectualized communication asks a lot of its audience; this is harder work than the formal pleasures of New Wave.

Much new typography is very quiet. Some of the most interesting, in fact, is impossible to show here because of its radically modest scale or its subtle development through a sequence of pages. Some is bold in scale but so matter-of-fact that it makes little in the way of a visual statement. (One designer calls these strictly linguistic intentions "nonallusive" typography.) Typefaces now range from the classics to banal, often industrial sans serifs. Copy is often treated as just that—undifferentiated blocks of words—without the mannered manipulations of New Wave, where sentences and words are playfully exploded to express their parts. Text is no longer the syntactic playground of Weingart's descendants.

These cryptic, poker-faced juxtapositions of text and image do not always strive for elegance or refinement, although they may achieve it inadvertently. The focus now is on expression through semantic content, utilizing the intellectual software of visual language as well as the structural hardware and graphic grammar of Modernism. It is an interactive process that—as art always anticipates social evolution—heralds our emerging information economy, in which meanings are as important as materials.

"I came to view this desire for 'cleanliness' as not much more than housekeeping"

Rethinking Modernism, Revising Functionalism
1994

....

When I think of the undercurrents that shape my graphic design, I think of ideas about language and form. Ideas about coding and reading visual form, about challenging the viewer to construct individual interpretations, about layers of form and layers of meaning. These are at the forefront of my mind, but behind that lie other deeper and older concerns that go back to my earliest years of design. Perhaps these are what could be called a philosophy or an ethic, a personal set of values and criteria, a thread that winds through the lifetime of work and sustains its rigor, the continuity in the cycles of change.

Undergraduate school in industrial design was a very idealistic time. The strong emphasis on problem-solving and a *form follows function*alism struck a resonance with my personal approach toward the opportunities and problems of daily life. As a college junior, I enthusiastically embraced the rationalism of the Museum of Modern Art's Permanent Design Collection, abandoning the ambiguously intuitive territory of fine art. This somewhat vague midwestern American Modernist ethic had its roots in the Bauhaus, and our group of students gained a dim understanding of its application by the Ulm School of Germany. Added to this was a reverence for the insights of George Nelson, Marshall McLuhan and Buckminster Fuller. In hindsight I continue to appreciate the foundation built by those years of industrial design training. At that time, in the middle 1960s, even the best American education in graphic design would not have gone much further than an intuitive "*ah ha*" method of conceptualizing design solutions and an emulation of the design masters of the moment.

This faith in rational functionalism (and not a polished portfolio) found me my first job, at Unimark International, then the American missionary for European Modernism, the graphic heir of the Bauhaus. There I had the opportunity to learn graphic design from "real" Swiss and to have my junior design work critiqued by Massimo Vignelli, the greatest missionary of them all, the master of Helvetica and the grid. Our ethic then was one of discipline, clarity and cleanliness. The highest praise for a piece of graphic design was, "*This is really clean.*" We saw ourselves as sweeping away the clutter and confusion of American advertising design with a professional rationality and objectivity that would define a new American design. This approach was fairly foreign to American clients, and in 1968 it was remarkably difficult to convince corporate clients that a grid-ordered page with only two weights of Helvetica was appropriate to their needs. Now, of course, one can hardly persuade them to give up their hold on "Swiss," so completely has the corporate world embraced rationalist Modernism in graphic design.

But after a few years of striving to design as "purely" as possible, employing a minimalist typographic vocabulary, strongly gridded page structures and contrast in scale for visual interest, I came to view this desire for "cleanliness" as not much more than housekeeping. A number of us, mainly graphic designers in the "Swiss" method, began to search for a more expressive design, paralleling a similar movement in architecture now known as Post Modernism. Eventually what came to be called "New Wave," for lack of a better term, emerged in the 1970s as a new operating mode of graphic design. This included a new permission to employ historical and vernacular elements, something prohibited by "Swiss" Modernism. Then in the mid 1980s at Cranbrook we found a new interest in verbal language in graphic design, as well as fine art. Text can be animated with voices and images can be read, as well as seen, with an emphasis on audience interpretation and participation in the construction of meaning. But now, as the cycles of change continue, Modernism may be reemerging somewhat, a renewed minimalism that is calming down the visual outburst of activity of the past fifteen years.

Through these years of continual change and new possibilities, where does the ethic lie? Does not the idea of ethic imply some sort of unshakable bedrock impervious to the winds of change? For me, there seems to be a habit of functionalism that shapes my process at the beginning of every design project, the rational analysis of the message and the audience, the objective structuring of the text. Each cycle of change during the passing years seems to have added another visual or conceptual layer laid upon that foundation of functionalism, but inside of every project it is always there. Although this emphasis on rationalism would seem to be at odds with recent experimentation at Cranbrook, in fact it has been the provocation to question accepted norms in graphic design, stimulating the search for new communications theories and visual languages. I have never lost my faith in rational functionalism, in spite of appearances to the contrary. The only thing lost was an absolute dedication to minimalist form, which is a completely different issue from rationalist process.

Part of this ethic is a strong conviction and enthusiasm that design is important, that it matters in life, not just mine, but in the lives of our audiences and users of designed communications. Graphic design can be a contribution to our audiences. It can enrich as it informs and communicates. And there is a faith in not only the possibility but the necessity for advancement and growth in our field, an imperative for change. That only through change can we continue to push ahead in knowledge and expertise, theory and expression, continually building our collective knowledge of the process of communication. These convictions were formed early and sustain me today.

4-4

Milton Glaser

Some Thoughts on Modernism: Past, Present, and Future

1994

"*a corporation can represent itself through the vehicle of modernism as being progressive and above the human squabble without ever having to deal with human sweat. if we look at history, it is not surprising that the utopian ideals of modernism would be captured by people who want to use it for their own purposes*"

Milton Glaser (1929–) is an iconic American graphic designer who created the I♥NY logo and the ubiquitous and often-copied psychedelic poster image of Bob Dylan, among many other designs. In 1954 he cofounded Push Pin Studios with Seymour Chwast and Edward Sorel, and in 1968 he cofounded New York *magazine with Clay Felker.*

....

Growing up in the thirties and forties one could not be immune to Modernism. It was the pervasive *zeitgeist*, the spirit of the time. It was the beginning of post-Bauhaus thought, the International School of architecture, the idea that beauty is the inevitable consequence of appropriate form. We were products of a Modernist age without ever thinking about it. We ingested the philosophy of Modernism and accepted the idea of reducing everything to its most expressive form. There was really very little to counter it as a proposition.

Yet I have never felt that there was any "single" truth. Modernism offered me a set of conventions to work with or against, because in the absence of beliefs (even temporary beliefs), it is just much harder to act. Anyway, I tend to view all philosophical notions as sometimes useful and sometimes not.

My own training was not very doctrinaire. I went to the High School of Music and Art in New York where I received one body of instruction, and then on to Cooper Union where I got another, then to the Art Students League for yet another. I had a variety of educational experiences before I ever realized that design existed as a profession.

When I was growing up, there was a real struggle between notions of what was called "abstraction" and "reality." The question of how to view the world and represent it most convincingly is art's oldest question. More than any other artist in history, Picasso demonstrated clearly that you could, in fact, represent the world from innumerable vantage points, all of which turn out to be equally compelling. Understanding that I could change my vantage point was one of the instructive lessons of my life. It meant that I did not have to be loyal to a single belief.

There is a certain arrogance in the idea that one can develop a universal methodology that works in every case for every person. It does not make any sense. I have never been able to simply subscribe to the idea that any one principle, such as simplicity or reductiveness, can be universally applied to every problem. Life and people are too complicated. I must admit to one belief about design: first, you have to accomplish your intended task. Then, if you are lucky and talented, you may also create something extraordinary that goes beyond the objective task.

The responsibility of reflecting our time is another idea inherent in Modernist thought. The truth is that people with talent do good things which last, and people without talent, no matter how much they follow the rules, do work that is discarded by history. There is no way to avoid being in your time. I do not think that anybody should worry about being timeless but rather be concerned about doing the job at hand.

I wonder if one had to define Modern graphic design for the last twenty years as opposed to the previous twenty years whether we would find much difference. Much of contemporary graphic design is a reiteration of fifties design thinking in terms of its appearance and vocabulary of form. Along these lines, one of the things that binds a lot of designers to a certain way of working is the fact that they cannot draw. As a result, they are limited in terms of their ability to create form. One way to deal with this limitation is to rely on geometric forms or existing materials.

Drawing was discouraged during the Modernist era, and this impulse still continues. Imagine, that designers should not be able to represent form through drawing. What stupidity! This is an example of ideology gone crazy. It is the aesthetic equivalent of eating yogurt, tofu, and wheat germ for life. The result of this constraint results in a specific working method—collage. Finding things, cutting them out, and assembling them in new combinations is the basic design methodology of our time. It is a way of working that had its parallels in the fifties.

The Modernist idea was not to imitate anything that existed in reality. Talk about limitation. It seems to me that the power of visual work is transmitted through the metaphors and re-creation of existing imagery. The idea that you cannot use the visible world as a subject is like saying you can only eat brown rice. Undernourishment comes from eating only one thing; you can become undernourished from having only one aspect of the visual world as a diet.

It is true that you can take a very narrow piece of the world and produce extraordinary things. The collage method can produce remarkable imagery. A whole generation of people are basically working off that idea. Drawing skills are technically significant and help in the understanding that occurs when you attempt to represent the world in some way. You cannot reject the body's form or the swell of a breast or thigh. Life is erotic, and the only thing that is missing from most Modernist work is eroticism. You really want to feel that a work has passion and sexuality. Why give it up? This has to do with the idea of purity. The idea that Modernism refuses to use the symbols and archetypes of history is its greatest limitation.

It is therefore understandable why Modernism became a useful tool for corporate representation. Corporations do not want to deal with issues of individuals, or eroticism, or the messy side of life. So Modernism became a wonderful way of detoxifying dirty people and dirty ideas. A corporation can represent itself through the vehicle of Modernism as being progressive and above the human squabble without ever having to deal with human sweat. If we look at history, it is not surprising that the utopian ideals of Modernism would be captured by people who want to use it for their own purposes. With all of that, the extraordinary unity of vision that Modernism provided us with is beginning to erode. Its all-encompassing principles are being questioned. Post-modernism has been officially announced but has not quite found its philosophical base. At the moment, it is addressing questions of style and fashion. Conversely, Modernism is powerful and pervasive. Although I've had my own problems with Modernism, I believe our world view is still a Modernist view.

Modernism is about progress, the endless frontier, and ceaseless development. Modernism is essentially utopian. Its origins are in the idea of good coming from boundless technology. Despite its contradictions and the erosion of its strength, the announcement of its death is premature.

4-5

Rick Poynor

Did We Ever Stop Being Postmodern?
2011

"could it be, then, that postmodernism's most basic problem in terms of public perception is the conundrum presented by its name?

Rick Poynor (1957–) is a writer, critic, lecturer and curator, specializing in design, photography, and visual culture. He founded Eye, *co-founded* Design Observer, *and contributes columns to* Eye *and* Print. *He is Professor of Design and Visual Culture at the University of Reading in the UK.*

The exhibition about postmodernism and design now running at the Victoria and Albert Museum in London ends with a defiant assertion: "like it or not we are all postmodern now." And before *Postmodernism: Style and Subversion, 1970–1990* had even opened at the end of September, the novelist and critic Hari Kunzru concluded a preview essay with much the same kind of observation: "We have lived through the end of postmodernism and the dawning of postmodernity."

Do you think of yourself that way—as a postmodern person? Most probably you don't. Postmodernism may have dominated the academy for more than a decade, but it was never a term that commanded much public understanding, let alone affection. I have a file full of semi-baffled think pieces published in the British press in the 1980s in an attempt to explain what this then fashionable buzzword was all about. The day the exhibition opened, the *Observer* newspaper dispatched its man to the V&A to find out "exactly what po-mo means." Claiming to have discovered only a mood of "pre-emptive ennui" and puzzlement among the exhibition's early visitors, he filed his report apparently none the wiser.

It certainly doesn't help that even postmodernism's proponents, who tended to be theorists rather than artists or designers, were always at pains to say how slippery the concept was, and hard to define. The exhibition's curators, Glenn Adamson and Jane Pavitt, offer the same disclaimer in their foreword to the exhibition book: "the reader will not find anywhere in this book, or the exhibition it accompanies, a single handy definition of postmodernism." That doesn't mean that the book and (in a necessarily simpler way) the show avoid the issue—they offer many rewarding perspectives on the subject. But any attempt to reduce such an intricate set of cultural factors across so many kinds of art, design and media to a brief, all-encompassing definition would be a misrepresentation. We like to think we are complex people living in a complex world. So why would we expect an explanation of our many-layered culture to be easy?

The added complication is the entirely valid distinction that Kunzru draws between post-modernism as a movement in the arts and postmodernity as an epoch with implications for every area of culture and society. Postmodernism in the stylistic sense might be over as movement, though there was no unitary postmodern style, but postmodernity is arguably still our cultural condition, as Adamson and Pavitt also imply. This divide was always going to be a tricky issue for the curators to negotiate and they make it clear from the outset that their subject is "postmodernism rather than postmodernity in general—that is a set of intentional design strategies, not the overarching condition that made them possible." One probable reason for this decision is that postmodernity is simply too complicated to reference and explain in short introductory wall texts, which would have to be loaded with great gobbets of Jameson and Lyotard. Large-scale exhibitions in public museums must always strike a balance between doing a subject adequate intellectual justice and appealing to ordinary visitors who are likely to know little or nothing about the theme.

For visitors of a certain age—my teens and 20s fell within the exhibition's time span—walking around Postmodernism is like seeing key signposts in your early cultural life flash before your eyes, though not necessarily in the original order. It's entirely fitting that architecture, one of the strongest and most compelling sections, comes first (there's a terrific room devoted to Venturi and Scott Brown in Las Vegas), but for many visitors it will be pop and rock music, album covers and videos, that first signaled the postmodern "turn." In 1978, I tuned into the retro-constructivist references on the cover of Kraftwerk's *The Man Machine*, the mournful yet oddly exhilarating sense that some version of the future had already occurred, several years before I knew that such a thing as postmodern architecture existed.

A room titled "Strike a Pose"—surely there was more to it than that self-loving line from Madonna implies?—has big screens with performances by Grace Jones (magisterial), David Byrne in his Big Suit ("If postmodernism means anything is allowed, then I was all for it"), and an operatic Klaus Nomi sporting black lipstick, triangular jacket and pointy po-mo hair. With one eye on sardonic Weimar cabaret and the other on the polymorphous future, Nomi carries off this identity experiment with fabulous assurance; he would have looked right at home lounging in a Memphis living room decorated with George Sowden's all-over b&w patterns (though the Memphis section of Postmodernism is one point where the curatorial balance seems skewed: there is just too much of it). Back on the video screens there are clips of Kraftwerk, Devo in red "energy dome" hats, Visage (how good "Fade to Grey" still sounds) and Laurie Anderson's monumentally haunting "O Superman."

If this seems like a lot of emphasis on pop music, then I should report that the V&A has released a CD and DVD set to accompany the show, with key tracks from the 1980s and sleeve notes by Adamson, who cautions us against nostalgia—sure!—while proving to be no slouch in the pop-crit department. The curators even use New Order's "Bizarre Love Triangle" video—"Why can't we be ourselves like we were yesterday?"—at the end as a kind of melancholy/upbeat finale.

Most of the graphic work in the exhibition is gathered in a section titled "Style Wars." This is the aspect of postmodern design I know best and I was one of the advisers consulted early in the process at a study day at the V&A. I also lent some pieces to the show so I can't claim detachment here. As with the music, I encountered many of these designs as they appeared, and any understanding I have is strongly tinted by experiencing first-hand how their stylistic codes communicated at the time. The curators zero in on work by Wolfgang Weingart, April Greiman, Emigre, Ed Fella, Paula Scher, Johanna Drucker, Barney Bubbles, Peter Saville, Neville Brody, Malcolm Garrett, and Vaughan Oliver, drawing attention to its bricolage, fragmentation and use of quotation, while arguing that it seamlessly blends avant-garde influences with the commercial sphere. However, few of these record covers, posters and magazines are very commercial and their audiences, though still consumers, tended to share the work's ambivalence. Postmodernism was, nevertheless, an integral expression of the late capitalist economy and the show progresses with inexorable (if depressing) cultural logic toward a section titled "Money."

Little is said about how the graphic pieces were seen in their day as such a controversial departure from the discipline's norms — older designers still loyal to a romantic but outmoded idea of modernism often voiced an almost visceral hatred of these innovations. What do visitors make of these once troubling experiments now? On my third visit, I saw a man on his own looking at Barney Bubbles' cover for *Music for Pleasure* (1977) by The Damned. "Oh, wow, that is so cool," he sighed out loud, forgetting himself. A friend told me had seen someone making a careful drawing of a magazine I had lent. A copy of New Socialist magazine (1986) with a cover by Brody has been commodified as a T-shirt in the V&A's shop apparently with the designer's approval—postmodern irony in action. I suspect that the graphic exhibits, like other parts of the show, are ripe for postmodern plunder by a new Gaga generation of viewers who will savor these artifacts not in terms of cultural ideas that were absorbed long ago, but as a cookie jar of exciting retro styles that can be dipped into at will because that's the kind of sampling and mashing up we do now as a matter of course.

There is a view of postmodernism—Kunzru expresses it in his essay and the show appears to endorse it by ending in 1990—that it is essentially a pre-digital phenomenon. Concentrating on postmodernism as temporal style rather than postmodernity as a condition that persists makes it easier to sustain this argument, but developments in 1980s postmodern graphic design undermine the thesis. April Greiman and the designers at Emigre, Rudy VanderLans and Zuzana Licko, embraced the Macintosh in 1984 as soon as it appeared (as work in the show demonstrates), seeing its possibilities not only for increased control of production but as a tool for generating new kinds of visual communication. As processing power increased in the early 1990s, these experiments became more ambitious and complex and this was the period when postmodern ideas about communication were most intensely debated. In those years, the American designer Jeffery Keedy, who isn't included in the exhibition, was one of postmodernism's most vigorous and polemical champions, and a scourge of "zombie modernists" who, in his view, continued to think and design as though postmodernism hadn't happened.

Is this the moment to try to rethink or reclaim postmodernism? The movement still arouses a surprising amount of disdain, as though it had been entirely indulgent, frivolous, wasteful, aesthetically misconceived and unnecessary. I confess myself to feeling close to disgust looking at the Alessi tea and coffee services designed by superstar architects—less for the overworked form than for the total vacuity of these over-gilded status symbols. The postmodernism that still seems rich, valuable and durable can be seen in some of the examples I have mentioned, or in the exhibition's adroitly chosen film clips from *Blade Runner* and Godfrey Reggio's *Koyaanisqatsi*, which portray the city as a sublime illuminated matrix of beauty and terror. The curators' concluding observation that postmodernism was "marked by a sense of loss, even destructiveness, but also a radical expansion of possibilities" feels right to me. At the end of a grim century, we had lost our illusions, our faith in scientific progress and our belief in the shaping power of "grand narratives." Yet we continue to benefit from and to explore postmodernism's expanded cultural terrain.

Could it be, then, that postmodernism's most basic problem in terms of public perception is the conundrum presented by its name? David Byrne touches on this in a post-script to the exhibition book. "Postmodernism" announces what it isn't, but it doesn't tell you what it is, and what the word appears to say isn't the whole story anyway because, as many theorists have noted, elements of modernism continue within the postmodern. The image it conjures is too negative, while modernism still sounds optimistic and far-seeing, like a cause you could join. No one wants to feel like the superfluous inhabitant of an aftermath. It's comforting to believe we are post postmodernism. But in a digital world, postmodernity has become everyone's inescapable reality—"like it or not." The V&A's show and book are vital investigations of how we arrived here and the part played by design in the journey.

PROCESS 5A

Auteurism
| Authority and Authenticity

PROCESS 5B

Design Ethics
| Ideology and Faith

The debate over the significance of the author emerged in the second half of the twentieth century and lingered into the twenty-first. Emerging from film theory, auteurism was first associated with French New Wave cinema of the 1950s and '60s, as well as with the film critics who contributed to the seminal journal *Cahiers du Cinéma*. It was most famously advocated by the director and critic François Truffaut.

Some contend that auteurism subjects work to limitations by superimposing onto it the details of the author's own life, ideals, and creative vision instead of letting the work breathe for itself. In contrast, poststructuralist literary theory privileged the reader's perceptions over the author's intentions. The philosopher and theorist Roland Barthes, in his 1967 essay "The Death of the Author," concluded that "the birth of the reader must be ransomed by the death of the Author." The philosopher and social theorist Michel Foucault weighed in, responding indirectly to Barthes through a lecture he gave in 1969—titled "What Is an Author?"—in which he argued for the emancipation of literature from the expression of the author.

Barthes's theory addressed literature, but it can be applied to art and design in ways that help to differentiate the two fields. Both rely on communication. In the realm of art, a signature declares the artist's authorship, but the piece can still be joyfully examined and interpreted by a viewer despite or in ignorance of the artist-author's intentions. Artists need not rely on direct communication with the viewer in order to create a successful work of art.

A designer is wholly different, being required to set aside ego and personal expression in the service of effective communication. Further, while in art the primary value lies in the original, the primary value of design is in reproduction. Design can reach an incredibly broad audience, but most designers seldom receive wider recognition for their work. The job of the designer is to be the parent of a thankless child, to go unrecognized as offspring receive acclaim. Instead of working under conditions of utopian autonomy, designers labor in an autonomous heteronomy, a creation process with restrictions. As design is always practiced within a culture or cultures, practitioners must always honor their responsibility to society.

The dilemma common to designers, then, is how to maintain a sense of personal ethics while fulfilling their duty as egoless communicators. André Bazin, cofounder of *Cahiers du Cinéma,* addressed this condition by questioning the role and value of the individual filmmaker—the would-be author—within the highly collaborative milieu of industrial film production under capitalism.

Visual communication is one of the most advanced forms of rhetoric, and communicators must recognize the social role of design and the ideological weight behind every message they transmit. The balance between mechanical transmission and subjective expression of a message in each project belongs to the designer, but the designer must also analyze with rigor the social and cultural influences and the larger implications of the design.

Designers are not culture consumers but, indeed, culture creators.

5A-1

André Bazin

On the Auteur Theory
1957

"the cinema is an art which is both popular and industrial. These conditions, which are necessary to its existence, in no way constitute a collection of hindrances—no more than in architecture"

"it is simply a question of the appearance of a clash between the subjective inspiration of the creator and the objective situation of the cinema"

André Bazin (1918–1958) was an influential French film critic who cofounded the film magazine Cahiers du Cinéma. *Many critics and filmmakers involved in the French New Wave considered him an important mentor.*

....

> Goethe? Shakespeare? Everything they put their name to is supposed to be good, and people rack their brains to find beauty in the silliest little thing they bungled. All great talents, like Goethe, Shakespeare, Beethoven and Michelangelo, created not only beautiful works, but things that were less than mediocre, quite simply awful.—Leo Tolstoy, *Diary* 1895–99.

I realise my task is fraught with difficulties. *Cahiers du Cinéma* is thought to practise the *politique des auteurs*. This opinion may perhaps not be justified by the entire output of articles, but it has been true of the majority, especially for the last two years. It would be useless and hypocritical to point to a few scraps of evidence to the contrary, and claim that our magazine is a harmless collection of wishywashy reviews.

Nevertheless, our readers must have noticed that this critical standpoint—whether implicit or explicit—has not been adopted with equal enthusiasm by all the regular contributors to *Cahiers*, and that there might exist serious differences in our admiration, or rather in the degree of our admiration. And yet the truth is that the most enthusiastic among us nearly always win the day. Eric Rohmer put his finger on the reason in his reply to a reader in *Cahiers du Cinéma* no. 64: 'When opinions differ on an important film, we generally prefer to let the person who likes it most to write about it.' It follows that the strictest adherents of the *politique des auteurs* get the best of it in the end, for, rightly or wrongly, they always see in their favourite directors the manifestation of the same specific qualities. So it is that Alfred Hitchcock, Jean Renoir, Roberto Rossellini, Fritz Lang, Howard Hawks or Nicholas Ray, to judge from the pages of *Cahiers*, appear as almost infallible directors who could never make a bad film.

I would like to avoid one misunderstanding from the start. I beg to differ with those of my colleagues who are the most firmly convinced that the *politique des auteurs* is well founded, but this in no way compromises the general policy of the magazine. Whatever our differences of opinion about films or directors, our common likes and dislikes are numerous enough and strong enough to bind us together; and although I do not see the role of the *auteur* in cinema in the same way as François Truffaut or Rohmer for example, it does not stop me believing to a certain extent in the concept of the *auteur* and very often sharing their opinions, although not always their passionate loves. I fall in with them more reluctantly in the case of their hostile reactions; often they are fiercely critical of films I find defensible—and I do so precisely because I find that the work transcends the director (they dispute this phenomenon, which they consider to be a critical contradiction). In other words, almost our only difference concerns the relationship between the work and its creator. I have never regretted that one of my colleagues has stuck up for such and such director, although I have not always agreed about the qualities of the film under examination. Finally, I would like to add that although it seems to me that the *politique des auteurs* has led its supporters to make a number of mistakes, its total results have been fertile enough to justify them in the face of their critics. It is very rare that the arguments drawn upon to attack them do not make me rush to their defence.

So it is within these limits, which, if you like, are those of a family quarrel, that I would like to tackle what seems to me to represent not so much a critical mistranslation as a critical 'false nuance of meaning'. My point of departure is an article by my friend Jean Domarchi on Vincente Minnelli's *Lust for Life*, which tells the story of Vincent van Gogh. His praise was very intelligent and sober, but it struck me that such an article should not have been published in a magazine, which, only one month previously, had allowed Rohmer to demolish John Huston. The relentless harshness of the latter, and the indulgent admiration of the former, can be explained only by the fact that Minnelli is one of Domarchi's favourites and that Huston is not a *Cahiers auteur*. This partiality is a good thing, up to a certain point, as it leads us to stick up for a film that illustrates certain facets of American culture just as much as Minnelli's personal talent. I could get Domarchi caught up in a contradiction, by pointing out to him that he ought to have sacrificed Minnelli in favour of Renoir, since it was the shooting of *Lust for Life* that forced the director of *French Cancan* to give up his own project on Van Gogh. Can Domarchi claim that a *Van Gogh* by Renoir would not have brought more prestige to the politique des auteurs than a film by Minnelli? What was needed was a painter's son, and what we get was a director of filmed ballets!

But whatever the case, this example is only a pretext. Many a time I have felt uneasy at the subtlety of an argument, which completely failed to camouflage the naïveté of the assumption whereby, for example, the intentions and the coherence of a deliberate and well-thought-out film are read into some little B-feature.

And of course as soon as you state that the film-maker and his or her films are one, there can be no minor films, as the worst of them will always be in the image of their creator. But let's see what the facts of the matter are. In order to do so, we must go right back to the beginning.

Of course, the *politique des auteurs* is the application to the cinema of a notion that is widely accepted in the individual arts. Truffaut likes to quote Jean Giraudoux's remark: 'There are no works, there are only *auteurs*'—a polemical sally which seems to me of limited significance. The opposite statement could just as well be set as an exam question. The two formulae, like the maxims of La Rochefoucauld and Chamfort, would simply reverse their proportion of truth and error. As for Rohmer, he states (or rather asserts) that in art it is the *auteurs*, and not the works, that remain; and the programmes of film societies would seem to support this critical truth.

But one should note that Rohmer's argument does not go nearly as far as Giraudoux's aphorism, for, if *auteurs* remain, it is not necessarily because of their output as a whole. There is no lack of examples to prove that the contrary is true. Maybe Voltaire's name is more important than his bibliography, but now that he has been put in perspective it is not so much his *Dictionnaire philosophique* that counts nowadays as his Voltairean wit, a certain style of thinking and writing. But today where are we to find the principle and the example? In his abundant and atrocious writings for the theatre? Or in the slim volume of short stories? And what about Beaumarchais? Are we to go looking in *La Mère coupable*?

In any case, the authors of that period were apparently themselves aware of the relativity of their worth, since they willingly disowned their works, and sometimes even did not mind being the subject of lampoons whose quality they took as a compliment. For them, almost the only thing that mattered was the work itself, whether their own or another's, and it was only at the end of the eighteenth century, with Beaumarchais in fact, that the concepts of the *auteur* finally crystallised legally, with his or her royalties, duties and responsibilities. Of course I am making allowances for historical and social contingencies; political and moral censorship has made anonymity sometimes inevitable and always excusable. But surely the anonymity of the writings of the French Resistance in no way lessened the dignity or responsibility of the writer. It was only in the nineteenth century that copying or plagiarism really began to be considered a professional breach that disqualified its perpetrator.

The same is true of painting. Although nowadays any old splash of paint can be valued according to its measurements and the celebrity of the signature, the objective quality of the work itself was formerly held in much higher esteem. Proof of this is to be found in the difficulty there is in authenticating many old pictures. What emerged from a studio might simply be the work of a pupil, and we are now unable to *prove* anything one way or another. If one goes back even further, one has to take into consideration the anonymous works that have come down to us as the products not of an artist, but of an art, not of a person, but of a society.

I can see how I will be rebutted. We should not objectify our ignorance or let it crystallise into a reality. All these works of art, from the Venus de Milo to the African mask, did in fact have an *auteur*; and the whole of modern historical science is tending to fill in the gaps and give names to these works of art. But did one really have to wait for such erudite addenda before being able to admire and enjoy them? Biographical criticism is but one of many possible critical dimensions—people are still arguing about the identity of Shake-speare or Molière.

But that's just the point! People *are* arguing. So their identity is not a matter of complete indifference. The evolution of Western art towards greater personalisation should defi-nitely be considered as a step forward, as a refinement of culture, but only as long as this individualisation remains only a final perfection and does not claim to *define* culture. At this point, we should remember the irrefutable commonplace we learned at school: the individual transcends society, but society is also and above all *within* the individual. So there can be no definitive criticism of genius or talent which does not first take into consideration the social determinism, the historical combination of circumstances and the technical background which to a large extent determine it. That is why the anonymity of a work of art is a handicap that impinges only very slightly on our understanding of it. In any case, much depends on the particular branch of art in question, the style adopted and the sociological context. African does not suffer by remaining anonymous—although of course it is unfortunate we know so little about the societies that gave birth to it.

But *The Man Who Knew Too Much*, *Europa '51* and *Bigger Than Life* are contemporary with the paintings of Picasso, Matisse and Singier! Does it follow that one should see in them the same degree of individualisation? I for one do not think so.

If you will excuse yet another commonplace, the cinema is an art which is both popular and industrial. These conditions, which are necessary to its existence, in no way constitute a collection of hindrances—no more than in architecture—they rather represent a group of positive and negative circumstances which have to be reckoned with. And this is especially true of the American cinema, which the theoreticians of the *politique des auteurs* admire so much. What makes Hollywood so much better than anything else in the world is not only the quality of certain directors, but also the vitality and, in a certain sense, the excellence of tradition. Hollywood's superiority is only incidentally technical; it lies much more in what one might call the American cinematic genius, something which should be analysed, then defined, by a sociological approach to its production. The American cinema has been able, in an extraordinarily competent way, to show American society just as it wanted to see itself; but not at all passively, as a simple act of satisfaction and escape, but dynamically, i.e. by participating with the means at its disposal in the building of that society. What is so admirable in the American cinema is that it cannot help being spontaneous. Although the fruit of free enterprise and capitalism—and harbouring their active or still only virtual defects—it is in a way the truest and most realistic cinema of all because it does not shrink from depicting even the contradictions of that society.

But it follows that directors are swept along by this powerful surge; naturally their artistic course has to be plotted according to the currents—it is not as if they were sailing as their fancy took them on the calm waters of a lake.

In fact it is not even true of the most individual artistic disciplines that genius is free and always self-dependent. And what is genius anyway if not a certain combination of unquestionable personal talents, a gift of the gods and a moment in history? Genius is an H-bomb. The fission of uranium triggers off the fusion of hydrogen pulp. But a sun cannot be born from the disintegration of an individual alone unless this disintegration has repercussions on the art that surrounds it. Whence the paradox of Arthur Rimbaud's life. His poetic flash in the pan suddenly died out, and Rimbaud the adventurer became more and more distant like a star, still glowing but heading towards extinction. Probably Rimbaud did not change at all. There was simply nothing left to feed the flames that had reduced the whole of literature to ashes. Generally speaking, the rate of this combination in the cycles of great art is usually greater than the lifespan of a man. Literature's step is measured in centuries. It will be said that genius foreshadows that which comes after it. This is true, but only dialectically. For one could also say that every age has the geniuses it needs in order to define, repudiate and transcend itself. Consequently, Voltaire was a horrible playwright when he thought he was Jean Racine's successor and a storyteller of genius when he made the parable a vehicle for the ideas which were going to shatter the eighteenth century.

And even without having to use as examples the utter failures which had their causes almost entirely in the sociology of art, creative psychology alone could easily account for a lot of patchiness even in the best authors. Victor Hugo's *Notre-Dame-de-Paris* is pretty slight compared with *La Légende des siècles*, Gustav Flaubert's *Salammbô* does not come up to *Madame Bovary*, or André Gide's *Corydon* to *Le Journal des faux-monnayeurs*. There is no point in quibbling about these examples; there will always be others to suit everyone's tastes. Surely one can accept the permanence of talent without confusing it with some kind of artistic infallibility or immunity against making mistakes, which could only be divine attributes. But God, as Jean-Paul Sartre has already pointed out, is not an artist! Were one to attribute to creative man, in the face of all psychological probability, an unflagging richness of inspiration, one would have to admit that this inspiration always comes up against a whole complex of particular circumstances, which make the result, in the cinema, a thousand times more chancy than in painting or in literature.

Conversely, there is no reason why there should not exist—and sometimes they do—flashes in the pan in the work of otherwise mediocre film-makers. Results of a fortunate combination of circumstances in which there is a precarious moment of balance between talent and milieu, these fleeting brilliances do not prove all that much about personal creative qualities; but they are not, however, intrinsically inferior to others—and probably would not seem so if the critics had not begun by reading the signature at the bottom of the painting.

Well, what is true of literature is even truer of the cinema, to the extent that this art, the last to come onto the scene, accelerates and multiplies the evolutionary factors that are common to all the others. In fifty years, the cinema, which started with the crudest forms of spectacle (primitive but not inferior) has had to cover the same ground as the play or the novel and is often on the same level as they are. Within that same period, its technical development has been of a kind that cannot compare with that of any traditional art within a comparable period (except perhaps architecture, another industrial art). Under such conditions, it is hardly surprising that genius will burn itself out ten times as fast, and that a director who suffers no loss of ability may cease to be swept along by the wave. This was the case with Erich von Stroheim, Abel Gance and Orson Welles. We are now beginning to see things in enough perspective to notice a curious phenomenon: a film-maker can, within his or her own lifetime, be refloated by the following wave. This is true of Gance and Stroheim, whose modernity is all the more apparent nowadays. I am fully aware that this only goes to prove their quality of *auteur*, but their eclipse still cannot be entirely explained away by the contradictions of capitalism or the stupidity of producers. If one keeps a sense of proportion, one sees that the same thing has happened to people of genius in the cinema as would have happened to a 120-year-old Racine writing Racinian plays in the middle of the eighteenth century. Would his tragedies have been better than Voltaire's? That answer is by no means clear-cut; but I bet they would not have been.

One can justifiably point to Charles Chaplin, Renoir or René Clair. But each of them was endowed with further gifts that have little to do with genius and which were precisely those that enabled them to adapt themselves to the predicament of film production. Of course, the case of Chaplin was unique, since, as both *auteur* and producer, he has been able to be both the cinema and its evolution.

It follows, then, according to the most basic laws of the psychology of creation, that, as the objective factors of genius are much more likely to modify themselves in the cinema than in any other art, a rapid maladjustment between the film-maker and the cinema can occur, and this can abruptly affect the quality of his or her films as a result. Of course I admire Welles's *Confidential Report,* and I can see the same qualities in it as I see in *Citizen Kane.* But *Citizen Kane* opened up a new era of American cinema, and *Confidential Report* is a film of only secondary importance.

But let's pause a moment on this assertion—it may, I feel, allow us to get to the heart of the matter. I think that not only would the supporters of the *politique des auteurs* refuse to agree that *Confidential Report* is an inferior film to *Citizen Kane;* they would be more eager to claim the contrary, and I can easily see how they would go about it. As *Confidential Report* is Welles's sixth film, one can assume that a certain amount of progress has already been made. Not only did the Welles of 1953 have more experience of himself and of his art than in 1941, but however great the freedom he was able to obtain in Hollywood *Citizen Kane* cannot help remaining to a certain extent an RKO product. The film would never have seen the light of day without co-operation of some superb technicians and their just as admirable technical apparatus. Gregg Toland, to mention only one, was more than a little responsible for the final result. On the other hand, *Confidential Report* is completely the work of Welles. Until it can be proved to the contrary, it will be considered *a priori* a superior film because it is more personal and because Welles's personality can only have matured as he grew older.

As far as this question is concerned, I can only agree with my young firebrands when they state that age as such cannot diminish the talent of a film-maker and react violently to that critical prejudice which consists of always finding the works of a young or mature film-maker superior to the films of an old director. It has been said that Chaplin's *Monsieur Verdoux* was not up to *The Gold Rush*; people have criticised Renoir's *The River* and

Le Carrosse d'or, saying they miss the good old days of *La Règle du jeu*. Eric Rohmer has found an excellent answer to this: 'The history of art offers no example, as far as I know, of an authentic genius who has gone through a period of true decline at the end of his career; this should encourage us rather to detect, beneath what seems to be clumsy or bald, the traces of that desire for simplicity that characterises the "last manner" of painters such as Titian, Rembrandt, Matisse, or Bonnard, composers such as Beethoven and Stravinsky…' (*Cahiers du Cinéma* no. 8, 'Renoir américain'). What kind of absurd discrimination has decided that film-makers alone are victims of a senility that other artists are protected from? There do remain the exceptional cases of dotage, but they are much rarer than is sometimes supposed. When Charles Baudelaire was paralysed and unable to utter anything other than his 'cré nom', was he any less Baudelairean? Robert Mallet tells us how Valéry Larbaud, Joyce's translator into French, struggling against paralysis after twenty years of immobility and silence, had managed to build up for himself a vocabulary of twenty simple words. With these, he was still able to bring out some extraordinarily shrewd literary judgements. In fact, the few exceptions one could mention only go to prove the rule. A great talent matures but does not grow old. There is no reason why this law of artistic psychology should not also be valid for the cinema. Criticism that is based implicitly on the hypothesis of senility cannot hold water. It is rather the opposite postulate that ought to be stated: we should say that when we think we can discern a decline it is our own critical sense that is at fault, since an impoverishment of inspiration is a very unlikely phenomenon. From this point of view, the bias of the *politique des auteurs* is very fruitful, and I will stick up for them against the naiveté, the foolishness even, of the prejudices they are fighting.

But, always remembering this, one has nevertheless to accept that certain indisputable 'greats' have suffered an eclipse or a loss of their powers. I think what I have already said in this article may point to the reason for this. The problem has to do with the ageing not of people but of the cinema itself: those who do not know how to age *with* it will be overtaken by its evolution. This is why it has been possible for there to have been a series of failures leading to complete catastrophe without it being necessary to suppose that the genius of yesterday has become an imbecile. Once again, it is simply a question of the appearance of a clash between the subjective inspiration of the creator and the objective situation of the cinema, and this is what the *politique des auteurs* refuses to see. To its supporters *Confidential Report* is a more important film than *Citizen Kane* because they justifiably see more of Orson Welles in it. In other words, all they want to retain in the equation *auteur* plus *subject* = *work* is the *auteur*, while the subject is reduced to zero. Some of them will pretend to grant me that, all things being equal as far as the *auteur* is concerned, a good subject is naturally better than a bad one, but the more outspoken and foolhardy among them will admit that it very much looks as if they prefer minor B-films, where the banality of the scenario leaves more room for the personal contribution of the *auteur*.

Of course I will be challenged on the very concept of *auteur*. I admit that the equation I have just used is artificial, just as much so in fact as the distinction one learned at school between form and content. To benefit from the *politique des auteurs* one first has to be worthy of it, and as it happens this school of criticism claims to distinguish between true *auteurs* and directors, even talented ones: Nicholas Ray is an *auteur*, John Huston is supposed to be only a metteurs-en-scene; Robert Bresson and Roberto Rossellini are *auteurs*, Rene Clément is only a great director, and so on. So this conception of the author is not compatible with the *auteur*/subject distinction, because it is of greater importance to find out if a director is worthy of entering the select group of *auteurs* than it is to judge how well he or she has used the material to hand. To a certain extent at least, *auteurs* are a subject to themselves; whatever the scenario, they always tell the same story, or, in case the word 'story' is confusing, let's say they have the same attitude and pass the same moral judgements on the action and on the characters. Jacques Rivette has said that an *auteur* is someone who speaks in the first person. It's a good definition; let's adopt it.

The *politique des auteurs* consists, in short, of choosing the personal factor in artistic creation as a standard of reference, and then of assuming that it continues and even progresses from one film to the next. It is recognised that there do exist certain important films of quality that escape this test, but these will systematically be considered inferior to those in which the personal stamp of the *auteur*, however run-of-the-mill the scenario, can be perceived even infinitesimally.

It is far from my intention to deny the positive attitude and methodological qualities of this bias. First of all, it has the great merit of treating the cinema as an adult art and of reacting against the impressionistic relativism that still reigns over the bulk of film criticism. I admit that the explicit or admitted pretension of a critic to reconsider the production of a film-maker with every new film in the light of his or her judgment has something presumptuous about it that recalls Ubu. I am also quite willing to admit that if one is human one cannot help doing this, and, short of giving up the whole idea of actually criticising, one might as well take as a starting point the feelings, pleasant or unpleasant, one feels personally when in contact with a film. Okay, but only on condition that these first impressions are kept in their proper place. We have to take them into consideration, but we should not use them as a basis. In other words, every critical act should consist of referring the film in question to a scale of values, but this reference is not merely a matter of intelligence; the sureness of one's judgement arises also, or perhaps even first of all (in the chronological sense of the word), from a general impression experienced during the film. I feel there are two symmetrical heresies, which are (a) objectively applying to a film a critical all-purpose yardstick; and (b) considering it sufficient simply to state one's pleasure or disgust. The first denies the role of taste; the second presupposes the superiority of the critic's taste over that of the author. Coldness…or presumption!

What I like about the *politique des auteurs* is that it reacts against the impressionist approach while retaining the best of it. In fact the scale of values it proposes is not ideological. Its starting point is an appreciation largely composed of taste and sensibility: it has to discern the contribution of the artist as such, quite apart from the qualities of the subject or the technique: i.e. the person behind the style. But once one has made this distinction, this kind of criticism is doomed to beg the question, for it assumes at the start of its analysis that the film is automatically good since it has been made by an *auteur*. And so the yardstick applied to the film is the aesthetic portrait of the film-maker deduced from his or her previous films. This is all right so long as there has been no mistake about promoting this film-maker to the status of *auteur*. For it is objectively speaking safer to trust in the genius of the artist than in one's own critical intelligence. And this is where the *politique des auteurs* falls in line with the system of 'criticism by beauty'; in other words, when one is dealing with a genius, it is always a good method to presuppose that a supposed weakness in a work of art is nothing other than a beauty that one has not yet managed to understand. But as I have shown, this method had its limitations even in traditionally individualistic arts such as literature, and all the more so in the cinema where the sociological and historical cross-currents are countless. By giving such importance to B-films, the *politique des auteurs* recognises and confirms this dependence *a contrario*.

Another point is that as the criteria of the *politique des auteurs* are very difficult to formulate, the whole thing becomes highly hazardous. It is significant that our finest writers on *Cahiers* have been practising it for three or four years now and have yet to produce the main corpus of its theory. Nor is one particularly likely to forget how Rivette suggested we should admire Hawks: 'The mark of Hawks's genius is its statement of fact; *Monkey Business* is the work of a genius, and it impresses itself on one's mind through this statement of fact. Some people resist against this, they demand more than simple affirmations. And perhaps the failure to appreciate his talent arises quite simply from this....' You can see the danger: an aesthetic personality cult.

But that is not the main point, at least to the extent that the *politique des auteurs* is practised by people of taste who know how to watch their step. It is its negative side that seems the most serious to me. It is unfortunate to praise a film that in no way deserves it, but the dangers are far less far-reaching than when a worthwhile film is rejected because its director has made nothing good up to that point. I am not denying that the champions of the *politique des auteurs* discover or encourage a budding talent when they get the chance. But they do systematically look down on anything in a film that comes from a common fund and which can sometimes be entirely admirable, just as it can be utterly detestable. Thus, a certain kind of popular American culture lies at the basis of Minnelli's *Lust for Life*, but another more spontaneous kind of culture is also the principle of American comedy, the Western and the film noir. And its influence is here beneficial, for it is this that gives these cinematic genres their vigour and richness, resulting as they do from an artistic evolution that has always been in wonderfully close harmony with its public. And so one can read a review in *Cahiers* of a Western by Anthony Mann—and God knows I like Anthony Mann's Westerns!—as if it were not above all a Western, i.e. a whole collection of conventions in the script, the acting and the direction. I know very well that in a film magazine one may be permitted to skip such mundane details; but they should at least be implied, whereas what in fact happens is that their existence is glossed over rather sheepishly, as though they were a rather ridiculous necessity that it would be incongruous to mention. In any case, the supporters of the *politique des auteurs* will look down on, or treat condescendingly, any Western by a director who is not yet approved, even if it is as round and smooth as an egg. Well, what is *Stagecoach* if not an ultra-classical Western in which the art of John Ford consists simply of raising characters and situations to an absolute degree of perfection? And while sitting on the Censorship Committee I have seen some admirable Westerns, more or less anonymous and off the beaten track, but displaying a wonderful knowledge of the conventions of the genre and respecting that style from beginning to end.

ANDRÉ BAZIN, ON THE AUTEUR THEORY

Paradoxically, the champions of the *politique des auteurs* admire the American cinema, where production restrictions are heavier than anywhere else. It is also true that it is the country where the greatest technical possibilities are offered to the director. But the one does not cancel out the other. I do, however, admit that freedom is greater in Hollywood than it is said to be, as long as one knows how to detect its manifestations, and I will go so far as to say that the tradition of genres is a base of operations for creative freedom. The American cinema is a classical art, but why not then admire in it what is most admirable, i.e. not only the talent of this or that film-maker, but the genius of the system, the richness of its ever-vigorous tradition, and its fertility when it comes into contact with new elements—as has been proved, if proof there need be, in such films as *An American in Paris*, *The Seven Year Itch* and *Bus Stop*. True, Joshua Logan is lucky enough to be considered an *auteur*, or at least a budding auteur. But then when *Picnic* or *Bus Stop* get good reviews the praise does not go to what seems to me to be the essential point, i.e. the social truth, which of course is not offered as a goal that suffices in itself, but is integrated into a style of cinematic narration just as pre-war America was integrated into American comedy.

To conclude: the *politique des auteurs* seems to me to hold and defend an essential critical truth that the cinema is in need of more than the other arts, precisely because an act of true artistic creation is more uncertain and vulnerable in the cinema than elsewhere. But its exclusive practice leads to another danger: the negation of the film to the benefit of praise of its *auteur*. I have tried to show why mediocre *auteurs* can, by accident, make admirable films, and how, conversely, a genius can fall victim to an equally accidental sterility. I feel that this useful and fruitful approach, quite apart from its polemical value, should be complemented by other approaches to the cinematic phenomenon which will restore to a film its quality as a work of art. This does not mean one has to deny the role of *auteurs*, but simply give them back the preposition without which the noun *auteur* remains but a halting concept. *Auteur*, yes, but what *of*?

5A-2

Andrew Sarris

Notes on the Auteur Theory
1962

"ultimate premise of the auteur *theory is concerned with interior meaning, the ultimate glory of the cinema as an art. interior meaning is extrapolated from the tension between a director's personality and his material"*

Andrew Sarris (1928–2012) was an American film critic who popularized the concept of auteur theory, inspired by the critics who wrote for the French journal Cahiers du Cinéma. *He was a film critic for the* Village Voice, *a professor of film at Columbia University, and a founding member of the National Society of Film Critics.*

....

As far as I know, there is no definition of the *auteur* theory in the English language, that is, by any American or British critic. Truffaut has recently gone to great pains to emphasize that the *auteur* theory was merely a polemical weapon for a given time and a given place, and I am willing to take him at his word. But, lest I be accused of misappropriating a theory no one wants anymore, I will give the *Cahiers* critics full credit for the original formulation of an idea that reshaped my thinking on the cinema. First of all, how does the auteur theory differ from a straightforward theory of directors. Ian Cameron's article "Films, Directors, and Critics," in *Movie* of September, 1962, makes an interesting comment on this issue: "The assumption that underlies all the writing in *Movie* is that the director is the author of a film, the person who gives it any distinctive quality. There are quite large exceptions, with which I shall deal later." So far, so good, at least for the *auteur* theory, which even allows for exceptions. However, Cameron continues: "On the whole, we accept the cinema of directors, although without going to the farthest-out extremes of the *la politique des auteurs*, which makes it difficult to think of a bad director making a good film and almost impossible to think of a good director making a bad one." We are back to Bazin again, although Cameron naturally uses different examples. That three otherwise divergent critics like Bazin, Roud, and Cameron make essentially the same point about the *auteur* theory suggests a common fear of its abuses. I believe there is a misunderstanding here about what the *auteur* theory actually claims, particularly since the theory itself is so vague at the present time.

First of all, the *auteur* theory, at least as I understand it and now intend to express it, claims neither the gift of prophecy nor the option of extracinematic perception. Directors,

ANDREW SARRIS, NOTES ON THE AUTEUR THEORY

even *auteurs*, do not always run true to form, and the critic can never assume that a bad director will always make a bad film. No, not always, but almost always, and that is the point. What is a bad director, but a director who has made many bad films?

What is the problem then? Simply this: The badness of a director is not necessarily considered the badness of a film. If Joseph Pevney directed Garbo, Cherkassov, Olivier, Belmondo, and Harriet Andersson in *The Cherry Orchard*, the resulting spectacle might not be entirely devoid of merit with so many subsidiary *auteurs* to cover up for Joe. In fact, with this cast and this literary property, a Lumet might be safer than a Welles. The realities of casting apply to directors as well as to actors, but the *auteur* theory would demand the gamble with Welles, if he were willing.

Marlon Brando has shown us that a film can be made without a director. Indeed, *One-Eyed Jacks* is more entertaining than many films with directors. A director-conscious critic would find it difficult to say anything good or bad about direction that is nonexistent. One can talk here about photography, editing, acting, but not direction. The film even has personality, but, like *The Longest Day* and *Mutiny on the Bounty,* it is a cipher directorially. Obviously, the *auteur* theory cannot possibly cover every vagrant charm of the cinema. Nevertheless, the first premise of the *auteur* theory is the technical competence of a director as a criterion of value. A badly directed or an undirected film has no importance in a critical scale of values, but one can make interesting conversation about the subject, the script, the acting, the color, the photography, the editing, the music, the costumes, the decor, and so forth. That is the nature of the medium. You always get more for your money than mere art. Now, by the *auteur* theory, if a director has no technical competence, no elementary flair for the cinema, he is automatically cast out from the pantheon of directors. A great director has to be at least a good director. This is true in any art. What constitutes directorial talent is more difficult to define abstractly. There is less disagreement, however, on this first level of the *auteur* theory than there will be later.

The second premise of the *auteur* theory is the distinguishable personality of the director as a criterion of value. Over a group of films, a director must exhibit certain recurrent characteristics of style, which serve as his signature. The way a film looks and moves should have some relationship to the way a director thinks and feels. This is an area where American directors are generally superior to foreign directors. Because so much of the American cinema is commissioned, a director is forced to express his personality through the visual treatment of material rather than through the literary content of the material. A Cukor, who works with all sorts of projects, has a more developed abstract style than a Bergman, who is free to develop his own scripts. Not that Bergman lacks personality, but his work has declined with the depletion of his ideas largely because his technique never equaled his sensibility. Joseph L. Mankiewicz and Billy Wilder are other examples of writer-directors without adequate technical mastery. By contrast, Douglas Sirk and Otto Preminger have moved up the scale because their miscellaneous projects reveal a stylistic consistency.

The third and ultimate premise of the *auteur* theory is concerned with interior meaning, the ultimate glory of the cinema as an art. Interior meaning is extrapolated from the tension between a director's personality and his material. This conception of interior meaning comes close to what Astruc defines as *mise en scène*, but not quite. It is not quite the vision of the world a director projects nor quite his attitude toward life. It is ambiguous, in any literary sense, because part of it is imbedded in the stuff of the cinema and cannot be rendered in noncinematic terms. Truffaut has called it the temperature of the director on the set, and that is a close approximation of its professional aspect. Dare I come out and say what I think it to be is an *élan* of the soul?

Lest I seem unduly mystical, let me hasten to add that all I mean by "soul" is that intangible difference between one personality and another, all other things being equal. Sometimes, this difference is expressed by no more than a beat's hesitation in the rhythm of a film. In one sequence of *La Régle du Jeu*, Renoir gallops up the stairs, turns to his right with a lurching movement, stops in hoplike uncertainty when his name is called by a coquettish maid, and, then, with marvelous postreflex continuity, resumes his bearishly shambling journey to the heroine's boudoir. If I could describe the musical grace note of that momentary suspension, and I can't, I might be able to provide a more precise definition of the *auteur* theory. As it is, all I can do is point at the specific beauties of interior meaning on the screen and, later, catalogue the moments of recognition.

The three premises of the *auteur* theory may be visualized as three concentric circles: the outer circle as technique; the middle circle, personal style; and the inner circle, interior meaning. The corresponding roles of the director may be designated as those of a technician, a stylist, and an *auteur*. There is no prescribed course by which a director passes through the three circles. Godard once remarked that Visconti had evolved from a *metteur en scène* to an *auteur*, whereas Rossellini had evolved from an *auteur* to a *metteur en scène*. From opposite directions, they emerged with comparable status. Minnelli began and remained in the second circle as a stylist; Buñuel was an *auteur* even before he had assembled the technique of the first circle. Technique is simply the ability to put a film together with some clarity and coherence. Nowadays, it is possible to become a director without knowing too much about the technical side, even the crucial functions of photography and editing. An expert production crew could probably cover up for a chimpanzee in the director's chair. How do you tell the genuine director from the quasichimpanzee? After a given number of films, a pattern is established.

In fact, the *auteur* theory itself is a pattern theory in constant flux. I would never endorse a Ptolemaic constellation of directors in a fixed orbit. At the moment, my list of *auteurs* runs something like this through the first twenty: Ophüls, Renoir, Mizoguchi, Hitchcock, Chaplin, Ford, Welles, Dreyer, Rossellini, Murnau, Griffith, Sternberg, Eisenstein, von Stroheim, Buñuel, Bresson, Hawks, Lang, Flaherty, Vigo. This list is somewhat weighted toward seniority and established reputations. In time, some of these *auteurs* will rise, some will fall, and some will be displaced either by new directors or rediscovered ancients. Again, the exact order is less important than the specific definitions of these and as many as two hundred other potential *auteurs*. I would hardly expect any other critic in the world fully to endorse this list, especially on faith. Only after thousands of films have been revaluated will any personal pantheon have a reasonably objective validity. The task of validating the *auteur* theory is an enormous one, and the end will never be in sight. Meanwhile, the *auteur* habit of collecting random films in directorial bundles will serve posterity with at least a tentative classification.

Although the *auteur* theory emphasizes the body of a director's work rather than isolated masterpieces, it is expected of great directors that they make great films every so often. The only possible exception to this rule I can think of is Abel Gance, whose greatness is largely a function of his aspiration. Even with Gance, *La Roue* is as close to being a great film as any single work of Flaherty's. Not that single works matter that much. As Renoir has observed, a director spends his life on variations of the same film.

Two recent films—*Boccaccio '70* and *The Seven Capital Sins*—unwittingly reinforced the *auteur* theory by confirming the relative standing of the many directors involved. If I had not seen either film, I would have anticipated that the order of merit in *Boccaccio '70* would be Visconti, Fellini, and De Sica, and in *The Seven Capital Sins* Godard, Chabrol, Demy, Vadim, De Broca, Molinaro. (Dhomme, Ionesco's stage director and an unknown quantity in advance, turned out to be the worst of the lot.) There might be some argument about the relative badness of De Broca and Molinaro, but, otherwise, the directors ran true to form by almost any objective criterion of value. However, the main point here is that even in these frothy, ultracommercial servings of entertainment, the contribution of each director had less in common stylistically with the work of other directors on the project than with his own previous work.

Sometimes, a great deal of corn must be husked to yield a few kernels of internal meaning. I recently saw *Every Night at Eight,* one of the many maddeningly routine films Raoul Walsh has directed in his long career. This 1935 effort featured George Raft, Alice Faye, Frances Langford, and Patsy Kelly in one of those familiar plots about radio shows of the period. The film keeps moving along in the pleasantly unpretentious manner one would expect of Walsh until one incongruously intense scene with George Raft thrashing about in his sleep, revealing his inner fears in mumbling dream-talk. The girl he loves comes into the room in the midst of his unconscious avowals of feeling and listens sympathetically. This unusual scene was later amplified in *High Sierra* with Humphrey Bogart and Ida Lupino. The point is that one of the screen's most virile directors employed an essentially feminine narrative device to dramatize the emotional vulnerability of his heroes. If I had not been aware of Walsh in *Every Night at Eight*, the crucial link to *High Sierra* would have passed unnoticed. Such are the joys of the *auteur* theory.

Roland Barthes

The Death of the Author

1968

"the birth of the reader must be the cost of the death of the author"

Roland Barthes (1915–1980) was a French literary theorist and philosopher whose interdisciplinary work influenced the realms of semiology, existentialism, poststructuralism, and design theory. He was particularly fascinated by photography and explored this medium extensively in his writing.

In his story *Sarrasine* Balzac, describing a castrato disguised as a woman, writes the following sentence: '*This was woman herself, with her sudden fears, her irrational whims, her instinctive worries, her impetuous boldness, her fussings and her delicious sensibility.*' Who is speaking thus? Is it the hero of the story bent on remaining ignorant of the castrato hidden beneath the woman? Is it Balzac the individual, furnished by his personal experience with a philosophy of Woman? Is it Balzac the author professing 'literary' ideas on femininity? Is it universal wisdom? Romantic psychology? We shall never know, for the good reason that writing is the destruction of every voice, of every point of origin. Writing is that neutral, composite, oblique space where our subject slips away, the negative where all identity is lost, starting with the very identity of the body writing.

No doubt it has always been that way. As soon as a fact is *narrated* no longer with a view to acting directly on reality but intransitively, that is to say, finally outside of any function other than that of the very practice of the symbol itself, this disconnection occurs, the voice loses its origin, the author enters into his own death, writing begins. The sense of this phenomenon, however, has varied; in ethnographic societies the responsibility for a narrative is never assumed by a person but by a mediator, shaman or relator whose 'performance'—the mastery of the narrative code—may possibly be admired but never his 'genius'. The author is a modern figure, a product of our society insofar as, emerging from the Middle Ages with English empiricism, French rationalism and the personal faith of the Reformation, it discovered the prestige of the individual, of, as it is more nobly put, the 'human person'. It is thus logical that in literature it should be this positivism, the epitome and culmination of capitalist ideology, which has attached the greatest importance to the 'person' of the author. The *author* still reigns in histories of literature, biographies of writers, interviews, magazines, as in the very consciousness of men of letters anxious to unite their person and their work through diaries and memoirs. The image of literature to be found in contemporary culture is tyrannically centred on the author, his person, his life, his tastes, his passions, while criticism still consists for the most part in saying that Baudelaire's work is the failure of Baudelaire the man, Van Gogh's his madness, Tchaikovsky's his vice. The *explanation* of the work is always sought in the man or woman who produced it, as if it were always in the end, through the more or less transparent allegory of the fiction, the voice of a single person, the *author* 'confiding' in us.

Though the sway of the Author remains powerful (the new criticism has often done no more than consolidate it), it goes without saying that certain writers have long since attempted to loosen it. In France, Mallarmé was doubtless the first to see and to foresee in its full extent the necessity to substitute language itself for the person who until then had been supposed to be its owner. For him, for us too, it is language which speaks, not the author; to write us, through a prerequisite impersonality (not at all to be confused with the castrating objectivity of the realistic novelist), to reach that point where only language acts, 'performs,' and not 'me'. Mallarmé's entire poetics consists in suppressing the author in the interests of writing (which is, as will be seen, to restore the place of the reader). Valéry, encumbered with a psychology of the Ego, considerably diluted Mallarmé's theory but, his taste for classicism leading him to turn to the lessons of rhetoric, never stopped calling into question and deriding the Author; he stressed the linguistic and, as it were, 'hazardous' nature of his activity, and throughout his prose works he militated in favour of the essentially verbal condition of literature, in the face of which all recourse to the writer's interiority seemed to him pure superstition. Proust himself, despite the apparent psychological character of what are called his *analyses*, was visibly concerned with the task of inexorably blurring, by an extreme subtilization, the relation between the writer and his characters; by making of the narrator not he who has seen or felt nor even he who is writing, but he who *is going to write* (the young man in the novel—but, in fact, how old is he, and who is he?—wants to write but cannot; the novel ends when writing at last becomes possible), Proust gave modern writing its epic. By radical reversal, instead of putting his life into his novel, as is so often maintained, he made of his very life a work for which his own book was the model; so that it is clear to us that Charlus does not imitate Montesquiou but that Montesquiou—in his anecdotal, historical reality—is no more than a secondary fragment, derived from Charlus. Lastly, to go no further than this prehistory of modernity, Surrealism, though unable to accord language a supreme place (language being system and the aim of the movement being, romantically, a direct subversion of codes—itself moreover illusory: a code cannot be destroyed, only 'played off'), contributed to the desacrilization of the image of the Author by ceaselessly recommending the abrupt disappointment of expectations of meaning (the famous surrealist "jolt"), by entrusting the hand with the task of writing as quickly as possible what the head itself is unaware of (automatic writing), by accepting the principle and the experience of a several writing together. Leaving aside literature itself (such distinctions really becoming invalid), linguistics has recently provided the destruction of the Author with a valuable analytical tool by showing that the whole of the enunciation is an empty process, functioning perfectly without there being any need for it to be filled with the person of the interlocutors. Linguistically, the author is never more than the instance writing, just as *I* is nothing more than the instance saying *I*: language knows a 'subject', not a 'person', and this subject, empty outside of the very utterance which defines it, suffices to make language 'hold together', suffices, that is to say, to exhaust it.

The removal of the Author (one could talk here with Brecht of a veritable 'distancing', the Author diminishing like a figurine at the far end of the literary stage) is not merely an historical fact or an act of writing: it utterly transforms the modern text (or—which is the same thing—the text is henceforth made and read in such a way that at all its levels, the Author is absent). The temporality is different. The Author, when believed in, is always conceived of as the past of his own book: book and author stand automatically on a single line divided into a *before* and an *after*. The Author is thought to *nourish* the book, which is to say that he exists before it, thinks, suffers, lives for it, is in the same relation of antecedence to his work as a father to his child. In complete contrast, the modern scriptor is born simultaneously with the text, is in no way equipped with a being preceding or exceeding the writing, is not the subject with the book is predicate; there is no other time than that of the enunciation and every text is eternally written *here and now*. The fact is (or, it follows) that *writing* can no longer designate an operation of recording, notation, representation, 'depiction' (as the Classics would say); rather, it designates exactly what linguists, referring to Oxford philosophy, call a performative, a rare verbal form (exclusively given in the first person and in the present tense), in which the enunciation has no other content (contains no other proposition) than the act by which it is uttered—something like the *I declare* of kings or the *I sing* of very ancient poets. Having buried the Author, the modern scriptor can thus no longer believe, as according to the pathetic view of his predecessors, that this hand is too slow for his thought or passion, and that consequently, making a law of necessity, he must emphasize this delay and indefinitely 'polish' his form. For him, on the contrary, the hand, cut off from any voice, borne by a pure gesture of inscription (and not of expression), traces a field without origin—or which, at least, has no other origin than language itself, language which ceaselessly calls into question all origins.

We know now that a text is not a line of words releasing a single 'theological' meaning (the 'message' of the Author-God), but a multi-dimensional space in which a variety of writings, none of them original, blend and clash. The text is a tissue of quotations drawn from the innumerable centres of culture. Similar to Bouvard and Pecuchet, those eternal copyists, at once sublime and comic and whose profound ridiculousness indicates precisely the truth, of writing, the writer can only imitate a gesture that is always anterior, never original. His only power is to mix writings, to counter the ones with the others, in such a way as never to rest on any one of them. Did he wish to *express himself*, he ought at least to know that the inner 'thing' he things to 'translate' is itself only a ready formed dictionary, its words only explainable through other words, and so on indefinitely; something experienced in exemplary fashion by the young Thomas de Quincey, he who was so good at Greek that in order to translate absolutely modern ideas and images into that dead language, he had, so Baudelaire tells us (in *Paradis Artificiels*), 'created for himself an unfailing dictionary, vastly more extensive and complex than those resulting from the ordinary patience of purely literary themes'. Succeeding the Author, the scriptor no longer bears within him passions, humours, feelings, impressions, but rather this emense dictionary from which he draws a writing that can know no halt: life never does more than imitate the book, and the book itself is only a tissue of signs, an imitation that is lost, infinitely deferred.

ROLAND BARTHES, THE DEATH OF THE AUTHOR

Once the Author is removed, the claim to decipher a text becomes quite futile. To give a text an Author is to impose a limit on that text, to furnish it with a final significed, to close the writing. Such a conception suits criticism very well, the latter then allotting itself the important task of discovering the Author (or its hypostases: society, history, psyche, liberty) beneath the work: when the Author has been found, the text is 'explained'—victory to the critic. Hence there is no surprise in the fact that, historically, the reign of the Author has also been that of the Critic, nor again in the fact that criticism (be it new) is today undermined along with the Author. In a multiplicity of writing, everything is to be *disentangled*, nothing *deciphered*; the structure can be followed, 'run' (like the thread of a stocking) at every point and at every level, but there is nothing beneath; the space of the writing is to be ranged over, not pierced; writing ceaselessly posits meaning ceaselessly to evaporate it, carrying out a systematic exemption of meaning. In precisely this way literature (it would be better from now on to say *writing*), by refusing to assign a 'secret', an ultimate meaning, to the text (and to the world as text) liberates what may be called an anti-theological activity, an activity that is truly revolutionary since to refuse to fix meaning is finally, in the end, to refuse God and his hypostases—reason, science, law.

Let us come back to the Balzac sentence. No one, no 'person', says it: its source, its voice, is not the true place of the writing, which is reading. Another—very precise—example will help to make this clear: recent research (J.-P. Vernant) has demonstrated the constitutively ambiguous nature of Greek tragedy, its texts being woven from with words with double meanings that each character understands unilaterally (this perpetual misunderstanding is exactly the 'tragic'); there is, however, someone who understands each word in its duplicity and who, in addition, hears the very deafness of the characters speaking in front of him— this someone being precisely the reader (or here, the listener). Thus is revealed the total existence of writing: a text is made of multiple writings, drawn from many cultures and entering into mutual relations of dialogue, parody, contestation, that there is one place where this multiplicity is focused and that place is the reader, not, as was hitherto said, the author. The reader is the space on which all the quotations that make up a writing are inscribed without any of them being lost; a text's unity lies not in its origin but in its destination. Yet this destination cannot any longer be personal: the reader is without history, biography, psychology; he is simply that *someone* who holds together in a single field all the traces by which the written text is constituted. This is why it is derisory to condemn the new writing in the name of a humanism hypocritically turned champion of the reader's rights. Classic criticism has never paid any attention to the reader; for it, the writer is the only person in literature. We are now beginning to let ourselves be fooled no longer by the arrogant antiphrasical recriminations of good society in favour of the very thing it sets aside, ignores, smothers, or destroys; we know that to give writing its future, it is necessary to overthrow the myth: the birth of the reader must be the cost of the death of the Author.

Michel Foucault

What Is an Author?

1969

*"it is obvious that even within the realm of discourse a person can
be the author of much more than a book.... For convenience, we
could say that such authors occupy a 'transdiscursive' position"*

*Michel Foucault (1926–1984) was a French academic and writer associated with the structur-
alist movement (though he frequently rejected this categorization). He wrote on a variety of
subjects, such as the architecture of incarceration, the history of sexuality, and representation in
Western art. His work strongly influenced the disciplines of the humanities and social sciences.*

In proposing this slightly odd question, I am conscious of the need for an explanation. To
this day, the 'author' remains an open question both with respect to its general function
within discourse and in my own writings; that is, this question permits me to return to
certain aspects of my own work which now appear ill-advised and misleading. In this
regard, I wish to propose a necessary criticism and reevaluation.

For instance, my objective in *The Order of Things* had been to analyse verbal clusters as
discursive layers which fall outside the familiar categories of a book, a work, or an author.
But while I considered "natural history," the "analysis of wealth," and 'political economy'
in general terms, I neglected a similar analysis of the author and his works; it is perhaps
due to this omission that I employed the names of authors throughout this book in a
naive and often crude fashion. I spoke of Buffon, Cuvier, Ricardo, and others as well, but
failed to realize that I had allowed their names to function ambiguously. This has proved
an embarrassment to me in that my oversight has served to raise two pertinent objections.

It was argued that I had not properly described Buffon or his work and that my handling
of Marx was pitifully inadequate in terms of the totality of his thought. Although these
objections were obviously justified, they ignored the task I had set myself: I had no
intention of describing Buffon or Marx or of reproducing their statements or implicit
meanings, but, simply stated, I wanted to locate the rules that formed a certain number
of concepts and theoretical relationships in their works. In addition, it was argued that
I had created monstrous families by bringing together names as disparate as Buffon and
Linnaeus or in placing Cuvier next to Darwin in defiance of the most readily observable
family resemblances and natural ties. This objection also seems inappropriate since I had

never tried to establish a genealogical table of exceptional individuals, nor was I concerned in forming an intellectual daguerreotype of the scholar or naturalist of the seventeenth and eighteenth century. In fact, I had no intention of forming any family, whether holy or perverse. On the contrary, I wanted to determine—a much more modest task—the functional conditions of specific discursive practices.

Then why did I use the names of authors in *The Order of Things*? Why not avoid their use altogether, or, short of that, why not define the manner in which they were used? These questions appear fully justified and I have tried to gauge their implications and consequences in a book that will appear shortly. These questions have determined my effort to situate comprehensive discursive units, such as "natural history" or "political economy," and to establish the methods and instruments for delimiting, analysing, and describing these unities. Nevertheless, as a privileged moment of individualization in the history of ideas, knowledge, and literature, or in the history of philosophy and science, the question of the author demands a more direct response. Even now, when we study the history of a concept, a literary genre, or a branch of philosophy, these concerns assume a relatively weak and secondary position in relation to the solid and fundamental role of an author and his works.

For the purposes of this paper, I will set aside a sociohistorical analysis of the author as an individual and the numerous questions that deserve attention in this context: how the author was individualized in a culture such as ours; the status we have given the author, for instance, when we began our research into authenticity and attribution; the systems of valorization in which he was included; or the moment when the stories of heroes gave way to an author's biography; the conditions that fostered the formulation of the fundamental critical category of 'the man and his work.' For the time being, I wish to restrict myself to the singular relationship that holds between an author and a text, the manner in which a text apparently points to this figure who is outside and precedes it.

Beckett supplies a direction: "What matter who's speaking, someone said, what matter who's speaking." In an indifference such as this we must recognize one of the fundamental ethical principles of contemporary writing. It is not simply 'ethical' because it characterizes our way of speaking and writing, but because it stands as an immanent rule, endlessly adopted and yet never fully applied. As a principle, it dominates writing as an ongoing practice and slights our customary attention to the finished product. For the sake of illustration, we need only consider two of its major themes. First, the writing of our day has freed itself from the necessity of "expression"; it only refers to itself, yet it is not restricted to the confines of interiority On the contrary, we recognize it in its exterior deployment. This reversal transforms writing into an interplay of signs, regulated less by the content it signifies than by the very nature of the signifier. Moreover, it implies an action that is always testing the limits of its regularity, transgressing and reversing an order that it accepts and manipulates. Writing unfolds like a game that inevitably moves beyond its own rules and finally leaves them behind. Thus, the essential basis of this writing is not the exalted emotions related to the act of composition or the insertion of a subject into language. Rather, it is primarily concerned with creating an opening where the writing subject endlessly disappears.

The second theme is even more familiar: it is the kinship between writing and death. This relationship inverts the age-old conception of Greek narrative or epic, which was designed to guarantee the immortality of a hero. The hero accepted an early death because his life, consecrated and magnified by death, passed into immortality; and the narrative redeemed his acceptance of death. In a different sense, Arabic stories, and *The Arabian Nights* in particular, had as their motivation, their theme and pretext, this strategy for defeating death. Storytellers continued their narratives late into the night to forestall death and to delay the inevitable moment when everyone must fall silent. Scheherazade's story is a desperate inversion of murder; it is the effort, throughout all those nights, to exclude death from the circle of existence. This conception of a spoken or written narrative as a protection against death has been transformed by our culture. Writing is now linked to sacrifice and to the sacrifice of life itself; it is a voluntary obliteration of the self that does not require representation in books because it takes place in the everyday existence of the writer. Where a work had the duty of creating immortality, it now attains the right to kill, to become the murderer of its author. Flaubert, Proust, and Kafka are obvious examples of this reversal. In addition, we find the link between writing and death manifested in the total effacement of the individual characteristics of the writer; the quibbling and confrontations that a writer generates between himself and his text cancel out the signs of his particular individuality. If we wish to know the writer in our day, it will be through the singularity of his absence and in his link to death, which has transformed him into a victim of his own writing. While all of this is familiar in philosophy, as in literary criticism, I am not certain that the consequences derived from the disappearance or death of the author have been fully explored or that the importance of this event has been appreciated. To be specific, it seems to me that the themes destined to replace the privileged position accorded the author have merely served to arrest the possibility of genuine change. Of these, I will examine two that seem particularly important.

To begin with, the thesis concerning a work. It has been understood that the task of criticism is not to reestablish the ties between an author and his work or to reconstitute an author's thought and experience through his works and, further, that criticism should concern itself with the structures of a work, its architectonic forms, which are studied for their intrinsic and internal relationships. Yet, what of a context that questions the concept of a work? What, in short, is the strange unit designated by the term, work? What is necessary to its composition, if a work is not something written by a person called an "author"? Difficulties arise on all sides if we raise the question in this way. If an individual is not an author, what are we to make of those things he has written or said, left among his papers or communicated to others? Is this not properly a work? What, for instance, were Sade's papers before he was consecrated as an author? Little more, perhaps, than rolls of paper on which he endlessly unravelled his fantasies while in prison.

Assuming that we are dealing with an author, is everything he wrote and said, everything he left behind, to be included in his work? This problem is both theoretical and practical. If we wish to publish the complete works of Nietzsche, for example, where do we draw the line? Certainly, everything must be published, but can we agree on what "everything" means? We will, of course, include everything that Nietzsche himself published, along with the drafts of his works, his plans for aphorisms, his marginal notations and corrections. But what if, in a notebook filled with aphorisms, we find a reference, a remainder of an appointment, an address, or a laundry bill, should this be included in his works?

Why not? These practical considerations are endless once we consider how a work can be extracted from the millions of traces left by an individual after his death. Plainly, we lack a theory to encompass the questions generated by a work and the empirical activity of those who naively undertake the publication of the complete works of an author often suffers from the absence of this framework. Yet more questions arise. Can we say that *The Arabian Nights*, and *Stromates* of Clement of Alexandria, or the *Lives* of Diogenes Laertes constitute works? Such questions only begin to suggest the range of our difficulties, and, if some have found it convenient to bypass the individuality of the writer or his status as an author to concentrate on a work, they have failed to appreciate the equally problematic nature of the word "work" and the unity it designates.

Another thesis has detained us from taking full measure of the author's disappearance. It avoids confronting the specific event that makes it possible and, in subtle ways, continues to preserve the existence of the author. This is the notion of *écriture*. Strictly speaking, it should allow us not only to circumvent references to an author, but to situate his recent absence. The conception of *écriture*, as currently employed, is concerned with neither the act of writing nor the indications, as symptoms or signs within a text, of an author's meaning; rather, it stands for a remarkably profound attempt to elaborate the conditions of any text, both the conditions of its spatial dispersion and its temporal deployment.

It appears, however, that this concept, as currently employed, has merely transposed the empirical characteristics of an author to a transcendental anonymity. The extremely visible signs of the author's empirical activity are effaced to allow the play, in parallel or opposition, of religious and critical modes of characterization. In granting a primordial status to writing, do we not, in effect, simply reinscribe in transcendental terms the theological affirmation of its sacred origin or a critical belief in its creative nature? To say that writing, in terms of the particular history it made possible, is subjected to forgetfulness and repression, is this not to reintroduce in transcendental terms the religious principle of hidden meanings (which require interpretation) and the critical assumption of implicit significations, silent purposes, and obscure contents (which give rise to commentary)? Finally, is not the conception of writing as absence a transposition into transcendental terms of the religious belief in a fixed and continuous tradition or the aesthetic principle that proclaims the survival of the work as a kind of enigmatic supplement of the author beyond his own death? This conception of *écriture* sustains the privileges of the author through the safeguard of the a priori; the play of representations that formed a particular image of the author is extended within a gray neutrality. The disappearance of the author—since Mallarme, an event of our time—is held in check by the transcendental. Is it not necessary to draw a line between those who believe that we can continue to situate our present discontinuities within the historical and transcendental tradition of the nineteenth century and those who are making a great effort to liberate themselves, once and for all, from this conceptual framework?

❧

It is obviously insufficient to repeat empty slogans: the author has disappeared; God and man died a common death. Rather, we should reexamine the empty space left by the author's disappearance; we should attentively observe, along its gaps and fault lines, its new demarcations, and the reapportionment of this void; we should await the fluid functions released by this disappearance. In this context we can briefly consider the problems that arise in the use of an author's name. What is the name of an author? How does it function? Far from offering a solution, I will attempt to indicate some of the difficulties related to these questions.

The name of an author poses all the problems related to the category of the proper name. (Here, I am referring to the work of John Searle, among others.) Obviously not a pure and simple reference, the proper name (and the author's name as well) has other than indicative functions. It is more than a gesture, a finger pointed at someone; it is, to a certain extent, the equivalent of a description. When we say "Aristotle," we are using a word that means one or a series of definite descriptions of the type: "the author of the *Analytics*," or "the founder of ontology," and so forth. Furthermore, a proper name has other functions than that of signification: when we discover that Rimbaud has not written *La Chasse spirituelle*, we cannot maintain that the meaning of the proper name or this author's name has been altered. The proper name and the name of an author oscillate between the poles of description and designation, and, granting that they are linked to what they name, they are not totally determined either by their descriptive or designative functions.18 Yet—and it is here that the specific difficulties attending an author's name appear—the link between a proper name and the individual being named and the link between an author's name and that which it names are not isomorphous and do not function in the same way; and these differences require clarification.

To learn, for example, that Pierre Dupont does not have blue eyes, does not live in Paris, and is not a doctor does not invalidate the fact that the name, Pierre Dupont, continues to refer to the same person; there has been no modification of the designation that links the name to the person. With the name of an author, however, the problems are far more complex. The disclosure that Shakespeare was not born in the house that tourists now visit would not modify the functioning of the author's name, but, if it were proved that he had not written the sonnets that we attribute to him, this would constitute a significant change and affect the manner in which the author's name functions. Moreover, if we establish that Shakespeare wrote Bacon's *Organon* and that the same author was responsible for both the works of Shakespeare and those of Bacon, we would have introduced a third type of alteration which completely modifies the functioning of the author's name. Consequently, the name of an author is not precisely a proper name among others.

Many other factors sustain this paradoxical singularity of the name of an author. It is altogether different to maintain that Pierre Dupont does not exist and that Homer or Hermes Trismegistes have never existed. While the first negation merely implies that there is no one by the name of Pierre Dupont, the second indicates that several individuals have been referred to by one name or that the real author possessed none of the traits traditionally associated with Homer or Hermes. Neither is it the same thing to say that Jacques Durand, not Pierre Dupont, is the real name of *X* and that Stendhal's name was Henri Beyle. We could also examine the function and meaning of such statements as 'Bourbaki is this or that person,' and 'Victor Eremita, Climacus, Anticlimacus, Frater Taciturnus, Constantin Constantius, all of these are Kierkegaard.'

These differences indicate that an author's name is not simply an element of speech (as a subject, a complement, or an element that could be replaced by a pronoun or other parts of speech). Its presence is functional in that it serves as a means of classification. A name can group together a number of texts and thus differentiate them from others. A name also establishes different forms of relationships among texts. Neither Hermes not Hippocrates existed in the sense that we can say Balzac existed, but the fact that a number of texts were attached to a single name implies that relationships of homogeneity, filiation, reciprocal explanation, authentification, or of common utilization were established among them. Finally, the author's name characterizes a particular manner of existence of discourse. Discourse that possesses an author's name is not to be immediately consumed and forgotten; neither is it accorded the momentary attention given to ordinary, fleeting words. Rather, its status and its manner of reception are regulated by the culture in which it circulates.

We can conclude that, unlike a proper name, which moves from the interior of a discourse to the real person outside who produced it, the name of the author remains at the contours of texts—separating one from the other, defining their form, and characterizing their mode of existence. It points to the existence of certain groups of discourse and refers to the status of this discourse within a society and culture. The author's name is not a function of a man's civil status, nor is it fictional; it is situated in the breach, among the discontinuities, which gives rise to new groups of discourse and their singular mode of existence. Consequently, we can say that in our culture, the name of an author is a variable that accompanies only certain texts to the exclusion of others: a private letter may have a signatory, but it does not have an author; a contract can have an underwriter, but not an author; and, similarly, an anonymous poster attached to a wall may have a writer, but he cannot be an author. In this sense, the function of an author is to characterize the existence, circulation, and operation of certain discourses within a society.

༈

In dealing with the "author" as a function of discourse, we must consider the characteristics of a discourse that support this use and determine its difference from other discourses. If we limit our remarks to only those books or texts with authors, we can isolate four different features.

First, they are objects of appropriation; the form of property they have become is of a particular type whose legal codification was accomplished some years ago. It is important to notice, as well, that its status as property is historically secondary to the penal code controlling its appropriation. Speeches and books were assigned real authors, other than mythical or important religious figures, only when the author became subject to punishment and to the extent that his discourse was considered transgressive. In our culture—undoubtedly in others as well—discourse was not originally a thing, a product, or a possession, but an action situated in a bipolar field of sacred and profane, lawful and unlawful, religious and blasphemous. It was a gesture charged with risks long before it became a possession caught in a circuit of property values. But it was at the moment when a system of ownership and strict copyright rules were established (toward the end of the eighteenth and beginning of the nineteenth century) that the transgressive properties always intrinsic to the act of writing became the forceful imperative of literature. It is as if the author, at the moment he was accepted into the social order of property which governs our culture, was compensating for his new status by reviving the older bipolar field of discourse in a systematic practice of transgression and by restoring the danger of writing which, on another side, had been conferred the benefits of property.

Secondly, the "author-function" is not universal or constant in all discourse. Even within our civilization, the same types of texts have not always required authors; there was a time when those texts which we now call 'literary' (stories, folk tales, epics, and tragedies) were accepted, circulated, and valorized without any question about the identity of their author. Their anonymity was ignored because their real or supposed age was a sufficient guarantee of their authenticity. Texts, however, that we now call 'scientific' (dealing with cosmology and the heavens, medicine or illness, the natural sciences or geography) were only considered truthful during the Middle Ages if the name of the author was indicated. Statements on the order of "Hippocrates said…" or "Pliny tells us that…" were not merely formulas for an argument based on authority; they marked a proven discourse. In the seventeenth and eighteenth centuries, a totally new conception was developed when scientific texts were accepted on their own merits and positioned within an anonymous and coherent conceptual system of established truths and methods of verification. Authentification no longer required reference to the individual who had produced them; the role of the author disappeared as an index of truthfulness and, where it remained as an inventor's name, it was merely to denote a specific theorem or proposition, a strange effect, a property, a body, a group of elements, or pathological syndrome.

At the same time, however, "literary" discourse was acceptable only if it carried an author's name; every text of poetry or fiction was obliged to state its author and the date, place, and circumstance of its writing. The meaning and value attributed to the text depended on this information. If by accident or design a text was presented anonymously, every effort was made to locate its author. Literary anonymity was of interest only as a puzzle to be solved as, in our day, literary works are totally dominated by the sovereignty of the author. (Undoubtedly, these remarks are far too categorical. Criticism has been concerned for some time now with aspects of a text not fully dependent on the notion of an individual creator; studies of genre or the analysis of recurring textual motifs and their variations from a norm other than the author. Furthermore, where in mathematics the author has become little more than a handy reference for a particular theorem or group of propositions, the reference to an author in biology and medicine, or to the date of his research has a substantially different bearing. This latter reference, more than simply indicating the source of information, attests to the 'reliability' of the evidence, since it entails an appreciation of the techniques and experimental materials available at a given time and in a particular laboratory.)

The third point concerning this "author-function" is that it is not formed spontaneously through the simple attribution of a discourse to an individual. It results from a complex operation whose purpose is to construct the rational entity we call an author. Undoubtedly, this construction is assigned a "realistic" dimension as we speak of an individual's "profundity" or "creative" power, his intentions or the original inspiration manifested in writing. Nevertheless, these aspects of an individual, which we designate as an author (or which comprise an individual as an author), are projections, in terms always more or less psychological, of our way of handling texts: in the comparisons we make, the traits we extract as pertinent, the continuities we assign, or the exclusions we practice. In addition, all these operations vary according to the period and the form of discourse concerned. A "philosopher" and a "poet" are not constructed in the same manner; and the author of an eighteenth-century novel was formed differently from the modern novelist. There are, nevertheless, transhistorical constants in the rules that govern the construction of an author.

In literary criticism, for example, the traditional methods for defining an author—or, rather, for determining the configuration of the author from existing texts—derive in large part from those used in the Christian tradition to authenticate (or to reject) the particular texts in its possession. Modern criticism, in its desire to "recover" the author from a work, employs devices strongly reminiscent of Christian exegesis when it wished to prove the value of a text by ascertaining the holiness of its author. In *De Viris Illustribus*, Saint Jerome maintains that homonymy is not proof of the common authorship of several works, since many individuals could have the same name or someone could have perversely appropriated another's name. The name, as an individual mark, is not sufficient as it relates to a textual tradition. How, then, can several texts be attributed to an individual author? What norms, related to the function of the author, will disclose the involvement of several authors? According to Saint Jerome, there are four criteria: the texts that must be eliminated from the list of works attributed to a single author are those inferior to the others (thus, the author is defined as a standard level of quality); those whose ideas conflict with the doctrine expressed in the others (here the author is defined as a certain field of conceptual or theoretical coherence); those written in a different style and containing words and phrases not ordinarily found in the other works (the author is seen as a stylistic uniformity); and those referring to events or historical figures subsequent to the death of the author (the author is thus a definite historical figure in which a series of events converge). Although modern criticism does not appear to have these same suspicions concerning authentication, its strategies for defining the author present striking similarities. The author explains the presence of certain events within a text, as well as their transformations, distortions, and their various modifications (and this through an author's biography or by reference to his particular point of view, in the analysis of his social preferences and his position within a class or by delineating his fundamental objectives). The author also constitutes a principle of unity in writing where any unevenness of production is ascribed to changes caused by evolution, maturation, or outside influence. In addition, the author serves to neutralize the contradictions that are found in a series of texts. Governing this function is the belief that there must be—at a particular level of an author's thought, of his conscious or unconscious desire—a point where contradictions are resolved, where the incompatible elements can be shown to relate to one another or to cohere around a fundamental and originating contradiction. Finally, the author is a particular source of expression who, in more or less finished forms, is manifested equally well, and with similar validity, in a text, in letters, fragments, drafts, and so forth. Thus, even while Saint Jerome's four principles of authenticity might seem largely inadequate to modern critics, they, nevertheless, define the critical modalities now used to display the function of the author.

However, it would be false to consider the function of the author as a pure and simple reconstruction after the fact of a text given as passive material, since a text always bears a number of signs that refer to the author. Well known to grammarians, these textual signs are personal pronouns, adverbs of time and place, and the conjugation of verbs. But it is important to note that these elements have a different bearing on texts with an author and on those without one. In the latter, these "shifters" refer to a real speaker and to an actual deictic situation, with certain exceptions such as the case of indirect speech in the first person. When discourse is linked to an author, however, the role of "shifters" is more complex and variable. It is well known that in a novel narrated in the first person, neither the first person pronoun, the present indicative tense, nor, for that matter, its signs of localization refer directly to the writer, either to the time when he wrote, or to the specific act of writing; rather, they stand for a "second self" whose similarity to the author is never fixed and undergoes considerable alteration within the course of a single book. It would be as false to seek the author in relation to the actual writer as to the fictional narrator; the "author-function" arises out of their scission—in the division and distance of the two. One might object that this phenomenon only applies to novels or poetry, to a context of "quasi-discourse," but, in fact, all discourse that supports this 'author-function' is characterized by this plurality of egos. In a mathematical treatise, the ego who indicates the circumstances of composition in the preface is not identical, either in terms of his position or his function, to the "I" who concludes a demonstration within the body of the text. The former implies a unique individual who, at a given time and place, succeeded in completing a project, whereas the latter indicates an instance and plan of demonstration that anyone could perform provided the same set of axioms, preliminary operations, and an identical set of symbols were used. It is also possible to locate a third ego: one who speaks of the goals of his investigation, the obstacles encountered, its results, and the problems yet to be solved and this 'I' would function in a field of existing or future mathematical discourses. We are not dealing with a system of dependencies where a first and essential use of the "I" is reduplicated, as a kind of fiction, by the other two. On the contrary, the 'author-function' in such discourses operates so as to effect the simultaneous dispersion of the three egos.

Further elaboration would, of course, disclose other characteristics of the "author-function," but I have limited myself to the four that seemed the most obvious and important. They can be summarized in the following manner: the 'author-function' is tied to the legal and institutional systems that circumscribe, determine, and articulate the realm of discourses; it does not operate in a uniform manner in all discourses, at all times, and in any given culture; it is not defined by the spontaneous attribution of a text to its creator, but through a series of precise and complex procedures; it does not refer, purely and simply, to an actual individual insofar as it simultaneously gives rise to a variety of egos and to a series of subjective positions that individuals of any class may come to occupy.

※

I am aware that until now I have kept my subject within unjustifiable limits; I should also have spoken of the 'author-function' in painting, music, technical fields, and so forth. Admitting that my analysis is restricted to the domain of discourse, it seems that I have given the term 'author' an excessively narrow meaning. I have discussed the author only in the limited sense of a person to whom the production of a text, a book, or a work can be legitimately attributed. However, it is obvious that even within the realm of discourse a person can be the author of much more than a book—of a theory, for instance, of a tradition or a discipline within which new books and authors can proliferate. For convenience, we could say that such authors occupy a 'transdiscursive' position.

Homer, Aristotle, and the Church Fathers played this role, as did the first mathematicians and the originators of the Hippocratic tradition. This type of author is surely as old as our civilization. But I believe that the nineteenth century in Europe produced a singular type of author who should not be confused with 'great' literary authors, or the authors of canonical religious texts, and the founders of sciences. Somewhat arbitrarily, we might call them "initiators of discursive practices."

The distinctive contribution of these authors is that they produced not only their own work, but the possibility and the rules of formation of other texts. In this sense, their role differs entirely from that of a novelist, for example, who is basically never more than the author of his own text. Freud is not simply the author of *The Interpretation of Dreams* or of *Wit and its Relation to the Unconscious* and Marx is not simply the author of the *Communist Manifesto* or *Capital*: they both established the endless possibility of discourse. Obviously, an easy objection can be made. The author of a novel may be responsible for more than his own text; if he acquires some 'importance' in the literary world, his influence can have significant ramifications. To take a very simple example, one could say that Ann Radcliffe did not simply write *The Mysteries of Udolpho* and a few other novels, but also made possible the appearance of Gothic Romances at the beginning of the nineteenth century. To this extent, her function as an author exceeds the limits of her work. However, this objection can be answered by the fact that the possibilities disclosed by the initiators of discursive practices (using the examples of Marx and Freud, whom I believe to be the first and the most important) are significantly different from those suggested by novelists. The novels of Ann Radcliffe put into circulation a certain number of resemblances and analogies patterned on her work—various characteristic signs, figures, relationships, and structures that could be integrated into other books. In short, to say that Ann Radcliffe created the Gothic Romance means that there are certain elements common to her works and to the nineteenth-century Gothic romance: the heroine ruined by her own innocence, the secret fortress that functions as a counter-city, the outlaw-hero who swears revenge on the world that has cursed him, etc. On the other hand, Marx and Freud, as "initiators of discursive practices," not only made possible a certain number of analogies that could be adopted by future texts, but, as importantly, they also made possible a certain number of differences. They cleared a space for the introduction of elements other than their own, which, never-theless, remain within the field of discourse they initiated. In saying that Freud founded psychoanalysis, we do not simply mean that the concept of libido or the techniques of dream analysis reappear in the writings of Karl Abraham or Melanie Klein, but that he made possible a certain number of differences with respect to his books, concepts, and hypotheses, which all arise out of psychoanalytic discourse.

Is this not the case, however, with the founder of any new science or of any author who successfully transforms an existing science? After all, Galileo is indirectly responsible for the texts of those who mechanically applied the laws he formulated, in addition to having paved the way for the production of statements far different from his own. If Cuvier is the founder of biology and Saussure of linguistics, it is not because they were imitated or that an organic concept or a theory of the sign was uncritically integrated into new texts, but because Cuvier, to a certain extent, made possible a theory of evolution diametrically opposed to his own system and because Saussure made possible a generative grammar radically different from his own structural analysis. Superficially, then, the initiation of discursive practices appears similar to the founding of any scientific endeavor, but I believe there is a fundamental difference.

In a scientific program, the founding act is on an equal footing with its future transforma-tions: it is merely one among the many modifications that it makes possible. This interde-pendence can take several forms. In the future development of a science, the founding act may appear as little more than a single instance of a more general phenomenon that has been discovered. It might be questioned, in retrospect, for being too intuitive or empirical and submitted to the rigors of new theoretical operations in order to situate it in a formal domain. Finally, it might be thought a hasty generalization whose validity should be restricted. In other words, the founding act of a science can always be rechanneled through the machinery of transformations it has instituted.

On the other hand, the initiation of a discursive practice is heterogeneous to its ulterior transformations. To extend psychoanalytic practice, as initiated by Freud, is not to presume a formal generality that was not claimed at the outset; it is to explore a number of possible applications. To limit it is to isolate in the original texts a small set of propositions or statements that are recognized as having an inaugurative value and that mark other Freudian concepts or theories as derivative. Finally, there are no "false" statements in the work of these initiators; those statements considered inessential or 'prehistoric,' in that they are associated with another discourse, are simply neglected in favor of the more pertinent aspects of the work. The initiation of a discursive practice, unlike the founding of a science, overshadows and is necessarily detached from its later developments and transformations. As a consequence, we define the theoretical validity of a statement with respect to the work of the initiator, whereas in the case of Galileo or Newton, it is based on the structural and intrinsic norms established in cosmology or physics. Stated schematically, the work of these initiators is not situated in relation to a science or in the space it defines; rather, it is science or discursive practice that relate to their works as the primary points of reference.

In keeping with this distinction, we can understand why it is inevitable that practitioners of such discourses must 'return to the origin.' Here, as well, it is necessary to distinguish a "return" from scientific "rediscoveries" or "reactivations." "Rediscoveries" are the effects of analogy or isomorphism with current forms of knowledge that allow the perception of forgotten or obscured figures. For instance, Chomsky in his book on Cartesian grammar 'rediscovered' a form of knowledge that had been in use from Cordemoy to Humboldt. It could only be understood from the perspective of generative grammar because this later manifestation held the key to its construction: in effect, a retrospective codification of an historical position. 'Reactivation' refers to something quite different: the insertion of discourse into totally new domains of generalization, practice, and transformations. The history of mathematics abounds in examples of this phenomenon as the work of Michel Serres on mathematical anamnesis shows.

The phrase, "return to," designates a movement with its proper specificity, which characterizes the initiation of discursive practices. If we return, it is because of a basic and constructive omission, an omission that is not the result of accident or incomprehension. In effect, the act of initiation is such, in its essence, that it is inevitably subjected to its own distortions; that which displays this act and derives from it is, at the same time, the root of its divergences and travesties. This nonaccidental omission must be regulated by precise operations that can be situated, analysed, and reduced in a return to the act of initiation. The barrier imposed by omission was not added from the outside; it arises from the discursive practice in question, which gives it its law. Both the cause of the barrier and the means for its removal, this omission—also responsible for the obstacles that prevent returning to the act of initiation—can only be resolved by a return. In addition, it is always a return to a text in itself, specifically, to a primary and unadorned text with particular attention to those things registered in the interstices of the text, its gaps and absences. We return to those empty spaces that have been masked by omission or concealed in a false and misleading plenitude. In these rediscoveries of an essential lack, we find the oscillation of two characteristic responses: "This point was made—you can't help seeing it if you know how to read"; or, inversely, "No, that point is not made in any of the printed words in the text, but it is expressed through the words, in their relationships and in the distance that separates them." It follows naturally that this return, which is a part of the discursive mechanism, constantly introduces modifications and that the return to a text is not a historical supplement that would come to fix itself upon the primary discursivity and redouble it in the form of an ornament which, after all, is not essential. Rather, it is an effective and necessary means of transforming discursive practice. A study of Galileo's works could alter our knowledge of the history, but not the science, of mechanics; whereas, a re-examination of the books of Freud or Marx can transform our understanding of psychoanalysis or Marxism.

A last feature of these returns is that they tend to reinforce the enigmatic link between an author and his works. A text has an inaugurative value precisely because it is the work of a particular author, and our returns are conditioned by this knowledge. The rediscovery of an unknown text by Newton or Cantor will not modify classical cosmology or group theory; at most, it will change our appreciation of their historical genesis. Bringing to light, however, *An Outline of Psychoanalysis*, to the extent that we recognize it as a book by Freud, can transform not only our historical knowledge, but the field of psychoanalytic theory— if only through a shift of accent or of the center of gravity. These returns, an important component of discursive practices, form a relationship between 'fundamental' and mediate authors, which is not identical to that which links an ordinary text to its immediate author.

These remarks concerning the initiation of discursive practices have been extremely schematic, especially with regard to the opposition I have tried to trace between this initiation and the founding of sciences. The distinction between the two is not readily discernible; moreover, there is no proof that the two procedures are mutually exclusive. My only purpose in setting up this opposition, however, was to show that the "author-function," sufficiently complex at the level of a book or a series of texts that bear a definite signature, has other determining factors when analysed in terms of larger entities—groups of works or entire disciplines.

❧

Unfortunately, there is a decided absence of positive propositions in this essay, as it applies to analytic procedures or directions for future research, but I ought at least to give the reasons why I attach such importance to a continuation of this work. Developing a similar analysis could provide the basis for a typology of discourse. A typology of this sort cannot be adequately understood in relation to the grammatical features, formal structures, and objects of discourse, because there undoubtedly exist specific discursive properties or relationships that are irreducible to the rules of grammar and logic and to the laws that govern objects. These properties require investigation if we hope to distinguish the larger categories of discourse. The different forms of relationships (or nonrelationships) that an author can assume are evidently one of these discursive properties.

This form of investigation might also permit the introduction of an historical analysis of discourse. Perhaps the time has come to study not only the expressive value and formal transformations of discourse, but its mode of existence: the modifications and variations, within any culture, of modes of circulation, valorization, attribution, and appropriation. Partially at the expense of themes and concepts that an author places in his work, the "author-function" could also reveal the manner in which discourse is articulated on the basis of social relationships.

Is it not possible to reexamine, as a legitimate extension of this kind of analysis, the privileges of the subject? Clearly, in undertaking an internal and architectonic analysis of a work (whether it be a literary text, a philosophical system, or a scientific work) and in delimiting psychological and biographical references, suspicions arise concerning the absolute nature and creative role of the subject. But the subject should not be entirely abandoned. It should be reconsidered, not to restore the theme of an originating subject, but to seize its functions, its intervention in discourse, and its system of dependencies. We should suspend the typical questions: how does a free subject penetrate the density of things and endow them with meaning; how does it accomplish its design by animating the rules of discourse from within? Rather, we should ask: under what conditions and through what forms can an entity like the subject appear in the order of discourse; what position does it occupy; what functions does it exhibit; and what rules does it follow in each type of discourse? In short, the subject (and its substitutes) must be stripped of its creative role and analysed as a complex and variable function of discourse.

The author—or what I have called the "author-function"—is undoubtedly only one of the possible specifications of the subject and, considering past historical transformations, it appears that the form, the complexity, and even the existence of this function are far from immutable. We can easily imagine a culture where discourse would circulate without any need for an author. Discourses, whatever their status, form, or value, and regardless of our manner of handling them, would unfold in a pervasive anonymity. No longer the tiresome repetitions:

> "Who is the real author?"
> "Have we proof of his authenticity and originality?"
> "What has he revealed of his most profound self in his language?"

New questions will be heard:
> "What are the modes of existence of this discourse?"
> "Where does it come from; how is it circulated; who controls it?"
> "What placements are determined for possible subjects?"
> "Who can fulfill these diverse functions of the subject?"

Behind all these questions we would hear little more than the murmur of indifference:
> "What matter who's speaking?"

Michael Rock

The Designer as Author
1996

"the entrepreneurial arm of authorship affords the possibility of personal voice and wide distribution. The challenge is that most in this category split the activities into three recognizable and discrete actions: editing, writing and designing"

Michael Rock (1959–) is an American graphic designer and educator. He is a founding partner and creative director of the international design consultancy 2x4 and teaches design at the Yale School of Art and Columbia University.

....

What does it mean to call a graphic designer an author?
Authorship, in one form or another, has been a popular term in graphic design circles, especially those at the edge of the profession, the design academies and the murky territories that exist between design and art. The word authorship has a ring of importance: it connotes seductive ideas of origination and agency. But the question of how designers become authors is a difficult one, and exactly who the designer/authors are and what authored design looks like depends entirely on how you define the term and the criteria you choose to grant entrance into the pantheon.

Authorship may suggest new approaches to understanding design process in a profession traditionally associated more with the communication than the origination of messages. But theories of authorship may also serve as legitimizing strategies, and authorial aspirations may actually end up reinforcing certain conservative notions of design production and subjectivity—ideas that run counter to recent critical attempts to overthrow the perception of design based on individual brilliance. The implications deserve careful evaluation. What does it really mean to call for a graphic designer to be an author?

What is an author?
That question has been an area of intense scrutiny over the last forty years. The meaning of the word itself has shifted significantly over time. The earliest definitions are not associated with writing; in fact the most inclusive is a "person who originates or gives existence to anything." Other usages clearly index authoritarian—even patriarchal—connotations: "father of all life," "any inventor, constructor or founder," "one who begets," and a "director, commander, or ruler."

All literary theory, from Aristotle on, has in some form or another been theory of authorship. Since this is not a history of the author but a consideration of the author as metaphor, I'll start with recent history. Wimsatt and Beardsley's seminal text, "The Intentional Fallacy" (1946), drove an early wedge between the author and the text, dispelling the notion that a reader could ever really know an author through his writing. The so-called death of the author, proposed most succinctly by Roland Barthes in 1968 in an essay of that title, is closely linked to the birth of critical theory, especially theory based in reader response and interpretation rather than intentionality. Michel Foucault used the rhetorical question "What is an author?" as the title of his influential essay of 1969 which, in response to Barthes, outlines the basic taxonomy and functions of the author and the problems associated with conventional ideas of authorship and origination.

Foucauldian theory holds that the connection between author and text has transformed and that there exist a number of author-functions that shape the way readers approach a text. These stubbornly persistent functions are historically determined and culturally specific categories.

Foucault posits that the earliest sacred texts were authorless, their origins lost in ancient history (the Vedas, the Gospels, etc.). The very anonymity of the text served as a certain kind of authentication. The author's name was symbolic, rarely attributable to an individual. (The Gospel of Luke, for instance, is a diversity of texts gathered under the rubric of Luke, someone who may indeed have lived and written parts, but not the totality, of what we now think of as the complete work.)

Scientific texts, at least through the Renaissance, demanded an author's name as validation. Far from *objective* truth, science was based in subjective invention and the authority of the scientist. This changed with the rise of the scientific method. Scientific discoveries and mathematical proofs were no longer in need of authors because they were perceived as discovered truths rather than authored ideas. The scientist revealed extant phenomena, facts anyone faced with the same conditions would discover. The scientist and the mathematician could claim to have been first to discover a paradigm, and lend their name to the phenomenon, but could never claim authorship over it. (The astronomer who discovers a new star may name it but does not conjure it.) Facts were universal and thus eternally preexisiting.

By the 18th century, Foucault suggests, the situation had reversed: literature was authored and science became the product of anonymous objectivity. When authors came to be punished for their writing—i.e. when a text could be transgressive—the link between author and text was firmly established.

The codification of ownership over a text is often dated to the adoption of the Statute of Anne (1709) by the British Parliament, generally considered the first real copyright act. The first line of the law is revealing: "Whereas Printers, Booksellers, and other Persons, have of late frequently taken the Liberty of Printing...Books, and other Writings, without the Consent of the Authors...to their very great Detriment, and too often to the Ruin of them and their Families..." The statute secures the right to benefit financially from a work and for the author to preserve its textual integrity. That authorial right was deemed irrevocable. Text came to be seen as a form of private property. A romantic criticism arose that reinforced that relationship, searching for critical keys in the life and intention of the writer.

By laying a legal ground for ownership, the Statute of Anne defines who is, and isn't, an author. It was a thoroughly modern problem. No one had *owned* the sacred texts. The very fact that the origins of sacred texts were lost in history, their authors either composites or anonymous, gave them their authority. The gospels in their purest form were public domain. Any work to be done, and any arguments to have, were interpretive. The authors referred to in the Statute were living, breathing—and apparently highly litigious—beings. The law granted them authority over the meaning and use of their own words.

Ownership of the text, and the authority granted to authors at the expense of the creative reader, fueled much of the 20th century's obsession with authorship. Post-structuralist reading of authorship tends to critique the prestige attributed to the figure of the author and to suggest or speculate about a time after his fall from grace.

Barthes ends his essay supposing that "the birth of the reader comes at the cost of the death of the author." Foucault imagines a time when we might ask, "What difference does it make who is speaking?" Both attempt to overthrow the notion that a text is a line of words that releases a single, predetermined meaning, the central message of an author/god, and refocus critical attention on the activity of reading and readers. The focus shifts from the author's intention to the internal workings of the writing itself, not what it means but *how* it means.

Postmodernity turns on what Fredric Jameson identified as a "fragmented and schizophrenic decentering and dispersion" of the subject. Decentered text—a text that is skewed from the direct line of communication from sender to receiver, severed from the authority of its origin, a free-floating element in a field of possible significations—figures heavily in constructions of a design based in reading and readers. But Katherine McCoy's prescient image of designers moving beyond problem solving and by "authoring additional content and a self-conscious critique of the message, adopting roles associated with art and literature," is often misconstrued. Rather than working to incorporate theory into their methods of production, many self-proclaimed deconstructivist designers literally illustrated Barthes' image of a reader-based text—a "tissue of quotations drawn from innumerable centers of culture"—by scattering fragments of quotations across the surface of their "authored" posters and book covers. (This technique went something like: "Theory is complicated, so my design is complicated.") The rather dark implications of Barthes' theory, note Ellen Lupton and J. Abbott Miller, were refashioned into a "romantic theory of self-expression."

After years in the somewhat thankless position of the faceless facilitator, many designers were ready to speak out. Some designers may be eager to discard the internal affairs of formalism—to borrow Paul de Man's metaphor—and branch out to the foreign affairs of external politics and content. By the '70s, design began to discard some of the scientistic approach that held sway for several decades. (As early as the '20s, Trotsky was labeling formalist artists the "chemists of art.") That approach was evident in the design ideology that preached strict adherence to an eternal grid and a kind of rational approach to design. (Keep in mind that although this example is a staple of critiques of modernism, in actuality the objectivists represented a small fragment of the design population at the time.)

Müller-Brockmann's evocation of the "aesthetic quality of mathematical thinking" is certainly the clearest and most cited example of this approach. Müller-Brockmann and a slew of fellow researchers like Kepes, Dondis and Arnheim worked to uncover preexisting order and form in the manner a scientist reveals a natural "truth." But what is most peculiar and revealing in Müller-Brockmann's writing is his reliance on tropes of submission: the designer submits to the will of the system, forgoes personality and withholds interpretation.

In his introduction to *Compendium for Literates*, which attempts a highly formal dissection of writing, Karl Gerstner claims about the organization of his book that "all the components are atomic, i.e. in principle they are irreducible. In other words, they establish a principle."

The reaction to that drive for an irreducible theory of design is well documented. On the surface at least, contemporary designers were moving from authorless, scientific text—in which inviolable visual principles were carefully revealed through extensive visual research—toward a more textual position in which the designer could claim some level of ownership over the message. (This at the time literary theory was trying to move away from that very position.) But some of the basic, institutional features of design practice have a way of getting tangled up in zealous attempts at self-expression. The idea of a decentered message does not necessarily sit well in a professional relationship in which the client is paying a designer to convey specific information or emotions. In addition, most design is done in some kind of collaborative setting, either within a client relationship or in the context of a design studio that utilizes the talents of numerous creative people. Thus the origin of any particular idea is clouded. And the ever-present pressure of technology and electronic communication only further muddies the water.

Is there an auteur in the house?
It is not surprising to find that Barthes' essay, "Death of the Author," was written in Paris in 1968, the year students joined workers on the barricades in the general strikes and the year the Western world flirted with social revolution. To call for the overthrow of authority—in the form of the author—in favor of the reader—read: the masses—had real resonance in 1968. But to lose power you must have already worn the mantle, and so designers had a bit of a dilemma overthrowing a power they may never have possessed.

On the other hand, the figure of the author implies a total control over creative activity and seemed an essential ingredient of high art. If the relative level of genius was the ultimate measure of artistic achievement, activities that lacked a clear central authority figure were necessarily devalued. The development of film theory in the 1950s serves as an interesting example.

Almost ten years before Barthes made his famous proclamation, film critic and budding director François Truffaut proposed "La politique des auteurs," a polemical strategy to reconfigure a critical theory of the cinema. The problem facing the auteur theorists was how to create a theory that imagined the film, necessarily a work of broad collaboration, as a work of a single artist and thus a singular work of art. The solution was to develop a set of criteria that allowed a critic to decree certain directors *auteurs*. In order to establish the film as a work of art, auteur theory required that the director—heretofore merely a third of the creative troika of director, writer and cinematographer—had the ultimate control of the entire project.

Auteur theory—especially as espoused by American critic Andrew Sarris—held that directors must meet three essential criteria in order to pass into the sacred hall of the auteur. Sarris proposed that the director must demonstrate technical expertise, have a stylistic signature that is demonstrated over the course of several films and, most important, through choice of projects and cinematic treatment, demonstrate a consistent vision and evoke a palpable interior meaning through his work. Since the film director often had little control over the choice of the material—especially in the Hollywood studio system that assigned directors to projects—the signature way he treated a varying range of scripts and subjects was especially important in establishing a director's auteur credentials. As Roger Ebert summed up the idea: "A film is not what it is about, it's how it is about it."

The interesting thing about the auteur theory was that, unlike literary critics, film theorists, like designers, had to construct the notion of the author. It was a legitimizing strategy, a method to raise what was considered low entertainment to the plateau of fine art. By crowning the director the author of the film, critics could elevate certain subjects to the status of high art. That elevation, in turn, would grant the director new freedoms in future projects. (Tantrums could be thrown in the name of artistic vision. "I'm an artist, dammit, not a butcher!" Expensive wines could be figured into overhead to satisfy rarefied palates.)

The parallel to design practice is useful. Like the film director, the art director or designer is often assigned his or her material and often works collaboratively in a role directing the activity of a number of other creative people. In addition, the designer works on a number of diverse projects over the course of a career, many of which have widely varying levels of creative potential; any inner meaning must come through the aesthetic treatment as much as from the content.

If we apply the auteur criteria to graphic designers we find a body of work that may be elevated to auteur status. Technical proficiency could be fulfilled by any number of practitioners, but couple technical proficiency with a signature style and the field narrows. The list of names that meet those two criteria would be familiar, as that work is often published, awarded and praised. (And, of course, that selective republishing of certain work to the exclusion of other work constructs a unified and stylistically consistent oeuvre.) But great technique and style alone do not an auteur make. If we add the third requirement of interior meaning, how does that list fare? Are there graphic designers who, by special treatment and choice of projects, approach the realm of deeper meaning the way a Bergman, Hitchcock or Welles does?

In these cases the graphic auteur must both seek projects that fit his or her vision and then tackle a project from a specific, recognizable critical perspective. For example, Jan van Toorn might be expected to approach a brief for a corporate annual report from a critical socioeconomic position.

But how do you compare a film poster with the film itself? The very scale of a cinematic project allows for a sweep of vision not possible in graphic design. Therefore, as the design of a single project lacks weight, graphic auteurs, almost by definition, have long, established bodies of work in which discernable patterns emerge. The auteur uses very specific client vehicles to attain a consistency of meaning. (Renoir observed that a director spends his whole career making variations on the same film.) Think of the almost fetishistic way a photographer like Helmut Newton returns to a particular vision of class and sexuality—no matter what he is assigned to shoot.

Conversely, many great stylists don't seem to make the cut, as it is difficult to discern a larger message in their work—a message that transcends stylistic elegance. (You have to ask yourself, "What's the work about?") Perhaps it's an absence or presence of an overriding philosophy or individual spirit that diminishes some designed works and elevates others.

We may have been applying a modified graphic auteur theory for years without really paying attention. What has design history been, if not a series of critical elevations and demotions as our attitudes about style and inner meaning evolve? In trying to describe interior meaning, Sarris finally resorts to the "intangible difference between one personality and another." That retreat to intangibility—"I can't say what it is but I know it when I see it"—is the Achilles heel of the auteur theory, which has long since fallen into disfavor in film-criticism circles. It never dealt adequately with the collaborative nature of the cinema and the messy problems of movie-making. But while the theory is passé, its effect is still with us: to this day, when we think of film structure, the director is squarely in the middle.

The application of auteur theory may be too limited an engine for our current image of design authorship, but there are a variety of other ways to frame the issue, a number of paradigms on which we could base our practice: the artist book, concrete poetry, political activism, publishing, illustration.

The general authorship rhetoric seems to include any work by a designer that is self-motivated, from artist books to political activism. But artist books easily fall within the realm and descriptive power of art criticism. Activist work may be neatly explicated using allusions to propaganda, graphic design, public relations and advertising.

Perhaps the graphic author is actually one who writes and publishes material about design. This category would include Josef Müller-Brockmann and Rudy VanderLans, Paul Rand and Eric Spiekermann, William Morris and Neville Brody, Robin Kinross and Ellen Lupton—rather strange bedfellows. The entrepreneurial arm of authorship affords the possibility of personal voice and wide distribution. The challenge is that most in this category split the activities into three recognizable and discrete actions: editing, writing and designing. Design remains the vehicle for their written thought even when they are acting as their own clients. (Kinross, for example, works as a historian and then changes hats and becomes a typographer.) Rudy VanderLans is perhaps the purest of the entrepreneurial authors. *Emigre* is a project in which the content is the form—i.e. the formal exploration is as much the content of the magazine as the articles. The three actions blur into one contiguous whole. VanderLans expresses his message through the selection of material (as an editor), the content of the writing (as a writer), and the form of the pages and typography (as a form-giver).

Ellen Lupton and her partner J. Abbott Miller are an interesting variation on this model. "The Bathroom, the Kitchen and the Aesthetics of Waste," an exhibition at MIT and a book, seems to approach a kind of graphic authorship. The message is explicated equally through graphic/visual devices as well as text panels and descriptions. The design of the exhibition and the book evoke design issues that are also the content: it is clearly self-reflexive.

Lupton and Miller's work is primarily critical. It forms and represents a reading of exterior social or historical phenomena and explicates that message for a specific audience. But there is a subset of work often overlooked by the design community, the illustrated book, that is almost entirely concerned with the generation of creative narrative. Books for children have been one of the most successful venues for the author/artist, and bookshops are packed with the fruits of their labors. Many illustrators have used the book in wholly inventive ways and produced serious work. Illustrator/authors include Sue Coe, Art Spiegelman, Charles Burns, David Macaulay, Chris Van Allsburg, Edward Gorey, Maurice Sendak, and many others. In addition, the comic book and the graphic novel have generated a renewed interest both in artistic and critical circles. Spiegelman's *Maus* and Coe's *X* and *Porkopolis* suggest expanded possibilities.

Power ploys
If the ways a designer can be an author are myriad, complex and often confusing, the way designers have used the term and the value attributed to it are equally so. Any number of recent statements claim authorship as the panacea to the woes of the browbeaten designer. In an article in *Emigre*, author Anne Burdick proposed that "designers must consider themselves authors, not facilitators. This shift in perspective implies responsibility, voice, action... With voice comes a more personal connection and opportunity to explore individual options." A recent call-for-entries for a design exhibition titled "Designer as Author: Voices and Visions" sought to identify "graphic designers who are engaged in work that transcends the traditional service-oriented commercial production, and who pursue projects that are personal, social or investigative in nature." In the rejection of the role of the facilitator and in the call for transcendence lies the implication that authored design holds some higher, purer purpose. The amplification of the personal voice compels designers to take possession of their texts and legitimizes design as an equal of the more traditionally privileged forms of authorship.

But if, as a chorus of contemporary theorists have convinced us, the proclivity of the contemporary designer is toward open reading and free textual interpretation, that desire is thwarted by oppositional theories of authorship. The cult of the author narrows interpretation and places the author at the center of the work. Foucault noted that the figure of the author is not a particularly liberating one. By transferring the authority of the text back to the author, by focusing on voice, presence becomes a limiting factor, containing and categorizing the work. The author as origin and ultimate owner of the text guards against the free will of the reader. The figure of the author reconfirms the traditional idea of the genius creator, and the esteem or status of the man frames the work and imbues it with some mythical value.

While some claims for authorship may be as simple as a renewed sense of responsibility, at times they seem to be ploys for property rights, attempts to finally exercise some kind of agency where traditionally there has been none. The author = authority. The longing for graphic authorship may be the longing for a kind of legitimacy, or a kind of power that has so long eluded the obedient designer. But do we get anywhere by celebrating the designer as some central character? Isn't that what fueled the last fifty years of design history? If we really want to move beyond the designer-as-hero model of history, we may have to imagine a time when we can ask, "What difference does it make who designed it?"

Perhaps, in the end, authorship is not a very convincing metaphor for the activity we understand as design. There are a few examples of work that is clearly the product of design authors and not designer/authors, and these tend to be exceptions to the rule.

Rather than glorify the act and sanctify the practice, I propose three alternative models for design that attempt to describe the activity as it exists and as it could evolve: designer as translator, designer as performer, and designer as director.

Designer as translator
This is based on the assumption that the act of design is, in essence, the clarification of material or the remodeling of content from one form to another. The ultimate goal is the expression of a given content rendered in a form that reaches a new audience. I am drawn to this metaphor by Ezra Pound's translations of Chinese character poetry. Pound translated not only the meaning of the characters but the visual component of the poem as well. Thus the original is rendered as a raw material reshaped into the conventions of Western poetry. The translation becomes a second art. Translation is neither scientific nor ahistorical. Every translation reflects both the character of the original and the spirit of the contemporary as well as the individuality of the translator: An 1850s translation of the *Odyssey* will be radically different from a 1950s translation.

In certain works, the designer remolds the raw material of given content, rendering it legible to a new audience. Like the poetic translator, the designer transforms not only the literal meaning of the elements but the spirit, too. For example, Bruce Mau's design of a book version of Chris Marker's 1962 film, *La Jetée*, attempts to translate the original material from one form to another. Mau is certainly not the author of the work but the translator of form and spirit. The designer is the intermediary.

Designer as performer
The performer metaphor is based on theater and music. The actor is not the author of the script, the musician is not the composer of the score, but without actor or musician, the art cannot be realized. The actor is the physical expression of the work; every work has an infinite number of physical expressions. Every performance re-contextualizes the original work. (Imagine the range of interpretations of Shakespeare's plays.) Each performer brings a certain reading to the work. No two actors play the same role in the same way.

In this model, the designer transforms and expresses content through graphic devices. The score or script is enhanced and made whole by the performance. And so the designer likewise becomes the physical manifestation of the content, not author but performer, the one who gives life to, who speaks the content, contextualizing it and bringing it into the frame of the present.

MICHAEL ROCK, THE DESIGNER AS AUTHOR

Examples abound, from early Dada, Situationist, and Fluxus experiments to more recent typographic scores like Warren Lehrer's performance typography or experimental typography from Edward Fella or David Carson. The most notable example is perhaps Quentin Fiore's *performance* of McLuhan. It was Fiore's graphic treatment as much as McLuhan's words that made *The Medium Is the Massage* a worldwide phenomena. (Other examples include any number of "graphic interpretations," such as Allen Hori's reinvention of Beatrice Warde's Crystal Goblet essay, or P. Scott Makela's improvisation on Tucker Viemeister's lecture, both originally printed in Michael Bierut's *Rethinking Design*.)

Designer as director
This model is a function of bigness. Meaning is manufactured by the arrangement of elements, so there must be many elements at play. Only in large-scale installations, advertising campaigns, mass-distribution magazines and very large books do we see evidence of this paradigm.

In such large projects, the designer orchestrates masses of materials to shape meaning, working like a film director, overseeing a script, a series of performances, photographers, artists, and production crews. The meaning of the work results from the entire production. Large-scale, mass-distribution campaigns like those for Nike or Coca-Cola are examples of this approach. Curatorial projects such as Sean Perkins' catalogue, *Experience*, which creates an exhibition of other design projects, is another example.

One of the clearest examples is Irma Boom's project for SHV Corporation. Working in conjunction with an archivist for more than five years, Boom created narrative from a mass of data, a case of the designer creating meaning almost exclusively via the devices of design: the narrative is not a product of words but almost exclusively of the sequence of pages and the cropping of images. The scale of the book allows for thematic development, contradiction, and coincidence.

The value of these models is that they accept the multivalent activity of design without resorting to totalizing description. The problem with the authorship paradigm alone is that it encourages both ahistorical and acultural readings of design. It grants too much agency, too much control to the lone artist/genius, and discourages interpretation by validating a "right" reading of a work.

On the other hand, work is made by someone. And the difference between the way different writers or designers approach situations and make sense of the world is at the heart of a certain criticism. The challenge is to accept the multiplicity of methods that comprise design language. Authorship is only one device to compel designers to rethink process and expand their methods.

If we really need to coin a phrase to describe an activity encompassing imaging, editing, narration, chronicling, performing, translating, organizing and directing, I'll conclude with a suggestion:

designer = designer.

PROCESS 5A

Auteurism
| Authority and Authenticity

PROCESS 5B

Design Ethics
| Ideology and Faith

Situationist International

Situationist Manifesto

1960

"at a higher stage, everyone will become an artist, i.e., inseparably a producer-consumer of total culture creation, which will help the rapid dissolution of the linear criteria of novelty"

The Situationist International (1957–72) was an influential group of Paris-based avant-garde artists and revolutionary theorists, including Guy Debord, Constant Nieuwenhuys, and Michèle Bernstein. Their conceptual art engaged in Marxist critique at a time of mass-media expansion and postwar reconstruction.

....

The existing framework cannot subdue the new human force that is increasing day by day alongside the irresistible development of technology and the dissatisfaction of its possible uses in our senseless social life.

Alienation and oppression in this society cannot be distributed amongst a range of variants, but only rejected *en bloc* with this very society. All real progress has clearly been suspended until the revolutionary solution of the present multiform crisis.

What are the organizational perspectives of life in a society which authentically "reorganizes production on the basis of the free and equal association of the producers"? Work would more and more be reduced as an exterior necessity through the automation of production and the socialization of vital goods, which would finally give complete liberty to the individual. Thus liberated from all economic responsibility, liberated from all the debts and responsibilities from the past and other people, humankind will exude a new surplus value, incalculable in money because it would be impossible to reduce it to the measure of waged work. The guarantee of the liberty of each and of all is in the value of the game, of life freely constructed. The exercise of this ludic recreation is the framework of the only guaranteed equality with non-exploitation of man by man. The liberation of the game, its creative autonomy, supersedes the ancient division between imposed work and passive leisure.

The church has already burnt the so-called witches to repress the primitive ludic tendencies conserved in popular festivities. Under the existing dominant society, which produces the miserable pseudo-games of non-participation, a true artistic activity is necessarily classed as criminality. It is semi-clandestine. It appears in the form of scandal.

So what really is the situation? It's the realization of a better game, which more exactly is provoked by the human presence. The revolutionary gamesters of all countries can be united in the S.I. to commence the emergence from the prehistory of daily life.

Henceforth, we propose an autonomous organization of the producers of the new culture, independent of the political and union organizations which currently exist, as we dispute their capacity to organize anything other than the management of that which already exists.

From the moment when this organization leaves the initial experimental stage for its first public campaign, the most urgent objective we have ascribed to it is the seizure of U.N.E.S.C.O. United at a world level, the bureaucratization of art and all culture is a new phenomenon which expresses the deep inter-relationship of the social systems co-existing in the world on the basis of eclectic conservation and the reproduction of the past. The riposte of the revolutionary artists to these new conditions must be a new type of action. As the very existence of this managerial concentration of culture, located in a single building, favors a seizure by way of putsch; and as the institution is completely destitute of any sensible usage outside our subversive perspective, we find our seizure of this apparatus justified before our contemporaries. And we will have it. We are resolved to take over U.N.E.S.C.O., even if only for a short time, as we are sure we would quickly carry out work which would prove most significant in the clarification of a long series of demands.

What would be the principle characteristics of the new culture and how would it compare with ancient art?

Against the spectacle, the realized situationist culture introduces total participation.

Against preserved art, it is the organization of the directly lived moment.

Against particularized art, it will be a global practice with a bearing, each moment, on all the usable elements. Naturally this would tend to collective production which would be without doubt anonymous (at least to the extent where the works are no longer stocked as commodities, this culture will not be dominated by the need to leave traces.) The minimum proposals of these experiences will be a revolution in behavior and a dynamic unitary urbanism capable of extension to the entire planet, and of being further extensible to all habitable planets.

Against unilateral art, situationist culture will be an art of dialogue, an art of interaction. Today artists—with all culture visible—have been completely separated from society, just as they are separated from each other by competition. But faced with this impasse of capitalism, art has remained essentially unilateral in response. This enclosed era of primitivism must be superseded by complete communication.

At a higher stage, everyone will become an artist, i.e., inseparably a producer-consumer of total culture creation, which will help the rapid dissolution of the linear criteria of novelty. Everyone will be a situationist so to speak, with a multidimensional inflation of tendencies, experiences, or radically different "schools"—not successively, but simultaneously.

We will inaugurate what will historically be the last of the crafts. The role of amateur-professional situationist—of anti-specialist—is again a specialization up to the point of economic and mental abundance, when everyone becomes an "artist," in the sense that the artists have not attained the construction of their own life. However, the last craft of history is so close to the society without a permanent division of labor, that when it appeared amongst the SI, its status as a craft was generally denied.

To those who don't understand us properly, we say with an irreducible scorn: "The situationists of which you believe yourselves perhaps to be the judges, will one day judge you. We await the turning point which is the inevitable liquidation of the world of privation, in all its forms. Such are our goals, and these will be the future goals of humanity."

Ken Garland

First Things First: A Manifesto

1964

"we do not advocate the abolition of high pressure consumer advertising: this is not feasible"

Ken Garland (1929–) is a British graphic designer, photographer, writer, and educator. His call for a more humanistic, less consumerist design practice has influenced graphic designers internationally.

We, the undersigned, are graphic designers, photographers and students who have been brought up in a world in which the techniques and apparatus of advertising have persistently been presented to us as the most lucrative, effective and desirable means of using our talents. We have been bombarded with publications devoted to this belief, applauding the work of those who have flogged their skill and imagination to sell such things as: cat food, stomach powders, detergent, hair restorer, striped toothpaste, aftershave lotion, beforeshave lotion, slimming diets, fattening diets, deodorants, fizzy water, cigarettes, roll-ons, pull-ons and slip-ons.

By far the greatest time and effort of those working in the advertising industry are wasted on these trivial purposes, which contribute little or nothing to our national prosperity.

In common with an increasing number of the general public, we have reached a saturation point at which the high pitched scream of consumer selling is no more than sheer noise. We think that there are other things more worth using our skill and experience on. There are signs for streets and buildings, books and periodicals, catalogues, instructional manuals, industrial photography, educational aids, films, television features, scientific and industrial publications and all the other media through which we promote our trade, our education, our culture and our greater awareness of the world.

We do not advocate the abolition of high pressure consumer advertising: this is not feasible. Nor do we want to take any of the fun out of life. But we are proposing a reversal of priorities in favour of the more useful and more lasting forms of communication. We hope that our society will tire of gimmick merchants, status salesmen and hidden persuaders, and that the prior call on our skills will be for worthwhile purposes. With this in mind we propose to share our experience and opinions, and to make them available to colleagues, students and others who may be interested.

Signed:

Edward Wright	Bernard Higton	Harriet Crowder
Geoffrey White	Brian Grimbly	Anthony Clift
William Slack	John Garner	Gerry Cinamon
Caroline Rawlence	Ken Garland	Robert Chapman
Ian McLaren	Anthony Froshaug	Ray Carpenter
Sam Lambert	Robin Fior	Ken Briggs
Ivor Kamlish	Germano Facetti	
Gerald Jones	Ivan Dodd	

5B-3

Victor Papanek

What Is Design?
1972

"should I design it to be functional… or to be aesthetically pleasing?"

"do you want it to look good, or to work?"

Victor Papanek (1923–1998) was an American designer, theorist, and educator. In his highly influential Design for the Real World *and other books, he was a strong advocate of socially and ecologically responsible design. His collaborator Buckminster Fuller (and Fuller's concept of "comprehensive anticipatory design science") largely inspired his own philosophy.*

....

A Definition of Design and the Function Complex

> The wheel's hub holds thirty spokes
> Utility depends on the hole through the hub.
> The potter's clay forms a vessel.
> It is the space within that serves.
> A house is built with solid walls
> The nothingness of window and door alone
> renders it useable,
> That which exists may be transformed
> What is non-existent has boundless uses.
>
> Lao-Tse

All men are designers. All that we do, almost all the time, is design, for design is basic to all human activity. The planning and patterning of any act towards a desired, foreseeable end constitutes the design process. Any attempt to separate design, to make it a thing-by-itself, works counter to the inherent value of design as the primary underlying matrix of life. Design is composing an epic poem, executing a mural, painting a masterpiece, writing a concerto. But design is also cleaning and reorganizing a desk drawer, pulling an impacted tooth, baking an apple pie, choosing sides for a back-lot baseball game, and educating a child.

Design is the conscious effort to impose meaningful order.

The order and delight we find in frost flowers on a window pane, in the hexagonal perfection of a honeycomb, in leaves, or in the architecture of a rose, reflect man's preoccupation with pattern, the constant attempt to understand an ever-changing, highly complex existence by imposing order on it—but these things are not the product of design. They possess only the order we ascribe to them. The reason we enjoy these and other things in nature is that we see an economy of means, simplicity, elegance and an essential rightness in them. But they are not design. Though they have pattern, order, and beauty, they lack conscious intention. If we call them design, we artificially ascribe our own values to an accidental side issue. The streamlining of a trout's body is aesthetically satisfying to us, but to the trout it is a by-product of swimming efficiency. The aesthetically satisfying spiral growth pattern found in sunflowers, pineapples, pine cones, or the arrangement of leaves on a stem can be explained by the Fibonacci sequence (each member is the sum of the two previous members: 1, 1, 2, 3, 5, 8, 13, 21, 34...), but the plant is only concerned with improving photosynthesis by exposing a maximum of its surface. Similarly, the beauty we find in the tail of a peacock, although no doubt even more attractive to a peahen, is the result of intraspecific selection (which, in the case cited, may even ultimately prove fatal to the species).

Intent is also missing from the random order system of a pile of coins. If, however, we move the coins around and arrange them according to size and shape, we add the element of intent and produce some sort of symmetrical alignment. This symmetrical order system is a favorite of small children, unusually primitive peoples, and some of the insane, because it is so easy to understand. Further shifting of the coins will produce an infinite number of asymmetrical arrangements which require a higher level of sophistication and greater participation on the part of the viewer to be understood and appreciated. While the aesthetic values of the symmetrical and asymmetrical designs differ, both can give ready satisfaction, since the underlying intent is clear. Only marginal patterns (those lying in the threshold area between symmetry and asymmetry) fail to make the designer's intent clear. The ambiguity of these "threshold cases" produces a feeling of unease in the viewer. But apart from these threshold cases there are an infinite number of possible satisfactory arrangements of the coins. Importantly, none of these is the one right answer, though some may seem better than others.

Shoving coins around on a board is a design act in miniature because design as a problem-solving activity can never, by definition, yield the one right answer: it will always produce an infinite number of answers, some "righter" and some "wronger." The "rightness" of any design solution will depend on the meaning with which we invest the arrangement. Design must be meaningful. And "meaningful" replaces the semantically loaded noise of such expressions as "beautiful," "ugly," "cool," "cute," "disgusting," "realistic," "obscure," "abstract," and "nice," labels convenient to a bankrupt mind when confronted by Picasso's *Guernica*, Frank Lloyd Wright's Fallingwater, Beethoven's *Eroica*, Stravinsky's *Le Sacre du printemps*, Joyce's *Finnegans Wake*. In all of these we respond to that which has meaning.

The mode of action by which a design fulfils its purpose is its function.

"Form follows function," Louis Sullivan's battle cry of the 1880's and 1890's, was followed by Frank Lloyd Wright's "Form and function are one." But semantically, all the statements from Horatio Greenough to the German Bauhaus are meaningless. The concept that what *works* well will of necessity *look* well has been the lame excuse for all the sterile, operating-room-like furniture and implements of the twenties and thirties. A dining table of the period might have a top, well proportioned in glistening white marble, the legs carefully nurtured for maximum strength with minimum materials in gleaming stainless steel. And the first reaction on encountering such a table is to lie down on it and have your appendix extracted. Nothing about the table says: "Dine off me." *Le style international* and *die neue Sachlichkeit* have let us down rather badly in terms of human value. Le Corbusier's house as *la machine à habiter* and the packing-crate houses evolved in the Dutch *De Stijl* movement reflect a perversion of aesthetics and utility.

"Should I design it to be functional," the students say, "or to be aesthetically pleasing?" This is the most heard, the most understandable, and the most mixed-up question in design today. "Do you want it to look good, or to work ?" Barricades erected between what are really just two of the many aspects of function. It is all quite simple: aesthetic value is an inherent *part* of function. A simple diagram will show the dynamic actions and relationships that make up the function complex:

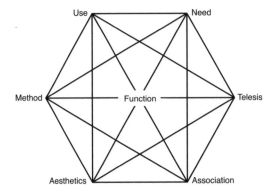

The Function Complex

It is now possible to go through the six parts of the function complex (above) and to define every one of its aspects.

METHOD: The interaction of *tools*, *processes*, and *materials*. An honest use of materials, never making the material seem that which it is not, is good method. Materials and tools must be used optimally, never using one material where another can do the job less expensively and/or more efficiently. The steel beam in a house, painted a fake wood grain; the moulded plastic bottle designed to look like expensive blown glass; the 1967 New England cobbler's bench reproduction ("worm holes $1 extra") dragged into a twentieth-century living room to provide dubious footing for martini glass and ash tray: these are all perversions of materials, tools, and processes. And this discipline of using a suitable method extends naturally to the field of the fine arts as well. Alexander Calder's "The Horse," a compelling sculpture at the Museum of Modern Art in New York, was shaped by the particular material in which it was conceived. Calder decided that boxwood would give him the specific color and texture he desired in his sculpture. But boxwood comes only in rather narrow planks of small sizes. (It is for this reason that it traditionally has been used in the making of small boxes: hence its name.) The only way he could make a fair-sized piece of sculpture out of a wood that only comes in small pieces was to interlock them somewhat in the manner of a child's toy. "The Horse," then, is a piece of sculpture, the aesthetic of which was largely determined by method. For the final execution at the Museum of Modern Art, Calder chose to use thin slats of walnut, a wood similar in texture.

When early Swedish settlers in what is now Delaware decided to build, they had at their disposal trees and axes. The *material* was a round tree trunk, the *tool* an ax, and the *process* a simple kerf cut into the log. The inevitable result of this combination of tools, materials, and process is a log cabin.

From the log cabin in the Delaware Valley of 1680 to Paolo Soleri's desert home in twentieth-century Arizona is no jump at all. Soleri's house is as much the inevitable result of tools, materials, and processes as is the log cabin. The peculiar viscosity of the desert sand where Soleri built his home made his unique method possible. Selecting a mound of desert sand, Soleri criss-crossed it with V-shaped channels cut into the sand, making a pattern somewhat like the ribs of a whale. Then he poured concrete in the channels, forming, when set, the roof-beams of the house-to-be. He added a concrete skin for the roof and bulldozed the sand out from underneath to create the living space itself. He then completed the structure by setting in car windows garnered from automobile junkyards. Soleri's creative use of tools, materials, and processes was a *tour de force* that gave us a radically new building method.

Dow Chemical's "self-generating" styrofoam dome is the product of another radical approach to building methods. The foundation of the building can be a 12-inch-high circular retaining wall. To this wall a 4-inch wide strip of styrofoam is attached, which raises as it goes around the wall from zero to 4 inches in height, forming the base for the spiral dome. On the ground in the center, motorized equipment operates two spinning booms, one with an operator and the other holding a welding machine. The booms move around, somewhat like a compass drawing a circle, and they rise with a spiraling motion at about 30 feet a minute. Gradually they move in towards the center. A man sitting in the saddle feeds an "endless" 4 × 4-inch strip of styrofoam into the welding machine, which heat-welds it to the previously hand-laid styrofoam. As the

Alexander Calder: The Horse (1928). Walnut 15½ × 34¾. Collection of the Museum of Modern Art, New York. Acquired through the Lillie P. Bliss Bequest.

Paolo Soleri: Carved earth form for the original drafting room and interior of the ceramics workshop.

feeding mechanism follows its circular, rising, but ever-diminishing diameter path, this spiral process creates the dome. Finally, a hole 36 inches in diameter is left in the top, through which man, mast, and movement arm can be removed. The hole is then closed with a clear plastic pop-in bubble or a vent. At this point the structure is translucent, soft, but still entirely without doors or windows. The doors and windows are then cut (with a minimum of effort; in fact the structure is still so soft that openings could be cut with one's fingernail), and the structure is sprayed inside and out with latex-modified concrete. The dome is ultra-lightweight, is secured to withstand high wind speeds and great snow loads, is vermin-proof, and inexpensive. Several of these 54-foot-diameter domes can be easily joined together into a cluster.

All these building methods demonstrate the elegance of solution possible with a creative interaction of tools, materials, and processes.

USE: "Does it work?" A vitamin bottle should dispense pills singly. An ink bottle should not tip over. A plastic-film package covering sliced pastrami should withstand boiling water. As in any reasonably conducted home, alarm clocks seldom travel through the air at speeds approaching five hundred miles per hour, "streamlining" clocks is out of place. Will a cigarette lighter designed like the tail fin of an automobile (the design of that automobile was copied from a pursuit plane of the Korean War) give more efficient service? Look at some hammers: they are all different in weight, material, and form. The sculptor's mallet is fully round, permitting constant rotation in the hand. The jeweler's chasing hammer is a precision instrument used for fine work on metal. The prospector's pick is delicately balanced to add to the swing of his arm when cracking rocks.

The ball-point pen with a fake polyethylene orchid surrounded by fake styrene carrot leaves sprouting out of its top, on the other hand, is a tawdry perversion of design for use.

But the results of the introduction of a new device are never predictable. In the case of the automobile, a fine irony developed. One of the earliest criticisms of the car was that, unlike "old Dobbin," it didn't have the sense "to find its way home" whenever its owner was incapacitated by an evening of genteel drinking. No one foresaw that mass acceptance of the car would put the American bedroom on wheels, offering everyone a new place to copulate (and privacy from supervision by parents and spouses). Nobody expected the car to accelerate our mobility, thereby creating the exurban sprawl and the dormitory suburbs that strangle our larger cities; or to sanction the killing of fifty thousand people per annum, brutalizing us and making it possible, as Philip Wylie says, "to see babies with their jaws ripped off on the corner of Maine and Maple"; or to dislocate our societal groupings, thus contributing to our alienation; and to put every yut, yahoo, and prickamouse from sixteen to sixty in permanent hock to the tune of $80 a month. In the middle forties, no one foresaw that, with the primary use function of the automobile solved, it would emerge as a combination status symbol and disposable, chrome-plated codpiece. But two greater ironies were to follow. In the early sixties, when people began to fly more, and to rent standard cars at their destination, the businessman's clients no longer saw the car he owned and therefore could not judge his "style of life" by it. Most of Detroit's baroque exuberance subsided, and the automobile again came closer to being a transportation device. Money earmarked for status demonstration was now spent on boats, color television sets, and other ephemera. The last irony is still to come: with carbon monoxide fumes poisoning our atmosphere, the electric car, driven at low speeds and with a cruising range of less than one hundred miles, reminiscent of the turn of the century, may soon make an anachronistic comeback. Anachronistic because the days of individual transportation devices are numbered.

The automobile gives us a typical case history of seventy years of the perversion of design for *use*.

NEED: Much recent design has satisfied only evanescent wants and desires, while the genuine needs of man have often been neglected by the designer. The economic, psychological, spiritual, technological, and intellectual needs of a human being are usually more difficult and less profitable to satisfy than the carefully engineered and manipulated "wants" inculcated by fad and fashion.

In a highly mobile, throw-away society, the psychological need for security and permanence is often viciously exploited by manufacturer, advertising agency, and salesman by turning the consumer's interest onto the superficial trappings of a transitory "in-group."

People seem to prefer the ornate to the plain as they prefer day-dreaming to thinking and mysticism to rationalism. As they seek crowd pleasures and choose widely traveled roads rather than solitude and lonely paths, they seem to feel a sense of security in crowds and crowdedness. *Horror vacui* is horror of inner as well as outer vacuum.

The need for security-through-identity has been perverted into role-playing. The consumer, unable or unwilling to live a strenuous life, can now act out the role by appearing caparisoned in Naugahyde boots, pseudo-military uniforms, voyageur's shirts, little fur jackets, and all the other outward trappings of Davy Crockett, Foreign Legionnaires, and Cossack Hetmans. (The apotheosis of the ridiculous: a "be-your-own-Paul-Bunyan-kit, beard included," neglecting the fact that Paul Bunyan is the imaginary creature of an advertising firm early in this century.) The furry parkas and elk-hide boots are obviously only role-playing devices, since climatic control makes their real use redundant anywhere except, possibly, in Bismarck, North Dakota.

A short ten months after the Scott Paper Company introduced disposable paper dresses for 99¢, it was possible to buy throw-away paper dresses ranging from $20 to $149.50. With increased consumption, the price of the 99¢ dress could have dropped to 40¢. And a 40¢ paper dress is a good idea. Typically, industry perverted the idea and chose to ignore an important need-fulfilling function of the design: disposable dresses inexpensive enough to make disposability economically feasible for the consumer.

Greatly accelerated technological change has been used to create technological obsolescence. This year's product often incorporates enough technical changes to make it really superior to last year's offering. The economy of the market place, however, is still geared to a static philosophy of "purchasing-owning" rather than a dynamic one of "leasing-using," and price policy has not resulted in lowered consumer cost. If a television set, for instance, is to be an every-year affair, rather than a once-in-a-lifetime purchase, the price must reflect it. Instead, the real values of real things have been driven out by false values of false things, a sort of Gresham's Law of Design.

As an attitude, "Let them eat cake" has been thought of as a manufacturer's basic right. And by now people, no longer "turned on" by a loaf of bread, can differentiate only between frostings. Our profit-oriented and consumer-oriented Western society has become so over specialized that few people experience the pleasures and benefits of full life, and many never participate in even the most modest forms of creative activity which might help to keep their sensory and intellectual faculties alive. Members of a "civilized" community or nation depend on the hands, brains, and imaginations of experts. But however well trained these experts may be, unless they have a sense of ethical, intellectual, and artistic responsibility, then morality and an intelligent, "beautiful," and elegant quality of life will suffer in astronomical proportions under our present-day system of mass production and private capital.

TELESIS: "The deliberate, purposeful utilization of the processes of nature and society to obtain particular goals" (*American College Dictionary*, 1961). The telesic content of a design must reflect the times and conditions that have given rise to it, and must fit in with the general human socio-economic order in which it is to operate.

The uncertainties and the new and complex pressures in our society make many people feel that the most logical way to regain lost values is to go out and buy Early American furniture, put a hooked rug on the floor, buy ready-made phony ancestor portraits, and hang a flint-lock rifle over the fireplace, and vote for Ronald Reagan. The gas-light so popular in our subdivisions is a dangerous and senseless anachronism that only reflects an insecure striving for the "good old days" by consumer and designer alike.

Our twenty-year love affair with things Japanese—Zen Buddhism, the architecture of the Ise Shrine and Katsura Imperial Palace, haiku poetry, Hiroshige and Hokusai blockprints, the music of koto and samisen, lanterns and sake sets, green tea liqueur and sukiyaki and tempura—has triggered an intemperate demand by consumers who disregard telesic aptness.

By now it is obvious that our interest in things Japanese is not just a passing fad or fashion but rather the result of a major cultural confrontation. As Japan was shut off for nearly two hundred years from the Western world under the Tokugawa Shogunate, its cultural expressions flourished in a pure (although somewhat inbred) form in the imperial cities of Kyoto and Edo (now Tokyo). The Western world's response to an in-depth knowledge of things Japanese is comparable only to the European reaction to things classical, which we are now pleased to call the Renaissance. Nonetheless, it is not possible to translate things from one culture to another.

The floors of traditional Japanese homes are covered by floor mats. These mats are 3 × 6 feet in size and consist of rice straw closely packed inside a cover of woven rush. The long sides are bound with black linen tape. While tatami mats impose a module (homes are spoken of as six-, eight-, or twelve-mat homes), their primary purposes are to absorb sounds and to act as a sort of wall-to-wall vacuum cleaner which filters particles of dirt through the woven surface and retains them in the inner core of rice straw. Periodically these mats (and the dirt within them) are discarded, and new ones are installed. Japanese feet encased in clean, sock-like tabi (the sandal-like street shoe, or *geta*, having been left at the door) are also designed to fit in with this system. Western-style leather-soled shoes and spike heels would destroy the surface of the mats and also carry much more dirt into the house. The increasing use of regular shoes and industrial precipitation make the use of tatami difficult enough in Japan and absolutely ridiculous in the United States, where high cost makes periodic disposal and re-installation ruinously expensive.

But a tatami-covered floor is only part of the larger design system of the Japanese house. Fragile, sliding paper walls and tatami give the house definite and significant acoustical properties that have influenced the design and development of musical instruments and even the melodic structure of Japanese speech, poetry, and drama. A piano, designed for the reverberating insulated walls and floors of Western homes and concert halls, cannot be introduced into a Japanese home without reducing the brilliance of a Rachmaninoff concerto to a shrill cacophony. Similarly, the fragile quality of a Japanese samisen cannot be fully appreciated in the reverberating box that constitutes the American house. Americans who try to couple a Japanese interior with an American living experience in their search for exotica find that elements cannot be ripped out of their telesic context with impunity.

Some products, unlike the tatami, are developed without regard for their aptness. The American automobile is an example. It is built for roads not yet constructed, super-fuels still unrefined, and drivers with fast reaction speeds (yet unborn).

ASSOCIATION: Our psychological conditioning, often going back to earliest childhood memories, comes into play and predisposes us, or provides us with antipathy against a given value.

Increased consumer resistance in many product areas testifies to design neglect of the associational aspect of the function complex. After two decades, the television set industry, for instance, has not yet resolved the question of whether a television set should carry the associational values of a piece of furniture (a lacquered mah-jongg chest of the Ming Dynasty) or of technical equipment (a portable tube tester). Television receivers that carry new associations (sets for children's rooms in bright colors and materials, enhanced by tactilely pleasant but non-working controls and pre-set for given times and channels, clip-on swivel sets for hospital beds, etc., etc.) might not only clear up the astoundingly large back inventory of sets in warehouses, but also *create* new markets. The tiny transistor pocket radio is still stuck on the threshold of the *trichotomy*: "camera?" "jewelry?" "purse?" which may account for the monotonous sameness of the many models now on view. While it is eminently possible to tailor these pocket radios to the differing needs and wants of various socio-economic groups and thus force new acceptance areas into being, as it is, transistor radios are still selling almost exclusively to the teen-age crowd.

And what shape is most appropriate to a vitamin bottle: a candy jar of the Gay Nineties, a perfume bottle, or a "Danish modern" style salt shaker ?

The response of many designers has been like that so unsuccessfully practiced by Hollywood: the public has been pictured as totally unsophisticated, possessed of neither taste nor discrimination. A picture emerges of a moral weakling with an IQ of about 70, ready to accept whatever specious values the unholy trinity of Motivation Research, Market Analysis, and Sales have decided is good for him. In short, the associational values of design have degenerated to the lowest common denominator, determined more by inspired guesswork and piebald graphic charts rather than by the genuinely felt wants of the consumer.

Since mass production and automation impose both volume and great similarity of types, it becomes increasingly important to extend two basic design approaches:

1. A clear-cut decision as to what the meaning of an object should be. Is an automobile, for instance, a piece of sports equipment, transportation, a living-room-cum-bordello on wheels, or a chrome-plated marshmallow predesigned to turn itself into a do-it-yourself coffin?

2. Greater variety of product sub-types. Can we really expect a Fuller Brush salesman, a university president, a shipyard welder, or a Westchester garden club matron to buy television sets that are identical except for surface finish and the fabric of the speaker grille?

Fixing the product image will demand greater research into the basics of color, form, tactility, visual organization, etc., as well as greater insight into man's perceptual sets and his self-image. The synthesis of these studies, coupled with a greater degree of empathy on the part of the designer, should provide products truer to their intrinsic meaning.

Many products already successfully embody values of high associational content, either accidentally or "by design."

The Sucaryl bottle by Raymond Loewy Associates for Abbott Laboratories communicates both table elegance and sweetening agent without any suggestion of being medicine-like.[1] The Lettera 22 portable typewriter by Olivetti establishes an immediate aura of refined elegance, precision, extreme portability, and business-like efficiency, while its two-toned carrying case of canvas and leather connotes "all-climate-proof."

---

1   To this, one must add that other bottles manufactured by Abbott Laboratories proved to be insufficiently medicine-like: as of March, 1971, Abbott's infected intravenous-fluid bottles for hospitals had killed nine persons.

Gestalt Comparison
Takete Maluma

Abstract values can be communicated directly to everyone, and this can be simply demonstrated.

If the reader is asked to choose which one of the figures above he would rather call *Takete* or *Maluma* (both are words devoid of all meaning in any known language), he will easily call the one on the right *Takete* (W. Koehler, *Gestalt Psychology*).

Many associational values are really universal, providing for unconscious, deep-seated drives and compulsions. Even totally meaningless sounds and shapes can, as demonstrated, mean the same thing to all of us. The unconscious relationship between spectator expectation and the configuration of the object can be experimented with and manipulated. This will not only enhance the "chair-ness" of a chair, for instance, but also load it with associational values of, say, elegance, formality, portability, or what-have-you.

AESTHETICS: Here dwells the traditionally bearded artist, mythological figure, equipped with sandals, mistress, garret, and easel, pursuing his dream-shrouded designs. The cloud of mystery surrounding aesthetics can (and should be) dispelled. The dictionary definition, "*a theory of the beautiful, in taste and art,*" leaves us not much better off than before. Nonetheless we know that aesthetics is a tool, one of the most important ones in the repertory of the designer, a tool that helps in shaping his forms and colors into entities that move us, please us, and are beautiful, exciting, filled with delight, meaningful.

Because there is no ready yardstick for the analysis of aesthetics, it is simply considered to be a personal expression fraught with mystery and surrounded with nonsense. We "know what we like" or dislike and let it go at that. Artists themselves begin to look at their productions as auto-therapeutic devices of self-expression, confuse license and liberty, and forsake all discipline. They are often unable to agree on the various elements and attributes of design aesthetics. If we contrast the "Last Supper" by Leonardo da Vinci with an ordinary piece of wallboard, we will understand how both operate in the area of aesthetics. In the work of so-called "pure" art, the main job is to operate on a level of inspiration, delight, beauty, catharsis…in short, to serve as a propagandistic communications device for the Holy Church at a time when a largely pre-literate population was exposed to a few non-verbal stimuli. But the "Last Supper" also had to fill the other requirements of function; aside from the spiritual, its *use* was to cover a wall. In terms of method it had to reflect the material (pigment and vehicle), tools (brushes and painting knives), and

The Last Supper *by Leonardo da Vinci*

processes (individualistic brushwork) employed by Leonardo. It had to fulfill the human need for spiritual satisfaction. And it had to work on the *associational* and *telesic* plane, providing reference points from the Bible. Finally, it had to make identification through association easier for the beholder through such clichés as the racial type, garb, and posture of the Saviour.

Earlier "Last Supper" versions, painted during the sixth and seventh centuries, saw Christ *lying* or reclining in the place of honor. For nearly a thousand years, the well-mannered did not *sit* at the table. Leonardo da Vinci disregarded the reclining position followed by earlier civilisations and painters for Jesus and the Disciples. To make the "Last Supper" acceptable to Italians of his time, on an associational plane, Leonardo sat the crowd around the last supper table on chairs or benches in the proper positions of his (Leonardo's) time. Unfortunately the scriptural account of St. John resting his head on the Saviour's bosom presented an unsolvable positioning problem to the artist, once everybody was seated according to the Renaissance custom.

On the other hand, the primary use of wallboard is to cover a wall. But an increased choice of textures and colors applied by the factory shows that it, too, must fulfil the *aesthetic* aspect of function. No one argues that in a great work of art such as the "Last Supper," prime functional emphasis is aesthetic, with *use* (to cover a wall) subsidiary. The main job of wallboard is its use in covering a wall, and the aesthetic assumes a highly subsidiary position. But both examples must operate in all *six* areas of the function complex.

We can "feed" any designed object through the filter of our six-sided function complex and understand it better. We can take a certain cologne bottle and examine it on the same basis as the "Last Supper." We will find that it works as well: *aesthetically* we have clear, general form. The surface color used is aquamarine blue ("Aquamarine" is also the name of the cologne), which contrasts well with the shiny brass top. Texture is soft and feels pleasantly yielding to the hand, proportion is excellent, giving the whole bottle unity-with-variety. Satisfying aspects of rhythm, repetition, proportion, and balance can also be observed in the size, placement, and type-face of the lettering. If we continue to the other five aspects of function, we find that the bottle reflects *method* through the good use of materials, tools, and processes. It reflects both the material (glass dipped in vinyl) and the process employed in machine -blown glass. It doesn't topple, and the vinyl coating protects the bottle to some extent from breakage, so that the *use* factor is well satisfied. It answers *need* areas: biological (sex), economic, and psychological (status). Hidden biological needs have been answered by the overall phallic shape. This also operates in the field of *association*. Further examples of the associational field: the color and the name of the cologne are identical; the color moreover has the fragility of the fragrance expected of it. The burnished brass top looks expensively golden; sophistication is powerfully denoted by the use of a script type-face. Its *telesic* content certainly fits some current myths that women are flower-like, expensive sexual playthings.

Designers often attempt to go beyond the primary functional requirements of *method, use, need, telesis, association,* and *aesthetics*; they strive for a more concise statement: precision, simplicity. In a statement so conceived, we find a degree of aesthetic satisfaction comparable to that found in the logarithmic spiral of a chambered nautilus, the ease of a seagull's flight, the strength of a gnarled tree trunk, the colour of a sunset. The particular satisfaction derived from the simplicity of a thing can be called *elegance*. When we speak of an "elegant" solution, we refer to something consciously evolved by men which reduces the complex to the simple:

> Euclid's Proof that the number of primes is infinite, from the field of mathematics, will serve: 'Primes' are numbers which are not divisible, like 3, 17, 23, etc. One would imagine as we get higher in the numerical series, primes would get rarer, crowded out by the ever-increasing products of small numbers, and that we would finally arrive at a very high number which would be the highest prime, the last numerical virgin.

> Euclid's Proof demonstrates in a simple and elegant way that this is not true and that to whatever astronomical regions we ascend, we shall always find numbers which are not the product of smaller ones but are generated by immaculate conceptions, as it were. Here is the proof: assume that P is the hypothetically highest prime; then imagine a number equal to 1 ×2 × 3 × 4...x P. This number is expressed by the numerical symbol (P!). Now add to it 1: (P! + 1). This number is obviously not divisible by P or any number less than P (because they are all contained in (P!); hence (P! + 1) is either a prime higher than P or it contains a prime factor higher than P...Q.E.D.

The deep satisfaction evoked by this proof is aesthetic as well as intellectual: a type of enchantment with the near-perfect.

5B-4

Régis Debray

Socialism and Print

2007

"typographers, intellectuals and teachers were the three supports of the socialist movement, each corresponding to one leg of the mediological tripod"

Régis Debray (1940–) is a French journalist and academic known for his theory of mediology, the study of the transmission of culture within and across societies. He implemented his radical theories as an important figure in the socialist movements of South America in the 1960s and '70s.

Impossible to grasp the nature of conscious collective life in any epoch without an understanding of the material forms and processes through which its ideas were transmitted—the communication networks that enable thought to have a social existence. Indeed, the successive stages of development of these means and relations of transmission—whose ensemble we might term the mediasphere—suggest a new periodization for the history of ideas.[1] First, what we may call the logosphere: that long period stretching from the invention of writing (and of clay tablets, papyrus, parchment scrolls) to the coming of the printing press. The age of the *logos*, but also that of theology, in which writing is, first and foremost, the inscription of the word of God, the 'sacred carving' of the hieroglyph. God dictates, man transcribes—in the Bible or the Koran—and dictates in his turn. Reading is done aloud, in company; man's task is not to invent but to transmit received truths.

A second period, the graphosphere, runs from 1448 to around 1968: from the Gutenberg Revolution to the rise of TV. The age of reason and of the book, of the newspaper and political party. The poet or artist emerges as guarantor of truth, invention flourishes amid an abundance of written references; the image is subordinate to the text. The third, still expanding today, is the era of the videosphere: the age of the image, in which the book is knocked off its pedestal and the visible triumphs over the great invisibles—God, History, Progress—of the previous epochs.

1 See Cours de médiologie générale, *Paris 1991; this essay is drawn from the 'Neuvième leçon: Vie et mort d'un écosystème: le socialisme'.*

This mediological periodization allows us to situate the life-cycle of socialism, that great fallen oak of political endeavour, within the last 150 years of the graphosphere; and to explore its ecosystem, so to speak, through its processes of propagation. Socialism will not be treated here in terms of the intrinsic value of any of its branches. Rather, the aim will be to grasp the common mediological basis that underlies all its doctrinal ramifications—from Fourier to Marx, Owen to Mao, Babeuf to Blum—by approaching it as an ensemble composed of men (militants, leaders, theoreticians), tools of transmission (books, schools, newspapers), and institutions (factions, parties, associations). The ecosystem takes the form of a particular sociotope, a milieu for the reproduction of certain kinds of life and thought. The professional typographer occupies a special niche within it, the key link between proletarian theory and the working-class condition; herein lay the best technical means of intellectualizing the proletariat and proletarianizing the intellectual, the double movement that constituted the workers' parties. For a printer is quintessentially a 'worker intellectual or an intellectual worker', the very ideal of that human type who would become the pivot of socialism: 'the conscious proletarian'.

The life-cycle of this ecosystem begins, in France at least, soon after the July Revolution. Organized Saint-Simonism was born one winter evening in 1831, when the carpenter Gauny met the bookseller Thierry in Paris. Propaganda work for the Saint-Simonian 'family' was planned for every *arrondissement*, and local directors were charged with the workers' education. Hence a new series of encounters between hatters, drapers, cabinet-makers, tilers, and the clerks, printers, engravers and type-founders responsible for running their evening classes and, most importantly, producing their newspapers: *Le Globe*, then *LaRuche populaire*, *L'Union*, and more. The cycle comes to an end in the aftermath of May 1968, Year One of the videosphere. But the life-span of socialism may best be understood within a vaster arc of time: the age of the graphosphere. Dawning with the early-modern era—the 'coming of the book'—the graphosphere itself comprises three successive chapters: reformation, republic, revolution.

Genetic Helix

The inventor of the word 'socialism' was the genial typographer, encyclopaedist and 1848-er, Pierre Leroux. Born in 1797, a bartender's son, Leroux attended the Ecole Polytechnique, then joined a printshop where he perfected a new process, the pianotype. He founded the *Globe* newspaper in 1824 and, with George Sand, the *Revue Indépendante* in 1841. Moving to Boussac, he set up his own publishing house and attracted a small community of disciples and readers. He was elected to the Constituent Assembly in 1848, and formally honoured by the Commune upon his death in 1871. The combination—book, newspaper, school—that would be the genetic helix of the workers' movement is prefigured in Leroux. Socialism was born with a printers' docket around its neck.

Book, newspaper, school: a reminder of the practical culture that preceded the political programmes. Socialism was a craft formation before it became a mentality. Its take-off came with a specific historical moment—1864, the First International founded in London; 1866, the Education League founded in Paris; 1867, the rotary press invented by Marinoni, permitting a tenfold rise in impressions—but also with a particular form of consciousness. 'The 19th-century working class harbours three aspirations,' wrote the foreman Pierre Bruno in his memoirs, published on the eve of the Commune. 'The first is to combat ignorance, the second, to combat poverty, and the third, to help one another.'[2] The first and most important was the fight against ignorance, rallying cry of the forces of reason. Working-class socialism, too, was a creature of reason—ruling spirit of the age of the graphosphere.

Typographers, intellectuals and teachers were the three supports of the socialist movement, each corresponding to one leg of the mediological tripod. What was on offer at any workers' lodge or *maison du peuple*? A library, newspapers, evening classes and lectures. Today, there are still platforms, books and newspapers. But the central axis of transmission has moved elsewhere, taking with it the apparatus of celebration, prestige and values that formerly conferred such an aura upon the books, teachers or peripatetic lecturers at workers' educational associations and *universités populaires*.

A powerful oral culture also played a large part in the workers' movement, of course: harangues at rallies, congress speeches, conferences; Jaurès at Pré-Saint-Gervais, Lenin on Red Square, Blum at Tours or the Place de la Nation in 1936—all spoke without benefit of microphones, shouting themselves hoarse, to the brink of exhaustion, before tens of thousands of listeners. But if the spokesmen of socialism relied as much on their public pulpits as on their presses, their rhetoric was nevertheless stamped by a bookish culture and a long familiarity with the written word. Even their extemporizations have the feel of the reader or the scholar. Many were great parliamentarians, orators and tribunes in the classical republican tradition; but their addresses were formally founded upon the written word, the real basis of law both in their own eyes and in those of the rank and file.

Powers of the Invisible

'Since 1789, ideas alone have constituted the strength and salvation of the proletariat. It owes to them its every victory', wrote Blanqui (one of those who passed the ideas of 1789 on to the Paris Commune). Abstract concepts were the ABC of a militant's apprenticeship. The notions of proletariat and bourgeoisie, like those of labour power, surplus value, relations of production, etc., that underlie them, are not apprehensible by the senses. Secondly, whether project or myth, the idea of the Revolution as 'what should be' is the denial and transcendence of the immediate, the overcoming of the present. Both as logical discourse and as moral undertaking, the socialist utopia demanded an inner break with the 'stream of everyday life', an act of faith that mobilized the powers of conceptual analysis to break the accepted social imagery down into elemental abstracts, like 'exploitation'.

Writing collectivizes individual memory; reading individualizes collective memory. The back-and-forth between them fosters the sense for history by unearthing potentials within the present, creating backdrops and foregrounds; it is fundamental for the idea of socialism. When it is cold outside and the night is long, memory means that we are not alone. Alphabetical memory, as Hegel would put it. Contrasting 'the inestimable educational value' of learning to read and write with alphabetical characters, as opposed to hieroglyphics, he described how the very process of alphabetical writing helps to turn the mind's attention from immediate ideas and sense impressions to 'the more formal structure of the

---

2   *Cited in Georges Duveau,* La pensée ouvrière sur l'éducation pendant la Seconde République et le Second Empire, *Paris 1947.*

word and its abstract components', in a way that 'gives stability and independence to the interior realm of mental life'.[3]

All the revolutionary men of action I have met, from Che Guevara to Pham van Dong by way of Castro (not the autocrat, but the one-time rebel), to say nothing of the walking encyclopaedias known as Trotskyists, were compulsive readers, as devoted to books as they were unreceptive to images. A Hegelian would explain this by saying that reading leads to critical detachment, and—given that there is 'no science that is not hidden', nor future without 'rehearsal' of the past—to utopian anticipation. Abstraction encourages action, as remembrance leads to innovation. The greatest modernizers inaugurate their career with a backward leap, and a renaissance proceeds through a return to the past, a recycling, and hence a revolution. Columbus discovered America in a library, through the perusal of arcane texts and cosmographies. The Ancien Régime in France was overthrown by admirers not of Montgolfier or Washington, but of Lycurgus and Cato. Chateaubriand and Hugo revolutionized literature by dint of Gothic ruins, Nietzsche vaulted over Jules Verne with the aid of the pre-Socratics, and Freud revisited Aeschylus.

The misfortune of revolutionaries is to have inherited a little more than most people. The written word is vital for these transmitters of collective memory, since their analytical tools are forged from its traditions. A legacy of ideas is not automatically transmissible; there are better or worse historical environments for conveying abstractions, just as there are better and worse conductors of electricity. The revolutionary act *par excellence* starts from a sense of nostalgia, the return to a forgotten text, a lost ideal. Behind the 're' of reformation, republic or revolution—of rehearsing, recommencing, rereading—there is a hand flicking through the pages of a book, from the end back to the beginning. Whereas the finger that presses a button, fast-forwarding a tape or disc, will never pose a danger to the establishment.

Parchment Batons

If news bulletins are the medium for history as spectacle, the archive is the medium for history as practice. The story of communism—as revolutionary utopia, not bureaucratic dictatorship—has been a tale of archivists and old papers. Communism was the bookish invention of Gracchus Babeuf, a specialist in feudal law, who extracted its central ideas from Rousseau, Mably and antique parchments. It flourished in the great storehouses of the written word. For Michelet: 'My history of the French Revolution was born in the archives. I am writing it in this central depot'—the official records office. Men wove between texts, texts wove between men. Myths beget acts which beget myths, and the movement of narratives spurs the movement of peoples. Histories of Rome had their effects on the deputies of 1789, Lamartine's *History of the Girondins* and Louis Blanc's *History of the French Revolution* on the 1848-ers, Hugo's *Les Misérables* on the Commune and his *Ninety-Three* on the birth of the Third Republic.

The baton was passed round the world, hand to hand: from the Society of Equals, founded by the medievalist Babeuf, to the Society of New Citizens, founded by the young librarian, Mao Zedong. Buonarroti (1761–1837), a year younger than Babeuf (1760–97),

3   G. W. F. Hegel, Encyclopaedia, § 459. *Passage analysed in Jacques Derrida*, De la grammatologie, *Paris 1967, pp. 36–45.*

dodged the Directory's police and survived his friend by forty years. In 1837 Buonarroti's account of the history they had lived, *Babeuf's Conspiracy for Equality*, was published in Brussels, where Marx would take refuge after his expulsion from Paris in 1845, and would find his first apostle in the young Philippe Gigot, paleographer and archivist. Exile in Brussels functioned as a turn-table after the 1815 Restoration. Here Buonarroti met up with the former Convention delegates, Barère and Vadier, who would organize the *carbonari*, seedbed for the secret societies that sprang up under the July Monarchy, and from which would emerge the League of the Just; which would in turn be refashioned into the Communist League in 1847 by Marx and Engels, along with delegates from Blanqui, 'the head and the heart of the proletarian party in France'. Thirty-nine years in jail and four death sentences: it was via Blanqui (1805–81), 'the prisoner', that the passage was made from Jacobinism to socialism, from 1793 to the Paris Commune; Blanqui who handed the torch to Vaillant, who would pass it to Jaurès, whose byline on his column in *La Dépêche de Toulouse* was 'The Reader', and who was succeeded by Blum, literary critic for *La Revue Blanche*.

An Olympic marathon: the glow of a letter—more firefly than flame—passing from runner to runner, as if the revolutionary was a forwarding agent, and the heart of the message lay precisely in its transmission: a telegraph flashing from peak to peak, via such human semaphores. Not forgetting the whispering in the valleys, some two hundred years of stories handed down from grandmothers to toddlers. 'My childhood was full of stories about the long march of the poor, across the ages', recalls the old French Communist Gérard Belloin.

> Tales prompted by a crust of bread on the floor, a drop of soup left in a bowl.
> They were told by the grandmothers, who had heard them told when they were
> young themselves. Like underground streams whose course cannot be mapped
> because their waters seem to disappear completely, then come up further on,
> the chronicle of peasant suffering knew little of its sources. But it too had run
> on underground, carried by anonymous voices, each generation confiding its
> trials to the next. At times it grew more insistent or seemed to fade, but it never
> went away. It constantly mixed up the past and the present, for isn't speaking of
> the troubles of the past a way of drawing attention to those of today? Did that
> happen long ago? Oh yes, my child, a very long time ago. But how can you be
> sure? For a child, how far back is long ago?[4]

The workers' press and the socialist library were crucibles for anarchists, Proudhonists, Leninists and reformists alike. Saint-Simon was a copyist, proof-corrector and bookseller; Proudhon, a typographer. So was Pablo Iglesias (1850–1925), founder of the Spanish Socialist Party. It was a Spanish journalist and typographer, José Mesa, who, exiled in Paris, passed on the heritage of the First International to Jules Guesde, recruiting sergeant of French socialism. Anarchists and socialists were the warring siblings of one family; pamphlets, articles, newpapers, literary supplements, filled their lives. Both followed Luther's order, to spare neither hardship nor money to set up 'good libraries and bookshops' everywhere. The sons of Marx and of Bakunin shared the same gospel: to read and to get others reading. Everywhere they went, they left a library. Hobsbawm could

4 *Gérard Belloin,* Nos rêves, camarades, *Paris 1979.*

measure the precise degree of socialism's penetration in Europe between 1890 and 1905 by comparing the number of annual publications.[5]

The cult of the book had its preacherly moments. Hugo to the illiterate worker:

> Have you forgotten that your liberator
> Is the book? The book is there on the heights;
> It gleams; because it shines and illuminates,
> It destroys the scaffold, war and famine;
> It speaks: No more slaves and no more pariahs.[6]

But it had its triumphal version too, gaily insurrectional in Jules Vallès's bulletin to his editor, warning of 'galleys within the fortnight, and "pass for press" in two months'. 'I breathe deep, I swell out. "Pass for press", it's as good as the order to fire! On the barricades, it's a gun-barrel poked out between the slats.' And Hugo himself had written: 'Nothing so much resembles the mouth of a cannon as an open bottle of ink.'[7]

Eastern Clandestinity

After 1945, this alphabetical heroism migrated to the Third World, equipped with hurricane lamp, exercise books and biros. Emancipation through literacy, the dark shadows of superstition gradually buried under millions of white pages—this Eluardesque symbolism of Europe's 19th century found a haven, in the mid-20th, in the struggle against the 'imperialist West'. The first action of any anti-colonial revolution was to launch a mass literacy campaign.[8] The Little Red Book was the talisman of Mao's China.

The process was frozen in the post-war period in Eastern Europe's huge conservatory of obsolete forms—a museum of the word, in which the living sources of the past lay fossilized. Yet, studious and scholarly, 'actually existing socialism' had a typographic soul. A glance at UNESCO indicators for number of books per head, quantity of public libraries, average household spending on books, etc., shows that during the Cold War, Communist countries—where the economy was struggling and audiovisual culture had barely arrived—held all the records for printed paper. To journey through those old-world provinces, where Western Europe's 19th century still lived on, was to witness a universal cult of books and an idolization of writers—Soviet stars were more likely to be novelists or poets than actors or musicians. With the atrophy of the image came a hypertrophy of the text, its aura enhanced by censorship.

Party-States had such respect for the power of words that they kept them under perpetual surveillance, yet this repression made a live grenade of every samizdat, in line with the 'best' Tsarist traditions. Everything was repeated, but upside-down. Under the Stalinist state, the Russian intelligentsia resumed its time-honoured typographical combat, its old mole's labours. For what else is told in the long history of the Russian underground, from

5   Eric Hobsbawm, 'La diffusione del marxismo (1890–1905)', Studi storici, vol. 15, no. 2 (1974), pp. 241–69.

6   Victor Hugo, 'A qui la faute?', L'Année terrible (1872).

7   Jules Vallès, L'Insurgé, Lausanne 1968, pp. 48–9; Victor Hugo, Œuvres complètes, Paris 1968, vol. VII, p. 678.

8   To participate, in 1961, in the Cuban national campaign that brought a million illiterate peasants into contact with writing was like a physical encounter with the progressive imaginary of the book.

Herzen's *Kolokol* (1855) to Lenin's *Iskra* (1900), but stories of clandestine presses, illicit news-sheets, books sewn into greatcoats? In Dostoevsky's *The Possessed*, Verkhovensky lures Shatov into a trap by sending him to retrieve a printing press buried in a schoolyard.

Between the various opposition groups, as between dissidents and the state, the battle-lines were drawn in print, above all through the journal. Russian populists (direct ancestors of Marxist study groups and parties) placed even greater emphasis on the importance of the press than did the secret societies and *carbonari* in the West. Lenin defined himself as a publicist,[9] in the mould of Chernyshevsky or Herzen, who moved to London for the sake of the cyrillic characters unavailable in Russia. In contrast to the Brezhnev era—better organized and hence less bloodthirsty than the Tsarist autocracy—written propaganda preceded, and alternated with, the propaganda of deeds. In 1880s Russia, the profession closest to 'editor' was 'terrorist'. The Tsarist police's litany was: 'Where's the printing press? The first link in the courier chain? The dispatch office?' The mastermind of a conspiracy was inevitably a bookseller or a printer. The most vexing problem was always how to move things (subversive literature or bombs), deep in travellers' bags.[10]

The fall of Communism in the East thus witnessed the extinction of the last literate societies in Europe—the triumph of showbiz extravagance over cheap editions and a dwindling readership for the classics, as the old European culture of printing segued into the 'mass culture' imported from America. The totalitarian hijacking of the Enlightenment, set against the new global imagery, could even make the defeat of Diderot at the hand of Disneyland look like emancipation. In a remarkable historical irony, the political victory of humanism spelled the cultural defeat of the humanities. Prosperous times for television and advertising in Eastern Europe; lean times for bookshops and publishers.

Alma Mater

If the history of the school has always been charged with political significance, political history has in turn carried scholastic implications. The 'battle for education' always featured high on the left's agenda; socialism, as the pedagogy of a world-view, knew that its own survival was at stake here. Any militant enrolling in a school of socialist thought must first have absorbed the habits of the schoolroom. The socialist's code of honour was modelled on that of the good schoolboy: he who can put up with the boredom of the classroom will triumph over the class enemy.

The early workers' movements arose before the advent of mass education; silk workers' uprisings, weavers' strikes and mutual insurance companies did not wait for universal schooling in order to exist. But trade unionism and 'workers' power' are self-limiting in their ideas, and philanthropy alone would have spawned no more than adult-learning centres. It was the educational project of socialism that lifted its vision beyond that of

---

9 We theoreticians, or, as I would rather say, publicists of Social Democracy': V. I. Lenin, 'Two Tactics of Social Democracy in the Democratic Revolution' (1905), Collected Works, Moscow 1965, vol. 9, pp. 15–140.

10 Let us note in passing how foreign the manners of 'actually existing socialism' were to Pol Pot's Cambodia, how remote the urban mystique of literacy and learning from that savage cult of rural ignorance. The Khmer Rouge decreed: no books, no schools. They ransacked the presses and libraries of Phnom Penh, closed the university, padlocked the high schools. The only medium allowed was the radio. A party without a paper! Pol Pot's back-to-the-jungle system was consistent: slaughter of the educated, a term encompassing anyone who had got beyond primary school; wholesale xenophobia; rejection of urban civilization, and gerontophobia as a political axiom (no one over 23 could belong to the Organization).

unions and guilds. Its parties were created on the strength of the conviction that class is an instinct, but socialism is a raising of consciousness. The job of the school was thus not incubation but production. This accounts for the intensive focus on educational questions. 'For every school that opens, a prison is closed'. The mystique of the emancipated and emancipatory school was a tribute rendered by the working-class parties to the bourgeois state.

Numerous teachers (Guesde and Jaurès among them) once hurried back and forth between blackboard and rostrum. The First International (1864) and the Workers' Educational League (1867) pooled their staff, premises and periodicals. One of the first acts of the Paris Commune was to appoint a Commission of Education, headed by Edouard Vaillant. Louise Michel, deported to New Caledonia with the Commune's suppression, immediately opened a school there for the Kanaks (had she enjoyed access to pulp and typeface, she would no doubt have launched the island's first newspaper). From its inception in 1920, the French Communist Party recruited its star cadres from the ranks of schoolteachers and professors. The best-established branch of the International between the wars was the education workers' section headed by Georges Cogniot, a practising Latinist.

Mill workers had provided a focus for the communist imaginary during the first industrial revolution; miners and steel workers took over that role during the second. But it is the primary schoolteacher, with his spartan or sententious modesty, who reveals the extent to which organized socialism's roots lie in the pre-industrial culture of the Enlightenment. Former Communist Gérard Belloin, a child of the field and the page, a self-educated man enlightened by the Resistance, provides an arresting sample of militant ecology in his memoirs: 'When in small groups we'd spent the night slipping tracts under doors or into letterboxes, we felt as uplifted on the way home as a schoolmaster at the end of the lesson.' Belloin went forth, not to earn party points but out of pure devotion. In those days (we are in the 1950s, by the banks of the Loire):

> one would not dream of casting aspersions on the teacher's social standing, or doubting the degree of personal effort this had cost him. According to the commonly accepted scale of values that substituted for an explanation of social class, it was quite the opposite. Repositories of knowledge, they were just about the only people locally acknowledged as such, along with doctors, priests, tax inspectors, notaries and chemists... We were imbued with the hallowed popular respect for learning, books and intellectuals.[11]

The ritual nature of this respect informed both the best—Belloin and his ilk—and the worst, who were to encircle and then crush them. A germ of Stalinism lay in the frankness of encyclopaedism, stupidity inside intelligence. A fatal distinction prevailed between the leaders and the led. Intellectual authority became the grounds for political domination. Knowledge became nationalized, because doctrines, like temples or countries, need frontiers, and armed clerics to guard them. The most philistine despot found himself wreathed in the laurels of knowledge. Academism, museomania and the general smell of mothballs impregnating Soviet societies became endemic when the 'tradition'-form was held up as the norm of the future: the archive's posthumous revenge on invention. The didacticism,

11 *Belloin,* Nos rêves, camarades.

ponderousness and rigidity of Soviet discourse, its moralistic gloom, are what ensue when a school turns upon thinking, and subdues it with an iron fist. The handbook becomes the curriculum, and the result is crude simplification, stereotypes and cant.

Socialist culture is paradoxically attached to an elitist curriculum reflecting 'bourgeois', not to say 'aristocratic' values, whose decline considerably hastened that of socialism. Socialism was marked during the first half of the 20th century by an educational universe that despised technical knowledge, commerce, industry and even maths, but taught Latin and Greek as living languages. For today's reader, to scour the archives of the French workers' movement prior to its 'Bolshevization' by the Communists, and standardization by the Socialists, is like moving from *Hello!* magazine to the *Metaphysics and Ethics Review*. Jaurès and Blum possessed the same cultural baggage as Marx and Trotsky, as did their opponents Barrès and Maurras. There are deeper affinities between Jaurès and Barrès than between Jaurès and any current Socialist leader. This is because Jaurès's holiday reading was *De natura rerum* in the original; Blum liked to relax with a translation of Lucretius; today's socialist elephant will pick up a seasonal blockbuster and a newspaper written in franglais. If he chose Lucretius over the latest opinion polls, he would soon lose his leadership. The biotope makes the animal, rather than the other way around.

Holy Morning Paper

Book, school, newspaper: for the party militant, the greatest emphasis lay on the third. The first, short-lived, working-class publications in France appeared between 1830 and 1840. Indeed it was *L'Atelier*, Buchez's paper, that in 1840 coined the expression 'working class'. The intervening period was crucial, for it was then that 'creating a school' mutated into 'creating a party'. For the Church, a daily paper is a plus; for the party, it is a must. *L'Humanité* was strategic for the PCF in a way *La Croix* would never be for the clergy. Churches came and went long before the invention of printing, but no workers' parties existed before the appearance of popular broadsheets around 1860. Socialist ideology lasted for the duration of the form called party, and the party-form lasted as long as the party dailies—roughly a hundred years. *Le Peuple*, for example, the Belgian Socialists' organ, expired with dignity in 1979, at the age of 94. It had fought for universal suffrage, the emancipation of women and human rights with Jaurès, Vandervelde and Huysmans. After that it merely survived, a different entity under the same name.

'The paper is not only a collective propagandist and agitator, but also a collective organizer' (Lenin). Its dissemination unites, creating a network of exchanges and liaisons. Jaurès, Trotsky and Lenin performed the same tasks (writing, typesetting, printing, posting) as Vallès did at *Le Cri du peuple*, Elisée Reclus at *Le Révolté*, Jean Grave at *Temps nouveaux*. Whether the reference was Marx, Bakunin or Fourier, printed words were sown in order to harvest activists. Lenin established his party with *Iskra*, Guesde with *L'Egalité* and Jaurès with *La Petite République*. Cabet propagated his Icarian dream with the tools and methods employed by Marx and Engels.

The political news-sheet carried serious implications, attesting to the active mediation of an idea of Man in the midst of men; the long-shot in the short term. Mainstream newspapers, product of a media conglomerate, are conceived as black boxes: events come in and information comes out. A class or party newspaper plays a different role: transforming a conception of the world into small change, a philosophical system into everyday slogans. Events are centralized by, and under, the idea; individual energies by the leadership. In contrast to the paper-as-mirror, the paper-as-guide fulfils the role assigned by Kant to the schema: intermediary and interpreter between the pure concept and the appearance of things. In the tradition of the socialist press, the author of the doctrine is his own intermediary; this is what distinguishes him from his contemporary, the belle-lettriste. 'For "intellectuals", the other profession that they should always practise alongside their own is surely that of printer,' wrote Andler, in his *Life of Lucien Herr*. 'A time will certainly come when writers and scientists know how to operate a linotype. If they wish to publish a book, they will be able to rent a rotary press, just as one hires a motor car to drive oneself.'[12]

Herr himself was a pioneer in this regard. Librarian at the Ecole Normale, prompter to Jaurès and Blum, he was for several years the anonymous editor of the foreign news page at *L'Humanité* (a name he coined). Aragon, Nizan or D'Astier did as much in their way. Until very recently, a knowledge of print and management of a press were indispensable to the work of intellectuals who never delegated such chores to others, preferring to be their own leader-writers, copy-writers, proofreaders, designers and managers. Running the paper and running the party often overlapped; it was unthinkable for the leader to be illiterate. While the political journal served as the internal organ for the intellectuals' power struggles, the newspaper was intended for laymen and amateurs. It formed a bridge between 'the theory of the vanguard' and the 'spontaneous movement of the class', in Lenin's idiom, or between 'metaphysics' and 'the world', in Jaurès's. It reunited the thinker and the worker, providing for socialism that day-to-day hyphen between the intellectual and the people that the school supplied for republicans.

So long as print remained the central meeting-ground for this type of interchange, the profession of politics and that of the intellectual—from the great writer to the typographer—had a common base. In its absence, the pen and the lathe have turned their backs on each other. The specialization of politicians—as vote-chasing technicians—has matched that of the printing sector, journalism and publishing. From the 17th century until the 20th, presses were meeting places, points of contact between people from different professions and classes, where cross-pollination was almost unavoidable. Writers and parliamentarians no longer share a common set of tools. A relationship that once was practical and professional has decayed into cocktail-party irrelevance.

The Party
Much has been written on the decline of the political party, and thus of the socialist project. But one factor that has been largely ignored is the transition from the written (flexible, decentralized, affordable) to the audio-visual (industrial, expensive); the diminishing stature of print and the modification of printing techniques. Photocomposition destroyed the last cultural bases of the workers' movement; both the bookmakers' craft and its traditional caste of pundits and commentators were rendered technologically redundant. Print lost its lead, the critical intellectual his milieu, socialist politics its reference; all three were thrown into crisis. If 'the first freedom of the press is that it is

12   *Charles Andler,* La Vie de Lucien Herr, *Paris 1977.*

not an industry', it should be added that, from 1881 to 1970, the press was *also* an industry. Now it is an industry first and foremost. It is hard to conceive that, in 1904, Herr, Blum and Lévy-Bruhl—a librarian, a lawyer and an academic—could have launched a daily paper such as *L'Humanité*, with a first edition of 138,000 copies, on a single subscription drive of 850,000 francs. Media companies have changed their nature along with their size. The concentration of titles, the determining weight of advertising budgets and the size of investment needed have pushed the price of a newspaper directorship well beyond the wallet and technical capacities of a handful of penniless intellectuals.

The separation of the print producer from his means of production in the journalistic sphere coincides with that of theory from practice in the political domain. Although there are electoral machines—still called 'parties', out of inertia—that issue internal bulletins to their indifferent representatives, the arc that once linked action and the future, parties and intellectuals, has been broken. The parties have ceased to be issuers of alternative ideas, while writers and thinkers must throw in their lot with the broadcasting networks that have acquired an industrial and commercial life of their own, as foreign to intellectual creation as to utopian ideology. The shift from graphosphere to videosphere has dissolved the connection between the party's technical base and its doctrinal logic. The distinction between left and right in politics relied upon a means of dissidence production: a craft-based network of newspapers, reviews, research institutes, book clubs, conferences, societies and so on. No class struggle without social classes; but no factional struggle without a clash of opinions, no politics without polemics; and no battle of ideas, when money has become the only sinew in the war of airwaves. In its stead comes the struggle of images and personalities, the battles of the scoop and the soundbite. No need for parties here.

The proceedings of socialist congresses were formerly published in full, six months later—those of the 1879 Congress of Marseille, which united the French workers' movement, took up 800 pages—in a volume that would become the Bible until the next sitting. The political world has never seen as many forums, conferences, conventions as there are today, but you would search the bookshops in vain for their bound record. Participants 'talk' ideas as one talks clothes. The (printed) motions are mere pretexts for tactical alliances between telegenic champions. In mediological terms, it would be only a slight exaggeration to say that because the debates are not published, there is no call for ideas; television—the new test of performance—has no need for them. Hence the new 'anti-ideological' ideology and the substitution of individual proposals for party programmes, personal positions for theoretical ones.

Quantitatively, of course, books, schools and newspapers are doing better than ever. There have never been so many volumes, students, authors and publishers. But mediaspheres are not a matter of statistics. Indeed, there may well be an inverse relation between the eclipse of form and the proliferation of content; between the scale of output and its status. Mass education first diluted, then obliterated, the symbolism of the university or school. Education is now a public service, like the subway or electricity provider, dealing with customers rather than disciples. There are many more public libraries under the videosphere than under the graphosphere, but what used to be 'the workshop of the human spirit' (Abbé Grégoire) is becoming a place of transit, of access to information. Never have so many books appeared—35,000 new titles a year in France—or in so many copies. But the readership is shrinking, and the aura of the book, or what remains of it, has been transferred to the face of the author, since that is what appears on TV. The printed word can still, exceptionally, kill. But can it still give birth to anything? And if so, to what?

Time, Speed, and Environment

The first element of a reply: temporality. Metaphors for diffusion, whether of heat or liquids, tend to imply a fairly slow process. In 1850 or 1880, an idea that at first went unremarked was not lost forever. The chemistry had time to work. A message could survive on the shelf, awaiting a later encounter. The best example of this delayed-action mechanism is the propagation of Marx's œuvre. It took twenty or thirty years for his published works to take effect, and the lag separating production from transmission proved crucial to the doctrine's ultimate influence. The first French edition of *Capital* Volume I took twenty-five years to sell out. In the famous letter to 'Citizen Maurice Lechâtre' of 1872 that prefaces the book, Marx wrote: 'I approve your idea of publishing the translation of *Das Kapital* by instalments. In that form, the work will be more accessible to the working class, and this consideration outweighs all others for me.' It took some time for the said working class to gain 'access' to the knowledge of its own exploitation. Between 1872 and 1875, Lechâtre took delivery of 44 sections of 40 pages each. The first instalment was boldly brought out in 10,000 copies, and priced at ten centimes. Sales peaked the first day: 234 copies were sold. Then disaster struck. There was no money for advertising, nor support from any political organization. It was not until 25 years later, with help from Jules Guesde's Parti Ouvrier, that the remaining booklets were sold.[13] In fact, it was not until 1890—seven years after Marx's death—that *Capital* began to be taken seriously among a handful of militant and scientific groups. Until then, it had only been read in condensed form (Delville's abridgement of 1883 numbered 253 pages), or presented in seminars such as Lafargue's.

The *Communist Manifesto*, published in London in German, caused hardly a ripple. By the time of the Commune, in 1871, it was regarded as a 'bibliographical curiosity'. Only in 1872 did it appear in French, 24 years after it was written, courtesy of Marx's daughter Laura Lafargue; by 1885, it was just beginning to enjoy a modest success. *The Poverty of Philosophy* was self-published in Paris, in June 1847. Six months later, 96 copies had been bought. The publisher dispatched free samples to the author's friends, asking only for the 15 sous it cost him for packing and postage: every one of them was returned to him. Alfred Sudre's *Histoire du Communisme* (1848) had not a word on Marx or Engels in its 532 pages. The first edition of Capital merited two reviews in French, both in obscure high-brow magazines. One was by Maurice Bloch, in the *Journal des Economistes*; the other was by Roberty in *Philosophie Positive*, and reproached the author for 'doing nothing but criticize, without offering concrete proposals for the future'. An article on his work in an English journal was still a rare enough event that in the winter of 1881 Marx would show it to his wife on her deathbed, 'to illuminate her final moments', as he wrote. Looking back from a world in which the life and status of the author sustain whole schools of theoretical research in the human sciences, the question is how a practically unknown writer of difficult books, none of which caused a stir, could subsequently have 'informed' the entire world for a hundred years.

13   See Maurice Dommanget, L'Introduction du marxisme en France, Lausanne 1969.

A second element: the environment. Mammals were unable to spread across the planet during the 140 million years of the Mesozoic era; only the abrupt extinction of the dinosaurs at the end of the Cretaceous allowed them to venture out from their highly specialized niches and multiply over dry land. Until the geophysical upheaval of the continental masses provoked an auspicious climate change (and so of flora and fauna), competition with flying reptiles and 50-ton brachiosaurs was unthinkable, such was the disproportion of the means of survival between the species.

Cultural biotopes are no less delicately balanced, and in the jungle of social ideas the survival of the fittest presupposes a certain proportion in the means of struggle. Marx benefited from the unusually temperate conditions of the pre-industrial graphosphere: a smaller world population and restricted literacy in the West meant fewer books on the market and thus an easier battle for recognition, all weapons being more or less equal. In the days of Marx, Hugo or Michelet, the circulation of a 'difficult' book compared to a best-seller stood at an approximate ratio of one to ten, or more commonly one to five. Today, it is one to a thousand. Around 1848, the young Marx was publishing around a thousand copies of each pamphlet or periodical (800 copies of *The Poverty of Philosophy*; 1,000 of the *Franco-German Yearbook*, in which 'On The Jewish Question' and 'Contribution to the Critique of Hegel's Philosophy of Right' appeared). But first-rank writers did not go beyond three or four thousand. Despite the huge growth of the reading public, that figure is still the average for works on political theory, economic history or sociology; the author of a piece of critical research that goes against the grain can feel blessed with two thousand readers. But the massive media launch-pads at the disposal of those who dominate the sales also serve to pulverize the small, scholarly productions, more complex and thus more vulnerable, and which have no time to carve a niche for themselves due to the drastic reduction in the average life-expectancy of books—three months for a successful publication; the rest might be in bookshop windows for three weeks. Publishers' figures have been inflated, but the mortality rate has risen too.

The Marxist critique of capitalism would not have been able to spread, it seems, had industrial capitalism already annexed the sphere of symbolic goods. Marx profited from the backwardness of cultural circuits in relation to those of market production. A hundred years later, he would have missed his chance. All things being equal on other fronts, within the logic of image and markets (literary talkshows, weekly top-tens), *Das Kapital* would have remained what it was when it first appeared: a scholarly extravagance for book-lovers, not the source of a mass political current. Marx and Engels were writing at the juncture of two technological eras, that of the 'mechanical machine', alleviating muscular effort, and the 'energetic machine', harnessing natural forces. State socialism developed at a second juncture: the moving machine and the information machine, car and television. In the same way, the century of Communist waxing and waning also pivoted around two eras: two kinds of memory, literal and analogical. 'Scientific socialism' would not survive the shift from electro-mechanical transmission (rotary printing press, telegraph) to electronic broadcasting. The single party did not fit well with the telephone; it survived the wireless, but the transistor radio was the limit. The cathode tube and the silicon chip spelt wholesale crisis. Cross-border radio transmissions swept away the relics, and the live-broadcast satellite presided over the funeral.

A crisis of cultural reproduction such as socialism's tends to cast the laws governing other cultures in a similar light. We should beware of emulating the American Trotskyist who, recording the extinction of Trotskyism in the United States in the post-war era, postulated the death of all ideologies on the planet. To confuse culture with one culture, the end of an era with the end of time, is the traditional mistake of the traditionalist. Every fall is the herald of a renaissance, and the gods who fled through the front door will come back, sooner or later, through the window.

Prison, Exile, Phone

An ecology of socialism must also take into account the extra-cultural, not to say anti-cultural factors that once ensured the community's cohesion. Like a Muslim or a Christian, a militant is never really isolated; he is always a member of the collective. Political engagement proceeds through a transfer of the group's image onto the individual, and the intensity of the militant's sense of belonging is the measure of his capacities for initiative. Ethology has taught us that a society of primates is close-knit in proportion to the hostility of its environment; in this respect revolutionaries, like all believers, are a bit more primate than most.[14] They have a visceral need for banishment and prison. Such were the historical conditions for the creation of milieux of stubbornly refractory thinking. Promoted to officialdom, the 'workers' movement' fell apart, for its brain ceased to function the moment it traded its enviable oppressed status for the fatal position of oppressor. Hence the immense spiritual superiority of the East European dissidents over the ruling bureaucrats, as the former regained all the resources of the old secessionist intelligentsia, prison and exile foremost among them. The lesson to be drawn from the century-long expansion and contraction of socialism: as long as there was repression, there was hope.

To explain: socialism was an attempt to establish a counter-medium of dissemination within a hostile milieu. Could the idea have become an 'ideology' if micro-circuits of solidarity had not established a mini-milieu for themselves, within this formless space? Cheap, sustainable information networks, alternative communities and counter-cultures that owed their capacity for resistance to the forces that besieged them from without. To jump the spark from written myth to social action, the electricians of workers' emancipation had to disconnect the main cables and rig up makeshift wiring of their own. Methods of underground organizing served as a protective casing, to shield proletarian telegraphy from bourgeois jamming and interference. The romance of clandestinity was essentially a communicative pragmatism. Tracking the footpaths of the revolution over the past two centuries would take one by the sheltering walls and shadowy corners that Rabelais evoked as inevitable sites for 'murmur and plot'.

But with all eyes and ears occupied every evening by the same news bulletin in four versions, the walls of the cell or sect are first perforated, then blown away by the airwaves. Hitherto, they had more or less succeeded in maintaining a difference of pressure or temperature from the outside world. The homogenization of symbolic flows tends to dissolve non-conformist nuclei into a common hegemonic gas. Television, now the principal interface of all social groups, erodes the boundaries between inside and out, and levels access to information. As a grass-roots militant, why should I bother to attend party meetings when the TV news will give me the essence of eight hours' debate, and when my neighbour

14   Primate: placentary mammal with full dentition and prehensile hands.

across the hall will find out as much as I could about my party, without wasting his time? As for the journalist, he knows as much and often more than the party leader, since he speaks to everyone and they to him. The ideological hold of television overrides the hold of the party, because its mode of organizing the populace engulfs and homogenizes all specialist groups.

By contrast, the two privileged evolutionary niches of the revolutionary socialist were prison and exile. Prison, to concentrate; exile, to campaign. Reading and writing are luxury pursuits by definition, since they imply leisure time. Where could one enjoy more time to oneself than in the police jails of the 19th century? Prison was the dissident's second university, his seat of higher learning and greatest moral awareness. 'When a man knows he is to be hanged in a fortnight,' said Samuel Johnson, 'it concentrates his mind wonderfully'. And Proudhon: 'All that I am I owe to despair.' Bureaucrat, beware the intellectuals that emerge from prison: they have matured and have muscles. Against capitalism in the West and communism in the East, the laboratories of social protest were the detention centres and prison camps of dictators. Right and left, revolutionaries and counter-revolutionaries (Joseph de Maistre or Solzhenitsyn, Dostoevsky or Maurras) have benefited in turn from these mediological privileges. The Orthodox religion emerged from the Soviet penal colonies in far better shape than it had entered them.

The honours list of European prisons from 1840 to 1930 provides a rollcall of Marxist laureates. It ends in the East with the Stalinist labour camp (and Victor Serge). In the West, the prisoners of capital form the links of an anti-capitalist chain, from Babeuf to Proudhon to Gramsci, Blanqui to Bebel to Guesde. It was deportation to Siberia that allowed Lenin to finish his first major work, *The Development of Capitalism in Russia*, begun in a St. Petersburg prison. Liebknecht, Luxemburg, Trotsky, Blum (who wrote his greatest work in prison): nearly all who left their mark on socialist thought spent time behind bars. Exile brought us 'Marx-and-Engels' banished in their youth. For half a century, most of the Russian intelligentsia was forced into clandestinity—and so into organizing—by the Tsarist regime. French socialism was born in England; Italian, Chinese and Vietnamese communism were born in France. Chased out of everywhere, the old socialism grew adept at border-crossing and emerged as a pure product of European culture. The level of a civilization, said Lucien Herr, can be measured by its degree of cosmopolitanism. To be uprooted awakens reason by suggesting comparison—always a good start.

Stalin and Mao are absent from the roll-call of exile: Stalin rarely left Russia, or Mao China (except to go to Moscow, where he shut himself away to avoid seeing the outside world). The despots of social-feudalism had sedentary souls. As a rule, the great paranoiacs only speak their mother tongue. Riveted to their soil, they lack all curiosity about the other, all impulse to challenge it or fuse with it. Autocrats fear to travel, shrinking from disorientation and unsavoury encounters.

Yet the mediasphere seems to have stripped the diasporas of their former productivity. Dispersion used to favour intellectual creativity by stimulating written exchange. Bodies met less frequently but minds were in closer contact. Consider the debt owed by socialist writing to the epistolary art: Marx and Engels worked out half their theories in letters, and virtually all their political activity had to pass through a pillarbox; the First

	Logosphere (Writing)	Graphosphere (Print)	Videosphere (Audiovisual)
Group ideal; political tendency	The One (City, Empire, Kingdom); absolutism	All (Nation, People, State); nationalism and totalitarianism	Each (population, society, world); individualism and anomie
Figure of time; vector	Circle (the Eternal, repetition); past-oriented	Line (history, Progress); future-oriented	Point (current events); self-oriented: cult of the present
Canonical generation	Elder	Adult	Youth
Spiritual class	Church (prophets, clerics)	Intelligentsia (professors, doctors)	Media (broadcasters, producers)
Legitimating reference	The divine (because it's sacred)	The ideal (because it's true)	The effective (because it works)
Driving force	Faith (fanaticism)	Law (dogmatism)	Opinion (relativism)
Status of the individual	Subject (to be commanded)	Citizen (to be persuaded)	Consumer (to be seduced)
Identifying myth	The saint	The hero	The celebrity
Maxim for personal authority	'God told me'	'I read it'	'I saw it on TV'
Basis of symbolic authority	The invisible	The legible	The visible
Subjective centre of gravity	The soul	The consciousness	The body

International was conceived by Marx as a central correspondence bureau of the working class. Nowadays the militants socialize more and know less of each other's ideas. More conversation means less controversy. The telephone destroyed the art of correspondence, and in the process diminished the moral stature of attempts at rational systematization; email has not restored it. Rarely do we pick up the phone to impart a complex sequence of principles and themes: we use it to chat. The general discourse has become indexed to the trappings of intimacy and private life. The cellphone, internet, laptop and plane are good for internationalization, but they render solidarity less organic—lethal for internationalism. They enlarge the sphere of individual relations but privatize them at the same time; they particularize even as they globalize. The cellphone is a permanent one-to-one. It drives the universal from our heads.

The crisis for socialism, then, is that even if it can resume its founding principles it cannot return to its founding cultural logic, its circuits of thought-production and dissemination. The collapse of the graphosphere has forced it to pack up its weapons and join the video-sphere, whose thought-networks are fatal for its culture. A practical example: to find out what is going on one has to watch TV, and so stay at home. A bourgeois house arrest, for beneath 'a man's home is his castle' there always lurks, 'every man for himself'. The demobilization of the citizen begins with the physical immobilization of the spectator.

What further implications for social thought might we draw from the 'three estates' of logosphere, graphosphere, videosphere—the word, the press, the screen? It would be possible to tabulate a series of norms and functions inherent in any social collectivity, and map out the particular modes and forms that have answered to them in each successive age (see opposite). Thus, the symbolic authority for the logosphere is the invisible; for the graphosphere, the printed word; for the videosphere, the visible. Status of the individual: subject; citizen; consumer. Maxim for personal authority: 'God told me'; 'I read it'; 'I saw it on TV'.

Yet although these three regimes succeed each other in historical time, each asserting its own predominant forms and modes, it should go without saying that any one of us contains all the ages at once. Inside each of us there lies a calligraphic East, a printed Europe, a widescreen America; and the continents negotiate within us without losing their respective place. Each one of us is, simultaneously, God, Reason and Emotion; theocrat, ideocrat, videocrat; saint, hero and star. We dream of ourselves as standing outside time; we think about our century; we wonder what to do with our evening.

Experimental Jetset

Design and Ideology

2008

"we don't see ideology as something that has to be 'haved', that has to be owned or studied in order to design. To us, ideology is something that can be generated during the actual act of designing"

Experimental Jetset is a Dutch graphic design studio founded in 1997 by Marieke Stolk, Erwin Brinkers, and Danny van den Dungen. Their linguistically playful body of work, centering on printed matter, emerges from a modernist sensibility.

....

00. Discussing design and ideology is of course rather difficult because it's such a big and complex issue.

We agree; it's an incredibly large subject. Thinking about how to tackle it, we came to the conclusion that there are two possible ways how to approach the issue: we could either investigate the notion of ideology-as-design, or the notion of design-as-ideology.

The first notion, ideology-as-design, would lead us to explore the idea of ideologies as designed entities in themselves. This is not a farfetched notion at all; in fact, most ideologies did not evolve organically, but were clearly constructed, in limited amounts of time, by limited amounts of people. In other words, these ideologies were designed.

The most obvious examples of designed ideologies are of course the many art movements that sprung up around the beginning of the 20th century. Many of these movements (Surrealism, Dada, Futurism, etc.) did not solely propagate a specific artistic program, but very often, within their carefully crafted manifestos, offered a very complete view on the world ('Weltanschauung'). In that sense, many of the 'isms' coming from the realms of literature, painting and design can be seen as full-fledged ideologies.

In the context of designed ideologies we can also mention the way in which Régis Debray, in his marvellous 'Socialism and Print' (more about that essay later), describes socialism: as a movement fabricated by printers, typographers, publicists and librarians. In other words, in Debray's essay, socialism is not only designed; it is graphically designed.

And, to mention just one more example, let us not forget how many religions and belief systems are designed as well. Take for instance the First Council of Nicaea (325 AD), in which a small group of religious leaders compiled and edited the Bible into the form we now know it, during a brief cut-and-paste session that can only be seen as an act of design.

In fact, it is precisely the fact that many ideologies and belief systems are fully based on texts (scriptures, manifestos) that shows us the construction of ideology-as-design. Just as texts only exist in their designed form, ideologies only exist as designed entities as well.

The second notion, design-as-ideology, leads us down an interesting path as well. After all, the notion of design is intrinsically linked to the ideology of 'makeability': the idea that we are living in a world that can be understood by people, interpreted by people, and thus can also be consciously shaped by people.

In English, the word 'makeability' might not have the same resonance as the Dutch translation 'maakbaarheid'; but we can assure you that, in the Netherlands, the word 'maakbaarheid' is loaded with ideology, inextricably associated with social-democracy and the welfare state.

The notion of makeability and the notion of design cannot be seen apart from each other; there is no possible way that they can be separated (nor should they). It is only logical that the awareness of the fact that the world around us can be shaped by people (makeability) will automatically lead to the actual act of shaping the world around us (design), and vice versa.

In that sense, every designed object, every cultural artefact, is a manifestation of the ideology of makeability, an ideology summed up best by Marx' famous axiom "If man is shaped by his surroundings, his surroundings must be made human". (Or, to speak with Devo, "whip it / into shape").

Following this line of thought, every designer is an ideologist, whether he/she likes it or not.

It is this line of thinking ('design-as-ideology') that we would like to follow to its logical conclusion in this interview.

01. What is an ideological designer? What does ideology as an idea mean to you as graphic designers? Are you driven by ideology or are you just interested in the notion of ideology? Is ideology important in design?

As we already established in the above introduction, design is intrinsically linked with ideology, so in our view, every designer is ideological, whether he/she is aware of it or not. This has been our opinion from the very beginning of our career. However, precisely a year ago, we read an essay that reaffirmed our beliefs, in a very enthusing and energizing way. That essay was 'Socialism and Print' by Régis Debray, published in issue 46 (July/August 2007) of *New Left Review* (this essay was later placed online, under the title 'Socialism: A Life-Cycle').

'Socialism and Print' is the best article about graphic design that we read in a very long time, taking into consideration that Debray nowhere actually mentions the word 'graphic design'. No wonder, as during the period that Debray describes (the birth and early years of socialism) the word 'graphic design' was still non-existent. However, when Debray describes the versatile subculture of printers, typographers, librarians and publishers that turned out to be the cradle of socialism, it is not hard to see that the not-named-yet heart of this "craft-based network" (as Debray himself describes it) is what later became widely known as 'graphic design'.

It is a rollercoaster-ride of a read, in which Debray repeatedly shows the many ways in which socialism grew from a particular ecosystem, an ecosystem consisting of printing and typography. Debray calls this system the 'graphosphere', and situates this sphere in the period running from 1448 to 1968; in fact, in our own interpretation of his text, the word 'graphosphere' could as well be a synonym for 'modernism', a modernism starting with the Gutenberg Revolution, and ending with the rise of postmodernism.

In Debray's 'graphosphere', ideology is a product of design, rather than design being a product of ideology, which is an exhilarating revelation. Debray's enthusiasm is contaminating: it is not hard to suddenly see socialism as the political manifestation of graphic design, and modernism as the social manifestation of graphic design. Design is not a tool to spread ideology; it is the other way around.

"An Olympic marathon: the glow of a letter (…) passing from runner to runner, the heart of the message laying precisely in its transmission". The glow of a letter, the transmission as the heart of the message… Debray is talking about something eerily close to the modern notion of graphic design, and he places it right at the center of the socialist project.

At first sight, Debray's essay seems quite straight-forward. Debray sets out to explain the demise of the socialist project, and concludes that this demise is caused by the collapse of the 'graphosphere' and the emergence of the 'videosphere': the age of the image. Seen in this light, Debray's message is all-too-familiar: the end of history, the end of print, the end of socialism, the end of modernism—the dreaded mantra of postmodernism. But sprinkled throughout the essay, there are endless glimmers of hope. Many times, Debray suggests that his simplified time line ('logosphere, graphosphere, videosphere') doesn't have to be as linear and definite as it seems. Debray leaves a lot of room for a more dialectical model of progress—a model in which the future can be shaped by the ghosts of the past. Debray mentions words such as memory ("when it is cold outside, and the night is long, memory means that we are not alone"), the archive ("the medium of history as practice"), and most significantly, includes the following paragraph:

"The greatest modernizers inaugurate their career with a backward leap, and a renaissance proceeds through a return to the past, a recycling, and hence a revolution. (…) Behind the 're' of reformation, republic or revolution, there is a hand flicking through the pages of a book, from the end back to the beginning. Whereas the finger that pushes a button, fast-forwarding a tape or disc, will never pose a danger to the establishment".

The ghost of the past as an active agent of change, as a specter of the future. The very concept of hauntology (as described by Derrida in 'Specters of Marx') invoked. The notion of dialectical progress: a future being shaped through a active dialogue with the past. Our hope, our drive, all that we believe in; it's all encapsulated in this simple paragraph.

02. Do you find it important to have a well-formulated ideology when working with design?

As we already described a few paragraphs earlier, we see ideology as a product of design rather than the other way around. We don't see ideology as something that has to be 'haved', that has to be owned or studied in order to design. To us, ideology is something that can be generated during the actual act of designing.

What we find so fascinating about graphic design is precisely that, in its ideal form, it is a perfect example of 'praxis': a synthesis of theory and practice in which each informs the other, simultaneously. In the true practice of graphic design, the artificial borders between manual labor and intellectual labor are torn down. Thinking becomes a form of making, and making becomes a form of thinking.

In 'Socialism and Print', Debray hints at a similar model of praxis, when he refers to both the professional typographer and the professional printer as quintessentially a "'worker intellectual or intellectual worker', the very ideal of that human type who would become the pivot of socialism: 'the conscious proletarian'".

03. How does your relation to ideology affect your methodology?

Right after we graduated, there was a short period in which we were truly obsessed with Guy Debord's 'Society of the Spectacle'. In retrospect, it might have been a somewhat childish obsession, but it did influence our methodology profoundly, to this very day.

We are sure that most of you are familiar with Debord's famous essay, but if we had to explain it very briefly: in 'Society of the Spectacle', Debord critiques what he calls the 'society spectacle' (Debray would call it 'the videosphere', others would call it the postmodernist condition): a world dominated by images, representations, projections. A society of alienation, in which images are completely separated from their material base.

This essay was quite an eye-opener for us, and we responded in a very literal way: our aim became to create objects, not images. Our goal was to design pieces of printed matter that would refer to their own materiality, their own physical dimension. We wanted to design posters that would never imprison the reader in some sort of false illusion, some sort of floating image; instead, we wanted to design posters that would constantly refer to their own material base.

We tried to achieve this by literally showing the poster as 'just' a piece of printed matter, a sheet of paper with some ink on it. By using methods such as overprint, perforation, folding, etc., we wanted to focus on the poster as nothing more (but certainly nothing less) than a physical construction. Through a specific use of white, empty space, we wanted to reveal the paper, the material base of the poster. We also tried to make the poster point to its own materiality by way of 'self-referentiality': through employing references to graphic design itself, we tried to let the poster be totally honest about its role as a piece of printed matter; we really wanted to show the construction of graphic design as a medium.

(It is interesting: self-referentiality is often seen as a postmodern, ironic device; we see it as anything but. In our view, self-referentiality is essentially a modernist gesture, making transparent the conceptual construction of the designed object. After all, what can be more modernist than the wish to make a construction transparent?)

While we are writing all this, we notice that we are using the past tense, while in fact the above paragraph perfectly encapsulates the way we still work. We may have drifted from Debord a bit, but we still believe in this principle of showing the designed object as primarily a human-made construction. This methodology is indeed very closely related to the idea of makeability ('maakbaarheid') that we discussed in the first paragraph of this interview.

"If man is shaped by his surroundings, his surroundings must be made human": we absolutely believe in this. For us, 'human surroundings' are not surroundings that try to represent or reflect humans, or surroundings that are overtly responsive to humans, but surroundings that show their own physical and conceptual construction, surroundings that show that they are human-made. Everything that is made by humans, can be changed by humans: that's why the human-made always carries with it the possibility of change. To show surroundings as human-made is to constantly open the horizon of change.

04. Are there any particular commissions that you turn down because of ideological reasons?

There have been numerous commissions that we turned down because of ideological reasons, political reasons, personal reasons. emotional reasons, sometimes downright silly reasons. We have certainly made mistakes: in retrospect, we have done a couple of assignments that we shouldn't have done, while we also might have rejected a few assignments that we should have done.

So we are certainly no saints. But in general, there are a couple of types of assignments that we always turn down. First of all, in our 11 years of existence, we have always refused to work for advertising agencies. And secondly, as long-time vegetarians/vegans, we have always turned down any assignment that is connected with the meat industry. Just to give two examples.

However, we don't think it is things like these that make a designer political or not. The way in which a designer selects his/her assignments, the question whether a design carries a political or commercial message, the political orientation of the client, etc. etc.—for us, things like these do not automatically affect the true political potential of the designed object. In our opinion, the true political potential of a designed object is foremost located in its aesthetic dimension. It is the aesthetical that makes the design political. (And just to be absolutely clear: when we say 'aesthetic', we are not just referring to the composition of forms, but also to the composition of ideas, of references, of concepts).

05. Can design make the world a better place to live in? Do you think that graphic designers in particular have an important role to play here?

David Carson (whose work we admire, by the way) once said that "graphic design will save the world, right after rock & roll does", which was supposedly meant as an ironic remark. However, this remark is only ironic when you assume that rock & roll won't save the world. We actually think rock & roll can save the world, and so can graphic design. To put it more concretely, we absolutely believe in the transformative, utopian potential of aesthetics.

As we already explained, our world view is somewhat shaped by Debord's idea of the 'spectacle society', and also by a slightly Marxist notion of alienation. In short, this means that we actually think we are living in a state of constant alienation. This state of alienation is not just one of many problems; we see it as the underlying problem, of which all other problems are, to a greater or lesser extent, merely symptoms. The only way out of this alienation is the "liberation of the senses", as Marx called it. In our opinion, this "liberation of the senses" can certainly be found in the de-alienating power of aesthetics.

Let us be clear that we are absolutely convinced that we are living in a world of extreme misery. Billions of people are starving to death. Day after day, innocent men, women and children are being killed, tortured, raped. There is no justice, no meaning, no logic. We are living in a valley of utter darkness. The fact that we are stupidly lucky enough to be part of the small percentage of people who live in considerable wealth doesn't make us feel better at all; the continuous feeling of guilt is a torture in itself, and we do carry it around like a shadow. Add to that the unspeakable cruelty that we, as humans, inflict on animals. Millions of living creatures are abused, mutilated and slaughtered everyday. Pigs, who are supposedly smarter and more sensible than cats and dogs, are born into a living nightmare: they are robbed from any love and affection, kicked around, castrated without anaesthetic, locked into brutally small cages, electrocuted, and skinned while they are barely dead. What we, as humans, do to each other is one thing; but what we do to animals is so extremely sadistic, so merciless; it's impossible to capture in words. These are the things that really keep us awake, night after night.

So how can we justify, to ourselves, the fact that we are spending all of our time on the micro-aesthetics of graphic design? How can we explain to ourselves all the hours, days, months and years that we put into wordplay, abstract composition and obscure pop-cultural references?

Herbert Marcuse asks himself the very thing in the beginning of his marvellous essay 'The Aesthetic Dimension'. His first sentence is this: "In a situation where the miserable reality can be changed only through radical political praxis, the concern with aesthetics demands justification". In the rest of the essay, he explains in crystal clear words why the concern with aesthetics is fully justified; more than that, he shows that aesthetics is a form of radical political praxis in itself. In fact, Marcuse states that, in order for an aesthetic practice (Marcuse uses literature as an example) to be truly political, it should stay clear of explicit political messages:

"Literature is not revolutionary because it is written for the working class or for 'the revolution'. Literature can be called revolutionary in a meaningful sense only with reference to itself, as content having become form. The political potential of art lies only in its own aesthetic dimension (…) The more immediately political the work of art, the more it reduces the power of estrangement and the radical, transcendent goals of change. In this sense, there may be more subversive potential in the poetry of Baudelaire and Rimbaud than in the didactic plays of Brecht".

Note that, when Marcuse says 'estrangement', he actually suggests 'de-estrangement'. In a world that is already alienated, the truly de-alienating will appear as something alienating. Or, better said: only alienating art has the power to de-alienate. In the words of Marcuse: "On the basis of aesthetic sublimation, a de-sublimation takes place in the perception of individuals—in their feelings, judgments, thoughts; an invalidation of dominant norms, needs and values". For us, Marcuse is talking here about Marx' "liberation of the senses". And we do think that what Marcuse describes here not only holds true for literature, but for any aesthetic practice, including graphic design.

This idea, of the transformative, utopian (and thus subversive) potential of aesthetics, is often ridiculed, obviously by critics, but also by designers themselves. Designers are generally very good at self-depreciation: "I'm just drawing pictures", "what do I know?", "it's not rocket science". In contrast, it is interesting to note that it is exactly those with concrete political power, the leaders and rulers, who are very much aware (and afraid) of the subversive power of aesthetics.

We recently read the autobiography of the musician Caetano Veloso ('Tropical Truth', a very inspiring book), and in it, Veloso describes (among a lot of other things) his detention: in 1969, both he and Gilberto Gil were arrested by the right-wing Junta of Brazil. Ironically, Tropicalia, the musical movement started by Gil and Veloso, was often attacked by the Brazilian Left for not making any explicit political statements; and yet it was Gil and Veloso who were captured, and later exiled from Brazil. In a startling passage, Veloso describes being interrogated by one of the military captains: "He [the captain] alluded to some of my statements to the press in which the term 'deconstruct' had appeared, and using it as the keyword, he denounced the insidious subversive power of our work. He said he understood clearly that what Gil and I were doing was much more dangerous than the work of artists who were engaged in explicit protests and political activity".

In other words, those who dabble in very concrete political power (the leaders, the rulers) are all-too-well aware of the subversive potential of aesthetics; it's surprising that not more designers are.

06. Do you think that art and design have a similar function here?

We see both art and design as aesthetic practices, so we certainly think that both have the same subversive potential, the same transformative power. We realize this is a leap of faith, as nowhere in 'The Aesthetic Dimension' Marcuse actually mentions graphic design; he focuses very specifically on literature. But then again, when we look at Marcuse's definition of aesthetics, we think he is describing something that is very close to graphic design as we know it. Marcuse describes aesthetics as "the result of the transformation of a given content (an actual or historical, personal or social fact) into a self-contained whole", and we certainly see graphic design as the act of transforming given content into self-contained entities.

Moreover, in the beginning of the 'The Aesthetic Dimension', there is a page containing acknowledgments in which Marcuse thanks his son Peter, "whose work in urban planning led us to common problems". If the premise is that literature and urban planning both deal with common aesthetic problems, it is fair to say that graphic design deals with aesthetic problems as well.

But then again, Marcuse might have been horrified by the idea of graphic design as an aesthetic practice. In the end, we are dealing with our own interpretation of his writings. In the same way the book shapes the reader, the reader also shapes the book.

07. Can you see that your background, being brought up in the Netherlands/Sweden (as two welfare states with similarities in its politics) has influenced your attitude to ideology in relation to your practice as designers?

Absolutely. Our work is a direct result of the welfare state, a clear manifestation of it, and we are very aware of that. This whole notion of social-democracy, of makeability (maakbaarheid) is encapsulated in the inner-cells of our work.

This we also recognize in Nille's work. He might disagree, but when we look at his work, we really see the language of Swedish social-democracy in the 60s and 70s, the context in which we assume Nille grew up. In the same way, our work is formed by the language of the Dutch social-democracy in which we grew up.

In that sense, we really are children of the welfare state. We shouldn't shy away from that incredibly interesting cultural heritage.

Many designers and critics coming from countries unfamiliar with this typical Scandinavian/Dutch model of the welfare state have a very one-dimensional take on the relationship between design and social-democracy. In their view, the design mentality that exists in our countries is the direct result of government funding and subsidy systems. Needless to say, this view is completely misguided.

In fact, the situation is the other way around: our collective design mentality is not a product of our subsidy system; our subsidy system is a product of our collective design mentality. Subsidy and funding are very conscious acts of design, committed by the welfare state to shape itself, a tremendous process in which the designer becomes part of the collective, and the collective becomes part of the designer. This process is definitely not something to be cynical about.

We think it is significant that both we and Nille are now experiencing the dismantling of the welfare state, which basically means the destruction of the things our childhood memories were filled with.

In our case, this dismantling only strengthens our desire to keep referring to the language of social-democracy, against the tide of neo-liberalism. We want our graphic design to serve as a sort of memory, a subjective archive, of social-democratic aesthetics.

Debray writes in 'Socialism and Print' about the archive as a "medium for history as practice", and argues that "the story of communism—as revolutionary utopia, not bureaucratic dictatorship—has been a tale of archivists and old papers". The story of social-democracy—as aesthetic language, and as childhood memory—will be a tale of old papers as well; we are designing those papers right now, in the form of posters, catalogs and t-shirt prints.

08. Are you modernists? What kind of relation do you have to modernist design?

There was a time that we were a bit reluctant to call ourselves modernists: the designation 'modernist' always felt too much like a honorary title, something you had to deserve rather than something you can just call yourself. Also, 'modernism' always seemed so hard to define; there are so many interpretations of it.

However, if we take our own interpretation of modernism as a starting point, we certainly think we can be considered modernists of some sort. For us, modernism can be defined by two propositions: the assumption that we are shaped by our material environment, and the assumption that it is possible, even desirable, for us to shape this material environment. Since we can safely say that these are the principles we work and live by, we would definitely place ourselves in the modernist camp.

Our relationship with past modernist design is more complicated than some people might think. It is certainly not so that we believe that our work is automatically modernist because of a certain choice of typefaces, or a certain way of placing the type. Referring to the aesthetic language of past modernism is not a modernist gesture per se; but in our work, we think it is.

The reason why, in our work, we often refer to the aesthetic language of past modernist movements (and especially the language of so-called 'late modernism') is twofold. On the one hand, referring to historical modernism is for us a way to achieve the 'self-referentiality' we already discussed a few paragraphs earlier. In our opinion, by letting graphic design refer to its own modernist history, the construction of the medium becomes visible, which we see as a modernist gesture.
On the other hand, the references to late modernism in our work have a clear emotional undertone. For us, late modernism is the context in which we grew up, our childhood, our natural language, our mother tongue. In our work, we are actively investigating late modernism, because it is the material environment that shaped us. This makes our emotional motive also a modernist one.

09. Do you think that our rapidly changing society (influenced by 'the market', rapid globalization and dismantling of the welfare state etc.) has created a new situation and platform for an ideological discussion in design? Are we at a paradigm shift? Can we compare the present situation with what was going on in the sixties and seventies?

A paradigm shift for sure. As we have seen, Debray places this schism in 1969, with the rise of what he calls 'the videosphere'. Others situate this rupture around 1989: the fall of the Berlin Wall, and the evaporation of the Iron Curtain.

It was inevitable that, after the age of modernism, we would experience a backlash, almost a regression to pre-modern times. Because that is how we ultimately see post-modernism: as a slight return to the period before modernism. (Of course, it isn't an actual return; in true dialectical fashion, it's more of a synthesis of modern means and pre-modern ideals).

If we had to sketch, in a couple of seconds, in a few simple sentences, a general time line, it would look roughly like this:

1. Pre-modern times, in which we are governed by untouchable forces from above: the laws of the jungle, gods, superstition, Platonic ideas floating high in the sky.

2. The age of modernism, in which we free ourselves from these forces from above, and see the world around us as something that could and should be interpreted and shaped by ourselves.

3. The postmodernist condition, in which we believe again in the laws of the jungle (free market capitalism) and untouchable forces from above (the 'market', the 'public', the 'target audience', the 'shareholders', etc.). Not surprisingly, this age is also characterized by a new uprising of religiosity (Islam Fundamentalism, the Christian Right).

To get back to your question, we are definitely aware that we entered the age of post-modernism. What does this, in concrete terms, mean for graphic design as a practice, as a craft?

First of all, we see the rise of the advertising agency in the cultural sphere. In areas that used to be the natural habitats of independent designers and small design studios (areas such as art institutes, book publishing, theatre, etc.), we see that the role of the graphic designer is getting increasingly marginalised. In an attempt to shed their ideological ballast, more and more of these cultural commissioners turn to advertising agencies (dressed up as hip communication agencies). This institutional desire to shed ideological weight cannot be seen separately from the widespread phenomenon of privatization, and the dismantling of the welfare state.

Secondly, we see more and more attempts to rename graphic design: 'visual communication', 'branding', 'innovation', 'design research', 'service design', 'concept

EXPERIMENTAL JETSET, DESIGN AND IDEOLOGY

development', 'image building', etc. etc. All these labels deny the material base of graphic design (printed matter) by cutting the ties that bind us to graphic production methods. These are deliberate attempts to let graphic design dissolve into a visual culture without memory, without ideological weight, without material ground, without terra firma.

Thirdly, we see that the role of printed matter is under attack, not only by the obvious online ('virtual') means of distribution, but also by methods coming from the sphere of printing itself: printing-on-demand, digital printing and other quick print media. With this, it looks as if we are at risk of losing the stubborn permanence of printed matter, its universal dimension and ideological weight, its 'slowness' so to speak (Debray speaks of the "delayed-action mechanism" of printed matter).

This is a very bleak picture indeed. What can we do? (And when we say 'we', we specifically mean us three; we aren't so vain that we automatically expect others to share our concerns).

As Debray writes, the 'graphosphere' (modernism) collapsed "when print lost its lead", which we think is a very interesting metaphor. Obviously, lead refers to typesetting, but it can also refer to a weight, a counterbalance, a sort of anchor needed to keep culture grounded to its material base. Print might have lost its lead in a literal way, but we think it is still possible to let graphic design function as a ballast, as a weight to keep culture grounded.

For Debray, the 'graphosphere' might be over, but for us, the struggle has just begun. We do believe we can keep the 'graphosphere' alive, if not as a dominant force, then at least as an underground movement, as an undercurrent. True, graphic design is being marginalised, but let's not forget that margins are in fact graphic spaces; the margins are ours.

Essential Design
| Toward Timelessness

The appearance is trendiness—but the essence is timeless.

Massimo Vignelli   2014

From the rubble left by deconstructionism emerged design that cultivated clarity of communication, tempered by a measure of humanism,
valuing honesty over manipulation and simplicity over complexity.
A new iteration of modernism was born: essential design.

Emphasizing clean execution resulting from logical consideration allowed designers to revisit the discourse of modern design through a new lens. Essential design relied on understanding the physical and psychological interactions of the user in order to create designs that work. Design became about identifying a problem and creating a focused solution without any extraneous clutter—an approach that opposed the deconstructivist method of expression. A minimalist aesthetic allowed design to transcend the designer, but as designers used individually constructed processes to produce designs rather than adhering to what had previously been considered overarching, infallible principles, the individuality of the designer was able to sneak through to create subtle but undeniably recognizable styles. Now, past the turn of the twenty-first century and in the midst of the digital age, it has again become imperative to further define the role of the designer.

Visualization systems and the collection and analysis of big data sped into overdrive with the spread of the internet, and designers have had to respond and adapt—by relinquishing formal authority in designing flexible and responsive systems. Designers must now anticipate user interaction and experience as part of their communication strategy, and this has led to a similarly essentialist aesthetic. It has also unmistakably prompted a reevaluation of the role of the designer.

Visual simplicity and adaptive structures led designers to create system-atized and self-generating designs that are endlessly adaptable. Into the digital arena have been introduced grids that stabilize design elements across platforms, and typography has been reconsidered to function in a digital world. Designers are no longer in complete control of their designs, but instead must create designs that reflect the current and potential needs of their clients. Designers now work in what-ifs instead of absolutes. The designer today must employ a fluidity not necessary in previous generations. The hand of the designer may be less evident, but more important, than ever before.

Favor oscillates once again between expression and reason. In the words of Sir Isaac Newton, "When one body exerts a force on a second body, the second body simultaneously exerts a force equal in magnitude and opposite in direction on the first body."

Dieter Rams

Ten Principles for Good Design
1970

Omit the Unimportant
1989

"back to purity, back to simplicity"

Dieter Rams (1932–) is a German industrial designer closely associated with the electronics company Braun and the furniture company Vitsœ. His minimal and functional designs have influenced many products and companies, including Apple.

....

Ten Principles for Good Design
1970

1. Good design is innovative
The possibilities for innovation are not, by any means, exhausted. Technological development is always offering new opportunities for innovative design. But innovative design always develops in tandem with innovative technology, and can never be an end in itself.

2. Good design makes a product useful
A product is bought to be used. It has to satisfy certain criteria, not only functional, but also psychological and aesthetic. Good design emphasises the usefulness of a product whilst disregarding anything that could possibly detract from it.

3. Good design is aesthetic
The aesthetic quality of a product is integral to its usefulness because products we use every day affect our person and our well-being. But only well-executed objects can be beautiful.

4. Good design makes a product understandable
It clarifies the product's structure. Better still, it can make the product talk. At best, it is self-explanatory.

5. Good design is unobtrusive
Products fulfilling a purpose are like tools. They are neither decorative objects nor works of art. Their design should therefore be both neutral and restrained, to leave room for the user's self-expression.

6. Good design is honest
It does not make a product more innovative, powerful or valuable than it really is. It does not attempt to manipulate the consumer with promises that cannot be kept.

7. Good design is long-lasting
It avoids being fashionable and therefore never appears antiquated. Unlike fashionable design, it lasts many years—even in today's throwaway society.

8. Good design is thorough down to the last detail
Nothing must be arbitrary or left to chance. Care and accuracy in the design process show respect towards the user.

9. Good design is environmentally-friendly
Design makes an important contribution to the preservation of the environment. It conserves resources and minimises physical and visual pollution throughout the lifecycle of the product.

10. Good design is as little design as possible
Less, but better—because it concentrates on the essential aspects, and the products are not burdened with non-essentials.

Back to purity, back to simplicity.

"I don't support dull or boring design but I do take a stand against the ruthless exploitation of people's weaknesses for visual and haptic signals, which many designers are engaged in"

Omit the Unimportant

1989

....

Every industrial product serves a specific purpose. People do not buy a specific product just to look at it, rather because it performs certain functions. Its design must conform in the best possible way to the expectations that result from the function the product fulfills. The more intensive and explicit the product's use, the clearer the demands on design. That all sounds very obvious, but anyone who looks at our environment will discover a host of products whose design is not substantiated by any functional necessities. Often you can count yourself lucky if the design is not disturbing during use. Rigid functionalism of the past has been somewhat discredited in recent years. Perhaps justly so because the functions a product had to fulfill were often seen too narrowly and with too much puritanism. The spectrum of people's needs is often greater than designers are willing, or sometimes able, to admit. Functionalism may well be a term with a multitude of definitions; however, there is no alternative.

One of the most significant design principles is to omit the unimportant in order to emphasize the important. The time has come for us to discover our environment anew and return to the simple basic aspects, for example, to items that have unconstructed obvious-seeming functionalism in both the physical and the psychological sense. Therefore, products should be well designed and as neutral and open as possible, leaving room for the self-expression of those using them.

Good design means as little design as possible. Not for reasons of economy or convenience. Arriving at a really convincing, harmonious form by employing simple means is surely a difficult task. The other way is easier and, as paradoxical as it may seem, often cheaper, but also more thoughtless with respect to production. Complicated, unnecessary forms are nothing more than designers' escapades that function as self-expression instead of expressing the product's functions. The reason is often that design is used to gain a superficial redundancy.

The economy of Braun design is a rejection of this type of approach. Braun products eliminate the superfluous to emphasize that which is more important. For example, the contours of the object become more placid, soothing, perceptible, and long-living. Much design today is modish sensation, and the rapid change of fashion outdates products quickly. The choices are sensible: disciplined simplicity or forced, oppressive, stupifying expression. For me there is only one way: discipline.

Every manufactured item sends out signals to the mind or emotions. These signals—strong or weak, wanted or unwanted, clear or hidden—create feelings. But the most important factor is whether the item can communicate its use. Of course, a product's effect is also important. What sentiments does it evoke? People are very much directly influenced and emotionally moved by the design of items surrounding them, often without realizing this immediately.

My own experience can be summarized in two theses. First, items should be designed in such a way that their function and attributes are directly understood. For design, this is an opportunity and a challenge. Until recently, this task hasn't been taken very seriously and the opportunity hasn't been used enough. The self-explanatory quality of most products is low especially in innovative fields where it is very important that a product's utility is understood without the frustrating continuous studies of user's instructions. Design riddles are impudent, and products that are informative, understandable, and clear are pleasant and agreeable. Of course, getting products to "talk" by means of design is a demanding task. Creativity, experience, tenacity, ability, and diligence are necessary.

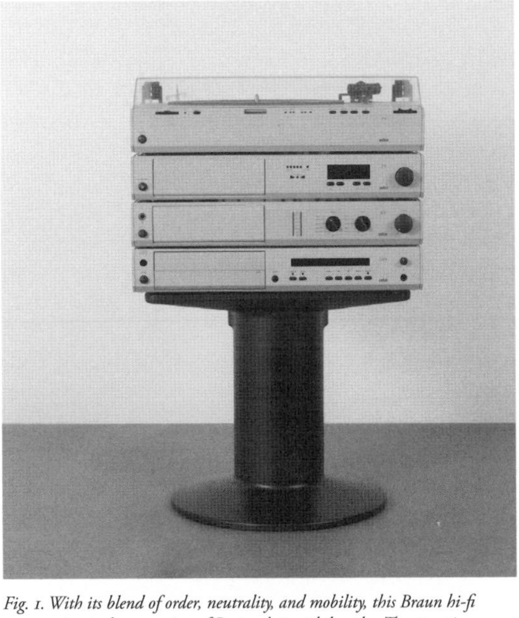

Second, the fewer the opportunities used to create informative design, the more design serves to evoke emotional responses. This is not always conscious but more or less instinctive, created by fireworks of signals that the products send out. Often these responses are so intense that they are confusing. I try to fight against them. I don't want to be dominated, nor do I want to be excited, stupified or amazed. I refuse to be surprised

Fig. 1. With its blend of order, neutrality, and mobility, this Braun hi-fi construction is the expression of Braun design philosophy. The operating components that are seldom used are set in the back of the stereo. The entanglement of wires is concealed behind a cover so that the stereo may be placed in an open space. Design: Peter Hartwein.

by the steadily increasing dynamic of taste. I refuse, as well, to submit to widespread demands or structures, of the market without asking for the product's use.

The latest design trends are intended to evoke emotions by trivial, superficial means. It is not a question of information for use, nor a problem of insight and perception in a broader sense. The issue is stimuli: new, strong, exciting, and therefore aggressive signals. The primary aim is to be recognized as intensely as possible. The aggressiveness of design is expressed in the harshness of combat to attain first place in people's perception and awareness and to win the fight for a front place in store display windows.

I don't support dull or boring design, but I do take a stand against the ruthless exploitation of people's weaknesses for visual and haptic signals, which many designers are engaged in. The festival of colors and forms and the entertainment of form sensations enlarges the world's chaos. To outdo each other with new design sensations leads nowhere. The alternative is to return to simplicity. And that requires working hard and seriously.

This task is not only for designers. Participation is required by all those involved in developing new products, and by the public as well. Aggressive individuality must be abandoned. We should not forego innovation, but reject novelty as the sole aim. Our culture is our home, especially the everyday culture expressed in items for whose forms I am responsible. It would be a great help if we could feel more at home in this everyday culture, if alienation, confusion and sensory overload would lessen.

Fig. 2. Input functions of this Braun pocket calculator are coded in green, output functions are in red. The clear legible display and the arched keys facilitate fast computations. If the power switch is left on, it automatically turns itself off after six minutes. Design: Dietrich Lubs.

Instead of trying to outdo our rivals, we designers should work together more seriously and thoughtfully. Designers are critics of civilization, technology, and society. But contrary to the many qualified and unqualified critical minds of our time, designers cannot stop there. They must continue to look for something new, something that ensues from the criticism and that can stand up against it. In addition, they cannot remain at the level of words, reflections, considerations, warnings, accusations, or slogans. They must transpose their insights into concrete, three-dimensional objects.

Of the many issues that confront designers, the increase of violence seems to be the most threatening. Destructive, aggressive tendencies are gaining momentum and counteract the idea on which design was founded. It is a frontal attack. I work in the hope of designing objects that are useful and convincing enough to be accepted and lived with for a long time in a very obvious, natural way. But such objects do not fit into a world of vandalism, aggression, and cynicism. In this kind of world, there is not room for design or culture of any type.

Design is the effort to make products in such a way that they are useful to people. It is more rational than irrational, optimistic and projected toward the future rather than resigned, cynical, and indifferent. Design means being steadfast and progressive rather than escaping and giving up. In a historical phase in which the outer world has become less natural and increasingly artificial and commercial, the value of design increases. The work of designers can contribute more concretely and effectively toward a more humane existence in the future.

Fig. 3. This Braun wall clock exemplified aesthetic functionality and adaptability with an economical use of its resources and a distinctly legible clock face. It has a metal casing and a plexiglass cover. Design: Dietrich Lubs.

6-2

Jürgen Habermas

Modernity versus Postmodernity
1981

"in the history of modern art one can detect a trend toward ever greater autonomy in the definition and practice of art"

"let me briefly distinguish the antimodernism of the young conservatives from the premodernism of the old conservatives and from the postmodernism of the neoconservatives"

Jürgen Habermas (1929–) is a German sociologist and critical theorist. He is known for engaging in public debates on resisting the normalization of Germany's Nazi past, as well as for his writings on communicative action and pragmatism. His writings on art examine the links between rationality and aesthetics.

....

Last year, architects were admitted to the Biennial in Venice, following painters and film-makers. The note sounded at this first Architecture Biennial was one of disappointment. I would describe it by saying that those who exhibited in Venice formed an avant-garde of reversed fronts. I mean that they sacrificed the tradition of modernity in order to make room for a new historicism. Upon this occasion, a critic of the German newspaper, *Frankfurter Allgemeine Zeitung*, advanced a thesis whose significance reaches beyond this particular event; it is a diagnosis of our times: "Postmodernity definitely presents itself as Antimodernity." This statement describes an emotional current of our times which has penetrated all spheres of intellectual life. It has placed on the agenda theories of post-enlightenment, postmodernity, even of posthistory.

From history we know the phrase:

"The Ancients and the Moderns"

Let me begin by defining these concepts. The term "modern" has a long history, one which has been investigated by Hans Robert Jauss. The word "modern" in its Latin form "modernus" was used for the first time in the late 5th century in order to distinguish the present, which had become officially Christian, from the Roman and pagan past. With varying content, the term "modern" again and again expresses the consciousness of an epoch that relates itself to the past of antiquity, in order to view itself as the result of a transition from the old to the new.

Some writers restrict this concept of "modernity" to the Renaissance, but this is historically too narrow. People considered themselves modern during the period of Charles the Great, in the 12th century, as well as in France of the late 17th century, at the time of the famous "Querelle des Anciens et des Modernes." This is to say, the term "modern" appeared and reappeared exactly during those periods in Europe when the consciousness of a new epoch formed itself through a renewed relationship to the ancients—whenever, moreover, antiquity was considered a model to be recovered through some kind of imitation.

The spell which the classics of the ancient world cast upon the spirit of later times was first dissolved with the ideals of the French Enlightenment. Specifically, the idea of being "modern" by looking back to the ancients changed with the belief, inspired by modern science, in the infinite progress of knowledge and in the infinite advance towards social and moral betterment. Another form of modernist consciousness was formed in the wake of this change. The romantic modernist sought to oppose the antique ideals of the classicists; he looked for a new historical epoch, and found it in the idealized Middle Ages. However, this new ideal age, established early in the 19th century, did not remain a fixed ideal. In the course of the 19th century, there emerged out of this romantic spirit that radicalized consciousness of modernity which freed itself from all specific historical ties. This most recent modernism simply makes an abstract opposition between tradition and the present; and we are, in a way, still the contemporaries of that kind of aesthetic modernity which first appeared in the midst of the 19th century. Since then, the distinguishing mark of works, which count as modern, is the "new." The characteristic of such works is "the new" which will be overcome and made obsolete through the novelty of the next style. But, while that which is merely "stylish" will soon become out-moded, that which is modern preserves a secret tie to the classical. Of course, whatever can survive time has always been considered to be a classic. But the emphatically modern document no longer borrows this power of being a classic from the authority of a past epoch; instead, a modern work becomes a classic because it has once been authentically modern. Our sense of modernity creates its own self-enclosed canons of being classic. In this sense we speak, e.g., in view of the history of modern art, of classical modernity. The relation between "modern" and "classical" has definitely lost a fixed historical reference.

The Discipline of Aesthetic Modernity

The spirit and discipline of aesthetic modernity assumed clear contours in the work of Baudelaire. Modernity then unfolded in various avant-garde movements, and finally reached its climax in the Café Voltaire of the Dadaists, and in Surrealism. Aesthetic modernity is characterized by attitudes which find a common focus in a changed consciousness of time. This time consciousness expresses itself through metaphors of the vanguard and the avant-garde. The avant-garde understands itself as invading unknown territory, exposing itself to the dangers of sudden, of shocking encounters, conquering an as yet unoccupied future. The avant-garde must find a direction in a landscape into which no one seems to have yet ventured.

But these forward gropings, this anticipation of an undefined future and the cult of the new, mean in fact the exaltation of the present. The new time consciousness, which enters philosophy in the writings of Bergson, does more than express the experience of mobility in society, acceleration in history, of discontinuity in everyday life. The new value placed on the transitory, the elusive, and the ephemeral, the very celebration of dynamism, discloses the longing for an undefiled, an immaculate and stable present.

This explains the rather abstract language in which the modernist temper has spoken of the "past." Individual epochs lose their distinct forces. Historical memory is replaced by the heroic affinity of the present with the extremes of history: a sense of time wherein decadence immediately recognizes itself in the barbaric, the wild and the primitive. We observe the anarchistic intention of blowing up the continuum of history, and we can account for it in terms of the subversive force of this new aesthetic consciousness. Modernity revolts against the normalizing functions of tradition; modernity lives on the experience of rebelling against all that is normative. This revolt is one way to neutralize the standards of both morality and utility. This aesthetic consciousness continuously stages a dialectical play between secrecy and public scandal; it is addicted to the fascination of that horror which accompanies the act of profaning, and is yet always in flight from the trivial results of profanation.

On the other hand, the time consciousness articulated in avant-garde art is not simply ahistorical; it is directed against what might be called a false normativity in history. The modern, avant-garde spirit has sought, instead, to use the past in a different way; it disposes over those pasts which have been made available by the objectifying scholarship of historicism, but it opposes at the same time a neutralized history, which is locked up in the museum of historicism.

Drawing upon the spirit of surrealism, Walter Benjamin constructs the relationship of modernity to history, in what I would call a post-historicist attitude. He reminds us of the self-understanding of the French Revolution: "The Revolution cited ancient Rome, just as fashion cites an antiquated dress. Fashion has a scent for what is current, whenever this moves within the thicket of what was once." This is Benjamin's concept of the *Jetztzeit*, of the present as a moment of revelation; a time, in which splinters of a messianic presence are enmeshed. In this sense, for Robespierre, the antique Rome was a past laden with momentary revelations.

Now, this spirit of aesthetic modernity has recently begun to age. It has been recited once more in the 1960s; after the 1970s, however, we must admit to ourselves that this modernism arouses a much fainter response today than it did fifteen years ago. Octavio Paz, a fellow traveller of modernity, noted already in the middle of the 1960s that "the avant-garde of 1967 repeats the deeds and gestures of those of 1917. We are experiencing the end of the idea of modern art." The work of Peter Bürger has since taught us to speak of "post-avant-garde" art; this term is chosen to indicate the failure of the surrealist rebellion. But, what is the meaning of this failure? Does it signal a farewell to modernity? Thinking more generally, does the existence of a post-avant-garde mean there is a transition to that broader phenomenon called postmodernity?

This is in fact how Daniel Bell, the most brilliant of the American neoconservatives, interprets matters. In his book, *The Cultural Contradictions of Capitalism*, Bell argues that the crises of the developed societies of the West are to be traced back to a split between culture and society. Modernist culture has come to penetrate the values of everyday life; the life-world is infected by modernism. Because of the forces of modernism, the principle of unlimited self-realization, the demand for authentic self-experience and the subjectivism of a hyperstimulated sensitivity have come to be dominant. This temperament unleashes hedonistic motives irreconcilable with the discipline of professional life in society, Bell says. Moreover, modernist culture is altogether incompatible with the moral basis of a purposive rational conduct of life. In this manner, Bell places the burden of responsibility for the dissolution of the Protestant ethic (a phenomenon which has already disturbed Max Weber) on the "adversary culture." Culture, in its modern form, stirs up hatred against the conventions and virtues of an everyday life, which has become rationalized under the pressures of economic and administrative imperatives.

I would call your attention to a complex wrinkle in this view. The impulse of modernity, we are told on the other hand, is exhausted; anyone who considers himself avant-garde can read his own death warrant. Although the avant-garde is still considered to be expanding, it is supposedly no longer creative. Modernism is dominant but dead. For the neoconservative, the question then arises: how can norms arise in society which will limit libertinism, reestablish the ethic of discipline and work? What new norms will put a brake on the levelling caused by the social welfare state, so that the virtues of individual competition for achievement can again dominate? Bell sees a religious revival to be the only solution. Religious faith tied to a faith in tradition will provide individuals with clearly defined identities, and with existential security.

Cultural Modernity and Societal Modernization

One can certainly not conjure up by magic the compelling beliefs which command authority. Analyses like Bell's, therefore, only result in an attitude which is spreading in Germany no less than here in the States: an intellectual and political confrontation with the carriers of cultural modernity. I cite Peter Steinfells, an observer of the new style which the neoconservatives have imposed upon the intellectual scene in the 1970s.

> The struggles takes the form of exposing every manifestation of what could be considered an oppositionist mentality and tracing its "logic" so as to link it to various forms of extremism: drawing the connection between modernism and nihilism…between government regulation and totalitarianism, between criticism of arms expenditures and subservience to communism, between Women's liberation or homosexual rights and the destruction of the family…between the Left generally and terrorism, anti-semitism, and fascism.…(Steinfells, *The Neoconservatives*, p. 65)

The *ad hominem* approach and the bitterness of these intellectual accusations have also been trumpeted loudly in Germany. They should not be explained so much in terms of the psychology of neoconservative writers; rather, they are rooted in the analytical weaknesses of neoconservative doctrine itself.

Neoconservatism shifts onto cultural modernism the uncomfortable burdens of a more or less successful capitalist modernization of the economy and society. The neoconservative doctrine blurs the relationship between the welcomed process of societal modernization on the one hand, and the lamented cultural development on the other. The neoconservative does not uncover the economic and social causes for the altered attitudes towards work, consumption, achievement, and leisure. Consequently, he attributes all of the following—hedonism, the lack of social identification, the lack of obedience, narcissism, the withdrawal from status and achievement competition—to the domain of "culture." In fact, however, culture is intervening in the creation of all these problems in only a very indirect and mediated fashion.

In the neoconservative view, those intellectuals who still feel themselves committed to the project of modernity are then presented as taking the place of those unanalyzed causes. The mood which feeds neoconservatism today in no way originates from the discontents about the antinomian consequences of a culture breaking from the museums into the stream of ordinary life. These discontents have not been called into life by modernist intellectuals. They are rooted in deep-seated reactions against the process of *societal* modernization. Under the pressures of the dynamics of economic growth and the organizational accomplishments of the state, this social modernization penetrates deeper and deeper into previous forms of human existence. I would describe this subordination of the life-worlds under system's imperatives as a matter of disturbing the communicative infrastructure of everyday life.

Thus, for example, neo-populist protests only bring to expression in pointed fashion a widespread fear regarding the destruction of the urban and natural environment, and of forms of human sociability. There is a certain irony about these protests in terms of neoconservatism. The tasks of passing on a cultural tradition, of social integration, and of socialization require the adherence to a criterion of communicative rationality. The occasions for protest and discontent originate exactly when spheres of communicative action, centered on the reproduction and transmission of values and norms, are penetrated by a form of modernization guided by standards of economic and administrative rationality; however, those very spheres are dependent on quite different standards of rationalization on the standards of what I would call communicative rationality. But, neoconservative doctrines turn our attention precisely away from such societal processes: they project the causes, which they do not bring to light, onto the plane of a subversive culture and its advocates.

To be sure, cultural modernity generates its own aporias as well. Independently from the consequences of *societal* modernization, and from *within the perspective* of *cultural* development itself, there originate motives for doubting the project of modernity. Having dealt with a feeble kind of criticism of modernity—that of neoconservatism—let me now move our discussion of modernity and its discontents into a different domain that touches on these aporias of cultural modernity, issues which often serve only as a pretense for those positions (which either call for a postmodernity, or recommend a return to some form of premodernity, or which throw modernity radically overboard).

The Project of Enlightenment

The idea of modernity is intimately tied to the development of European art; but what I call "the project of modernity" comes only into focus when we dispense with the usual concentration upon art. Let me start a different analysis by recalling an idea from Max Weber. He characterized cultural modernity as the separation of the substantive reason expressed in religion and metaphysics into three autonomous spheres. They are: science, morality and art. These came to be differentiated because the unified world conceptions of religion and metaphysics fell apart. Since the 18th century, the problems inherited from these older world-views could be rearranged so as to fall under specific aspects of validity: truth, normative rightness, authenticity and beauty. They could then be handled as questions of knowledge, or of justice and morality, or of taste. Scientific discourse, theories of morality, jurisprudence, the production and criticism of art, could in turn be institutionalized. Each domain of culture could be made to correspond to cultural professions, in which problems could be dealt with as the concern of special experts. This professionalized treatment of the cultural tradition brings to the fore the intrinsic structures of each of the three dimensions of culture. There appear the structures of cognitive-instrumental, moral-practical, and of aesthetic-expressive rationality, each of these under the control of specialists who seem more adept at being logical in these particular ways than other people are. As a result, the distance has grown between the culture of the experts and that of the larger public. What accrues to culture through specialized treatment and reflexion does not immediately and necessarily become the property of everyday praxis. With cultural rationalization of this sort, the threat increases that the life-world, whose traditional substance has already been devaluated, will become more and more impoverished.

The project of modernity formulated in the 18th century by the philosophers of the Enlightenment consisted in their efforts to develop objective science, universal morality and law, and autonomous art, according to their inner logic. At the same time, this project intended to release the cognitive potentials of each of these domains to set them free from their esoteric forms. The Enlightenment philosophers wanted to utilize this accumulation of specialized culture for the enrichment of everyday life, that is to say, for the rational organization of everyday social life.

Enlightenment thinkers of the cast of mind of Condorcet still had the extravagant expectation that the arts and the sciences would promote not only the control of natural forces, but would also further understanding of the world and of the self, would promote moral progress, the justice of institutions, and even the happiness of human beings. The 20th century has shattered this optimism. The differentiation of science, morality, and art has come to mean the autonomy of the segments treated by the specialist and at the same time letting them split off from the hermeneutics of everyday communication. This splitting off is the problem that has given rise to those efforts to "negate" the culture of expertise. But the problem won't go away: should we try to hold on to the *intentions* of the Enlightenment, feeble as they may be, or should we declare the entire project of modernity a lost cause? I now want to return to the problem of artistic culture, having explained why, historically, that aesthetic modernity is a part only of cultural modernity in general.

The False Programs of the Negation of Culture

Greatly oversimplifying, I would say in the history of modern art one can detect a trend toward ever greater autonomy in the definition and practice of art. The category of "beauty" and the domain of beautiful objects were first constituted in the Renaissance. In the course of the 18th century, literature, the fine arts and music were institutionalized as activities independent from sacred and courtly life. Finally, around the middle of the 19th century an aestheticist conception of art emerged, which encouraged the artist to produce his work according to the distinct consciousness of art for art's sake. The autonomy of the aesthetic sphere could then become a deliberate project: the talented artist could lend authentic expression to those experiences he had in encountering his own de-centered subjectivity, detached from the constraints of routinized cognition and everyday action.

In the mid-19th century, in painting and literature, a movement began which Octavio Paz finds epitomized already in the art criticism of Baudelaire. Color, lines, sounds and movement ceased to serve primarily the cause of representation; the media of expression and the techniques of production themselves became the aesthetic object. Theodor W. Adorno could therefore begin his *Aesthetic Theory* with the following sentence: "It is now taken for granted that nothing which concerns art can be taken for granted any more: neither art itself, nor art in its relationship to the whole, nor even the right of art to exist." And this is what surrealism then denied: *das Existenzrecht der Kunst als Kunst*. To be sure, surrealism would not have challenged the right of art to exist, if modern art no longer had advanced a promise of happiness concerning its own relationship "to the whole" of life. For Schiller, such a promise was delivered by aesthetic intuition, but not fulfilled by it. Schiller's *Letters on the Aesthetic Education of Man* speak to us of a utopia reaching beyond art itself. But by the time of Baudelaire, who repeated this *promesse de bonheur*, via art, the utopia of reconciliation with society had gone sour. A relation of opposites had come into being; art had become a critical mirror, showing the irreconcilable nature of the aesthetic and the social world. This modernist transformation was all the more painfully realized, the more art alienated itself from life and withdrew into the untouchableness of complete autonomy. Out of such emotional currents finally gathered those explosive energies which unloaded themselves in the surrealist attempt to blow up the autarkical sphere of art and to force a reconciliation of art and life.

But all those attempts to level art and life, fiction and praxis, appearance and reality to one plane; the attempts to remove the distinction between artifact and object of use, between conscious staging and spontaneous excitement; the attempts to declare every-thing to be art and everyone to be artist, to retract all criteria and to equate aesthetic judgement with the expression of subjective experiences—all these undertakings have proved themselves to be sort of nonsense experiments. These experiments have served to bring back to life, and to illuminate all the more glaringly, exactly those structures of art which they were meant to dissolve. They gave a new legitimacy, as an end in itself, to appearance as the medium of fiction, to the transcendence of the art work over society, to the concentrated and planned character of artistic production as well as to the special cognitive status of judgements of taste. The radical attempt to negate art has ended up ironically by giving due exactly to these categories through which Enlightenment aesthetics had circumscribed its object domain. The surrealists waged the most extreme warfare, but two mistakes in particular destroyed their revolt. First, when the containers of an autonomously developed cultural sphere are shattered, the contents get dispersed. Nothing remains from a desublimated meaning or a destructured form; an emancipatory effect does not follow.

Their second mistake has more important consequences. In everyday communication, cognitive meanings, moral expectations, subjective expressions and evaluations must relate to one another. Communication processes need a cultural tradition covering all spheres— cognitive, moral-practical and expressive. A rationalized everyday life, therefore, could hardly be saved from cultural impoverishment through breaking open a single cultural sphere—art—and so providing access to just one of the specialized knowledge complexes. The surrealist revolt would have replaced only one abstraction.

In the sphere of theoretical knowledge and morality as well, there are parallels to this failed attempt of what we might call the false negation of culture. Only they are less pro-nounced. Since the days of the Young Hegelians, there has been talk about the negation of philosophy. Since Marx, the question of the relationship of theory and practice has been posed. However, Marxist intellectuals joined a social movement; and only at its peripheries were there sectarian attempts to carry out a program of the negation of phi-losophy similar to the surrealist program to negate art. A parallel to the surrealist mistakes becomes visible in these programs when one observes the consequences of dogmatism and of moral rigorism.

A reified everyday praxis can be cured only by creating unconstrained interaction of the cognitive with the moral-practical and the aesthetic expressive elements. Reification cannot be overcome by forcing just one of those highly stylized cultural spheres to open up and become more accessible. Instead, we see under certain circumstances a relation-ship emerge between terroristic activities and the over-extension of any one of these spheres into other domains: examples would be tendencies to aestheticize politics, or to replace politics by moral rigorism or to submit it to the dogmatism of a doctrine. These phenomena should not lead us, however, into denouncing the intentions of the surviving Enlightenment tradition as intentions rooted in a "terroristic reason." Those who lump together the very project of modernity with the state of consciousness and the spectacular action of the individual terrorist are no less short-sighted than those who would claim that the incomparably more persistent and extensive bureaucratic terror practiced in the dark, in the cellars of the military and secret police, and in camps and institutions, is the *raison d'etre* of the modern state, only because this kind of administrative terror makes use of the coercive means of modern bureaucracies.

Alternatives

I think that instead of giving up modernity and its project as a lost cause, we should learn from the mistakes of those extravagant programs which have tried to negate modernity. Perhaps the types of reception of art may offer an example which at least indicates the direction of a way out.

Bourgeois art had two expectations at once from its audiences. On the one hand, the lay-man who enjoyed art should educate himself to become an expert. On the other hand, he should also behave as a competent consumer who uses art and relates aesthetic experiences to his own life problems. This second, and seemingly harmless, manner of experiencing art has lost its radical implications, exactly because it had a confused relation to the attitude of being expert and professional.

To be sure, artistic production would dry up, if it were not carried out in the form of a specialized treatment of autonomous problems, and if it were to cease to be the concern of experts who do not pay so much attention to exoteric questions. Both artists and critics accept thereby the fact that such problems fall under the spell of what I earlier called the "inner logic" of a cultural domain. But this sharp delineation, this exclusive concentration on one aspect of validity alone, and the exclusion of aspects of truth and justice, breaks down as soon as aesthetic experience is drawn into an individual life history and is absorbed into ordinary life. The reception of art by the layman, or by the "everyday expert," goes in a rather different direction than the reception of art by the professional critic.

Albrecht Wellmer has drawn my attention to one way that an aesthetic experience which is not framed around the experts' critical judgements of taste can have its significance altered: as soon as such an experience is used to illuminate a life-historical situation and is related to life problems, it enters into a language game which is no longer that of the aesthetic critic. The aesthetic experience then not only renews the interpretation of our needs in whose light we perceive the world. It permeates as well our cognitive significations and our normative expectations and changes the manner in which all these moments refer to one another. Let me give an example of this process.

This manner of receiving and relating to art is suggested in the first volume of the work *The Aesthetics of Resistance* by the German-Swedish writer Peter Weiss. Weiss describes the process of reappropriating art by presenting a group of politically motivated, knowledge-hungry workers in 1937 in Berlin. These were young people, who, through an evening high school education, acquired the intellectual means to fathom the general and the social history of European art. Out of the resilient edifice of the objective mind, embodied in works of art which they saw again and again in the museums in Berlin, they started removing their own chips of stone, which they gathered together and reassembled in the context of their own milieu. This milieu was far removed from that of traditional education as well as from the then existing regime. These young workers went back and forth between the edifice of European art and their own milieu until they were able to illuminate both.

In examples like this which illustrate the reappropriation of the expert's culture from the standpoint of the life-world, we can discern an element which does justice to the intentions of the hopeless surrealist revolts, perhaps even more to Brecht's and Benjamin's interests in how art works, which lost their aura, could yet be received in illuminating ways. In sum, the project of modernity has not yet been fulfilled. And the reception of art is only one of at least three of its aspects. The project aims at a differentiated relinking of modern culture with an everyday praxis that still depends on vital heritages, but would be impoverished through mere traditionalism. This new connection, however, can only be established under the condition that societal modernization will also be steered in a different direction. The life-world has to become able to develop institutions out of itself which sets limits to the internal dynamics and to the imperatives of an almost autonomous economic system and its administrative complements.

If I am not mistaken, the chances for this today are not very good. More or less in the entire Western world, a climate has developed that furthers capitalist modernization processes as well as trends critical of cultural modernism. The disillusionment with the very failures of those programs that called for the negation of art and philosophy has come to serve as a pretense for conservative positions. Let me briefly distinguish the antimodernism of the young conservatives from the premodernism of the old conservatives and from the postmodernism of the neoconservatives.

The *Young Conservatives* recapitulate the basic experience of aesthetic modernity. They claim as their own the revelations of a decentered subjectivity, emancipated from the imperatives of work and usefulness, and with this experience they step outside the modern world. On the basis of modernistic attitudes, they justify an irreconcilable anti-modernism. They remove into the sphere of the far away and the archaic the spontaneous powers of imagination, of self-experience and of emotionality. To instrumental reason, they juxtapose in manichean fashion a principle only accessible through evocation, be it the will to power or sovereignty, Being or the dionysiac force of the poetical. In France this line leads from Bataille via Foucault to Derrida.

The *Old Conservatives* do not allow themselves to be contaminated by cultural modernism. They observe the decline of substantive reason, the differentiation of science, morality and art, the modern world view and its merely procedural rationality, with sadness and recommend a withdrawal to a position anterior to modernity.

Neo-Aristotelianism, in particular, enjoys a certain success today. In view of the problematic of ecology, it allows itself to call for a cosmological ethic. As belonging to this school, which orginates with Leo Strauss, one can count for example the interesting works of Hans Jonas and Robert Spaemann.

Finally, the *Neoconservatives* welcome the development of modern science, as long as this only goes beyond its sphere to carry forward technical progress, capitalist growth and rational administration. Moreover, they recommend a politics of defusing the explosive content of cultural modernity. According to one thesis, science, when properly understood, has become irrevocably meaningless for the orientation of the life-world. A further thesis is that politics must be kept as far aloof as possible from the demands of moral-practical justification. And a third thesis asserts the pure immanence of art, disputes that it has a utopian content, and points to its illusory character in order to limit the aesthetic experience to privacy. One could name here the early Wittgenstein, Carl Schmitt of the middle period, and Gottfried Benn of the late period. But with the decisive confinement of science, morality and art to autonomous spheres separated from the life-world and administered by experts, what remains from the project of cultural modernity is only what we would have if we were to give up the project of modernity altogether. As a replacement one points to traditions, which, however, are held to be immune to demands of (normative) justification and validation.

This typology is like any other, of course, a simplification; but it may not prove totally useless for the analysis of contemporary intellectual and political confrontations. I fear that the ideas of anti-modernity, together with an additional touch of premodernity, are becoming popular in the circles of alternative culture. When one observes the transformations of consciousness within political parties in Germany, a new ideological shift (*Tendenzwende*) becomes visible. And this is the alliance of postmodernists with pre-modernists. It seems to me that there is no party in particular that monopolizes the abuse of intellectuals and the position of neoconservatism. I therefore have good reason to be thankful for the liberal spirit in which the city of Frankfurt offers me a prize bearing the name of Theodor Adorno. Adorno, a most significant son of this city, who as philosopher and writer has stamped the image of the intellectual in our country in incomparable fashion; even more, who has become the very image of emulation for the intellectual.

6-3

Massimo Vignelli

Long Live Modernism!
1991

Schematic Chart of Ideological and Design Changes from the 60s to the Present
2012

"modernism was and still is the search for the truth, the search for integrity, the search for cultural stimulation and enrichment of the mind. Modernism was never a style, but an attitude"

Massimo Vignelli (1931–2014) was an Italian-born designer whose work encompassed packaging, furniture, signs, showrooms, publications, and buildings. He is known for a strong and consistent belief in the modernist tradition, expressed in all his works. His most iconic design is his New York City subway map for the Metropolitan Transit Authority.

....

Long Live Modernism!
1991

I was raised to believe that an architect should be able to design everything from a spoon to a city. At the root, this belief is a commitment to improve the design of everything that can be made—to make it better. To make it better not only from a functional or mechanical point of view, but to design it to reflect cultural and ethical values, ethical integrity. Integrity of purpose, materials and of the manufacturing process.

Integrity of purpose implies a severe analysis of what the problem is: its meaning, what the possibilities for a range of solutions are: solutions that have to be sifted through to determine the most appropriate for the specific problem—not just alternatives I may like, but one that answers all of the questions posed by the problem. The solutions to a problem are in the problem itself. To solve all the questions posed by the problem, however, is not enough. The solutions should reflect the approach taken, and by virtue of its configuration, stimulate cultural reactions in the viewer, rather than emotional titillations. In this process, nothing is taken for granted, no dogmas are accepted, no preconceived ideas are assumed or adopted without questioning them in the context of the project.

I was raised to believe that, as a designer, I have the responsibility to improve the world around us, to make it a better place to live, to fight and oppose trivia, kitsch and all norms of subculture that are visually polluting our world. The ethics of Modernism, or I should say the ideology of Modernism, was an ideology of the fight, the ongoing battle to combat all the wrongs developed by industrialization during the last century. Modernism was and still is the search for the truth, the search for integrity, the search for cultural stimulation and enrichment of the mind. Modernism was never a style, but an attitude. This is often misunderstood by those designers who dwell on revivals of the form rather than on the content of Modernism. From the beginning, Modernism had the urgency of Utopianism: to make a world better by design. Today we know better. It takes more than design to change things. But the cultural thrust of the Modernist belief is still valid, because we still have too much trash around us, not only material trash but intellectual trash as well. In that respect, I value, endorse and promote the continued relevance of the Modern movement as the cultural mainstream of our century.

The cultural events of the last 20 years have expanded and deepened the issues and values promoted by the modern movement. The revision of many of the Modernist issues has enriched our perception and contributed to improving the quality of work. The increased number of architects and designers with good training has a positive effect on our society and our environment. Much still has to be done to convince industry and government that design is an integral part of the production process and not a last-minute embellishment.

The cultural energy of the Modern movement is still burning, fueling intellects against shallow trends, transitory values, superficial titillations brought forward by the media, whose very existence depends on ephemera. Many of the current modes are created, supported and discarded by the very media that generates that change and documents it to survive. It is a vicious circle. It has always been, only now it is bigger than ever.

As seen in a broad historical perspective, Modernism's ascetic, Spartan look still has a towering position of strength and dignity. Modernism's inherent notion of timeless values as opposed to transient values still greatly appeals to my intellectual being.

The best architects in the world today are all Modernists at the core, and so are the best designers. The followers of the Post-Modernist fad are gone, reduced to caricatures of the recent past. Post-Modernism should be regarded at best as a critical evaluation of the issues of Modernism. In that perspective, it has been extremely helpful to correct, expand and improve the issues of Modernism. None of us would be the same without it. However, the lack of a profound ideology eventually brought Post-Modernism to its terminal stage. In the cultural confusion produced by pluralism and its eclectic manifestations, Modernism finds its raison d'être in its commitment to the original issues of its ideology and its energy to change the world into a better place in which to live.

Long live the Modern movement!

"choosing is easy today, so choose wisely"

Schematic Chart of Ideological and Design Changes from the 1960s to the Present
2012

Much has changed since the original version of this chart (on the following page) first appeared at the Alliance Graphique Internationale in 1985. The advent of the computer has brought about profound changes over the last 20 years, providing a wider spectrum of creative options than ever before. Today, just about anything is possible, so it's up to the designer to choose what is appropriate. In the past, there were specific trends; now, there is infinite variety. What before was just fantasy can easily become reality, from the sublime to the banal (or worse). In this new climate, the responsibilities of the designer—toward the client, toward the user, toward society at large—have increased manyfold. We have more powerful tools, but must be more disciplined and discerning in how we use them. This technical facility is both an opportunity and a trap. Choosing is easy today, so choose wisely.

We live in an interesting time, a period of profound change brought about by technologies, which are shaping our ways of thinking, communicating, and behaving. It's a great era for the younger generation, which seems much better equipped than previous ones to tackle the challenges ahead.

Schematic chart of ideological and design changes from the 60s to the present

by Massimo Vignelli

We can say today that all experiences of the past are available for use, since everything is reinterpreted according to our contemporary sensibility.

The advent of the computer in the last twenty years has brought about profound changes and provided a wider spectrum of possibilities never experienced before.

Today just about everything is possible: it is up to the designer to choose what is appropriate or to choose a particular discipline. If in the past there were specific trends, today everything is available and made possible by the new technologies. What before was just a fantasy today could be a reality, from the worst to the sublime. In this new climate the responsibility of the designer has increased manyfold, toward the client, toward the user, toward society at large. Since everything can be done, it is important to set up some personal boundaries to contain a sense of decency, perhaps more than before, when operating within a set of rules helped to structure the actions. Many contrasting issues of the past have found the possibility of coexistence, playing together in the same artifact. For example: identity & diversity, loose & tight, less & more, absolute & relative, and so on. We live in a very interesting time, a time of profound changes brought about by technologies which are affecting our way of thinking, communicating and behaving. A great time for the young generation, who seem to be so much better than the previous ones...

1960s	1970s
Discipline	Appropriateness
Idealism	Pluralism
Objectivity	Aspecificity
Simplicity	Complex simplicity
Structure	Program
Absolute	Consistent
Geometry	Articulate geometry
One stylistic code	Contrasting stylistic codes
Form follows function	Form and function
No symbolism	Controlled symbolism
No humor	Surprise as humor
Anti-metaphor	Towards metaphors
Anti-ornament	Structure as ornament
Orthodox grid	Loose grid
One typeface (Helvetica)	Few typefaces
One type size	Few type sizes
Primary colors, black, and red	Rainbow
High gloss	Soft
Asymmetry	Dynamic symmetry
Sameness	Identity
Rigid systems	Modular systems
Less is more	Less is a bore

1980s	1990s	2000s
Ambiguity	Ad hoc-ism	Restraint
Semiotics	Deconstructivism	Minimalism as style
Subjectivity	Complacency	Responsibility
Complexity	Fragmentation	Consistency
Meaning	Randomness	Logic
Relative	Ephemeral	Timeless
Contradicting geometry	Chaos theory	Order
Double-stylistic codes	Visual noise	Codes
Semiotic form	Function follows form	Alternative forms
Expressive symbolism	Legitimization of the absurd	Return to sanity
Contradiction as humor	Provocation as food for the media	Humor as seriousness
Metaphors	Arbitrariness	Search for clarity
Ornament	Shock value as ornament	Contempt for shock values
Complex grid	No grid	Grids are back
Variety of typefaces	Any typeface	Few typefaces
Hierarchy concept	Any size	Limited type sizes
Muted colors	Any color	Lots of white and black
Contrasting textures	Any texture	Gloss & matte
Symmetry plus asymmetry	No symmetry	Symmetry & asymmetry
Diversity	Change for the sake of change	Identity & diversity
Accidental systems	No systems	Modular systems
The more the better	Less is less, more is more	Less & more

Paul Rand

Confusion and Chaos

1992

"'It is no secret,' asserts the author of Tenured Radicals, *'that the academic study of the humanities in this country is in a state of crisis'"*

Paul Rand (1914–1996) was an American designer who created often-playful variations on Swiss Style graphic design. He was a professor at Yale University and is best known for the design of logos for corporations such as IBM, UPS, *Enron, Westinghouse,* ABC, *and NeXT.*

....

In the torturous history of painting and design, from Cimabue (1240–1302) to Cassandre (1901–1968), communications between artist and spectator—even if one disagreed with what was being communicated—was rarely a problem. Today, with emphasis on self, on style, rather than on content or idea, and in much of what is alleged to be graphic design, communication at best, is puzzling. Order out of chaos, it seems, is not the order of the day.

The deluge of design that colors our lives, our print, and video screens is synchronous with the spirit of our time. No less than drugs and pollution, and all the fads and -isms that have plagued our communities, the big brush of graffiti for example, has been blanketing our cities from Basel to Brooklyn. Much of graphic design today is a grim reminder of this overwhelming presence. The qualities which evoke this bevy of depressing images are a collage of confusion and chaos, swaying between high tech and low art, and wrapped in a cloak of arrogance: squiggles, pixels, doodles, dingbats, ziggurats; boudoir colors: turquoise, peach, pea green, and lavender; corny woodcuts on moody browns and russets; Art Deco rip-offs, high gloss finishes, sleazy textures; tiny color photos surrounded by acres of white space; indecipherable, zany typography with miles of leading; text in all caps (despite indisputable proof that lowercase letters are more readable); omnipresent, decorative letterspaced caps; visually annotated typography and revivalist caps and small caps; pseudo-Dada and Futurist collages; and whatever 'special effects' a computer makes possible. These *inspirational decorations* are, apparently, convenient stand-ins for real ideas and genuine skills. And all this is a reflection, less of the substance, than of the spirit of graffiti—less of the style, than of the quality.

That these cliches are used repeatedly, irrespective of needs, is what defines trendiness. The 'Memphis' fad was also based on cliches and on outrageous, kitschy notions. (Occasionally, however, some potentially useful ideas seeped through—only proving that it takes talent to make something out of nothing.) The huge investments involved in the manufacture and storage of Memphis products have probably helped speed its demise. Trendy printed ephemera, on the other hand, which involves less capital, may take a bit longer.

There is something about graffiti and graffiti-like design that smacks of WWI Dada. But that was a revolt against the lopsided conventions of the time. The participants were often great artists and reformers: Arp, Grosz, Heartfield, Duchamp, Ernst, Schwitters, etc. And the work was not, in any way, trendy; it was serious, often amusing, and always interesting. Today's Dada, if it can be called that, is a revolt against anything that is deemed old hat. Faddish and frivolous, it harbors its own built-in boredom.

'I feel that the ideas I tried to outline...will strike many of you as consisting too much of the atrabiliar grumblings of a disgruntled elder,' is how Roger Fry,[1] the distinguished British critic, expressed the fear that his message might be falling on deaf ears.

Most of this 'new' style of design is confined to pro bono work, small boutiques, fledgling studios, trendy publishers, misguided educational institutions, anxious graphic arts associations, and a few innocent paper manufacturers, who produce beautiful papers, but then spoil them with 'the latest' graphics, and who, undoubtedly, see themselves as the avant-garde—and are comforted by the illusion that this must be progress. Unhappily, this is infecting some of the graphics of the corporate world: annual reports, identity programs, direct mail, etc. Trendiness is seductive, especially to the young and inexperienced, for the principal reason that it offers no restraints, is lots of 'fun', permits unlimited possibilities for 'self-expression,' and doesn't require conforming to the dictates of reason or aesthetics. 'Self-expression is real only after the means to it have been acquired,'[2] comments the author of a brilliant commentary on the foibles of education, 'Begin Here.'

Lack of humility and originality and the obsession with style, is what seem to encourage these excesses. The absence of restraint, the equation of simplicity with shallowness, complexity with depth of understanding, and obscurity with innovation, distinguishes the quality of work of these times. The focus on freedom is just another sign that suggests a longing to reject the past—'the infinite greatness of the past,'[3] is how Walt Whitman put it. All this, of course, carries little weight with critics who, out of hand, reject the styles of their predecessors, and respond to reason with disdain.

Added to this is the obsession with theory which, instead of being fuel for action as it was at other times, during the Renaissance, for example, is merely the vehicle for fathomless language, variously described as 'extravagantly obscure, modish, opaque verbal shenanigans—and the authors as masters of impenetrability.'[4] Although these descriptions are aimed at architects, they seem equally appropriate for graphic design theorists of the

1   Roger Fry, Art and Commerce (London, 1925), 23.
2   Jacques Barzun, 'The Centrality of Reading.' Begin Here (Chicago, 1991), 24.
3   Walt Whitman, Passage to India (1868).
4   Roger Kimball, 'Deconstruction Comes to America,' Tenured Radicals (New York, 1990), 123.

'new', (a buzzword often seen in advertising sometimes preceded by the expression 'amazing'.) Reaching for the new is tilting at windmills; the goal is not what is new (original), as Mies put it, but what is good.

Twenty-eight years ago, my friend Charles Eames (1908–1977) spoke at the Pasadena Art Museum concerning a growing preoccupation with the problem of creativity. 'This preoccupation in itself', said Eames, 'suggests that we are in some special kind of trouble—and indeed we are.' A look at graphic design today suggests that, perhaps, we are even in greater trouble now than we were twenty-eight years ago. As a matter of fact, design today is reminiscent of the trials of an earlier era in which Edward Gibbon, author of *The History of the Decline and Fall of the Roman Empire* (1776), astutely described the arts in theatre, music, and painting as 'freakishness pretending to originality, enthusiasm masquerading as vitality'.[5]

Eames would probably turn in his grave if he knew what was happening even in academia today. 'It is no secret,' asserts the author of *Tenured Radicals*, 'that the academic study of the humanities in this country is in a state of crisis'…'Every special interest—women's studies, black studies, gay studies, and the like—and every modish interpretive gambit— deconstructivism, post structuralism, new historicism {postmodernism},…has found a welcome roost in the academy {and in many studios}, while the traditional curriculum and modes of intellectual inquiry are excoriated as sexist, racist, or just plain reactionary.'[6] 'It is also necessary,' adds another critic, 'to remind oneself of the dangers that ensue when metaphors substitute for facts, when words lose their meaning, and when signifiers and signifieds part company, with the deconstructionists' blessing.'[7]

Today, the popular sport is to put down whatever isn't perceived as change—the very latest—subjects like: the classics, the curriculum, Modernism, functionalism and, for example, the Bauhaus, into whose history is woven the very fabric of Modernism, is seen as a style rather than as an idea, a cultural manifestation. Socially aware, and like neoplasticism and constructivism, it harbored a strain of the ascetic. To say that the Bauhaus (1919) and its ideology are defunct is to cast aspersions on its antecedents: on Ruskin and Morris, on the Arts and Crafts movement, on the Secessionists, on Hoffman and Moser, on Muthesius and the Werkbund (1907), on Behrens, on the predecessor of the Bauhaus—van de Velde—the director of the Weimar Academy, on Gropius, Klee, Kandinsky, Moholy-Nagy, Albers, Mies, and on outsiders like Malevich, Mondrian, Van Doesburg and Lissitzky. Cubism and some of its progeny, suprematism, neoplasticism, constructivism, futurism, were its aesthetic foundation. The Bauhaus Archives in Berlin, the refurbished building in Dessau, and original products now available to all, are stark evidence that the Bauhaus is breathing vigorously.

'There are two principles inherent in the very nature of things…' writes Whitehead,[8] 'the spirit of change, and the spirit of conservation. There can be nothing real without both. Mere change without conservation is a passage from nothing to nothing. Mere conser-

5   *Alistair Cooke,* America Observed *(New York, 1990), 14*
6   *Roger Kimball,* Tenured Radicals *(New York, 1990), xl. xiii.*
7   *David Lehman, 'A Scandal of Academe,'* Signs of the Times *(New York, 1991), 243.*
8   *Alfred North Whitehead, 'Requisites for Social Progress,'* Science and the Modern World *(New York, 1925), 289.*

vation without change cannot conserve.' Elsewhere he says, 'Mere change before the attainment of adequacy of achievement, either in quality or output, is destructive of greatness.'

Interminable disputes about whether or not design at the Kunstgewerbeschule of Basel is focused too much on form at the expense of other goals is to deny what Mies espoused: 'Form is not the goal but the result of our work.' Fads are governed by the same immutable laws of form as are other visual phenomena. Wishful thinking will not make them go away; and one can no more escape from the exigencies of form than from one's shadow. To poke fun at form or formalism is to poke fun at Roger Fry, Clive Bell, John Dewey, and the philosophy called aesthetics. Ironically, it also pokes fun at trendy design, since the devices which characterize this style of 'decoration' are, primarily, formal. Furthermore, it denies what the great historian, painter, and architect of the Renaissance, Vasari,[9] had already stated about design (form): 'It is the animating principle of all creative processes.'

The quality of teaching in the university and art school is rarely taken to task. To teach in a university, practical experience, it seems, is not one of the prerequisites (at least, not long-term experience). Experience in the work place, and a thorough knowledge of the history of one's specialization is indispensable, both for imparting information and for one's well being. But such experience, with some exceptions, is rare among students as well as among faculty. Absence of these disciplines can only help perpetuate mediocrity, and insure the continual flow of questionable work in the marketplace.

But for the familiarity with a few obvious names and facts about the history of painting and design, history is a subject not taken too seriously. This does not imply that just because some work is a product of the past it is privileged, willy-nilly, to join the ranks of the immortals. The historical process is (or should be), a process of distillation and not accumulation. In a certain sense it is related to natural selection—survival of the fittest. Furthermore, to shun history is to reinvent the wheel—the probability of repeating what has already been done.

Gutenberg, Picasso, Cubism, Futurism, Lissitzky and Tschichold are among the historical facts and figures that a student or teacher may be aware of. But what about the history of art pre-Renaissance, which is so well documented? What about the history of design, largely a product of journals and a few isolated books, which is not so well documented?

Even though artists of the 1890s, like Lautrec, Bonnard, and the Beggarstaff Brothers, may be familiar to some schools, designers of the 20s and 30s are little known. If the artist happens to wear two hats—a painter as well as a designer—more time is spent discussing the relative merits of 'fine' as opposed to 'applied' arts, than on intrinsic values. Mention of some of the Europeans (not necessarily linked with the avant-garde), whose work appeared in periodicals like *Gebrauchsgraphik* and *Arts et Métiers Graphiques* (before wwii) will probably be greeted with silence. With few exceptions, a blank stare is the usual reaction when some of these names are ticked off, from students and teachers alike.

This, by no means, is a complete roster: Ehmeke, Parzinger, Klinger, Arpke, Schulpig, Bernhard, Dexel, Buchartz, Leistikow, Zietara, Deffke, Mahlau, Goedecker, Ahlers, Hadank,

9   T. S. R. Boase, 'The Critic,' Giorgio Vasari *(Washington, D.C., 1971), 124.*

Fuss, Koerner, Gipkens, Boehm, Corty, Garretto, Brissaud, Benito, Renner, Depero, Schleger, Koch, Schwichtenberg, Trump, Colin, Martin, Satomi, Scheurich, Boutet de Monvel, Berzny, Kozma—designers, illustrators, fashion artists, and others too numerous to list. And among Americans, in the 30s and 40s, there were Jensen, Trafton, Bobri, Sinel, Switzer, and others like McKnight Kauffer, who spent most of his life in England. Designers like Dwiggins or Gill occupy a different category.

The purpose of listing these names should not be seen as mere pedantry; rather it provides an opportunity to learn by example, by studying the work of an extraordinary number of out-of-the-ordinary talents.

Both in education and in business graphic design is often a case of the blind leading the blind. To make the classroom a perpetual forum for political and social issues for instance is wrong; and to see aesthetics as sociology, is grossly misleading. A student whose mind is cluttered with matters which have nothing directly to do with design; whose goal is to learn doing and making; who is thrown into the fray between learning how to use a computer at the same time that he or she is learning design basics; and being overwhelmed with social problems and political issues is a bewildered student; this is not what he or she bargained for, nor, indeed, paid for.

'Schools are not intended to moralize a wicked world,' says Barzun,[10] 'but to impart knowledge and develop intelligence, with only two social ends in mind: prepare to take on one's share in the world's work and, perhaps in addition, lend a hand in improving society after schooling is done. Anything else is the nonsense we have been living with.' Further on he continues, 'All that such good samaritan courses amount to is pieties. They present moralizing mixed with anecdotes, examples of good and bad, discussions of that catch-all word "values"'…and finally, he admonishes, 'Make the school a place for academic vocational instruction, not social reform…'[11]

This does not suggest that social or political issues are mere trivia. On the contrary, they are of real significance and deserve the kind of forum that is free of interference. Even though common decency implies continuing concern for human needs—social issues are not aesthetic issues, nor can they be the basis for aesthetic judgments. Where, for example, would Caravaggio, Lautrec, or even Degas be if work were judged on issues other than aesthetics? And where, today, would so many schools, studios, and advertising agencies be if important decisions depended on aesthetic priorities?

Coping with the problems relating to the understanding of design in business depends a great deal on how well informed, genuinely interested, and experienced a businessman is. Managers responsible for design are chosen, not for their aesthetic judgments, nor for their impeccable taste, but for their administrative skills. Few, if any, understand the intricacies of design, or even the role, beyond the obvious, that design and designers play.

10   Jacques Barzun, 'Ideas vs. Notions,' Begin Here (Chicago, 1991), 50.
11   Ibid., 208.

Most see the designer as a set of hands—a supplier—not as a strategic part of a business. Their background is primarily that of marketers, purchasing agents, or advertising specialists, not of connoisseurs of design. It is their uninformed, unfocused preferences or prejudices, their likes or dislikes that too often determine the look of things. Yet, much of the time, they are not even discriminating enough to distinguish between good and bad, between trendy and original, nor can they always recognize talent or specialized skills. In the field of design theirs is the dichotomy of being privileged but not necessarily being qualified—after all, design is not their business.

Bureaucrats largely responsible for the administration of design spend endless hours at meetings allegedly about design, in which miscellaneous subjects are discussed; and in which marketing, production, and administration problems are treated as if they were design problems. Whether or not the participants really understand the nature of the problems, or the implication of design, is questionable. If quality, for example, is the subject for discussion, it is dealt with only as an abstraction, with participants assuming the other person understands what is being discussed, when, in fact, nobody can be sure. Since perception is so intimately a part of taste and design, it is the experienced designer who might possibly point the way to meaningful solutions, and smooth the path for an administrator's needs.

Even though there are comparatively few experienced and really innovative designers around, there are, regrettably, even fewer administrators who are receptive to innovative work.

6-5

Billy Childish and Charles Thomson

Remodernism
1999

The Stuckist Manifesto
1999

"remodernism discards and replaces post-modernism because of its failure to answer or address any important issues of being a human being"

Billy Childish (1959–) and Charles Thomson (1953–) are English artists, painters, and photographers. Their art movement, Stuckism, was conceived after Childish's ex-lover, the artist Tracey Emin, told him that his art was "stuck stuck stuck." Their movement is anticonceptual and emphasizes figurative painting.

Remodernism
1999

'towards a new spirituality in art'

Through the course of the 20th-century Modernism has progressively lost its way, until finally toppling into the pit of Postmodern balderdash. At this appropriate time, The Stuckists, the first Remodernist Art Group, announce the birth of Remodernism.

1. Remodernism takes the original principles of Modernism and reapplies them, highlighting vision as opposed to formalism.

2. Remodernism is inclusive rather than exclusive and welcomes artists who endeavour to know themselves and find themselves through art processes that strive to connect and include, rather than alienate and exclude. Remodernism upholds the spiritual vision of the founding fathers of Modernism and respects their bravery and integrity in facing and depicting the travails of the human soul through a new art that was no longer subservient to a religious or political dogma and which sought to give voice to the gamut of the human psyche.

3. Remodernism discards and replaces Post-Modernism because of its failure to answer or address any important issues of being a human being.

4. Remodernism embodies spiritual depth and meaning and brings to an end an age of scientific materialism, nihilism and spiritual bankruptcy.

5. We don't need more dull, boring, brainless destruction of convention, what we need is not new, but perennial. We need an art that integrates body and soul and recognises enduring and underlying principles which have sustained wisdom and insight throughout humanity's history. This is the proper function of tradition.

6. Modernism has never fulfilled its potential. It is futile to be 'post' something which has not even 'been' properly something in the first place. Remodernism is the rebirth of spiritual art.

7. Spirituality is the journey of the soul on earth. Its first principle is a declaration of intent to face the truth. Truth is what it is, regardless of what we want it to be. Being a spiritual artist means addressing unflinchingly our projections, good and bad, the attractive and the grotesque, our strengths as well as our delusions, in order to know ourselves and thereby our true relationship with others and our connection to the divine.

8. Spiritual art is not about fairyland. It is about taking hold of the rough texture of life. It is about addressing the shadow and making friends with wild dogs. Spirituality is the awareness that everything in life is for a higher purpose.

9. Spiritual art is not religion. Spirituality is humanity's quest to understand itself and finds its symbology through the clarity and integrity of its artists.

10. The making of true art is man's desire to communicate with himself, his fellows and his God. Art that fails to address these issues is not art.

11. It should be noted that technique is dictated by, and only necessary to the extent to which it is commensurate with, the vision of the artist.

12. The Remodernist's job is to bring God back into art but not as God was before. Remodernism is not a religion, but we uphold that it is essential to regain enthusiasm (from the Greek, *en theos*, to be possessed by God).

13. A true art is the visible manifestation, evidence and facilitator of the soul's journey. Spiritual art does not mean the painting of Madonnas or Buddhas. Spiritual art is the painting of things that touch the soul of the artist. Spiritual art does not often look very spiritual, it looks like everything else because spirituality includes everything.

14. Why do we need a new spirituality in art? Because connecting in a meaningful way is what makes people happy. Being understood and understanding each other makes life enjoyable and worth living.

Summary
It is quite clear to anyone of an uncluttered mental disposition that what is now put forward, quite seriously, as art by the ruling elite, is proof that a seemingly rational development of a body of ideas has gone seriously awry. The principles on which Modernism was based are sound, but the conclusions that have now been reached from it are preposterous.

We address this lack of meaning, so that a coherent art can be achieved and this imbalance redressed.

Let there be no doubt, there will be a spiritual renaissance in art because there is nowhere else for art to go. Stuckism's mandate is to initiate that spiritual renaissance now.

The Stuckist Manifesto

1999

"Your paintings are stuck, you are stuck! Stuck! Stuck! Stuck!"
Tracey Emin

Against conceptualism, hedonism and the cult of the ego-artist.

1. Stuckism is the quest for authenticity. By removing the mask of cleverness and admitting where we are, the Stuckist allows him/herself uncensored expression.

2. Painting is the medium of self-discovery. It engages the person fully with a process of action, emotion, thought and vision, revealing all of these with intimate and unforgiving breadth and detail.

3. Stuckism proposes a model of art which is holistic. It is a meeting of the conscious and unconscious, thought and emotion, spiritual and material, private and public. Modernism is a school of fragmentation—one aspect of art is isolated and exaggerated to detriment of the whole. This is a fundamental distortion of the human experience and perpetrates an egocentric lie.

4. Artists who don't paint aren't artists.

5. Art that has to be in a gallery to be art isn't art.

6. The Stuckist paints pictures because painting pictures is what matters.

7. The Stuckist is not mesmerised by the glittering prizes, but is wholeheartedly engaged in the process of painting. Success to the Stuckist is to get out of bed in the morning and paint.

8. It is the Stuckist's duty to explore his/her neurosis and innocence through the making of paintings and displaying them in public, thereby enriching society by giving shared form to individual experience and an individual form to shared experience.

9. The Stuckist is not a career artist but rather an amateur (*amare*, Latin, to love) who takes risks on the canvas rather than hiding behind ready-made objects (e.g. a dead sheep). The amateur, far from being second to the professional, is at the forefront of experimentation, unencumbered by the need to be seen as infallible. Leaps of human endeavour are made by the intrepid individual, because he/she does not have to protect their status. Unlike the professional, the Stuckist is not afraid to fail.

10. Painting is mysterious. It creates worlds within worlds, giving access to the unseen psychological realities that we inhabit. The results are radically different from the materials employed. An existing object (e.g. a dead sheep) blocks access to the inner world and can only remain part of the physical world it inhabits, be it moorland or gallery. Ready-made art is a polemic of materialism.

11. Post Modernism, in its adolescent attempt to ape the clever and witty in modern art, has shown itself to be lost in a cul-de-sac of idiocy. What was once a searching and provocative process (as Dadaism) has given way to trite cleverness for commercial exploitation. The Stuckist calls for an art that is alive with all aspects of human experience; dares to communicate its ideas in primeval pigment; and possibly experiences itself as not at all clever!

12. Against the jingoism of Brit Art and the ego-artist. Stuckism is an international non-movement.

13. Stuckism is anti 'ism'. Stuckism doesn't become an 'ism' because Stuckism is not Stuckism, it is stuck!

14. Brit Art, in being sponsored by Saachis [sic], main stream conservatism and the Labour government, makes a mockery of its claim to be subversive or avant-garde.

15. The ego-artist's constant striving for public recognition results in a constant fear of failure. The Stuckist risks failure wilfully and mindfully by daring to transmute his/her ideas through the realms of painting. Whereas the ego-artist's fear of failure inevitably brings about an underlying self-loathing, the failures that the Stuckist encounters engage him/her in a deepening process which leads to the understanding of the futility of all striving. The Stuckist doesn't strive—which is to avoid who and where you are—the Stuckist engages with the moment.

16. The Stuckist gives up the laborious task of playing games of novelty, shock and gimmick. The Stuckist neither looks backwards nor forwards but is engaged with the study of the human condition. The Stuckists champion process over cleverness, realism over abstraction, content over void, humour over wittiness and painting over smugness.

17. If it is the conceptualist's wish to always be clever, then it is the Stuckist's duty to always be wrong.

18. The Stuckist is opposed to the sterility of the white wall gallery system and calls for exhibitions to be held in homes and musty museums, with access to sofas, tables, chairs and cups of tea. The surroundings in which art is experienced (rather than viewed) should not be artificial and vacuous.

19. Crimes of education: instead of promoting the advancement of personal expression through appropriate art processes and thereby enriching society, the art school system has become a slick bureaucracy, whose primary motivation is financial. The Stuckists call for an open policy of admission to all art schools based on the individual's work regardless of his/her academic record, or so-called lack of it. We further call for the policy of entrapping rich and untalented students from at home and abroad to be halted forthwith. We also demand that all college buildings be available for adult education and recreational use of the indigenous population of the respective catchment area. If a school or college is unable to offer benefits to the community it is guesting in, then it has no right to be tolerated.

20. Stuckism embraces all that it denounces. We only denounce that which stops at the starting point—Stuckism starts at the stopping point!

Experimental Jetset

Design & Art Reader

2006

"we are firm believers in the utopian dimension of design"

"we don't see graphic design as art, but we do see art as a form of design"

Experimental Jetset is a Dutch graphic design studio founded in 1997 by Marieke Stolk, Erwin Brinkers, and Danny van den Dungen. Their linguistically playful body of work, centering on printed matter, emerges from a modernist sensibility.

....

01. Education and inspiration

All three of us studied at the Gerrit Rietveld Academy (Amsterdam). Marieke and Danny graduated in 1997; Erwin, who was in another year, graduated in 1998. At that time, Linda van Deursen was definitely a very influential person; she was one of our favorite teachers. She still is very inspirational to us.

A person that also had a huge impact on us was Richard Prince; we were introduced to his work through Linda. We especially liked his 'joke paintings'. We remember that seeing these paintings, displaying a few simple sentences in Helvetica, was really a breath of fresh air in a time when graphic design was more about layered compositions, techno- and grunge-typography, and clogged lay-outs. Prince's work (not only his 'joke paintings', but also his 'gangs', his grouped photographs) showed that it was possible to analyse/deconstruct pop-culture, but without the 'deconstructivist' aesthetics (that were so fashionable in graphic design around that time, and that we disliked so much). His work had a hard and cool 'punk-minimalist' sensibility that had a huge influence on us. (It's funny; some people assume our work to be heavily influenced by Swiss late-modernists such as Josef Müller-Brockmann and designers like that, but actually, we only learned about these designers quite recently. Richard Prince had a much larger influence on us).

Another person that influenced us was Bob Gill. In the library of the Rietveld Academy we discovered a dusty copy of 'Forget All The Rules You Ever Learned About Graphic Design—Including The Ones In This Book'. Gill's work had an immediate impact on us. What impressed us most was his consistent use of the 'problem/solution' model. It's a dialectical model that some might find outdated, rigid, one-dimensional, didactic, archaic.

To us, the problem/solution model is most of all beautiful. Of course, it has a tragic side, as every solution only brings forth more problems; and besides, we all know there is no such thing as one perfect solution. But it is exactly this inherent tragic side which makes this model so beautiful and useful to us.

Last but not least, we would like to mention Wim Crouwel. What influenced us most is the fact that, in his work, you can't distinguish between his form and his approach. In Crouwel's work, form and approach are the same. There's an idiosyncratic quality in his designs: Crouwel's work is highly systematic, but it's a highly personal system, organized according to Crouwel's own logic. From the smallest logo to his body of work as a whole, his pieces are systematic worlds in itself. To be confronted with such systematic work is quite powerful; it's ecstatic and disturbing at the same time. To feel your own logic clash with another logic, to be suddenly drawn into another rhythm, another rationality, a different set of rules: it's a profound experience, causing you to see the world with different eyes. Crouwel's work can certainly trigger experiences like that. (It is often thought that design, to have a subversive potential, has to be unexpected, irrational, rebellious; anything as long as it's not 'boring'. We very much disagree: in our view, it is consistency, and an iron logic, that can really throw you off your feet, and change your way of thinking).

02. Modernism and functionalism
Whether we consider ourselves modernists or not is an impossible question. The answer would depend completely on the definition of modernism one employs.

For example, there's the idea of modernism as a very defined, historical classification, starting, let's say, in the 1850s, peaking around 1910, and rapidly fading away after that. That's quite a feasible definition.

Another definition would be the more 'Habermasian' idea of modernism, as something yet to be fulfilled, linked to the notion of modernity as a project that started with the Enlightment. That's also a very plausible definition.

In between these two definitions, there are hundreds of others. And since we are torn between all of them, it's quite difficult for us to answer this question.

What we do know, though, is that we aren't functionalists (in the common use of the word), as we aren't just interested in the 'narrow' definition of the word 'function'. To us, a chair isn't simply something to just sit on; it also functions as the embodiment of a certain way of thinking. This 'broad' definition of function is actually closer to early modernism than to late modernism.

To give a simple example of this, in the brilliant 'Theory and Design in the First Machine Age', Reyner Banham shows that Rietveld's arm-chair is in fact a highly symbolic structure. The design of the chair cannot be simply justified as being 'functional'; the chair is also a statement about the infinity of space. This is something we're quite interested in: the function of design as an embodiment of ideology.

03. Aesthetics and utopia

We are firm believers in the utopian dimension of design. It's something we're absolutely convinced of. It's our main drive. But we aren't sure if this utopian dimension can be found in utilitarianism, or social messages. Those particular forms of engagement can be strong sources of inspiration for the designer, and in that sense they certainly play an important role, but they often lack a real dialectical potential. In our view, a true utopian design should change people's way of thinking, not just their opinions.

If we are indeed living in a fragmented society (and we believe we are), then perhaps the only way to shock us out of this alienation is to counter the fragmentation of society with the wholeness of design. In that sense, the utopian dimension is to be found in the internal organization of the designed object, its inner-logic. Which brings us back to the idiosyncratic quality of Crouwel's work which we mentioned earlier, or the example of Rietveld's chair as an embodiment of ideology. You can define it in many different ways: Herbert Marcuse speaks of 'the aesthetic dimension' (in a very good essay of the same name, 'The Aesthetic Dimension', published by Beacon Press, 1978), you can also refer to it as the dialectical dimension, or the critical dimension, or the inner-logic, or the internal whole. In our view, these are all names for the same thing.

We recently stumbled across a quote by the artist John McCracken, who said 'I've always felt that it was possible that a piece could change or transform reality, or the world. A work being so tuned that it somehow alters the constitution of things'. This almost musical idea of 'tuning' is precisely where we locate the utopian potential of design. (We know, this probably sounds hopelessly idealistic, but that's exactly what we are).

To elaborate on this last remark, we see the work of minimal artists such as McCracken and Donald Judd as profoundly political. The modularity in the work of Judd is especially subversive. Modularity, which is the repetition of standard units, always seems to point towards the idea of infinity; after all, repetition is a phenomenon that suggests a movement 'ad infinitum'. And in our view, it is exactly this idea of infinity that has the potential to shock us out of the alienation of the everyday. It is no wonder that some of the most radical artworks share this sense of infinity, and therefore possess the subversive potential to let us see the world in a different way. Interestingly enough, we think it is precisely his modularity (and not necessarily his attempts to produce furniture) that caused Judd to touch the world of design. To put it boldly, we think that design, intrinsically linked to diverse processes of repetition (serial production, graphic multiplication, etc.), is closely related to the modularity of minimal art.

04. Advil and Excedrin

Graphic design is enormously important to us. It occupies every minute of our lives. We have to admit that every single thing that we do, even when seemingly unrelated to graphic design, we immediately try to place in the context of graphic design. Watching a documentary on TV, listening to pop music, taking a walk, going to a rock show, teaching, hanging out with friends, even sleeping: it all becomes part of the design process.

Recently, we wrote a short text for U.K. graphic design magazine *Grafik*, to answer their question '2004: How was it for you?' In that text, we wrote that 'since we started in 1997, the usual rhythm of weeks, months and years gradually disappeared. We're now marching to the beat of deadline after deadline. The only constants are the daily pressure to perform, and a steady diet of Advil 400 (against common headache), Excedrin (against tension headache) and Maxalt (against migraine).'

So your question if it's worth it is a good one. Because the practice of graphic design is causing us a lot of physical discomfort. All three of us are slightly dysfunctional, and slightly oversensitive. Which means that we don't have the right personalities to deal with the deadlines we have to deal with on a daily basis. The responsibility that comes with working on large projects, and the constant pressure to perform and to live up to expectations, is really killing us, resulting in headaches, overeating, dizziness and sleeplessness.

But we still think it is worth it. We're living a world that seems dominated by post-modern tendencies (movements such as neo-conservatism, right-wing populism and religious fundamentalism). Working in graphic design, a discipline born out of modernism, gives us the chance to explore values and themes that we can't find anywhere else. For us, there is a lot of consolation to be found in graphic design.

In our answer to one of your earlier questions (about the political dimension of graphic design), we wrote that, in our opinion, 'the only way to shock us out of this alienation is to counter the fragmentation of society with the wholeness of design'. This is not just a rhetoric statement; for us this is quite personal. The practice of graphic design is also a way to shock us out of our own alienation.

05. Design and art
We don't see graphic design as art, but we do see art as a form of design. Although it's hard to define art, it's not difficult to define its context: there exists a clear infrastructure of exhibition spaces, galleries, museums, art magazines, art publishers, art history, art theory, etc. Art can be seen as the production of objects, concepts and activities intended to function within this specific infrastructure. In our view, this production can certainly be seen as a specific form of design.

Speaking about art and design, it's interesting to see how the view on the relationship between art and design changed during the course of modernism. Striving towards a synthesis of art and design was quite an essential characteristic of early modernism, quite possibly its most defining one. Early modernists such as László Moholy-Nagy and El Lissitzky were absolutely driven by the idea to unite art and the everyday; the idea of art, not as an added, decorative layer, but as something fully integrated in modern life. While late-modernists, such as Wim Crouwel and the late Gerrit Rietveld (as opposed to the early Gerrit Rietveld) were (and in the case of Wim Crouwel, still are) radically against such a synthesis of art and design.

In the conclusion of 'Theory and Design in the First Machine Age', Reyner Banham seems to suggest that the late modernists more or less sacrificed the early-modernist ideal of synthesis (of art and the everyday) in favour of late-modernist ideals such as functionalism and utilitarianism. Which is an interesting observation. Nevertheless, in our view, there is certainly a necessity to restore the historical, modernist link between design and art.

Afterword: when we wrote about seeing 'art as a form of design', we weren't necessarily talking about 'arty' design, or 'designy' art. We were simply trying to recognize the material conditions of art, trying to define art as a form of cultural production (and thus as a specific form of design). It was in no way an attempt to belittle art; in fact, it was quite the opposite. By 'grounding' art in its material context, its cultural infrastructure, we were trying to show art as what it is: a concrete activity, in a concrete world. Too often, art is seen as this sphere of floating, disconnected images, almost as a form of branding or advertising. We view art as something completely different than that: we see it as a very conscious act of shaping the material world around us. And in that sense, we do see it as a specific manifestation of design. Because, after all, that is exactly what design is: the conscious act of shaping the material world around us.

Naoto Fukasawa and Jasper Morrison

Super Normal

2007

"design is refining that 'normal' core existence bit by bit so that it fits in with our lives today. Then this exceeds normal and becomes Super Normal. Those things that never change can also be called Super Normal. I think that Super Normal indicates our 'realization' of what is good in 'normal'"

Naoto Fukasawa (1956–) is a Japanese industrial designer and Jasper Morrison (1959–) is an English product and furniture designer. Together they examine how examples of iconic industrial design can become "ordinary" through repeated use.

....

Francesca Picchi: Super Normal has been received as a kind of manifesto of what design should be according to you. Today there is a certain ambiguity about the term design (about its meaning); generally it is perceived as something to "make nicer things." Can Super Normal be considered as a sort of theory? Or an attempt at theorizing what good design is or should be?

Naoto Fukasawa: Super Normal is not a theory. I believe it's re-realizing something that you already knew, re-acknowledging what you naturally thought was good in something. It's true that design is all about improving what already exists, but there's also the danger that things that were already good get changed. Design is expected to provide something "new" or "beautiful" or "special." When we look at the things around us with such a mindset, those things outside "design" are viewed as being "normal" or "ugly" in contrast. Super Normal consists of the things that we overlook when we focus too much on "design"—I think it points to those things in our everyday lives that we naturally hold an affinity for. I believe Super Normal is the inevitable form that results from the lengthy use of a thing—shall we say, a core of awareness. Design is refining that "normal" core existence bit by bit so that it fits in with our lives today. Then this exceeds normal and becomes Super Normal. Those things that never change can also be called Super Normal. I think that Super Normal indicates our "realization" of what is good in "normal."

Jasper Morrison: I don't mind the definition to "make nicer things." If design achieved this occasionally, it would be fine! I agree Super Normal isn't a theory, it's more of a "noticing." Super Normal has been around for a long time, probably since the first pots were made. It's an aspect of how we live with and relate to objects rather than a system for designing better things, although I think there's a lot to be learnt from that. Objects become Super Normal through use rather than design, although their design is a key factor. You might not know something was Super Normal simply by looking at it, nor would you know it by using it once. It's more of a long-term discovery of the quality of an object, which goes beyond the initial visual judgment and basic assessment that we make of things when we first notice them. Super Normal may belong more to everyday life than it does to design.

FP: What could be a possible definition of Super Normal?

NF: It refers to something that already exists, something so ordinary or normal that everybody points to it and says, "That's really normal!" It can also mean something that has been newly designed, which people look at with the expectation of being blown away by its newness or by something special about it. Instead they say, "Huh?! That's just so... normal!" So it's something that packs a surprise at odds with our expectations.

JM: An even more basic definition could be something that's good to have around, that you use in a completely satisfactory way without having to think about its shape or decipher any hidden message or trickiness. If you went into a shop looking for a dining plate, it would be the most plate-like plate you could find. Even more plate-like than you could imagine a plate to be. What's good about a more than plate-like plate is that it will do its job without messing up the atmosphere in the way that designer tableware might do. The same can be applied to almost any category of object.

FP: Normal is a term that has to do with the idea of conforming to a standard (*norma* = rules in Latin). Super Normal could be taken as meaning something that goes beyond the rules (if we consider the Latin meaning: *super*=above, beyond) but also as something that is really, really normal, that concentrates all quality on normality, and expresses a kind of extra normality (if we consider the Anglo-Saxon use of super as an adjective). How did the definition of Super Normal come about? How should we interpret the term Super Normal and how did you come up with the idea of formalizing Super Normal by gathering real examples?

NF: "Normal" is the situation where something has blended comfortably into our lives. One would venture to say that such things are used unconsciously. I understand it as a term that indicates an entity that is integrated into our lifescape. Within this normal is a particularly symbolic archetype that is "really normal," and this is what has been termed "Super Normal." Super Normal is the normal within the normal.

Jasper and I started collecting things without really talking over beforehand what kinds of things Super Normal defined. I gathered together a lot of things using my own criteria; when I showed these to Jasper, our agreement as to them being Super Normal was almost total. And I agreed completely with all the things Jasper had chosen. Those things at the center of normal may be termed "standard," but when people choose a particular item, I believe that they choose something that is the very epitome of that item. And I believe it's because people know that that's the thing that feels right, that doesn't make waves in their lives. By gathering together and showing these things, we hoped to discover their focal point.

JM: I guess we are talking about the modern sense of the term. I like Francesca's description of concentrating all quality on normality, because I think that within what could be described as normal form or normal character in objects, there are enormous possibilities for creating things that are positive influences on the man-made environment. The term itself can be used various ways. An object can be Super Normal by being so extremely normal that its presence is taken entirely for granted, or it can take its influence from normality and seek to go beyond it by "concentrating all quality on normality," a kind of distilled, concentrated form of normality or summary of everyone's expectations of an object. As for the exhibition and why we decided to do it, it was a natural way to visualize something that at first was rather a vague notion. We knew that Super Normal existed in different guises and gathering together examples was the easiest and most direct way of understanding it. Proposing different objects to each other became a 3-dimensional dialogue before we put any words to it, like two aliens in outer space finding a way to communicate!

FP: What place does Super Normal occupy in your work as designers?

NF: When I start a project these days, I tend to check what is normal or archetypal in the category, because I believe that Super Normal is about extracting the essence of this normality. Once the archetypal character of the category is discovered, I refine it to suit today's lifestyle. This may only involve very slight changes, but I think that when the essence of normal is found and refined, the result is naturally something Super Normal. I try to avoid the pressures of trying to create something new and better, ignoring existing perfections in a category.

JM: Once you notice something Super Normal it becomes a bit of an obsession, it occupies a lot of time. I find myself asking if a thing seems Super Normal before buying it, or comparing two models of a product to decide which might be more Super Normal, or sitting in restaurants turning plates upside down. These moments have always been an important part of how I design, and at the start of a project I've noticed myself asking whether it's appropriate to aim for a Super Normal result, but I think an awareness of Super Normal can only be good for one's design. I think most designers get inspiration from looking at life, and this is no different; it's just concentrated on normality.

FP: Why did you feel the need at this point in your careers to develop an idea like Super Normal? Where does this attempt at theorizing come from? Does Super Normal express a reaction against someone or something? And if so, against what?

NF: Whenever I evaluate an object or when I ask myself what part of a design I don't like, I always get hung up on the creator's intentions or the self-expression being at odds with the functions or the harmony inherent in that object. I don't like this aspect of the designs of others, and I try to ensure that such things don't appear in my own designs. The idea of designs that result when we take ourselves a little less seriously and do what comes naturally overlaps with Super Normal. I think this comes from a desire to share the pleasurable sensation that comes with realizing the hint of "goodness" in an object that is sensed with the entire body, apart from one's consciousness.

Perhaps both Jasper and myself were tired of the same thing, of designs that are "designed." Perhaps we both felt some kind of intense appeal in things in our daily lives that were not designed, the kind of things that in a certain sense could be called unstylish. Both the "Déjà-vu" stool that I designed for Magis and the cutlery Jasper designed for Alessi are things that play on the feeling cultivated in day-to-day life. Re-designing something that was normal to start with: that is exactly what the term "Super Normal" expressed. Takashi Okutani came up with the term "Super Normal" when Jasper was talking to him about the cutlery and the "Déjà-vu" stool; I think Jasper was jubilant to have a single term that so precisely expressed his thoughts and feelings. At that moment, the thought took on a concrete form.

It's true that it is a backlash against the kind of design that creates things that do not blend in with people, with the environment and circumstances, or with lifestyles. But it's not a backlash that manifests itself in our movement; I believe that it is a backlash by consumers themselves with respect to their own penchant for a jolt to the senses, when they wake up having found a new feeling of comfort in something, when they realize that what they have been looking for so far are designs that pack a punch. But the punch I'm talking about here is the kind that far exceeds what's required in an object, and it goes without saying that it's necessary only where a design would be inadequate without it.

JM: For me it is a reaction, a reaction to noticing how much better most normal things are than most design things. I think design is in danger of becoming something false and out of tune with real life, when it could be doing something worthwhile. It's degenerating into a marketing tool to promote the identity of companies and to sell magazines. That's not the profession I admired as a student. There's lots of good design going on, maybe more than when I was a student, but unfortunately it's heavily outweighed by what can only be described as visual pollution, atmospheric interference, designs with nothing more in mind than getting noticed, and on balance I'd have to say we would be better off without it. Super Normal is a reminder of more genuine motives for designing something.

FP: Is Super Normal related to your personal idea of beauty? I think it would be interesting to understand your personal point of view on beauty. What is beauty for you in an object? What is a beautiful object?

NF: Beauty can refer to form or shape, but in this case we're thinking in terms of the beauty of the relationship between people, the environment, and circumstances. In other words it's the echo of beauty that arises when we use something. Because the beauty of this relationship lies in the fact that people often use things in similar ways, in similar environments, and under similar circumstances. The beauty of the relationship is therefore naturally narrowed down to certain situations. For example, the way everyone holds the soy sauce dispenser when pouring is the same, and the action of pouring has become part of the atmosphere of enjoying sushi, so that a newer design most likely would not be able to re-create this atmosphere. I think that this beauty arises with the natural, unconscious use of something.

JM: I think Super Normal is wrapped up in a debate about beauty, not just beauty quickly perceived but beauty on other levels, the beauty which takes time to be noticed, which may become beautiful through use, the beauty of the everyday, the beauty of the ugly and the useful, long-term beauty. A beautiful object is not necessarily one with the best shape, and an object may start out ugly and become beautiful over time. Sometimes I'm struck by something beautiful; I buy it, thinking it'll be useful, and discover later on that it never got used and it doesn't seem so beautiful anymore. Actually I think beauty is over-rated.

FP: Jasper, Enzo Mari suggests that the most important thing you did, from a theoretical point of view—the one that best conveyed your personal design philosophy—is the volume *A World Without Words*. Compare to *A World Without Words*, what does Super Normal represent? What is the relationship between the two? And what leads you today to feel the need to formalize your thought with words?

JM: Before it became a book, "A World without Words" was a slide show lecture, a collection of images which meant something to me, put together to get around the difficulty of speaking in public, and perhaps to show that some things don't need to be said. Super Normal could also have been left unsaid, but I think there's a lack of discourse in the design world, a kind of noisy silence in which we have all been working. Something had to be said. It probably bothers some people that we're saying it, but I believe Super Normal is a way out of the hole that design has got itself into. There may be other ways, or maybe some people prefer to stay in the hole, but for anyone who cares about it, I hope it will lead to a better understanding of what makes a good object.

FP: I have the impression that Super Normal is essentially confused or taken as a "call to order" regarding the proliferation of signs and forms that produce the visual pollution that surrounds us. On the one hand it has been perceived as a Calvinistic stance with respect to homogenized forms and, on the other, as an excess of narcissistic expression. Furthermore, I think the most interesting aspect is the one related to the perception of form vis-à-vis use, which is related to your contesting the prevalence of seeing over the other senses that are more directly involved in the use of an object. What do you think about that?

JM: In the 70s design was all about function, but it was the function of the moment, the kind of function you test while opening a can of peas, asking yourself in that moment how good the can opener is. These days we take function for granted and for the most part things work well enough not to complain about them. So taking a purely functional approach to design would be disastrous. Super Normal's about how things work in relation to our living with them. Not just in one-off use but interactively, over the long term, in relation to everything else we own and use and the atmospheric influence all these things have on our lives. It's interesting to discover, after five years of using a chopping board, that we've been making use of aspects of its design without even noticing them. The slightly curved profile of its sides, which helps us pick it up and stops the wood grain absorbing water while it dries upright on the kitchen counter, and beyond this realization, the sudden appreciation of a form so subtly adapted to its job as to be almost invisibly integrated into the object, allowing it to perform naturally and without any call for praise until we are ready to notice it…I'm getting carried away, but what I mean to say is this discovery is a real wake-up call for what we think of as design. There are levels of sophistication in the object world, achieved most often through the evolutionary forces of an object's development, which make our attempts at design laughable. We can learn a lot from them.

FP: Can you explain your personal relationship to objects? What kind of relationship do you normally establish with the objects that are part of your daily life?

NF: A great deal of our time is taken up with the job of designing, constantly attempting to seek the existence and the shape of things that can be in harmony with, and appropriate for our lives. Within the profusion of signs and forms that get designed, there are occasions when we discover the existence of something that gives us a feeling of comfort, something Super Normal. By evaluating the necessity, the appropriateness of a thing's existence in this world, we may discover an intense appeal in an object, which may at first have seemed ugly. I believe that the emotion we feel when we come into contact with the essence of such useful beauty is stronger than the emotion we may feel when we look at something that has been "designed."

JM: I have to confess to being quite obsessive about objects. They are the main subject of my work and occupy a good deal of my day, either in planning them or in studying them. The studying part is all about seeing how they fit in with everything else, what kind of atmospheric influence they have, how they work and how well they work. When coming across a well-balanced object that does everything it should do, it seems to me that it possesses something more than the sum of its parts, a kind of completeness that qualifies it as Super Normal.

FP: In our relationship with objects we are all used to thinking in terms of use, value, and function. However, I recall that some time ago you spoke about a kind of "psychoanalysis of objects," meaning that they could be considered to have a kind of personality, or "objectality," as you called it. Could your research on Super Normal be considered the ongoing development of that idea? And how does it relate to your previous research?

JM: Objectality may have been the first noticing of something Super Normal in objects. I guess you can break down our perception of objects as follows: the first encounter may well be based more on an evaluation of the object's cost, the quality of the object relating to the cost, the perceived usefulness of the object to us, and the object's desirability. But later on, when it comes to living with an object, we forget all about the cost and we have in mind the object's usefulness in relation to certain tasks, how much we enjoy using it, and how much we appreciate it as a possession. It becomes a part of our lives, which we may not think about much but which nevertheless exists, as witnessed when we move house and may be forced to confront the relationship we have with the object in deciding whether to keep it or not. I think this is true no matter how many objects we possess. I remember seeing Gandhi's worldly possessions laid out in the room he occupied in Ahmedabad: a pair of spectacles, a rice bowl, and a piece of cloth, I think that was about it, but it was obvious, thinking about it now, that these objects were Super Normal to him and he needed no others.

FP: Super Normal seems to suggest that objects may be endowed with their own soul, rather than being inanimate objects. This perspective is probably closer to Japanese culture and its world populated by a divine being, connected to the presences of the Kami. What do you think?

NF: There is a kind of beauty, a purity to brand-new objects that have been untouched by human hands. In the Shinto faith, there is a philosophy that links the beauty of such untouched objects to God and that searches for a beauty removed from those things tainted by the real world in which we live, this being the world of God. Another idea is that an implement that has been newly created and not yet used has no soul. In contrast, something used by many people (this doesn't mean just one item; it means a number of the same implements used by many) has a soul to it. Through many people using it, an object is substantiated and attains a brilliance; the weight of the soul within this object shows its worth. Wabisabi is a beauty that arises after useful beauty has been mastered.

FP: I recently read an article in an old issue of *Domus*, written by Yusaku Kamekura (a graphic designer and a pioneer of modernity in postwar Japan) about form and tradition in Japan. He talks about the concept of "pure" form—form that is not subject to market pressures or any other pressure—using the term *katachi*, a quality expressing a particular aspect of form, connected to a specific emotional and rational quality. He writes: "a form that is present both in the matter and in the action…" and "In Japan form still expresses simplicity, elegance and splendor…" and "I think it is of the utmost importance to fight against what is possible and achieve the impossible."

NF: I believe that in Japan, there is a tendency to take the actual act of using a thing as beauty. This is precisely the beauty of the relationship between objects and people. For example, a chair might have a backrest with a shape that invites me to lean on it when I'm standing behind it, so it's not the beauty of the shape as such that is appreciated but rather a form's presence that sparks off actions and contributes to the atmosphere around it. A form that beautifies behavior and actions, or a form that beautifies the relationship between itself and the things around it, has to be something that does not fix action and environment, but something you might call a generic, overall beauty that grants a degree of freedom. So there is a tendency towards objects inevitably taking on a simplicity. Or there is a tendency for things to become easier to use function-wise. I believe that representations of decorativeness or ornateness for the sake of appreciation are far-removed and separate from useful beauty.

FP: I don't really understand the deep meaning or the significance of this culture of form, but I would like to understand, Naoto, how you relate to that tradition. More generally, how does your idea of Super Normal relate respectively to good design and the Modern, on the one hand and the Japanese, on the other—both implicitly referring to an idea of simplicity and formal clarity?

NF: I think that beauty of function is the kind of beauty where all attention is focused on the function of an object, instead of forms with decorative or ornamental nuances or expressions. And any expression of self on the part of the creator is also done away with; by focusing on function, any emotion that may be attached to an object and its uses is eliminated, and the object can thus fulfill its function perfectly. That's the way I see it. It's like people being respected for getting down to it and focusing on their own particular role, so that an unseen yet cohesive relationship is built up. It's the same with objects: a focus on function and a lack of emotion in the equation means that our connection to the object becomes more attractive and we develop an affinity for it. In a sense, it's where an object is perfect and uncompromising in function, even though it is modest and doesn't make a personal statement. A relationship where there is no flattery on either side is the base of the Japanese aesthetic consciousness. But focusing on function also means that objects allow us to use them in many different ways. Instead of a hammer whose rubber grip has four grooves for fingers molded into it, one with a simple, easy-to-use round wooden handle is a form that comes to feel comfortable in one's hand, as its shape changes slowly with use; it's one that has a lot of freedom to it and can be used when hammering in any type of nail. Like a hammer, we're talking about objects that don't advertise "Hey, I'm easy to use" just with their shape. Super Normal refers exactly to that simple, straightforward hammer icon.

FP: The selection of Super Normal objects comprises objects of known authors (for example, world famous designers like Sori Yanagi, Enzo Mari, and Konstantin Grcic) and anonymous, everyday products without specific aesthetic intent. What do they share that makes them all Super Normal?

NF: There is a feeling of comfort in using anonymous things that have been around for a long time. Out-living other things, which proved less enduring, they have become so familiar to us that we rarely ask ourselves who their creator might have been. Designers often hold the greatest respect for such objects, aware of the undeniable beauty within these normal things. They frequently derive great inspiration from them. The Super Normal that already existed and the Super Normal that has been achieved more recently have a unified value; the only difference is how long they have been used and the presence or absence of the creator's name.

JM: I couldn't say it any better than that, except to add that what unites the two categories may be a motivation to put the object ahead of the individual creative ego as opposed to the urge to have it noticed. The evolutionary step instead of the creative leap. Not that a Super Normal object is uncreative, but the creativity is less focused on the visual aspect of an object's character and more on creating an object in balance with its role and with its likely environment.

FP: I believe that the goose egg, especially if compared to the chicken egg we are all more familiar with, seems to be the form allowing us to immediately understand the concept of Super Normal. This idea of a slight deviation from the standard—a minimal intervention that acts as a shift in meaning—is one of the concepts that clearly emerges from both Super Normal and your activity in general. I am thinking for example about Jasper's Glo Ball; in this lamp the deviation from the pure geometrical shape is evident. Can you tell us something more about this? Are there other Super Normal objects that could be perceived in terms of this perspective?

JM: The minimal intervention or subtle change could be a change of scale or proportion, just as it could be a slight simplification or the adaptation of a successful feature of an object to a new form, or the concentration of an object's character. Many of the exhibits are examples of these possibilities, and I agree that the goose egg demonstrates this very well. Some other obvious ones are N° 1, the tables on which everything is displayed (designed by Jean Nouvel); N° 21, Enzo Mari's Mariolina chair; N° 118, the paper clip; N° 166, Fiskar scissors; and N°205, the *Herald Tribune* newspaper.

FP: Some anonymous Japanese objects can be found in the exhibition, such as the salt cellar from the Japanese state monopoly. This object is obviously experienced in a different way by Naoto and Jasper. For Naoto it probably belongs to his memory/history. To what extent does the history of an object effect the way it is perceived when used? What is the impact of the history of an object or of its author's personality on the way it is perceived when used?

JM: I think there's a sub-group of Super Normal objects, which is a very subjective one. They are Super Normal through familiarity and even nostalgic memories. I think everyone could point to at least one item in their home and describe it as an object they love to have around for the memory of past atmosphere that it evokes. Our appreciation of atmosphere is often linked or cross referenced with the past, and objects that played a part in some previous atmospheric memories have a powerful hold on us. For me N° 29 bicycle handlebars could easily be included in this category, as my first serious bicycle had very similar ones, or N° 203 Alvar Aalto stool, which a childhood friend had at his house.

FP: All the objects in your selection—whether designed or anonymous, of eastern or western origins, modern or contemporary—show a common spirit, and I really appreciate that. Nowadays, many people talk about the risks connected to cultural homogeneity and globalization; your exhibition is a selection of industrial objects mirroring some aspects of a consistency that can not be clearly explained but that can be clearly seen in practice. Do you think Super Normal can be considered as a catalogue of examples of a possible idea of modernity shared by the East and the West? Can Super Normal be generally considered as a rejection of the "design style"?

JM: I hadn't thought of it before, but now that you mention it, I can see it as a kind of spirit of things, which is both modern and old fashioned and which I think could be understood by anyone. They might not all be everyone's idea of good taste, but then they are not objects that need to be judged in terms of taste. I think they represent an advanced level of object precisely because they reject design as an issue of taste.

FP: Is what I heard about Sori Yanagi true, about his visiting the exhibition in Tokyo and asking who had designed an object that he forgot he'd designed many years before? That would be extraordinary evidence of the detachment from one's ego as an author. However, it also suggests that the object has achieved that specific level of sophistication mentioned by Jasper. Jasper states that objects achieve a consistent shape after a formal process of adjustment that can only be appraised on the long term and that results from the efforts of many designers—often anonymous—over time.

NF: Through the years, objects are created and then used; any deficiencies are corrected; the object is used again…then corrected again—the relationship between people and objects reaches an end point. This also means that the form reaches an end form. This does not mean that designers picked out this end form, but rather that the shape has resulted from the use of that object in day-to-day life by many people and over time. Who designed the object is no longer that important. If a designer believes that people and time have created a form, then they want to get rid of the ego that says, "I designed this object"—I think this is a modest, natural turn of events. Like the flow of water or the wind smoothing the edges of rocks so they take on a roundness. When people use something that leads to a particular form, the result is something normal. The end point of this is Super Normal.

FP: It seems that some designers have been able to interfere in that process of evolution and give a positive shift to it. For instance, Enzo Mari says that the designer is the guardian of a collective knowledge and that the project often "involves the slight adjustment of details, because the structural functionality of objects has been regulated by ancient use."

JM: I think he's quite right, although the amount of shift may vary. I like the idea that we are guardians of a collective knowledge, and the passing on of it could be seen as a parallel to the evolutionary process, whereby things that don't work are discarded and things that do work are built upon. Looking at the development of objects from the first tool until recently, this has been the case, but the modern creative urge in humankind is strong enough to override this commonsense approach, even though in most cases the result is a failure. The entertainment provided by these formal gymnastics seems to be enough to justify the exercise. The bigger the shift that Enzo Mari speaks of, the less likely it is to stick.

FP: Naoto mentioned the *wabi-sabi* principle, which implies an idea of beauty or serenity that comes with age, when the life of the object is evidenced in its patina and wear, or in any visible repairs. With the concept of Super Normal you are suggesting that the use is a relation that strengthens over time. You also mentioned a kind of relation to the objects that does not necessarily involve the fact that an object is "nice" (Naoto speaks about the "beauty of the ugly"). How do aspects of imperfection or use-dependent transformation of the material state of the object contribute to the definition of a Super Normal quality?

NF: In Japan, we have the word *shutaku*. A literal translation would be "polished by hand." It is a metaphor for something that's been used and become better after having been touched again and again; *shutaku* is a polished luster; it is also a metaphor for something that has taken on a personality of its own, or improved with age. It fits comfortably in one's hand, a metaphor for something that has come to fit in our lifestyle. This same meaning is included in *wabi* and *sabi*, but the awkward beauty of something decaying over time indicates an overall beauty, which human hands cannot touch directly; nature in its entirety has weathered that thing. *Shutaku* expresses the beauty that occurs with time when an object survives constant use, undergoes a metamorphosis and becomes more beautiful than something that is new. It's talking about the deepening of a relationship. Something that isn't found in an object that graces a shelf; the form and luster an object gains as people use it deepens its beauty: it invites people to get attached to it.

So both *shutaku* and *wabi-sabi* refer to things that aren't cool design-wise but rather normal with nothing special about them except that they have the potential for becoming great with use. Something that was normal gains *shutaku* and has the potential for acquiring the beauty of *wabi-sabi*. That's because with something that has been created not with beauty but with function in mind, this modesty becomes even more *wabi* and *sabi*.

Super Normal means things that move towards this normal—it's talking about awkward beauty.

JM: That sums up the physical side of Super Normal very well, and I'd only add that I think there is also a less physical transformation that objects we possess go through with time. For example, the accumulated use of a hammer or a teapot (separately, of course) creates a relationship between user and object which may be parallel to its material change but nevertheless independent. We come to appreciate an object through using it, and the more we use a good object, the more we are able to appreciate its qualities, and we may discover its beauty not just in how it ages but in how we age with it.

Kenya Hara

What Is Design?

2007

"today's designers are beginning to realize that endless possibilities for design lie dormant not just in the new situations brought on by technology, but also in the common circumstances of our daily lives"

Kenya Hara (1958–) grew up in Tokyo and studied design at Musashino Art University. He has been the art director of the home goods and apparel store Muji since 2001 and is a prolific writer. Hara's book Designing Design *elaborates on the importance of emptiness in both the visual and philosophical traditions of Japan, and its application to design.*

....

The Prank of Postmodernism

On the brink of the explosive spread of personal computers, we were bound to head into the infancy of yet another new economic culture, but on the eve of that birth, for just a bit, design strayed into a bizarre labyrinth. In the '8os, the term "postmodern" was introduced in the world of design, developing into a trendy phenomenon that spread across the fields of architecture, interior design and product design. Originating in Italy, it spread like wildfire to the rest of the developed world. As the term indicates, postmodernism was conceived as the ideological conflict between modernism and the new era, but if we review it with a little broader perspective today, in the 21st century, we recognize that postmodernism cannot be seen as a turning point in design history. It was just a fleeting commotion that occurred during the hand-off of the concept of modernism from one generation to the next. If we look carefully, we can even see postmodernism as an event symbolizing the aging of the generation of designers that sustained modernism.

From the trends in the plastic arts, it is clear that postmodernism was a small, manipulated system of icons and something of a fad. Photos of people in old-fashioned clothes of any past era make us laugh because of the strangeness of an entire society's participation in this empty agreement called fashion. Viewed from the 21st century, postmodernism makes us laugh for the same reason. It seems like a revival of the Streamline Style. However, it's worth noting that those who initiated the movement included designers like Ettore Sottsass, whose brilliant accomplishments include products and corporate identity for Olivetti created within the tide of modernism. What distinguishes this movement from the streamline boom is the fact that the designers were not overwhelmed by the plastic, representational nature of postmodernism, but those who perceived the limitations and possibilities of modernism through their own experience played with design, creating an empty iconic system with full knowledge of what they were doing. At the same time we can't forget the germination, among ordinary people, the recipients of design, of a kind of maturity and worldliness that recognized and accepted the fictitious nature of this kind of design.

However, I question reading postmodernism as the aging of a certain generation, because this is a world of pranks, directed by designers weary of spending time with modernism and ordinary people who have attained some sophistication regarding information. In the generation tired of pouring its pure passion into modernism, I sense a phase of mature insight.

The forms attending the playfulness of postmodernism are like the sophisticated jokes cracked by the designers of our grandparents' generation, an epoch of design's dissolution that we should cherish. The world should have let postmodernism pass with a smile, but the economy alone was serious, trying to use it to revitalize the market, and spreading it into the world much more than was necessary. For a bit, young designers were tossed about in the melee too. Even critics acclaimed postmodernism as a duel between modernism and a new era. Here lies the cause of postmodernism's wandering, its bewilderment and its bitterness.

From these events we should recognize that modernism isn't over yet. Even if the power of the impact it had at its inception has been lost, modernism is not the kind of thing that can turn into a trend or a fashion.

Modernism has temporarily suffered from the experience of being ironically shrugged off as a parody by designers of a certain generation who were tired of pursuing it. If the intellect that understands the quality of life through the practice of making things is an essential energy that can inspire modernism to evolve and grow, designers born afresh among the younger generation who are exposed to the idea of modernism will direct a new modernism that transcends the work of the senior generation that grew so tired of the mainstream.

Computer Technology and Design

Where does design stand today? The remarkable progress of information technology has thrown our society into great turmoil. The computer promises, we believe, to dramatically increase human ability, and the world has overreacted to potential environmental change in that computer-filled future. In spite of the fact that our rockets have only gone as far as the moon, the world busies itself with worries and preparations for intergalactic travel.

The Cold War between East and West is over, and the world long ago began revolving on the unspoken standard of economic might. In a world in which economic power accounts for the majority of our values, people believe that the best plan for preserving that power is to respond quickly to forecasted changes to the environment. Convinced of a paradigm shift to rival the Industrial Revolution, people are so worried about missing the bus that they beat their brains out trying to get to a new place, but are only acting on precepts of precomputer education.

In a world in which the motive force is the desire to get the jump on the next person, to reap the wealth computer technology is expected to yield, people have no time to leisurely enjoy the actual benefits and treasures already available, and in leaning so far forward in anticipation of the possibilities, they've lost their balance and are in a highly unstable situation, barely managing to stay upright as they fall forward into their next step.

Apparently, people think they shouldn't criticize technological progress. It may be that deeply seated in the consciousness of our contemporaries is an obsession of a sort, to the effect that those who contradicted the Industrial Revolution or the machine civilization were thought of as lacking in foresight and were looked down upon. That's why people have such a hard time speaking out against flaws that are likely felt by everyone. This is probably because they're afraid that anyone who grumbles about technology will be thought an anachronism. Society has no mercy for those who can't keep up with the times.

However, at the risk of being misunderstood, I have to say that technology ought to evolve more slowly and steadily. It would be best if it took the time to mature, through trial and error. We are so excessively and frantically competitive that we have repeatedly planted unsteady system in unsteady ground, which have evolved into a variety of trunk systems that are weak and liable to fail, but have been left to develop anyway. Having no way to stop, they barrel down the track, completely exhausted. People have wrapped themselves in this unhealthy technological environment and are accumulating more stress every day. Technology continues to advance and has multiplied beyond the amount knowable by a single individual; its entirety can be neither grasped nor seen, and it's so vast its edges fade from view. There is nothing aesthetically appealing about communication or the practice of making things when their ideology and education remain unable to cope with this situation, but just continue on their familiar trodden paths.

The computer is not a tool but a material. So says John Maeda, a professor at the Massachusetts Institute of Technology. The implication is that we shouldn't use computers in the manner of just swallowing whatever software comes along, but need to think deeply and carefully about what kind of intellectual world can be cultivated based on this new material that operates with numbers. I think his suggestion deserves our respect. For any material to become a superb material, we need to purify its distinguishing attributes as much as possible. As a material for modeling and carving, clay has endless plasticity, but that limitless plasticity is not unrelated to the material's development. If it were filled with nails or other shards of metal, we wouldn't be able to knead it to a usable consistency. These days it's as if we're kneading the clay until our hands bleed. I have trouble believing that anything generated in this kind of impossible situation is going to bring any satisfaction to our lives.

Design today has been given the role of presenting the latest innovations of technology and here, too, is strained. Design, which is accustomed to showing its strength in "making what's fresh today look old tomorrow" as well as bringing novel fruits to a table full of curious diners, is further exacerbating its contortions, in obedience to the new technology.

Radical Dash

When technology moves society, we call the society "technology driven," but there is one country whose design conforms to this situation more than that of any other country. It's the Netherlands. The cradle of Europe's most recent design epoch isn't always Italy or Germany.

In 2000, the World Exposition was held in Hanover, Germany. Ecology was the theme, with presentations of programs about issues like natural resources and environmental preservation. Only the Netherlands' message differed from the rest. I remember it went something like this: "Our country's land, the forests, the varieties of flowers, energy, even beer: we've made it all, on our own." The Dutch pavilion, nicknamed "Big Mac" and designed by the architect group MVRDV, comprised six layers. The rooftop held a plateau-like area with a small lake and several windmills that generated the building's power. The lower level was a forest of natural trees. Natural wood pillars supported the floors and ceilings. A tremendous number of fluorescent lights were installed at random all over the ceilings, and it looked as if they had helped the trees to perform photosynthesis. On the sub-level was a flower garden. I seem to remember hearing the sound of honeybees from small monitors scattered in the carpet of flowers. Fundamentally, visitors to the pavilion were richly rewarded with a direct experience of the Dutch way of communing with Nature.

Now that I think about it, I recall that the Netherlands reclaimed its land by drainage and a quarter of its land lies below sea level. This is the origin of the saying "God created the world. Netherlanders created the Netherlands." Saying that they made the land means they made the forests, the fields and the canals. The Dutch canals are very geometric, as if they were drawn with a ruler, and the houses stand neatly along their banks. Once tremendously enthusiastic about improving tulip varieties, the Netherlands is now the hub of the flower seedling industry. Its technique for generating energy through windmills is superb; it's possible to conclude that the nation has some pride in having intervened in nature and created its own environment through man's artifice.

Simply put, the tradition of Dutch modern design is radicalism, probably partly reflecting this cultural disposition. The artists who took an active part in the De Stijl movement in the first half of the previous century included the graphic designer Piet Zwart, who taught at the Bauhaus, the architect Gerrit T. Rietveld, noted for designing the Red and Blue Chair as well as the Schroder House, and the painter Piet Mondrian. The distinguishing feature of the De Stijl artists can be interpreted as frank and fundamentalist. The De Stijl gave origin to the tradition of Dutch modernism exemplified by fastidiousness as well as wholeheartedness, and marked by the sort of attitude that, once one decides to do something, he'd better commit to it until the end. Rem Koolhaas, who shines with particular brilliance in the world of architecture, is the emblematic figure of this Dutch radicalism; a floor turns directly into walls and the walls immediately into ceilings. Pillars do not necessarily stand upright. The color selection for the seats in an auditorium is random. Ceiling lamps are spaced randomly as well. To pursue a rational space apportionment, he comes up with the solution of a building designed as if it were raised from a ground plan made of a pie graph. His design approach, presenting modern brilliant touches against his dry, candid solutions, which at first glance look aggressive, seems to be a product of the technology-driven context.

The Dutch product design collective, Droog Design, also entails a nihilistic criticism of modernism. Though their pranks differ a bit from postmodernism's, the radical sensibility at their core has the same root as Koolhaas's. The aesthetics cultivated in this land of no mountains and much human ingenuity, fighting a bit with the jarring rhythm of an immature technology, has had no small effect on today's design around the world. It blows a breeze of originality into the blocked mind. Before complaining about the rapid progress of technology, it might be a good idea to learn something from the straightforward, positive dash the Dutch have been on. There must be something for us to learn from it, even if the greater part of this book's message is an antithesis to this kind of context.

Beyond Modernism

So far, this tale of design has covered design absorbed in style-changing techniques and design that clings closely to new technologies, but design is not going to end up as a servant to the economy or technology. While leaning towards that tendency on the one hand, design has done a consistently good job as a rational indicator for giving form to objects. Within its innermost parts, design carries an extra gene of idealistic thought: the pursuit of shape and function, and even while operating on economic energy, it maintains some semblance of a cool, pious way-seeker. That is, within industrial society, design has steadily acted as the rational and efficient indicator, planning for optimal objects and environments. Every time technological progress reveals a new possibility for creating new products or communication infrastructures, design plays a role in persistently and consistently pursuing the best possible solution. I am writing this on a plane bound to Buenos Aires from New York; not only the improvement of aircraft safety, but also the comfort of the seats and other interior furnishings can be recognized as the results of design's assiduous efforts. And from the simplified, ergonomic form of my computer's keyboard, I also see clearly design's role in manufacturing. In other words, one of the achievements of modernism is design's firmly rooted place in our daily lives.

Today's designers are beginning to realize that endless possibilities for design lie dormant not just in the new situations brought on by technology, but also in the common circumstances of our daily lives. Creation of novel things is not the only creativity. The sensibility that allows one to rediscover the unknown in the familiar is equally creative. We hold a great accumulation of culture in our own hands, yet we remain unaware of its value. The ability to make use of these cultural assets as a virgin resource is no less creative than the ability to produce something out of nothing. Beneath our feet lies a gigantic, untouched vein of ore. Just as simply donning sunglasses makes the world look fresher to us, there is an unlimited number of ways of looking at things, and most of them haven't been discovered yet. To awaken and activate those new ways of perceiving things is to enrich our cognitive faculty, and this relates to the enrichment of the relationship between objects and human beings. Design is not the act of amazing an audience with the novelty of forms or materials; it is the originality that repeatedly extracts astounding ideas from the crevices of the very commonness of everyday life. Designers who have inherited the legacy of modernism and shoulder the new century have gradually begun to explore their consciousness of that fact.

The same is true of communication. To create an indicator that can be trusted in chaotic circumstances is to amass sensible, practical observations on the real state of affairs. Today we have come to understand the real state of affairs as follows. The conventional is not replaced by new technologies. The old accepts the new, resulting in more options. What we need for that to happen is not to cling to the new, but to rationally analyze the options we've got. For example, in the e-commerce market, newly established companies have not been as successful as existing companies that entered the same field after painstaking analysis. Internet news services haven't eliminated newspapers. The development of e-mail service and cell phones hasn't reduced the number of postal objects. Clearly, an increase in the number and complexity of media leads to multipolarization of our communication channels.

Communication design is the sensibility that efficiently organizes these media. The sensitivity cultivated by conventional media is not going to be made redundant by the emergence of new media. One medium may be the one that cultivates our communication sense, but others will make use of it as well. Design is the vocation of taking both old and new media, favoring neither, putting them into a cross-disciplinary perspective, and making full use of all. Design is not subordinate to media; design explores the essence of media. In fact, within the labyrinthine complexity of today's media, we can expect people to more clearly understand the genuine value of design.

Digging a little deeper into the relationship between technology and communication, some designers have begun to rethink the possibilities of the quality of information; putting aside the rough information that swirls around like dust on the internet and clings to our monitors, they have recognized the profundity of the quality of information perceptible only when the senses become mobilized. A symbolic example is the attention in recent years that the field of cognitive science (which studies virtual reality) has showered on the "haptic" senses—those besides sight and hearing. The very delicate human senses have begun to become very important in the forefront of technology. Human beings and the environment being equally tangible, the comfort as well as the satisfaction we sense is based on how we appreciate and cherish our communication with the world via our diverse sensory organs. In terms of this perspective, the paired fields of design and technology and of design and science are headed in the same direction. I specialize in communication but have come to think that the ideal of this discipline is not trying to catch the audience's eye with an arresting image, but having the image permeate the five senses. This is communication that is very elusive yet solid and therefore tremendously powerful, which succeeds before we even realize it's there.

Well, we took a roundabout path, but here we are. This spot where we stand together now is where we think about design and practice design. Design is not merely the art of making things. Our brief jaunt through history proved that. No, design is the occupation of straining our ears and eyes to discover new questions from the midst of everyday life. People create their environments by living. Beyond the rational observation of this fact lie the future of technology and the future of design. Somewhere near their loose intersection, we'll find the future of modernism.

PROCESS 7

Structural Process of Design
| Consilience and Concrescence

Art is the imposing of a pattern on experience,
and our aesthetic enjoyment is recognition of the pattern.

Alfred North Whitehead   1929

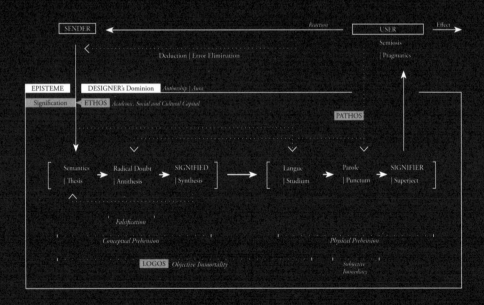

The evolution of graphic design has been driven by available media and defined by the aesthetics of the artifacts of those media. Most design methodologies have developed through a process of continuous and practical application of design principles to achieve a desired outcome. However, a strong awareness of the true meaning and value of design as a process[AW] of problem solving[MV] demands a more sophisticated and rational methodology that employs theoretical interpretation within the overall system of visual communication. Thus, creating a systematic[FS] process[AW] is essential for professional graphic designers to be able to consistently produce satisfactory outcomes.

It is all about the process![AW]

Every step of the process is an important anchor point. The whole process is the nexus of individual, though interrelated, events, including the jelling of the designer's prehension[AW] of the subject, and the visualization process. Intuitive or spontaneous processes that skip some or all of these points could result in a flawed outcome. Completion of the entire process will guarantee the concrescence[AW] of each participant's prehensions,[AW] the ultimate outcome of consilience.[EW] The designer creates an aura,[WB] or the spirit of authorship[RB MF2] through this patterned process in their work.

Design should be understood and practiced as a philanthropic profession aimed at the efficient dissemination of information and communication of messages, not necessarily the designer's own. While André Bazin positioned the concept of the auteur in relation to the restrictions of film production[AB] and Roland Barthes declared the death of author,[RB] Michel Foucault's self-identification as a transdiscursive author[MF2] could be the most accurate and honest acknowledgment of the designer's process.[AW] We give birth to our designs by drawing from multiple discourses and sources. Thus the first step in the process of any design should be to develop a firm understanding of the sender[FS] (the person, people, group, thing, information, message, or meaning), which requires the designer to employ a systematic methodology. Comprehending early examples of critical thinking, such as those offered by Immanuel Kant and Georg Wilhelm Friedrich Hegel, is essential to all designers.

< "Concrescence of Ontological Design Principles" by Henry Hongmin Kim.
See page 437 for details.

A rational analysis of prehension[AW] and the communication process is not just a modern concept. In the fourth century BCE, Aristotle outlined three modes of persuasion[AT] in his treatise on discourse, Rhetoric:

Ethos:[AT] confidence in the ethical credentials of the communicator, based in part on academic, cultural, and social capital[PB]
Logos:[AT] the logical[RD IK GH] interpretation of the message
Pathos:[AT] appealing to the recipient's emotional reaction[RB2] to the communication process

These values are still relevant to the ethical and effective dissemination of information. For designers, they are also closely connected and mirror the relationship among the sender, the designer, and, ultimately, the user.

Still, many designers and artists use antithesis (negative reasoning)[GH] or confrontation[FM] against a given thesis (abstract or concept),[FH] as their main communication tactic without having a good understanding of thesis (abstract or concept).[FH] Thus, the stage of synthesis (concrete, science)[FH] or symbolism is still far off. More design-related theories can be found in cognitive philosophy—including ontology, epistemology, semiotics, and linguistics. Without being able to analyze our culture and language from a structural or post-structural approach, visualization will remain elementary.

(Continue to page 461, "Concrescence of Ontological Design Principles")

AT | Aristotle. *Rhetoric. 4th century BCE.*
RD | Descartes, René. *The Discourse on Method; And, Metaphysical Meditations.* 1635.
IK | Kant, Immanuel. *Critique of Pure Reason.* 1781.
GH | Hegel, Georg Wilhelm Friedrich. *Science of Logic.* 1812.
KM | Marx, Karl. *Manifesto of the Communist Party.* 1848.
FM | Marinetti, F. T. *The Joy of Mechanical Force: Futuristic Manifesto.* 1909.
FS | Saussure, Ferdinand de. *Course in General Linguistics.* 1916.
JT | Tschichold, Jan. *The New Typography.* 1928.
AW | Whitehead, Alfred North. *Process and Reality: An Essay in Cosmology.* 1929.
KP | Popper, Karl. *The Logic of Scientific Discovery.* 1934.
WB | Benjamin, Walter. *Illuminations.* 1936.
AB | Bazin, André. *On the Auteur Theory.* 1957.
JI | Itten, Johannes. *The Art of Color: The Subjective Experience and Objective Rationale of Color.* 1960.
JL | Lacan, Jacques. *The Seminar. Book XI. The Four Fundamental Concepts of Psychoanalysis.* 1964.
MF | Foucault, Michel. *The Order of Things: An Archaeology of the Human Sciences.* 1966.
RB | Barthes, Roland. "The Death of the Author." 1968.
MF2| Foucault, Michel. "What Is an Author?" 1969.
RB2 | Barthes, Roland. *Camera Lucida: Reflections of Photography.* 1980.
JB | Baudrillard, Jean. *For a Critique of the Political Economy of the Sign.* 1981.
JM | Müller-Brockmann, Josef. *Grid and Design Philosophy.* 1981.
PB | Bourdieu, Pierre. "The Forms of Capital." 1986.
VM | Margolin, Victor. *Design Discourse.* 1989.
EW | Wilson, Edward O. *Consilience: The Unity of Knowledge.* 1998.
MV | Vignelli, Massimo. *The Vignelli Canon.* 2010.

7-1

Aristotle

Rhetoric

4TH CENTURY BCE

"(1) to reason logically, (2) to understand human character and goodness in their various forms, and (3) to understand the emotions"

Aristotle (384–322 BCE) was an ancient Greek philosopher who studied under Plato. His thinking covered logic, metaphysics, mathematics, physics, biology, botany, ethics, politics, agriculture, medicine, dance, and theater. He is generally credited with developing a fundamental discourse on rhetoric, politics, and persuasion.

....

Book I

Chapter 1

Rhetoric is the counterpart of Dialectic. Both alike are concerned with such things as come, more or less, within the general ken of all men and belong to no definite science. Accordingly all men make use, more or less, of both; for to a certain extent all men attempt to discuss statements and to maintain them, to defend themselves and to attack others. Ordinary people do this either at random or through practice and from acquired habit. Both ways being possible, the subject can plainly be handled systematically, for it is possible to inquire the reason why some speakers succeed through practice and others spontaneously; and every one will at once agree that such an inquiry is the function of an art.

Now, the framers of the current treatises on rhetoric have constructed but a small portion of that art. The modes of persuasion are the only true constituents of the art: everything else is merely accessory. These writers, however, say nothing about enthymemes, which are the substance of rhetorical persuasion, but deal mainly with non-essentials. The arousing of prejudice, pity, anger, and similar emotions has nothing to do with the essential facts, but is merely a personal appeal to the man who is judging the case. Consequently if the rules for trials which are now laid down in some states—especially in well-governed states—were applied everywhere, such people would have nothing to say. All men, no doubt, think that the laws should prescribe such rules, but some, as in the court of Areopagus, give practical effect to their thoughts and forbid talk about non-essentials. This is sound law and custom. It is not right to pervert the judge by moving him to anger or envy or pity—one might as well warp a carpenter's rule before using it. Again, a litigant has clearly nothing to do but to show that the alleged fact is so or is not so, that it has or has not happened. As to whether a thing is important or unimportant, just or unjust, the judge must surely refuse to take his instructions from the litigants: he must decide for himself all such points as the law-giver has not already defined for him.

Now, it is of great moment that well-drawn laws should themselves define all the points they possibly can and leave as few as may be to the decision of the judges; and this for several reasons. First, to find one man, or a few men, who are sensible persons and capable of legislating and administering justice is easier than to find a large number. Next, laws are made after long consideration, whereas decisions in the courts are given at short notice, which makes it hard for those who try the case to satisfy the claims of justice and expediency. The weightiest reason of all is that the decision of the lawgiver is not particular but prospective and general, whereas members of the assembly and the jury find it their duty to decide on definite cases brought before them. They will often have allowed themselves to be so much influenced by feelings of friendship or hatred or self-interest that they lose any clear vision of the truth and have their judgement obscured by considerations of personal pleasure or pain. In general, then, the judge should, we say, be allowed to decide as few things as possible. But questions as to whether something has happened or has not happened, will be or will not be, is or is not, must of necessity be left to the judge, since the lawgiver cannot foresee them. If this is so, it is evident that any one who lays down rules about other matters, such as what must be the contents of the "introduction" or the "narration" or any of the other divisions of a speech, is theorizing about non-essentials as if they belonged to the art. The only question with which these writers here deal is how to put the judge into a given frame of mind. About the orator's proper modes of persuasion they have nothing to tell us; nothing, that is, about how to gain skill in enthymemes.

Hence it comes that, although the same systematic principles apply to political as to forensic oratory, and although the former is a nobler business, and fitter for a citizen, than that which concerns the relations of private individuals, these authors say nothing about political oratory, but try, one and all, to write treatises on the way to plead in court. The reason for this is that in political oratory there is less inducement to talk about nonessentials. Political oratory is less given to unscrupulous practices than forensic, because it treats of wider issues. In a political debate the man who is forming a judgement is making a decision about his own vital interests. There is no need, therefore, to prove anything except that the facts are what the supporter of a measure maintains they are. In forensic oratory this is not enough; to conciliate the listener is what pays here. It is other people's affairs that are to be decided, so that the judges, intent on their own satisfaction and listening with partiality, surrender themselves to the disputants instead of judging between them. Hence in many places, as we have said already, irrelevant speaking is forbidden in the law-courts: in the public assembly those who have to form a judgement are themselves well able to guard against that.

It is clear, then, that rhetorical study, in its strict sense, is concerned with the modes of persuasion. Persuasion is clearly a sort of demonstration, since we are most fully persuaded when we consider a thing to have been demonstrated. The orator's demonstration is an enthymeme, and this is, in general, the most effective of the modes of persuasion. The enthymeme is a sort of syllogism, and the consideration of syllogisms of all kinds, without distinction, is the business of dialectic, either of dialectic as a whole or of one of its branches. It follows plainly, therefore, that he who is best able to see how and from what elements a syllogism is produced will also be best skilled in the enthymeme, when he has further learnt what its subject-matter is and in what respects it differs from the syllogism of strict logic. The true and the approximately true are apprehended by the same faculty; it may also be noted that men have a sufficient natural instinct for what is true, and usually do arrive at the truth. Hence the man who makes a good guess at truth is likely to make a good guess at probabilities.

It has now been shown that the ordinary writers on rhetoric treat of non-essentials; it has also been shown why they have inclined more towards the forensic branch of oratory.

Rhetoric is useful (1) because things that are true and things that are just have a natural tendency to prevail over their opposites, so that if the decisions of judges are not what they ought to be, the defeat must be due to the speakers themselves, and they must be blamed accordingly. Moreover, (2) before some audiences not even the possession of the exactest knowledge will make it easy for what we say to produce conviction. For argument based on knowledge implies instruction, and there are people whom one cannot instruct. Here, then, we must use, as our modes of persuasion and argument, notions possessed by everybody, as we observed in the Topics when dealing with the way to handle a popular audience. Further, (3) we must be able to employ persuasion, just as strict reasoning can be employed, on opposite sides of a question, not in order that we may in practice employ it in both ways (for we must not make people believe what is wrong), but in order that we may see clearly what the facts are, and that, if another man argues unfairly, we on our part may be able to confute him. No other of the arts draws opposite conclusions: dialectic and rhetoric alone do this. Both these arts draw opposite conclusions impartially. Nevertheless, the underlying facts do not lend themselves equally well to the contrary views. No; things that are true and things that are better are, by their nature, practically always easier to prove and easier to believe in. Again, (4) it is absurd to hold that a man ought to be ashamed of being unable to defend himself with his limbs, but not of being unable to defend himself with speech and reason, when the use of rational speech is more distinctive of a human being than the use of his limbs. And if it be objected that one who uses such power of speech unjustly might do great harm, that is a charge which may be made in common against all good things except virtue, and above all against the things that are most useful, as strength, health, wealth, generalship. A man can confer the greatest of benefits by a right use of these, and inflict the greatest of injuries by using them wrongly.

It is clear, then, that rhetoric is not bound up with a single definite class of subjects, but is as universal as dialectic; it is clear, also, that it is useful. It is clear, further, that its function is not simply to succeed in persuading, but rather to discover the means of coming as near such success as the circumstances of each particular case allow. In this it resembles all other arts. For example, it is not the function of medicine simply to make a man quite healthy, but to put him as far as may be on the road to health; it is possible to give excellent treatment even to those who can never enjoy sound health. Furthermore, it is plain that it is the function of one and the same art to discern the real and the apparent means of persuasion, just as it is the function of dialectic to discern the real and the apparent syllogism. What makes a man a "sophist" is not his faculty, but his moral purpose. In rhetoric, however, the term "rhetorician" may describe either the speaker's knowledge of the art, or his moral purpose. In dialectic it is different: a man is a "sophist" because he has a certain kind of moral purpose, a "dialectician" in respect, not of his moral purpose, but of his faculty.

Let us now try to give some account of the systematic principles of Rhetoric itself—of the right method and means of succeeding in the object we set before us. We must make as it were a fresh start, and before going further define what rhetoric is.

Chapter 2

Rhetoric may be defined as the faculty of observing in any given case the available means of persuasion. This is not a function of any other art. Every other art can instruct or persuade about its own particular subject-matter; for instance, medicine about what is healthy and unhealthy, geometry about the properties of magnitudes, arithmetic about numbers, and the same is true of the other arts and sciences. But rhetoric we look upon as the power of observing the means of persuasion on almost any subject presented to us; and that is why we say that, in its technical character, it is not concerned with any special or definite class of subjects.

Of the modes of persuasion some belong strictly to the art of rhetoric and some do not. By the latter I mean such things as are not supplied by the speaker but are there at the outset—witnesses, evidence given under torture, written contracts, and so on. By the former I mean such as we can ourselves construct by means of the principles of rhetoric. The one kind has merely to be used, the other has to be invented.

Of the modes of persuasion furnished by the spoken word there are three kinds. The first kind depends on the personal character of the speaker; the second on putting the audience into a certain frame of mind; the third on the proof, or apparent proof, provided by the words of the speech itself. Persuasion is achieved by the speaker's personal character when the speech is so spoken as to make us think him credible. We believe good men more fully and more readily than others: this is true generally whatever the question is, and absolutely true where exact certainty is impossible and opinions are divided. This kind of persuasion, like the others, should be achieved by what the speaker says, not by what people think of his character before he begins to speak. It is not true, as some writers assume in their treatises on rhetoric, that the personal goodness revealed by the speaker contributes nothing to his power of persuasion; on the contrary, his character may almost be called the most effective means of persuasion he possesses. Secondly, persuasion may come through the hearers, when the speech stirs their emotions. Our judgements when we are pleased and friendly are not the same as when we are pained and hostile. It is towards producing these effects, as we maintain, that present-day writers on rhetoric direct the whole of their efforts. This subject shall be treated in detail when we come to speak of the emotions. Thirdly, persuasion is effected through the speech itself when we have proved a truth or an apparent truth by means of the persuasive arguments suitable to the case in question.

There are, then, these three means of effecting persuasion. The man who is to be in command of them must, it is clear, be able (1) to reason logically, (2) to understand human character and goodness in their various forms, and (3) to understand the emotions—that is, to name them and describe them, to know their causes and the way in which they are excited. It thus appears that rhetoric is an offshoot of dialectic and also of ethical studies. Ethical studies may fairly be called political; and for this reason rhetoric masquerades as political science, and the professors of it as political experts—sometimes from want of education, sometimes from ostentation, sometimes owing to other human failings. As a matter of fact, it is a branch of dialectic and similar to it, as we said at the outset. Neither rhetoric nor dialectic is the scientific study of any one separate subject: both are faculties for providing arguments. This is perhaps a sufficient account of their scope and of how they are related to each other.

With regard to the persuasion achieved by proof or apparent proof: just as in dialectic there is induction on the one hand and syllogism or apparent syllogism on the other, so it is in rhetoric. The example is an induction, the enthymeme is a syllogism, and the apparent enthymeme is an apparent syllogism. I call the enthymeme a rhetorical syllogism, and the example a rhetorical induction. Every one who effects persuasion through proof does in fact use either enthymemes or examples: there is no other way. And since every one who proves anything at all is bound to use either syllogisms or inductions (and this is clear to us from the *Analytics*), it must follow that enthymemes are syllogisms and examples are inductions. The difference between example and enthymeme is made plain by the passages in the *Topics* where induction and syllogism have already been discussed. When we base the proof of a proposition on a number of similar cases, this is induction in dialectic, example in rhetoric; when it is shown that, certain propositions being true, a further and quite distinct proposition must also be true in consequence, whether invariably or usually, this is called syllogism in dialectic, enthymeme in rhetoric. It is plain also that each of these types of oratory has its advantages. Types of oratory, I say: for what has been said in the *Methodics* applies equally well here; in some oratorical styles examples prevail, in others enthymemes; and in like manner, some orators are better at the former and some at the latter. Speeches that rely on examples are as persuasive as the other kind, but those which rely on enthymemes excite the louder applause. The sources of examples and enthymemes, and their proper uses, we will discuss later. Our next step is to define the processes themselves more clearly.

A statement is persuasive and credible either because it is directly self-evident or because it appears to be proved from other statements that are so. In either case it is persuasive because there is somebody whom it persuades. But none of the arts theorize about individual cases. Medicine, for instance, does not theorize about what will help to cure Socrates or Callias, but only about what will help to cure any or all of a given class of patients: this alone is business: individual cases are so infinitely various that no systematic knowledge of them is possible. In the same way the theory of rhetoric is concerned not with what seems probable to a given individual like Socrates or Hippias, but with what seems probable to men of a given type; and this is true of dialectic also. Dialectic does not construct its syllogisms out of any haphazard materials, such as the fancies of crazy people, but out of materials that call for discussion; and rhetoric, too, draws upon the regular subjects of debate. The duty of rhetoric is to deal with such matters as we deliberate upon without arts or systems to guide us, in the hearing of persons who cannot take in at a glance a complicated argument, or follow a long chain of reasoning. The subjects of our deliberation are such as seem to present us with alternative possibilities: about things that could not have been, and cannot now or in the future be, other than they are, nobody who takes them to be of this nature wastes his time in deliberation.

It is possible to form syllogisms and draw conclusions from the results of previous syllogisms; or, on the other hand, from premisses which have not been thus proved, and at the same time are so little accepted that they call for proof. Reasonings of the former kind will necessarily be hard to follow owing to their length, for we assume an audience of untrained thinkers; those of the latter kind will fail to win assent, because they are based on premisses that are not generally admitted or believed.

The enthymeme and the example must, then, deal with what is in the main contingent, the example being an induction, and the enthymeme a syllogism, about such matters. The enthymeme must consist of few propositions, fewer often than those which make up the normal syllogism. For if any of these propositions is a familiar fact, there is no need even to mention it; the hearer adds it himself. Thus, to show that Dorieus has been victor in a contest for which the prize is a crown, it is enough to say "For he has been victor in the Olympic games," without adding "And in the Olympic games the prize is a crown," a fact which everybody knows.

There are few facts of the 'necessary' type that can form the basis of rhetorical syllogisms. Most of the things about which we make decisions, and into which therefore we inquire, present us with alternative possibilities. For it is about our actions that we deliberate and inquire, and all our actions have a contingent character; hardly any of them are determined by necessity. Again, conclusions that state what is merely usual or possible must be drawn from premisses that do the same, just as 'necessary' conclusions must be drawn from 'necessary' premisses; this too is clear to us from the *Analytics*. It is evident, therefore, that the propositions forming the basis of enthymemes, though some of them may be 'necessary,' will most of them be only usually true. Now the materials of enthymemes are Probabilities and Signs, which we can see must correspond respectively with the propositions that are generally and those that are necessarily true. A Probability is a thing that usually happens; not, however, as some definitions would suggest, anything whatever that usually happens, but only if it belongs to the class of the 'contingent' or 'variable.' It bears the same relation to that in respect of which it is probable as the universal bears to the particular. Of Signs, one kind bears the same relation to the statement it supports as the particular bears to the universal, the other the same as the universal bears to the particular. The infallible kind is a 'complete proof' (*tekmerhiou*); the fallible kind has no specific name. By infallible signs I mean those on which syllogisms proper may be based: and this shows us why this kind of Sign is called 'complete proof': when people think that what they have said cannot be refuted, they then think that they are bringing forward a 'complete proof,' meaning that the matter has now been demonstrated and completed (*peperhasmeuou*); for the word *perhas* has the same meaning (of 'end' or 'boundary') as the word *tekmarh* in the ancient tongue. Now the one kind of Sign (that which bears to the proposition it supports the relation of particular to universal) may be illustrated thus. Suppose it were said, "The fact that Socrates was wise and just is a sign that the wise are just." Here we certainly have a Sign; but even though the proposition be true, the argument is refutable, since it does not form a syllogism. Suppose, on the other hand, it were said, "The fact that he has a fever is a sign that he is ill," or, "The fact that she is giving milk is a sign that she has lately borne a child." Here we have the infallible kind of Sign, the only kind that constitutes a complete proof, since it is the only kind that, if the particular statement is true, is irrefutable. The other kind of Sign, that which bears to the proposition it supports the relation of universal to particular, might be illustrated by saying, "The fact that he breathes fast is a sign that he has a fever." This argument also is refutable, even if the statement about the fast breathing be true, since a man may breathe hard without having a fever.

It has, then, been stated above what is the nature of a Probability, of a Sign, and of a complete proof, and what are the differences between them. In the *Analytics* a more explicit description has been given of these points; it is there shown why some of these reasonings can be put into syllogisms and some cannot.

The 'example' has already been described as one kind of induction; and the special nature of the subject-matter that distinguishes it from the other kinds has also been stated above. Its relation to the proposition it supports is not that of part to whole, nor whole to part, nor whole to whole, but of part to part, or like to like. When two statements are of the same order, but one is more familiar than the other, the former is an "example." The argument may, for instance, be that Dionysius, in asking as he does for a bodyguard, is scheming to make himself a despot. For in the past Peisistratus kept asking for a bodyguard in order to carry out such a scheme, and did make himself a despot as soon as he got it; and so did Theagenes at Megara; and in the same way all other instances known to the speaker are made into examples, in order to show what is not yet known, that Dionysius has the same purpose in making the same request: all these being instances of the one general principle, that a man who asks for a bodyguard is scheming to make himself a despot. We have now described the sources of those means of persuasion which are popularly supposed to be demonstrative.

There is an important distinction between two sorts of enthymemes that has been wholly overlooked by almost everybody—one that also subsists between the syllogisms treated of in dialectic. One sort of enthymeme really belongs to rhetoric, as one sort of syllogism really belongs to dialectic; but the other sort really belongs to other arts and faculties, whether to those we already exercise or to those we have not yet acquired. Missing this distinction, people fail to notice that the more correctly they handle their particular subject the further they are getting away from pure rhetoric or dialectic. This statement will be clearer if expressed more fully. I mean that the proper subjects of dialectical and rhetorical syllogisms are the things with which we say the regular or universal Lines of Argument are concerned, that is to say those lines of argument that apply equally to questions of right conduct, natural science, politics, and many other things that have nothing to do with one another. Take, for instance, the line of argument concerned with 'the more or less'. On this line of argument it is equally easy to base a syllogism or enthymeme about any of what nevertheless are essentially disconnected subjects—right conduct, natural science, or anything else whatever. But there are also those special Lines of Argument which are based on such propositions as apply only to particular groups or classes of things. Thus there are propositions about natural science on which it is impossible to base any enthymeme or syllogism about ethics, and other propositions about ethics on which nothing can be based about natural science. The same principle applies throughout. The general Lines of Argument have no special subject-matter, and therefore will not increase our understanding of any particular class of things. On the other hand, the better the selection one makes of propositions suitable for special Lines of Argument, the nearer one comes, unconsciously, to setting up a science that is distinct from dialectic and rhetoric. One may succeed in stating the required principles, but one's science will be no longer dialectic or rhetoric, but the science to which the principles thus discovered belong. Most enthymemes are in fact based upon these particular or special Lines of Argument; comparatively few on the common or general kind. As in the *Topics*, therefore, so in this work, we must distinguish, in dealing with enthymemes, the special and the general Lines of Argument on which they are to be founded. By special Lines of Argument I mean the propositions peculiar to each several class of things, by general those common to all classes alike. We may begin with the special Lines of Argument. But, first of all, let us classify rhetoric into its varieties. Having distinguished these we may deal with them one by one, and try to discover the elements of which each is composed, and the propositions each must employ.

Georg Wilhelm Friedrich Hegel

The Doctrine of Essence: Appearance

1812

"appearance is the existent mediated by its negation, which constitutes its subsistence"

Georg Wilhelm Friedrich Hegel (1770–1831) was a German philosopher whose writings codified German idealist philosophy. Many scholars consider his unique systematic thinking to be the successor to Kantian thought.

....

Volume One. The Objective Logic
Book Two. The Doctrine of Essence
Appearance

A. The Law of Appearance

1088

1. Appearance is the existent mediated by its negation, which constitutes its subsistence. This its negation is, indeed, another self-subsistence; but this is equally essentially a sublated self-subsistence. The existent is accordingly the return of itself into itself through its negation and through the negation of this its negation; it has, therefore, essential self-subsistence; just as it is equally immediately a sheer positedness which has a ground and an other for its subsistence. In the first place, therefore, Appearance is Existence along with its essentiality, positedness with its ground; but this ground is a negation; and the other self-subsistent, the ground of the first is likewise only a positedness. In other words, the existent is, as an Appearance, reflected into an other which it has for its ground, which other is itself only this, to be reflected into an other. The essential self-subsistence which belongs to it because it is a return-into-self is the return of the nothing through nothing back to itself on account of the negativity of the moments; the self-subsistence of the existent is, therefore, only the essential illusory show [wesentliche Schein]. The connection of the reciprocally grounding existents consists therefore in this reciprocal negation, namely, that the subsistence of the one is not the subsistence of the other, but is its positedness, which relation of the positedness alone constitutes the subsistence of the existents. The ground is present as it is in truth, namely, to be a first that is only presupposed.

1089

Now this constitutes the negative side of Appearance. But in this negative mediation is immediately contained the positive identity of the existent with itself. For it is not a positedness relatively to an essential ground, or is not an illusory being in a self-subsistent; it is positedness that is related to a positedness, or is an illusory being only in an illusory being. It relates itself in this its negation or in its other, which is itself a sublated moment, to itself, and is therefore self-identical or positive essentiality. This identity of the existent is not the immediacy that belongs to Existence as such, the merely unessential which subsists in an other. On the contrary, it is the essential content of Appearance which has two sides, first, to be in the form of positedness or external immediacy, secondly, to be positedness as self-identical. According to the first side it is a determinate being, but one which is contingent, unessential and, in keeping with its immediacy, is subject to transition, coming-to-be and ceasing-to-be. According to the other side, it is the simple content determination exempt from this flux, the enduring element of it.

1090

This content in general, besides being the simple element in that which is transitory, is also a determinate, inwardly diverse content. It is the reflection of Appearance into itself, of negative determinate being, and therefore essentially contains determinateness. But Appearance is the simply affirmative manifold variety which wantons in unessential manifoldness; its reflected content, on the other hand, is its manifoldness reduced to simple difference. The determinate essential content is, more precisely, not merely simply determinate, but, as the essential moment of Appearance, is complete determinateness; the one and its other. In Appearance each of these two has its subsistence in the other in such a manner that at the same time it is only in the other's non-subsistence. This contradiction sublates itself; and its reflection-into-self is the identity of their double-sided subsistence: the positedness of the one is also the positedness of the other. They constitute one subsistence, but at the same time as a diverse, mutually indifferent content. Hence in the essential side of Appearance, the negative aspect of the unessential content, its self-sublation, has returned into identity; it is an indifferent subsistence, which is not the sublatedness, but rather the subsistence, of the other.

This unity is the law of Appearance.

1091

2. The law is therefore the positive side of the mediation of what appears. Appearance is at first Existence as negative self-mediation, so that the existent is mediated with itself through its own non-subsistence, through an other, and, again, through the non-subsistence of this other. In this is contained first, the mere illusory being and the vanishing of both, the unessential Appearance; secondly, also their permanence or law; for each of the two exists in this sublating of the other; and their positedness as their negativity is at the same time the identical, positive positedness of both.

This permanent subsistence which Appearance has in law, is therefore, conformable to its determination, first, opposed to the immediacy of being which Existence has.

True, this immediacy is in itself reflected immediacy, namely the ground which has withdrawn into itself; but now in Appearance this simple immediacy is distinguished from the reflected immediacy which first started to separate itself in the thing. The existent thing in its dissolution has become this opposition; the positive side of its dissolution is that identity-with-self of what appears, as positedness, in its other positedness. Secondly, this reflected immediacy is itself determined as positedness over against the simply affirmative immediacy of Existence. This positedness [Gesetztsein] is now the essential and the truly positive. The German expression Gesetz [law] likewise contains this determination. In this positedness lies the essential relation of the two sides of the difference which law contains; they are a diverse content, each side being immediate with respect to the other, and they are this as the reflection of the vanishing content belonging to Appearance. As essential diversity, the different sides are simple self-related content-determinations. But equally, neither is immediate on its own, but each is essentially a positedness, or is, only in so far as the other is.

1092

Thirdly, Appearance and law have one and the same content. Law is the reflection of Appearance into identity-with-self; Appearance, as the null immediate, thus stands opposed to that which is reflected into itself, and they are distinguished according to this form. But the reflection of Appearance by virtue of which this difference is, is also the essential identity of Appearance itself and of its reflection, which is, in general, the nature of reflection; it is the self-identical in the positedness and is indifferent to that difference which is the form, or positedness; a content, therefore, which continues itself from Appearance into law, the content of law and Appearance.

1093

Accordingly, this content constitutes the substrate of Appearance; law is this substrate itself, Appearance is the same content, but contains still more, namely, the unessential content of its immediate being. The form-determination, too, by which Appearance as such is distinguished from law, is, namely, a content and is likewise a content distinguished from the content of the law. For Existence, as immediacy in general, is likewise a self-identity of matter and form which is indifferent to its form determinations and therefore a content; it is thinghood with its properties and matters. But it is the content whose self-subsistent immediacy is, at the same time, only as a non-subsistence. But the identity of the content with itself in this its non-subsistence is the other, essential content. This identity, the substrate of Appearance, which constitutes law is Appearance's own moment; it is the positive side of essentiality by virtue of which Existence is Appearance.

1094

Accordingly, law is not beyond Appearance but is immediately present in it; the realm of laws is the stable image of the world of Existence or Appearance. But the fact is rather that both form a single totality, and the existent world is itself the realm of laws, which, as that which is simply identical, is also identical with itself in positedness or in the self-dissolving self-subsistence of Existence.

Existence withdraws into law as into its ground; Appearance contains these two, the simple ground, and the dissolving movement of the manifested [erscheinenden] universe whose essentiality it is.

3. Law is therefore essential Appearance; it is the latter's reflection-into-self in its posited-ness, the identical content of itself and of unessential Existence. Now first, this identity of law with its Existence is at first only the immediate, simple identity, and law is indifferent to its Existence; Appearance has a further content other than the content of law. The former content is, indeed, unessential and is the withdrawal into the latter; but for law it is a first which is not posited by it; as content, therefore, it is externally connected with law. Appearance is a host of more precise determinations which belong to the 'this' or the concrete, and are not contained in law but are determined by an other.

Secondly, that which Appearance contains distinct from law, determined itself as a positive or as another content; but it is essentially a negative; it is form and its movement as such, which belongs to Appearance. The realm of laws is the stable content of Appearance; Appearance is the same content but presenting itself in restless flux and as reflection-into-other.

It is law as the negative, simply alterable Existence, the movement of transition into the opposite, of self-sublation and withdrawal into unity. Law does not contain this side of restless form or negativity; Appearance, therefore, as against law is the totality, for it contains law, but also more, namely, the moment of self-moving form.

Thirdly, this defect is present in law in this way, that the content of law is at first only diverse and so indifferent to itself; therefore the identity of its sides with one another is at first only immediate and therefore internal, or not yet necessary. In law two content determinations are essentially connected (for instance, in the law of descent of a falling body, spatial and temporal magnitudes: spaces passed through vary as the squares of the times elapsed); they are connected; this relation is at first only an immediate one. It is, therefore, likewise at first only a posited relation, the immediate in general having obtained in Appearance the meaning of positedness. The essential unity of the two sides of the law would be their negativity, that is to say, the one would contain its other within itself; but this essential unity has not yet emerged in the law. (That is why the Notion of the space traversed by a falling body does not itself imply that time corresponds to it as a square. Because fall is a sensible movement it is the relation of time and space; but first, the determination of time—that is, time as it is commonly imagined-does not itself imply its relationship to space, and vice versa; it is said that time can quite well be imagined without space and space without time; thus the one comes only externally into relation with the other, which external relation is motion. Secondly, the further determination is indifferent, namely, the magnitudes in accordance with which space and time are related in motion. The law of this relationship is empirically ascertained and in so far it is only immediate; it still demands a proof, that is, a mediation for cognition, showing that the law not only occurs but is necessary; the law as such does not contain this proof and its objective necessity.) Law is, therefore, only the positive, and not the negative, essentiality of Appearance. In the latter, the content determinations are moments of form, as such passing over into their other and in themselves are equally not themselves but their other.

Accordingly, though in law the positedness of one side of it is the positedness of the other, their content is indifferent to this relation: the content does not itself therefore contain this positedness. Law, therefore, is indeed essential form, but not as yet real form, which is reflected into its sides as content.

B. The World of Appearance and the World-in-Itself

1098

1. The existent world tranquilly raises itself to a realm of laws; the null content of its manifold being has its subsistence in an other; its subsistence is therefore its dissolution. But in this other the world of Appearance also unites with itself; thus Appearance in its changing is also an enduring, and its positedness is law. Law is this simple identity of Appearance with itself and therefore its substrate, not its ground; for it is not the negative unity of Appearance but, as its simple identity, the immediate, that is abstract unity, alongside which therefore its other content also occurs. The content is this content, internally coherent, or has its negative reflection within itself. It is reflected into an other; this other is itself an Existence of Appearance; phenomenal things have their grounds and conditions in other phenomenal things.

1099

But law is, in fact, also the other of Appearance as such and its negative reflection as into its other. The content of Appearance which is distinct from the content of law is the existent, which has its negativity for its ground or is reflected into its non-being. But this other, which is also an existent, is likewise reflected into its non-being; it is therefore the same and the phenomenon is therefore in fact reflected not into an other but into itself; it is just this reflection of positedness into itself that is law. But as a phenomenon it is essentially reflected into its non-being, or its identity is itself essentially no less its negativity and its other. Therefore the reflection-into-self of Appearance, namely law, is not only the identical substrate of Appearance, but the latter also has its opposite in law and law is its negative unity.

1100

Now through this, the determination of law has been altered in law itself. At first, it is merely a diverse content and the formal reflection of positedness into itself, so that the positedness of one of its sides is the positedness of the other. But because it is also negative reflection-into-self, its sides are in their relationship not merely different but are negatively related to each other. Or, when law is considered merely on its own, the sides of its content are indifferent to each other; but equally they are sublated by their identity; the positedness of one is the positedness of the other, and therefore the subsistence of each is also the non-subsistence of itself. This positedness of one in the other is their negative unity and each is not only the positedness of itself but also of the other, or, each is itself this negative unity. The positive identity which they have in law as such is at first only their inner unity which stands in need of proof and mediation, because this negative is not as yet posited in them. But since the different sides of law are now determined as being different in their negative unity, or such that each of them contains its other within it, and at the same time, as a self-subsistent side, repels this its otherness from itself, the identity of law is therefore now also a posited and real identity.

Consequently, law likewise has obtained the moment of the negative form of its sides which was lacking, the moment, that is, which previously belonged still to Appearance. Existence has thus completely withdrawn into itself and has reflected itself into its absolute otherness in and for itself. That which was previously law is accordingly no longer only one side of the whole whose other side was Appearance as such, but is itself the whole. Existence is the essential totality of Appearance, so that it now contains the moment of unessentiality which still belonged to Appearance, but as reflected, implicit unessentiality, that is, as essential negativity. As an immediate content, law is determinate in general, distinguished from other laws, and of these there is an indeterminable number. But since it now has within it essential negativity it no longer contains such a merely indifferent, contingent content determination; on the contrary, its content is all determinateness whatsoever, in an essential relation developing itself into totality. Thus Appearance which is reflected into itself is now a world, which reveals itself as a world in and for itself above the world of Appearance.

The realm of laws contains only the simple, changeless but varied content of the existent world. But now since it is the total reflection of this world it also contains the moment of its essenceless manifoldness. This moment of alterableness and alteration as reflected into self, as essential, is absolute negativity or pure form as such, whose moments, however, in the world in and for itself have the reality of self-subsistent but reflected Existence; just as, conversely, this reflected self-subsistence now has form within itself, by virtue of which its content is not a merely manifold, but an essentially self-coherent, content.

This world in and for itself is also called the supersensuous world; in so far as the existent world is characterised as sensuous, namely, as determined for intuition, for the immediate attitude of consciousness. The supersensuous world likewise has immediacy, Existence, but reflected, essential Existence. Essence has as yet no determinate being; but it is, and in a profounder sense than being; the thing is the beginning of reflected Existence; it is an immediacy that is not yet posited as essential or reflected; but it is in truth not a simply affirmative [seiendes] immediate. It is only as things of another, supersensuous world that things are posited first, as veritable Existences, and secondly as the true in contrast to what has simply affirmative being; in them it is acknowledged that there is a being distinct from immediate being, a being that is veritable Existence. On the one hand, the sensuous representation which ascribes Existence only to the immediate being of feeling and intuition is overcome in this determination; but, on the other hand, there is also in it unconscious reflection which, though having the conception of things, forces, the inner, and so on, does not know that such determinations are not sensuous or simply affirmative immediacies, but reflected Existences.

2. The world in and for itself is the totality of Existence; outside it there is nothing. But since it is in its own self absolute negativity or form, its reflection-into-self is a negative relation to itself. It contains opposition and repels itself within itself into the essential world and into the world of otherness or the world of Appearance. Thus, because it is totality, it is also only one side of it, and in this determination constitutes a self-subsistence distinct from the world of Appearance. The world of Appearance has in the essential world its negative unity in which it falls to the ground and into which it withdraws as into its ground. Further, the essential world is also the positing ground of the world of Appearance; for, containing the absolute form in its essentiality, its identity sublates itself, makes itself into positedness and as this posited immediacy is the world of Appearance.

1105

Further it is not merely ground as such of the world of Appearance, but its determinate ground. As the realm of laws, it is already a manifold content, namely, the essential content of the world of Appearance, and as ground with a content, the determinate ground of the other world, but only in respect of this content; for the world of Appearance still had other manifold content than the realm of laws, because the negative moment was still peculiarly its own. But since the realm of laws now likewise contains this moment, it is the totality of the content of the world of Appearance and the ground of all its manifoldness. But it is at the same time the negative of this totality and as such is the world opposed to it. That is to say, in the identity of both worlds, one of them is determined in respect of form as essential and the other as the same world but as posited and unessential, so that the ground relation has, it is true, been restored; but it is also the ground relation of Appearance, namely, as relation not of an identical content, nor of a merely diverse one, as is law, but as total relation, or as negative identity and essential relation of the opposed sides of the content. The realm of laws is not only this, that the positedness of a content is the positedness of another, but this identity is essentially, as we have seen, also a negative unity; each of the two sides of law is, in the negative unity, in its own self its other content; accordingly the other is not an indeterminate other in general, but is its other, or, it too contains the content determination of the first; and thus the two sides are opposed. Now since the realm of Laws contains within it this negative moment and opposition, and hence as totality repels itself from itself into a world in and for itself and a world of Appearance, the identity of both is thus the essential relation of opposition. The ground relation as such is the opposition which, in its contradiction, has fallen to the ground; and Existence is the ground that has united with itself. But Existence becomes Appearance; ground is sublated in Existence; it reinstates itself as the return of Appearance into itself, but at the same time as sublated ground, namely, as ground relation of opposed determinations; but the identity of such determinations is essentially a becoming and a transition, no longer the ground relation as such.

1106

The world in and for itself is, therefore, itself a world distinguished within itself into the totality of a manifold content; it is identical with the world of Appearance or the posited world and in so far its ground; but its identical relationship is at the same time determined as opposition, because the form of the world of Appearance is reflection into its otherness and this world has therefore veritably withdrawn into itself in the world in and for itself in such a manner that the latter is its opposite. The relation is, therefore, specifically this, that the world in and for itself is the inversion of the manifested world.

C. Dissolution of Appearance

The world in and for itself is the determinate ground of the world of Appearance and is this only in so far as it is within itself the negative moment, and hence the totality of the content determinations and their alterations which corresponds to the world of Appearance but at the same time constitutes its completely opposed side.

The two worlds are therefore in such a relationship that what is positive in the world of Appearance is negative in the world in and for-itself, and conversely, what is negative in the former is positive in the latter. The north pole in the world of Appearance is in and for itself the south pole, and conversely; positive electricity is in itself negative, and so on. What is evil, a misfortune and so on, in manifested existence is in and for itself, good and a piece of good fortune.

In point of fact it is just in this opposition of the two worlds that their difference has vanished, and what was supposed to be the world in and for itself is itself world of Appearance, while this conversely in its own self is the essential world. The world of Appearance is in the first instance determined as reflection into otherness, so that its determinations and Existences have their ground and subsistence in an other; but since this other is likewise a reflection-into-an-other they are related therein only to a self-sublating other, hence to themselves; the world of Appearance is thus in its own self the law which is identical with itself. Conversely, the world in and for itself is at first the self-identical content exempt from otherness and change; but this, as complete reflection of the world of Appearance into itself, or, because its diversity is difference reflected into itself and absolute, contains the negative moment and relation to itself as to otherness; it thereby becomes essenceless content, self-opposed and self-inverting. Further, this content of the world in and for itself has thereby also received the form of immediate Existence. For it is in the first instance ground of the world of Appearance; but since it has opposition within it, it is equally sublated ground and immediate Existence.

Thus the world of Appearance and the essential world are each in themselves the totality of self-identical reflection and reflection-into-an-other, or of being-in-and-for-self and Appearance. Both are self-subsistent wholes of Existence the one is supposed to be only reflected Existence, the other immediate Existence; but each continues itself in its other and is therefore in its own self the identity of these two moments. What is present, therefore, is this totality which repels itself from itself into two totalities, one the reflected, the other the immediate, totality. Both, in the first instance, are self-subsistents, but they are self-subsistent only as totalities, and they are this in so far as each essentially contains within it the moment of the other. Accordingly the distinct self-subsistence of each, of that determined as immediate and that as reflected, is now so posited that each is only as essential relation to the other and has its self-subsistence in this unity of both.

We started from the law of Appearance; this is the identity of a varied content with another content, so that the positedness of the one is the positedness of the other. In law, this difference is still present, in that the identity of its sides is at first only an inner identity which these sides do not yet have within themselves. Thus first, this identity is not realised; the content of law is not as an identical, but an indifferent, varied content; and secondly, the content is thereby only implicitly determined such that the positedness of the one is the positedness of the other; this is not yet present in the content. Now, however, law is realised; its inner identity is also determinately present, and conversely the content of law is raised into ideality; for it is a content sublated within itself, reflected into itself, in that each side has its other within it and is therefore veritably identical with it and with itself.

Thus law is essential relation. The truth of the unessential world is, at first, a world in and for itself and other to it; but this world is a totality since it is itself and that first world. Thus both are immediate Existences and hence reflections into their otherness, and also for this same reason veritably reflected into self.

"World" expresses in general the formless totality of manifoldness; this world, both as essential and as manifested, has fallen to the ground in that the manifoldness has ceased to be a mere variety; as such it is still a totality or universe, but as essential relation. There have arisen two totalities of the content in the world of Appearance; at first they are determined as mutually indifferent self-subsistents and each has the form within itself, but not as against the other; but the form has also shown itself to be their relation, and the essential relation is the consummation of their unity of form.

Alfred North Whitehead

Process and Reality

1929

"'concrescence' is the name for the process in which the universe of many things acquires an individual unity in a determinate relegation of each item of the 'many' to its subordination in the constitution of the novel 'one'"

Alfred North Whitehead (1861–1947) was first a British mathematician, later a philosopher of science, and eventually a philosopher of metaphysics. He was the central figure of the philosophical movement process philosophy and taught at Trinity College, the University of London, and Harvard University.

....

Chapter X
Process

Section I
Fluency and Permanence; Generation and Substance; Spatialization; Two Kinds of Fluency: Macroscopic and Microscopic, from Occasion to Occasion and within Each Occasion.

That 'all things flow' is the first vague generalization which the unsystematized, barely analysed, intuition of men has produced. It is the theme of some of the best Hebrew poetry in the Psalms; it appears as one of the first generalizations of Greek philosophy in the form of the saying of Heraclitus; amid the later barbarism of Anglo-Saxon thought it reappears in the story of the sparrow flitting through the banqueting[1] hall of the Northumbrian king; and in all stages of civilization its recollection lends its pathos to poetry. Without doubt, if we are to go back to that ultimate, integral experience, unwarped by the sophistications of theory, that experience whose elucidation is the final aim of philosophy, the flux of things is one ultimate generalization around which we must weave our philosophical system.

At this point we have transformed the phrase, 'all things flow' into the alternative phrase, 'the flux of things.' In so doing, the notion of the 'flux' has been held up before our thoughts as one primary notion for further analysis. But in the sentence 'all things flow,' there are three words—and we have started by isolating the last word of the three. We

1 changed 'banquetting' to 'banqueting' (M 317.11; C 295.10)

move backward to the next word 'things' and ask, What sort of things flow? Finally we reach the first word 'all' and ask, What is the meaning of the 'many' things engaged in this common flux, and in what sense, if any, can the word 'all' refer to a definitely indicated set of these many things?

The elucidation of meaning involved in the phrase 'all things flow'[2] is one chief task of metaphysics.

But there is a rival notion, antithetical to the former. I cannot at the moment recall one immortal phrase which expresses it with the same completeness as that with which[3] the alternative notion has been rendered by Heraclitus. This other notion dwells on permanences of things—the solid earth, the mountains, the stones, the Egyptian Pyramids, the spirit of man, God.

The best rendering of integral experience, expressing its general form divested of irrelevant details, is often to be found in the utterances of religious aspiration. One of the reasons of the thinness of so much modern metaphysics is its neglect of this wealth of expression of ultimate feeling. Accordingly we find in the first two lines of a famous hymn a full expression of the union of the two notions in one integral experience:

> Abide with me;
> Fast falls the eventide.

Here the first line expresses the permanences, 'abide,' 'me' and the 'Being' addressed; and the second line sets these permanences amid the inescapable flux. Here at length we find formulated the complete problem of metaphysics. Those philosophers who start with the first line have given us the metaphysics of 'substance'; and those who start with the second line have developed the metaphysics of 'flux.' But, in truth, the two lines cannot be torn apart in this way; and we find that a wavering balance between the two is a characteristic of the greater number of philosophers. Plato found his permanences in a static, spiritual heaven, and his flux in the entanglement of his forms amid the fluent imperfections of the physical world. Here I draw attention to the word 'imperfection.' In any assertion as to Plato I speak under correction; but I believe that Plato's authority can be claimed for the doctrine that the things that flow are imperfect in the sense of 'limited' and of 'definitely exclusive of much that they might be and are not.' The lines quoted from the hymn are an almost perfect expression of the direct intuition from which the main position of the Platonic philosophy is derived. Aristotle corrected his Platonism into a somewhat different[4] balance. He was the apostle of 'substance and attribute' and of the classificatory logic which this notion suggests. But, on the other side, he makes a masterly analysis of the notion of 'generation.' Aristotle in his own person expressed a useful protest against the Platonic tendency to separate a static spiritual world from a fluent world of superficial experience. The later Platonic schools stressed this tendency: just as the mediaeval Aristotelian thought allowed the static notions of Aristotle's logic to formulate some of the main metaphysical problems in terms which have lasted till today.

2 *deleted comma after 'flow' (M 317.32; C 295.31)*
3 *inserted 'that with which' after 'as' (M 318.3)*
4 *changed 'difference' to 'different' (M 319.3)*

On the whole, the history of philosophy supports Bergson's charge that the human intellect 'spatializes the universe'; that is to say, that it tends to ignore the fluency, and to analyse the world in terms of static categories. Indeed Bergson went further and conceived this tendency as an inherent necessity of the intellect. I do not believe this accusation; but I do hold that 'spatialization' is the shortest route to a clear-cut philosophy expressed in reasonably familiar language. Descartes gave an almost perfect example of such a system of thought. The difficulties of Cartesianism with its three clear-cut substances, and with its 'duration' and 'measured time' well in the background, illustrate the result of the subordination of fluency. This subordination is to be found in the unanalysed longing of the hymn, in Plato's vision of heavenly perfection, in Aristotle's logical concepts, and in Descartes' mathematical mentality. Newton, that Napoleon of the world of thought, brusquely ordered fluency back into the world, regimented into his 'absolute mathematical time, flowing equably without regard to anything external.' He also gave it a mathematical uniform in the shape of his Theory of Fluxions.

At this point the group of seventeenth- and eighteenth- century philosophers practically made a discovery, which, although it lies on the surface of their writings, they only half-realized. The discovery is that there are two kinds of fluency. One kind is the *concrescence*[5] which, in Locke's language, is 'the real internal constitution of a particular existent.' The other kind is the *transition* from particular existent to particular existent. This transition, again in Locke's language, is the 'perpetually perishing' which is one aspect of the notion of time; and in another aspect the transition is the origination of the present in conformity with the 'power' of the past.

The phrase 'the real internal constitution of a particular existent,' the description of the human understanding as a process of reflection upon data, the phrase 'perpetually perishing,' and the word 'power' together with its elucidation are all to be found in Locke's *Essay*. Yet owing to the limited scope of his investigation Locke did not generalize or put his scattered ideas together. This implicit notion of the two kinds of flux finds further unconscious illustration in Hume. It is all but explicit in Kant, though—as I think— misdescribed. Finally, it is lost in the evolutionary monism of Hegel and of his derivative schools. With all his inconsistencies, Locke is the philosopher to whom it is most useful to recur, when we desire to make explicit the discovery of the two kinds of fluency, required for the description of the fluent world. One kind is the fluency inherent in the constitution of the particular existent. This kind I have called 'concrescence.' The other kind is the fluency whereby the perishing of the process, on the completion of the particular existent, constitutes that existent as an original element in the constitutions of other particular existents elicited by repetitions of process. This kind I have called 'transition.' Concrescence moves towards its final cause, which is its subjective aim; transition is the vehicle of the efficient cause, which is the immortal past.

The discussion of how the actual particular occasions become original elements for a new creation is termed the theory of objectification. The objectified particular occasions together have the unity of a datum for the creative concrescence. But in acquiring this measure of connection, their inherent presuppositions of each other eliminate certain

---

5   italicized 'concrescence' (M 320.4; C 297.36)—It is parallel with 'transition' (and both terms are put in quotation marks in the following paragraph).

elements in their constitutions, and elicit into relevance other elements. Thus objectification is an operation of mutually adjusted abstraction, or elimination, whereby the many occasions of the actual world become one complex datum. This fact of the elimination by reason of synthesis is sometimes termed the perspective of the actual world from the standpoint of that concrescence. Each actual occasion defines its own actual world from which it originates. No two occasions can have identical actual worlds.

Section II
Concrescence, Novelty, Actuality; Microscopic Concrescence.
'Concrescence' is the name for the process in which the universe of many things acquires an individual unity in a determinate relegation of each item of the 'many' to its subordination in the constitution of the novel 'one.'

The most general term 'thing'—or, equivalently, 'entity'—means nothing else than to be one of the 'many' which find their niches in each instance of concrescence. Each instance of concrescence *is itself* the novel individual 'thing' in question. There are not 'the concrescence' *and* 'the[6] novel thing': when we analyse the novel thing we find nothing but the concrescence. 'Actuality' means nothing else than this ultimate entry into the concrete, in abstraction from which there is mere nonentity. In other words, abstraction from the notion of 'entry into the concrete' is a self-contradictory notion, since it asks us to conceive a thing as not a thing.

An instance of concrescence is termed an 'actual entity'—or, equivalently, an 'actual occasion.' There is not one completed set of things which are actual occasions. For the fundamental inescapable fact is the creativity in virtue of which there can be no 'many things' which are not subordinated in a concrete unity. Thus a set of all actual occasions is by the nature of things a standpoint for another concrescence which elicits a concrete unity from those many actual occasions. Thus we can never survey the actual world except from the standpoint of an immediate concrescence which is falsifying the presupposed completion. The creativity in virtue of which any relative[7] complete actual world is, by the nature of things, the datum for a new concrescence[8] is termed 'transition.' Thus, by reason of transition, 'the actual world' is always a relative term, and refers to that basis of presupposed actual occasions which is a datum for the novel concrescence.

An actual occasion is analysable. The analysis discloses operations transforming entities which are individually alien[9] into components of a complex which is concretely one. The term 'feeling' will be used as the generic description of such operations. We thus say that an actual occasion is a concrescence effected by a process of feelings.

A feeling can be considered in respect to (i) the actual occasions felt, (ii) the eternal objects felt, (iii) the feelings felt, and (iv) its own subjective forms of intensity. In the process of concrescence the diverse feelings pass on to wider generalities of integral feeling.

---

6   put quotation mark before 'the' instead of before 'novel' (M 321.26)
7   It has been suggested that 'relative' ought to read 'relatively,' but we believe that this change would be incorrect.
8   deleted comma after 'concrescence' (M 322.10; C 300.l)
9   deleted comma after 'alien' (M 322.17; C 300.7)—This change was made by Whitehead in his Macmillan copy.

Such a wider generality is a feeling of a complex of feelings, including their specific elements of identity and contrast. This process of the integration of feeling proceeds until the concrete unity of feeling is obtained. In this concrete unity all indetermination as to the realization of possibilities has been eliminated. The many entities of the universe, including those originating in the concrescence itself, find their respective roles in this final unity. This final unity is termed the 'satisfaction.' The 'satisfaction' is the culmination of the concrescence into a completely determinate matter of fact. In any of its antecedent stages the concrescence exhibits sheer indetermination as to the nexus between its many components.

Section III
Three Stages of Microscopic Concrescence;
Vector Characters Indicate Macroscopic Transition;
Emotion, and Subjective Form Generally,
Is Scalar in Microscopic Origination and Is the Datum for Macroscopic
Transition.

An actual occasion is nothing but the unity to be ascribed to a particular instance of concrescence. This concrescence is thus nothing else than the 'real internal constitution' of the actual occasion in question. The analysis of the formal constitution of an actual entity has given three stages in the process of feeling: (i) the responsive phase, (ii) the supplemental stage, and (iii) the satisfaction.

The satisfaction is merely the culmination marking the evaporation of all indetermination; so that, in respect to all modes of feeling and to all entities in the universe, the satisfied actual entity embodies a determinate attitude of 'yes' or 'no.' Thus the satisfaction is the attainment of the private ideal which is the final cause of the concrescence. But the process itself lies in the two former phases. The first phase is the phase of pure reception of the actual world in its guise of objective datum for aesthetic synthesis. In this phase there is the mere reception of the actual world as a multiplicity of private centres of feeling, implicated in a nexus of mutual presupposition. The feelings are felt as belonging to the external centres, and are not absorbed into the private immediacy. The second stage is governed by the private ideal, gradually shaped in the process itself; whereby the many feelings, derivatively felt as alien, are transformed into a unity of aesthetic appreciation immediately felt as private. This is the incoming of 'appetition' which in its higher exemplifications we term 'vision.' In the language of physical science, the 'scalar' form overwhelms the original 'vector' form: the origins become subordinate to the individual experience. The vector form is not lost, but is submerged as the foundation of the scalar superstructure.

In this second stage the feelings assume an emotional character by reason of this influx of conceptual feelings. But the reason why the origins are not lost in the private emotion is that there is no element in the universe capable of pure privacy. If we could obtain a complete analysis of meaning, the notion of pure privacy would be seen to be self-contradictory. Emotional feeling is still subject to the third metaphysical principle, that to be 'something' is 'to have the potentiality for acquiring real unity with other entities.' Hence, 'to be a real component of an actual entity' is in some way 'to realize this potentiality.' Thus 'emotion' is 'emotional feeling' and 'what is felt' is the presupposed vector situation. In physical science this principle takes the form which should never be lost sight of in fundamental speculation, that scalar quantities are constructs derivative from vector quantities. In more familiar language, this principle can be expressed by the statement that the notion of 'passing on' is more fundamental than that of a private individual fact. In the abstract language here adopted for metaphysical statement, 'passing on' becomes 'creativity' in the dictionary sense of the verb *creare*, 'to bring forth, beget, produce.' Thus, according to the third principle, no entity can be divorced from the notion of creativity. An entity is at least a particular form capable of infusing its own particularity into creativity. An actual entity, or a phase of an actual entity, is more than that; but, at least, it is that.

Locke's 'particular ideas' are merely the antecedent actual entities exercising their function of infusing with their own particularity the 'passing on' which is the primary phase of the 'real internal constitution' of the actual entity in question. In obedience to a prevalent misconception, 'Locke termed this latter entity the 'mind'; and discussed its 'furniture' when he should have discussed 'mental operations' in their capacity of later phases in the constitutions of actual entities. Locke himself flittingly expresses this fundamental vector function of his 'ideas.' In a paragraph, forming a portion of a quotation already made, he writes: "I confess power includes in it some kind of relation,—a relation to action or change; as, indeed, which of our ideas, of what kind soever, when attentively considered, does not?"[10]

Section IV
Higher Phases of Microscopic Concrescence.

The second phase, that of supplementation, divides itself into two subordinate phases. Both of these phases may be trivial; also they are not truly separable, since they interfere with each other by intensification or inhibition. If both phases are trivial, the whole second phase is merely the definite negation of individual origination; and the process passes passively to its satisfaction. The actual entity is then the mere vehicle for the transference of inherited constitutions of feeling. Its private immediacy passes out of the picture. Of these two sub-phases, the former—so far as there is an order—is that of aesthetic supplement, and the latter is that of intellectual supplement.

In the aesthetic supplement there is an emotional appreciation of the contrasts and rhythms inherent in the unification of the objective content in the concrescence of one actual occasion. In this phase perception is heightened by its assumption of pain and pleasure, beauty and distaste. It is the phase of inhibitions and intensifications. It is the phase in which blue becomes more intense by reason of its contrasts, and shape acquires dominance by reason of its loveliness. What was received as alien has been re-created as private. This is the phase of perceptivity, including emotional reactions to perceptivity. In this phase, private immediacy has welded the data into a new fact of blind feeling. Pure aesthetic supplement has solved its problem. This phase requires an influx of conceptual feelings and their integration with the pure physical feelings.

But 'blindness' of the process, so far, retains an indetermination. There must be either a determinate negation of intellectual 'sight' or an admittance of intellectual 'sight.' The

10   changed 'II, XXI, I' to 'Essay, II, XXI, 3' (M 325 fn.1; C 302 fn.1)

negation of intellectual sight is the dismissal into irrelevance of eternal objects in their abstract status of pure potentials. 'What might be' has the capability of relevant contrast with 'what is.' If the pure potentials, in this abstract capacity, are dismissed from relevance, the second sub-phase is trivial. The process then constitutes a blind actual occasion, 'blind' in the sense that no intellectual operations are involved; though conceptual operations are always involved. Thus there is always mentality in the form of 'vision' but not always mentality in the form of conscious 'intellectuality.'

But if some eternal objects, in their abstract capacity, are realized as relevant to actual fact, there is an actual occasion with intellectual operations. The complex of such intellectual operations is sometimes termed the 'mind' of the actual occasion; and the actual occasion is also termed 'conscious.' But the term 'mind' conveys the suggestion of independent substance. This is not meant here: a better term is the 'consciousness' belonging to the actual occasion.

An eternal object realized in respect to its pure potentiality as related to *determinate* logical subjects is termed a 'prepositional feeling' in the mentality of the actual occasion in question. The consciousness belonging to an actual occasion is its sub-phase of intellectual supplementation, when that sub-phase is not purely trivial. This sub-phase is the eliciting, into feeling, of the full contrast between mere propositional potentiality and realized fact.

Section V
Summary
To sum up: There are two species of process, macroscopic process, and microscopic process. The macroscopic process is the transition from attained actuality to actuality in attainment; while the microscopic process is the conversion of conditions which are merely real into determinate actuality. The former process effects the transition from the 'actual' to the 'merely real'; and the latter process effects the growth from the real to the actual. The former process is efficient; the latter process is teleological. The future is merely real, without being actual; whereas the past is a nexus of actualities. The actualities are constituted by their real genetic phases. The present is the immediacy of teleological process whereby reality becomes actual. The former process provides the conditions which really govern attainment; whereas the latter process provides the ends actually attained. The notion of 'organism' is combined with that of 'process' in a twofold manner. The community of actual things is an organism; but it is not a static organism. It is an incompletion in process of production. Thus the expansion of the universe in respect to actual things is the first meaning of 'process'; and the universe in any stage of its expansion is the first meaning of 'organism.' In this sense, an organism is a nexus.

Secondly, each actual entity is itself only describable as an organic process. It repeats in microcosm what the universe is in macrocosm. It is a process proceeding from phase to phase, each phase being the real basis from which its successor proceeds towards the completion of the thing in question. Each actual entity bears in its constitution the 'reasons' why its conditions are what they are. These 'reasons' are the other actual entities objectified for it.

An 'object' is a transcendent element characterizing that *definiteness* to which our 'experience' has to conform. In this sense, the future has *objective* reality in the present, but no *formal* actuality. For it is inherent in the constitution of the immediate, present actuality that a future will supersede it. Also conditions to which that future must conform, including real relationships to the present, are really objective in the immediate actuality.

Thus each actual entity, although complete so far as concerns its microscopic process, is yet incomplete by reason of its objective inclusion of the macroscopic process. It really experiences a future which must be actual, although the completed actualities of that future are undetermined. In this sense, each actual occasion experiences its own objective immortality.

Karl R. Popper

The Logic of Scientific Discovery: Falsifiability
1935

What Is Dialectic?
1963

"a system as empirical or scientific only if it is capable of being tested by experience. These considerations suggest that not the verifiability but the falsifiability of a system is to be taken as a criterion of demarcation"

Karl Popper (1902–1994) was an Austrian-British sociopolitical philosopher. His work as a proponent of critical rationalism influenced a generation of scientists and philosophers.

....

Part I
Introduction to the Logic of Science

I. A Survey of Some Fundamental Problems
[...]
4. The Problem of Demarcation
Of the many objections which are likely to be raised against the view here advanced, the most serious is perhaps the following. In rejecting the method of induction, it may be said, I deprive empirical science of what appears to be its most important characteristic; and this means that I remove the barriers which separate science from metaphysical speculation. My reply to this objection is that my main reason for rejecting inductive logic is precisely that it *does not provide a suitable distinguishing mark* of the empirical, non-metaphysical, character of a theoretical system; or in other words, that it *does not provide a suitable 'criterion of demarcation'*.

The problem of finding a criterion which would enable us to distinguish between the empirical sciences on the one hand, and mathematics and logic as well as 'metaphysical' systems on the other, I call the *problem of demarcation*.

This problem was known to Hume who attempted to solve it. With Kant it became the central problem of the theory of knowledge. If, following Kant, we call the problem of induction 'Hume's problem', we might call the problem of demarcation 'Kant's problem'.

Of these two problems—the source of nearly all the other problems of the theory of knowledge—the problem of demarcation is, I think, the more fundamental. Indeed, the main reason why epistemologists with empiricist leanings tend to pin their faith to the 'method of induction' seems to be their belief that this method alone can provide a suitable criterion of demarcation. This applies especially to those empiricists who follow the flag of 'positivism'.

The older positivists wished to admit, as scientific or legitimate, only those *concepts* (or notions or ideas) which were, as they put it, 'derived from experience'; those concepts, that is, which they believed to be logically reducible to elements of sense-experience, such as sensations (or sense-data), impressions, perceptions, visual or auditory memories, and so forth. Modern positivists are apt to see more clearly that science is not a system of concepts but rather a system of *statements*. Accordingly, they wish to admit, as scientific or legitimate, only those statements which are reducible to elementary (or 'atomic') statements of experience—to 'judgments of perception' or 'atomic propositions' or 'protocol-sentences' or what not. It is clear that the implied criterion of demarcation is identical with the demand for an inductive logic.

Since I reject inductive logic I must also reject all these attempts to solve the problem of demarcation. With this rejection, the problem of demarcation gains in importance for the present inquiry. Finding an acceptable criterion of demarcation must be a crucial task for any epistemology which does not accept inductive logic.

Positivists usually interpret the problem of demarcation in a *naturalistic way*; they interpret it as if it were a problem of natural science. Instead of taking it as their task to propose a suitable convention, they believe they have to discover a difference, existing in the nature of things, as it were, between empirical science on the one hand and metaphysics on the other. They are constantly trying to prove that metaphysics by its very nature is nothing but nonsensical twaddle—'sophistry and illusion', as Hume says, which we should 'commit to the flames'.

If by the words 'nonsensical' or 'meaningless' we wish to express no more, by definition, than 'not belonging to empirical science', then the characterization of metaphysics as meaningless nonsense would be trivial; for metaphysics has usually been defined as non-empirical. But of course, the positivists believe they can say much more about metaphysics than that some of its statements are non-empirical. The words 'meaningless' or 'nonsensical' convey, and are meant to convey, a derogatory evaluation; and there is no doubt that what the positivists really want to achieve is not so much a successful demarcation as the final overthrow and the annihilation of metaphysics. However this may be, we find that each time the positivists tried to say more clearly what 'meaningful' meant, the attempt led to the same result—to a definition of 'meaningful sentence' (in contradistinction to 'meaningless pseudo-sentence') which simply reiterated the criterion of demarcation of their *inductive logic*.

This 'shows itself' very clearly in the case of Wittgenstein, according to whom every meaningful proposition must be *logically reducible* to elementary (or atomic) propositions, which he characterizes as descriptions or 'pictures of reality' (a characterization, by the way, which is to cover all meaningful propositions). We may see from this that Wittgenstein's criterion of meaningfulness coincides with the inductivists' criterion of demarcation, provided we replace their words 'scientific' or 'legitimate' by 'meaningful'. And it is precisely over the problem of induction that this attempt to solve the problem of demarcation comes to grief: positivists, in their anxiety to annihilate metaphysics, annihilate natural science along with it. For scientific laws, too, cannot be logically reduced to elementary statements of experience. If consistently applied, Wittgenstein's criterion of meaningfulness rejects as meaningless those natural laws the search for which, as Einstein says, is 'the supreme task of the physicist': they can never be accepted as genuine or legitimate statements. Wittgenstein's attempt to unmask the problem of induction as an empty pseudo-problem was formulated by Schlick in the following words: 'The problem of induction consists in asking for a logical justification of *universal statements* about reality... We recognize, with Hume, that there is no such logical justification: there can be none, simply because *they are not* genuine statements.'

This shows how the inductivist criterion of demarcation fails to draw a dividing line between scientific and metaphysical systems, and why it must accord them equal status; for the verdict of the positivist dogma of meaning is that both are systems of meaningless pseudo-statements. Thus instead of eradicating metaphysics from the empirical sciences, positivism leads to the invasion of metaphysics into the scientific realm.

In contrast to these anti-metaphysical stratagems—anti-metaphysical in intention, that is— my business, as I see it, is not to bring about the overthrow of metaphysics. It is, rather, to formulate a suitable characterization of empirical science, or to define the concepts 'empirical science' and 'metaphysics' in such a way that we shall be able to say of a given system of statements whether or not its closer study is the concern of empirical science.

My criterion of demarcation will accordingly have to be regarded as a *proposal for an agreement or convention*. As to the suitability of any such convention opinions may differ; and a reasonable discussion of these questions is only possible between parties having some purpose in common. The choice of that purpose must, of course, be ultimately a matter of decision, going beyond rational argument.

Thus anyone who envisages a system of absolutely certain, irrevocably true statements as the end and purpose of science will certainly reject the proposals I shall make here. And so will those who see 'the essence of science... in its dignity', which they think resides in its 'wholeness' and its 'real truth and essentiality'. They will hardly be ready to grant this dignity to modern theoretical physics in which I and others see the most complete realization to date of what I call 'empirical science'.

The aims of science which I have in mind are different. I do not try to justify them, however, by representing them as the true or the essential aims of science. This would only distort the issue, and it would mean a relapse into positivist dogmatism. There is only *one* way, as far as I can see, of arguing rationally in support of my proposals. This is to analyse their logical consequences: to point out their fertility—their power to elucidate the problems of the theory of knowledge.

Thus I freely admit that in arriving at my proposals I have been guided, in the last analysis, by value judgments and predilections. But I hope that my proposals may be acceptable to those who value not only logical rigour but also freedom from dogmatism; who seek practical applicability, but are even more attracted by the adventure of science, and by discoveries which again and again confront us with new and unexpected questions, challenging us to try out new and hitherto undreamed-of answers.

The fact that value judgments influence my proposals does not mean that I am making the mistake of which I have accused the positivists—that of trying to kill metaphysics by calling it names. I do not even go so far as to assert that metaphysics has no value for empirical science. For it cannot be denied that along with metaphysical ideas which have obstructed the advance of science there have been others—such as speculative atomism— which have aided it. And looking at the matter from the psychological angle, I am inclined to think that scientific discovery is impossible without faith in ideas which are of a purely speculative kind, and sometimes even quite hazy; a faith which is completely unwarranted from the point of view of science, and which, to that extent, is 'metaphysical'.

Yet having issued all these warnings, I still take it to be the first task of the logic of knowledge to put forward a *concept of empirical science*, in order to make linguistic usage, now somewhat uncertain, as definite as possible, and in order to draw a clear line of demarcation between science and metaphysical ideas—even though these ideas may have furthered the advance of science throughout its history.

5. Experience as a Method

The task of formulating an acceptable definition of the idea of an 'empirical science' is not without its difficulties. Some of these arise from *the fact that there must be many theoretical systems* with a logical structure very similar to the one which at any particular time is the accepted system of empirical science. This situation is sometimes described by saying that there is a great number—presumably an infinite number—of 'logically possible worlds'. Yet the system called 'empirical science' is intended to represent only *one* world: the 'real world' or the 'world of our experience'.

In order to make this idea a little more precise, we may distinguish three requirements which our empirical theoretical system will have to satisfy. First, it must be *synthetic*, so that it may represent a non-contradictory, a *possible* world. Secondly, it must satisfy the criterion of demarcation, i.e. it must not be metaphysical, but must represent a world of possible *experience*. Thirdly, it must be a system distinguished in some way from other such systems as the one which represents *our* world of experience.

But how is the system that represents our world of experience to be distinguished? The answer is: by the fact that it has been submitted to tests, and has stood up to tests. This means that it is to be distinguished by applying to it that deductive method which it is my aim to analyse, and to describe.

'Experience', on this view, appears as a distinctive *method* whereby one theoretical system may be distinguished from others; so that empirical science seems to be characterized not only by its logical form but, in addition, by its distinctive *method*. (This, of course, is also the view of the inductivists, who try to characterize empirical science by its use of the inductive method.)

The theory of knowledge, whose task is the analysis of the method or procedure peculiar to empirical science, may accordingly be described as a theory of the empirical method— *a theory of what is usually called 'experience'*.

6. Falsifiability as a Criterion of Demarcation

The criterion of demarcation inherent in inductive logic—that is, the positivistic dogma of meaning—is equivalent to the requirement that all the statements of empirical science (or all 'meaningful' statements) must be capable of being finally decided, with respect to their truth and falsity; we shall say that they must be '*conclusively decidable*'. This means that their form must be such that *to verify them and to falsify them* must both be logically possible. Thus Schlick says: '... a genuine statement must be capable of *conclusive verification*'; and Waismann says still more clearly: 'If there is no possible way to *determine whether a statement is true* then that statement has no meaning whatsoever. For the meaning of a statement is the method of its verification.'

Now in my view there is no such thing as induction. Thus inference to theories, from singular statements which are 'verified by experience' (whatever that may mean), is logically inadmissible. Theories are, therefore, never empirically verifiable. If we wish to avoid the positivist's mistake of eliminating, by our criterion of demarcation, the theoretical systems of natural science, then we must choose a criterion which allows us to admit to the domain of empirical science even statements which cannot be verified.

But I shall certainly admit a system as empirical or scientific only if it is capable of being tested by experience. These considerations suggest that not the verifiability but the falsifiability of a system is to be taken as a criterion of demarcation. In other words: I shall not require of a scientific system that it shall be capable of being singled out, once and for all, in a positive sense; but I shall require that its logical form shall be such that it can be singled out, by means of empirical tests, in a negative sense: it must be possible for an empirical scientific system to be refuted by experience.

(Thus the statement, 'It will rain or not rain here tomorrow' will not be regarded as empirical, simply because it cannot be refuted; whereas the statement, 'It will rain here tomorrow' will be regarded as empirical.)

Various objections might be raised against the criterion of demarcation here proposed. In the first place, it may well seem somewhat wrong-headed to suggest that science, which is supposed to give us positive information, should be characterized as satisfying a negative requirement such as refutability. However, I shall show that this objection has little weight, since the amount of positive information about the world which is conveyed by a scientific statement is the greater the more likely it is to clash, because of its logical character, with possible singular statements. (Not for nothing do we call the laws of nature 'laws': the more they prohibit the more they say.)

Again, the attempt might be made to turn against me my own criticism of the inductivist criterion of demarcation; for it might seem that objections can be raised against falsifiability as a criterion of demarcation similar to those which I myself raised against verifiability.

This attack would not disturb me. My proposal is based upon an *asymmetry* between verifiability and falsifiability; an asymmetry which results from the logical form of universal statements. For these are never derivable from singular statements, but can be contradicted by singular statements. Consequently it is possible by means of purely deductive inferences (with the help of the *modus tollens* of classical logic) to argue from the truth of singular statements to the falsity of universal statements. Such an argument to the falsity of universal statements is the only strictly deductive kind of inference that proceeds, as it were, in the 'inductive direction'; that is, from singular to universal statements.

A third objection may seem more serious. It might be said that even if the asymmetry is admitted, it is still impossible, for various reasons, that any theoretical system should ever be conclusively falsified. For it is always possible to find some way of evading falsification, for example by introducing *ad hoc* an auxiliary hypothesis, or by changing *ad hoc* a definition. It is even possible without logical inconsistency to adopt the position of simply refusing to acknowledge any falsifying experience whatsoever. Admittedly, scientists do not usually proceed in this way, but logically such procedure is possible; and this fact, it might be claimed, makes the logical value of my proposed criterion of demarcation dubious, to say the least.

I must admit the justice of this criticism; but I need not therefore withdraw my proposal to adopt falsifiability as a criterion of demarcation. For I am going to propose that the *empirical method* shall be characterized as a method that excludes precisely those ways of evading falsification which, as my imaginary critic rightly insists, are logically possible. According to my proposal, what characterizes the empirical method is its manner of exposing to falsification, in every conceivable way, the system to be tested. Its aim is not to save the lives of untenable systems but, on the contrary, to select the one which is by comparison the fittest, by exposing them all to the fiercest struggle for survival.

The proposed criterion of demarcation also leads us to a solution of Hume's problem of induction—of the problem of the validity of natural laws. The root of this problem is the apparent contradiction between what may be called 'the fundamental thesis of empiricism'—the thesis that experience alone can decide upon the truth or falsity of scientific statements—and Hume's realization of the inadmissibility of inductive arguments. This contradiction arises only if it is assumed that all empirical scientific statements must be 'conclusively decidable', i.e. that their verification and their falsification must both in principle be possible. If we renounce this requirement and admit as empirical also statements which are decidable in one sense only—unilaterally decidable and, more especially, falsifiable—and which may be tested by systematic attempts to falsify them, the contradiction disappears: the method of falsification presupposes no inductive inference, but only the tautological transformations of deductive logic whose validity is not in dispute.

7. The Problem of the 'Empirical Basis'
If falsifiability is to be at all applicable as a criterion of demarcation, then singular statements must be available which can serve as premises in falsifying inferences. Our criterion therefore appears only to shift the problem—to lead us back from the question of the empirical character of theories to the question of the empirical character of singular statements.

Yet even so, something has been gained. For in the practice of scientific research, demarcation is sometimes of immediate urgency in connection with theoretical systems, whereas in connection with singular statements, doubt as to their empirical character rarely arises. It is true that errors of observation occur and that they give rise to false singular statements, but the scientist scarcely ever has occasion to describe a singular statement as non-empirical or metaphysical.

Problems of the empirical basis—that is, problems concerning the empirical character of singular statements, and how they are tested—thus play a part within the logic of science that differs somewhat from that played by most of the other problems which will concern us. For most of these stand in close relation to the *practice* of research, whilst the problem of the empirical basis belongs almost exclusively to the *theory* of knowledge. I shall have to deal with them, however, since they have given rise to many obscurities. This is especially true of the relation between *perceptual experiences* and *basic statements*. (What I call a 'basic statement' or a 'basic proposition' is a statement which can serve as a premise in an empirical falsification; in brief, a statement of a singular fact.)

Perceptual experiences have often been regarded as providing a kind of justification for basic statements. It was held that these statements are 'based upon' these experiences; that their truth becomes 'manifest by inspection' through these experiences; or that it is made 'evident' by these experiences, etc. All these expressions exhibit the perfectly sound tendency to emphasize the close connection between basic statements and our perceptual experiences. Yet it was also rightly felt that *statements can be logically justified only by statements*. Thus the connection between the perceptions and the statements remained obscure, and was described by correspondingly obscure expressions which elucidated nothing, but slurred over the difficulties or, at best, adumbrated them through metaphors.

Here too a solution can be found, I believe, if we clearly separate the psychological from the logical and methodological aspects of the problem. We must distinguish between, on the one hand, *our subjective experiences or our feelings of conviction*, which can never justify any statement (though they can be made the subject of psychological investigation) and, on the other hand, the *objective logical relations* subsisting among the various systems of scientific statements, and within each of them.

The problems of the empirical basis will be discussed in some detail in sections 25 to 30. For the present I had better turn to the problem of scientific objectivity, since the terms 'objective' and 'subjective' which I have just used are in need of elucidation.

8. Scientific Objectivity and Subjective Conviction

The words 'objective' and 'subjective' are philosophical terms heavily burdened with a heritage of contradictory usages and of inconclusive and interminable discussions.

My use of the terms 'objective' and 'subjective' is not unlike Kant's. He uses the word 'objective' to indicate that scientific knowledge should be *justifiable*, independently of anybody's whim: a justification is 'objective' if in principle it can be tested and understood by anybody. 'If something is valid', he writes, 'for anybody in possession of his reason, then its grounds are objective and sufficient.'

Now I hold that scientific theories are never fully justifiable or verifiable, but that they are nevertheless testable. I shall therefore say that the *objectivity* of scientific statements lies in the fact that they can be *inter-subjectively tested*.

The word 'subjective' is applied by Kant to our feelings of conviction (of varying degrees). To examine how these come about is the business of psychology. They may arise, for example, 'in accordance with the laws of association'. Objective reasons too may serve as 'subjective *causes* of judging', in so far as we may reflect upon these reasons, and become convinced of their cogency.

Kant was perhaps the first to realize that the objectivity of scientific statements is closely connected with the construction of theories—with the use of hypotheses and universal statements. Only when certain events recur in accordance with rules or regularities, as is the case with repeatable experiments, can our observations be tested—in principle—by anyone. We do not take even our own observations quite seriously, or accept them as scientific observations, until we have repeated and tested them. Only by such repetitions can we convince ourselves that we are not dealing with a mere isolated 'coincidence', but with events which, on account of their regularity and reproducibility, are in principle inter-subjectively testable.

Every experimental physicist knows those surprising and inexplicable apparent 'effects' which in his laboratory can perhaps even be reproduced for some time, but which finally disappear without trace. Of course, no physicist would say in such a case that he had made a scientific discovery (though he might try to rearrange his experiments so as to make the effect reproducible). Indeed the scientifically significant *physical effect* may be defined as that which can be regularly reproduced by anyone who carries out the appropriate experiment in the way prescribed. No serious physicist would offer for publication, as a scientific discovery, any such 'occult effect', as I propose to call it—one for whose reproduction he could give no instructions. The 'discovery' would be only too soon rejected as chimerical, simply because attempts to test it would lead to negative results. (It follows that any controversy over the question whether events which are in principle unrepeatable and unique ever do occur cannot be decided by science: it would be a meta-physical controversy.)

We may now return to a point made in the previous section: to my thesis that a subjective experience, or a feeling of conviction, can never justify a scientific statement, and that within science it can play no part except that of an object of an empirical (a psychological) inquiry. No matter how intense a feeling of conviction it may be, it can never justify a statement. Thus I may be utterly convinced of the truth of a statement; certain of the evidence of my perceptions; overwhelmed by the intensity of my experience: every doubt may seem to me absurd. But does this afford the slightest reason for science to accept my statement? Can any statement be justified by the fact that K. R. P. is utterly convinced of its truth? The answer is, 'No'; and any other answer would be incompatible with the idea of scientific objectivity. Even the fact, for me so firmly established, that I am experiencing this feeling of conviction, cannot appear within the field of objective science except in the form of a *psychological hypothesis* which, of course, calls for intersubjective testing: from the conjecture that I have this feeling of conviction the psychologist may deduce, with the help of psychological and other theories, certain predictions about my behaviour; and these may be confirmed or refuted in the course of experimental tests. But from the epistemological point of view, it is quite irrelevant whether my feeling of conviction was strong or weak; whether it came from a strong or even irresistible impression of indubitable certainty (or 'selfevidence'), or merely from a doubtful surmise. None of this has any bearing on the question of how scientific statements can be justified.

Considerations like these do not of course provide an answer to the problem of the empirical basis. But at least they help us to see its main difficulty. In demanding objectivity for basic statements as well as for other scientific statements, we deprive ourselves of any logical means by which we might have hoped to reduce the truth of scientific statements to our experiences. Moreover we debar ourselves from granting any favoured status to statements which describe experiences, such as those statements which describe our perceptions (and which are sometimes called 'protocol sentences'). They can occur in science only as psychological statements; and this means, as hypotheses of a kind whose standards of inter-subjective testing (considering the present state of psychology) are certainly not very high.

Whatever may be our eventual answer to the question of the empirical basis, one thing must be clear: if we adhere to our demand that scientific statements must be objective, then those statements which belong to the empirical basis of science must also be objective, i.e. inter-subjectively testable. Yet inter-subjective testability always implies that, from the statements which are to be tested, other testable statements can be deduced. Thus if the basic statements in their turn are to be inter-subjectively testable, *there can be no ultimate statements in science*: there can be no statements in science which cannot be tested, and therefore none which cannot in principle be refuted, by falsifying some of the conclusions which can be deduced from them.

We thus arrive at the following view. Systems of theories are tested by deducing from them statements of a lesser level of universality. These statements in their turn, since they are to be inter-subjectively testable, must be testable in like manner—and so *ad infinitum*.

It might be thought that this view leads to an infinite regress, and that it is therefore untenable. In section 1, when criticizing induction, I raised the objection that it may lead to an infinite regress; and it might well appear to the reader now that the very same objection can be urged against that procedure of deductive testing which I myself advocate. However, this is not so. The deductive method of testing cannot establish or justify the statements which are being tested; nor is it intended to do so. Thus there is no danger of an infinite regress. But it must be admitted that the situation to which I have drawn attention—testability *ad infinitum* and the absence of ultimate statements which are not in need of tests—does create a problem. For, clearly, tests cannot in fact be carried on *ad infinitum*: sooner or later we have to stop. Without discussing this problem here in detail, I only wish to point out that the fact that the tests cannot go on forever does not clash with my demand that every scientific statement must be testable. For I do not demand that every scientific statement must have in fact been tested before it is accepted. I only demand that every such statement must be capable of being tested; or in other words, I refuse to accept the view that there are statements in science which we have, resignedly, to accept as true merely because it does not seem possible, for logical reasons, to test them.

"Hegel's philosophy of identity, 'That which is reasonable is real, and that which is real is reasonable; thus, reason and reality are identical', was undoubtedly an attempt to re-establish rationalism an a new basis"

What Is Dialectic?

1963

....

2. Hegelian Dialectic

So far I have tried to outline the idea of dialectic in a way which I hope makes it intelligible, and it was my aim not to be unjust about its merits. In this outline dialectic was presented as a way of describing developments; as one way among others, not fundamentally important, but sometimes quite suitable. As opposed to t his, a theory of dialectic has been put forward, for example by Hegel and his school, which exaggerates its significance, and which is dangerously misleading.

In order to make Hegel's dialectic intelligible it may be useful to refer briefly to a chapter in the history of philosophy—in my opinion not a very creditable one.

A major issue in the history of modern philosophy is the struggle between Cartesian rationalism (mainly continental) an the one hand, and empiricism (mainly British) an the other. The sentence from Descartes which I have used as a motto for this paper was not intended by its author, the founder of the rationalist school, in the way in which I have made use of it. It was not intended as a hint that the human mind has to try everything in order to arrive at something—i.e. at some useful solution—but rather as a hostile criticism of those who dare to try out such absurdities. What Descartes had in mind, the main idea behind his sentence, is that the real philosopher should carefully avoid absurd and foolish ideas. In order to find truth he has only to accept those rare ideas which appeal to reason by their lucidity, by their clarity and distinctness, which are, in short, 'self-evident'. The Cartesian view is that we can construct the explanatory theories of science without any reference to experience, just by making use of our reason; for every reasonable proposition (i.e. one recommending itself by its lucidity) must be a true description of the facts. This, in brief outline, is the theory which the history of philosophy has called 'rationalism'. (A better name would be `intellectualism'.) It can be summed up (using a formulation of a much later period, namely that of Hegel) in the words: 'That which is reasonable must be real.'

Opposed to this theory, empiricism maintains that only experience enables us to decide upon the truth or falsity of a scientific theory. Pure reasoning alone, according to empiricism, can never establish factual truth; we have to make use of observation and experiment. It can safely be said that empiricism, in some form or other, although perhaps in a modest and modified form, is the only interpretation of scientific method which can be taken seriously in our day. The struggle between the earlier rationalists and empiricists was thoroughly discussed by Kant, who tried to offer what a dialectician (but not Kant) might describe as a synthesis of the two opposing views, but what was, more precisely, a modified form of empiricism. His main interest was to reject pure rationalism. In his Critique of Pure Reason he asserted that the scope of our knowledge is limited to the field of possible experience, and that speculative reasoning beyond this field—the attempt to build up a metaphysical system out of pure reason—has no justification whatever. This criticism of pure reason was felt as a terrible blow to the hopes of nearly all continental philosophers; yet German philosophers recovered and, far from being convinced by Kant's rejection of metaphysics, hastened to build up new metaphysical systems based an 'intellectual intuition'. They tried to use certain features of Kant's system, hoping thereby to evade the main force of his criticism. The school which developed, usually called the school of the German idealists, culminated in Hegel.

There are two aspects of Hegel's philosophy which we have to discuss his idealism and his dialectic. In both cases Hegel was influenced by some of Kant's ideas, but tried to go further. In order to understand Hegel we must therefore show how his theory made use of Kant's.

Kant started from the fact that science exists. He wanted to explain this fact; that is, he wanted to answer the question, 'How is science possible?' or, 'How are human minds able to gain knowledge of the world', or, 'How can our minds grasp the world?' (We might call this question the epistemological problem.)

His reasoning was somewhat as follows. The mind can grasp the world, or rather the world as it appears to us, because this world is not utterly different from the mind—because it is mind-like. And it is so, because in the process of obtaining knowledge, of grasping the world, the mind is, so to speak, actively digesting all that material which enters it by the senses. It is forming, moulding this material; it impresses an it its own intrinsic forms or laws—the forms or laws of our thought. What we call 'nature'—the world in which we live, the world as it appears to us—is already a world digested, a world formed, by our minds. And being thus assimilated by the mind, it is mind-like.

The answer, 'The mind can grasp the world because the world as it appears to us is mind-like' is an idealistic argument; for what idealism asserts is just that the world has something of the character of mind.

I do not intend to argue here for or against this Kantian epistemology and I do not intend to discuss it in detail. But I want to point out that it certainly is not entirely idealistic. It is, as Kant himself points out, a mixture or a synthesis, of some sort of realism and some sort of idealism—its realist element being the assertion that the world, as it appears to us, is some sort of material formed by our mind, whilst its idealist element is the assertion that it is some sort of material formed by our mind.

So much for Kants rather abstract but certainly ingenious epistemology. Before I proceed to Hegel, I must beg those readers (I like them best) who are not philosophers and who are used to relying an their common sense to bear in mind the sentence which I chose as a motto for this paper; for what they will hear now will probably appear to them—in my opinion quite rightly—absurd.

As I have said, Hegel in his idealism went further than Kant. Hegel, too, was concerned with the epistemological question, 'How can our minds grasp the world?' With the other idealists, he answered: 'Because the world is mind-like.' But his theory was more radical than Kant's. He did not say, like Kant, 'Because the mind digests or forms the world'. He said, 'Because the mind is the world'; or in another formulation, 'Because the reasonable is the real; because reality and reason are identical'.

This is Hegel's so-called 'philosophy of the identity of reason and reality', or, for short, his 'philosophy of identity'. It may be noted in passing that between Kant's epistemological answers, 'Because the mind forms the world', and Hegels philosophy of identity, 'Because the mind is the world', there was, historically, a bridge—namely Fichte's answer, 'Because the mind creates the world'.[1]

Hegel's philosophy of identity, 'That which is reasonable is real, and that which is real is reasonable; thus, reason and reality are identical', was undoubtedly an attempt to re-establish rationalism an a new basis. It permitted the philosopher to construct a theory of the world out of pure reasoning and to maintain that this must be a true theory of the real world. Thus it allowed exactly what Kant had said to be impossible. Hegel, therefore, was bound to try to refute Kant's arguments against metaphysics. He did this with the help of his dialectic.

To understand his dialectic, we have to go back to Kant again. To avoid too much detail, I shall not discuss the triadic construction of Kant's table of categories, although no doubt it inspired Hegel.[2] But I have to refer to Kant's method of rejecting rationalism. I mentioned above that Kant maintained that the scope of our knowledge is limited to the field of possible experience and that pure reasoning beyond this field is not justified. In a section of the Critique which he headed 'Transcendental Dialectic' he showed this as follows. If we try to construct a theoretical system out of pure reason—for instance, if we try to argue that the world in which we live is infinite (an idea which obviously goes beyond possible experience)—then we can do so; but we shall find to our dismay that we can always argue, with the help of analogous arguments, to the opposite effect as well. In other words, given such a metaphysical thesis, we could always construct and defend an exact antithesis; and for any argument which supports the thesis, we can easily construct its opposite argument in favour of the antithesis. And both arguments will carry with them a similar force and conviction—both arguments will appear to be equally, or almost equally, reasonable. Thus, Kant said, reason is bound to argue against itself and to contradict itself, if used to go beyond possible experience.

1   This answer was not even original, because Kant had considered it previously; but he of course rejected it.
2   MacTaggart has made this point the centre of his interesting Studies in Hegelian Dialectic.

If I were to give some sort of modernized reconstruction, or reinterpretation, of Kant, deviating from Kant's own view of what he had done, I should say that Kant showed that the metaphysical principle of reasonableness or self-evidence does not lead unambiguously to one and only one result or theory. It is always possible to argue, with similar apparent reasonableness, in favour of a number of different theories, and even of opposite theories. Thus if we get no help from experience, if we cannot make experiments or observations which at least tell us to eliminate certain theories—namely those which although they may seem quite reasonable, are contrary to the observed facts—then we have no hope of ever settling the claims of competing theories.

How did Hegel overcome Kant's refutation of rationalism? Very easily, by holding that contradictions do not matter. They just have to occur in the development of thought and reason. They only show the insufficiency of a theory which does not take account of the fact that thought, that is reason, and with it (according to the philosophy of identity) reality, is not something fixed once and for all, but is developing—that we live in a world of evolution. Kant, so says Hegel, refuted metaphysics, but not rationalism. For what Hegel calls 'metaphysics', as opposed to 'dialectic', is only such a rationalistic system as does not take account of evolution, motion, development, and thus tries to conceive of reality as something stable, unmoved and free of contradictions. Hegel, with his philosophy of identity, infers that since reason develops, the world must develop, and since the development of thought or reason is a dialectic one, the world must also develop in dialectic triads.

Thus we find the following three elements in Hegel's dialectic.

(a) An attempt to evade Kant's refutation of what Kant called 'dogmatism' in metaphysics. This refutation is considered by Hegel to hold only for systems which are metaphysical in his more narrow sense, but not for dialectical rationalism, which takes account of the development of reason and is therefore not afraid of contradictions. In evading Kant's criticism in this way, Hegel embarks an an extremely dangerous venture which must lead to disaster, for he argues something like this: 'Kant refuted rationalism by saying that it must lead to contradictions. I admit that. But it is clear that this argument draws its force from the law of contradiction: it refutes only such systems as accept this law, i.e. such as try to be free from contradictions. It is not dangerous for a system like mine which is prepared to put up with contradictions—that is, for a dialectic system.' It is clear that this argument establishes a dogmatism of an extremely dangerous kind—a dogmatism which need no longer be afraid of any sort of attack. For any attack, any criticism of any theory whatsoever, must be based an the method of pointing out some sort of contradiction, either within the theory itself or between the theory and some facts, as I said above. Hegel's method of superseding Kant, therefore, is effective, but unfortunately too effective. It makes his system secure against any sort of criticism or attack and thus it is dogmatic in a very peculiar sense, so that I should like to call it a 'reinforced dogmatism'. (It may be remarked that similar reinforced dogmatisms help to support the structures of other dogmatic systems as well.)

(b) The description of the development of reason in terms of dialectic is an element in Hegel's philosophy which, had a good deal of plausibility. This becomes clear if we remember that Hegel uses the word 'reason' not only in the subjective sense, to denote a certain mental capacity, but also in the objective sense, to denote all sorts of theories, thoughts, ideas and so on. Hegel, who holds that philosophy is the highest expression of reasoning, has in mind mainly the development of philosophical thought when he speaks of the development of reasoning. And indeed hardly anywhere can the dialectic triad be more successfully applied than in the study of the development of philosophical theories, and it is therefore not surprising that Hegel's most successful attempt at applying his dialectic method was his History of Philosophy.

In order to understand the danger connected with such a success, we have to remember that in Hegel's time—and even much later—logic was usually described and defined as the theory of reasoning or the theory of thinking, and accordingly the fundamental laws of logic were usually called the 'laws of thought'. It is therefore quite understandable that Hegel, believing that dialectic is the true description of our actual procedure when reasoning and thinking, held that he must alter logic so as to make dialectic an important, if not the most important, part of logical theory. This made it necessary to discard the 'law of contradiction', which clearly was a grave obstacle to the acceptance of dialectic. Here we have the origin of the view that dialectic is 'fundamental' in the sense that it can compete with logic, that it is an improvement upon logic. I have already criticized this view of dialectic, and I only want to repeat that any sort of logical reasoning, whether before or after Hegel, and whether in science or in mathematics or in any truly rational philosophy, is always based an the law of contradiction. But Hegel writes (Logic, Section 81, (1)): 'It is of the highest importance to ascertain and understand rightly the nature of Dialectic. Wherever there is movement, wherever there is life, wherever anything is carried into effect in the actual world, there Dialectic is at work. It is also the soul of all knowledge which is truly scientific.'

But if by dialectic reasoning Hegel means a reasoning which discards the law of contradiction, then he certainly would not be able to give any instance of such reasoning in science. (The many instances quoted by dialecticians are without exception an the level of Engel's examples referred to above—the grain and $(-a)2 = a2$—or even worse.) It is not scientific reasoning itself which is based an dialectic; it is only the history and development of scientific theories which can with some success be described in terms of the dialectic method. As we have seen, this fact cannot justify the acceptance of dialectic as something fundamental, because it can be explained without leaving the realm of ordinary logic if we remember the working of the trial and error method.

The main danger of such a confusion of dialectic and logic is, as I said, that it helps people to argue dogmatically. For we find only too often that dialecticians, when in logical difficulties, as a last resort tell their opponents that their criticism is mistaken because it is based an logic of the ordinary type instead of an dialectic; if they would only use dialectic, they would see that the contradictions which they have found in some arguments of the dialecticians are quite legitimate (namely from the dialectic point of view).

(c) A third element in Hegelian dialectic is based an his philosophy of identity. If reason and reality are identical and reason develops dialectically (as is so well exemplified by the development of philosophical thought) then reality must develop dialectically too. The world must be ruled by the laws of dialectical logic. (This standpoint has been called 'pentagram'.) Thus, we must find in the world the same contradictions as are permitted by dialectic logic. It is this very fact that the world is full of contradictions which shows us from another angle that the law of contradiction has to be discarded. For this law says that no self-contradictory proposition, or no pair of contradictory propositions, can be true, that is, can correspond to the facts. In other words, the law implies that a contradiction can never occur in nature, i.e. in the world of facts, and that facts can never contradict each other. But an the basis of the philosophy of the identity of reason and reality, it is asserted that facts can contradict each other since ideas can contradict each other and that facts develop through contradictions, just as ideas do; so that the law of contradiction has to be abandoned.

But apart from what appears to me to be the utter absurdity of the philosophy of identity (about which I shall say something later), if we look a little closer into these so-called contradictory facts, then we find that all the examples proffered by dialecticians just state that the world in which we live shows, sometimes, a certain structure which could perhaps be described with the help of the word 'polarity'. An instance of that structure would be the existence of positive and negative electricity. It is only a metaphorical and loose way of speaking to say, for instance, that positive and negative electricity are contradictory to each other. An example of a true contradiction would be two sentences: 'This body here was, an the 1st of November, 1938, between 9 and 10 a.m., positively charged', and an analogous sentence about the same body, saying that it was at the same time not positively charged.

This would be a contradiction between two sentences and the corresponding contradictory fact would be the fact that a body is, as a whole, at the same time both positively and not positively charged, and thus at the same time both attracts and does not attract certain negatively charged bodies. But we need not say that such contradictory facts do not exist. (A deeper analysis might show that the non-existence of such facts is not a law which is akin to laws of physics, but is based an logic, that is, an the rules governing the use of scientific language.)

So there are three points: (a) the dialectic opposition to Kant's anti-rationalism, and consequently the re-establishment of rationalism supported by a reinforced dogmatism; (b) the incorporation of dialectic in logic, grounded an the ambiguity of expressions like 'reason', 'laws of thought', and so on; (c) the application of dialectic to 'the whole world', based an Hegel's panlogism and his philosophy of identity. These three points seem to me to be the main elements within Hegelian dialectic. Before I proceed to outline the fate of dialectic after Hegel, I should like to express my personal opinion about Hegel's philosophy, and especially about his philosophy of identity. I think it represents the worst of all those absurd and incredible philosophic theories to which Descartes refers in the sentence which I have chosen as the motto for this paper. It is not only that philosophy of identity is offered without any sort of serious argument; even the problem which it has been invented to answer—the question, 'How can our minds grasp the world?'—seems to me not to be at all clearly formulated. And the idealist answer, which has been varied by different idealist philosophers but remains fundamentally the same, namely, 'Because the world is mind-like', has only the appearance of an answer. We shall see clearly that it is not a real answer if we only consider some analogous argument, like: 'How can this mirror reflect my face?' 'Because it is face-like.' Although this sort of argument is obviously utterly unsound, it has been formulated again and again. We find it formulated by Jeans, for instance, in our own time, along lines like these: 'How can mathematics grasp the world?'—Because the world is mathematics-like.' He argues thus that reality is of the very nature of mathematics—that the world is a mathematical thought (and therefore ideal). This argument is obviously no sounder than the following: 'How can language describe the world?'—'Because the world is language-like—it is linguistic', and no sounder than: 'How can the English language describe the world?—'Because the world is intrinsically British.' That this latter argument really is analogous to the one advanced by Jeans is easily seen if we recognize that the mathematical description of the world is just a certain way of describing the world and nothing else, and that mathematics supplies us with the means of description—with a particularly rich language.

Perhaps one can show this most easily with the help of a trivial example. There are primitive languages which do not employ numbers but try to express numerical ideas with the help of expressions for one, two, and many. It is clear that such a language is unable to describe some of the more complicated relationships between certain groups of objects, which can easily be described with the help of the numerical expressions 'three', 'four', 'five', and so on. It can say that A has many sheep, and more than B, but it cannot say that A has 9 sheep and 5 more than B. In other words, mathematical symbols are introduced into a language in order to describe certain more complicated relationships which could not be described otherwise; a language which contains the arithmetic of natural numbers is simply richer than a language which lacks the appropriate symbols. All that we can infer about the nature of the world from the fact that we have to use mathematical language if we want to describe it is that the world has a certain degree of complexity, so that there are certain relationships in it which cannot be described with the help of too primitive instruments of description.

Jeans was uneasy about the fact that our world happens to suit mathematical formulae originally invented by pure mathematicians who did not intend at all to apply their formulae to the world. Apparently he originally started off as what I should call an 'inductivist'; that is, he thought that theories are obtained from experience by some more or less simple procedure of inference. If one starts from such a position it obviously is astonishing to find that a theory which has been formulated by pure mathematicians, in a purely speculative manner, afterwards proves to be applicable to the physical world. But for those who are not inductivists, this is not astonishing at all. They know that it happens quite often that a theory put forward originally as a pure speculation, as a mere possibility, later proves to have its empirical applications. They know that often it is this speculative anticipation which prepares the way for the empirical theories. (In this way the problem of induction, as it is called, has a bearing an the problem of idealism with which we are concerned here.)

3. Dialectic after Hegel

The thought that facts or events might mutually contradict each other appears to me as the very paradigm of thoughtlessness.
David Hilbert

Hegel's philosophy of the identity of reason and reality is sometimes characterized as (absolute) idealism, because it states that reality is mind-like or of the character of reason. But clearly such a dialectical philosophy of identity can easily be turned round so as to become a kind of materialism. Its adherents would then argue that reality is in fact of material or physical character, as the ordinary man thinks it is; and by saying that it is identical with reason, or mind, one would imply that the mind is also a material or physical phenomenon—or if not, that the difference between the mental and the physical cannot be of great importance.

This materialism can be regarded as a revival of certain aspects of Cartesianism, modified by links with dialectic. But in discarding its original idealistic basis, dialectic loses everything which made it plausible and understandable; we have to remember that the best arguments in favour of dialectic lay in its applicability to the development of thought, especially of philosophical thought. Now we are faced blankly with the statement that physical reality develops dialectically—an extremely dogmatic assertion with so little scientific support that materialistic dialecticians are forced to make a very extensive use of the dangerous method we have already described whereby criticism is rejected as non-dialectical. Dialectical materialism is thus in agreement which points (a) and (b) discussed above, but it alters point (c) considerably, although I think with no advantage to its dialectic features. In expressing this opinion, I want to stress the point that although I should not describe myself as a materialist, my criticism is not directed against materialism, which I personally should probably prefer to idealism if I were forced to choose (which happily I am not). It is only the combination of dialectic and materialism that appears to me to be even worse than dialectic idealism.

These remarks apply particularly to the 'Dialectical Materialism' developed by Marx. The materialistic element in this theory could be comparatively easily reformulated in such a way that no serious objections to it could be made. As far as I can see the main point is this: there is no reason to assume that whilst the natural sciences can proceed an the basis of the common man's realistic outlook the social sciences need an idealist background like the one offered by Hegelianism. Such an assumption was often made in Marx's time, owing to the fact that Hegel with his idealist theory of the State appeared strongly to influence, and even to further, the social sciences, while the futility of views which he held within the field of the natural sciences was—at least for natural scientists—only too obvious.[3] I think it is a fair Interpretation of the ideas of Marx and Engels to say that one of

---

3   At least it should be obvious to everybody who considers, as an instance, the following surprising analysis of the essence of electricity which I have translated as well as I could, even to the extent of trying to render it more understandable than Hegel's original: 'Electricity... is the purpose of the form from which it emancipates itself, it is the form that is just about to overcome its own indifference; for, electricity is the immediate emergence, or the actuality just emerging, from the proximity of the form, and still determined by it-not yet the dissolution, however, of the form itself, but rather the more superficial process by which the differences desert the form which, however, they still retain, as their condition, having not yet grown into independence of and

their chief interests in emphasizing materialism was to dismiss any theory which, referring to the rational or spiritual nature of man, maintains that sociology has to be based on an idealist or spiritualist basis, or an the analysis of reason. In opposition they stressed the material side of human nature—such as our need for food and other material goods—and its importance for sociology.

This view was undoubtedly sound; and I hold Marx's contributions an this point to be of real significance and lasting influence. Everyone learned from Marx that the development even of ideas cannot be fully understood if the history of ideas is treated (although such a treatment may often have its great merits) without mentioning the conditions of their origin and the situation of their originators, among which conditions the economic aspect is highly significant. Nevertheless I personally think that Marx's economism—his emphasis an the economic background as the ultimate basis of any sort of development— is mistaken and in fact untenable. I think that social experience clearly shows that under certain circumstances the influence of ideas (perhaps supported by propaganda) can outweigh and supersede economic forces. Besides, granted that it is impossible fully to understand mental developments without understanding their economic background, it is at least as impossible to understand economic developments without understanding the development of, for instance, scientific or religious ideas.

For our present purpose it is not so important to analyse Marx's materialism and econom- ism as to see what has become of the dialectic within his system. Two points seem to me important. One is Marx's emphasis an historical method in sociology, a tendency which I have called 'historicism'. The other is the anti-dogmatic tendency of Marx's dialectic.

As for the first point, we have to remember that Hegel was one of the inventors of the historical method, a founder of the school of thinkers who believed that in describing a development historically one has causally explained it. This school believed that one could, for example, explain certain social institutions by showing how mankind has slowly developed them. Nowadays it is often recognized that the significance of the historical method for social theory has been much over-rated; but the belief in this method has by no means disappeared. I have tried to criticize this method elsewhere (especially in my book The Poverty of Historicism). Here I merely want to stress that Marx's sociology adopted from Hegel not only the view that its method has to be historical, and that sociology as well as history have to become theories of social development, but also the view that this development has to be explained in dialectical terms. To Hegel history was the history of ideas. Marx dropped idealism but retained Hegel's doctrine that the dynamic forces of historical development are the dialectical 'contradictions', 'negations', and 'negations of negations'. In this respect Marx and Engels followed Hegel very closely indeed, as may be shown by the following quotations. Hegel in his Encyclopaedia (Part I ch. VI p. 81) described Dialectic as 'the universal and irresistible power before which nothing can stay, however secure and stable it may deem itself'. Similarly, Engels writes (Anti-Dühring, Part i, 'Dialectics: Negation of the Negation'): 'What therefore is the

---

through them.' (No doubt it ought to have been 'of and through it'; but I do not wish to suggest that this would have made much difference to the differences.) The passage is from Hegel's Philosophy of Nature. See also the passages an Sound and an Heat, quoted in my Open Society, note 4 to ch. 12, and text.

negation of the negation? An extremely genera…law of development of Nature, history and thought; a law which…holds good in the animal and plant kingdom, in geology, in mathematics, in history, and in philosophy.'

In Marx's view it is the main task of sociological science to show how these dialectic forces are working in history, and thus to prophesy the course of history; or, as he says in the preface to Capital, 'It is the ultimate aim of this work to lay bare the economic law of motion of modern society'. And this dialectic law of motion, the negation of the negation, furnishes the basis of Marx's prophecy of the impending end of capitalism (Capital, I, ch. XXIV, p. 7): 'The capitalist mode of production…is the first negation… But capitalism begets, with the inexorability of a law of Nature, its own negation. It is the negation of the negation.

Prophecy certainly need not be unscientific, as predictions of eclipses and other astronomical events show. But Hegelian dialectic, or its materialistic version, cannot be accepted as a sound basis for scientific forecasts. ('But all Marx's predictions have come true,' Marxists usually answer. They have not. To quote one example out of many: In Capital, immediately after the last passage quoted, Marx said that the transition from capitalism to socialism would naturally be a process incomparably less 'protracted, violent, and difficult' than the industrial revolution, and in a footnote he amplified this forecast by referring to the 'irresolute and non-resisting bourgeoisie'. Few Marxists will say nowadays that these predictions were successful.) Thus if forecasts based an dialectic are made, some will come true and some will not. In the latter case, obviously, a situation will arise which has not been foreseen. But dialectic is vague and elastic enough to interpret and to explain this unforeseen situation just as well as it interpreted and explained the Situation which it predicted and which happened not to come true. Any development whatever will fit the dialectic scheme; the dialectician need never be afraid of any refutation by future experience.[4] As mentioned before, it is not just the dialectical approach, it is, rather, the idea of a theory of historical development—the idea that scientific sociology aims at large-scale historical forecasts—which is mistaken. But this does not concern us here.

Apart from the role dialectic plays in Marx's historical method, Marx's anti-dogmatic attitude should be discussed. Marx and Engels strongly insisted that science should not be interpreted as a body of final and well-established knowledge, or of 'eternal truth', but rather as something developing, progressive. The scientist is not the man who knows a lot but rather the man who is determined not to give up the search for truth. Scientific systems develop; and they develop, according to Marx, dialectically.

There is not very much to be Said against this point—although personally I think that the dialectical description of scientific development is not always applicable unless it is forced, and that it is better to describe scientific development in a less ambitious and ambiguous way, as for example, in terms of the trial and error theory. But I am prepared

---

4   *In L.Sc.D. I have tried to show that the scientific content of a theory is the greater the more the theory conveys, the more it risks, the more it is exposed to refutation by future experience. If it takes no such risks, its scientific content is zero-it has no scientific content, it is metaphysical. By this standard we can say that dialectic is unscientific: it is metaphysical.*

to admit that this criticism is not of great importance. It is, however, of real moment that Marx's progressive and anti-dogmatic view of science has never been applied by orthodox Marxists within the field of their own activities. Progressive, anti-dogmatic science is critical—criticism is its very life. But criticism of Marxism, of dialectical materialism, has never been tolerated by Marxists.

Hegel thought that philosophy develops; yet his own system was to remain the last and highest stage of this development and could not be superseded. The Marxists adopted the same attitude towards the Marxism system. Hence, Marx's anti-dogmatic attitude exists only in the theory and not in the practice of orthodox Marxism, and dialectic is used by Marxists, following the example of Engels Anti-Dühring, mainly for the purposes of apologetics-to defend the Marxist system against criticism. As a rule critics are denounced for their failure to understand the dialectic, or proletarian science, or for being traitors. Thanks to dialectic the anti-dogmatic attitude has disappeared, and Marxism has established itself as a dogmatism which is elastic enough, by using its dialectic method, to evade any further attack. It has thus become what I have called a reinforced dogmatism.

Yet there can be no worse obstacle to the growth of science than a reinforced dogmatism. There can be no scientific development without the free competition of thought—this is the essence of the anti-dogmatic attitude once so strongly supported by Marx and Engels; and in general there cannot be free competition in scientific thought without freedom for all thought.

Thus dialectic has played a very unfortunate role not only in the development of philosophy, but also in the development of political theory. A full understanding of this unfortunate role will be easier if we try to See how Marx originally came to develop such a theory. We have to consider the whole situation. Marx, a young man who was progressive, evolutionary and even revolutionary in his thought, came under the influence of Hegel, the most famous German philosopher. Hegel had been a representative of Prussian reaction. He had used his principle of the identity of reason and reality to support the existing powers—for what exists, is reasonable—and to defend the idea of the Absolute State (an idea nowadays called 'Totalitarianism'). Marx, who admired him, but who was of a very different political temperament, needed a philosophy an which to base his own political opinions. We can understand his elation at discovering that Hegel's dialectical philosophy could easily be turned against its own master—that dialectic was in favour of a revolutionary political theory, rather than of a conservative and apologetic one. Besides this, it was excellently adapted to his need for a theory which should be not only revolutionary, but also optimistic—a theory forecasting progress by emphasizing that every new step is a step upwards.

This discovery, although undeniably fascinating for a disciple of Hegel and in an era dominated by Hegel, has now, together with Hegelianism, lost all significance, and can hardly be considered to be more than the clever tour de force of a brilliant young student revealing a weakness in the speculations of his undeservedly famous master. But it became the theoretical basis of what is called 'Scientific Marxism'. And it helped to turn Marxism into a dogmatic system by preventing the scientific development of which it might have been capable. So Marxism has for decades kept its dogmatic attitude, repeating against its opponents just the Same arguments as were originally used by its founders. It is sad but illuminating to See how orthodox Marxism today officially recommends, as a basis for the study of scientific methodology, the reading of Hegel's Logic—which is not merely obsolete but typical of pre-scientific and even pre-logical ways of thinking. It is worse than recommending Archimedes' mechanics as a basis for modern engineering.

The whole development of dialectic should be a warning against the dangers inherent in philosophical system-building. It should remind us that philosophy must not be made a basis for any sort of scientific system and that philosophers should be much more modest in their claims. One task which they can fulfill quite usefully is the study of the critical methods of science.

7-5

Walter Benjamin

The Work of Art in the Age of Mechanical Reproduction

1936

"one might subsume the eliminated element in the term 'aura' and go on to say: that which withers in the age of mechanical reproduction is the aura of the work of art. This is a symptomatic process whose significance points beyond the realm of art"

Walter Benjamin (1892–1940) was a German-Jewish philosopher and cultural critic whose work set the foundations of the movement of social and political philosophy known as the Frankfurt School. His essays and criticism touched on materialism, the advent of modernity, and film theory.

....

Preface

When Marx undertook his critique of the capitalistic mode of production, this mode was in its infancy. Marx directed his efforts in such a way as to give them prognostic value. He went back to the basic conditions underlying capitalistic production and through his presentation showed what could be expected of capitalism in the future. The result was that one could expect it not only to exploit the proletariat with increasing intensity, but ultimately to create conditions which would make it possible to abolish capitalism itself.

The transformation of the superstructure, which takes place far more slowly than that of the substructure, has taken more than half a century to manifest in all areas of culture the change in the conditions of production. Only today can it be indicated what form this has taken. Certain prognostic requirements should be met by these statements. However, theses about the art of the proletariat after its assumption of power or about the art of a classless society would have less bearing on these demands than theses about the developmental tendencies of art under present conditions of production. Their dialectic is no less noticeable in the superstructure than in the economy. It would therefore be wrong to underestimate the value of such theses as a weapon. They brush aside a number of outmoded concepts, such as creativity and genius, eternal value and mystery—concepts whose uncontrolled (and at present almost uncontrollable) application would lead to a processing of data in the Fascist sense. The concepts which are introduced into the theory of art in what follows differ from the more familiar terms in that they are completely useless for the purposes of Fascism. They are, on the other hand, useful for the formulation of revolutionary demands in the politics of art.

I

In principle a work of art has always been reproducible. Man-made artifacts could always be imitated by men. Replicas were made by pupils in practice of their craft, by masters for diffusing their works, and, finally, by third parties in the pursuit of gain. Mechanical reproduction of a work of art, however, represents something new. Historically, it advanced intermittently and in leaps at long intervals, but with accelerated intensity. The Greeks knew only two procedures of technically reproducing works of art: founding and stamping. Bronzes, terra cottas, and coins were the only art works which they could produce in quantity. All others were unique and could not be mechanically reproduced. With the woodcut graphic art became mechanically reproducible for the first time, long before script became reproducible by print. The enormous changes which printing, the mechanical reproduction of writing, has brought about in literature are a familiar story. However, within the phenomenon which we are here examining from the perspective of world history, print is merely a special, though particularly important, case. During the Middle Ages engraving and etching were added to the woodcut; at the beginning of the nineteenth century lithography made its appearance.

With lithography the technique of reproduction reached an essentially new stage. This much more direct process was distinguished by the tracing of the design on a stone rather than its incision on a block of wood or its etching on a copperplate and permitted graphic art for the first time to put its products on the market, not only in large numbers as hitherto, but also in daily changing forms. Lithography enabled graphic art to illustrate everyday life, and it began to keep pace with printing. But only a few decades after its invention, lithography was surpassed by photography. For the first time in the process of pictorial reproduction, photography freed the hand of the most important artistic functions which henceforth devolved only upon the eye looking into a lens. Since the eye perceives more swiftly than the hand can draw, the process of pictorial reproduction was accelerated so enormously that it could keep pace with speech. A film operator shooting a scene in the studio captures the images at the speed of an actor's speech. Just as lithography virtually implied the illustrated newspaper, so did photography foreshadow the sound film. The technical reproduction of sound was tackled at the end of the last century. These convergent endeavors made predictable a situation which Paul Valery pointed up in this sentence: "Just as water, gas, and electricity are brought into our houses from far off to satisfy our needs in response to a minimal effort, so we shall be supplied with visual or auditory images, which will appear and disappear at a simple movement of the hand, hardly more than a sign." Around 1900 technical reproduction had reached a standard that not only permitted it to reproduce all transmitted works of art and thus to cause the most profound change in their impact upon the public; it also had captured a place of its own among the artistic processes. For the study of this standard nothing is more revealing than the nature of the repercussions that these two different manifestations—the reproduction of works of art and the art of the film—have had on art in its traditional form.

II

Even the most perfect reproduction of a work of art is lacking in one element: its presence in time and space, its unique existence at the place where it happens to be. This unique existence of the work of art determined the history to which it was subject throughout the time of its existence. This includes the changes which it may have suffered in physical condition over the years as well as the various changes in its ownership. The traces of the first can be revealed only by chemical or physical analyses which it is impossible to perform on a reproduction; changes of ownership are subject to a tradition which must be traced from the situation of the original.

The presence of the original is the prerequisite to the concept of authenticity. Chemical analyses of the patina of a bronze can help to establish this, as does the proof that a given manuscript of the Middle Ages stems from an archive of the fifteenth century. The whole sphere of authenticity is outside technical—and, of course, not only technical—reproducibility. Confronted with its manual reproduction, which was usually branded as a forgery, the original preserved all its authority; not so vis-à-vis technical reproduction. The reason is twofold. First, process reproduction is more independent of the original than manual reproduction. For example, in photography, process reproduction can bring out those aspects of the original that are unattainable to the naked eye yet accessible to the lens, which is adjustable and chooses its angle at will. And photographic reproduction, with the aid of certain processes, such as enlargement or slow motion, can capture images which escape natural vision. Secondly, technical reproduction can put the copy of the original into situations which would be out of reach for the original itself. Above all, it enables the original to meet the beholder halfway, be it in the form of a photograph or a phonograph record. The cathedral leaves its locale to be received in the studio of a lover of art; the choral production, performed in an auditorium or in the open air, resounds in the drawing room.

The situations into which the product of mechanical reproduction can be brought may not touch the actual work of art, yet the quality of its presence is always depreciated. This holds not only for the art work but also, for instance, for a landscape which passes in review before the spectator in a movie. In the case of the art object, a most sensitive nucleus—namely, its authenticity—is interfered with, whereas no natural object is vulnerable on that score. The authenticity of a thing is the essence of all that is transmissible from its beginning, ranging from its substantive duration to its testimony to the history which it has experienced. Since the historical testimony rests on the authenticity, the former, too, is jeopardized by reproduction when substantive duration ceases to matter. And what is really jeopardized when the historical testimony is affected is the authority of the object.

One might subsume the eliminated element in the term "aura" and go on to say: that which withers in the age of mechanical reproduction is the aura of the work of art. This is a symptomatic process whose significance points beyond the realm of art. One might generalize by saying: the technique of reproduction detaches the reproduced object from the domain of tradition. By making many reproductions it substitutes a plurality of copies for a unique existence. And in permitting the reproduction to meet the beholder or listener in his own particular situation, it reactivates the object reproduced. These two processes lead to a tremendous shattering of tradition which is the obverse of the contemporary crisis and renewal of mankind. Both processes are intimately connected with the contemporary mass movements. Their most powerful agent is the film. Its social significance, particularly in its most positive form, is inconceivable without its destructive, cathartic aspect, that is, the liquidation of the traditional value of the cultural heritage. This phenomenon is most palpable in the great historical films. It extends to ever new positions. In 1927 Abel Gance exclaimed enthusiastically: "Shakespeare, Rembrandt, Beethoven will make films...all

legends, all mythologies and all myths, all founders of religion, and the very religions…
await their exposed resurrection, and the heroes crowd each other at the gate."
Presumably without intending it, he issued an invitation to a far-reaching liquidation.

III

During long periods of history, the mode of human sense perception changes with
humanity's entire mode of existence. The manner in which human sense perception is
organized, the medium in which it is accomplished, is determined not only by nature but
by historical circumstances as well. The fifth century, with its great shifts of population,
saw the birth of the late Roman art industry and the Vienna Genesis, and there developed
not only an art different from that of antiquity but also a new kind of perception. The
scholars of the Viennese school, Riegl and Wickhoff, who resisted the weight of classical
tradition under which these later art forms had been buried, were the first to draw
conclusions from them concerning the organization of perception at the time. However
far-reaching their insight, these scholars limited themselves to showing the significant,
formal hallmark which characterized perception in late Roman times. They did not
attempt—and, perhaps, saw no way—to show the social transformations expressed by
these changes of perception. The conditions for an analogous insight are more favorable
in the present. And if changes in the medium of contemporary perception can be comprehended as decay of the aura, it is possible to show its social causes.

The concept of aura which was proposed above with reference to historical objects may
usefully be illustrated with reference to the aura of natural ones. We define the aura of the
latter as the unique phenomenon of a distance, however close it may be. If, while resting
on a summer afternoon, you follow with your eyes a mountain range on the horizon or a
branch which casts its shadow over you, you experience the aura of those mountains, of
that branch. This image makes it easy to comprehend the social bases of the contemporary
decay of the aura. It rests on two circumstances, both of which are related to the increasing significance of the masses in contemporary life. Namely, the desire of contemporary
masses to bring things "closer" spatially and humanly, which is just as ardent as their bent
toward overcoming the uniqueness of every reality by accepting its reproduction. Every
day the urge grows stronger to get hold of an object at very close range by way of its like-
ness, its reproduction. Unmistakably, reproduction as offered by picture magazines and
newsreels differs from the image seen by the unarmed eye. Uniqueness and permanence
are as closely linked in the latter as are transitoriness and reproducibility in the former. To
pry an object from its shell, to destroy its aura, is the mark of a perception whose "sense of
the universal equality of things" has increased to such a degree that it extracts it even from
a unique object by means of reproduction. Thus is manifested in the field of perception
what in the theoretical sphere is noticeable in the increasing importance of statistics. The
adjustment of reality to the masses and of the masses to reality is a process of unlimited
scope, as much for thinking as for perception.

IV

The uniqueness of a work of art is inseparable from its being imbedded in the fabric of
tradition. This tradition itself is thoroughly alive and extremely changeable. An ancient
statue of Venus, for example, stood in a different traditional context with the Greeks,
who made it an object of veneration, than with the clerics of the Middle Ages, who

viewed it as an ominous idol. Both of them, however, were equally confronted with its uniqueness, that is, its aura. Originally the contextual integration of art in tradition found its expression in the cult. We know that the earliest art works originated in the service of a ritual—first the magical, then the religious kind. It is significant that the existence of the work of art with reference to its aura is never entirely separated from its ritual function. In other words, the unique value of the "authentic" work of art has its basis in ritual, the location of its original use value. This ritualistic basis, however remote, is still recognizable as secularized ritual even in the most profane forms of the cult of beauty. The secular cult of beauty, developed during the Renaissance and prevailing for three centuries, clearly showed that ritualistic basis in its decline and the first deep crisis which befell it. With the advent of the first truly revolutionary means of reproduction, photography, simultaneously with the rise of socialism, art sensed the approaching crisis which has become evident a century later. At the time, art reacted with the doctrine of *l'art pour l'art*, that is, with a theology of art. This gave rise to what might be called a negative theology in the form of the idea of "pure" art, which not only denied any social function of art but also any categorizing by subject matter. (In poetry, Mallarmé was the first to take this position.)

An analysis of art in the age of mechanical reproduction must do justice to these relationships, for they lead us to an all-important insight: for the first time in world history, mechanical reproduction emancipates the work of art from its parasitical dependence on ritual. To an ever greater degree the work of art reproduced becomes the work of art designed for reproducibility. From a photographic negative, for example, one can make any number of prints; to ask for the "authentic" print makes no sense. But the instant the criterion of authenticity ceases to be applicable to artistic production, the total function of art is reversed. Instead of being based on ritual, it begins to be based on another practice—politics.

V

Works of art are received and valued on different planes. Two polar types stand out; with one, the accent is on the cult value; with the other, on the exhibition value of the work. Artistic production begins with ceremonial objects destined to serve in a cult. One may assume that what mattered was their existence, not their being on view. The elk portrayed by the man of the Stone Age on the walls of his cave was an instrument of magic. He did expose it to his fellow men, but in the main it was meant for the spirits. Today the cult value would seem to demand that the work of art remain hidden. Certain statues of gods are accessible only to the priest in the cella; certain Madonnas remain covered nearly all year round; certain sculptures on medieval cathedrals are invisible to the spectator on ground level. With the emancipation of the various art practices from ritual go increasing opportunities for the exhibition of their products. It is easier to exhibit a portrait bust that can be sent here and there than to exhibit the statue of a divinity that has its fixed place in the interior of a temple. The same holds for the painting as against the mosaic or fresco that preceded it. And even though the public presentability of a mass originally may have been just as great as that of a symphony, the latter originated at the moment when its public presentability promised to surpass that of the mass.

With the different methods of technical reproduction of a work of art, its fitness for exhibition increased to such an extent that the quantitative shift between its two poles turned into a qualitative transformation of its nature. This is comparable to the situation of the work of art in prehistoric times when, by the absolute emphasis on its cult value, it was, first and foremost, an instrument of magic. Only later did it come to be recognized as a work of art. In the same way today, by the absolute emphasis on its exhibition value the work of art becomes a creation with entirely new functions, among which the one we are conscious of, the artistic function, later may be recognized as incidental. This much is certain: today photography and the film are the most serviceable exemplifications of this new function.

VI

In photography, exhibition value begins to displace cult value all along the line. But cult value does not give way without resistance. It retires into an ultimate retrenchment: the human countenance. It is no accident that the portrait was the focal point of early photography. The cult of remembrance of loved ones, absent or dead, offers a last refuge for the cult value of the picture. For the last time the aura emanates from the early photographs in the fleeting expression of a human face. This is what constitutes their melancholy, incomparable beauty. But as man withdraws from the photographic image, the exhibition value for the first time shows its superiority to the ritual value. To have pinpointed this new stage constitutes the incomparable significance of Atget, who, around 1900, took photographs of deserted Paris streets. It has quite justly been said of him that he photographed them like scenes of crime. The scene of a crime, too, is deserted; it is photographed for the purpose of establishing evidence. With Atget, photographs become standard evidence for historical occurrences, and acquire a hidden political significance. They demand a specific kind of approach; free-floating contemplation is not appropriate to them. They stir the viewer; he feels challenged by them in a new way. At the same time picture magazines begin to put up signposts for him, right ones or wrong ones, no matter. For the first time, captions have become obligatory. And it is clear that they have an altogether different character than the title of a painting. The directives which the captions give to those looking at pictures in illustrated magazines soon become even more explicit and more imperative in the film where the meaning of each single picture appears to be prescribed by the sequence of all preceding ones.

VII

The nineteenth-century dispute as to the artistic value of painting versus photography today seems devious and confused. This does not diminish its importance, however; if anything, it underlines it. The dispute was in fact the symptom of a historical transformation the universal impact of which was not realized by either of the rivals. When the age of mechanical reproduction separated art from its basis in cult, the semblance of its autonomy disappeared forever. The resulting change in the function of art transcended the perspective of the century; for a long time it even escaped that of the twentieth century, which experienced the development of the film. Earlier much futile thought had been devoted to the question of whether photography is an art. The primary question— whether the very invention of photography had not transformed the entire nature of art— was not raised. Soon the film theoreticians asked the same ill-considered question with regard to the film. But the difficulties which photography caused traditional aesthetics were mere child's play as compared to those raised by the film. Whence the insensitive and forced character of early theories of the film. Abel Gance, for instance, compares the film with hieroglyphs: "Here, by a remarkable regression, we have come back to the level of expression of the Egyptians...Pictorial language has not yet matured because our eyes have not yet adjusted to it. There is as yet insufficient respect for, insufficient cult of, what it expresses." Or, in the words of Séverin-Mars: "What art has been granted a dream more poetical and more real at the same time! Approached in this fashion the film might represent an incomparable means of expression. Only the most high-minded persons, in the most perfect and mysterious moments of their lives, should be allowed to enter its ambience." Alexandre Arnoux concludes his fantasy about the silent film with the question: "Do not all the bold descriptions we have given amount to the definition of prayer?" It is instructive to note how their desire to class the film among the "arts" forces these theoreticians to read ritual elements into it—with a striking lack of discretion. Yet when these speculations were published, films like *L'Opinion Publique* and *The Gold Rush* had already appeared. This, however, did not keep Abel Gance from adducing hieroglyphs for purposes of comparison, nor Séverin-Mars from speaking of the film as one might speak of paintings by Fra Angelico. Characteristically, even today ultra reactionary authors give the film a similar contextual significance—if not an outright sacred one, then at least a supernatural one. Commenting on Max Reinhardt's film version of *A Midsummer Night's Dream*, Werfel states that undoubtedly it was the sterile copying of the exterior world with its streets, interiors, railroad stations, restaurants, motorcars, and beaches which until now had obstructed the elevation of the film to the realm of art. "The film has not yet realized its true meaning, its real possibilities...these consist in its unique faculty to express by natural means and with incomparable persuasiveness all that is fairy like, marvelous, supernatural."

VIII

The artistic performance of a stage actor is definitely presented to the public by the actor in person; that of the screen actor, however, is presented by a camera, with a twofold consequence. The camera that presents the performance of the film actor to the public need not respect the performance as an integral whole. Guided by the cameraman, the camera continually changes its position with respect to the performance. The sequence of positional views which the editor composes from the material supplied him constitutes the completed film. It comprises certain factors of movement which are in reality those of the camera, not to mention special camera angles, close-ups, etc. Hence, the performance of the actor is subjected to a series of optical tests. This is the first consequence of the fact that the actor's performance is presented by means of a camera. Also, the film actor lacks the opportunity of the stage actor to adjust to the audience during his performance, since he does not present his performance to the audience in person. This permits the audience to take the position of a critic, without experiencing any personal contact with the actor. The audience's identification with the actor is really an identification with the camera. Consequently the audience takes the position of the camera; its approach is that of testing. This is not the approach to which cult values may be exposed.

IX

For the film, what matters primarily is that the actor represents himself to the public before the camera, rather than representing someone else. One of the first to sense the actor's metamorphosis by this form of testing was Pirandello. Though his remarks on the subject in his novel *Si Gira* were limited to the negative aspects of the question and to the silent film only, this hardly impairs their validity. For in this respect, the sound film did not change anything essential. What matters is that the part is acted not for an audience but for a mechanical contrivance—in the case of the sound film, for two of them. "The film actor," wrote Pirandello, "feels as if in exile—exiled not only from the stage but also from himself. With a vague sense of discomfort he feels inexplicable emptiness: his body loses its corporeality, it evaporates, it is deprived of reality, life, voice, and the noises caused by his moving about, in order to be changed into a mute image, flickering an instant on the screen, then vanishing into silence.... The projector will play with his shadow before the public, and he himself must be content to play before the camera." This situation might also be characterized as follows: for the first time—and this is the effect of the film—man has to operate with his whole living person, yet forgoing its aura. For aura is tied to his presence; there can be no replica of it. The aura which, on the stage, emanates from Mac-beth, cannot be separated for the spectators from that of the actor. However, the singular-ity of the shot in the studio is that the camera is substituted for the public. Consequently, the aura that envelops the actor vanishes, and with it the aura of the figure he portrays.

It is not surprising that it should be a dramatist such as Pirandello who, in characteriz-ing the film, inadvertently touches on the very crisis in which we see the theater. Any thorough study proves that there is indeed no greater contrast than that of the stage play to a work of art that is completely subject to or, like the film, founded in, mechanical reproduction. Experts have long recognized that in the film "the greatest effects are almost always obtained by 'acting' as little as possible..." In 1932 Rudolf Arnheim saw "the latest trend...in treating the actor as a stage prop chosen for its characteristics and...inserted at the proper place." With this idea something else is closely connected. The stage actor identifies himself with the character of his role. The film actor very often is denied this opportunity. His creation is by no means all of a piece; it is composed of many separate performances. Besides certain fortuitous considerations, such as cost of studio, availability of fellow players, décor, etc., there are elementary necessities of equipment that split the actor's work into a series of mountable episodes. In particular, lighting and its installation require the presentation of an event that, on the screen, unfolds as a rapid and unified scene, in a sequence of separate shootings which may take hours at the studio; not to mention more obvious montage. Thus a jump from the window can be shot in the studio as a jump from a scaffold, and the ensuing flight, if need be, can be shot weeks later when outdoor scenes are taken. Far more paradoxical cases can easily be construed. Let us assume that an actor is supposed to be startled by a knock at the door. If his reaction is not satisfactory, the director can resort to an expedient: when the actor happens to be at the studio again he has a shot fired behind him without his being forewarned of it. The frightened reaction can be shot now and be cut into the screen version. Nothing more strikingly shows that art has left the realm of the "beautiful semblance" which, so far, had been taken to be the only sphere where art could thrive.

X

The feeling of strangeness that overcomes the actor before the camera, as Pirandello describes it, is basically of the same kind as the estrangement felt before one's own image in the mirror. But now the reflected image has become separable, transportable. And where is it transported? Before the public. Never for a moment does the screen actor cease to be conscious of this fact. While facing the camera he knows that ultimately he will face the public, the consumers who constitute the market. This market, where he offers not only his labor but also his whole self, his heart and soul, is beyond his reach. During the shooting he has as little contact with it as any article made in a factory. This may contribute to that oppression, that new anxiety which, according to Pirandello, grips the actor before the camera. The film responds to the shriveling of the aura with an artificial build-up of the "personality" outside the studio. The cult of the movie star, fostered by the money of the film industry, preserves not the unique aura of the person but the "spell of the personality," the phony spell of a commodity. So long as the movie-makers' capital sets the fashion, as a rule no other revolutionary merit can be accredited to today's film than the promotion of a revolutionary criticism of traditional concepts of art. We do not deny that in some cases today's films can also promote revolutionary criticism of social conditions, even of the distribution of property. However, our present study is no more specifically concerned with this than is the film production of Western Europe.

It is inherent in the technique of the film as well as that of sports that everybody who witnesses its accomplishments is somewhat of an expert. This is obvious to anyone listening to a group of newspaper boys leaning on their bicycles and discussing the outcome of a bicycle race. It is not for nothing that newspaper publishers arrange races for their delivery boys. These arouse great interest among the participants, for the victor has an opportunity to rise from delivery boy to professional racer. Similarly, the newsreel offers everyone the opportunity to rise from passer-by to movie extra. In this way any man might even find himself part of a work of art, as witness Vertov's *Three Songs About Lenin* or Ivens' *Borinage*. Any man today can lay claim to being filmed. This claim can best be elucidated by a comparative look at the historical situation of contemporary literature.

For centuries a small number of writers were confronted by many thousands of readers. This changed toward the end of the last century. With the increasing extension of the press, which kept placing new political, religious, scientific, professional, and local organs before the readers, an increasing number of readers became writers—at first, occasional ones. It began with the daily press opening to its readers space for "letters to the editor." And today there is hardly a gainfully employed European who could not, in principle, find an opportunity to publish somewhere or other comments on his work, grievances, documentary reports, or that sort of thing. Thus, the distinction between author and public is about to lose its basic character. The difference becomes merely functional; it may vary from case to case. At any moment the reader is ready to turn into a writer. As expert, which he had to become willy-nilly in an extremely specialized work process, even if only in some minor respect, the reader gains access to authorship. In the Soviet Union work itself is given a voice. To present it verbally is part of a man's ability to perform the work. Literary license is now founded on polytechnic rather than specialized training and thus becomes common property.

All this can easily be applied to the film, where transitions that in literature took centuries have come about in a decade. In cinematic practice, particularly in Russia, this change-over has partially become established reality. Some of the players whom we meet in Russian films are not actors in our sense but people who portray *themselves*—and primarily in their own work process. In Western Europe the capitalistic exploitation of the film denies consideration to modern man's legitimate claim to being reproduced. Under these circumstances the film industry is trying hard to spur the interest of the masses through illusion-promoting spectacles and dubious speculations.

XI

The shooting of a film, especially of a sound film, affords a spectacle unimaginable anywhere at any time before this. It presents a process in which it is impossible to assign to a spectator a viewpoint which would exclude from the actual scene such extraneous accessories as camera equipment, lighting machinery, staff assistants, etc.—unless his eye were on a line parallel with the lens. This circumstance, more than any other, renders superficial and insignificant any possible similarity between a scene in the studio and one on the stage. In the theatre one is well aware of the place from which the play cannot immediately be detected as illusionary. There is no such place for the movie scene that is being shot. Its illusionary nature is that of the second degree, the result of cutting. That is to say, in the studio the mechanical equipment has penetrated so deeply into reality that its pure aspect freed from the foreign substance of equipment is the result of a special procedure, namely, the shooting by the specially adjusted camera and the mounting of the shot together with other similar ones. The equipment-free aspect of reality here has become the height of artifice; the sight of immediate reality has become an orchid in the land of technology.

Even more revealing is the comparison of these circumstances, which differ so much from those of the theatre, with the situation in painting. Here the question is: How does the cameraman compare with the painter? To answer this we take recourse to an analogy with a surgical operation. The surgeon represents the polar opposite of the magician. The magician heals a sick person by the laying on of hands; the surgeon cuts into the patient's body. The magician maintains the natural distance between the patient and himself; though he reduces it very slightly by the laying on of hands, he greatly increases it by virtue of his authority. The surgeon does exactly the reverse; he greatly diminishes the distance between himself and the patient by penetrating into the patient's body, and increases it but little by the caution with which his hand moves among the organs. In short, in contrast to the magician—who is still hidden in the medical practitioner—the surgeon at the decisive moment abstains from facing the patient man to man; rather, it is through the operation that he penetrates into him.

Magician and surgeon compare to painter and cameraman. The painter maintains in his work a natural distance from reality, the cameraman penetrates deeply into its web. There is a tremendous difference between the pictures they obtain. That of the painter is a total one, that of the cameraman consists of multiple fragments which are assembled under a new law. Thus, for contemporary man the representation of reality by the film is incomparably more significant than that of the painter, since it offers, precisely because of the thoroughgoing permeation of reality with mechanical equipment, an aspect of reality which is free of all equipment. And that is what one is entitled to ask from a work of art.

XII

Mechanical reproduction of art changes the reaction of the masses toward art. The reactionary attitude toward a Picasso painting changes into the progressive reaction toward a

Chaplin movie. The progressive reaction is characterized by the direct, intimate fusion of visual and emotional enjoyment with the orientation of the expert. Such fusion is of great social significance. The greater the decrease in the social significance of an art form, the sharper the distinction between criticism and enjoyment by the public. The conventional is uncritically enjoyed, and the truly new is criticized with aversion. With regard to the screen, the critical and the receptive attitudes of the public coincide. The decisive reason for this is that individual reactions are predetermined by the mass audience response they are about to produce, and this is nowhere more pronounced than in the film. The moment these responses become manifest they control each other. Again, the comparison with painting is fruitful. A painting has always had an excellent chance to be viewed by one person or by a few. The simultaneous contemplation of paintings by a large public, such as developed in the nineteenth century, is an early symptom of the crisis of painting, a crisis which was by no means occasioned exclusively by photography but rather in a relatively independent manner by the appeal of art works to the masses.

Painting simply is in no position to present an object for simultaneous collective experience, as it was possible for architecture at all times, for the epic poem in the past, and for the movie today. Although this circumstance in itself should not lead one to conclusions about the social role of painting, it does constitute a serious threat as soon as painting, under special conditions and, as it were, against its nature, is confronted directly by the masses. In the churches and monasteries of the Middle Ages and at the princely courts up to the end of the eighteenth century, a collective reception of paintings did not occur simultaneously, but by graduated and hierarchized mediation. The change that has come about is an expression of the particular conflict in which painting was implicated by the mechanical reproducibility of paintings. Although paintings began to be publicly exhibited in galleries and salons, there was no way for the masses to organize and control themselves in their reception. Thus the same public which responds in a progressive manner toward a grotesque film is bound to respond in a reactionary manner to surrealism.

XIII

The characteristics of the film lie not only in the manner in which man presents himself to mechanical equipment but also in the manner in which, by means of this apparatus, man can represent his environment. A glance at occupational psychology illustrates the testing capacity of the equipment. Psychoanalysis illustrates it in a different perspective. The film has enriched our field of perception with methods which can be illustrated by those of Freudian theory. Fifty years ago, a slip of the tongue passed more or less unnoticed. Only exceptionally may such a slip have revealed dimensions of depth in a conversation which had seemed to be taking its course on the surface. Since the *Psychopathology of Everyday Life* things have changed. This book isolated and made analyzable things which had heretofore floated along unnoticed in the broad stream of perception. For the entire spectrum of optical, and now also acoustical, perception the film has brought about a similar deepening of apperception. It is only an obverse of this fact that behavior items shown in a movie can be analyzed much more precisely and from more points of view than those presented on paintings or on the stage. As compared with painting, filmed behavior lends itself more readily to analysis because of its incomparably more precise statements of the situation. In comparison with the stage scene, the filmed behavior item lends itself more readily to analysis because it can be isolated more easily. This circumstance derives its chief importance from its tendency to promote the mutual penetration of art and science. Actually, of a screened behavior item which is neatly brought out in a certain situation, like a muscle of a body, it is difficult to say which is more fascinating, its artistic value or its value for science. To demonstrate the identity of the artistic and scientific uses of photography which heretofore usually were separated will be one of the revolutionary functions of the film.

By close-ups of the things around us, by focusing on hidden details of familiar objects, by exploring common place milieus under the ingenious guidance of the camera, the film, on the one hand, extends our comprehension of the necessities which rule our lives; on the other hand, it manages to assure us of an immense and unexpected field of action. Our taverns and our metropolitan streets, our offices and furnished rooms, our railroad stations and our factories appeared to have us locked up hopelessly. Then came the film and burst this prison-world asunder by the dynamite of the tenth of a second, so that now, in the midst of its far-flung ruins and debris, we calmly and adventurously go traveling. With the close-up, space expands; with slow motion, movement is extended. The enlargement of a snapshot does not simply render more precise what in any case was visible, though unclear: it reveals entirely new structural formations of the subject. So, too, slow motion not only presents familiar qualities of movement but reveals in them entirely unknown ones "which, far from looking like retarded rapid movements, give the effect of singularly gliding, floating, supernatural motions." Evidently a different nature opens itself to the camera than opens to the naked eye—if only because an unconsciously penetrated space is substituted for a space consciously explored by man. Even if one has a general knowledge of the way people walk, one knows nothing of a person's posture during the fractional second of a stride. The act of reaching for a lighter or a spoon is familiar routine, yet we hardly know what really goes on between hand and metal, not to mention how this fluctuates with our moods. Here the camera intervenes with the resources of its lowerings and liftings, its interruptions and isolations, it extensions and accelerations, its enlargements and reductions. The camera introduces us to unconscious optics as does psychoanalysis to unconscious impulses.

XIV

One of the foremost tasks of art has always been the creation of a demand which could be fully satisfied only later. The history of every art form shows critical epochs in which a certain art form aspires to effects which could be fully obtained only with a changed technical standard, that is to say, in a new art form. The extravagances and crudities of art which thus appear, particularly in the so-called decadent epochs, actually arise from the nucleus of its richest historical energies. In recent years, such barbarisms were abundant in Dadaism. It is only now that its impulse becomes discernible: Dadaism attempted to create by pictorial—and literary—means the effects which the public today seeks in the film.

Every fundamentally new, pioneering creation of demands will carry beyond its goal. Dadaism did so to the extent that it sacrificed the market values which are so characteristic of the film in favor of higher ambitions—though of course it was not conscious of such intentions as here described. The Dadaists attached much less importance to the sales value of their work than to its uselessness for contemplative immersion. The studied degradation of their material was not the least of their means to achieve this uselessness.

Their poems are "word salad" containing obscenities and every imaginable waste product of language. The same is true of their paintings, on which they mounted buttons and tickets. What they intended and achieved was a relentless destruction of the aura of their creations, which they branded as reproductions with the very means of production. Before a painting of Arp's or a poem by August Stramm it is impossible to take time for contemplation and evaluation as one would before a canvas of Derain's or a poem by Rilke. In the decline of middle-class society, contemplation became a school for asocial behavior; it was countered by distraction as a variant of social conduct. Dadaistic activities actually assured a rather vehement distraction by making works of art the center of scandal. One requirement was foremost: to outrage the public.

From an alluring appearance or persuasive structure of sound the work of art of the Dadaists became an instrument of ballistics. It hit the spectator like a bullet, it happened to him, thus acquiring a tactile quality. It promoted a demand for the film, the distracting element of which is also primarily tactile, being based on changes of place and focus which periodically assail the spectator. Let us compare the screen on which a film unfolds with the canvas of a painting. The painting invites the spectator to contemplation; before it the spectator can abandon himself to his associations. Before the movie frame he cannot do so. No sooner has his eye grasped a scene than it is already changed. It cannot be arrested. Duhamel, who detests the film and knows nothing of its significance, though something of its structure, notes this circumstance as follows: "I can no longer think what I want to think. My thoughts have been replaced by moving images." The spectator's process of association in view of these images is indeed interrupted by their constant, sudden change. This constitutes the shock effect of the film, which, like all shocks, should be cushioned by heightened presence of mind. By means of its technical structure, the film has taken the physical shock effect out of the wrappers in which Dadaism had, as it were, kept it inside the moral shock effect.

XV

The mass is a matrix from which all traditional behavior toward works of art issues today in a new form. Quantity has been transmuted into quality. The greatly increased mass of participants has produced a change in the mode of participation. The fact that the new mode of participation first appeared in a disreputable form must not confuse the spectator. Yet some people have launched spirited attacks against precisely this superficial aspect. Among these, Duhamel has expressed himself in the most radical manner. What he objects to most is the kind of participation which the movie elicits from the masses. Duhamel calls the movie "a pastime for helots, a diversion for uneducated, wretched, worn-out creatures who are consumed by their worries a spectacle which requires no concentration and presupposes no intelligence which kindles no light in the heart and awakens no hope other than the ridiculous one of someday becoming a 'star' in Los Angeles." Clearly, this is at bottom the same ancient lament that the masses seek distraction whereas art demands concentration from the spectator. That is a commonplace.

The question remains whether it provides a platform for the analysis of the film. A closer look is needed here. Distraction and concentration form polar opposites which may be stated as follows: A man who concentrates before a work of art is absorbed by it. He enters into this work of art the way legend tells of the Chinese painter when he viewed his finished painting. In contrast, the distracted mass absorbs the work of art. This is most obvious with regard to buildings. Architecture has always represented the prototype of a work of art the reception of which is consummated by a collectivity in a state of distraction. The laws of its reception are most instructive.

Buildings have been man's companions since primeval times. Many art forms have developed and perished. Tragedy begins with the Greeks, is extinguished with them, and after centuries its "rules" only are revived. The epic poem, which had its origin in the youth of nations, expires in Europe at the end of the Renaissance. Panel painting is a creation of the Middle Ages, and nothing guarantees its uninterrupted existence. But the human need for shelter is lasting. Architecture has never been idle. Its history is more ancient than that of any other art, and its claim to being a living force has significance in every attempt to comprehend the relationship of the masses to art. Buildings are appropriated in a twofold manner: by use and by perception—or rather, by touch and sight. Such appropriation cannot be understood in terms of the attentive concentration of a tourist before a famous building. On the tactile side there is no counterpart to contemplation on the optical side. Tactile appropriation is accomplished not so much by attention as by habit. As regards architecture, habit determines to a large extent even optical reception. The latter, too, occurs much less through rapt attention than by noticing the object in incidental fashion. This mode of appropriation, developed with reference to architecture, in certain circumstances acquires canonical value. For the tasks which face the human apparatus of perception at the turning points of history cannot be solved by optical means, that is, by contemplation, alone. They are mastered gradually by habit, under the guidance of tactile appropriation.

The distracted person, too, can form habits. More, the ability to master certain tasks in a state of distraction proves that their solution has become a matter of habit. Distraction as provided by art presents a covert control of the extent to which new tasks have become soluble by apperception. Since, moreover, individuals are tempted to avoid such tasks, art will tackle the most difficult and most important ones where it is able to mobilize the masses. Today it does so in the film. Reception in a state of distraction, which is increasing noticeably in all fields of art and is symptomatic of profound changes in apperception, finds in the film its true means of exercise. The film with its shock effect meets this mode of reception halfway. The film makes the cult value recede into the background not only by putting the public in the position of the critic, but also by the fact that at the movies this position requires no attention. The public is an examiner, but an absent-minded one.

Epilogue

The growing proletarianization of modern man and the increasing formation of masses are two aspects of the same process. Fascism attempts to organize the newly created proletarian masses without affecting the property structure which the masses strive to eliminate. Fascism sees its salvation in giving these masses not their right, but instead a chance to express themselves. The masses have a right to change property relations; Fascism seeks to give them an expression while preserving property. The logical result of Fascism is the introduction of aesthetics into political life. The violation of the masses, whom Fascism, with its *Führer* cult, forces to their knees, has its counterpart in the violation of an apparatus which is pressed into the production of ritual values.

All efforts to render politics aesthetic culminate in one thing: war. War and war only can set a goal for mass movements on the largest scale while respecting the traditional property system. This is the political formula for the situation. The technological formula may be stated as follows: Only war makes it possible to mobilize all of today's technical resources while maintaining the property system. It goes without saying that the Fascist apotheosis of war does not employ such arguments. Still, Marinetti says in his manifesto on the Ethiopian colonial war:

"For twenty-seven years we Futurists have rebelled against the branding of war as anti-aesthetic...Accordingly we state:... War is beautiful because it establishes man's dominion over the subjugated machinery by means of gas masks, terrifying megaphones, flame throwers, and small tanks. War is beautiful because it initiates the dreamt-of metallization of the human body. War is beautiful because it enriches a flowering meadow with the fiery orchids of machine guns. War is beautiful because it combines the gunfire, the cannonades, the cease-fire, the scents, and the stench of putrefaction into a symphony. War is beautiful because it creates new architecture, like that of the big tanks, the geometrical formation flights, the smoke spirals from burning villages, and many others... Poets and artists of Futurism!...remember these principles of an aesthetics of war so that your struggle for a new literature and a new graphic art...may be illumined by them!"

This manifesto has the virtue of clarity. Its formulations deserve to be accepted by dialecticians. To the latter, the aesthetics of today's war appears as follows: If the natural utilization of productive forces is impeded by the property system, the increase in technical devices, in speed, and in the sources of energy will press for an unnatural utilization, and this is found in war. The destructiveness of war furnishes proof that society has not been mature enough to incorporate technology as its organ, that technology has not been sufficiently developed to cope with the elemental forces of society. The horrible features of imperialistic warfare are attributable to the discrepancy between the tremendous means of production and their inadequate utilization in the process of production—in other words, to unemployment and the lack of markets. Imperialistic war is a rebellion of technology which collects, in the form of "human material," the claims to which society has denied its natural material. Instead of draining rivers, society directs a human stream into a bed of trenches; instead of dropping seeds from airplanes, it drops incendiary bombs over cities; and through gas warfare the aura is abolished in a new way.

"*Fiat ars—pereat mundus*," says Fascism, and, as Marinetti admits, expects war to supply the artistic gratification of a sense perception that has been changed by technology. This is evidently the consummation of "*l'art pour l'art.*" Mankind, which in Homer's time was an object of contemplation for the Olympian gods, now is one for itself. Its self-alienation has reached such a degree that it can experience its own destruction as an aesthetic pleasure of the first order. This is the situation of politics which Fascism is rendering aesthetic. Communism responds by politicizing art.

Marshall McLuhan

The Medium Is the Message

1964

"it is the medium that shapes and controls the scale and form of human association and action"

Marshall McLuhan (1911–1980) was a Canadian philosopher of communication theory and a professor of English. His essays provided a framework for understanding advertising and mass media.

In a culture like ours, long accustomed to splitting and dividing all things as a means of control, it is sometimes a bit of a shock to be reminded that, in operational and practical fact, the medium is the message. This is merely to say that the personal and social consequences of any medium—that is, of any extension of ourselves—result from the new scale that is introduced into our affairs by each extension of ourselves, or by any new technology. Thus, with automation, for example, the new patterns of human association tend to eliminate jobs, it is true. That is the negative result. Positively, automation creates roles for people, which is to say depth of involvement in their work and human association that our preceding mechanical technology had destroyed. Many people would be disposed to say that it was not the machine, but what one did with the machine, that was its meaning or message. In terms of the ways in which the machine altered our relations to one another and to ourselves, it mattered not in the least whether it turned out corn flakes or Cadillacs. The restructuring of human work and association was shaped by the technique of fragmentation that is the essence of machine technology. The essence of automation technology is the opposite. It is integral and decentralist in depth, just as the machine was fragmentary, centralist, and superficial in its patterning of human relationships.

The instance of the electric light may prove illuminating in this connection. The electric light is pure information. It is a medium without a message, as it were, unless it is used to spell out some verbal ad or name. This fact, characteristic of all media, means that the "content" of any medium is always another medium. The content of writing is speech, just as the written word is the content of print, and print is the content of the telegraph. If it is asked, "What is the content of speech?," it is necessary to say, "It is an actual process of thought, which is in itself nonverbal." An abstract painting represents direct manifestation of creative thought processes as they might appear in computer designs. What we are considering here, however, are the psychic and social consequences of the designs or patterns as they amplify or accelerate existing processes. For the "message" of any medium or technology is the change of scale or pace or pattern that it introduces into human affairs. The railway did not introduce movement or transportation or wheel or road into human society, but it accelerated and enlarged the scale of previous human functions, creating totally new kinds of cities and new kinds of work and leisure. This happened whether the railway functioned in a tropical or a northern environment, and is quite independent of the freight or content of the railway medium. The airplane, on the other hand, by accelerating the rate of transportation, tends to dissolve the railway form of city, politics, and association, quite independently of what the airplane is used for.

Let us return to the electric light. Whether the light is being used for brain surgery or night baseball is a matter of indifference. It could be argued that these activities are in some way the "content" of the electric light, since they could not exist without the electric light. This fact merely underlines the point that "the medium is the message" because it is the medium that shapes and controls the scale and form of human association and action. The content or uses of such media are as diverse as they are ineffectual in shaping the form of human association. Indeed, it is only too typical that the "content" of any medium blinds us to the character of the medium. It is only today that industries have become aware of the various kinds of business in which they are engaged. When IBM discovered that it was not in the business of making office equipment or business machines, but that it was in the business of processing information, then it began to navigate with clear vision. The General Electric Company makes a considerable portion of its profits from electric light bulbs and lighting systems. It has not yet discovered that, quite as much as AT&T, it is in the business of moving information.

The electric light escapes attention as a communication medium just because it has no "content." And this makes it an invaluable instance of how people fail to study media at all.

For it is not till the electric light is used to spell out some brand name that it is noticed as a medium. Then it is not the light but the "content" (or what is really another medium) that is noticed. The message of the electric light is like the message of electric power in industry, totally radical, pervasive, and decentralized. For electric light and power are separate from their uses, yet they eliminate time and space factors in human association exactly as do radio, telegraph, telephone, and TV, creating involvement in depth.

A fairly complete handbook for studying the extensions of man could be made up from selections from Shakespeare. Some might quibble about whether or not he was referring to TV in these familiar lines from *Romeo and Juliet*:

> But soft! what light through yonder window breaks?
> It speaks, and yet says nothing.

In *Othello*, which, as much as *King Lear*, is concerned with the torment of people transformed by illusions, there are these lines that bespeak Shakespeare's intuition of the transforming powers of new media:

Is there not charms
By which the property of youth and maidhood
May be abused?
Have you not read Roderigo,
Of some such thing?

In Shakespeare's *Troilus and Cressida*, which is almost completely devoted to both a psychic and social study of communication, Shakespeare states his awareness that true social and political navigation depend upon anticipating the consequences of innovation:

The providence that's in a watchful state
Knows almost every grain of Plutus' gold,
Finds bottom in the uncomprehensive deeps,
Keeps place with thought, and almost like the gods
Does thoughts unveil in their dumb cradles.

The increasing awareness of the action of media, quite independently of their "content" or programming, was indicated in the annoyed and anonymous stanza:

In modern thought, (if not in fact)
Nothing is that doesn't act,
So that is reckoned wisdom which
Describes the scratch but not the itch.

The same kind of total, configurational awareness that reveals why the medium is socially the message has occurred in the most recent and radical medical theories. In his *Stress of Life*, Hans Selye tells of the dismay of a research colleague on hearing of Selye's theory:

When he saw me thus launched on yet another enraptured description
of what I had observed in animals treated with this or that impure,
toxic material, he looked at me with desperately sad eyes and said in
obvious despair: "But Selye try to realize what you are doing before it
is too late! You have now decided to spend your entire life studying the
pharmacology of dirt!"
(Hans Selye, *The Stress of Life*)

As Selye deals with the total environmental situation in his "stress" theory of disease, so the latest approach to media study considers not only the "content" but the medium and the cultural matrix within which the particular medium operates. The older unawareness of the psychic and social effects of media can be illustrated from almost any of the conventional pronouncements.

In accepting an honorary degree from the University of Notre Dame a few years ago, General David Sarnoff made this statement: "We are too prone to make technological instruments the scapegoats for the sins of those who wield them. The products of modern science are not in themselves good or bad; it is the way they are used that determines their value." That is the voice of the current somnambulism. Suppose we were to say, "Apple pie is in itself neither good nor bad; it is the way it is used that determines its value." Or, "The smallpox virus is in itself neither good nor bad; it is the way it is used that determines its value." Again, "Fire arms are in themselves neither good nor bad; it is the way they are used that determines their value." That is, if the slugs reach the right people firearms are good. If the TV tube fires the right ammunition at the right people it is good. I am not being perverse. There is simply nothing in the Sarnoff statement that will bear scrutiny, for it ignores the nature of the medium, of any and all media, in the true Narcissus style of one hypnotized by the amputation and extension of his own being in a new technical form. General Sarnoff went on to explain his attitude to the technology of print, saying that it was true that print caused much trash to circulate, but it had also disseminated the Bible and the thoughts of seers and philosophers. It has never occurred to General Sarnoff that any technology could do anything but add itself on to what we already are.

Such economists as Robert Theobald, W. W. Rostow, and John Kenneth Galbraith have been explaining for years how it is that "classical economics" cannot explain change or growth. And the paradox of mechanization is that although it is itself the cause of max-imal growth and change, the principle of mechanization excludes the very possibility of growth or the understanding of change. For mechanization is achieved by fragmenta-tion of any process and by putting the fragmented parts in a series. Yet, as David Hume showed in the eighteenth century, there is no principle of causality in a mere sequence. That one thing follows another accounts for nothing. Nothing follows from following, except change. So the greatest of all reversals occurred with electricity, that ended sequence by making things instant. With instant speed the causes of things began to emerge to awareness again, as they had not done with things in sequence and in concate-nation accordingly. Instead of asking which came first, the chicken or the egg, it suddenly seemed that a chicken was an egg's idea for getting more eggs.

Just before an airplane breaks the sound barrier, sound waves become visible on the wings of the plane. The sudden visibility of sound just as sound ends is an apt instance of that great pattern of being that reveals new and opposite forms just as the earlier forms reach their peak performance. Mechanization was never so vividly fragmented or sequential as in the birth of the movies, the moment that translated us beyond mechanism into the world of growth and organic interrelation. The movie, by sheer speeding up the mechan-ical, carried us from the world of sequence and connections into the world of creative configuration and structure. The message of the movie medium is that of transition from lineal connections to configurations. It is the transition that produced the now quite cor-rect observation: "If it works, it's obsolete." When electric speed further takes over from mechanical movie sequences, then the lines of force in structures and in media become loud and clear. We return to the inclusive form of the icon.

To a highly literate and mechanized culture the movie appeared as a world of triumphant illusions and dreams that money could buy. It was at this moment of the movie that cubism occurred and it has been described by E. H. Gombrich (*Art and Illusion*) as "the most radical attempt to stamp out ambiguity and to enforce one reading of the picture— that of a man-made construction, a colored canvas." For cubism substitutes all facets of an object simultaneously for the "point of view" or facet of perspective illusion. Instead of the specialized illusion of the third dimension on canvas, cubism sets up an interplay of planes and contradiction or dramatic conflict of patterns, lights, textures that "drives home the message" by involvement. This is held by many to be an exercise in painting, not in illusion.

In other words, cubism, by giving the inside and outside, the top, bottom, back, and front and the rest, in two dimensions, drops the illusion of perspective in favor of instant sensory awareness of the whole. Cubism, by seizing on instant total awareness, suddenly announced that the *medium is the message*. Is it not evident that the moment that sequence yields to the simultaneous, one is in the world of the structure and of configuration? Is that not what has happened in physics as in painting, poetry, and in communication? Specialized segments of attention have shifted to total field, and we can now say, "The medium is the message" quite naturally. Before the electric speed and total field, it was not obvious that the medium is the message. The message, it seemed, was the "content," as people used to ask what a painting was *about*. Yet they never thought to ask what a melody was about, nor what a house or a dress was about. In such matters, people retained some sense of the whole pattern, of form and function as a unity. But in the electric age this integral idea of structure and configuration has become so prevalent that educational theory has taken up the matter. Instead of working with specialized "problems" in arithmetic, the structural approach now follows the lines of force in the field of number and has small children meditating about number theory and "sets."

Cardinal Newman said of Napoleon, "He understood the grammar of gunpowder." Napoleon had paid some attention to other media as well, especially the semaphore telegraph that gave him a great advantage over his enemies. He is on record for saying that "Three hostile newspapers are more to be feared than a thousand bayonets."

Alexis de Tocqueville was the first to master the grammar of print and typography. He was thus able to read off the message of coming change in France and America as if he were reading aloud from a text that had been handed to him. In fact, the nineteenth century in France and in America was just such an open book to de Tocqueville because he had learned the grammar of print. So he, also, knew when that grammar did not apply. He was asked why he did not write a book on England, since he knew and admired England. He replied:

> One would have to have an unusual degree of philosophical folly to believe oneself able to judge England in six months. A year always seemed to me too short a time in which to appreciate the United States properly, and it is much easier to acquire clear and precise notions about the American Union than about Great Britain. In America all laws derive in a sense from the same line of thought. The whole of society, so to speak, is founded upon a single fact; everything springs from a simple principle. One could compare America to a forest pierced by a multitude of straight roads all converging on the same point. One has only to find the center and everything is revealed at a glance. But in England the paths run criss-cross, and it is only by travelling down each one of them that one can build up a picture of the whole.

De Tocqueville in earlier work on the French Revolution had explained how it was the printed word that, achieving cultural saturation in the eighteenth century, had homogenized the French nation. Frenchmen were the same kind of people from north to south. The typographic principles of uniformity, continuity, and lineality had overlaid the complexities of ancient feudal and oral society. The Revolution was carried out by the new literati and lawyers.

In England, however, such was the power of the ancient oral traditions of common law, backed by the medieval institution of Parliament, that no uniformity or continuity of the new visual print culture could take complete hold. The result was that the most important event in English history has never taken place; namely, the English Revolution on the lines of the French Revolution. The American Revolution had no medieval legal institutions to discard or to root out, apart from monarchy. And many have held that the American Presidency has become very much more personal and monarchical than any European monarch ever could be.

De Tocqueville's contrast between England and America is clearly based on the fact of typography and of print culture creating uniformity and continuity. England, he says, has rejected this principle and clung to the dynamic or oral common law tradition. Hence the discontinuity and unpredictable quality of English culture. The grammar of print cannot help to construe the message of oral and nonwritten culture and institutions. The English aristocracy was properly classified as barbarian by Matthew Arnold because its power and status had nothing to do with literacy or with the cultural forms of typography. Said the Duke of Gloucester to Edward Gibbon upon the publication of his *Decline and Fall*: "Another damned fat book, eh, Mr. Gibbon? Scribble, scribble, scribble, eh, Mr. Gibbon?" De Tocqueville was a highly literate aristocrat who was quite able to be detached from the values and assumptions of typography. That is why he alone understood the grammar of typography. And it is only on those terms, standing aside from any structure or medium, that its principles and lines of force can be discerned. For any medium has the power of imposing its own assumption on the unwary. Prediction and control consist in avoiding this subliminal state of Narcissus trance. But the greatest aid to this end is simply in knowing that the spell can occur immediately upon contact, as in the first bars of a melody.

A Passage to India by E. M. Forster is a dramatic study of the inability of oral and intuitive oriental culture to meet with the rational, visual European patterns of experience. "Rational," of course, has for the West long meant "uniform and continuous and sequential." In other words, we have confused reason with literacy, and rationalism with a single technology. Thus in the electric age man seems to the conventional West to become irrational. In Forster's novel the moment of truth and dislocation from the typographic trance of the West comes in the Marabar Caves. Adela Quested's reasoning powers cannot cope with the total inclusive field of resonance that is India. After the Caves: "Life went on as usual, but had no consequences, that is to say, sounds did not echo nor thought develop. Everything seemed cut off at its root and therefore infected with illusion."

A Passage to India (the phrase is from Whitman, who saw America headed Eastward) is a parable of Western man in the electric age, and is only incidentally related to Europe or the Orient. The ultimate conflict between sight and sound, between written and oral kinds of perception and organization of existence is upon us. Since understanding stops action, as Nietzsche observed, we can moderate the fierceness of this conflict by understanding the media that extend us and raise these wars within and without us.

Detribalization by literacy and its traumatic effects on tribal man is the theme of a book by the psychiatrist J. C. Carothers, *The African Mind in Health and Disease* (World Health Organization, Geneva, 1953). Much of his material appeared in an article in *Psychiatry* magazine, November, 1959: "The Culture, Psychiatry, and the Written Word." Again, it is electric speed that has revealed the lines of force operating from Western technology in the remotest areas of bush, savannah, and desert. One example is the Bedouin with his battery radio on board the camel. Submerging natives with floods of concepts for which nothing has prepared them is the normal action of all of our technology. But with electric media Western man himself experiences exactly the same inundation as the remote native. We are no more prepared to encounter radio and TV in our literate milieu than the native of Ghana is able to cope with the literacy that takes him out of his collective tribal world and beaches him in individual isolation. We are as numb in our new electric world as the native involved in our literate and mechanical culture.

Electric speed mingles the cultures of prehistory with the dregs of industrial marketeers, the nonliterate with semiliterate and the postliterate. Mental breakdown of varying degrees is the very common result of uprooting and inundation with new information and endless new patterns of information. Wyndham Lewis made this a theme of his group of novels called *The Human Age*. The first of these, *The Childermass*, is concerned precisely with accelerated media change as a kind of massacre of the innocents. In our own world as we become more aware of the effects of technology on psychic formation and manifestation, we are losing all confidence in our right to assign guilt. Ancient prehistoric societies regard violent crime as pathetic. The killer is regarded as we do a cancer victim. "How terrible it must be to feel like that," they say. J. M. Synge took up this idea very effectively in his *Playboy of the Western World*.

If the criminal appears as a nonconformist who is unable to meet the demand of technology that we behave in uniform and continuous patterns, literate man is quite inclined to see others who cannot conform as somewhat pathetic. Especially the child, the cripple, the woman, and the colored person appear in a world of visual and typographic technology as victims of injustice. On the other hand, in a culture that assigns roles instead of jobs to people—the dwarf, the skew, the child create their own spaces. They are not expected to fit into some uniform and repeatable niche that is not their size anyway. Consider the phrase "It's a man's world." As a quantitative observation endlessly repeated from within a homogenized culture, this phrase refers to the men in such a culture who have to be homogenized Dagwoods in order to belong at all. It is in our I.Q. testing that we have produced the greatest flood of misbegotten standards. Unaware of our typographic cultural bias, our testers assume that uniform and continuous habits are a sign of intelligence, thus eliminating the ear man and the tactile man.

C. P. Snow, reviewing a book of A. L. Rowse (The *New York Times Book Review*, December 24, 1961) on Appeasement and the road to Munich, describes the top level of British brains and experience in the 1930s. "Their I.Q.'s were much higher than usual among political bosses. Why were they such a disaster?" The view of Rowse, Snow approves: "They would not listen to warnings because they did not wish to hear." Being anti-Red made it impossible for them to read the message of Hitler. But their failure was as nothing compared to our present one. The American stake in literacy as a technology or uniformity applied to every level of education, government, industry, and social life is totally threatened by the electric technology. The threat of Stalin or Hitler was external. The electric technology is within the gates, and we are numb, deaf, blind, and mute about its encounter with the Gutenberg technology, on and through which the American way of life was formed. It is, however, no time to suggest strategies when the threat has not even been acknowledged to exist. I am in the position of Louis Pasteur telling doctors that their greatest enemy was quite invisible, and quite unrecognized by them. Our conventional response to all media, namely that it is how they are used that counts, is the numb stance of the technological idiot. For the "content" of a medium is like the juicy piece of meat carried by the burglar to distract the watchdog of the mind. The effect of the medium is made strong and intense just because it is given another medium as "content." The content of a movie is a novel or a play or an opera. The effect of the movie form is not related to its program content. The "content" of writing or print is speech, but the reader is almost entirely unaware either of print or of speech.

Arnold Toynbee is innocent of any understanding of media as they have shaped history, but he is full of examples that the student of media can use. At one moment he can seriously suggest that adult education, such as the Workers Educational Association in Britain, is a useful counterforce to the popular press. Toynbee considers that although all of the oriental societies have in our time accepted the industrial technology and its political consequences: "On the cultural plane, however, there is no uniform correspond-ing tendency." (Somervell, I. 267) This is like the voice of the literate man, floundering in a milieu of ads, who boasts, "Personally, I pay no attention to ads." The spiritual and cultural reservations that the oriental peoples may have toward our technology will avail them not at all. The effects of technology do not occur at the level of opinions or con-cepts, but alter sense ratios or patterns of perception steadily and without any resistance. The serious artist is the only person able to encounter technology with impunity, just because he is an expert aware of the changes in sense perception.

The operation of the money medium in seventeenth century Japan had effects not unlike the operation of typography in the West. The penetration of the money economy, wrote G. B. Sansom (in *Japan*, Cresset Press, London, 1931) "caused a slow but irresistible revo-lution, culminating in the breakdown of feudal government and the resumption of inter-course with foreign countries after more than two hundred years of seclusion." Money has reorganized the sense life of peoples just because it is an *extension* of our sense lives. This change does not depend upon approval or disapproval of those living in the society.

Arnold Toynbee made one approach to the transforming power of media in his concept of "etherialization," which he holds to be the principle of progressive simplification and efficiency in any organization or technology. Typically, he is ignoring the *effect* of the chal-lenge of these forms upon the response of our senses. He imagines that it is the response of our opinions that is relevant to the effect of media and technology in society, a "point of view" that is plainly the result of the typographic spell. For the man in a literate and homogenized society ceases to be sensitive to the diverse and discontinuous life of forms. He acquires the illusion of the third dimension and the "private point of view" as part of his Narcissus fixation, and is quite shut off from Blake's awareness or that of the Psalmist, that we become what we behold.

Today when we want to get our bearings in our own culture, and have need to stand aside from the bias and pressure exerted by any technical form of human expression, we have only to visit a society where that particular form has not been felt, or a historical period in which it was unknown. Professor Wilbur Schramm made such a tactical move in studying *Television in the Lives of Our Children.* He found areas where TV had not penetrated at all and ran some tests. Since he had made no study of the peculiar nature of the TV image, his tests were of "content"preferences, viewing time, and vocabulary counts. In a word, his approach to the problem was a literary one, albeit unconsciously so. Consequently, he had nothing to report. Had his methods been employed in 1500 A.D. to discover the effects of the printed book in the lives of children or adults, he could have found out nothing of the changes in human and social psychology resulting from typography. Print created individualism and nationalism in the sixteenth century. Program and "content" analysis offer no clues to the magic of these media or to their subliminal charge.

Leonard Doob, in his report *Communication in Africa,* tells of one African who took great pains to listen each evening to the BBC news, even though he could understand nothing of it. Just to be in the presence of those sounds at 7 P.M. each day was important for him. His attitude to speech was like ours to melody—the resonant intonation was meaning enough. In the seventeenth century our ancestors still shared this native's attitude to the forms of media, as is plain in the following sentiment of the Frenchman Bernard Lam expressed in *The Art of Speaking* (London, 1696):

> 'Tis an effect of the Wisdom of God, who created Man to be happy,
> that whatever is useful to his conversation (way of life) is agreeable to
> him...because all victual that conduces to nourishment is relishable,
> whereas other things that cannot be assimilated and be turned into
> our substance are insipid. A Discourse cannot be pleasant to the
> Hearer that is not easie to the Speaker; nor can it be easily pronounced
> unless it be heard with delight.

Here is an equilibrium theory of human diet and expression such as even now we are only striving to work out again for media after centuries of fragmentation and specialism.

Pope Pius XII was deeply concerned that there be serious study of the media today. On February 17, 1950, he said:

> It is not an exaggeration to say that the future of modern society and
> the stability of its inner life depend in large part on the maintenance of
> an equilibrium between the strength of the techniques of communica-
> tion and the capacity of the individual's own reaction.

Failure in this respect has for centuries been typical and total for mankind. Subliminal and docile acceptance of media impact has made them prisons without walls for their human users. As A. J. Liebling remarked in his book *The Press*, a man is not free if he cannot see where he is going, even if he has a gun to help him get there. For each of the media is also a powerful weapon with which to clobber other media and other groups. The result is that the present age has been one of multiple civil wars that are not limited to the world of art and entertainment. In *War and Human Progress*, Professor J. U. Nef declared: "The total wars of our time have been the result of a series of intellectual mistakes..."

If the formative power in the media are the media themselves, that raises a host of large matters that can only be mentioned here, although they deserve volumes. Namely that technological media are staples or natural resources, exactly as are coal and cotton and oil. Anybody will concede that society whose economy is dependent upon one or two major staples like cotton, or grain, or lumber, or fish, or cattle is going to have some obvious social patterns of organization as a result. Stress on a few major staples creates extreme instability in the economy but great endurance in the population. The pathos and humor of the American South are embedded in such an economy of limited staples. For a society configured by reliance on a few commodities accepts them as a social bond quite as much as the metropolis does the press. Cotton and oil, like radio and TV, become "fixed charges" on the entire psychic life of the community. And this pervasive fact creates the unique cultural flavor of any society. It pays through the nose and all its other senses for each staple that shapes its life.

That our human senses, of which all media are extensions, are also fixed charges on our personal energies, and that they also configure the awareness and experience of each one of us may be perceived in another connection mentioned by the psychologist C. G. Jung:

> Every Roman was surrounded by slaves. The slave and his psychology
> flooded ancient Italy, and every Roman became inwardly, and of
> course unwittingly, a slave. Because living constantly in the atmosphere
> of slaves, he became infected through the unconscious with their
> psychology. No one can shield himself from such an influence
> (*Contributions to Analytical Psychology*, London, 1928).

Roland Barthes

Myth Today
1956

Elements of Semiology
1964

Camera Lucida: Reflections on Photography
1980

"we shall therefore take language, discourse, speech, etc., to mean any significant unit or synthesis, whether verbal or visual: a photograph will be a kind of speech for us in the same way as a newspaper article; even objects will become speech, if they mean something"

Roland Barthes (1915–1980) was a French literary theorist and philosopher whose interdisciplinary work influenced the realms of semiology, existentialism, poststructuralism, and design theory. He was particularly fascinated by photography and explored this medium extensively in his writing.

What is a myth, today? I shall give at the outset a first, very simple answer, which is perfectly consistent with etymology: *myth is a type of speech.*[1]

Myth Is a Type of Speech
Of course, it is not *any* type: language needs special conditions in order to become myth: we shall see them in a minute. But what must be firmly established at the start is that myth is a system of communication, that it is a message. This allows one to perceive that myth cannot possibly be an object, a concept, or an idea; it is a mode of signification, a form. Later, we shall have to assign to this form historical limits, conditions of use, and reintroduce society into it: we must nevertheless first describe it as a form.

It can be seen that to purport to discriminate among mythical objects according to their substance would be entirely illusory: since myth is a type of speech, everything can be a myth provided it is conveyed by a discourse. Myth is not defined by the object of its message, but by the way in which it utters this message: there are formal limits to myth, there are no 'substantial' ones. Everything, then, can be a myth? Yes, I believe this, for the

---

1   *Innumerable other meanings of the word 'myth' can be cited against this. But I have tried to define things, not words.*

universe is infinitely fertile in suggestions. Every object in the world can pass from a closed, silent existence to an oral state, open to appropriation by society, for there is no law, whether natural or not, which forbids talking about things. A tree is a tree. Yes, of course. But a tree as expressed by Minou Drouet is no longer quite a tree, it is a tree which is decorated, adapted to a certain type of consumption, laden with literary self-indulgence, revolt, images, in short with a type of social *usage* which is added to pure matter.

Naturally, everything is not expressed at the same time: some objects become the prey of mythical speech for a while, then they disappear, others take their place and attain the status of myth. Are there objects which are *inevitably* a source of suggestiveness, as Baudelaire suggested about Woman? Certainly not: one can conceive of very ancient myths, but there are no eternal ones; for it is human history which converts reality into speech, and it alone rules the life and the death of mythical language. Ancient or not, mythology can only have an historical foundation, for myth is a type of speech chosen by history: it cannot possibly evolve from the 'nature' of things.

Speech of this kind is a message. It is therefore by no means confined to oral speech. It can consist of modes of writing or of representations; not only written discourse, but also photography, cinema, reporting, sport, shows, publicity, all these can serve as a support to mythical speech. Myth can be defined neither by its object nor by its material, for any material can arbitrarily be endowed with meaning: the arrow which is brought in order to signify a challenge is also a kind of speech. True, as far as perception is concerned, writing and pictures, for instance, do not call upon the same type of consciousness; and even with pictures, one can use many kinds of reading: a diagram lends itself to signification more than a drawing, a copy more than an original, and a caricature more than a portrait. But this is the point: we are no longer dealing here with a theoretical mode of representation: we are dealing with *this* particular image, which is given for *this* particular signification. Mythical speech is made of a material which has *already* been worked on so as to make it suitable for communication: it is because all the materials of myth (whether pictorial or written) presuppose a signifying consciousness, that one can reason about them while discounting their substance. This substance is not unimportant: pictures, to be sure, are more imperative than writing, they impose meaning at one stroke, without analysing or diluting it. But this is no longer a constitutive difference. Pictures become a kind of writing as soon as they are meaningful: like writing, they call for a *lexis*.

We shall therefore take *language, discourse, speech*, etc., to mean any significant unit or synthesis, whether verbal or visual: a photograph will be a kind of speech for us in the same way as a newspaper article; even objects will become speech, if they mean something. This generic way of conceiving language is in fact justified by the very history of writing: long before the invention of our alphabet, objects like the Inca *quipu*, or drawings, as in pictographs, have been accepted as speech. This does not mean that one must treat mythical speech like language; myth in fact belongs to the province of a general science, coextensive with linguistics, which is *semiology*.

Myth as a Semiological System

For mythology, since it is the study of a type of speech, is but one fragment of this vast science of signs which Saussure postulated some forty years ago under the name of *semiology*. Semiology has not yet come into being. But since Saussure himself, and sometimes independently of him, a whole section of contemporary research has constantly been referred to the problem of meaning: psycho-analysis, structuralism, eidetic psychology, some new types of literary criticism of which Bachelard has given the first examples, are no longer concerned with facts except inasmuch as they are endowed with significance. Now to postulate a signification is to have recourse to semiology. I do not mean that semiology could account for all these aspects of research equally well: they have different contents. But they have a common status: they are all sciences dealing with values. They are not content with meeting the facts: they define and explore them as tokens for something else.

Semiology is a science of forms, since it studies significations apart from their content. I should like to say one word about the necessity and the limits of such a formal science. The necessity is that which applies in the case of any exact language. Zhdanov made fun of Alexandrov the philosopher, who spoke of *'the spherical structure of our planet'*. *'It was thought until now'*, Zhdanov said, *'that form alone could be spherical.'* Zhdanov was right: one cannot speak about structures in terms of forms, and vice versa. It may well be that on the plane of 'life', there is but a totality where structures and forms cannot be separated. But science has no use for the ineffable: it must speak about 'life' if it wants to transform it. Against a certain quixotism of synthesis, quite Platonic incidentally, all criticism must consent to the *ascesis*, to the artifice of analysis; and in analysis, it must match method and language. Less terrorized by the spectre of 'formalism', historical criticism might have been less sterile; it would have understood that the specific study of forms does not in any way contradict the necessary principle of totality and History. On the contrary: the more a system is specifically defined in its forms, the more amenable it is to historical criticism. To parody a well-known saying, I shall say that a little formalism turns one away from History, but that a lot brings one back to it. Is there a better example of total criticism than the description of saintliness, at once formal and historical, semio-logical and ideological, in Sartre's *Saint-Genet*? The danger, on the contrary, is to consider forms as ambiguous objects, half-form and half-substance, to endow form with a sub-stance of form, as was done, for instance, by Zhdanovian realism. Semiology, once its lim-its are settled, is not a metaphysical trap: it is a science among others, necessary but not sufficient. The important thing is to see that the unity of an explanation cannot be based on the amputation of one or other of its approaches, but, as Engels said, on the dialectical co-ordination of the particular sciences it makes use of. This is the case with mythology: it is a part both of semiology inasmuch as it is a formal science, and of ideology inasmuch as it is an historical science: it studies ideas-in-forms.[2]

Let me therefore restate that any semiology postulates a relation between two terms, a signifier and a signified. This relation concerns objects which belong to different catego-ries, and this is why it is not one of equality but one of equivalence. We must here be on our guard for despite common parlance which simply says that the signifier *expresses* the signified, we are dealing, in any semiological system, not with two, but with three differ-

2   *The development of publicity, of a national press, of radio, of illustrated news, not to speak of the survival of a myriad rites of communication which rule social appearances, makes the development of a semiological science more urgent than ever. In a single day, how many really non-signifying fields do we cross? Very few, sometimes none. Here I am, before the sea; it is true that it bears no message. But on the beach, what material for semiology! Flags, slogans, signals, sign-boards, clothes, suntan even, which are so many messages to me.*

ent terms. For what we grasp is not at all one term after the other, but the correlation which unites them: there are, therefore, the signifier, the signified and the sign, which is the associative total of the first two terms. Take a bunch of roses: I use it to *signify* my passion. Do we have here, then, only a signifier and a signified, the roses and my passion? Not even that: to put it accurately, there are here only 'passionified' roses. But on the plane of analysis, we do have three terms; for these roses weighted with passion perfectly and correctly allow themselves to be decomposed into roses and passion: the former and the latter existed before uniting and forming this third object, which is the sign. It is as true to say that on the plane of experience I cannot dissociate the roses from the message they carry, as to say that on the plane of analysis I cannot confuse the roses as signifier and the roses as sign: the signifier is empty, the sign is full, it is a meaning. Or take a black pebble: I can make it signify in several ways, it is a mere signifier; but if I weigh it with a definite signified (a death sentence, for instance, in an anonymous vote), it will become a sign. Naturally, there are between the signifier, the signified and the sign, functional implications (such as that of the part to the whole) which are so close that to analyse them may seem futile; but we shall see in a moment that this distinction has a capital importance for the study of myth as semiological schema.

Naturally these three terms are purely formal, and different contents can be given to them. Here are a few examples: for Saussure, who worked on a particular but method-ologically exemplary semiological system—the language or *langue*—the signified is the concept, the signifier is the acoustic image (which is mental) and the relation between concept and image is the sign (the word, for instance), which is a concrete entity.[3] For Freud, as is well known, the human psyche is a stratification of tokens or representa-tives. One term (I refrain from giving it any precedence) is constituted by the manifest meaning of behaviour, another, by its latent or real meaning (it is, for instance, the sub-stratum of the dream); as for the third term, it is here also a correlation of the first two: it is the dream itself in its totality, the parapraxis (a mistake in speech or behaviour) or the neurosis, conceived as compromises, as economies effected thanks to the joining of a form (the first term) and an intentional function (the second term). We can see here how necessary it is to distinguish the sign from the signifier: a dream, to Freud, is no more its manifest datum than its latent content: it is the functional union of these two terms. In Sartrean criticism, finally (I shall keep to these three well-known examples), the signified is constituted by the original crisis in the subject (the separation from his mother for Baudelaire, the naming of the theft for Genet); Literature as discourse forms the signifier; and the relation between crisis and discourse defines the work, which is a signification. Of course, this tri-dimensional pattern, however constant in its form, is actualized in dif-ferent ways: one cannot therefore say too often that semiology can have its unity only at the level of forms, not contents; its field is limited, it knows only one operation: reading, or deciphering.

In myth, we find again the tri-dimensional pattern which I have just described: the signifier, the signified and the sign. But myth is a peculiar system, in that it is constructed from a semiological chain which existed before it: it is a *second-order semiological system*. That which is a sign (namely the associative total of a concept and an image) in the first system becomes a mere signifier in the second. We must here recall that the materials of

3 *The notion of word is one of the most controversial in linguistics. I keep it here for the sake of simplicity.*

mythical speech (the language itself, photography, painting, posters, rituals, objects, etc.), however different at the start, are reduced to a pure signifying function as soon as they are caught by myth. Myth sees in them only the same raw material; their unity is that they all come down to the status of a mere language. Whether it deals with alphabetical or pictorial writing, myth wants to see in them only a sum of signs, a global sign, the final term of a first semiological chain. And it is precisely this final term which will become the first term of the greater system which it builds and of which it is only a part. Everything happens as if myth shifted the formal system of the first significations sideways. As this lateral shift is essential for the analysis of myth, I shall represent it in the following way, it being understood, of course, that the spatialization of the pattern is here only a metaphor:

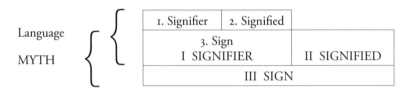

It can be seen that in myth there are two semiological systems, one of which is staggered in relation to the other: a linguistic system, the language (or the modes of representation which are assimilated to it), which I shall call the *language-object*, because it is the language which myth gets hold of in order to build its own system; and myth itself, which I shall call *metalanguage*, because it is a second language, *in which* one speaks about the first. When he reflects on a metalanguage, the semiologist no longer needs to ask himself questions about the composition of the language-object, he no longer has to take into account the details of the linguistic schema; he will only need to know its total term, or global sign, and only inasmuch as this term lends itself to myth. This is why the semiologist is entitled to treat in the same way writing and pictures: what he retains from them is the fact that they are both *signs*, that they both reach the threshold of myth endowed with the same signifying function, that they constitute, one just as much as the other, a language-object.

It is now time to give one or two examples of mythical speech. I shall borrow the first from an observation by Valéry.[4] I am a pupil in the second form in a French *lycée*. I open my Latin grammar, and I read a sentence, borrowed from Aesop or Phaedrus: *quia ego nominor leo*. I stop and think. There is something ambiguous about this statement: on the one hand, the words in it do have a simple meaning: *because my name is lion*. And on the other hand, the sentence is evidently there in order to signify something else to me. Inasmuch as it is addressed to me, a pupil in the second form, it tells me clearly: I am a grammatical example meant to illustrate the rule about the agreement of the predicate. I am even forced to realize that the sentence in no way *signifies* its meaning to me, that it tries very little to tell me something about the lion and what sort of name he has; its true and fundamental signification is to impose itself on me as the presence of a certain agreement of the predicate. I conclude that I am faced with a particular, greater, semiological system, since it is co-extensive with the language: there is, indeed, a signifier,

4 *Tel Quel, II, p. 191.*

but this signifier is itself formed by a sum of signs, it is in itself a first semiological system (*my name is lion*). Thereafter, the formal pattern is correctly unfolded: there is a signified (*I am a grammatical example*) and there is a global signification, which is none other than the correlation of the signifier and the signified; for neither the naming of the lion nor the grammatical example are given separately.

And here is now another example: I am at the barber's, and a copy of *Paris-Match* is offered to me. On the cover, a young Negro in a French uniform is saluting, with his eyes uplifted, probably fixed on a fold of the tricolour. All this is the *meaning* of the picture. But, whether naively or not, I see very well what it signifies to me: that France is a great Empire, that all her sons, without any colour discrimination, faithfully serve under her flag, and that there is no better answer to the detractors of an alleged colonialism than the zeal shown by this Negro in serving his so-called oppressors. I am therefore again faced with a greater semiological system: there is a signifier, itself already formed with a previous system (*a black soldier is giving the French salute*); there is a signified (it is here a purposeful mixture of Frenchness and militariness); finally, there is a presence of the signified through the signifier.

Before tackling the analysis of each term of the mythical system, one must agree on terminology. We now know that the signifier can be looked at, in myth, from two points of view: as the final term of the linguistic system, or as the first term of the mythical system. We therefore need two names. On the plane of language, that is, as the final term of the first system, I shall call the signifier: *meaning* (*my name is lion, a Negro is giving the French salute*); on the plane of myth, I shall call it: *form*. In the case of the signified, no ambiguity is possible: we shall retain the name *concept*. The third term is the correlation of the first two: in the linguistic system, it is the *sign*; but it is not possible to use this word again without ambiguity, since in myth (and this is the chief peculiarity of the latter), the signifier is already formed by the *signs* of the language. I shall call the third term of myth the *signification*. This word is here all the better justified, since myth has in fact a double function: it points out and it notifies, it makes us understand something and it imposes it on us.

"the signified is not 'a thing' but a mental representation of the 'thing'"

Elements of Semiology

1964

....

II. Signifier and Signified

1. The Sign

I-I

The classification of signs: The signified and the signifier, in Saussurean terminology, are the components of the *sign*. Now this term, *sign*, which is found in very different vocabularies (from that of theology to that of medicine), and whose history is very rich (running from the Gospels to cybernetics), is for these very reasons very ambiguous; so before we come back to the Saussurean acceptance of the word, we must say a word about the notional field in which it occupies a place, albeit imprecise, as will be seen. For, according to the arbitrary choice of various authors, the sign is placed in a series of terms which have affinities and dissimilarities with it: *signal, index, icon, symbol, allegory* are the chief rivals of *sign*. Let us first state the element which is common to all these terms: they all necessarily refer us to a *relation* between two *relata*. This feature cannot therefore be used to distinguish any of the terms in the series; to find a variation in meaning, we shall have to resort to other features, which will be expressed here in the form of an alternative (*presence/absence*): i) the relation implies, or does not imply, the mental representation of one of the *relata*; ii) the relation implies, or does not imply, an analogy between the *relata*; iii) the link between the two *relata* (the stimulus and its response) is immediate or is not; iv) the *relata* exactly coincide or, on the contrary, one overruns the other; v) the relation implies, or does not imply, an existential connection with the user. Whether these features are positive or negative (marked or unmarked), each term in the field is differentiated from its neighbours. It must be added that the distribution of the field varies from one author to another, a fact which produces terminological contradictions; these will be easily seen at a glance from a table of the incidence of features and terms in four different authors: Hegel, Peirce, Jung and Wallon (the reference to some features, whether marked or unmarked, may be absent in some authors). We see that the terminological contradiction bears essentially on *index* (for Peirce, the index is existential, for Wallon, it is not) and on *symbol* (for Hegel and Wallon there is a relation of analogy—or of 'motivation'—between the two *relata* of the symbol, but not for Peirce; moreover, for Peirce, the symbol is not existential, whereas it is for Jung). But we see also that these contradictions—which in this table are read vertically—are very well explained, or rather, that they compensate each other through transfers of meaning from term to term in the same author. These transfers can here be read horizontally: for instance, the symbol is analogical in Hegel as opposed to the sign which is not; and if it is not in Peirce, it is because the icon can absorb that feature. All this means, to sum up and talk in semiological terms (this being the point of this brief analysis which reflects, like a mirror, the subject and methods of our study), that the words in the field derive their meaning only from their opposition to one another (usually in pairs), and that if these oppositions are preserved, the meaning is unambiguous. In particular, *signal* and *index*, *symbol* and *sign*, are the terms of two different functions, which can themselves be opposed as a whole, as they do in Wallon, whose terminology is the clearest and the most complete (*icon* and *allegory* are confined to the vocabulary of Peirce and Jung). We shall therefore say, with Wallon, that the *signal* and the *index* form a group of *relata* devoid of mental representation, whereas in the opposite group, that of *symbol* and *sign*, this representation exists; furthermore, the *signal* is immediate and existential, whereas the *index* is not (it is only a trace); finally, that in the *symbol* the representation is analogical and inadequate (Christianity 'outruns' the cross), whereas in the *sign* the relation is unmotivated and exact (there is no analogy between the word *ox* and the image of an *ox*, which is perfectly covered by its *relatum*).

I-2

The linguistic sign: In linguistics, the notion of sign does not give rise to any competition between neighbouring terms. When he sought to designate the signifying relationship, Saussure immediately eliminated *symbol* (because the term implied the idea of motivation) in favour of *sign* which he defined as the union of a signifier and a signified (in the fashion of the recto and verso of a sheet of paper), or else of an acoustic image and a concept. Until he found the words *signifier* and *signified*, however, *sign* remained ambiguous, for it tended to become identified with the signifier only, which Saussure wanted at all costs to avoid; after having hesitated between *sôme* and *sème*, *form* and *idea*, *image* and *concept*, Saussure settled upon *signifier* and *signified*, the union of which forms the sign. This is a paramount proposition, which one must always bear in mind, for there is a tendency to interpret *sign* as signifier, whereas this is a two-sided Janus-like entity. The (important) consequence is that, for Saussure, Hjelmslev and Frei at least, since the signifieds are signs among others, semantics must be a part of structural linguistics, whereas for the American mechanists the signifieds are substances which must be expelled from linguistics and left to psychology. Since Saussure, the theory of the linguistic sign has been enriched by the *double articulation* principle, the importance of which has been shown by Martinet, to the extent that he made it the criterion which defines language. For among linguistic signs, we must distinguish between the *significant units*, each one of which is endowed with one meaning (the 'words', or to be exact, the 'monemes') and which form the first articulation, and the *distinctive units*, which are part of the form but do not have a direct meaning ('the sounds', or rather the phonemes), and which constitute the second articulation. It is this double articulation which accounts for the economy of human language; for it is a powerful gearing-down which allows, for instance, American Spanish to produce, with only 21 distinctive units, 100,000 significant units.

1-3

Form and substance: The sign is therefore a compound of a signifier and a signified. The plane of the signifiers constitutes the *plane of expression* and that of the signifieds the *plane of content*. Within each of these two planes, Hjelmslev has introduced a distinction which may be important for the study of the semiological (and no longer only linguistic) sign. According to him, each plane comprises two *strata*: *form* and *substance*; we must insist on the new definition of these two terms, for each of them has a weighty lexical past. The *form* is what can be described exhaustively, simply and coherently (epistemological criteria) by linguistics without resorting to any extra-linguistic premise; the *substance* is the whole set of aspects of linguistic phenomena which cannot be described without resorting to extra-linguistic premises. Since both *strata* exist on the plane of expression and the plane of content, we therefore have: i) a substance of expression: for instance the phonic, articulatory, non-functional substance which is the field of phonetics, not phonology; ii) a form of expression, made of the paradigmatic and syntactic rules (let us note that the same form can have two different substances, one phonic, the other graphic); iii) a substance of content: this includes, for instance, the emotional, ideological, or simply notional aspects of the signified, its 'positive' meaning; iv) a form of content: it is the formal organisation of the signified among themselves through the absence or presence of a semantic mark. This last notion is difficult to grasp, because of the impossibility of sep-arating the signifiers from the signifieds in human language; but for this very reason the subdivision *form/substance* can be made more useful and easier to handle in semiology, in the following cases: i) when we deal with a system in which the signifieds are substantified in a substance other than that of their own system (this is, as we have seen, the case with fashion as it is written about); ii) when a system of objects includes a substance which is not immediately and functionally significant, but can be, at a certain level, simply utilitar-ian: the function of a dish can be to signify a situation and also to serve as food.

1-4

The semiological sign: This perhaps allows us to foresee the nature of the semiological sign in relation to the linguistic sign. The semiological sign is also, like its model, compounded of a signifier and a signified (the colour of a light, for instance, is an order to move on, in the Highway Code), but it differs from it at the level of its substances. Many semiological systems (objects, gestures, pictorial images) have a substance of expression whose essence is not to signify; often, they are objects of everyday use, used by society in a derivative way, to signify something: clothes are used for protection and food for nourishment even if they are also used as signs. We propose to call these semiological signs, whose origin is utilitarian and functional, *sign-functions*. The sign-function bears witness to a double movement, which must be taken apart. In a first stage (this analysis is purely operative and does not imply real temporality) the function becomes pervaded with meaning. This semantisation is inevitable: *as soon as there is a society, every usage is converted into a sign of itself*; the use of a raincoat is to give protection from the rain, but this use cannot be dis-sociated from the very signs of an atmospheric situation. Since our society produces only standardised, normalised objects, these objects are unavoidably realisations of a model, the speech of a language, the substances of a significant form. To rediscover a non-signifying object, one would have to imagine a utensil absolutely improvised and with no similarity to an existing model (Lévi-Strauss has shown to what extent tinkering about is itself the search for a meaning): a hypothesis which is virtually impossible to verify in any society.

This universal semantisation of the usages is crucial: it expresses the fact that there is no reality except when it is intelligible, and should eventually lead to the merging of sociology with socio-logic. But once the sign is constituted, society can very well refunctionalise it, and speak about it as if it were an object made for use: a fur-coat will be described as if it served only to protect from the cold. This recurrent functionalisation, which needs, in order to exist, a second-order language, is by no means the same as the first (and indeed purely ideal) functionalisation: for the function which is re-presented does in fact correspond to a second (disguised) semantic institutionalisation, which is of the order of connotation. The sign-function therefore has (probably) an anthropological value, since it is the very unit where the relations of the technical and the significant are woven together.

2. The Signified

2-1

Nature of the signified: In linguistics, the nature of the signified has given rise to discussions which have centred chiefly on its degree of 'reality'; all agree, however, on emphasising the fact that the signified is not 'a thing' but a mental representation of the 'thing'. We have seen that in the definition of the sign by Wallon, this representative character was a relevant feature of the sign and the symbol (as opposed to the index and the signal). Saussure himself has clearly marked the mental nature of the signified by calling it a *concept*: the signified of the word *ox* is not the animal *ox*, but its mental image (this will prove important in the subsequent discussion on the nature of the sign). These discussions, however, still bear the stamp of psychologism, so the analysis of the Stoics will perhaps be thought preferable. They carefully distinguished the *phantasia logiki* (the mental representation), the *tinganon* (the real thing) and the *lekton* (the utterable). The signified is neither the *phantasia* nor the *tinganon* but rather the *lekton*; being neither an act of consciousness, nor a real thing, it can be defined only within the signifying process, in a quasi-tautological way: it is this 'something' which is meant by the person who uses the sign. In this way we are back again to a purely functional definition: the signified is one of the two *relata* of the sign; the only difference which opposes it to the signified is that the latter is a mediator. The situation could not be essentially different in semiology, where objects, images, gestures, etc., inasmuch as they are significant, refer back to something which can be expressed only through them, except that the semiological signified can be taken up by the linguistic signs. One can say, for instance, that a certain sweater means *long autumn walks in the woods*; in this case, the signified is mediated not only by its vestimentary signifier (the sweater), but also by a fragment of speech (which greatly helps in handling it). We could give the name of *isology* to the phenomenon whereby language wields its signifiers and signifieds so that it is impossible to dissociate and differentiate them, in order to set aside the case of the non-isologic systems (which are inevitably complex), in which the signified can be simply *juxtaposed* with its signifier.

2-2

Classification of the linguistic signifieds: How can we classify the signifieds? We know that in semiology this operation is fundamental, since it amounts to isolating the *form* from the content. As far as linguistic signifiers are concerned, two sorts of classification can be conceived. The first is external, and makes use of the 'positive' (and not purely differential) content of concepts: this is the case in the methodical groupings of Hallig and Wartburg, and in the more convincing notional fields of Trier and lexicological fields of Matoré.

But from a structural point of view, this classification (especially those of Hallig and Wartburg) has the defect of resting still too much on the (ideological) *substance* of the signifieds, and not on their *form*. To succeed in establishing a really formal classification, one would have to succeed in reconstituting oppositions of signifieds, and in isolating, within each one of these, a relevant commutative feature: this method has been advocated by Hjelmslev, Sørensen, Prieto and Greimas. Hjelmslev, for instance, decomposes a moneme like 'mare' into two smaller significant units: 'Horse' + 'female', and these units can be commutated and therefore used to reconstitute new monemes ('pig', + 'female' = 'sow', 'horse' + 'male' = 'stallion'); Prieto sees in 'vir' two commutable features 'homo' + 'masculus'; Sørensen reduces the lexicon of kinship to a combination of 'primitives' ('father' = male parent, 'parent' = first ascendant). None of these analyses has yet been developed. Finally, we must remind the reader that according to some linguists, the signifieds are not a part of linguistics, which is concerned only with signifiers, and that semantic classification lies outside the field of linguistics.

2-3

The semiological signifieds: Structural linguistics, however advanced, has not yet elaborated a semantics, that is to say a classification of the *forms* of the verbal signified. One may therefore easily imagine that it is at present impossible to put forward a classification of semiological signifieds, unless we choose to fall back on to known notional fields. We shall venture three observations only.

The first concerns the mode of actualisation of semiological signifieds. These can occur either isologically or not; in the latter case, they are taken up, through articulated language, either by a word (*week-end*) or by a group of words (*long walks in the country*); they are thereby easier to handle, since the analyst is not forced to impose on them his own metalanguage, but also more dangerous, since they ceaselessly refer back to the semantic classification of the language itself (which is itself unknown), and not to a classification having its bases in the system under observation. The signifieds of the fashion garment, even if they are mediated by the speech of the magazine, are not necessarily distributed like the signifieds of the language, since they do not always have the same 'length' (here a word, there a sentence). In the first case, that of the isologic systems, the signified has no materialisation other than its typical signifier; one cannot therefore handle it except by imposing on it a metalanguage. One can for instance ask some subjects about the meaning they attribute to a piece of music by submitting to them a list of verbalised signifieds (*anguished, stormy, sombre, tormented,* etc.); whereas in fact all these verbal signs for a single musical signified, which ought to be designated by one single cipher, which would imply no verbal dissection and no metaphorical small change. These metalanguages, issuing from the analyst in the former case, and the system itself in the latter, are probably inevitable, and this is what still makes the analysis of the signifieds, or ideological analysis, problematical; its place within the semiological project will at least have to be defined in theory.

Our second remark concerns the extension of the semiological signifieds. The whole of the signifieds of a system (once formalised) constitutes a great function; now it is probable that from one system to the other, the great semiological functions not only communicate, but also partly overlap; the form of the signified in the garment system is

ROLAND BARTHES, ELEMENTS OF SEMIOLOGY

probably partly the same as that of the signified in the food system, being, as they are, both articulated on the large-scale opposition of work and festivity, activity and leisure. One must therefore foresee a total ideological description, common to all the systems of a given synchrony.

Finally—and this will be our third remark—we may consider that to each system of magnifiers (lexicons) there corresponds, on the plane of the signifieds, a corpus of practices and techniques; these collections of signifieds imply on the part of system consumers (of 'readers', that is to say), different degrees of knowledge (according to differences in their 'culture'), which explains how the same 'lexie' (or large unit of reading) can be deciphered differently according to the individuals concerned, without ceasing to belong to a given 'language'. Several lexicons—and consequently several bodies of signifieds—can coexist within the same individual, determining in each one more or less 'deep' readings.

3. The Signifier
3-1

Nature of the signaller: The nature of the signifier suggests roughly the same remarks as that of the signified: it is purely a *relatum*, whose definition cannot be separated from that of the signified. The only difference is that the magnifier is a mediator: some matter is necessary to it. But on the one hand it is not sufficient to it, and on the other, in semiology, the signifier can, too, be relayed by a certain matter: that of words. This materiality of the signifier makes it once more necessary to distinguish clearly *matter* from *substance*: a substance can be immaterial (in the case of the substance of the content); therefore, all one can say is that the substance of the signifier is always material (sounds, objects, images). In semiology, where we shall have to deal with mixed systems in which different kinds of matter are involved (sound and image, object and writing, etc.), it may be appropriate to collect together all the signs, *inasmuch as they are home by one and the same matter*, under the concept of the *typical sign*: the verbal sign, the graphic sign, the iconic sign, the gestural sign are all typical signs.

3-2

Classification of the signifiers: The clarification of the signifiers is nothing but the structuralisation proper of the system. What has to be done is to cut up the 'endless' message constituted by the whole of the messages emitted at the level of the studied corpus, into minimal significant units by means of the commutation test, then to group these units into paradigmatic classes, and finally to classify the syntagmatic relations which link these units. These operations constitute an important part of the semiological undertaking which will be dealt with in chapter III; we anticipate the point in mentioning it here.

4. The Signification
4-1

The significant correlation: The sign is a (two-faced) slice of sonority, visuality, etc. The *signification* can be conceived as a process; it is the act which binds the signifier and the signified, an act whose product is the sign. This distinction has, of course, only a classifying (and not phenomenological) value: firstly, because the union of signifier and signified, as we shall see, does not exhaust the semantic act, for the sign derives its value also from its surroundings; secondly, because, probably, the mind does not proceed, in the semantic process, by conjunction but by carving out. And indeed the signification (*semiosis*) does not unite unilateral entities, it does not conjoin two terms, for the very good reason that signifier and signified are both at once term and relation. This ambiguity makes any graphic representation of the signification somewhat clumsy, yet this operation is necessary for any semiological discourse. On this point, let us mention the following attempts:

1. $\frac{Sr}{Sd}$: In Saussure, the sign appears, in his demonstration, as the vertical extension of a situation *in depth*: in the language, the signified is, as it were, *behind* the signifier, and can be reached only through it, although, on the one hand, these excessively spatial metaphors miss the dialectical nature of the signification, and on the other hand the 'closed' character of the sign is acceptable only for the frankly discontinuous systems, such as that of the language.

2. ERC: Hjelmslev has chosen in preference a purely graphic representation: there is a relation (R) between the plane of expression (E) and the plane of content (C). This formula enables us to account economically and without metaphorical falsification, for the metalanguages or derivative systems E R (ERC).

3. $\frac{S}{s}$: Lacan, followed by Laplanche and Leclaire, uses a spatialised writing which, however, differs from Saussure's representation on two points: i) the signifier (S) is global, made up of a multi-levelled chain (metaphorical chain): signifier and signified have only a floating relationship and coincide only at certain anchorage points; ii) the line between the signifier (S) and the signified (s) has its own value (which of course it had not in Saussure): it represents the repression of the signified.

4. Sr $\equiv$ Sd: Finally, in non-isologic systems (that is, those in which the signifieds are materialised through another system), it is of course legitimate to extend the relation in the form of an equivalence($\equiv$) but not of an identity($=$).

4-2
The arbitrary and the motivated in linguistics: We have seen that all that could be said about the signifier is that it was a (material) mediator of the signified. What is the nature of this mediation? In linguistics, this problem has provoked some discussion, chiefly about terminology, for all is fairly clear about the main issues (this will perhaps not be the case with semiology). Starting from the fact that in human language the choice of sounds is not imposed on us by the meaning itself (the ox does not determine the sound ox, since in any case the sound is different in other languages), Saussure had spoken of an *arbitrary* relation between signifier and signified. Benveniste has questioned the aptness of this word: what is arbitrary is the relation between the signifier and the 'thing' which is signified (of the sound ox and the animal the ox). But, as we have seen, even for Saussure, the sign is not the 'thing', but the mental representation of the thing (*concept*); the association of sound and representation is the outcome of a collective training (for instance the learning of the French tongue); this association—which is the signification—is by no means arbitrary (for no French person is free to modify it), indeed it is, on the contrary, necessary. It was therefore suggested to say that in linguistics the signification is *unmotivated*. This lack of motivation, is, by the way, only partial (Saussure speaks of a relative analogy): from signified to signifier, there is a certain motivation in the (restricted) case of onomatopoeia, as we shall see shortly, and also every time a series of signs is created

by the tongue through the imitation of a certain prototype of composition or derivation: this is the case with so-called proportional signs: *pommier, poirer, abricotier*, etc., once the lack of motivation in their roots and their suffix is established, show an analogy in their composition. We shall therefore say in general terms that in the language the link between signifier and signified is contractual in its principle, but that this contract is collective, inscribed in a long temporality (Saussure says that 'a language is always a legacy'), and that consequently it is, as it were, *naturalised*; in the same way, Lévi-Strauss specified that the linguistic sign is arbitrary *a priori* but non-arbitrary *a posteriori*. This discussion leads us to keep two different terms, which will be useful during the semiological extension. We shall say that a system is arbitrary when its signs are founded not by convention, but by unilateral decision: the sign is not arbitrary in the language but it is in fashion; and we shall say that a sign is *motivated* when the relation between its signified and its signifier is analogical (Buyssens has put forward, as suitable terms, *intrinsic semes* for motivated signs, and *extrinsic semes* for unmotivated ones). It will therefore be possible to have systems which are arbitrary and motivated, and others which are non-arbitrary and unmotivated.

4-3
The arbitrary and the motivated in semiology: In linguistics, motivation is limited to the partial plane of derivation or composition; in semiology, on the contrary, it will put to us more general problems. On the one hand, it is possible that outside language systems may be found, in which motivation plays a great part. We shall then have to establish in what way analogy is compatible with the discontinuous character which up to now has seemed necessary to signification; and afterwards how paradigmatic series (that is, in which the terms are few and discrete) can be established when the signifiers are *analogs*: this will probably be the case of 'images', the semiology of which is, for these reasons, far from being established. On the other hand, it is highly probable that a semiological inventory will reveal the existence of impure systems, comprising either very loose motivations, or motivations pervaded, so to speak, with secondary non-motivations, as if, often, the sign lent itself to a kind of conflict between the motivated and the unmotivated. This is already to some extent the case of the most 'motivated' zone of language, that of onomatopoeia. Martinet has pointed out that the onomatopoeic motivation was accompanied by a loss of the double articulation (ouch, which depends only on the second articulation, replaces the doubly articulated syntagm '*it hurts*'); yet the onomatopoeia which expresses pain is not exactly the same in French (*aie*) and in Danish (*au*), for instance. This is because in fact motivation here submits, as it were, to phonological models which of course vary with different languages: there is an impregnation of the analogical by the digital. Outside language, problematic systems, like the 'language' of the bees, show the same ambiguity: the honey-gathering dances have a vaguely analogical value; that at the entrance of the hive is frankly motivated (by the direction of the food), but the wriggly dance in a figure of eight is quite unmotivated (it refers to a distance). Finally, and as a last example of such ill-defined areas, certain trade-marks used in advertising consist of purely abstract (non-analogical) shapes; they can, however, express a certain impression (for instance one of 'power') which has a relation of affinity with the signified. The trade-mark of the Berliet lorries (a circle with a thick arrow across it) does not in any way 'copy' power—indeed, how could one 'copy' power?—and yet suggests it through a latent analogy; the same ambiguity is to be found in the signs of some ideographic writings (Chinese, for instance).

The coexistence of the analogical and the non-analogical therefore seems unquestionable, even within a single system. Yet semiology cannot be content with a description acknowledging this compromise without trying to systematise it, for it cannot admit a continuous differential, since, as we shall see, meaning is articulation. These problems have not yet been studied in detail, and it would be impossible to give a general survey of them. The outline of an economy of signification (at the anthropological level) can, however, be perceived: in the language, for instance, the (relative) motivation introduces a certain order at the level of the first (significant) articulation: the 'contract' is therefore in this case underpinned by a certain naturalisation of this *a priori* arbitrariness which Lévi-Strauss talks about; other systems, on the contrary, can go from motivation to non-motivation: for instance the set of the ritual puppets of initiation of the Senoufo, cited by Lévi-Strauss in *The Savage Mind*. It is therefore probable that at the level of the most general semiology, which merges with anthropology, there comes into being a sort of circularity between the analogical and the unmotivated: there is a double tendency (each aspect being complementary to the other) to naturalise the unmotivated and to intellectualise the motivated (that is to say, to culturalise it). Finally, some authors are confident that digitalism, which is the rival of the analogical, is itself in its purest form—binarism—a 'reproduction' of certain physiological processes, if it is true that sight and hearing, in the last analysis, function by alternative selections.

5. Value

5-1

Value in linguistics: We have said, or at least hinted, that to treat the sign 'in itself', as the only link between signifier and signified, is a fairly arbitrary (although inevitable) abstraction. We must, to conclude, tackle the sign, no longer by way of its 'composition', but of its 'setting': this is the problem of value. Saussure did not see the importance of this notion at the outset, but even as early as his second *Course in General Linguistics*, he increasingly concentrated on it, and value became an essential concept for him, and eventually more important than that of signification (with which it is not co-extensive). Value bears a close relation to the notion of the language (as opposed to speech); its effect is to de-psychologise linguistics and to bring it closer to economics; it is therefore central to structural linguistics. In most sciences, Saussure observes, there is no coexistence of synchrony and diachrony: astronomy is a synchronic science (although the heavenly bodies alter); geology is a diachronic science (although it can study fixed states); history is mainly diachronic (a succession of events), although it can linger over some 'pictures'. Yet there is a science in which these two aspects have an equal share: economics (which included economics proper, and economic history); the same applies to linguistics, Saussure goes on to say. This is because in both cases we are dealing with a system of equivalence between two different things: work and reward, a signifier and a signified (this is the phenomenon which we have up to now called *signification*). Yet, in linguistics as well as in economics, this equivalence is not isolated, for if we alter one of its terms, the whole system changes by degrees. For a sign (or an economic 'value') to exist, it must therefore be possible, on the one hand, to *exchange* dissimilar things (work and wage, signifier and signified), and on the other, to compare similar things with each other. One can exchange a five-franc note for bread, soap or a cinema ticket, but one can also compare this banknote with ten- or fifty-franc notes, etc.; in the same way, a 'word' can be 'exchanged' for an idea (that is, for something dissimilar), but it can also be compared with other words (that is, something similar): in English the word mutton derives its value only from its coexistence with *sheep;* the meaning is truly fixed only at the end of this double determination: signification and value. Value, therefore, is not signification; it comes, Saussure says, 'from the reciprocal situation of the pieces of the language'. It is even more important than signification: 'what quantity of idea or phonic matter a sign contains is of less import than what there is around it in the other signs': a prophetic sentence, if one realises that it already was the foundation of Lévi-Strauss's homology and of the principle of taxonomies. Having thus carefully distinguished, with Saussure, signification and value, we immediately see that if we return to Hjemslev's *strata* (substance and form), the signification partakes of the substance of the content, and value, of that of its form (*mutton* and *sheep* are in a paradigmatic relation *as signifieds* and not, of course, as signifiers).

5-2

The articulation: In order to account for the double phenomenon of signification and value, Saussure used the analogy of a sheet of paper: if we cut out shapes in it, on the one hand we get various pieces (A, B, C), each of which has a value in relation to its neighbours, and, on the other, each of these pieces has a recto and a verso *which have been cut out at the same time* (A-A', B-B', C-C'): this is the signification. This comparison is useful because it leads us to an original conception of the production of meaning: no longer as the mere correlation of a signifier and a signified, but perhaps more essentially *as an act of simultaneously cutting out* two amorphous masses, two 'floating kingdoms', as Saussure says. For Saussure imagines that at the (entirely theoretical) origin of meaning, ideas and sounds form two floating, labile, continuous and parallel masses of substances; meaning intervenes when one cuts at the same time and at a single stroke into these two masses. The signs (thus produced) are therefore *articuli*; meaning is therefore an order with chaos on either side, but this order is essentially a *division*. The language is an intermediate object between sound and thought: it consists in *uniting both while simultaneously decomposing them.* And Saussure suggests a new simile: signifier and signified are like two superimposed layers, one of air, the other of water; when the atmospheric pressure changes, the layer of water divides into waves: in the same way, the signifier is divided into *articuli*. These images, of the sheet of paper as well as of the waves, enable us to emphasise a fact which is of the utmost importance for the future of semiological analysis: that language is the domain of *articulations*, and the meaning is above all a cutting-out of shapes. It follows that the future task of semiology is far less to establish lexicons of objects than to rediscover the articulations which men impose on reality; looking into the distant and perhaps ideal future, we might say that semiology and taxonomy, although they are not yet born, are perhaps meant to be merged into a new science, arthrology, namely, the science of apportionment.

"in this habitually unary space, occasionally (but alas all too rarely) a 'detail' attracts me. I feel that its mere presence changes my reading, that I am looking at a new photograph, marked in my eyes with a higher value. This 'detail' is the punctum"

Camera Lucida: Reflections on Photography

1980

....

10. STUDIUM and PUNCTUM

My rule was plausible enough for me to try to name (as I would need to do) these two elements whose co-presence established, it seemed, the particular interest I took in these photographs.

The first, obviously, is an extent, it has the extension of a field, which I perceive quite familiarly as a consequence of my knowledge, my culture; this field can be more or less stylized, more or less successful, depending on the photographer's skill or luck, but it always refers to a classical body of information: rebellion, Nicaragua, and all the signs of both: wretched un-uniformed soldiers, ruined streets, corpses, grief, the sun, and the heavy-lidded Indian eyes. Thousands of photographs consist of this field, and in these photographs I can, of course, take a kind of general interest, one that is even stirred sometimes, but in regard to them my emotion requires the rational intermediary of an ethical and political culture. What I feel about these photographs derives from an *average* affect, almost from a certain training. I did not know a French word which might account for this kind of human interest, but I believe this word exists in Latin: it is *studium*, which doesn't mean, at least not immediately, 'study,' but application to a thing, taste for someone, a kind of general, enthusiastic commitment, of course, but without special acuity. It is by *studium* that I am interested in so many photographs, whether I receive them as political

"... the sheet carried by the weeping mother (why this sheet?)... Koen Wessing: Nicaragua. 1979

testimony or enjoy them as good historical scenes: for it is culturally (this connotation is present in *studium*) that I participate in the figures, the faces, the gestures, the settings, the actions.

The second element will break (or punctuate) the *studium*. This time it is not I who seek it out (as I invest the field of the *studium* with my sovereign consciousness), it is this element which rises from the scene, shoots out of it like an arrow, and pierces me. A Latin word exists to designate this wound, this prick, this mark made by a pointed instrument: the word suits me all the better in that it also refers to the notion of punctuation, and because the photographs I am speaking of are in effect punctuated, sometimes even speckled with these sensitive points; precisely, these marks, these wounds are so many *points*. This second element which will disturb the *studium* I shall therefore call *punctum*; for *punctum* is also: sting, speck, cut, little hole—and also a cast of the dice. A photograph's *punctum* is that accident which pricks me (but also bruises me, is poignant to me).

Having thus distinguished two themes in Photography (for in general the photographs I liked were constructed in the manner of a classical sonata), I could occupy myself with one after the other.

11. STUDIUM

Many photographs are, alas, inert under my gaze. But even among those which have some existence in my eyes, most provoke only a general and, so to speak, *polite* interest: they have no *punctum* in them: they please or displease me without pricking me: they are invested with no more than *studium*. The *studium* is that very wide field of unconcerned desire, of various interest, of inconsequential taste: *I like / I don't like*. The *studium* is of the order of *liking*, not of *loving*; it mobilizes a half desire, a demi-volition; it is the same sort of vague, slippery, irresponsible interest one takes in the people, the entertainments, the books, the clothes one finds "all right."

To recognize the *studium* is inevitably to encounter the photographer's intentions, to enter into harmony with them, to approve or disapprove of them, but always to understand them, to argue them within myself, for culture (from which the *studium* derives) is a contract arrived at between creators and consumers. The *studium* is a kind of education (knowledge and civility, "politeness") which allows me to discover the *Operator*, to experience the intentions which establish and animate his practices, but to experience them "in reverse," according to my will as a *Spectator*. It is rather as if I had to read the Photographer's myths in the Photograph, fraternizing with them but not quite believing in them. These myths obviously aim (this is what myth is for) at reconciling the Photograph with society (is this necessary?—Yes, indeed: the Photograph is *dangerous*) by endowing it with functions, which are, for the Photographer, so many alibis. These functions are: to inform, to represent, to surprise, to cause to signify, to provoke desire. And I, the *Spectator*, I recognize them with more or less pleasure: I invest them with my *studium* (which is never my delight or my pain).

[...]

18. Co-presence of the STUDIUM and the PUNCTUM

In this habitually unary space, occasionally (but alas all too rarely) a "detail" attracts me. I feel that its mere presence changes my reading, that I am looking at a new photograph, marked in my eyes with a higher value. This "detail" is the *punctum*.

It is not possible to posit a rule of connection between the *studium* and the *punctum* (when it happens to be there). It is a matter of a co-presence, that is all one can say: the nuns "happened to be there," passing in the background, when Wessing photographed the Nicaraguan soldiers; from the viewpoint of reality (which is perhaps that of the *Operator*), a whole causality explains the presence of the "detail": the Church implanted in these Latin American countries, the nuns allowed to circulate as nurses, etc.; but from my *Spectator's* viewpoint, the detail is offered by chance and for nothing; the scene is in no way "composed" according to a creative logic; the photograph is doubtless dual, but this duality is the motor of no "development," as happens in classical discourse. In order to perceive the *punctum*, no analysis would be of any use to me (but perhaps memory sometimes would as we shall see): it suffices that the image be large enough, that I do not have to study it (this would be of no help at all), that, given right there on the page, I should receive it right here in my eyes.

19. PUNCTUM: Partial Feature

Very often the *Punctum* is a "detail," *i.e.*, a partial object. Hence, to give examples of *punctum* is, in a certain fashion, to *give myself up*.

Here is a family of American blacks, photographed in 1926 by James van der Zee. The *studium* is clear: I am sympathetically interested, as a docile cultural subject, in what the photograph has to say, for it speaks (it is a "good" photograph): it utters respectability, family life, conformism, Sunday best, an effort of social advancement in order to assume the White Man's attributes (an effort touching by reason of its naïveté). The spectacle interests me but does not prick me. What does, strange to say, is the belt worn low by the sister (or daughter)—the "solacing Mammy"—whose arms are crossed behind her back like a schoolgirl, and above all her *strapped pumps* (Mary Janes—why does this dated fashion touch me? I mean: to what date does it refer me?). This particular *punctum* arouses great sympathy in me, almost a kind of tenderness. Yet the *punctum* shows no preference for morality or good taste: the *punctum* can be ill-bred. William Klein has photographed children of Little Italy in New York (1954); all very touching, amusing, but what I stubbornly see are one child's bad teeth. Kertész, in 1926, took young Tzara's portrait (with a monocle); but what I notice, by that additional vision which is in a sense the gift, the grace of the *punctum*, is Tzara's hand resting on the door frame: a large hand whose nails are anything but clean.

However lightning-like it may be, the *punctum* has, more or less potentially, a power of expansion. This power is often metonymic. There is a photograph by Kertész (1921) which shows a blind gypsy violinist being led by a boy; now what I see, by means of this "thinking eye" which makes me add something to the photograph, is the dirt road; its texture gives me the certainty of being in Central Europe; I perceive the referent (here, the photograph really transcends itself: is this not the sole proof of its art? To annihilate itself as *medium*, to be no longer a sign but the thing itself?), I recognize, with my whole body, the struggling villages I passed through on my long-ago travel in Hungary and Rumania.

There is another (less Proustian) expansion of the *punctum*: when, paradoxically, while remaining a "detail," it fills the whole picture. Duane Michals has photographed Andy Warhol: a provocative portrait, since Warhol hides his face behind both hands. I have no desire to comment intellectually on this game of hide-and-seek (which belongs to the *Studium*); since for me, Warhol hides nothing; he offers his hands to read, quite openly; and the *punctum* is not the gesture but the slightly repellent substance of those spatulate nails, at once soft and hard-edged.

The strapped pumps
James van der Zee: Family Portrait. 1926

"What I stubbornly see are one boy's bad teeth…"
William Klein: Little Italy. New York. 1954

Pierre Bourdieu

The Forms of Capital

1986

"economic capital is at the root of all the other types of capital and that these transformed, disguised forms of economic capital, never entirely reducible to that definition"

Pierre Bourdieu (1930–2002) was a sociologist and anthropologist who made significant contributions to economic sociological theory.

The social world is accumulated history, and if it is not to be reduced to a discontinuous series of instantaneous mechanical equilibria between agents who are treated as interchangeable particles, one must reintroduce into it the notion of capital and with it, accumulation and all its effects. Capital is accumulated labor (in its materialized form or its 'incorporated,' embodied form) which, when appropriated on a private, i.e., exclusive, basis by agents or groups of agents, enables them to appropriate social energy in the form of reified or living labor. It is a vis insita, a force inscribed in objective or subjective structures, but it is also a lex insita, the principle underlying the immanent regularities of the social world. It is what makes the games of society—not least, the economic game— something other than simple games of chance offering at every moment the possibility of a miracle. Roulette, which holds out the opportunity of winning a lot of money in a short space of time, and therefore of changing one's social status quasi-instantaneously, and in which the winning of the previous spin of the wheel can be staked and lost at every new spin, gives a fairly accurate image of this imaginary universe of perfect competition or perfect equality of opportunity, a world without inertia, without accumulation, without heredity or acquired properties, in which every moment is perfectly independent of the previous one, every soldier has a marshal's baton in his knapsack, and every prize can be attained, instantaneously, by everyone, so that at each moment anyone can become anything. Capital, which, in its objectified or embodied forms, takes time to accumulate and which, as a potential capacity to produce profits and to reproduce itself in identical or expanded form, contains a tendency to persist in its being, is a force inscribed in the objectivity of things so that everything is not equally possible or impossible.[1] And

---

1   *This inertia, entailed by the tendency of the structures of capital to reproduce themselves in institutions or in dispositions adapted to the structures of which they are the product, is, of course, reinforced by a specifically political action of concerted conservation, i.e., of demobilization and depoliticization. The latter tends to keep the dominated agents in the state of a practical group, united only by the orchestration of their dispositions and condemned to function as an aggregate repeatedly performing discrete, individual acts (such as consumer or electoral choices).*

the structure of the distribution of the different types and subtypes of capital at a given moment in time represents the immanent structure of the social world, i.e. , the set of constraints, inscribed in the very reality of that world, which govern its functioning in a durable way, determining the chances of success for practices.

It is in fact impossible to account for the structure and functioning of the social world unless one reintroduces capital in all its forms and not solely in the one form recognized by economic theory. Economic theory has allowed to be foisted upon it a definition of the economy of practices which is the historical invention of capitalism; and by reducing the universe of exchanges to mercantile exchange, which is objectively and subjectively oriented toward the maximization of profit, i.e., (economically) self-interested, it has implicitly defined the other forms of exchange as noneconomic, and therefore disinterested. In particular, it defines as disinterested those forms of exchange which ensure the transubstantiation whereby the most material types of capital—those which are economic in the restricted sense—can present themselves in the immaterial form of cultural capital or social capital and vice versa. Interest, in the restricted sense it is given in economic theory, cannot be produced without producing its negative counterpart, disinterestedness. The class of practices whose explicit purpose is to maximize monetary profit cannot be defined as such without producing the purposeless finality of cultural or artistic practices and their products; the world of bourgeois man, with his double-entry accounting, cannot be invented without producing the pure, perfect universe of the artist and the intellectual and the gratuitous activities of art-for-art's sake and pure theory. In other words, the con-stitution of a science of mercantile relationships which, inasmuch as it takes for granted the very foundations of the order it claims to analyze—private property, profit, wage labor, etc.—is not even a science of the field of economic production, has prevented the constitution of a general science of the economy of practices, which would treat mercan-tile exchange as a particular case of exchange in all its forms.

It is remarkable that the practices and assets thus salvaged from the 'icy water of egotistical calculation' (and from science) are the virtual monopoly of the dominant class—as if economism had been able to reduce everything to economics only because the reduction on which that discipline is based protects from sacrilegious reduction everything which needs to be protected. If economics deals only with practices that have narrowly eco-nomic interest as their principle and only with goods that are directly and immediately convertible into money (which makes them quantifiable), then the universe of bourgeois production and exchange becomes an exception and can see itself and present itself as a realm of disinterestedness. As everyone knows, priceless things have their price, and the extreme difficulty of converting certain practices and certain objects into money is only due to the fact that this conversion is refused in the very intention that produces them, which is nothing other than the denial (Verneinung) of the economy. A general science of the economy of practices, capable of reappropriating the totality of the practices which, although objectively economic, are not and cannot be socially recognized as economic, and which can be performed only at the cost of a whole labor of dissimulation or, more precisely, euphemization, must endeavor to grasp capital and profit in all their forms and to establish the laws whereby the different types of capital (or power, which amounts to the same thing) change into one another.[2]

2   This is true of all exchanges between members of different fractions of the dominant class, possessing different types of capital.

Depending on the field in which it functions, and at the cost of the more or less expensive transformations which are the precondition for its efficacy in the field in question, capital can present itself in three fundamental guises: as economic capital, which is immediately and directly convertible into money and may be institutionalized in the forms of property rights; as cultural capital, which is convertible, on certain conditions, into economic capital and may be institutionalized in the forms of educational qualifications; and as social capital, made up of social obligations ('connections'), which is convertible, in certain conditions, into economic capital and may be institutionalized in the forms of a title of nobility.[3]

CULTURAL CAPITAL

Cultural capital can exist in three forms: in the embodied state, i.e., in the form of long-lasting dispositions of the mind and body; in the objectified state, in the form of cultural goods (pictures, books, dictionaries, instruments, machines, etc.), which are the trace or realization of theories or critiques of these theories, problematics, etc.; and in the institutionalized state, a form of objectification which must be set apart because, as will be seen in the case of educational qualifications, it confers entirely original properties on the cultural capital which it is presumed to guarantee.

The reader should not be misled by the somewhat peremptory air which the effort at axiomization may give to my argument.[4] The notion of cultural capital initially presented itself to me, in the course of research, as a theoretical hypothesis which made it possible to explain the unequal scholastic achievement of children originating from the different social classes by relating academic success, i.e., the specific profits which children from the different classes and class fractions can obtain in the academic market, to the distribution of cultural capital between the classes and class fractions. This starting point implies a break with the presuppositions inherent both in the commonsense view, which sees academic success or failure as an effect of natural aptitudes, and in human capital theories. Economists might seem to deserve credit for explicitly raising the question of the relationship between the rates of profit on educational investment and on economic investment (and its evolution). But their measurement of the yield from scholastic investment takes account only of monetary investments and profits, or those directly convertible into money, such as the costs of schooling and the cash equivalent of time devoted to study; they are unable to explain the different proportions of their resources which different agents or different social classes allocate to economic investment and cultural investment because they fail to take systematic account of the structure of the

---

These range from sales of expertise, treatment, or other services which take the form of gift exchange and dignify themselves with the most decorous names that can be found (honoraria, emoluments, etc.) to matrimonial exchanges, the prime example of a transaction that can only take place insofar as it is not perceived or defined as such by the contracting parties. It is remarkable that the apparent extensions of economic theory beyond the limits constituting the discipline have left intact the asylum of the sacred, apart from a few sacrilegious incursions. Gary S. Becker, for example, who was one of the first to take explicit account of the types of capital that are usually ignored, never considers anything other than monetary costs and profits, forgetting the nonmonetary investments (inter alia, the affective ones) and the material and symbolic profits that education provides in a deferred, indirect way, such as the added value which the dispositions produced or reinforced by schooling (bodily or verbal manners, tastes, etc.) or the relationships established with fellow students can yield in the matrimonial market (Becker 1964a).

3   *Symbolic capital, that is to say, capital—in whatever form—insofar as it is represented, i.e., apprehended symbolically, in a relationship of knowledge or, more precisely, of misrecognition and recognition, presupposes the intervention of the habitus, as a socially constituted cognitive capacity.*

4   *When talking about concepts for their own sake, as I do here, rather than using them in research, one always runs the risk of being both schematic and formal, i.e., theoretical in the most usual and most usually approved sense of the word.*

differential chances of profit which the various markets offer these agents or classes as a function of the volume and the composition of their assets (see esp. Becker 1964b). Furthermore, because they neglect to relate scholastic investment strategies to the whole set of educational strategies and to the system of reproduction strategies, they inevitably, by a necessary paradox, let slip the best hidden and socially most determinant educational investment, namely, the domestic transmission of cultural capital. Their studies of the relationship between academic ability and academic investment show that they are unaware that ability or talent is itself the product of an investment of time and cultural capital (Becker 1964a, p. 63–66). Not surprisingly, when endeavoring to evaluate the profits of scholastic investment, they can only consider the profitability of educational expenditure for society as a whole, the 'social rate of return,' or the 'social gain of education as measured by its effects on national productivity' (Becker 1964b, pp. 121, 155). This typically functionalist definition of the functions of education ignores the contribution which the educational system makes to the reproduction of the social structure by sanctioning the hereditary transmission of cultural capital. From the very beginning, a definition of human capital, despite its humanistic connotations, does not move beyond economism and ignores, inter alia, the fact that the scholastic yield from educational action depends on the cultural capital previously invested by the family. Moreover, the economic and social yield of the educational qualification depends on the social capital, again inherited, which can be used to back it up.

The Embodied State

Most of the properties of cultural capital can be deduced from the fact that, in its fundamental state, it is linked to the body and presupposes embodiment. The accumulation of cultural capital in the embodied state, i.e., in the form of what is called culture, cultivation, Bildung, presupposes a process of embodiment, incorporation, which, insofar as it implies a labor of inculcation and assimilation, costs time, time which must be invested personally by the investor. Like the acquisition of a muscular physique or a suntan, it cannot be done at second hand (so that all effects of delegation are ruled out).

The work of acquisition is work on oneself (self-improvement), an effort that presupposes a personal cost (on paie de sa personne, as we say in French), an investment, above all of time, but also of that socially constituted form of libido, libido sciendi, with all the privation, renunciation, and sacrifice that it may entail. It follows that the least inexact of all the measurements of cultural capital are those which take as their standard the length of acquisition—so long, of course, as this is not reduced to length of schooling and allowance is made for early domestic education by giving it a positive value (a gain in time, a head start) or a negative value (wasted time, and doubly so because more time must be spent correcting its effects), according to its distance from the demands of the scholastic market.[5]

This embodied capital, external wealth converted into an integral part of the person, into a habitus, cannot be transmitted instantaneously (unlike money, property rights, or even titles of nobility) by gift or bequest, purchase or exchange. It follows that the use or

---

5 *This proposition implies no recognition of the value of scholastic verdicts; it merely registers the relationship which exists in reality between a certain cultural capital and the laws of the educational market. Dispositions that are given a negative value in the educational market may receive very high value in other markets—not least, of course, in the relationships internal to the class.*

exploitation of cultural capital presents particular problems for the holders of economic or political capital, whether they be private patrons or, at the other extreme, entrepreneurs employing executives endowed with a specific cultural competence (not to mention the new state patrons). How can this capital, so closely linked to the person, be bought without buying the person and so losing the very effect of legitimation which presupposes the dissimulation of dependence? How can this capital be concentrated—as some undertakings demand—without concentrating the possessors of the capital, which can have all sorts of unwanted consequences?

Cultural capital can be acquired, to a varying extent, depending on the period, the society, and the social class, in the absence of any deliberate inculcation, and therefore quite unconsciously. It always remains marked by its earliest conditions of acquisition which, through the more or less visible marks they leave (such as the pronunciations characteristic of a class or region), help to determine its distinctive value. It cannot be accumulated beyond the appropriating capacities of an individual agent; it declines and dies with its bearer (with his biological capacity, his memory, etc.). Because it is thus linked in numerous ways to the person in his biological singularity and is subject to a hereditary transmission which is always heavily disguised, or even invisible, it defies the old, deep-rooted distinction the Greek jurists made between inherited properties (ta patroa) and acquired properties (epikteta), i.e., those which an individual adds to his heritage. It thus manages to combine the prestige of innate property with the merits of acquisition. Because the social conditions of its transmission and acquisition are more disguised than those of economic capital, it is predisposed to function as symbolic capital, i.e., to be unrecognized as capital and recognized as legitimate competence, as authority exerting an effect of (mis)recognition, e.g., in the matrimonial market and in all the markets in which economic capital is not fully recognized, whether in matters of culture, with the great art collections or great cultural foundations, or in social welfare, with the economy of generosity and the gift. Furthermore, the specifically symbolic logic of distinction additionally secures material and symbolic profits for the possessors of a large cultural capital: any given cultural competence (e.g., being able to read in a world of illiterates) derives a scarcity value from its position in the distribution of cultural capital and yields profits of distinction for its owner. In other words, the share in profits which scarce cultural capital secures in class-divided societies is based, in the last analysis, on the fact that all agents do not have the economic and cultural means for prolonging their children's education beyond the minimum necessary for the reproduction of the labor-power least valorized at a given moment.[6]

Thus the capital, in the sense of the means of appropriating the product of accumulated labor in the objectified state which is held by a given agent, depends for its real efficacy on the form of the distribution of the means of appropriating the accumulated and objectively available resources; and the relationship of appropriation between an agent and the resources objectively available, and hence the profits they produce, is mediated by the relationship of (objective and/or subjective) competition between himself and the other possessors of capital competing for the same goods, in which scarcity—and through it social value—is generated. The structure of the field, i.e., the unequal distribution of

---

6 *In a relatively undifferentiated society, in which access to the means of appropriating the cultural heritage is very equally distributed, embodied culture does not function as cultural capital, i.e., as a means of acquiring exclusive advantages.*

capital, is the source of the specific effects of capital, i.e., the appropriation of profits and the power to impose the laws of functioning of the field most favorable to capital and its reproduction.

But the most powerful principle of the symbolic efficacy of cultural capital no doubt lies in the logic of its transmission. On the one hand, the process of appropriating objectified cultural capital and the time necessary for it to take place mainly depend on the cultural capital embodied in the whole family—through (among other things) the generalized Arrow effect and all forms of implicit transmission.[7] On the other hand, the initial accumulation of cultural capital, the precondition for the fast, easy accumulation of every kind of useful cultural capital, starts at the outset, without delay, without wasted time, only for the offspring of families endowed with strong cultural capital; in this case, the accumulation period covers the whole period of socialization. It follows that the transmission of cultural capital is no doubt the best hidden form of hereditary transmission of capital, and it therefore receives proportionately greater weight in the system of reproduction strategies, as the direct, visible forms of transmission tend to be more strongly censored and controlled.

It can immediately be seen that the link between economic and cultural capital is established through the mediation of the time needed for acquisition. Differences in the cultural capital possessed by the family imply differences first in the age at which the work of transmission and accumulation begins—the limiting case being full use of the time biologically available, with the maximum free time being harnessed to maximum cultural capital—and then in the capacity, thus defined, to satisfy the specifically cultural demands of a prolonged process of acquisition. Furthermore, and in correlation with this, the length of time for which a given individual can prolong his acquisition process depends on the length of time for which his family can provide him with the free time, i.e., time free from economic necessity, which is the precondition for the initial accumulation (time which can be evaluated as a handicap to be made up).

The Objectified State

Cultural capital, in the objectified state, has a number of properties which are defined only in the relationship with cultural capital in its embodied form. The cultural capital objectified in material objects and media, such as writings, paintings, monuments, instruments, etc., is transmissible in its materiality. A collection of paintings, for example, can be transmitted as well as economic capital (if not better, because the capital transfer is more disguised). But what is transmissible is legal ownership and not (or not necessarily) what constitutes the precondition for specific appropriation, namely, the possession of the means of 'consuming' a painting or using a machine, which, being nothing other than embodied capital, are subject to the same laws of transmission.[8]

7   What I call the generalized Arrow effect, i.e., the fact that all cultural goods—paintings, monuments, machines, and any objects shaped by man, particularly all those which belong to the childhood environment—exert an educative effect by their mere existence, is no doubt one of the structural factors behind the 'schooling explosion,' in the sense that a growth in the quantity of cultural capital accumulated in the objectified state increases the educative effect automatically exerted by the environment. If one adds to this the fact that embodied cultural capital is constantly increasing, it can be seen that, in each generation, the educational system can take more for granted. The fact that the same educational investment is increasingly productive is one of the structural factors of inflation of qualifications (together with cyclical factors linked to effects of capital conversion).

8   The cultural object, as a living social institution, is, simultaneously, a socially instituted material object and a particular class of habitus, to which it is addressed. The material object—for example, a work of art in its materiality—may be separated by

Thus cultural goods can be appropriated both materially—which presupposes economic capital—and symbolically—which presupposes cultural capital. It follows that the owner of the means of production must find a way of appropriating either the embodied capital which is the precondition of specific appropriation or the services of the holders of this capital. To possess the machines, he only needs economic capital; to appropriate them and use them in accordance with their specific purpose (defined by the cultural capital, of scientific or technical type, incorporated in them), he must have access to embodied cultural capital, either in person or by proxy. This is no doubt the basis of the ambiguous status of cadres (executives and engineers). If it is emphasized that they are not the possessors (in the strictly economic sense) of the means of production which they use, and that they derive profit from their own cultural capital only by selling the services and products which it makes possible, then they will be classified among the dominated groups; if it is emphasized that they draw their profits from the use of a particular form of capital, then they will be classified among the dominant groups. Everything suggests that as the cultural capital incorporated in the means of production increases (and with it the period of embodiment needed to acquire the means of appropriating it), so the collective strength of the holders of cultural capital would tend to increase—if the holders of the dominant type of capital (economic capital) were not able to set the holders of cultural capital in competition with one another. (They are, moreover, inclined to competition by the very conditions in which they are selected and trained, in particular by the logic of scholastic and recruitment competitions.)

Cultural capital in its objectified state presents itself with all the appearances of an autonomous, coherent universe which, although the product of historical action, has its own laws, transcending individual wills, and which, as the example of language well illustrates, therefore remains irreducible to that which each agent, or even the aggregate of the agents, can appropriate (i.e., to the cultural capital embodied in each agent or even in the aggregate of the agents). However, it should not be forgotten that it exists as symbolically and materially active, effective capital only insofar as it is appropriated by agents and implemented and invested as a weapon and a stake in the struggles which go on in the fields of cultural production (the artistic field, the scientific field, etc.) and, beyond them, in the field of the social classes—struggles in which the agents wield strengths and obtain profits proportionate to their mastery of this objectified capital, and therefore to the extent of their embodied capital.[9]

The Institutionalized State

The objectification of cultural capital in the form of academic qualifications is one way of neutralizing some of the properties it derives from the fact that, being embodied, it has the same biological limits as its bearer. This objectification is what makes the difference between the capital of the autodidact, which may be called into question at any time, or

---

space (e.g., a Dogon statue) or by time (e.g., a Simone Martini painting) from the habitus for which it was intended. This leads to one of the most fundamental biases of art history. Understanding the effect (not to be confused with the function) which the work tended to produce—for example, the form of belief it tended to induce—and which is the true basis of the conscious or unconscious choice of the means used (technique, colors, etc.), and therefore of the form itself, is possible only if one at least raises the question of the habitus on which it 'operated.'

9 The dialectical relationship between objectified cultural capital—of which the form par excellence is writing—and embodied cultural capital has generally been reduced to an exalted description of the degradation of the spirit by the letter, the living by the inert, creation by routine, grace by heaviness.

even the cultural capital of the courtier, which can yield only ill-defined profits, of fluctuating value, in the market of high-society exchanges, and the cultural capital academically sanctioned by legally guaranteed qualifications, formally independent of the person of their bearer. With the academic qualification, a certificate of cultural competence which confers on its holder a conventional, constant, legally guaranteed value with respect to culture, social alchemy produces a form of cultural capital which has a relative autonomy vis-à-vis its bearer and even vis-à-vis the cultural capital he effectively possesses at a given moment in time. It institutes cultural capital by collective magic, just as, according to Merleau-Ponty, the living institute their dead through the ritual of mourning. One has only to think of the concours (competitive recruitment examination) which, out of the continuum of infinitesimal differences between performances, produces sharp, absolute, lasting differences, such as that which separates the last successful candidate from the first unsuccessful one, and institutes an essential difference between the officially recognized, guaranteed competence and simple cultural capital, which is constantly required to prove itself. In this case, one sees clearly the performative magic of the power of instituting, the power to show forth and secure belief or, in a word, to impose recognition.

By conferring institutional recognition on the cultural capital possessed by any given agent, the academic qualification also makes it possible to compare qualification holders and even to exchange them (by substituting one for another in succession). Furthermore, it makes it possible to establish conversion rates between cultural capital and economic capital by guaranteeing the monetary value of a given academic capital.[10] This product of the conversion of economic capital into cultural capital establishes the value, in terms of cultural capital, of the holder of a given qualification relative to other qualification holders and, by the same token, the monetary value for which it can be exchanged on the labor market (academic investment has no meaning unless a minimum degree of reversibility of the conversion it implies is objectively guaranteed). Because the material and symbolic profits which the academic qualification guarantees also depend on its scarcity, the investments made (in time and effort) may turn out to be less profitable than was anticipated when they were made (there having been a de facto change in the conversion rate between academic capital and economic capital). The strategies for converting economic capital into cultural capital, which are among the short-term factors of the schooling explosion and the inflation of qualifications, are governed by changes in the structure of the chances of profit offered by the different types of capital.

SOCIAL CAPITAL

Social capital is the aggregate of the actual or potential resources which are linked to possession of a durable network of more or less institutionalized relationships of mutual acquaintance and recognition—or in other words, to membership in a group[11]—which provides each of its members with the backing of the collectivity-owned capital, a 'creden-

10   This is particularly true in France, where in many occupations (particularly the civil service) there is a very strict relationship between qualification, rank, and remuneration (translator's note).

11   Here, too, the notion of cultural capital did not spring from pure theoretical work, much less from an analogical extension of economic concepts. It arose from the need to identify the principle of social effects which, although they can be seen clearly at the level of singular agents—where statistical inquiry inevitably operates—cannot be reduced to the set of properties individually possessed by a given agent. These effects, in which spontaneous sociology readily perceives the work of 'connections,' are particularly visible in all cases in which different individuals obtain very unequal profits from virtually equivalent (economic or cultural) capital, depending on the extent to which they can mobilize by proxy the capital of a group (a family, the alumni of an elite school, a select club, the aristocracy, etc.) that is more or less constituted as such and more or less rich in capital.

tial' which entitles them to credit, in the various senses of the word. These relationships may exist only in the practical state, in material and/or symbolic exchanges which help to maintain them. They may also be socially instituted and guaranteed by the application of a common name (the name of a family, a class, or a tribe or of a school, a party, etc.) and by a whole set of instituting acts designed simultaneously to form and inform those who undergo them; in this case, they are more or less really enacted and so maintained and reinforced, in exchanges. Being based on indissolubly material and symbolic exchanges, the establishment and maintenance of which presuppose reacknowledgment of proximity, they are also partially irreducible to objective relations of proximity in physical (geographical) space or even in economic and social space.[12]

The volume of the social capital possessed by a given agent thus depends on the size of the network of connections he can effectively mobilize and on the volume of the capital (economic, cultural or symbolic) possessed in his own right by each of those to whom he is connected.[13] This means that, although it is relatively irreducible to the economic and cultural capital possessed by a given agent, or even by the whole set of agents to whom he is connected, social capital is never completely independent of it because the exchanges instituting mutual acknowledgment presuppose the reacknowledgment of a minimum of objective homogeneity, and because it exerts a multiplier effect on the capital he possesses in his own right.

The profits which accrue from membership in a group are the basis of the solidarity which makes them possible.[14] This does not mean that they are consciously pursued as such, even in the case of groups like select clubs, which are deliberately organized in order to concentrate social capital and so to derive full benefit from the multiplier effect implied in concentration and to secure the profits of membership—material profits, such as all the types of services accruing from useful relationships, and symbolic profits, such as those derived from association with a rare, prestigious group.

The existence of a network of connections is not a natural given, or even a social given, constituted once and for all by an initial act of institution, represented, in the case of the family group, by the genealogical definition of kinship relations, which is the characteristic of a social formation. It is the product of an endless effort at institution, of which institution rites—often wrongly described as rites of passage—mark the essential moments and which is necessary in order to produce and reproduce lasting, useful relationships that can secure material or symbolic profits (see Bourdieu 1982). In other words, the

12 Neighborhood relationships may, of course, receive an elementary form of institutionalization, as in the Bearn—or the Basque region—where neighbors, lous besis (a word which, in old texts, is applied to the legitimate inhabitants of the village, the rightful members of the assembly), are explicitly designated, in accordance with fairly codified rules, and are assigned functions which are differentiated according to their rank (there is a 'first neighbor,' a 'second neighbor,' and so on), particularly for the major social ceremonies (funerals, marriages, etc.). But even in this case, the relationships actually used by no means always coincide with the relationships socially instituted.

13 Manners (bearing, pronunciation, etc.) may be included in social capital insofar as, through the mode of acquisition they point to, they indicate initial membership of a more or less prestigious group.

14 National liberation movements or nationalist ideologies cannot be accounted for solely by reference to strictly economic profits, i.e., anticipation of the profits which may be derived from redistribution of a proportion of wealth to the advantage of the nationals (nationalization) and the recovery of highly paid jobs (see Breton 1964). To these specifically economic anticipated profits, which would only explain the nationalism of the privileged classes, must be added the very real and very immediate profits derived from membership (social capital) which are proportionately greater for those who are lower down the social hierarchy ('poor whites') or, more precisely, more threatened by economic and social decline.

network of relationships is the product of investment strategies, individual or collective, consciously or unconsciously aimed at establishing or reproducing social relationships that are directly usable in the short or long term, i.e., at transforming contingent relations, such as those of neighborhood, the workplace, or even kinship, into relationships that are at once necessary and elective, implying durable obligations subjectively felt (feelings of gratitude, respect, friendship, etc.) or institutionally guaranteed (rights). This is done through the alchemy of consecration, the symbolic constitution produced by social institution (institution as a relative—brother, sister, cousin, etc.—or as a knight, an heir, an elder, etc.) and endlessly reproduced in and through the exchange (of gifts, words, women, etc.) which it encourages and which presupposes and produces mutual knowledge and recognition. Exchange transforms the things exchanged into signs of recognition and, through the mutual recognition and the recognition of group membership which it implies, reproduces the group. By the same token, it reaffirms the limits of the group, i.e., the limits beyond which the constitutive exchange—trade, commensality, or marriage—cannot take place. Each member of the group is thus instituted as a custodian of the limits of the group: because the definition of the criteria of entry is at stake in each new entry, he can modify the group by modifying the limits of legitimate exchange through some form of misalliance. It is quite logical that, in most societies, the preparation and conclusion of marriages should be the business of the whole group, and not of the agents directly concerned. Through the introduction of new members into a family, a clan, or a club, the whole definition of the group, i.e., its fines, its boundaries, and its identity, is put at stake, exposed to redefinition, alteration, adulteration. When, as in modern societies, families lose the monopoly of the establishment of exchanges which can lead to lasting relationships, whether socially sanctioned (like marriage) or not, they may continue to control these exchanges, while remaining within the logic of laissez-faire, through all the institutions which are designed to favor legitimate exchanges and exclude illegitimate ones by producing occasions (rallies, cruises, hunts, parties, receptions, etc.), places (smart neighborhoods, select schools, clubs, etc.), or practices (smart sports, parlor games, cultural ceremonies, etc.) which bring together, in a seemingly fortuitous way, individuals as homogeneous as possible in all the pertinent respects in terms of the existence and persistence of the group.

The reproduction of social capital presupposes an unceasing effort of sociability, a continuous series of exchanges in which recognition is endlessly affirmed and reaffirmed. This work, which implies expenditure of time and energy and so, directly or indirectly, of economic capital, is not profitable or even conceivable unless one invests in it a specific competence (knowledge of genealogical relationships and of real connections and skill at using them, etc.) and an acquired disposition to acquire and maintain this competence, which are themselves integral parts of this capital.[15] This is one of the factors which explain why the profitability of this labor of accumulating and maintaining social capital rises in proportion to the size of the capital. Because the social capital accruing from a relationship is that much greater to the extent that the person who is the object of it is richly endowed with capital (mainly social, but also cultural and even economic capital), the possessors of an inherited social capital, symbolized by a great name, are able to transform all circumstantial relationships into lasting connections. They are sought after for their

15 *There is every reason to suppose that socializing, or, more generally, relational, dispositions are very unequally distributed among the social classes and, within a given class, among fractions of different origin.*

social capital and, because they are well known, are worthy of being known ('I know him well'); they do not need to 'make the acquaintance' of all their 'acquaintances'; they are known to more people than they know, and their work of sociability, when it is exerted, is highly productive.

Every group has its more or less institutionalized forms of delegation which enable it to concentrate the totality of the social capital, which is the basis of the existence of the group (a family or a nation, of course, but also an association or a party), in the hands of a single agent or a small group of agents and to mandate this plenipotentiary, charged with plena potestas agendi et loquendi,[16] to represent the group, to speak and act in its name and so, with the aid of this collectively owned capital, to exercise a power incommensurate with the agent's personal contribution. Thus, at the most elementary degree of institutionalization, the head of the family, the pater familias, the eldest, most senior member, is tacitly recognized as the only person entitled to speak on behalf of the family group in all official circumstances. But whereas in this case, diffuse delegation requires the great to step forward and defend the collective honor when the honor of the weakest members is threatened. The institutionalized delegation, which ensures the concentration of social capital, also has the effect of limiting the consequences of individual lapses by explicitly delimiting responsibilities and authorizing the recognized spokesmen to shield the group as a whole from discredit by expelling or excommunicating the embarrassing individuals.

If the internal competition for the monopoly of legitimate representation of the group is not to threaten the conservation and accumulation of the capital which is the basis of the group, the members of the group must regulate the conditions of access to the right to declare oneself a member of the group and, above all, to set oneself up as a representative (delegate, plenipotentiary, spokesman, etc.) of the whole group, thereby committing the social capital of the whole group. The title of nobility is the form par excellence of the institutionalized social capital which guarantees a particular form of social relationship in a lasting way. One of the paradoxes of delegation is that the mandated agent can exert on (and, up to a point, against) the group the power which the group enables him to concentrate. (This is perhaps especially true in the limiting cases in which the mandated agent creates the group which creates him but which only exists through him.) The mechanisms of delegation and representation (in both the theatrical and the legal senses) which fall into place—that much more strongly, no doubt, when the group is large and its members weak—as one of the conditions for the concentration of social capital (among other reasons, because it enables numerous, varied, scattered agents to act as one man and to overcome the limitations of space and time) also contain the seeds of an embezzlement or misappropriation of the capital which they assemble.

This embezzlement is latent in the fact that a group as a whole can be represented, in the various meanings of the word, by a subgroup, clearly delimited and perfectly visible to all, known to all, and recognized by all, that of the nobles, the 'people who are known,' the paradigm of whom is the nobility, and who may speak on behalf of the whole group, represent the whole group, and exercise authority in the name of the whole group. The noble is the group personified. He bears the name of the group to which he gives his name (the metonymy which links the noble to his group is clearly seen when Shakespeare calls

16 A 'full power to act and speak' (translator).

Cleopatra 'Egypt' or the King of France 'France,' just as Racine calls Pyrrhus 'Epirus'). It is by him, his name, the difference it proclaims, that the members of his group, the liegemen, and also the land and castles, are known and recognized. Similarly, phenomena such as the 'personality cult' or the identification of parties, trade unions, or movements with their leader are latent in the very logic of representation. Everything combines to cause the signifier to take the place of the signified, the spokesmen that of the group he is supposed to express, not least because his distinction, his 'outstandingness,' his visibility constitute the essential part, if not the essence, of this power, which, being entirely set within the logic of knowledge and acknowledgment, is fundamentally a symbolic power; but also because the representative, the sign, the emblem, may be, and create, the whole reality of groups which receive effective social existence only in and through representation.[17]

CONVERSIONS

The different types of capital can be derived from economic capital, but only at the cost of a more or less great effort of transformation, which is needed to produce the type of power effective in the field in question. For example, there are some goods and services to which economic capital gives immediate access, without secondary costs; others can be obtained only by virtue of a social capital of relationships (or social obligations) which cannot act instantaneously, at the appropriate moment, unless they have been established and maintained for a long time, as if for their own sake, and therefore outside their period of use, i.e., at the cost of an investment in sociability which is necessarily long-term because the time lag is one of the factors of the transmutation of a pure and simple debt into that recognition of nonspecific indebtedness which is called gratitude.[18] In contrast to the cynical but also economical transparency of economic exchange, in which equivalents change hands in the same instant, the essential ambiguity of social exchange, which pre-supposes misrecognition, in other words, a form of faith and of bad faith (in the sense of self-deception), presupposes a much more subtle economy of time.

So it has to be posited simultaneously that economic capital is at the root of all the other types of capital and that these transformed, disguised forms of economic capital, never entirely reducible to that definition, produce their most specific effects only to the extent that they conceal (not least from their possessors) the fact that economic capital is at their root, in other words—but only in the last analysis—at the root of their effects. The real logic of the functioning of capital, the conversions from one type to another, and the

17 It goes without saying that social capital is so totally governed by the logic of knowledge and acknowledgment that it always functions as symbolic capital.

18 It should be made clear, to dispel a likely misunderstanding, that the investment in question here is not necessarily conceived as a calculated pursuit of gain, but that it has every likelihood of being experienced in terms of the logic of emotional investment, i.e., as an involvement which is both necessary and disinterested. This has not always been appreciated by historians, who (even when they are as alert to symbolic effects as E. P. Thompson) tend to conceive symbolic practices—powdered wigs and the whole paraphernalia of office—as explicit strategies of domination, intended to be seen (from below), and to interpret generous or charitable conduct as 'calculated acts of class appeasement.' This naively Machiavellian view forgets that the most sincerely disinterested acts may be those best corresponding to objective interest. A number of fields, particularly those which most tend to deny interest and every sort of calculation, like the fields of cultural production, grant full recognition, and with it the conse-cration which guarantees success, only to those who distinguish themselves by the immediate conformity of their investments, a token of sincerity and attachment to the essential principles of the field. It would be thoroughly erroneous to describe the choices of the habitus which lead an artist, writer, or researcher toward his natural place (a subject, style, manner, etc.) in terms of rational strategy and cynical calculation. This is despite the fact that, for example, shifts from one genre, school, or speciality to another, quasi-religious conversions that are performed 'in all sincerity,' can be understood as capital conversions, the direction and moment of which (on which their success often depends) are determined by a 'sense of investment' which is the less likely to be seen as such the more skillful it is. Innocence is the privilege of those who move in their field of activity like fish in water.

law of conservation which governs them cannot be understood unless two opposing but equally partial views are superseded: on the one hand, economism, which, on the grounds that every type of capital is reducible in the last analysis to economic capital, ignores what makes the specific efficacy of the other types of capital, and on the other hand, semiologism (nowadays represented by structuralism, symbolic interactionism, or ethnomethodology), which reduces social exchanges to phenomena of communication and ignores the brutal fact of universal reducibility to economics.[19]

In accordance with a principle which is the equivalent of the principle of the conservation of energy, profits in one area are necessarily paid for by costs in another (so that a concept like wastage has no meaning in a general science of the economy of practices). The universal equivalent, the measure of all equivalences, is nothing other than labor-time (in the widest sense); and the conservation of social energy through all its conversions is verified if, in each case, one takes into account both the labor-time accumulated in the form of capital and the labor-time needed to transform it from one type into another.

It has been seen, for example, that the transformation of economic capital into social capital presupposes a specific labor, i.e., an apparently gratuitous expenditure of time, attention, care, concern, which, as is seen in the endeavor to personalize a gift, has the effect of transfiguring the purely monetary import of the exchange and, by the same token, the very meaning of the exchange. From a narrowly economic standpoint, this effort is bound to be seen as pure wastage, but in the terms of the logic of social exchanges, it is a solid investment, the profits of which will appear, in the long run, in monetary or other form. Similarly, if the best measure of cultural capital is undoubtedly the amount of time devoted to acquiring it, this is because the transformation of economic capital into cultural capital presupposes an expenditure of time that is made possible by possession of economic capital. More precisely, it is because the cultural capital that is effectively transmitted within the family itself depends not only on the quantity of cultural capital, itself accumulated by spending time, that the domestic group possess, but also on the usable time (particularly in the form of the mother's free time) available to it (by virtue of its economic capital, which enables it to purchase the time of others) to ensure the transmission of this capital and to delay entry into the labor market through prolonged schooling, a credit which pays off, if at all, only in the very long term.[20]

19 To understand the attractiveness of this pair of antagonistic positions which serve as each other's alibi, one would need to analyze the unconscious profits and the profits of unconsciousness which they procure for intellectuals. While some find in economism a means of exempting themselves by excluding the cultural capital and all the specific profits which place them on the side of the dominant, others can abandon the detestable terrain of the economic, where everything reminds them that they can be evaluated, in the last analysis, in economic terms, for that of the symbolic. (The latter merely reproduce, in the realm of the symbolic, the strategy whereby intellectuals and artists endeavor to impose the recognition of their values, i.e., their value, by inverting the law of the market in which what one has or what one earns completely defines what one is worth and what one is—as is shown by the practice of banks which, with techniques such as the personalization of credit, tend to subordinate the granting of loans and the fixing of interest rates to an exhaustive inquiry into the borrower's present and future resources.)

20 Among the advantages procured by capital in all its types, the most precious is the increased volume of useful time that is made possible through the various methods of appropriating other people's time (in the form of services). It may take the form either of increased spare time, secured by reducing the time consumed in activities directly channeled toward producing the means of reproducing the existence of the domestic group, or of more intense use of the time so consumed, by recourse to other people's labor or to devices and methods which are available only to those who have spent time learning how to use them and which (like better transport or living close to the place of work) make it possible to save time. (This is in contrast to the cash savings of the poor, which are paid for in time—do-it-yourself, bargain hunting, etc.) None of this is true of mere economic capital; it is possession of cultural capital that makes it possible to derive greater profit not only from labor-time, by securing a higher yield from the same time, but also from spare time, and so to increase both economic and cultural capital.

The convertibility of the different types of capital is the basis of the strategies aimed at ensuring the reproduction of capital (and the position occupied in social space) by means of the conversions least costly in terms of conversion work and of the losses inherent in the conversion itself (in a given state of the social power relations). The different types of capital can be distinguished according to their reproducibility or, more precisely, according to how easily they are transmitted, i.e., with more or less loss and with more or less concealment; the rate of loss and the degree of concealment tend to vary in inverse ratio. Everything which helps to disguise the economic aspect also tends to increase the risk of loss (particularly the intergenerational transfers). Thus the (apparent) incommensurability of the different types of capital introduces a high degree of uncertainty into all transactions between holders of different types. Similarly, the declared refusal of calculation and of guarantees which characterizes exchanges tending to produce a social capital in the form of a capital of obligations that are usable in the more or less long term (exchanges of gifts, services, visits, etc.) necessarily entails the risk of ingratitude, the refusal of that recognition of nonguaranteed debts which such exchanges aim to produce. Similarly, too, the high degree of concealment of the transmission of cultural capital has the disadvantage (in addition to its inherent risks of loss) that the academic qualification which is its institutionalized form is neither transmissible (like a title of nobility) nor negotiable (like stocks and shares). More precisely, cultural capital, whose diffuse, continuous transmission within the family escapes observation and control (so that the educational system seems to award its honors solely to natural qualities) and which is increasingly tending to attain full efficacy, at least on the labor market, only when validated by the educational system, i.e., converted into a capital of qualifications, is subject to a more disguised but more risky transmission than economic capital. As the educational qualification, invested with the specific force of the official, becomes the condition for legitimate access to a growing number of positions, particularly the dominant ones, the educational system tends increasingly to dispossess the domestic group of the monopoly of the transmission of power and privileges—and, among other things, of the choice of its legitimate heirs from among children of different sex and birth rank.[21] And economic capital itself poses quite different problems of transmission, depending on the particular form it takes. Thus, according to Grassby (1970), the liquidity of commercial capital, which gives immediate economic power and favors transmission, also makes it more vulnerable than landed property (or even real estate) and does not favor the establishment of long-lasting dynasties.

Because the question of the arbitrariness of appropriation arises most sharply in the process of transmission—particularly at the time of succession, a critical moment for all power—every reproduction strategy is at the same time a legitimation strategy aimed at consecrating both an exclusive appropriation and its reproduction. When the subversive critique which aims to weaken the dominant class through the principle of its perpetuation by bringing to light the arbitrariness of the entitlements transmitted and of their transmission (such as the critique which the Enlightenment philosophes directed, in the name of nature, against the arbitrariness of birth) is incorporated in institutionalized

21 It goes without saying that the dominant fractions, who tend to place ever greater emphasis on educational investment, within an overall strategy of asset diversification and of investments aimed at combining security with high yield, have all sorts of ways of evading scholastic verdicts. The direct transmission of economic capital remains one of the principal means of reproduction, and the effect of social capital ('a helping hand,' 'string-pulling,' the 'old boy network') tends to correct the effect of academic sanctions. Educational qualifications never function perfectly as currency. They are never entirely separable from their holders: their value rises in proportion to the value of their bearer, especially in the least rigid areas of the social structure.

mechanisms (for example, laws of inheritance) aimed at controlling the official, direct transmission of power and privileges, the holders of capital have an ever greater interest in resorting to reproduction strategies capable of ensuring better-disguised transmission, but at the cost of greater loss of capital, by exploiting the convertibility of the types of capital. Thus the more the official transmission of capital is prevented or hindered, the more the effects of the clandestine circulation of capital in the form of cultural capital become determinant in the reproduction of the social structure. As an instrument of reproduction capable of disguising its own function, the scope of the educational system tends to increase, and together with this increase is the unification of the market in social qualifications which gives rights to occupy rare positions.

Dieter Rams

Design for a More Human Environment

2013

"design is primarily an intellectual process. It's a procedure and an approach to create innovation and new meaning"

Dieter Rams (1932–) is a German industrial designer closely associated with the electronics company Braun and the furniture company Vitsœ. His minimal and functional designs have influenced many products and companies, including Apple.

Over the past six decades I have barely changed my conception and principles of design—and quite consciously so—because I believed them to be right back then and I believe them to be right right now.

The requirements for our living environment are still essentially human, but as society changes and therefore design changes, so too do the responsibilities of the professional designer.

Now, in my view, the term "design" is frequently wrongly applied. It is used too often to mean "mere otherness" or "conspicuousness at all cost."

The word "design" is increasingly associated with a growth-oriented consumer society. Instead of being degraded to a lifestyle term, I wish for [it] to stand for something that really helps human beings come to grips with our own world, to get along with each other and also to better our environment.

We want to contribute to the preservation of this planet. And in addition there is a very urgent and necessary need to minimize the physical and visual pollution. Good design is as little design as possible. As I said in my principles, "Less design is more." We want to go back to the pure and to the simple. And simplicity is the key to brilliance.

As my credo "Less But Better" implies: Do we really always need new things? In the face of economical and ecological challenges, the design of our environment is now confronted with fundamental changes in meaning.

We should consider that we need a design approach that thinks way beyond superficial and cosmetic consumption! And by that I also mean going beyond an exclusively consumer-oriented society.

Innovative, useful, aesthetic, understandable, honest, unobtrusive, long-lasting, thorough down to the last detail, environmentally-friendly and finally, as little design as possible—[these] were, and still are, the 10 principles that I first drew up some 30 years ago. But good design does not only come from fulfilling these basic requirements alone.

Good everyday design should also always involve a special kind of design that appears to speak for itself. They are rare, but these very special products provide the necessary incentive and the encouragement for the design of the entire living environment. They are the benchmark for the future.

During the course of my career I was fortunate enough to be able to work together with innovative, socially responsible and risk-friendly business personalities. But it wasn't just a case of lucky circumstances, we also shared the same vision for another kind of world. We wanted to produce things that were not aggressively conspicuous, but that were convincing through their use and through their sustainable aesthetic.

Tomorrow's world will be designed by the design students of today—by you—and while this is a great opportunity, this is also a great challenge and a great responsibility. And a great opportunity and chance for you.

For over 50 years I have been able to accompany the process both as a product designer and as a university professor. Back then we, too, wanted a different world and a better environment. Designers should always have the ambition to improve the world just a little—after all, it doesn't improve itself.

Today's main challenges are the protection of the natural environment and overcoming mindless consumption. And there are new, further-reaching challenges coming for the designers of tomorrow. It is no longer enough to think of products alone, designers also need to consider new behavior patterns and how to deal with cultural values and trans-cultural relationships. That requires a design ethos that goes way beyond complacency and arbitrariness.

I would like to identify five dimensions that are essential to design, from my point of view:

1. The Functional Dimension, or Is There an Alternative to Utility?
Concentrating on function, on product utility in the broadest sense of the word, has influenced my work from the very beginning.

It is true that we have amassed a great deal of precise design experience over the past years. And that completely new technologies have developed to facilitate the designer's work. Designers have increasingly learned to use the potential of these new technologies and production techniques, as well as the possibilities that the new materials have to offer.

Nonetheless, we rarely achieve perfect solutions. The more we dedicate ourselves to the problem, the more we realize how much still needs to be done.

At the same time, as I see it, the area that is described by the term "function" keeps growing and growing. We have learned how complex and manifold the functions of a product can be. Today we are acutely aware that what we create must also have psychological, ecological and social benefits.

Most certainly "functionality" is a multifaceted area. But in my eyes, there is no alternative.

2. The Communicative Dimension, or What Should Design Communicate?
Every design process is also about communication: It conveys all kinds of information. On the purpose of a product, on its basic structure, on how to use it, what it can do and what it is worth.

Making the information as accurate and easy to understand as possible is also an aspect of the functionality of a product. After all, the better I understand it, the better I can use it.

The challenge of designing understandable products has become much more urgent and more difficult. More and more products are being developed with innovative technology and innovative functions. Individual products are required to be able to do more and more, to perform more and more functions, by increasing and growing the area of function in itself.

Over the years it has become easier for clever designers to create illusions with design. And these illusions appear to promise even greater success.

We must not allow ourselves to exploit the manipulative potential of design. Why? Because I can't imagine that in the long-term interest of a company, that it would want to deliberately mislead its customers. And certainly that should not apply to society as a whole.

3. The Aesthetic Dimension, or How Much Chaos Can We Live with?
My idea of an aesthetically designed environment is, and has always been, one that is so restrained and unobtrusive that one hardly notices it.

But it should also be so appealing that one enjoys being part of it, that you're glad you have the chance to use it and have a sense of being part of it. It should be contemporary in a way that has nothing to do with ephemeral fashions, or any kind of flight from the present into something historical.

Imbuing products with these aesthetic qualities has never been easy. And it must always be emphasized that unobtrusive, restrained, matter-of-fact design is not an end in itself. Nor is it a deficiency.

To my mind, aesthetic quality in this sense is becoming increasingly important, since it has a lasting influence on the mood and atmosphere of one's surroundings.

We are surrounded by a seemingly unlimited supply of products that is not exhilarating in its diversity but chaotic, exhausting and even paralyzing in its excess.

That's why I see it as an important task—maybe as the most important task facing design today—is to help reduce the chaotic clutter that we are forced to live in.

That leads me to:

4. The Temporal Dimension, or How Much Waste Can We Afford?

There is an unpleasant expression "built-in obsolescence." It's introducing new products with the sole intention of devaluing existing ones and persuading consumers to replace them before their time.

But that's really a deliberate waste of money, of materials, of energy and time. Developing products nobody needs is often easier and quicker than developing products that we actually need. Design is often used—or "abused"—as the cheapest way to create an illusion of innovation.

Striving to achieve durability through design is one of the key aspects in my view of design. But durability cannot be achieved with design alone.

What is needed is an interplay of intelligent product ideas, successful engineering, high quality production as well as well thought-out design.

It shows again that design can only really be successful as part of a collective corporate effort.

Which brings us to:

5. The Ecological Dimension

In creating our artificial world, we humans have entered into what has now turned out to be a highly risky endeavor. For in the process we are destroying the natural world on which our survival depends—air, water, soil, plants and animals.

Nobody can deny that humankind, industrial production and the sheer diversity of products are threatening to our natural environment.

And equally, nobody can deny that industrial production must become "sustainable."

Being "sustainable" in the sense that our natural resources need to be preserved, not destroyed. In this respect, we are facing the greatest challenge that humanity has ever faced.

The question is, *What can we do?* My formula for sustainable production is: *Less but better! Much, much less, and much, much better.*

In dressing up products just to persuade people to buy them, design has contributed, and still contributes, to an everlasting flood of new products. But now design can play an active part in stemming that flood.

Many of today's products are often bought at a high price to the environment, but they are of little use. They don't last long. They don't age gracefully. They are so wrong that it is difficult to remain on good terms with them. And of course they all end up in a big rubbish heap, sucking ever new products behind them that are going to be produced.

It makes a huge difference if we use our products for one year, five years or for 10. That's why we need less and less products whose manufacture or use squanders resources or their existence harms the environment.

And we need less and less of products that are mere fashion and that are out of date and are thrown away when that fashion changes.

What we want instead are products that the consumers should expect. Which is they should make it easier, they should enhance and they should intensify life.

Design is primarily an intellectual process. It's a procedure and an approach to create innovation and new meaning.

That's why we also need a wide range of simple, yet real advances like, for example, intelligent redesign, not just for products but also for buildings before we tear them down.

In conclusion, I would like to come back to the importance of companies and entrepreneurs in this process.

For me, important constellations always involved an outstanding entrepreneurial relationship and entrepreneurial personalities that I had a chance to work with. At the beginning of the 20th century there was Peter Behrens and Emil Rathenau of AEG, later, in the mid '50s when I began my career, there was Adriano Olivetti with Nizzoli, Mario Bellini or Ettore Sottsass. I myself was fortunate enough to encounter the Braun brothers in 1955 and Niels Wiese Vitsoe in 1957.

"Simplicity is the ultimate sophistication." That's the maxim that Steve Jobs used. It's a quote of Leonardo da Vinci's. And of course Apple has been, in recent years, the company that most represented and constituted that aspect of design.

Both designers and entrepreneurs face an even greater social responsibility for today and for the future. Because it could really be said that we are moving away from competition between products but towards a new form of competition that involves communication, utility and sustainability.

Consumers will be more critical in the future of the corporate philosophies and aesthetics that are behind the brands.

If we say it differently, we can say that the credibility of a brand will depend on its real, qualitative and useful content and not on its media-projected message.

If changes in the social and behavioral values within a company do not occur hand in hand with changing values in society, dangerous value conflicts will ensue between a company and its environment.

This is a matter that must be taken seriously today. For utilitarian and ecological qualities will most definitely play a crucial role in positive product experience in our future.

Mahatma Gandhi once said: "We must be the change we want to see in the world." Let us start by changing attitudes.

Thank you for listening.

Henry Hongmin Kim

Concrescence of
Ontological Design Principles

2017

"successful visualization requires an in-depth understanding of linguistic process from ontology, epistemology, semiotics, linguistics, structuralism, poststructuralism and process philosophy"

Henry Hongmin Kim (1971–) is a Korean-born graphic designer, educator, and theorist in the United States. He is the founder and organizer of Graphic Design Discourse, a group of designers and educators formed within the graphic design department at Savannah College of Art and Design in Atlanta, Georgia, and is the global design director of The Coca-Cola company.

....

(Continued from page 323, "Structural Process of Design")

The continuation of graphic design is predicated on the need for open discourse based on relevant philosophical and political ideologies and faith in the ability of design to be impactful. From a discursive standpoint, it is not necessary to start anew, but instead to absorb, restructure, and revitalize existing discourses. To accomplish this, we can employ existing terminology within new structural systems.

Traditional communication involves a **sender** and a **user** in a simple and direct exchange of knowledge. However, in the age of information—in the age of complex, persistent, immediate, and individualized communication—there is a growing need for a professional to control this process: a mediator or communicator to facilitate understanding and guide the message from sender to user through the clearest, most effective means.

While it is being created, a design is in constant flux, as factors involved in a given situation are always evolving. Thus, a completed design is not static but a product of concrescence: a growing together of parts previously unlinked, an event, a whole that at its best must maintain the interconnection of all its constituent parts. A designer must focus on the overall event—the moment of concrescence embodied by a design—and have an understanding of the history of every step and consideration that will lead to that event. Thus a designer must also be an ontologist.

Concrescence of Ontological Design Principles

| Categorical Scheme and Descriptive Generalization
of Deductive Visual Communication Process

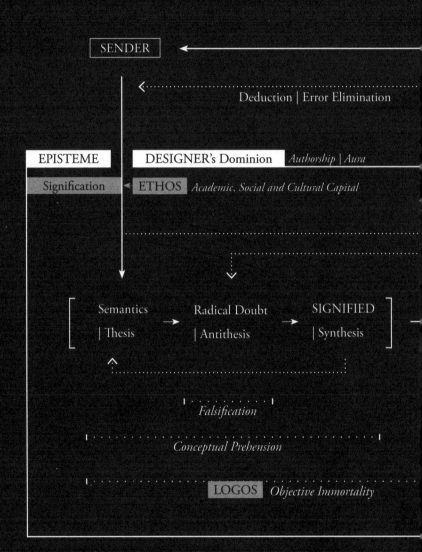

SENDER

Deduction | Error Elimination

EPISTEME   DESIGNER's Dominion   *Authorship | Aura*

Signification   ETHOS   *Academic, Social and Cultural Capital*

Semantics   Radical Doubt   SIGNIFIED
| Thesis | Antithesis | Synthesis

Falsification

Conceptual Prehension

LOGOS   *Objective Immortality*